The Business Environment
Sixth Edition

PEARSON

We work with leading authors to develop the strongest learning experiences, bringing cutting-edge thinking and best learning practice to a global market. We craft our print and digital resources to do more to help learners not only understand their content, but to see it in action and apply what they learn, whether studying or at work.

Pearson is the world's leading learning company. Our portfolio includes Penguin, Dorling Kindersley, the Financial Times and our educational business, Pearson International. We are also a leading provider of electronic learning programmes and of test development, processing and scoring services to educational institutions, corporations and professional bodies around the world.

Pearson Custom Publishing enables our customers to access a wide and expanding range of market-leading content from world-renowned authors and develop their own tailor-made book. You choose the content that meets your needs and Pearson Custom Publishing produces a high-quality printed book.

Every day our work helps learning flourish, and wherever learning flourishes, so do people.

To learn more please visit us at: www.pearsoncustom.co.uk

PEARSON CUSTOM PUBLISHING

The Business Environment
Sixth Edition

Compiled from:

Economics for Business
Fifth Edition
by John Sloman, Kevin Hinde and Dean Garratt

Law for Business Students
Sixth Edition
by Alix Adams

Economics
Eighth Edition
John Sloman, Dean Garratt and Alison Wride

Economics for Business
Eighth Edition
by John Sloman, Kevin Hinde and Dean Garratt

Pearson Education Limited
Edinburgh Gate
Harlow
Essex CM20 2JE

And associated companies throughout the world

Visit us on the World Wide Web at:
www.pearsoned.co.uk

First Published 2004
This Custom Book Edition © Pearson Education Limited 2012

Compiled from:

Economics for Business
Fifth Edition
John Sloman, Kevin Hinde and Dean Garratt
ISBN 978 0 273 72233 5
© John Sloman and Mark Sutcliffe 1998, 2001, 2004
© John Sloman and Kevin Hinde 2007
© John Sloman, Kevin Hinde and Dean Garratt 2010

Economics
Eighth Edition
John Sloman, Dean Garratt and Alison Wride
ISBN 978 0 273 76312 3
© John Sloman 1991
© John Sloman, Alison Bird and Mark Sutcliffe 1994, 1997
© John Sloman, Alison Sloman and Mark Sutcliffe 2000, 2003
© John Sloman 2006
© John Sloman, Alison Wride 2009
© John Sloman, Alison Wride and Dean Garratt 2012

Law for Business Students
Sixth Edition
Alix Adams
ISBN 978 1 4082 2545 5
© Pearson Professional Limited 1996
© Pearson Education Limited 2000, 2010

All rights reserved. No part of this publication may be reproduced, stored in a retrieval system, or transmitted in any form or by any means, electronic, mechanical, photocopying, recording or otherwise, without either the prior written permission of the publisher or a licence permitting restricted copying in the United Kingdom issued by the Licensing Agency Ltd, Saffron House, 6–10 Kirby Street, London EC1N 8TS.

ISBN 978 1 78236 292 0

Printed and bound by Clays Ltd, Bungay, Suffolk.

Contents

Section 1: Chapters from Sloman

Chapter 1   **Business Organisations**   2
Chapter 3 in *Economics for Business*
Fifth Edition
John Sloman, Kevin Hinde and Dean Garratt

Chapter 2   **The Working of Competitive Markets**   19
Chapter 4 in *Economics for Business*
Fifth Edition
John Sloman, Kevin Hinde and Dean Garratt

Chapter 3   **Business in a Market Environment**   39
Chapter 5 in *Economics for Business*
Fifth Edition
John Sloman, Kevin Hinde and Dean Garratt

Chapter 4   **Costs of Production**   63
Chapter 9 in *Economics for Business*
Fifth Edition
John Sloman, Kevin Hinde and Dean Garratt

Chapter 5   **Revenue and Profit**   89
Chapter 10 in *Economics for Business*
Fifth Edition
John Sloman, Kevin Hinde and Dean Garratt

Chapter 6   **Profit Maximisation Under Perfect Competition and Monopoly**   103
Chapter 11 in *Economics for Business*
Fifth Edition
John Sloman, Kevin Hinde and Dean Garratt

Chapter 7   **Profit Maximisation Under Imperfect Competition**   124
Chapter 12 in *Economics for Business*
Fifth Edition
John Sloman, Kevin Hinde and Dean Garratt

Chapter 8   **Alternative Theories of the Firm**   149
Chapter 14 in *Economics for Business*
Fifth Edition
John Sloman, Kevin Hinde and Dean Garratt

Chapter 9	**Reasons for Government Intervention in the Market**	163
	Chapter 20 in *Economics for Business* Fifth Edition John Sloman, Kevin Hinde and Dean Garratt	
Chapter 10	**Government and the Firm**	191
	Chapter 21 in *Economics for Business* Fifth Edition John Sloman, Kevin Hinde and Dean Garratt	
Chapter 11	**Government and the Market**	214
	Chapter 22 in *Economics for Business* Fifth Edition John Sloman, Kevin Hinde and Dean Garratt	
Chapter 12	**Macroeconomic Objectives**	244
	Section 26.1 in *Economics for Business* Fifth Edition John Sloman, Kevin Hinde and Dean Garratt	
Chapter 13	**Economic Growth**	245
	Section 26.2 in *Economics for Business* Fifth Edition John Sloman, Kevin Hinde and Dean Garratt	
Chapter 14	**Macroeconomic Issues and Analysis: an Overview**	253
	Section 15.1 in *Economics* Eighth Edition John Sloman, Alison Wride and Dean Garratt	
Chapter 15	**Inflation**	263
	Section 26.4 in *Economics for Business* Fifth Edition John Sloman, Kevin Hinde and Dean Garratt	
Chapter 16	**The Business Cycle and Macroeconomic Objectives**	269
	Section 26.5 in *Economics for Business* Fifth Edition John Sloman, Kevin Hinde and Dean Garratt	
Chapter 17	**The Circular Flow of Income**	270
	Section 26.6 in *Economics for Business* Fifth Edition John Sloman, Kevin Hinde and Dean Garratt	
Chapter 18	**Business Activity, Employment and Inflation**	275
	Chapter 29 in *Economics for Business* Fifth Edition John Sloman, Kevin Hinde and Dean Garratt	
Chapter 19	**Demand-side Policy**	305
	Chapter 30 in *Economics for Business* Fifth Edition John Sloman, Kevin Hinde and Dean Garratt	

| Chapter 20 | **Supply-side Policy** | 331 |

Chapter 31 in *Economics for Business*
Fifth Edition
John Sloman, Kevin Hinde and Dean Garratt

Section 2: Chapters from Adams

| Chapter 21 | **How the Law is Made** | 350 |

Chapter 2 in *Law for Business Students*
Sixth Edition
Alix Adams

| Chapter 22 | **The Law of Contract: Offer and Acceptance** | 374 |

Chapter 4 in *Law for Business Students*
Sixth Edition
Alix Adams

| Chapter 23 | **The Law of Contract: Consideration, Intention and Privity** | 394 |

Chapter 5 in *Law for Business Students*
Sixth Edition
Alix Adams

| Chapter 24 | **The Terms of the Contract** | 412 |

Chapter 6 in *Law for Business Students*
Sixth Edition
Alix Adams

| Chapter 25 | **Tort Liability for Defective Goods** | 438 |

Chapter 13 in *Law for Business Students*
Sixth Edition
Alix Adams

| Chapter 26 | **Tort Liability for Defective Services** | 458 |

Chapter 14 in *Law for Business Students*
Sixth Edition
Alix Adams

| **Index** | 497 |

Chapters from Sloman
Part One

Business organisations

> **Business issues covered in this chapter**
>
> - How are businesses organised and structured?
> - What are the aims of business?
> - Will owners, managers and other employees necessarily have the same aims? How can those working in the firm be persuaded to achieve the objectives of their employers?
> - What are the various legal categories of business and how do different legal forms suit different types of business?
> - How do businesses differ in their internal organisation? What are the relative merits of alternative forms of organisation?

If you decide to grow strawberries in your garden or allotment, or if you decide to put up a set of shelves in your home, then you have made a production decision. Most production decisions, however, are not made by the individuals who will consume the product. Most production decisions are made by firms: whether by small one-person businesses or by giant multinational corporations, such as General Motors or Sony.

In this chapter we are going to investigate the firm: what is its role in the economy; what are the goals of firms; how do firms differ in respect to their legal status; and in what ways are they organised internally?

3.1 THE NATURE OF FIRMS

Economists have traditionally paid little attention to the ways in which firms operate and to the different roles they might take. Firms were often seen merely as organisations for producing output and employing inputs in response to market forces. Virtually no attention was paid to just how firms were organised and how different forms of organisation would influence their behaviour. The firm was seen as a 'black box': inputs were fed in one end, they were used in the most efficient way, and output then emerged from the other end. But do firms have a more significant function to play in respect to resource allocation and production, and does their internal organisation affect their decisions? The answer to these questions is clearly yes.

Complex production

Very few goods or services are produced by one person alone. Most products require a complex production process that will involve many individuals. But how are these individuals to be organised in order to produce such goods and services? Two very different ways are:

- within markets via price signals;
- within firms via a hierarchy of managerial authority.

In the first of these two ways, each stage of production would involve establishing a distinct contract with each separate producer. Assume that you wanted to purchase a woollen jumper. You would need to enter a series of separate contracts: to have the jumper designed, to buy the wool, to get the wool spun, to get it dyed, to have the jumper knitted. There are many other stages in the production and distribution process that might also be considered. With each contract a price will have to be determined, and that price will reflect current market conditions. In most cases, such a form of economic organisation would prove to be highly inefficient and totally impractical. Consider the number of contracts that might be necessary if you wished to purchase a motor car!

With the second way of organising production, a single firm (or just a few firms) replaces the market. The coordination of the conversion of inputs into output takes place *within* the firm: not through the market mechanism, but by management issuing orders as to what to produce and the manner in which this is to take place. Hence the distinguishing feature of the firm is that the price mechanism plays little if any role in allocating resources within it.

The benefits of organising production within firms

The function of the firm is to bring together a series of production and distribution operations, doing away with the need for individuals to enter into narrowly specified contracts. If you want a woollen jumper, you go to a woollen jumper retailer.

According to Ronald Coase,[1] the key advantage of organising production and distribution through firms, as opposed to the market, is that it involves lower transaction costs. Transaction costs are the costs of making economic arrangements about production, distribution and sales.

> **Definitions**
>
> **The firm**
> An economic organisation that coordinates the process of production and distribution.
>
> **Transaction costs**
> Those costs incurred when making economic contracts in the marketplace.

Transactions costs. The costs incurred when firms buy inputs or services from other firms as opposed to producing them themselves. They include the costs of searching for the best firm to do business with, the costs of drawing up, monitoring and enforcing contracts, and the costs of transporting and handling products between the firms. These costs should be weighed against the benefits of outsourcing through the market.

---

[1] Ronald H. Coase, 'The Nature of the Firm', *Economica*, Vol. 4, No. 16, Nov. 1937, pp. 386–405.

The transaction costs associated with individual contracts made through the market are likely to be substantial for the following reasons:

- The *uncertainty* in framing contracts. It is unlikely that decision makers will have perfect knowledge of the production process. Given, then, that such contracts are established on imperfect information, they are consequently subject to error.
- The *complexity* of contracts. Many products require many stages of production. The more complex the product, the greater the number of contracts that would have to be made. The specifications within contracts may also become more complex, requiring high levels of understanding and knowledge of the production process, which raises the possibility of error in writing them. As contracts become more complex they raise a firm's costs of production and make it difficult to determine the correct price for a transaction.
- *Monitoring* contracts. Entering into a contract with another person may require that you monitor whether the terms of the contract are fulfilled. This may incur a significant time cost for the individual, especially if a large number of contracts require monitoring.
- *Enforcing* contracts. If one party breaks its contract, the legal expense of enforcing the contract or recouping any losses may be significant. Many individuals might find such costs prohibitive, and as a consequence be unable to pursue broken contracts through the legal system.

What is apparent is that, for most goods, the firm represents a superior way to organise production. The actions of management replace the price signals of the market and overcome many of the associated transaction costs.

Goals of the firm

Economists have traditionally assumed that firms will want to maximise profits. The 'traditional theory of the firm', as it is called, shows how much output firms should produce and at what price, in order to make as much profit as possible. But do firms necessarily want to maximise profits?

It is reasonable to assume that the *owners* of firms will want to maximise profits: this much most of the critics of the traditional theory accept. The question is, however, whether the owners make the decisions about how much to produce and at what price.

The divorce of ownership from control

As businesses steadily grew over the eighteenth and nineteenth centuries, many owner-managers were forced, however reluctantly, to devolve some responsibility for the running of the business to other individuals. These new managers brought with them technical skills and business expertise, a crucial prerequisite for a modern successful business enterprise. The managerial revolution that was to follow, in which business owners (shareholders) and managers became distinct groups, called into question what the precise goals of the business enterprise might now be. This debate was to be further fuelled by the development of the joint-stock company, in which the ownership of the enterprise was progressively dispersed over a large number of shareholders. The growth in the joint-stock company was a direct consequence of business owners looking to raise large amounts of investment capital in order to maintain or expand business activity.

> **Definition**
>
> **Joint-stock company**
> A company where ownership is distributed between a large number of shareholders.

This twin process of managerial expansion and widening share ownership led Berle and Means[2] to argue that the *ownership* of stocks and shares in an enterprise no longer meant *control* over its assets. They subsequently drew a distinction between 'nominal ownership', namely getting a return from investing in a business, and 'effective ownership', which is the ability to control and direct the assets of the business. The more dispersed nominal ownership becomes, the less and less likely it is that there will be effective ownership by shareholders. This issue will be considered in more detail in Chapter 14.

As you will discover in section 3.2, the modern company is *legally* separate from its owners. Hence the assets are legally owned by the business itself. Consequently, the group *in charge* of the business is that which controls the use of these assets: i.e. the group which determines the business's objectives and implements the necessary procedures to secure them. In most companies this group is the managers.

Berle and Means argued that, as a consequence of this transition from owner to manager control, conflicts are likely to develop between the goals of managers and those of the owners.

But what are the objectives of managers? Will they want to maximise profits, or will they have some other aim?

Managers may be assumed to want to maximise their *own* interests. This may well involve pursuits that conflict with profit maximisation. They may, for example, pursue higher salaries, greater power or prestige, greater sales, better working conditions or greater popularity with their subordinates. Different managers in the same firm may well pursue different aims.

Managers will still have to ensure that *sufficient* profits are made to keep shareholders happy, but that may be very different from *maximising* profits.

Alternative theories of the firm to those of profit maximisation, therefore, tend to assume that large firms are profit 'satisficers'. That is, managers strive hard for a minimum target level of profit, but are less interested in profits above this level.

Such theories fall into two categories: first, those theories that assume that firms attempt to maximise some other aim, provided that sufficient profits are achieved; and second, those theories that assume that firms pursue a number of potentially conflicting aims, of which sufficient profit is merely one. These alternative theories are examined more fully in Chapter 14.

> **Pause for thought**
>
> *Make a list of six possible aims that a manager of a high street department store might have. Identify some conflicts that might arise between these aims.*

The nature of institutions and organisations is likely to influence behaviour. There are various forces influencing people's decisions in complex organisations. Assumptions that an organisation will follow one simple objective (e.g. short-run profit maximisation) are thus too simplistic in many cases.

The principal–agent relationship

Can the owners of a firm ever be sure that their managers will pursue the business strategy most appropriate to achieving the owners' goals (which traditional economic theory tells us is the maximisation of profit)? This is an example of what is known as the principal–agent problem. One of the features of a complex modern economy

> **Definition**
>
> **Principal–agent problem**
> One where people (principals), as a result of lack of knowledge, cannot ensure that their best interests are served by their agents.

---

[2] A. A. Berle and G. C. Means, *The Modern Corporation and Private Property* (Macmillan, 1933).

is that people (principals) have to employ others (agents) to carry out their wishes. If you want to go on holiday, it is easier to go to a travel agent to sort out the arrangements than to do it all yourself. Likewise, if you want to buy a house, it is more convenient to go to an estate agent.

The crucial advantage that agents have over their principals is specialist knowledge and information. This is frequently the basis upon which agents are employed. For example, owners employ managers for their specialist knowledge of a market or their understanding of business practice. But this situation of asymmetric information – that one party (the agent) knows more than the other (the principal) – means that it will be very difficult for the principal to judge in whose interest the agent is operating. Are the manager's own goals rather than the goals of the owner being pursued? It is the same in other walks of life. The estate agent selling your house may try to convince you that it is necessary to accept a lower price, while the real reason is to save the agent time, effort and expense. A second-hand car dealer may 'neglect' to tell you about the rust on the underside of the car, or that it had a history of unreliability.

> **Definition**
>
> **Asymmetric information**
> A situation in which one party in an economic relationship knows more than another.

The principal–agent problem. Where people (principals), as a result of a lack of knowledge, cannot ensure that their best interests are served by their agents. Agents may take advantage of this situation to the disadvantage of the principals.

Principals may attempt to reconcile the fact that they have imperfect information, and are thus in an inherently weak position, in the following ways:

- *Monitoring* the performance of the agent. Shareholders could monitor the performance of their senior managers through attending annual general meetings. The managers could be questioned by shareholders and ultimately replaced if their performance is seen as unsatisfactory.
- Establishing a series of *incentives* to ensure that agents act in the principals' best interest. For example, managerial pay could be closely linked to business performance.

Within any firm there will exist a complex chain of principal–agent relationships – between workers and managers, between junior managers and senior managers, between senior managers and directors, and between directors and shareholders. All groups will hold some specialist knowledge which might be used to further their own distinct goals. Predictably, the development of effective monitoring and evaluation programmes and the creation of performance-related pay schemes have been two central themes in the development of business practices in recent years – a sign that the principal is looking to fight back.

Staying in business

Aiming for profits, sales, salaries, power, etc. will be useless if the firm does not survive! Trying to *maximise* any of the various objectives may be risky. For example, if a firm tries to maximise its market share by aggressive advertising or price cutting, it might invoke a strong response from its rivals. The resulting war may drive it out of business. Some of the managers may easily move to other jobs and may actually gain from the experience, but the majority are likely to lose. Concern with survival, therefore, may make firms cautious.

Not all firms, however, make survival the top priority. Some are adventurous and are prepared to take risks. Adventurous firms are most likely to be those dominated by a powerful and ambitious individual – an individual prepared to take gambles.

The more dispersed the decision-making power is in the firm, and the more worried managers are about their own survival, the more cautious are their policies likely to be: preferring 'tried and trusted' methods of production, preferring to stick with products that have proved to be popular, and preferring to expand slowly and steadily.

If a firm is too cautious, however, it may not after all survive. It may find that it loses markets to more aggressive competitors. Ultimately, therefore, if a firm is concerned to survive, it must be careful to balance caution against keeping up with competitors, ensuring that the customer is sufficiently satisfied and that costs are kept sufficiently low by efficient management and the introduction of new technology.

The efficient operation of the firm may be strongly influenced by its internal organisational structure. We will consider this in more detail in section 3.3, but first we must consider how the *legal* structure of the firm might influence its conduct within the market place.

THE FIRM AS A LEGAL ENTITY 3.2

The legal structure of the firm is likely to have a significant impact on its conduct, and subsequent performance, within the marketplace. In the UK, there are several types of firm, each with a distinct legal status.

The sole proprietor

This is where the business is owned by just one person. Usually such businesses are small, with only a few employees. Retailing, building and farming are typical areas to find sole proprietorships. Such businesses are easy to set up and may require only a relatively small initial capital investment. They may well flourish if the owner is highly committed to the business, and they can be very flexible to changing market conditions. They suffer two main disadvantages, however:

- *Limited scope for expansion.* Finance is limited to what the owner can raise personally. Also there is a limit to the size of an organisation that one person can effectively control.
- *Unlimited liability.* The owner is personally liable for any losses that the business might make. This could result in the owner's house, car and other assets being seized to pay off any outstanding debts.

The partnership

This is where two or more people own the business. In most partnerships there is a legal limit of 20 partners. Partnerships are common in the same fields as sole proprietorships. They are also common in the professions: solicitors, accountants, surveyors, etc. With more owners, there is more scope for expansion. More finance can be raised and the partners can each specialise in one aspect of the business.

BOX 3.1 MANAGERS AND PERFORMANCE

Are high CEO salaries justified?

In 2007, the average pay, including bonuses and long-term incentive plans, for a chief executive of the top 100 UK companies was some £2.8 million. Average earnings in the UK in the same year were just over £24 000. Thus, the average chief executive was paid 116 times more than an average UK worker. What is more, the average annual increase in executive pay from 2002 to 2007 was 31.4 per cent. This compares with a figure of just 13 per cent for average earnings over the same period.[1]

The awards given to executive 'fat cats' have met with considerable protest in recent years. So how can such high pay awards to top executives be justified? The two main arguments put forward to justify such generosity are as follows:

- 'The best cost money.' Failure to offer high rewards may encourage the top executives within an industry to move elsewhere.
- 'High rewards motivate.' High rewards are likely to motivate not only top executives, but also those below them. Managers, especially those in the middle of the business hierarchy, will compete for promotion and seek to do well with such high rewards on offer.

However, a report by the *Financial Times* highlighting the work of the International Labour Office argues otherwise.

> Soaring executive pay over the past few years has not only exacerbated income inequality but appears to have done little or nothing to improve company performance . . . A report by the International Labour Organisation . . . finds no justification for the sums paid to chief executives. 'Evidence suggests that developments in executive pay may have been both inequality-enhancing and economically inefficient,' it says.
>
> Performance-related and share-based compensation packages pushed up executive pay in the US by nearly 10 per cent a year between 2003 and 2007, adjusted for inflation, compared with 0.7 per cent for employees.
>
> In 2007 chief executives of the 15 largest US companies earned on average more than $24 m (€18 m, £14 m), 520 times the wage of the average worker, compared with 370 times four years earlier.

There were similar though less exaggerated trends in other countries for which data were available, including Australia, Germany, Hong Kong, the Netherlands and South Africa.

Yet empirical studies summarised in the report show 'only very moderate, if any, effects' of performance-related pay on company performance. The authors suggest that a more plausible explanation of chief executive remuneration is the strong bargaining position of executives in relation to boards and shareholders.

The report mentions various proposals for curbing excessive executive pay packages, including more say for shareholders and preventing companies from deducting executive compensation as a business expense.

The report warns that the market turmoil will hit the poor hardest and worsen inequality. Governments should adopt policies that combine redistribution with promotion of employment, it says.

Though 'a certain degree of income inequality' is useful in rewarding effort, talent and innovation, excessive differences are associated with more crime, worse health, reduced social mobility and more corruption.[2]

1. Explain how sky-high executive remuneration might illustrate the principal–agent problem.
2. In the UK, many of the highest-paid executives head former public utilities. Why might the giving of very high rewards to such individuals be a source of public concern?

---

[1] *Guardian*, 11 September 2008.

[2] *Financial Times*, 17 October 2008.

Although since 2001 it has been possible to form limited liability partnerships, many partnerships still have unlimited liability. This problem could be very serious. The mistakes of one partner could jeopardise the personal assets of all the other partners.

Where large amounts of capital are required and/or when the risks of business failure are relatively high, partnerships without limited liability are not an appropriate form of organisation. In such cases it is best to form a company (or 'joint-stock company' to give it its full title).

Companies

A company is legally separate from its owners. This means that it can enter into contracts and own property. Any debts are *its* debts, not the owners'.

Each owner has a share in the company. The size of their share holdings will vary from one shareholder to another and will depend on the amount they invest. Each shareholder will receive his or her share of the company's distributed profit. The payments to shareholders are called 'dividends'.

The owners have only *limited liability*. This means that, if the company goes bankrupt, the owners will lose the amount of money they have invested in the company, but no more. Their personal assets cannot be seized. This has the advantage of encouraging people to become shareholders, and indeed large companies may have thousands of shareholders – some with very small holdings and others, including institutional shareholders such as pension funds, with very large holdings. Without the protection of limited liability, many of these investors would never put their money into any company that involved even the slightest risk.

Shareholders often take no part in the running of the firm. They may elect a board of directors which decides broad issues of company policy. The board of directors in turn appoints managers who make the day-to-day decisions. There are two types of company: public and private.

Public limited companies. Don't be confused by the title. A public limited company is still a private enterprise: it is not a nationalised industry. It is 'public' because it can offer new shares publicly: by issuing a prospectus, it can invite the public to subscribe to a new share issue. In addition, many public limited companies are quoted on the Stock Exchange. This means that existing shareholders can sell some or all of their shares on the Stock Exchange. The prices of these shares will be determined by demand and supply. A public limited company must hold an annual shareholders' meeting. Examples of well-known UK public limited companies are Marks & Spencer, BP, Barclays, BSkyB and Tesco.

Private limited companies. Private limited companies cannot offer their shares publicly. Shares have to be sold privately. This makes it more difficult for private limited companies to raise finance, and consequently they tend to be smaller than public companies. They are, however, easier to set up than public companies. One of the most famous examples of a private limited company is Manchester United football club (which used to be a public limited company until it was bought out by the Glazer family in 2005).

Consortia of firms

It is common, especially in large civil engineering projects that involve very high risks, for many firms to work together as a consortium. The Channel Tunnel and Thames Barrier are products of this form of business organisation. Within the consortium one firm may act as the managing contractor, while the other members may provide specialist services. Alternatively, management may be more equally shared.

Cooperatives

These are of two types.

Consumer cooperatives. These, like the old high street Co-ops, are officially owned by the consumers. Consumers in fact play no part in the running of these cooperatives. They are run by professional managers.

Producer cooperatives. These are firms that are owned by their workers, who share in the firm's profit according to some agreed formula. They are sometimes formed by people in the same trade coming together: for example, producers of handicraft goods. At other times they are formed by workers buying out their factory from the owners; this is most likely if it is due to close, with a resultant loss of jobs. Producer cooperatives, although still relatively few in number, have grown in recent years. One of the most famous is the department store chain, John Lewis, with its supermarket division, Waitrose.

Public corporations

These are state-owned enterprises such as the BBC, the Bank of England and nationalised industries.

Public corporations have a legal identity separate from the government. They are run by a board, but the members of the board are appointed by the relevant government minister. The boards have to act within various terms of reference laid down by Act of Parliament. Profits of public corporations that are not reinvested accrue to the Treasury. Since 1980 most public corporations have been 'privatised': that is, they have been sold directly to other firms in the private sector (such as Austin Rover to British Aerospace) or to the general public through a public issue of shares (such as British Gas). However, in response to turmoil in the financial markets, the UK government nationalised two banks in 2008, Northern Rock (see Box 15.3) and Bradford and Bingley.

The issue of privatisation is considered in Chapter 22.

3.3 THE INTERNAL ORGANISATION OF THE FIRM

Pause for thought

Before you read on, consider in what ways technology might influence the organisational structure of a business.

The internal operating structures of firms are frequently governed by their size. Small firms tend to be centrally managed, with decision making operating through a clear managerial hierarchy. In large firms, however, the organisational structure tends to be more complex, although technological change is forcing many organisations to reassess the most suitable organisational structure for their business.

Definition

U-form business organisation
One in which the central organisation of the firm (the chief executive or a managerial team) is responsible both for the firm's day-to-day administration and for formulating its business strategy.

U-form

In small to medium-sized firms, the managers of the various departments – marketing, finance, production, etc. – are normally directly responsible to a chief executive, whose function is to coordinate their activities: relaying the firm's overall strategy to them and being responsible for interdepartmental communication. We call this type of structure U (unitary) form (see Figure 3.1).

When firms expand beyond a certain size, however, a U-form structure is likely to become inefficient. This inefficiency arises from difficulties in communication, coordination and control. It becomes too difficult to manage the whole organisation from the centre. The problem is that the chief executive suffers from bounded

Figure 3.1 U-form business organisation

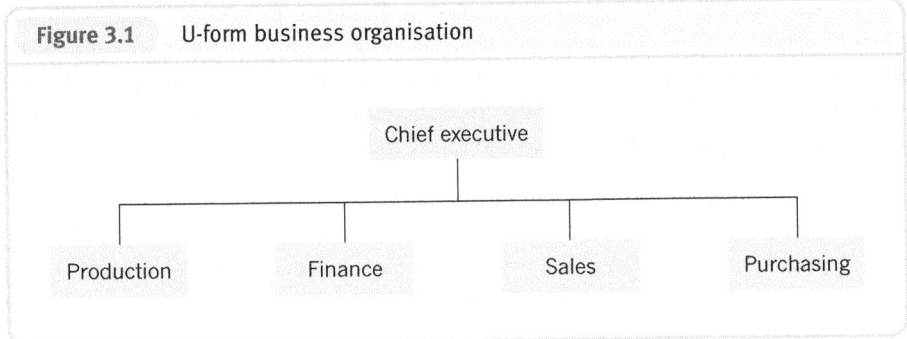

rationality – a limit on the rate at which information can be absorbed and processed. As the firm grows, more decisions are required. This leads to less time per decision and ultimately poorer decisions. The chief executive effectively loses control of the firm.

 Good decision making requires good information. Where information is poor, decisions and their outcomes may be poor.

In attempting to regain control, it is likely that a further managerial layer will be inserted. The chain of command thus becomes lengthened as the chief executive must now coordinate and communicate via this intermediate managerial level. This leads to the following problems:

- Communication costs increase.
- Messages and decisions may be misinterpreted and distorted.
- The firm experiences a decline in organisational efficiency as various departmental managers, freed from central control, seek to maximise their personal departmental goals.

M-form

To overcome these organisational problems, the firm can adopt an M (multi-divisional) form of managerial structure (see Figure 3.2).

> **Definitions**
>
> **Bounded rationality**
> Individuals are limited in their ability to absorb and process information. People think in ways conditioned by their experiences (family, education, peer groups, etc.).
>
> **M-form business organisation**
> One in which the business is organised into separate departments, such that responsibility for the day-to-day management enterprise is separated from the formulation of the business's strategic plan.

Figure 3.2 M-form business organisation

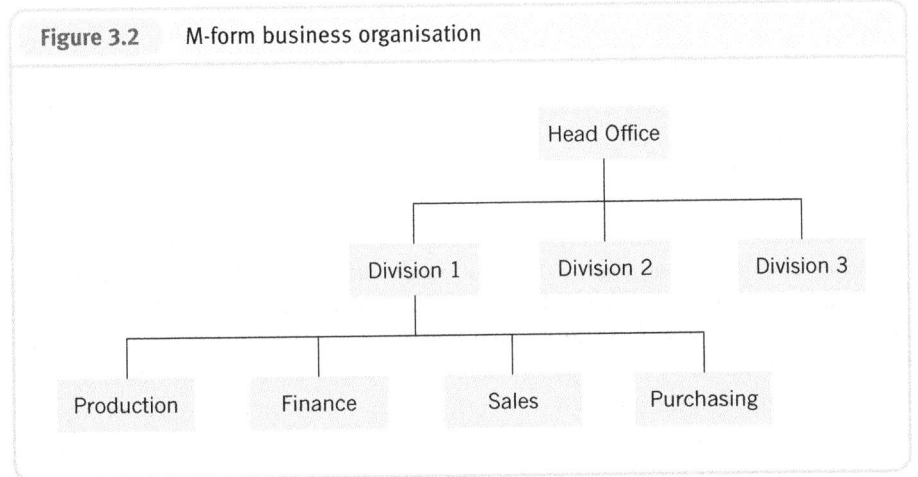

This suits medium to large firms. The firm is divided into a number of 'divisions'. Each division could be responsible for a particular product or group of products, or a particular market (e.g. a specific country). The day-to-day running and even certain long-term decisions of each division would be the responsibility of the divisional manager(s). This leads to the following benefits:

- Reduced length of information flows.
- The chief executive being able to concentrate on overall strategic planning.
- An enhanced level of control, with each division being run as a mini 'firm', competing with other divisions for the limited amount of company resources available.

The flat organisation

The shift towards the M-form organisational structure was primarily motivated by a desire to improve the process of decision making within the business. This involved adding layers of management. Recent technological innovations, especially in respect to computer systems such as e-mail and management information systems, have encouraged many organisations to think again about how to establish an efficient and effective organisational structure. The flat organisation is one that fully embraces the latest developments in information technology, and by so doing is able to reduce the need for a large group of middle managers. Senior managers, through these new information systems, can communicate easily and directly with those lower in the organisational structure. Middle managers are effectively bypassed.

The speed of information flows reduces the impact of bounded rationality on the decision-making process. Senior managers are able to re-establish and, in certain cases, widen their span of control over the business organisation.

In many respects the flat organisation represents a return to the U-form structure. It is yet to be seen whether we also have a return to the problems associated with this type of organisation.

Multinationals and business organisation

Further types of business organisation which we might identify are closely linked to the expansion and development of the multinational enterprise. Such organisational structures have developed as a response to these businesses attempting to control their business activities on a global scale. Three forms of multinational business organisation are identified below.

H-form. The H-form or holding company is in many respects a variation on the M-form structure. A holding company (or parent company) is one which owns a controlling interest in other subsidiary companies. These subsidiaries, in turn, may also have controlling interests in other companies.

H-form organisational structures can be highly complex. While the parent company has ultimate control over its various subsidiaries, it is likely that both tactical and strategic decision making is left to the individual companies within the organisation. Many multinationals are organised along the lines of an international holding company, where overseas subsidiaries pursue their own independent strategy. The Walt Disney Company (Holding Company) represents a good example of an H-form business organisation. Figure 3.3 shows the firm's organisational structure and the range of assets it owns.

> **Definitions**
>
> **Flat organisation**
> One in which technology enables senior managers to communicate directly with those lower in the organisational structure. Middle managers are bypassed.
>
> **Holding company**
> A business organisation in which the present company holds interests in a number of other companies or subsidiaries.

Business Organisations 13

Figure 3.3 Organisational structure of The Walt Disney Company (Holding Company)

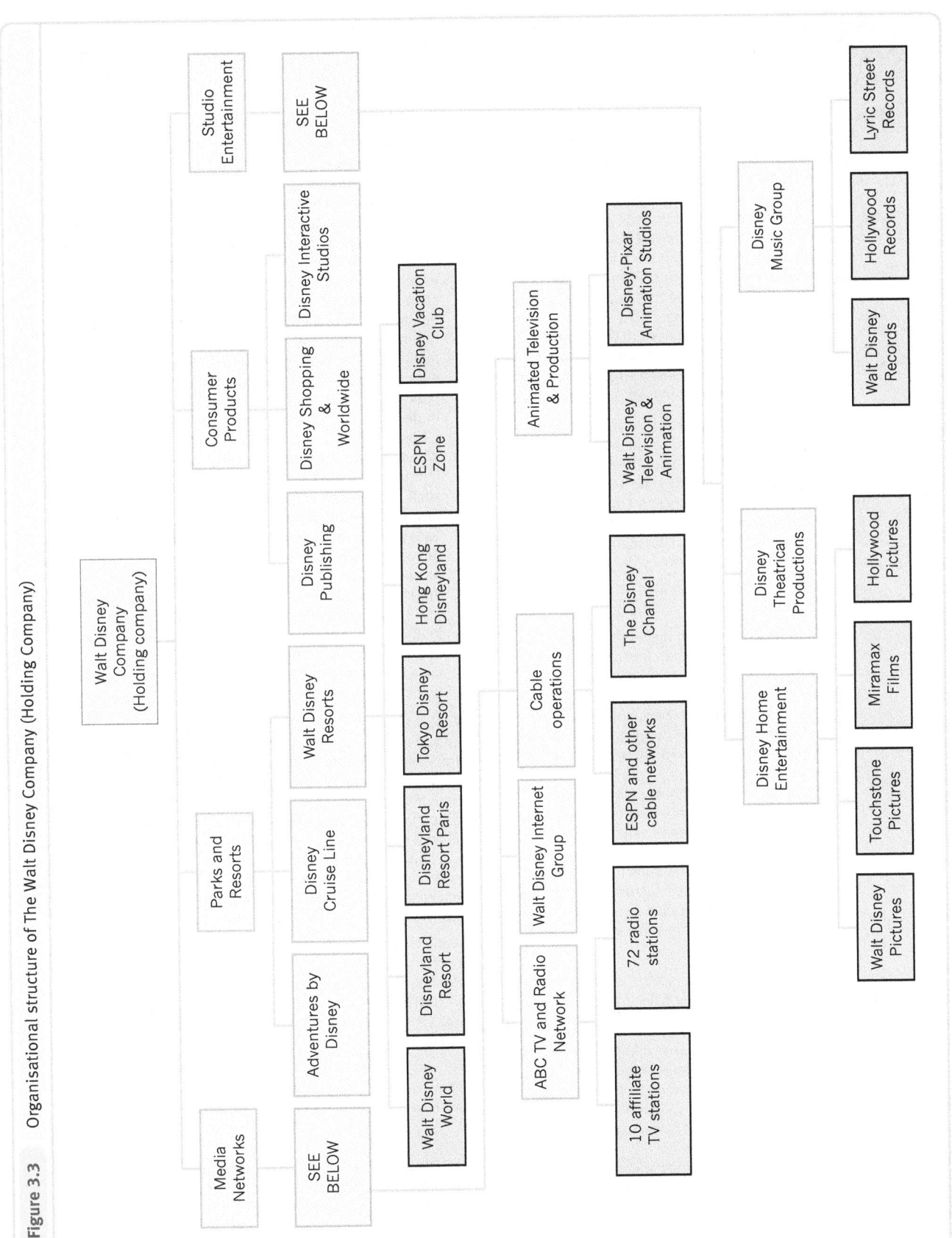

BOX 3.2 THE CHANGING NATURE OF BUSINESS

Knowledge rules

In the knowledge-driven economy, innovation has become central to achievement in the business world. With this growth in importance, organisations large and small have begun to re-evaluate their products, their services, even their corporate culture in the attempt to maintain their competitiveness in the global markets of today. The more forward-thinking companies have recognised that only through such root and branch reform can they hope to survive in the face of increasing competition.

European Commission, Directorate-General for Enterprise, *Innovation Management and the Knowledge-Driven Economy* (ECSC-EC-EAEC Brussels-Luxembourg, 2004)

Knowledge is fundamental to economic success in many industries, and for most firms, key knowledge resides in skilled members of the workforce. The result is a market in knowledge, with those having the knowledge being able to command high salaries and often being 'head hunted'. The 'knowledge economy' is affecting people from all walks of life, and fundamentally changing the nature, organisation and practice of business.

The traditional business corporation was based around five fundamental principles:

- Individual workers needed the business and the income it provided more than the business needed them. After all, employers could always find alternative workers. As such, the corporation was the dominant partner in the employment relationship.
- Employees who worked for the corporation tended to be full time, and depended upon the work as their sole source of income.
- The corporation was integrated, with a single management structure overseeing all the various stages of production. This was seen as the most efficient way to organise productive activity.
- Suppliers, and especially manufacturers, had considerable power over the customer by controlling information about their product or service.
- Technology relevant to an industry was developed within the industry.

In more recent times, with the advent of the knowledge economy, the principles above have all but been turned on their head.

- The key factor of production in a knowledge economy is knowledge itself, and the workers that hold such knowledge. Without such workers, the corporation is unlikely to succeed. As such, the balance of power between the business and the worker in today's economy is far more equal.
- Even though the vast majority of employees still work full time, the diversity in employment contracts, such as part-time and short-term contracts and consultancy, means that full-time work is not the only option. (We examine this in section 18.7.) The result is an increasing number of workers offering their services to business in non-conventional ways.
- As the domestic economy increasingly spills into the global economy, the complexity of the marketplace facing business means that few businesses have the expertise to provide an integrated product. With communication costs that are largely insignificant, businesses are likely to be more efficient and flexible if they outsource and de-integrate. Not only are businesses outsourcing various stages of production, but many are employing specialist companies to provide key areas of management, such as HRM (human resource management): hiring, firing, training, benefits, etc.
- Whereas in the past businesses controlled information, today access to information via sources such as the Internet means that power is shifting towards the consumer.
- Today, unlike in previous decades, technological developments are less specific to industries. Knowledge developments diffuse and cut across industry boundaries. What this means for business, in a knowledge-driven economy, is that they must look beyond their own industry if they are to develop and grow. We frequently see partnerships and joint ventures between businesses that cut across industry types and technology.

What is clear from the above is that the dynamics of the knowledge economy require a quite fundamental change in the nature of business. Organisationally it needs to be more flexible, helping it to respond to the ever-changing market conditions it faces. Successful companies draw upon their *core* competencies to achieve market advantage, and thus ultimately specialise in what they do best. Businesses must learn to work with others, either through outsourcing specialist tasks, or through more formal strategic partnerships.

Within this new business model the key assets are the specialist people in the organisation – its knowledge workers. How will businesses attract, retain and motivate the best? Will financial rewards be sufficient, or will workers seek more from their work and the organisation they work for?

With such issues facing the corporation we can expect to see a radical reinterpretation of what business looks like and how it is practised over the coming years.

How is the development of the knowledge economy likely to affect the distribution of wage income? Will it become more equal or less equal?

Integrated international enterprise. The integrated international enterprise is an organisational structure where a company's international subsidiaries, rather than pursuing independent business strategies, coordinate and integrate their activities in pursuit of shared corporate aims and objectives. The coordination of such activities can be either at a regional level – for example, within the European market – or on a truly global scale. In such an organisation, the distinction between parent company and subsidiary is of less relevance than the identification of a clear corporate philosophy which dominates business goals and policy.

Transnational association. A further form of multinational business organisation is the transnational association. Here the business headquarters holds little equity investment in its subsidiaries. These are largely owned and managed by local people. These subsidiaries receive from the headquarters managerial and technical assistance, in exchange for contractual agreements that output produced by the subsidiary is sold to the headquarters. Such output is most likely to take the form of product components rather than finished products. The headquarters then acts as an assembler, marketer or distributor of such output, or some combination of all three. The main advantage of organising international business in this way is that it reduces costs. This form of organisation is known as global sourcing and involves the international business using distinct production sites to produce large numbers of single components. With the transnational association, the headquarters still retains the decisive role in integrating business activity.

The organisational structures and issues surrounding multinational corporations will be investigated more fully in Chapter 23.

> **Definitions**
>
> **Integrated international enterprise**
> One in which an international company pursues a single business strategy. It coordinates the business activities of its subsidiaries across different countries.
>
> **Transnational association**
> A form of business organisation in which the subsidiaries of a company in different countries are contractually bound to the parent company to provide output to or receive inputs from other subsidiaries.
>
> **Global sourcing**
> Where a company uses production sites in different parts of the world to provide particular components for a final product.

SUMMARY

1a The firm's role in the economy is to eliminate the need for making individual contracts through the market, and to provide a more efficient way to organise production.

1b Using the market to establish a contract is not costless. Transaction costs will mean that the market is normally less efficient than the firm as an allocator of resources.

1c The divorce of ownership from control implies that the objectives of owners and managers may diverge, and similarly the objectives of one manager from another. Hence the goals of firms may be diverse. What is more, as ownership becomes more dispersed, so the degree of control by owners diminishes yet further.

1d Managers might pursue maximisation goals other than profit, or look to achieve a wide range of targets in which profit acts as a constraint on other business aims.

1e The problem of managers not pursuing the same goals as the owners is an example of the *principal–agent problem*. Agents (in this case the managers) may not always carry out the wishes of their principals (in this case the owners). Because of asymmetric information, managers are able to pursue their own aims, just so long as they produce results that will satisfy the owners. The solution for owners is for there to be better means of monitoring the performance of managers, and incentives for the managers to behave in the owners' interests.

2a The legal status of the firm will influence both its actions and performance within the marketplace.

2b There are several types of legal organisation of firms: the sole proprietorship, the partnership, the private limited company, the public limited company, consortia of firms, cooperatives and public corporations. In the first two cases, the owners have unlimited liability: the owners are personally liable for any losses the business might make. With companies, however, shareholders' liability is limited to the amount they have invested. This reduced risk encourages people to invest in companies.

3a The relative success of a business organisation will be strongly influenced by its organisational structure. As a firm grows, its organisational structure will need to evolve in order to account for the business's growing complexity. This is particularly so if the business looks to expand overseas.

3b As firms grow, so they tend to move from a U-form to an M-form structure. In recent years, however, with the advance of information technology, many firms have adopted a flat organisation – a return to U-form.

3c Multinational companies often adopt relatively complex forms of organisation. These vary from a holding company (H-form) structure, to the integrated international enterprise, to transnational associations.

REVIEW QUESTIONS

1 What is meant by the term 'transaction costs'? Explain why the firm represents a more efficient way of organising economic life than relying on individual contracts.

2 Explain why the business objectives of owners and managers are likely to diverge. How might owners attempt to ensure that managers act in their interests and not in the managers' own interests?

3 Compare and contrast the relative strengths and weaknesses of the partnership and the public limited company.

4 Conduct an investigation into a recent large building project, such as the 2012 London Olympics. Identify what firms were involved and the roles and responsibilities they had. Outline the advantages and disadvantages that such business consortia might have.

5 If a business is thinking of reorganisation, why and in what ways might new technology be an important factor in such considerations?

6 What problems are multinational corporations, as opposed to domestic firms, likely to have in respect to organising their business activity? What alternative organisational models might multinationals adopt? To what extent do they overcome the problems you have identified?

Additional Part A case studies on the *Economics for Business* website (www.pearsoned.co.uk/sloman)

A.1 **The UK defence industry.** A PEST analysis of the changes in the defence industry in recent years.

A.2 **Scarcity and abundance.** If scarcity is the central economic problem, is anything truly abundant?

A.3 **Global economics.** This examines how macroeconomics and microeconomics apply at the global level and identifies some key issues.

A.4 **Buddhist economics.** A different perspective on economic problems and economic activity.

A.5 **Downsizing and business reorganisation.** Many companies in recent years have 'downsized' their operations and focused on their core competencies. This looks particularly at the case of IBM.

Websites relevant to Part A

Numbers and sections refer to websites listed in the Web appendix and hotlinked from this book's website at **www.pearsoned.co.uk/sloman**

- For a tutorial on finding the best economics websites, see site C8 (*The Internet Economist*).
- For news articles relevant to Part A, see the *Economics News Articles* link from the book's website.
- For general economics news sources, see websites in section A of the Web appendix at the end of the book, and particularly A1–9, 24, 38, 39. See also A38, 39 and 43 for links to newspapers worldwide; and A42 for links to economics news articles from newspapers worldwide.
- For business news items, again see websites in section A of the Web appendix at the end of the book, and particularly A1–3, 20–26, 35, 36.
- For sources of economic and business data, see sites in section B and particularly B1–4, 33, 34.
- For general sites for students of economics for business, see sites in section C and particularly C1–7.
- For sites giving links to relevant economics and business websites, organised by topic, see sites I4, 7, 8, 11, 12, 17, 18.
- For details on companies, see sites B2 and A3.

Chapter 4

The working of competitive markets

> **Business issues covered in this chapter**
>
> - How do markets operate?
> - How are market prices determined and when are they likely to rise or fall?
> - Under what circumstances do firms have to accept a price given by the market rather than being able to set the price themselves?
> - What are the influences on consumer demand?
> - What factors determine the amount of supply coming on to the market?
> - How do markets respond to changes in demand or supply?

4.1 BUSINESS IN A COMPETITIVE MARKET

If a firm wants to increase its profits, should it raise its prices, or should it lower them? Should it increase its output, or should it reduce it? Should it modify its product, or should it keep the product unchanged? The answer to these and many other questions is that it depends on the market in which the firm operates. If the market is buoyant, it may well be a good idea for the firm to increase its output in anticipation of greater sales. It may also be a good idea to raise the price of its product in the belief that consumers will be willing to pay more. If, however, the market is declining, the firm may well decide to reduce output, or cut prices, or diversify across into an alternative product.

The firm is thus greatly affected by its market environment, an environment that is often outside the firm's control and subject to frequent changes. For many firms, prices are determined not by them, but by the market. Even where they do have some influence over prices, the influence is only slight. They may be able to put prices up a small amount, but if they raise them too much, they will find that they lose sales to their rivals.

The market dominates a firm's activities. The more competitive the market, the greater this domination becomes. In the extreme case, the firm may have no power at all to change its price: it is what we call a price taker. It has to accept the market price as given. If the firm attempts to raise the price above the market price, it will simply be unable to sell its product: it will lose all its sales to its competitors. Take the case of farmers selling wheat. They have to accept the price as dictated by the market. If individually they try to sell above the market price, no one will buy.

In competitive markets, consumers too are price takers. When we go into shops we have no control over prices. We have to accept the price as given. For example, when you get to the supermarket checkout, you cannot start haggling with the checkout operator over the price of a can of beans or a tub of margarine.

So how does a competitive market work? For simplicity we will examine the case of a perfectly competitive market. This is where both producers and consumers are too numerous to have any control over prices whatsoever: a situation where everyone is a price taker.

(Clearly, in other markets, firms will have some discretion over the prices they charge. For example, a manufacturing company such as Ford will have some discretion over the prices it charges for its Fiestas or Mondeos. In such cases the firm has some 'market power'. We will examine different degrees of market power in Chapters 11 and 12.)

The price mechanism

In a free market individuals are free to make their own economic decisions. Consumers are free to decide what to buy with their incomes: free to make demand decisions. Firms are free to choose what to sell and what production methods to use: free to make supply decisions. The resulting demand and supply decisions of consumers and firms are transmitted to each other through their effect on *prices*: through the price mechanism.

The price mechanism works as follows. Prices respond to *shortages* and *surpluses*. Shortages cause prices to rise. Surpluses cause prices to fall.

If consumers decide they want more of a good (or if producers decide to cut back supply), demand will exceed supply. The resulting *shortage* will cause *the price of the good to rise*. This will act as an incentive to producers to supply more, since production will now be more profitable. At the same time, it will discourage consumers from buying so much. *The price will continue rising until the shortage has thereby been eliminated*.

If, on the other hand, consumers decide they want less of a good (or if producers decide to produce more), supply will exceed demand. The resulting *surplus* will cause *the price of the good to fall*. This will act as a disincentive to producers, who will supply less, since production will now be less profitable. It will encourage consumers to buy more. *The price will continue falling until the surplus has thereby been eliminated*.

This price, where demand equals supply, is called the equilibrium price. By equilibrium we mean a point of balance or a point of rest: in other words, a point towards which there is a tendency to move.

The same analysis can be applied to labour (and other factor) markets, except that here the demand and supply roles are reversed. Firms are the demanders of labour. Households are the suppliers. If the demand for a particular type of labour exceeded its supply, the resulting shortage would drive up the wage rate (i.e. the price of labour), thus reducing firms' demand for that type of labour and encouraging more workers to take up that type of job. Wages would continue rising until demand equalled supply: until the shortage was eliminated.

Definitions

Price taker
A person or firm with no power to be able to influence the market price.

Perfectly competitive market (preliminary definition)
A market in which all producers and consumers of the product are price takers. (There are other features of a perfectly competitive market; these are examined in Chapter 11.)

Free market
One in which there is an absence of government intervention. Individual producers and consumers are free to make their own economic decisions.

The price mechanism
The system in a market economy whereby changes in price in response to changes in demand and supply have the effect of making demand equal to supply.

Equilibrium price
The price where the quantity demanded equals the quantity supplied: the price where there is no shortage or surplus.

Equilibrium
A position of balance. A position from which there is no inherent tendency to move away.

Likewise if there were a surplus of a particular type of labour, the wage would fall until demand equalled supply. As with price, the wage rate where the demand for labour equals the supply is known as the *equilibrium* wage rate.

The response of demand and supply to changes in price illustrates a very important feature of how economies work.

People respond to incentives. It is important, therefore, that incentives are appropriate and have the desired effect.

The effect of changes in demand and supply

How will the price mechanism respond to changes in consumer demand or producer supply? After all, the pattern of consumer demand changes over time. For example, people may decide they want more downloadable tracks and fewer CDs. Likewise the pattern of supply also changes. For example, changes in technology may allow the mass production of microchips at lower cost, while the production of hand-built furniture becomes relatively expensive.

In all cases of changes in demand and supply, the resulting changes in *price* act as both *signals* and *incentives*.

A change in demand

A rise in demand is signalled by a rise in price. This then acts as an incentive for firms to produce more of the good: the quantity supplied rises. Firms divert resources from goods with lower prices relative to costs (and hence lower profits) to those goods that are more profitable.

A fall in demand is signalled by a fall in price. This then acts as an incentive for firms to produce less: such goods are now less profitable to produce.

A change in supply

A rise in supply is signalled by a fall in price. This then acts as an incentive for consumers to buy more: the quantity demanded rises. A fall in supply is signalled by a rise in price. This then acts as an incentive for consumers to buy less: the quantity demanded falls.

Changes in demand or supply cause markets to adjust. Whenever such changes occur, the resulting 'disequilibrium' will bring an automatic change in prices, thereby restoring equilibrium (i.e. a balance of demand and supply).

The interdependence of markets

The interdependence of goods and factor markets

A rise in demand for a good will raise its price and profitability. Firms will respond by supplying more. But to do this they will require more inputs. Thus the demand for the inputs will rise, which, in turn, will raise the price of the inputs. The suppliers of inputs will respond to this incentive by supplying more. This can be summarised as follows:

Goods market

- Demand for the good rises.
- This creates a shortage.
- This causes the price of the good to rise.
- This eliminates the shortage by choking off some of the demand and encouraging firms to produce more.

Factor market

- The increased supply of the good causes an increase in the demand for factors of production (i.e. inputs) used in making it.
- This causes a shortage of those inputs.
- This causes their prices to rise.
- This eliminates their shortage by choking off some of the demand and encouraging the suppliers of inputs to supply more.

Goods markets thus affect factor markets. Figure 4.1 summarises this sequence of events. (It is common in economics to summarise an argument like this by using symbols.)

Interdependence exists in the other direction too: factor markets affect goods markets. For example, the discovery of raw materials will lower their price. This will lower the costs of production of firms using these raw materials and increase the supply of the finished goods. The resulting surplus will lower the price of the good, which, in turn, will encourage consumers to buy more.

The interdependence of different goods markets

A rise in the price of one good will encourage consumers to buy alternatives. This will drive up the price of alternatives. This in turn will encourage producers to supply more of the alternatives.

Let us now turn to examine each side of the market – demand and supply – in more detail.

Figure 4.1 The price mechanism: the effect of a rise in demand

Goods market

$D_g \uparrow \longrightarrow$ shortage $\longrightarrow P_g \uparrow \begin{array}{c} \nearrow S_g \uparrow \\ \searrow D_g \downarrow \end{array}$ until $D_g = S_g$
$(D_g > S_g)$

Factor market

$S_g \uparrow \longrightarrow D_i \uparrow \longrightarrow$ shortage $\longrightarrow P_i \uparrow \begin{array}{c} \nearrow S_i \uparrow \\ \searrow D_i \downarrow \end{array}$ until $D_i = S_i$
$(D_i > S_i)$

(where D = demand, S = supply, P = price, g = the good, i = inputs, $\longrightarrow$ means 'leads to')

DEMAND

4.2

The relationship between demand and price

The headlines announce, 'Major crop failures in Brazil and East Africa: coffee prices soar.' Shortly afterwards you find that coffee prices have doubled in the shops. What do you do? Presumably you will cut back on the amount of coffee you drink. Perhaps you will reduce it from, say, six cups per day to two. Perhaps you will give up drinking coffee altogether.

This is simply an illustration of the general relationship between price and consumption: *when the price of a good rises, the quantity demanded will fall*. This relationship is known as the law of demand. There are two reasons for this law:

- People will feel poorer. They will not be able to afford to buy so much of the good with their money. The purchasing power of their income (their *real income*) has fallen. This is called the income effect of a price rise.
- The good will now be dearer relative to other goods. People will thus switch to alternative or 'substitute' goods. This is called the substitution effect of a price rise.

Similarly, when the price of a good falls, the quantity demanded will rise. People can afford to buy more (the income effect), and they will switch away from consuming alternative goods (the substitution effect).

Therefore, returning to our example of the increase in the price of coffee, we will not be able to afford to buy as much as before, and we will probably drink more tea, cocoa, fruit juices or even water instead.

A word of warning: be careful about the meaning of the words quantity demanded. They refer to the amount consumers are willing and able to purchase at a given price over a given time period (for example, a week, or a month, or a year). They do *not* refer to what people would simply *like* to consume. You might like to own a luxury yacht, but your demand for luxury yachts will almost certainly be zero.

The demand curve

Consider the hypothetical data in Table 4.1. The table shows how many kilos of potatoes per month would be purchased at various prices.

Columns (2) and (3) show the demand schedules for two individuals, Tracey and Darren. Column (4), by contrast, shows the total market demand schedule. This is the total demand by all consumers. To obtain the market demand schedule for

> **Definitions**
>
> **The law of demand**
> The quantity of a good demanded per period of time will fall as the price rises and rise as the price falls, other things being equal (*ceteris paribus*).
>
> **Income effect**
> The effect of a change in price on quantity demanded arising from the consumer becoming better or worse off as a result of the price change.
>
> **Substitution effect**
> The effect of a change in price on quantity demanded arising from the consumer switching to or from alternative (substitute) products.
>
> **Quantity demanded**
> The amount of a good that a consumer is willing and able to buy at a given price over a given period of time.
>
> **Demand schedule for an individual**
> A table showing the different quantities of a good that a person is willing and able to buy at various prices over a given period of time.
>
> **Market demand schedule**
> A table showing the different total quantities of a good that consumers are willing and able to buy at various prices over a given period of time.

Table 4.1 The demand for potatoes (monthly)

	Price (pence per kg) (1)	Tracey's demand (kg) (2)	Darren's demand (kg) (3)	Total market demand (tonnes: 000s) (4)
A	20	28	16	700
B	40	15	11	500
C	60	5	9	350
D	80	1	7	200
E	100	0	6	100

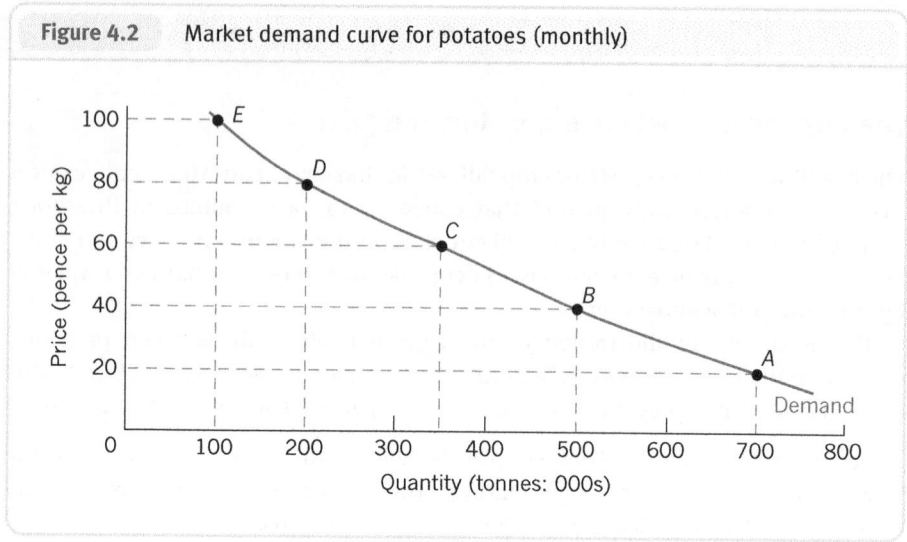

Figure 4.2 Market demand curve for potatoes (monthly)

potatoes, we simply add up the quantities demanded at each price by *all* consumers: i.e. Tracey, Darren and everyone else who demands potatoes. Notice that we are talking about demand *over a period of time* (not at a *point* in time). Thus we would talk about daily demand or weekly demand or annual demand or whatever.

The demand schedule can be represented graphically as a **demand curve**. Figure 4.2 shows the market demand curve for potatoes corresponding to the schedule in Table 4.1. The price of potatoes is plotted on the vertical axis. The quantity demanded is plotted on the horizontal axis.

Point *E* shows that at a price of 100p per kilo, 100 000 tonnes of potatoes are demanded each month. When the price falls to 80p we move down the curve to point *D*. This shows that the quantity demanded has now risen to 200 000 tonnes per month. Similarly, if price falls to 60p, we move down the curve again to point *C*: 350 000 tonnes are now demanded. The five points on the graph (*A–E*) correspond to the figures in columns (1) and (4) of Table 4.1. The graph also enables us to read off the likely quantities demanded at prices other than those in the table.

A demand curve could also be drawn for an individual consumer. Like market demand curves, individuals' demand curves generally slope downward from left to right (they have negative slope): the lower the price of a product, the more is a person likely to buy.

Two points should be noted at this stage:

- In textbooks, demand curves (and other curves too) are only occasionally used to plot specific data. More frequently they are used to illustrate general theoretical arguments. In such cases the axes will simply be price and quantity, with the units unspecified.
- The term 'curve' is used even when the graph is a straight line! In fact, when using demand curves to illustrate arguments we frequently draw them as straight lines – it's easier.

Other determinants of demand

Price is not the only factor that determines how much of a good people will buy. Demand is also affected by the following.

> **Definition**
>
> **Demand curve**
> A graph showing the relationship between the price of a good and the quantity of the good demanded over a given time period. Price is measured on the vertical axis; quantity demanded is measured on the horizontal axis. A demand curve can be for an individual consumer or a group of consumers, or more usually for the whole market.

Tastes. The more desirable people find the good, the more they will demand. Tastes are affected by advertising, by fashion, by observing other consumers, by considerations of health and by the experiences from consuming the good on previous occasions.

The number and price of substitute goods (i.e. competitive goods). The higher the price of substitute goods, the higher will be the demand for this good as people switch from the substitutes. For example, the demand for coffee will depend on the price of tea. If tea goes up in price, the demand for coffee will rise.

The number and price of complementary goods. Complementary goods are those that are consumed together: cars and petrol, shoes and polish, bread and butter. The higher the price of complementary goods, the fewer of them will be bought and hence the less the demand for this good. For example, the demand for compact discs will depend on the price of CD players. If the price of CD players goes up, so that fewer are bought, the demand for CDs will fall.

Income. As people's incomes rise, their demand for most goods will rise. Such goods are called normal goods. There are exceptions to this general rule, however. As people get richer, they spend less on inferior goods, such as cheap margarine, and switch to better-quality goods.

Distribution of income. If, for example, national income were redistributed from the poor to the rich, the demand for luxury goods would rise. At the same time, as the poor got poorer, they might have to turn to buying inferior goods, whose demand would thus rise too.

Expectations of future price changes. If people think that prices are going to rise in the future, they are likely to buy more now before the price does go up.

Movements along and shifts in the demand curve

A demand curve is constructed on the assumption that 'other things remain equal' (*ceteris paribus*). In other words, it is assumed that none of the determinants of demand, other than price, changes. The effect of a change in price is then simply illustrated by a movement along the demand curve: for example, from point *B* to point *D* in Figure 4.2 when price rises from 40p to 80p per kilo.

What happens, then, when one of these other determinants does change? The answer is that we have to construct a whole new demand curve: the curve shifts. If a change in one of the other determinants causes demand to rise – say, income rises – the whole curve will shift to the right. This shows that at each price more will be demanded than before. Thus in Figure 4.3 at a price of P, a quantity of Q_0 was originally demanded. But now, after the increase in demand, Q_1 is demanded. (Note that D_1 is not necessarily parallel to D_0.)

If a change in a determinant other than price causes demand to fall, the whole curve will shift to the left.

To distinguish between shifts in and movements along demand curves, it is usual to distinguish between a change in *demand* and a change in the *quantity demanded*. A shift in demand is referred to as a change in demand, whereas a movement along the demand curve as a result of a change in price is referred to as a change in the quantity demanded.

Definitions

Substitute goods
A pair of goods which are considered by consumers to be alternatives to each other. As the price of one goes up, the demand for the other rises.

Complementary goods
A pair of goods consumed together. As the price of one goes up, the demand for both goods will fall.

Normal goods
Goods whose demand rises as people's incomes rise.

Inferior goods
Goods whose demand falls as people's incomes rise.

Pause for thought

1 By referring to each of these six determinants of demand, consider what factors would cause a rise in the demand for butter.
2 Do all these six determinants of demand affect both an individual's demand and the market demand for a product?

Definitions

Change in demand
The term used for a shift in the demand curve. It occurs when a determinant of demand *other* than price changes.

Change in the quantity demanded
The term used for a movement along the demand curve to a new point. It occurs when there is a change in price.

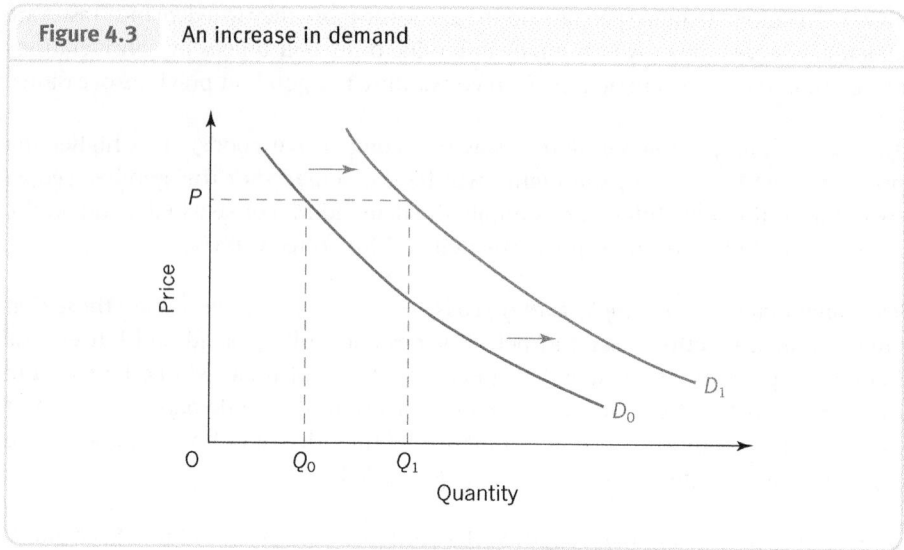

Figure 4.3 An increase in demand

4.3 SUPPLY

Supply and price

Imagine you are a farmer deciding what to do with your land. Part of your land is in a fertile valley. Part is on a hillside where the soil is poor. Perhaps, then, you will consider growing vegetables in the valley and keeping sheep on the hillside.

Your decision will depend to a large extent on the price that various vegetables will fetch in the market, and likewise the price you can expect to get from sheep and wool. As far as the valley is concerned, you will plant the vegetables that give the best return. If, for example, the price of potatoes is high, you will probably use a lot of the valley for growing potatoes. If the price gets higher, you may well use the whole of the valley, perhaps being prepared to run the risk of potato disease. If the price is very high indeed, you may even consider growing potatoes on the hillside, even though the yield per acre is much lower there. In other words, the higher the price of a particular crop, the more you are likely to grow in preference to other crops.

This illustrates the general relationship between supply and price: *when the price of a good rises, the quantity supplied will also rise.* There are three reasons for this:

- As firms supply more, they are likely to find that, beyond a certain level of output, costs rise more and more rapidly. Only if price rises will it be worth producing more and incurring these higher costs.

  In the case of the farm we have just considered, once potatoes have to be grown on the hillside, the costs of producing them will increase. Also if the land has to be used more intensively, say by the use of more and more fertilisers, again the cost of producing extra potatoes is likely to rise quite rapidly. It is the same for manufacturers. Beyond a certain level of output, costs are likely to rise rapidly as workers have to be paid overtime and as machines approach their full capacity. If higher output involves higher costs of production, producers will need to get a higher price if they are to be persuaded to produce extra output.

- The higher the price of the good, the more profitable it becomes to produce. Firms will thus be encouraged to produce more of it by switching from producing less profitable goods.
- Given time, if the price of a good remains high, new producers will be encouraged to set up in production. Total market supply thus rises.

The first two determinants affect supply in the short run. The third affects supply in the long run. We distinguish between short-run and long-run supply later, in section 5.4.

The supply curve

The amount that producers would like to supply at various prices can be shown in a **supply schedule**. Table 4.2 shows a monthly supply schedule for potatoes, both for an individual farmer (farmer X) and for all farmers together (the whole market).

The supply schedule can be represented graphically as a **supply curve**. A supply curve may be an individual firm's supply curve or a market supply curve (i.e. that of the whole industry).

Figure 4.4 shows the *market* supply curve of potatoes. As with demand curves, price is plotted on the vertical axis and quantity on the horizontal axis. Each of the points *a–e* corresponds to a figure in Table 4.2. Thus for example, a price rise from 60 p per kilogram to 80 p per kilogram will cause a movement along the supply

> **Definitions**
>
> **Supply schedule**
> A table showing the different quantities of a good that producers are willing and able to supply at various prices over a given time period. A supply schedule can be for an individual producer or group of producers, or for all producers (the market supply schedule).
>
> **Supply curve**
> A graph showing the relationship between the price of a good and the quantity of the good supplied over a given period of time.

Table 4.2 The supply of potatoes (monthly)

	Price of potatoes (pence per kg)	Farmer X's supply (tonnes)	Total market supply (tonnes: 000s)
a	20	50	100
b	40	70	200
c	60	100	350
d	80	120	530
e	100	130	700

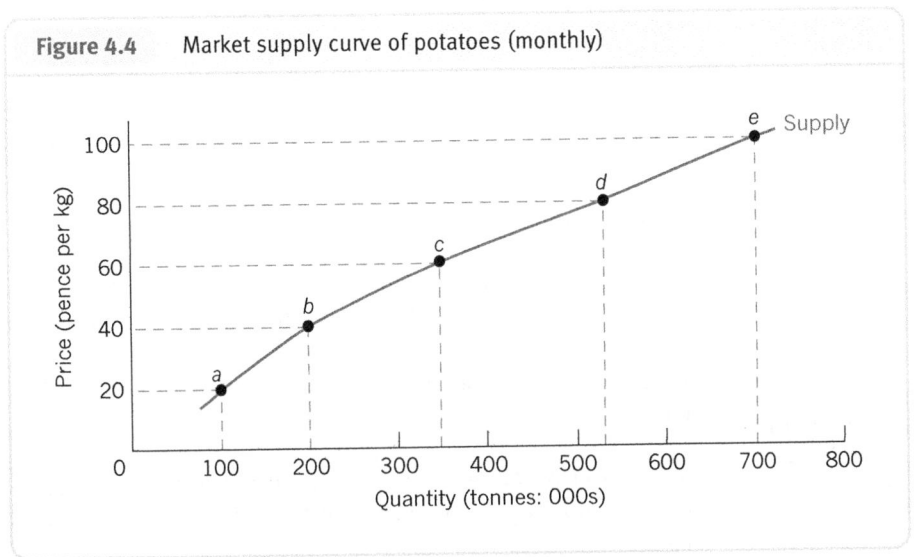

Figure 4.4 Market supply curve of potatoes (monthly)

> **Pause for thought**
>
> 1. How much would be supplied at a price of 70p per kilo?
> 2. Draw a supply curve for farmer X. Are the axes drawn to the same scale as in Figure 4.4?

curve from point *c* to point *d*: total market supply will rise from 350 000 tonnes per month to 530 000 tonnes per month.

Not all supply curves will be upward sloping (positively sloped). Sometimes they will be vertical, or horizontal, or even downward sloping. This will depend largely on the time period over which firms' response to price changes is considered. This question is examined in the next chapter (pages 89–91).

Other determinants of supply

Like demand, supply is not determined simply by price. The other determinants of supply are as follows.

The costs of production. The higher the costs of production, the less profit will be made at any price. As costs rise, firms will cut back on production, probably switching to alternative products whose costs have not risen so much.

The main reasons for a change in costs are as follows:

- Change in input prices: costs of production will rise if wages, raw material prices, rents, interest rates or any other input prices rise.
- Change in technology: technological advances can fundamentally alter the costs of production. Consider, for example, how the microchip revolution has changed production methods and information handling in virtually every industry in the world.
- Organisational changes: various cost savings can be made in many firms by reorganising production.
- Government policy: costs will be lowered by government subsidies and raised by various taxes.

> **Definitions**
>
> **Substitutes in supply**
> These are two goods where an increased production of one means diverting resources away from producing the other.
>
> **Goods in joint supply**
> These are two goods where the production of more of one leads to the production of more of the other.

The profitability of alternative products (substitutes in supply). If some alternative product (a **substitute in supply**) becomes more profitable to supply than before, producers are likely to switch from the first good to this alternative. Supply of the first good falls. Other goods are likely to become more profitable if their prices rise or their costs of production fall. For example, if the price of carrots goes up, or the cost of producing carrots comes down, farmers may decide to produce more carrots. The supply of potatoes is therefore likely to fall.

The profitability of goods in joint supply. Sometimes when one good is produced, another good is also produced at the same time. These are said to be **goods in joint supply**. An example is the refining of crude oil to produce petrol. Other grade fuels will be produced as well, such as diesel and paraffin. If more petrol is produced, due to a rise in demand, then the supply of these other fuels will rise too.

Nature, 'random shocks' and other unpredictable events. In this category we would include the weather and diseases affecting farm output, wars affecting the supply of imported raw materials, the breakdown of machinery, industrial disputes, earthquakes, floods and fire, etc.

> **Pause for thought**
>
> By reference to each of the above determinants of supply, identify what would cause (a) the supply of potatoes to fall and (b) the supply of leather to rise.

The aims of producers. A profit-maximising firm will supply a different quantity from a firm that has a different aim, such as maximising sales.

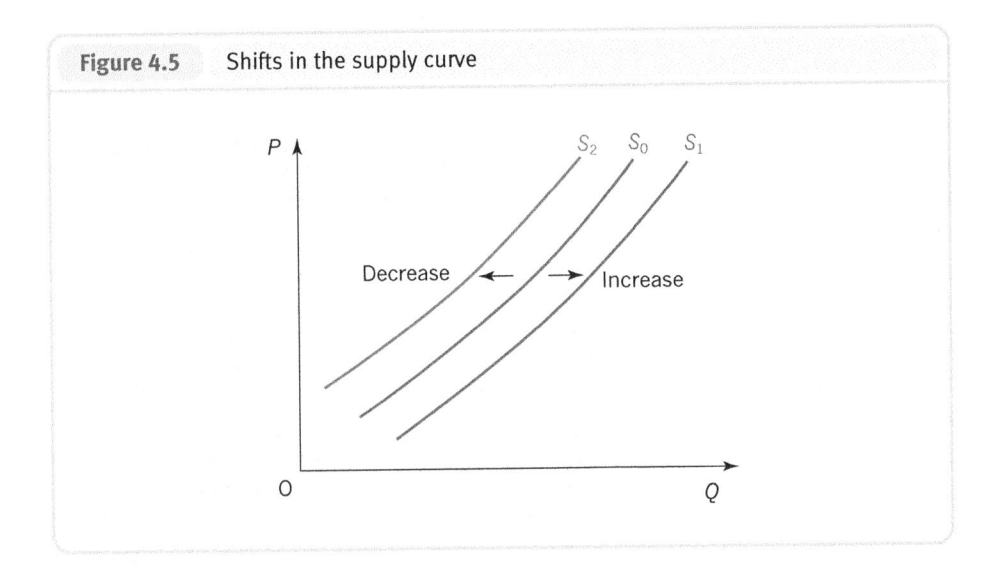

Figure 4.5 Shifts in the supply curve

Expectations of future price changes. If price is expected to rise, producers may temporarily reduce the amount they sell. Instead they are likely to build up their stocks and only release them on to the market when the price does rise. At the same time they may plan to produce more, by installing new machines, or taking on more labour, so that they can be ready to supply more when the price has risen.

The number of suppliers. If new firms enter the market, supply is likely to rise.

Movements along and shifts in the supply curve

The principle here is the same as with demand curves. The effect of a change in price is illustrated by a movement along the supply curve: for example, from point *d* to point *e* in Figure 4.4 when price rises from 80p to 100p. Quantity supplied rises from 530 000 to 700 000 tonnes.

If any other determinant of supply changes, the whole supply curve will shift. A rightward shift illustrates an increase in supply. A leftward shift illustrates a decrease in supply. Thus in Figure 4.5, if the original curve is S_0, the curve S_1 represents an increase in supply (more is supplied at each price), whereas the curve S_2 represents a decrease in supply (less is supplied at each price).

A movement along a supply curve is often referred to as a change in the quantity supplied, whereas a shift in the supply curve is simply referred to as a change in supply.

> **Definitions**
>
> **Change in the quantity supplied**
> The term used for a movement along the supply curve to a new point. It occurs when there is a change in price.
>
> **Change in supply**
> The term used for a shift in the supply curve. It occurs when a determinant other than price changes.

PRICE AND OUTPUT DETERMINATION 4.4

Equilibrium price and output

We can now combine our analysis of demand and supply. This will show how the actual price of a product and the actual quantity bought and sold are determined in a free and competitive market.

BOX 4.1 UK HOUSE PRICES

The ups and downs of the housing market

If you are thinking of buying a house sometime in the future, then you may well follow the fortunes of the housing market with some trepidation. In the late 1980s there was a housing price explosion in the UK: in fact, between 1984 and 1989 house prices doubled. After several years of falling or gently rising house prices in the early and mid-1990s, there was another boom from 1996 to 2007, with house prices tripling in value over that period. For those on low incomes, owning a home of their own was becoming increasingly difficult. However, in 2008 the return of falling house prices created uncertainty in the market with buyers postponing their purchases until the price falls slowed down.

House prices since the early 1980s

The diagram shows what happened to house prices in the period 1983 to 2009. Initially, there was rapid house price inflation up to 1989, reaching a peak in 1988.

In their rush to buy a house before prices rose any further, many people in this period borrowed as much as they were able. Building societies and banks at that time had plenty of money to lend and were only too willing to do so. Many people, therefore, took out very large mortgages. In 1983 the average new mortgage was 2.08 times average annual earnings. By 1989 this figure had risen to 3.44.

After 1989 there followed a period of *falling* prices. From 1990 to 1995, house prices fell by 12.2 per cent.

As a result of this, many people found themselves in a position of *negative equity*. This is the situation where the size of their mortgage is greater than the value of their house. In other words, if they sold their house, they would end up still owing money! For this reason many people found that they could not move house.

Then, in 1996, house prices began to recover and for the next three years rose moderately – by around 5 per cent per annum. But then they started rising rapidly again, and by 2003, house price inflation had returned to rates similar to those in the 1980s. Was this good news or bad news? For those trapped in negative equity, it was good news. It was good news also for old people who wished to move into a retirement home and who had a house to sell. It was bad news, however, for the first-time buyer! In the mid-1990s the gross house price to earnings ratio for first-time buyers was just over 2 but by 2007 the price of a house was over 5 times higher than a first-time buyer's earnings. It became increasingly difficult for younger people to get on to the housing ladder. As we shall see in many parts of this book, what is good news for one person is often bad news for another.

The determinants of house prices

House prices are determined by demand and supply. If demand rises (i.e. shifts to the right) or if supply falls (i.e. shifts to the left), the equilibrium price of houses will rise. Similarly, if demand falls or supply rises, the equilibrium price will fall.

UK house price inflation: annual percentage rates, adjusted quarterly (all houses, all buyers)

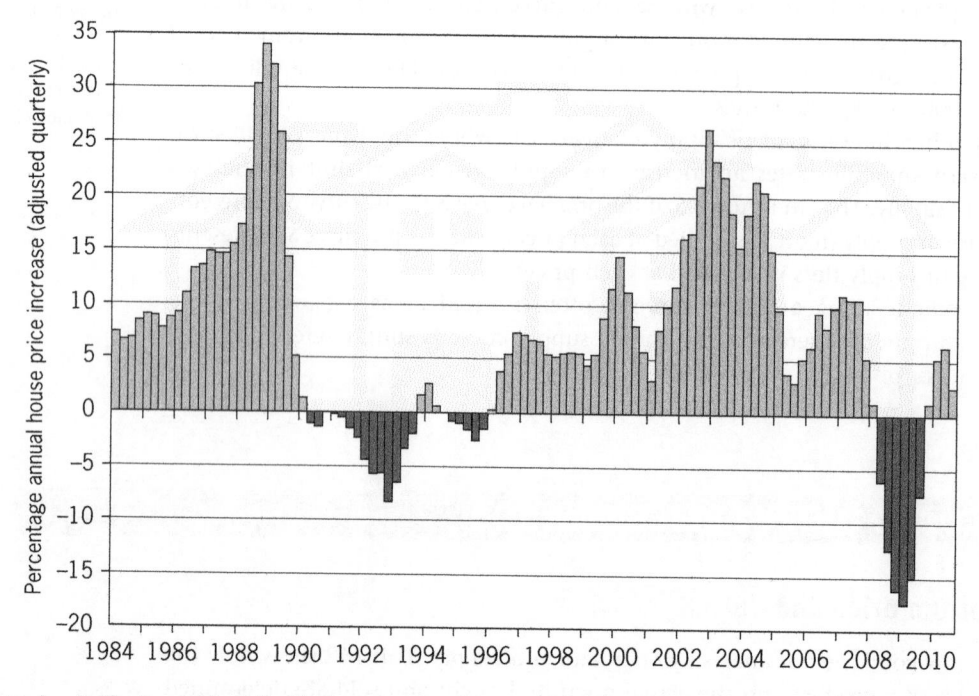

Source: based on *Halifax House Price Index* (Lloyds Banking Group)

So why did house prices rise so rapidly in the 1980s, only to fall in the early 1990s and then rise rapidly again in the late 1990s through to 2007? The answer lies primarily in changes in the *demand* for housing. Let us examine the various factors that affected the demand for houses.

Incomes (actual and anticipated). The second half of the 1980s and from 1996 to 2007 were periods of rapidly rising incomes. The economy was experiencing economic 'boom' during these times. Many people wanted to spend their extra incomes on housing: either buying a house for the first time, or moving to a better one. What is more, many people thought that their incomes would continue to grow, and were thus prepared to stretch themselves financially in the short term by buying an expensive house, confident that their mortgage payments would become more and more affordable over time.

The early 1990s, by contrast, was a period of recession, with rising unemployment and much more slowly growing incomes. People had much less confidence about their ability to afford large mortgages.

The desire for home ownership. The desire for home ownership has increased over the years. In recent times this has been fuelled by a host of television programmes focused on buying and selling property.

The cost of mortgages. During the second half of the 1980s, mortgage interest rates were generally falling. This meant that people could afford larger mortgages, and thus afford to buy more expensive houses. In 1989, however, this trend was reversed. Mortgage interest rates were now rising. Many people found it difficult to maintain existing payments, let alone to take on a larger mortgage. From 1996 to 2003 mortgage rates were generally reduced again, once more fuelling the demand for houses. From 2003 to 2007 interest rates rose again, but this was not enough to deter the demand for housing.

The availability of mortgages. In the late 1980s, mortgages were readily available. Banks and building societies were prepared to accept smaller deposits on houses, and to grant mortgages of $3^1/_2$ times a person's annual income, compared with $2^1/_2$ times in the early 1980s. In the early 1990s, however, banks and building societies were more cautious about granting mortgages. They were aware that, with falling house prices, rising unemployment and the growing problem of negative equity, there was a growing danger that borrowers would default on payments.

With the recovery of the economy in the mid-1990s, however, and with a growing number of mortgage lenders, mortgages became more readily available and for greater amounts relative to people's income. This pushed up prices. In 2001 the average house price was 3.4 times greater than a person's earnings, but this rose steadily to reach 5.74 times a person's earnings in 2007. From late 2007, however, problems in acquiring loans from the banking sector, falling house prices and rising unemployment all signalled a repeat of the early 1990s.

Speculation. In the 1980s and from the mid-1990s to 2007, people generally believed that house prices would continue rising. This encouraged people to buy as soon as possible, and to take out the biggest mortgage possible, before prices went up any further. There was also an effect on supply. Those with houses to sell held back until the last possible moment in the hope of getting a higher price. The net effect was for a rightward shift in the demand curve for houses and a leftward shift in the supply curve. The effect of this speculation, therefore, was to help bring about the very effect that people were predicting (see section 5.4).

In the early 1990s, the opposite occurred. People thinking of buying houses held back, hoping to buy at a lower price. People with houses to sell tried to sell as quickly as possible before prices fell any further. Again the effect of this speculation was to aggravate the change in prices – this time a fall in prices.

Then, in the late 1990s and early 2000s, the return of rapidly rising house prices encouraged people to buy more rapidly again, once more adding fuel to house price inflation. When prices started falling in 2008, again speculation occurred, this time pushing prices down even further.

A global dimension to falling house prices

The fall in UK house prices in 2008 had global origins. The dramatic growth in mortgage lending in the UK was also a feature of many other industrialised countries at this time, most notably the USA, where there had been similar dramatic rises in house prices.

Banks and other mortgage lenders bundled up these large mortgage debts into 'financial instruments' and sold them on to other global financial institutions so that they could meet their everyday liquidity requirements of paying bills and meeting customers' demands for cash. This worked well while there was economic prosperity and people could pay their mortgages. However, it became apparent in 2007 that many of the mortgages sold, notably in the USA, were to people who could not meet their repayments.

As the number of mortgage defaults increased, the value of the mortgage-laden financial instruments sold on to other financial institutions fell. As banks found it increasingly difficult to meet their liquidity requirements, they reduced the number of mortgages to potential home owners. By mid-2009, UK house prices had fallen by some 20 per cent. The uncertainty over how far house prices might fall was stopping consumers from moving home and, as the financial crisis turned into economic recession, house building fell dramatically and construction firms were laying off workers.

1. Draw supply and demand diagrams to illustrate what was happening to house prices (a) in the second half of the 1980s and from the late 1990s to 2007; (b) in the early 1990s and 2008–9.
2. Are there any factors on the supply side that contribute to changes in house prices? If so, what are they?
3. Find out what has happened to house prices over the past three years. Attempt an explanation of what has happened.

Table 4.3 The market demand and supply of potatoes (monthly)

Price of potatoes (pence per kg)	Total market demand (tonnes: 000s)	Total market supply (tonnes: 000s)
20	700 (A)	100 (a)
40	500 (B)	200 (b)
60	350 (C)	350 (c)
80	200 (D)	530 (d)
100	100 (E)	700 (e)

Let us return to the example of the market demand and market supply of potatoes, and use the data from Tables 4.1 and 4.2. These figures are given again in Table 4.3.

What will be the price and output that actually prevail? If the price started at 20p per kilogram, demand would exceed supply by 600 000 tonnes (A – a). Consumers would be unable to obtain all they wanted and would thus be willing to pay a higher price. Producers, unable or unwilling to supply enough to meet the demand, will be only too happy to accept a higher price. The effect of the shortage, then, will be to drive up the price. The same would happen at a price of 40p per kilogram. There would still be a shortage; price would still rise. But as the price rises, the quantity demanded falls and the quantity supplied rises. The shortage is progressively eliminated.

What would happen if the price started at a much higher level: say, at 100p per kilogram? In this case supply would exceed demand by 600 000 tonnes (e – E). The effect of this surplus would be to drive the price down as farmers competed against each other to sell their excess supplies. The same would happen at a price of 80p per kilogram. There would still be a surplus; price would still fall.

In fact, only one price is sustainable. This is the price where demand equals supply: namely 60p per kilogram, where both demand and supply are 350 000 tonnes. When supply matches demand the market is said to clear. There is no shortage and no surplus.

As we saw on page 60, the price, where demand equals supply, is called the *equilibrium price*. In Table 4.3, if the price starts at any level other than 60p per kilogram, there will be a tendency for it to move towards 60p. The equilibrium price is the only price at which producers' and consumers' wishes are mutually reconciled: where the producers' plans to supply exactly match the consumers' plans to buy.

> **Definition**
>
> **Market clearing**
> A market clears when supply matches demand, leaving no shortage or surplus.

> **KEY IDEA 11**
>
> *Equilibrium is the point where conflicting interests are balanced.* Only at this point is the amount that demanders are willing to purchase the same as the amount that suppliers are willing to supply. It is a point which will be automatically reached in a free market through the operation of the price mechanism.

Demand and supply curves

The determination of equilibrium price and output can be shown using demand and supply curves. Equilibrium is where the two curves intersect.

Figure 4.6 shows the demand and supply curves of potatoes corresponding to the data in Table 4.3. Equilibrium price is P_e (60p) and equilibrium quantity is Q_e (350 000 tonnes).

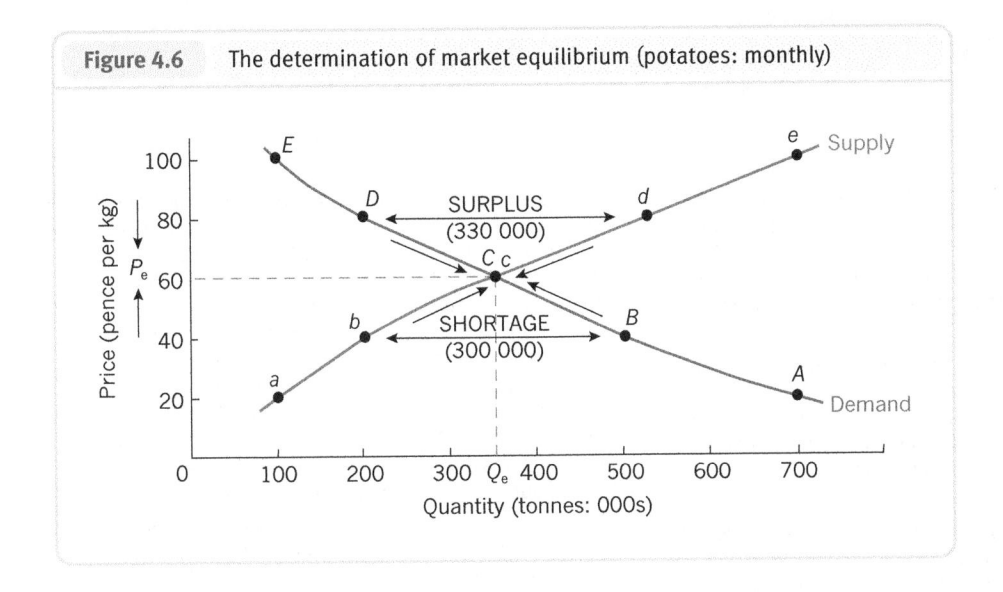

Figure 4.6 The determination of market equilibrium (potatoes: monthly)

At any price above 60p, there would be a surplus. Thus at 80p there is a surplus of 330 000 tonnes ($d - D$). More is supplied than consumers are willing and able to purchase at that price. Thus a price of 80p fails to clear the market. Price will fall to the equilibrium price of 60p. As it does so, there will be a movement along the demand curve from point D to point C, and a movement along the supply curve from point d to point c.

At any price below 60p, there would be a shortage. Thus at 40p there is a shortage of 300 000 tonnes ($B - b$). Price will rise to 60p. This will cause a movement along the supply curve from point b to point c and along the demand curve from point B to point C.

Point Cc is the equilibrium: where demand equals supply.

Movement to a new equilibrium

The equilibrium price will remain unchanged only so long as the demand and supply curves remain unchanged. If either of the curves shifts, a new equilibrium will be formed.

A change in demand

If one of the determinants of demand changes (other than price), the whole demand curve will shift. This will lead to a movement *along* the *supply* curve to the new intersection point.

For example, in Figure 4.7, if a rise in consumer incomes led to the demand curve shifting to D_2, there would be a shortage of $h - g$ at the original price P_{e_1}. This would cause price to rise to the new equilibrium P_{e_2}. As it did so there would be a movement along the supply curve from point g to point i, and along the new demand curve (D_2) from point h to point i. Equilibrium quantity would rise from Q_{e_1} to Q_{e_2}.

The effect of the shift in demand, therefore, has been a movement *along* the supply curve from the old equilibrium to the new: from point g to point i.

> **Pause for thought**
>
> What would happen to price and quantity if the demand curve shifted to the left? Draw a diagram to illustrate your answer.

BOX 4.2 STOCK MARKET PRICES

Demand and supply in action

Firms that are quoted on the stock market (see page 47 and section 19.5) can raise money by issuing shares. These are sold on the 'primary stock market'. People who own the shares receive a 'dividend' on them, normally paid six-monthly. This varies with the profitability of the company.

People or institutions that buy these shares, however, may not wish to hold on to them for ever. This is where the 'secondary stock market' comes in. It is where existing shares are bought and sold. There are stock markets, primary and secondary, in all the major countries of the world.

There are more than 3000 companies whose shares are listed on the London Stock Exchange and shares are traded each Monday to Friday (excluding bank holidays). The prices of shares depend on demand and supply. For example, if the demand for Tesco shares at any one time exceeds the supply on offer, the price will rise until demand and supply are equal. Share prices fluctuate throughout the trading day and sometimes price changes can be substantial.

To give an overall impression of share price movements, stock exchanges publish share price indices. The best known one in the UK is the FTSE 100, which stands for the 'Financial Times Stock Exchange' index of the 100 largest companies' shares. The index represents an average price of these 100 shares. The chart shows movements in the FTSE 100 from 1995 to 2009. The index was first calculated on 3 January 1984 with a base level of 1000 points. It reached a peak of 6930 points on 30 December 1999 and fell to 3287 on 12 March 2003. It then rose again, reaching a high of 6730 on 12 October 2007, but fell to 3781 on 21 November 2008.

But what causes share prices to change? Why were they so high in 1999, but only just over half that value just three years later, and why has this trend repeated itself recently? The answer lies in the determinants of the demand and supply of shares.

Demand

There are four main factors that affect the demand for shares.

Financial Times Stock Exchange Index (FTSE) (3/1/1984 = 1000)

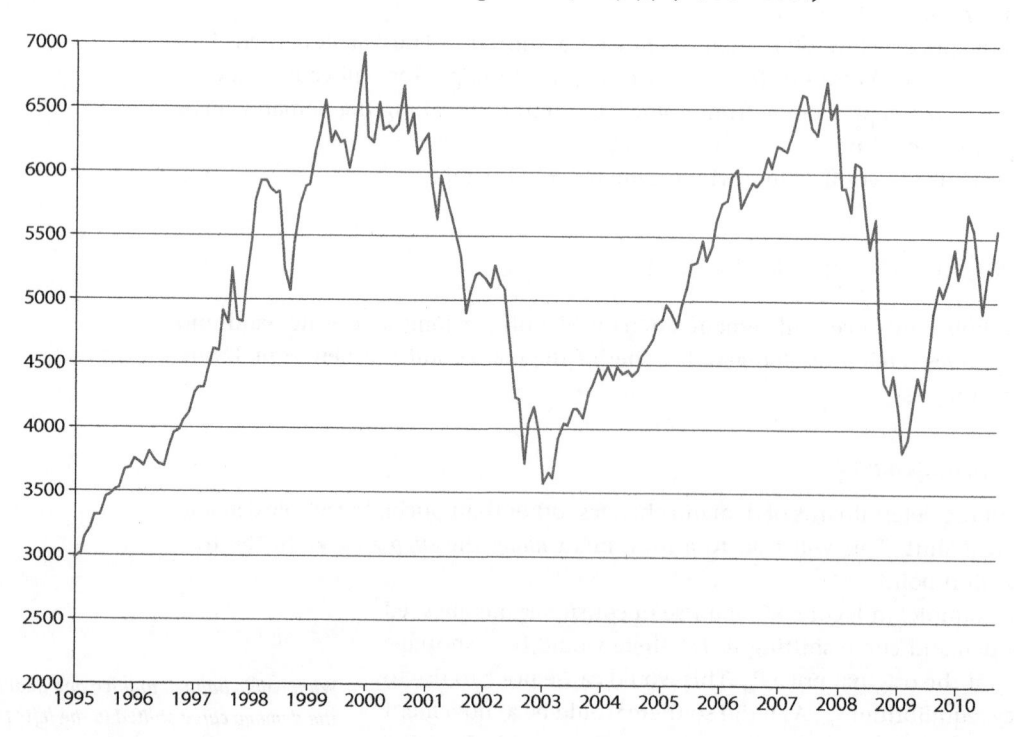

The price of and/or return on substitutes. The main substitutes for shares in specific companies are other shares. Thus if, in comparison with other shares, Tesco shares are expected to pay high dividends relative to the share price, people will buy Tesco shares. As far as shares in general are concerned, the main substitutes are other forms of saving. Thus if the interest rate on savings accounts in banks and building societies fell, people with such accounts would be tempted to take their money out and buy shares instead. Another major substitute is property. If house prices rise rapidly, as they did from the late 1990s to 2007, this will reduce the demand for shares as many people switch to buying property in anticipation of even higher prices. If house prices level off, this makes shares relatively more attractive as an investment and can boost the demand for them.

From late 2007, when house prices and share prices fell dramatically, investors looked towards other investments such as gold, buying government debt (Treasury bills and gilts) or even holding cash.

Incomes. If the economy is growing rapidly and people's incomes are thus rising rapidly, they are likely to buy more shares. Thus in the mid to late 1990s, when UK incomes were rising at an average annual rate of over 3 per cent, share prices rose rapidly (see chart). As growth rates fell in the early 2000s, so share prices fell. Similarly, when economic growth improved from 2003 to 2007 shares prices increased, but they fell back because of a global liquidity crisis and the onset of recession in 2008.

Wealth. 'Wealth' is people's accumulated savings and property. Wealth rose in the 1990s and 2000s, and many people used their increased wealth to buy shares.

Expectations. From 2003 to 2007 people expected share prices to go on rising. They were optimistic about continued growth in the economy. But as people bought shares, this pushed their prices up even more, thereby fuelling further speculation that they would go on rising and encouraging further share buying. In early 2008, by contrast, confidence was shaken. A global banking crisis and fears of impending recession started a dramatic fall in share prices. As people anticipated further price falls, so they held back from buying, thereby pushing prices even lower.

Supply

The factors affecting supply in the secondary market are largely the same as those affecting demand, but in the opposite direction.

If the return on alternative forms of saving falls, people with shares are likely to hold on to them, as they represent a better form of saving. The supply of shares to the market will fall. If incomes or wealth rise, people again are likely to want to hold on to their shares. As far as expectations are concerned, if people believe that share prices will rise, they will hold on to the shares they have. Supply to the market will fall, thereby pushing up prices. If, however, they believe that prices will fall (as they did in 2008), they will sell their shares now before prices do fall. Supply will increase, driving down the price.

Share prices and business

Companies are crucially affected by their share price. If a company's share price falls, this is taken as a sign that 'the market' is losing confidence in the company. This will make it more difficult to raise finance, not only by issuing additional shares in the primary market, but also from banks. It will also make the company more vulnerable to a takeover bid. This is where one company seeks to buy out another by offering to buy all its shares. A takeover will succeed if the owners of more than half of the company's shares vote to accept the offered price. Shareholders are more likely to agree to the takeover if the company's share price has not been performing very well.

Can you buck the market?

Many individuals like to play the market, thinking that they can make a fortune. However, beware! The 'efficient markets hypothesis' predicts that historical share price information, such as that shown in the chart or in the pages of today's financial press, provides no help whatsoever in determining future share prices. Why? Because the current share price *already* reflects what people anticipate will happen. Future share price movements will occur only as *new* (unanticipated) information arrives – and it's pure chance if you can predict the unanticipated! In this purist view, the market for shares is said to be a perfectly efficient market (see section 19.5 for further analysis).

If the rate of economic growth in the economy is 3 per cent in a particular year, why are share prices likely to rise by more than 3 per cent that year?

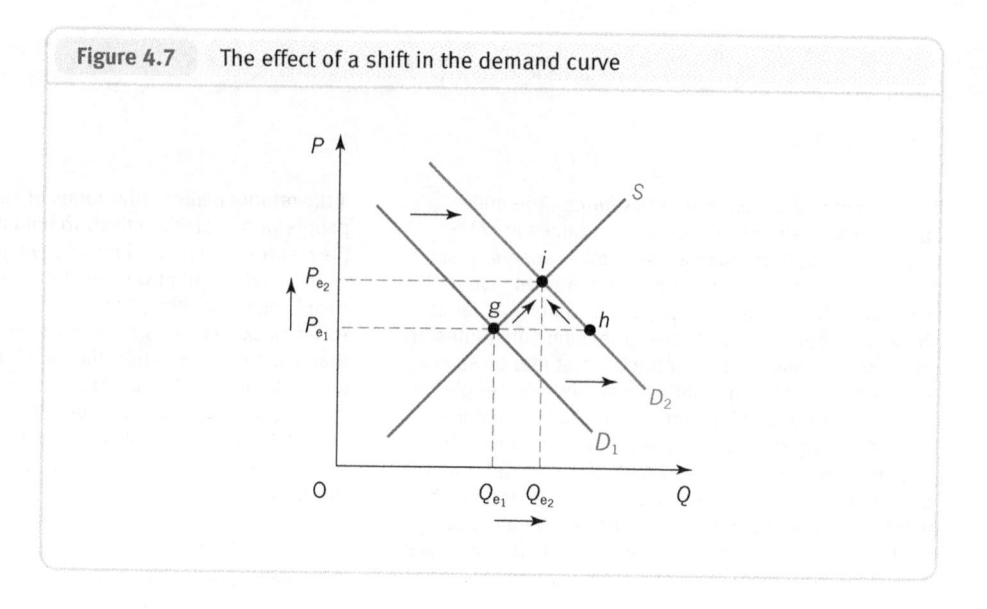

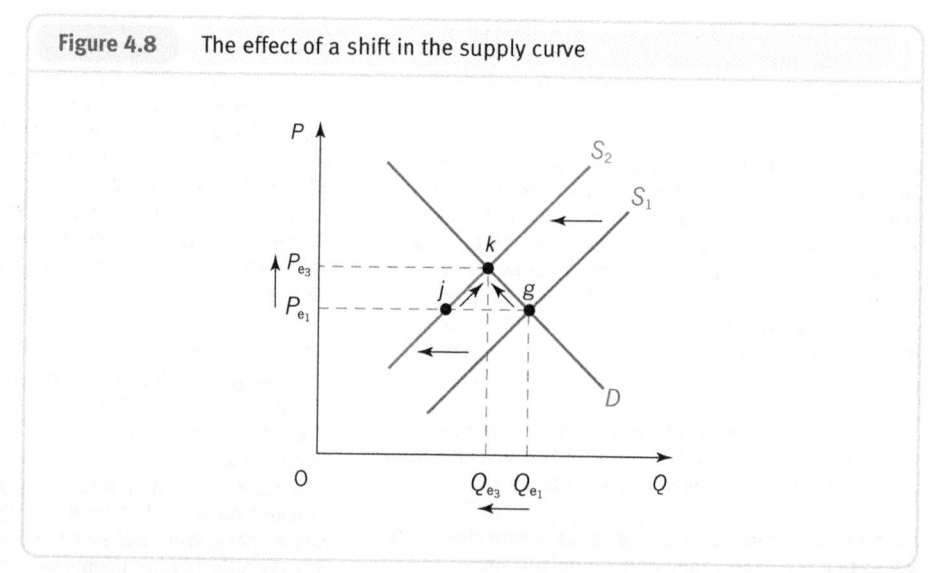

Figure 4.7 The effect of a shift in the demand curve

Figure 4.8 The effect of a shift in the supply curve

A change in supply

Likewise, if one of the determinants of supply changes (other than price), the whole supply curve will shift. This will lead to a movement *along* the *demand* curve to the new intersection point.

For example, in Figure 4.8, if costs of production rose, the supply curve would shift to the left: to S_2. There would be a shortage of $g - j$ at the old price of P_{e_1}. Price would rise from P_{e_1} to P_{e_3}. Quantity would fall from Q_{e_1} to Q_{e_3}. In other words, there would be a movement along the demand curve from point g to point k, and along the new supply curve (S_2) from point j to point k.

To summarise: a shift in one curve leads to a movement along the other curve to the new intersection point.

Sometimes a number of determinants might change. This may lead to a shift in *both* curves. When this happens, equilibrium simply moves from the point where the old curves intersected to the point where the new ones intersect.

SUMMARY

1a A firm is greatly affected by its market environment. The more competitive the market, the less discretion the firm has in determining its price. In the extreme case of a perfect market, the price is entirely outside the firm's control. The price is determined by demand and supply in the market, and the firm has to accept this price: the firm is a price taker.

1b In a perfect market, price changes act as the mechanism whereby demand and supply are balanced. If there is a shortage, price will rise until the shortage is eliminated. If there is a surplus, price will fall until that is eliminated.

2a When the price of a good rises, the quantity demanded per period of time will fall. This is known as the 'law of demand'. It applies both to individuals' demand and to the whole market demand.

2b The law of demand is explained by the income and substitution effects of a price change.

2c The relationship between price and quantity demanded per period of time can be shown in a table (or 'schedule') or as a graph. On the graph, price is plotted on the vertical axis and quantity demanded per period of time on the horizontal axis. The resulting demand curve is downward sloping (negatively sloped).

2d Other determinants of demand include tastes, the number and price of substitute goods, the number and price of complementary goods, income, the distribution of income and expectations of future price changes.

2e If price changes, the effect is shown by a movement along the demand curve. We call this effect 'a change in the quantity demanded'.

2f If any other determinant of demand changes, the whole curve will shift. We call this effect 'a change in demand'. A rightward shift represents an increase in demand; a leftward shift represents a decrease in demand.

3a When the price of a good rises, the quantity supplied per period of time will usually also rise. This applies both to individual producers' supply and to the whole market supply.

3b There are two reasons in the short run why a higher price encourages producers to supply more: (a) they are now willing to incur higher costs per unit associated with producing more; (b) they will switch to producing this product and away from now less profitable ones. In the long run there is a third reason: new producers will be attracted into the market.

3c The relationship between price and quantity supplied per period of time can be shown in a table (or schedule) or as a graph. As with a demand curve, price is plotted on the vertical axis and quantity per period of time on the horizontal axis. The resulting supply curve is upward sloping (positively sloped).

3d Other determinants of supply include the costs of production, the profitability of alternative products, the profitability of goods in joint supply, random shocks and expectations of future price changes.

3e If price changes, the effect is shown by a movement along the supply curve. We call this effect 'a change in the quantity supplied'.

3f If any determinant *other* than price changes, the effect is shown by a shift in the whole supply curve. We call this effect 'a change in supply'. A rightward shift represents an increase in supply; a leftward shift represents a decrease in supply.

4a If the demand for a good exceeds the supply, there will be a shortage. This will lead to a rise in the price of the good.

4b If the supply of a good exceeds the demand, there will be a surplus. This will lead to a fall in the price.

4c Price will settle at the equilibrium. The equilibrium price is the one that clears the market: the price where demand equals supply. This is shown in a demand and supply diagram by the point where the two curves intersect.

4d If the demand or supply curve shifts, this will lead either to a shortage or to a surplus. Price will therefore either rise or fall until a new equilibrium is reached at the position where the supply and demand curves *now* intersect.

REVIEW QUESTIONS

1. Using a diagram like Figure 4.1, summarise the effect of (a) a reduction in the demand for a good; (b) a reduction in the costs of production of a good.

2. Referring to Table 4.1, assume that there are 200 consumers in the market. Of these, 100 have schedules like Tracey's and 100 have schedules like Darren's. What would be the total market demand schedule for potatoes now?

3. Again referring to Table 4.1, draw Tracey's and Darren's demand curves for potatoes on one diagram. (Note that you will use the same vertical scale as in Figure 4.2, but you will need a quite different horizontal scale.) At what price is their demand the same? What explanations could there be for the quite different shapes of their two demand curves? (This question is explored in the next chapter.)

4. The price of pork rises and yet it is observed that the sales of pork increase. Does this mean that the demand curve for pork is upward sloping? Explain.

5. This question is concerned with the supply of oil for central heating. In each case consider whether there is a movement along the supply curve (and in which direction) or a shift in it (and whether left or right): (a) new oil fields start up in production; (b) the demand for central heating rises; (c) the price of gas falls; (d) oil companies anticipate an upsurge in the demand for central-heating oil; (e) the demand for petrol rises; (f) new technology decreases the costs of oil refining; (g) all oil products become more expensive.

6. For what reasons might the price of foreign holidays rise? In each case, identify whether these are reasons affecting demand or supply (or both).

7. The price of cod is much higher today than it was 20 years ago. Using demand and supply diagrams, explain why this should be so.

8. The number of owners of compact disc players has grown rapidly and hence the demand for compact discs has also grown rapidly. Yet the price of CDs has fallen. Why? Use a supply and demand diagram to illustrate your answer.

9. What will happen to the equilibrium price and quantity of butter in each of the following cases? You should state whether demand or supply or both have shifted and in which direction: (a) a rise in the price of margarine; (b) a rise in the demand for yoghurt; (c) a rise in the price of bread; (d) a rise in the demand for bread; (e) an expected increase in the price of butter in the near future; (f) a tax on butter production; (g) the invention of a new, but expensive, process of removing all cholesterol from butter, plus the passing of a law which states that butter producers must use this process. In each case, assume *ceteris paribus*.

10. If both demand and supply change, and if we know in which direction they have shifted but not by how much, why is it that we will be able to predict the direction in which *either* price or quantity will change, but not both? (Clue: consider the four possible combinations and sketch them if necessary: *D* left, *S* left; *D* right, *S* right; *D* left, *S* right; *D* right, *S* left.)

Chapter 5

Business in a market environment

> **Business issues covered in this chapter**
>
> - How responsive is consumer demand to changes in the market price? How responsive is it to changes in consumer incomes and to the prices of competitor products?
> - How is a firm's sales revenue affected by a change in price?
> - How responsive is business output to changes in price?
> - How does the responsiveness (or 'elasticity') of demand and supply to changes in price affect the working of markets?
> - Why are markets likely to be more responsive in the long run than in the short run to changes in demand or supply?
> - What is meant by 'risk' and 'uncertainty' and what is their significance to business?
> - How do firms deal with uncertainty about future market movements?

In Chapter 4 we examined how prices are determined in perfectly competitive markets: by the interaction of market demand and market supply. In such markets, although the *market* demand curve is downward sloping, the demand curve faced by the individual firm will be horizontal. This is illustrated in Figure 5.1.

The market price is P_m. The individual firm can sell as much as it likes at this market price: it is too small to have any influence on the market – it is a price taker. It will not force the price down by producing more because, in terms of the total market, this extra would be an infinitesimally small amount. If a farmer doubled the output of wheat sent to the market, it would be too small an increase to affect the world price of wheat!

In practice, however, many firms are not price takers; they have some discretion in choosing their price. Such firms will face a downward-sloping demand curve. If they raise their price, they will sell less; if they lower their price, they will sell more. But firms will want to know more than this. They will want to know just *how much* the quantity demanded will fall. In other words, they will want to know how *responsive* demand is to a rise in price. This responsiveness is measured using a concept called 'elasticity'.

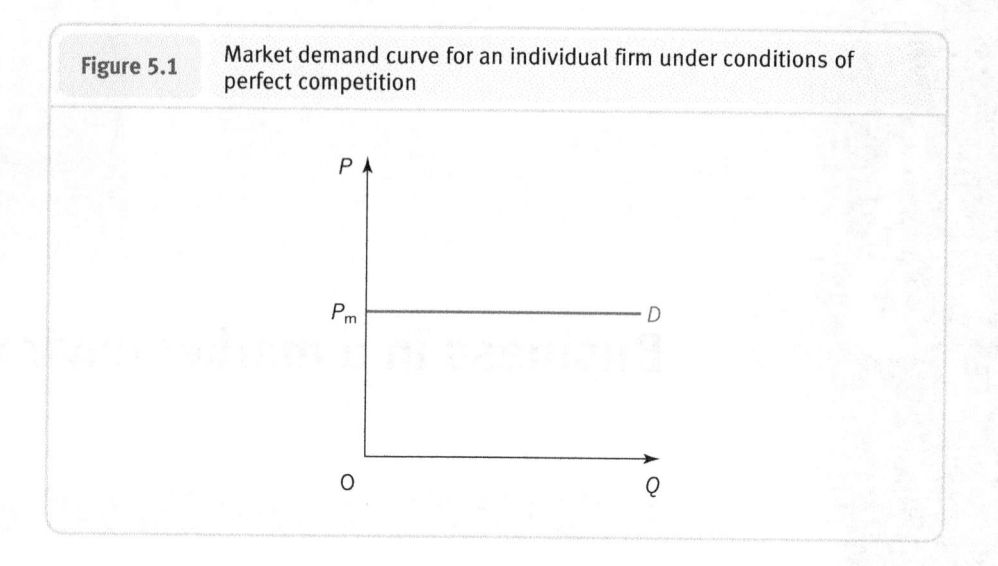

Figure 5.1 Market demand curve for an individual firm under conditions of perfect competition

> **KEY IDEA 12**
>
> *Elasticity.* The responsiveness of one variable (e.g. demand) to a change in another (e.g. price). This concept is fundamental to understanding how markets work. The more elastic variables are, the more responsive is the market to changing circumstances.

5.1 PRICE ELASTICITY OF DEMAND

The responsiveness of quantity demanded to a change in price

The demand for an individual firm

For any firm considering changing its price, it is vital to know the likely effect on the quantity demanded. Take the case of two firms facing very different demand curves. These are shown in Figure 5.2.

Firm A can raise its price quite substantially – from £6 to £10 – and yet its level of sales only falls by a relatively small amount – from 100 units to 90 units. This firm will probably be quite keen to raise its price. After all, it could make significantly

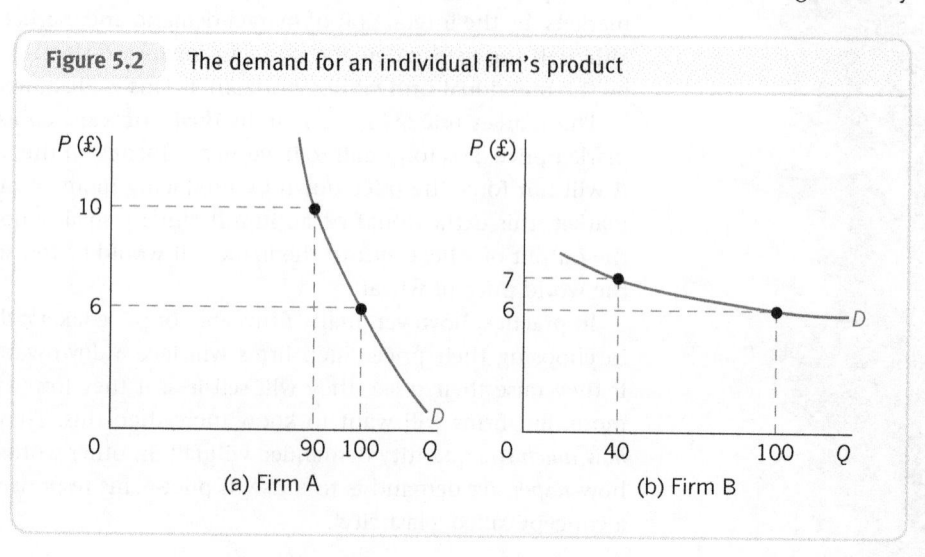

Figure 5.2 The demand for an individual firm's product

(a) Firm A

(b) Firm B

Figure 5.3 Market supply and demand

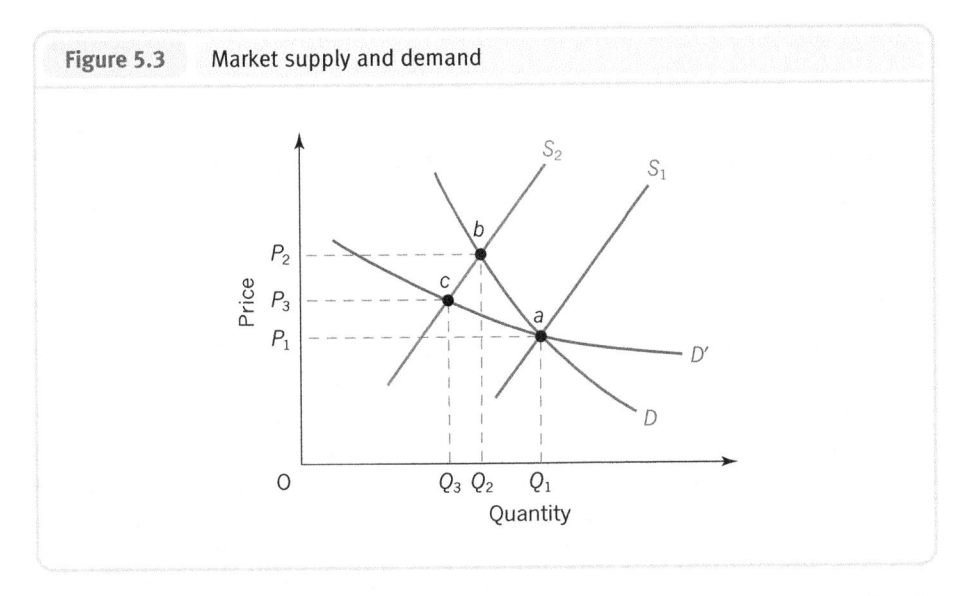

more profit on each unit sold (assuming no rise in costs per unit), and yet sell only slightly fewer units.

Firm B, however, will think twice about raising its price. Even a relatively modest increase in price – from £6 to £7 – will lead to a substantial fall in sales from 100 units to 40 units. What is the point of making a bit more profit on those units it manages to sell, if in the process it ends up selling a lot fewer units? In such circumstances the firm may contemplate lowering its price.

The responsiveness of market demand

Economists too will want to know how responsive demand is to a change in price: except in this case it is the responsiveness of *market* demand that is being considered. This information is necessary to enable them to predict the effects of a shift in supply on the market price of a product.

Figure 5.3 shows the effect of a shift in supply with two quite different demand curves (D and D'). Assume that initially the supply curve is S_1, and that it intersects with both demand curves at point a, at a price of P_1 and a quantity of Q_1. Now supply shifts to S_2. What will happen to price and quantity? Economists will want to know! The answer is that it depends on the shape of the demand curve. In the case of demand curve D, there is a relatively large rise in price (to P_2) and a relatively small fall in quantity (to Q_2): equilibrium is at point b. In the case of demand curve D', however, there is only a relatively small rise in price (to P_3), but a relatively large fall in quantity (to Q_3): equilibrium is at point c.

Given the importance of knowing the responsiveness of demand to a change in price, we will need some way of measuring this responsiveness. *Elasticity* is the measure we use.

Defining price elasticity of demand

What we will want to compare is the size of the change in quantity demanded of a given product with the size of the change in price. **Price elasticity of demand** does just this. It is defined as follows:

$$P\varepsilon_D = \frac{\text{proportionate (or percentage) change in quantity demanded}}{\text{proportionate (or percentage) change in price}}$$

Definition

Price elasticity of demand
A measure of the responsiveness of quantity demanded to a change in price.

If, for example, a 20 per cent rise in the price of a product causes a 10 per cent fall in the quantity demanded, the price elasticity of demand will be:

−10%/20% = −0.5

Three things should be noted at this stage about the figure that is calculated for elasticity.

The use of proportionate or percentage measures

Elasticity is measured in proportionate or percentage terms for the following reasons:

- It allows comparison of changes in two qualitatively different things, which are thus measured in two different types of unit: i.e. it allows comparison of quantity changes (quantity demanded) with monetary changes (price).
- It is the only sensible way of deciding *how big* a change in price or quantity is. Take a simple example. An item goes up in price by £1. Is this a big increase or a small increase? We can answer this only if we know what the original price was. If a can of beans goes up in price by £1, that is a huge price increase. If, however, the price of a house goes up by £1, that is a tiny price increase. In other words, it is the percentage or proportionate increase in price that we look at in deciding how big a price rise it is.

The sign (positive or negative)

If price increases (a positive figure), the quantity demanded will fall (a negative figure). If price falls (a negative figure), the quantity demanded will rise (a positive figure). Thus price elasticity of demand will be negative: a positive figure is being divided by a negative figure (or vice versa).

The value (greater or less than 1)

If we now ignore the sign and just concentrate on the value of the figure, this tells us whether demand is elastic or inelastic.

Elastic ($\varepsilon > 1$). This is where a change in price causes a proportionately larger change in the quantity demanded. In this case the price elasticity of demand will be greater than 1, since we are dividing a larger figure by a smaller figure.

Inelastic ($\varepsilon < 1$). This is where a change in price causes a proportionately smaller change in the quantity demanded. In this case the price elasticity of demand will be less than 1, since we are dividing a smaller figure by a larger figure.

Unit elastic ($\varepsilon = 1$). Unit elasticity is where the quantity demanded changes proportionately the same as price. This will give an elasticity equal to 1, since we are dividing a figure by itself.

The determinants of price elasticity of demand

The price elasticity of demand varies enormously from one product to another. But why do some products have a highly elastic demand, whereas others have a highly *in*elastic demand? What determines price elasticity of demand?

The number and closeness of substitute goods

This is the most important determinant. The more substitutes there are for a good, and the closer they are, the more will people switch to these alternatives

> **Definitions**
>
> **Elastic**
> If demand is (price) elastic, then any change in price will cause the quantity demanded to change proportionately more. (Ignoring the negative sign) it will have a value greater than 1.
>
> **Inelastic**
> If demand is (price) inelastic, then any change will cause the quantity demanded to change by a proportionately smaller amount. (Ignoring the negative sign) it will have a value less than 1.
>
> **Unit elasticity**
> When the price elasticity of demand is unity, this is where quantity demanded changes by the same proportion as the price. Price elasticity is equal to −1.

when the price of the good rises: the greater, therefore, will be the price elasticity of demand.

For example, the price elasticity of demand for a particular brand of a product will probably be fairly high, especially if there are many other, similar brands. If its price goes up, people can simply switch to another brand: there is a large substitution effect. By contrast, the demand for a product in general will normally be pretty inelastic. If the price of food in general goes up, demand for food will fall only slightly. People will buy a little less, since they cannot now afford so much: this is the *income* effect of the price rise. But there is no alternative to food that can satisfy our hunger: there is therefore virtually no *substitution* effect.

The proportion of income spent on the good

The higher the proportion of our income we spend on a good, the more we will be forced to cut consumption when its price rises: the bigger will be the income effect and the more elastic will be the demand.

Thus salt has a very low price elasticity of demand. This is because we spend such a tiny fraction of our income on salt that we would find little difficulty in paying a relatively large percentage increase in its price: the income effect of a price rise would be very small. By contrast, there will be a much bigger income effect when a major item of expenditure rises in price. For example, if mortgage interest rates rise (the 'price' of loans for house purchase), people may have to cut down substantially on their demand for housing – being forced to buy somewhere much smaller and cheaper, or to live in rented accommodation.

> **Pause for thought**
>
> *Think of two products and estimate which is likely to have the higher price elasticity of demand. Explain your answer.*

The time period

When price rises, people may take a time to adjust their consumption patterns and find alternatives. The longer the time period after a price change, then, the more elastic is the demand likely to be.

THE IMPORTANCE OF PRICE ELASTICITY OF DEMAND TO BUSINESS DECISION MAKING 5.2

A firm's sales revenue

One of the most important applications of price elasticity of demand concerns its relationship with a firm's sales revenue. The **total sales revenue (TR)** of a firm is simply price times quantity:

$$TR = P \times Q$$

For example, 3000 units (Q) sold at £2 per unit (P) will earn the firm £6000 (TR).

Let us assume that a firm wants to increase its total revenue. What should it do? Should it raise its price or lower it? The answer depends on the price elasticity of demand.

> **Definition**
>
> **Total (sales) revenue (TR)**
> The amount a firm earns from its sales of a product at a particular price. $TR = P \times Q$. Note that we are referring to *gross* revenue: that is, revenue before the deduction of taxes or any other costs.

Elastic demand and sales revenue

As price rises, so quantity demanded falls, and vice versa. When demand is elastic, quantity changes proportionately more than price. Thus the change in quantity has

Figure 5.4 Elastic demand between two points

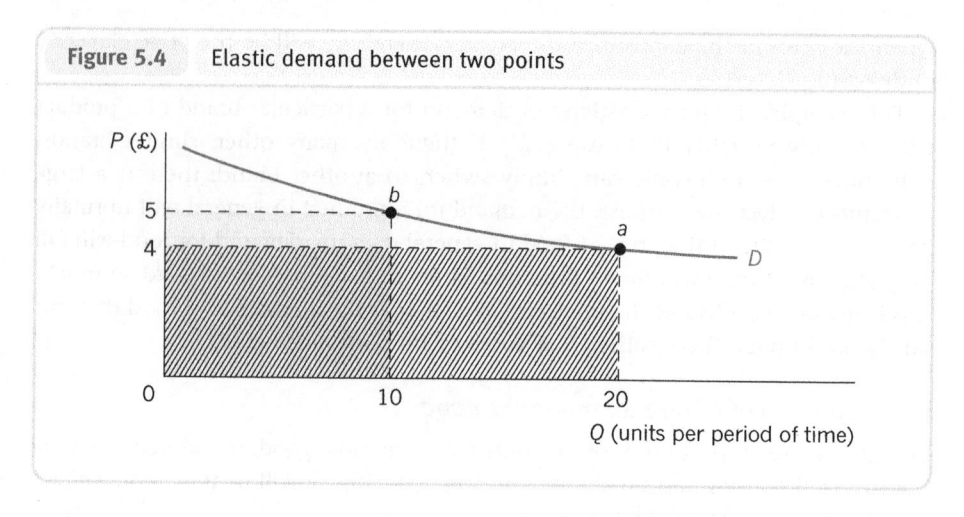

a bigger effect on total revenue than does the change in price. This can be summarised as follows:

P rises; *Q* falls proportionately more; therefore *TR* falls.
P falls; *Q* rises proportionately more; therefore *TR* rises.

In other words, total revenue changes in the same direction as *quantity*.

This is illustrated in Figure 5.4. The areas of the rectangles in the diagram represent total revenue. But why? The area of a rectangle is its height multiplied by its length. In this case, this is price multiplied by quantity purchased, which, as we have seen, gives total expenditure.

Demand is elastic between points *a* and *b*. A rise in price from £4 to £5 causes a proportionately larger fall in quantity demanded: from 20 to 10. Total revenue *falls* from £80 (the striped area) to £50 (the shaded area).

When demand is elastic, then, a rise in price will cause a fall in total revenue. If a firm wants to increase its revenue, it should *lower* its price.

> **Pause for thought**
>
> *If a firm faces an elastic demand curve, why will it not necessarily be in the firm's interests to produce more? (Clue: you will need to distinguish between revenue and profit. We will explore this relationship in the next chapter.)*

Inelastic demand and sales revenue

When demand is inelastic, it is the other way around. Price changes proportionately more than quantity. Thus the change in price has a bigger effect on total revenue than does the change in quantity. To summarise the effects:

P rises; *Q* falls proportionately less; *TR* rises.
P falls; *Q* rises proportionately less; *TR* falls.

In other words, total revenue changes in the same direction as *price*.

This is illustrated in Figure 5.5. Demand is inelastic between points *a* and *c*. A rise in price from £4 to £8 causes a proportionately smaller fall in quantity demanded: from 20 to 15. Total revenue *rises* from £80 (the striped area) to £120 (the shaded area).

If a firm wants to increase its revenue in this case, therefore, it should *raise* its price.

Special cases

Figure 5.6 shows three special cases: (a) a totally inelastic demand ($P\varepsilon_D = 0$), (b) an infinitely elastic demand ($P\varepsilon_D = \infty$) and (c) a unit elastic demand ($P\varepsilon_D = -1$).

Figure 5.5 Inelastic demand between two points

Totally inelastic demand

This is shown by a vertical straight line. No matter what happens to price, quantity demanded remains the same. It is obvious that the more the price is raised, the bigger will be the revenue. Thus in Figure 5.6(a), P_2 will earn a bigger revenue than P_1.

Infinitely elastic demand

This is shown by a horizontal straight line. At any price above P_1 demand is zero. But at P_1 (or any price below) demand is 'infinitely' large.

This seemingly unlikely demand curve is in fact relatively common. Many firms that are very small (like the small-scale grain farmer) are price takers. They have to accept the price as given by supply and demand in the *whole market*. If individual farmers were to try to sell above this price, they would sell nothing at all. At this price, however, they can sell to the market all they produce. (Demand is not *literally* infinite, but as far as the farmer is concerned it is.) In this case, the more the individual farmer produces, the more revenue will be earned. In Figure 5.6(b), more revenue is earned at Q_2 than at Q_1.

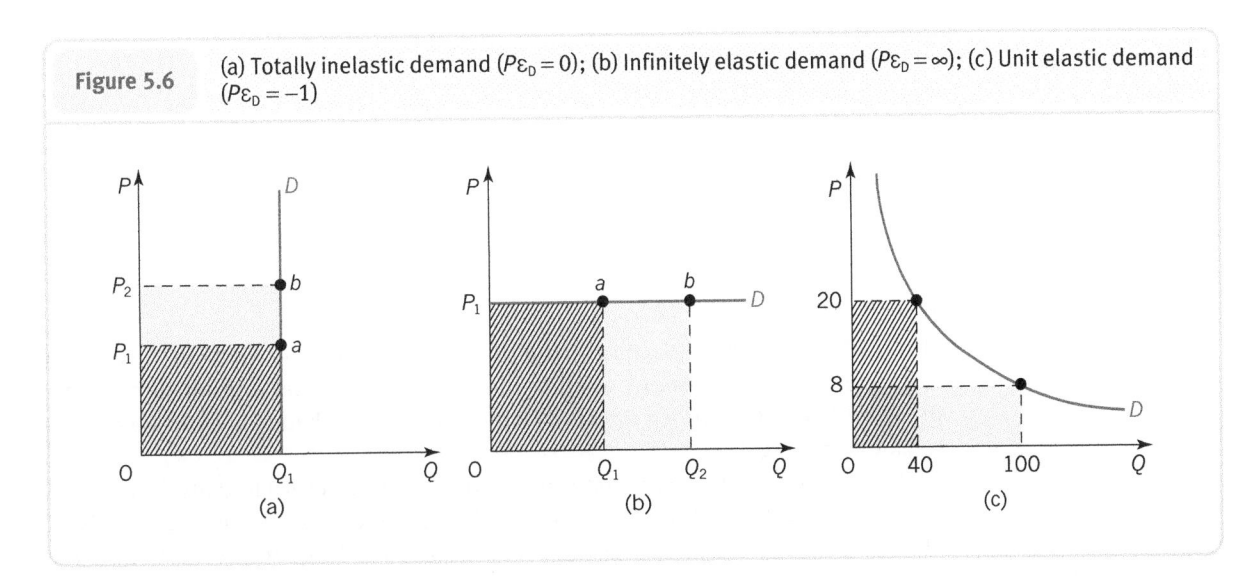

Figure 5.6 (a) Totally inelastic demand ($P\varepsilon_D = 0$); (b) Infinitely elastic demand ($P\varepsilon_D = \infty$); (c) Unit elastic demand ($P\varepsilon_D = -1$)

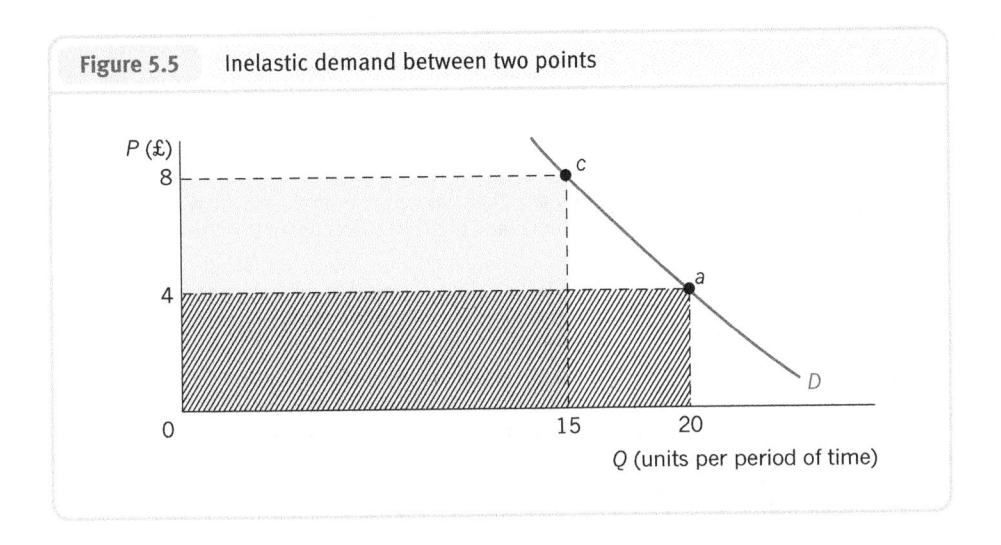

BOX 5.1 THE MEASUREMENT OF ELASTICITY

An optional technical box

We have defined price elasticity as the percentage or proportionate change in quantity demanded divided by the percentage or proportionate change in price. But how, in practice, do we measure these changes for a specific demand curve?

A common mistake that students make is to think that you can talk about the elasticity of a whole *curve*. The mistake here is that in most cases the elasticity will vary along the length of the curve.

Take the case of the demand curve illustrated in diagram (a). Between points *a* and *b*, total revenue rises ($P_2Q_2 > P_1Q_1$): demand is thus elastic between these two points. Between points *b* and *c*, however, total revenue falls ($P_3Q_3 < P_2Q_2$). Demand here is inelastic.

Normally, then, we can refer to the elasticity only of a *portion* of the demand curve, not of the *whole* curve.

There is, however, an exception to this rule. This is when the elasticity just so happens to be the same all the way along a curve, as in the three special cases illustrated in Figure 5.6.

Although we cannot normally talk about the elasticity of a whole curve, we can nevertheless talk about the elasticity between any two points on it. Remember the formula we used was:

$$\frac{\%\ or\ proportionate\ \Delta Q}{\%\ or\ proportionate\ \Delta P}$$

(where Δ means 'change in').

(a) Different elasticities along different portions of a demand curve

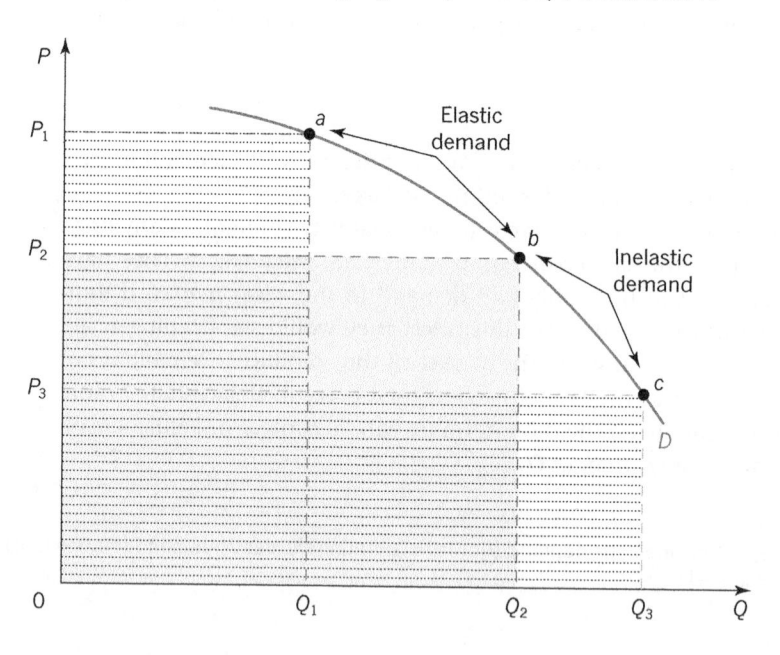

Unit elastic demand

This is where price and quantity change in exactly the same proportion. Any rise in price will be exactly offset by a fall in quantity, leaving total revenue unchanged. In Figure 5.6(c), the striped area is exactly equal to the shaded area: in both cases total revenue is £800.

You might have thought that a demand curve with unit elasticity would be a straight line at 45° to the axes. Instead it is a curve called a *rectangular hyperbola*. The reason for its shape is that the proportionate *rise* in quantity must equal the

(b) Measuring elasticity using the arc method

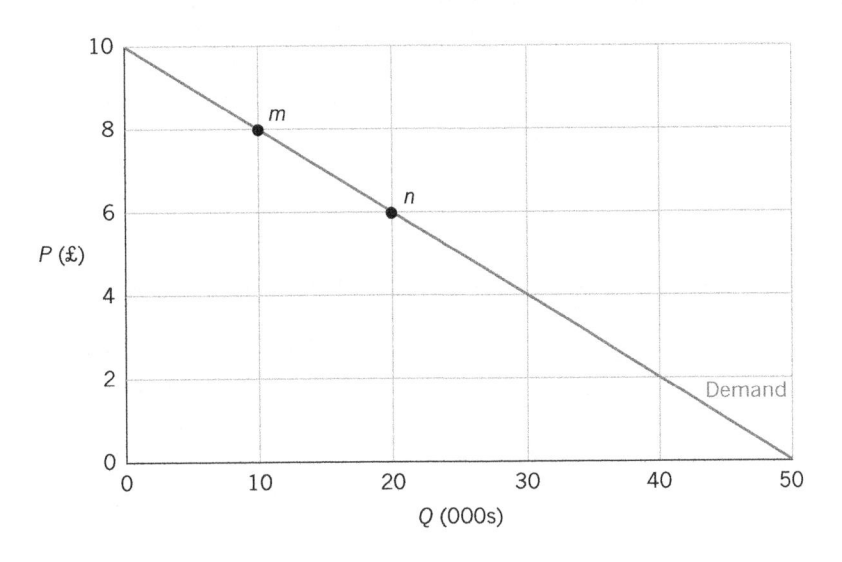

The way we measure a *proportionate* change in quantity is to divide that change by the level of Q: i.e. ΔQ/Q. Similarly, we measure a proportionate change in price by dividing that change by the level of P: i.e. ΔP/P. Price elasticity of demand can thus now be rewritten as:

$$\frac{\Delta Q}{Q} \div \frac{\Delta P}{P}$$

But just what value do we give to P and Q? Consider the demand curve in diagram (b). What is the elasticity of demand between points m and n? Price has fallen by £2 (from £8 to £6), but what is the proportionate change? Is it −2/8 or −2/6? The convention is to express the change as a proportion of the average of the two prices, £8 and £6: in other words to take the mid-point price, £7. Thus the proportionate change is −2/7.

Similarly the proportionate change in quantity between points m and n is 10/15, since 15 is mid-way between 10 and 20.

Thus using the *average (or 'mid-point') formula*, elasticity between m and n is given by:

$$\frac{\Delta Q}{\text{average } Q} \div \frac{\Delta P}{\text{average } P} = \frac{10}{15} \div \frac{-2}{7} = -2.33$$

Since 2.33 is greater than 1, demand is elastic between m and n.

> **?** Referring again to diagram (b), what is the price elasticity of demand between a price of (a) £6 and £4; (b) £4 and £2? What do you conclude about the elasticity of a straight-line demand curve as you move down it?

proportionate *fall* in price (and vice versa). As we move down the demand curve, in order for the *proportionate* (or percentage) change in both price and quantity to remain constant, there must be a bigger and bigger *absolute* rise in quantity and a smaller and smaller absolute fall in price. For example, a rise in quantity from 200 to 400 is the same proportionate change as a rise from 100 to 200, but its absolute size is double. A fall in price from £5 to £2.50 is the same percentage as a fall from £10 to £5, but its absolute size is only half.

> **Pause for thought**
>
> *Two customers go to the fish counter at a supermarket to buy some cod. Neither looks at the price. Customer A orders 1 kilo of cod. Customer B orders £3 worth of cod. What is the price elasticity of demand of each of the two customers?*

5.3 OTHER ELASTICITIES

> **Definitions**
>
> **Income elasticity of demand**
> The responsiveness of demand to a change in consumer incomes: the proportionate change in demand divided by the proportionate change in income.
>
> **Cross-price elasticity of demand**
> The responsiveness of demand for one good to a change in the price of another: the proportionate change in demand for one good divided by the proportionate change in price of the other.

Firms are interested to know the responsiveness of demand not just to a change in price: they will also want to know the responsiveness of demand to changes in other determinants, such as consumers' incomes and the prices of substitute or complementary goods to theirs. They will want to know the income elasticity of demand – the responsiveness of demand to a change in consumers' incomes (Y); and the cross-price elasticity of demand – the responsiveness of demand for their good to a change in the price of another (whether a substitute or a complement).

Income elasticity of demand ($Y\varepsilon_D$)

We define the income elasticity of demand for a good as follows:

$$Y\varepsilon_D = \frac{\text{proportionate (or percentage) change in quantity demanded}}{\text{proportionate (or percentage) change in income}}$$

For example, if a 2 per cent rise in consumer incomes causes an 8 per cent rise in a product's demand, then its income elasticity of demand will be:

$$8\%/2\% = 4$$

The major determinant of income elasticity of demand is the degree of 'necessity' of the good.

In a developed country, the demand for luxury goods expands rapidly as people's incomes rise, whereas the demand for more basic goods, such as bread, rises only a little. Thus items such as cars and foreign holidays have a high income elasticity of demand, whereas items such as potatoes and bus journeys have a low income elasticity of demand.

The demand for some goods actually decreases as income rises. These are inferior goods such as cheap margarine. As people earn more, so they switch to butter or better-quality margarine. Unlike normal goods, which have a positive income elasticity of demand, inferior goods have a negative income elasticity of demand (a rise in income leads to a *fall* in demand).

Income elasticity of demand and the firm

Income elasticity of demand is an important concept to firms considering the future size of the market for their product. If the product has a high income elasticity of demand, sales are likely to expand rapidly as national income rises, but may also fall significantly if the economy moves into recession.

Firms may also find that some parts of their market have a higher income elasticity of demand than others, and may thus choose to target their marketing campaigns on this group. For example, middle-income groups may have a higher income elasticity of demand for certain high-tech products than lower-income groups (who are unlikely to be able to afford such products even if their incomes rise somewhat) or higher-income groups (who can probably afford them anyway, and thus would not buy much more if their incomes rose).

> **Pause for thought**
>
> *Assume that you decide to spend a quarter of your income on clothes. What is (a) your income elasticity of demand; (b) your price elasticity of demand?*

Cross-price elasticity of demand ($C\varepsilon_{D_{ab}}$)

This is often known by its less cumbersome title of 'cross elasticity of demand'. It is a measure of the responsiveness of demand for one product to a change in the price of another (either a substitute or a complement). It enables us to predict how much the demand curve for the first product will shift when the price of the second product changes. For example, knowledge of the cross elasticity of demand for Coca-Cola with respect to the price of Pepsi would allow Coca-Cola to predict the effect on its own sales if the price of Pepsi were to change.

We define cross-price elasticity as follows:

$$C\varepsilon_D = \frac{\text{proportionate (or percentage) change in demand for good a}}{\text{proportionate (or percentage) change in price of good b}}$$

If good b is a *substitute* for good a, a's demand will *rise* as b's price rises. For example, the demand for bicycles will rise as the price of public transport rises. In this case, cross elasticity will be a positive figure. If b is *complementary* to a, however, a's demand will *fall* as b's price rises and thus as the quantity of b demanded falls. For example, the demand for petrol falls as the price of cars rises. In this case, cross elasticity will be a negative figure.

Cross-price elasticity of demand and the firm

The major determinant of cross elasticity of demand is the closeness of the substitute or complement. The closer it is, the bigger will be the effect on the first good of a change in the price of the substitute or complement, and hence the greater will be the cross elasticity – either positive or negative.

Firms will wish to know the cross elasticity of demand for their product when considering the effect on the demand for their product of a change in the price of a rival's product (a substitute). If firm b cuts its price, will this make significant inroads into the sales of firm a? If so, firm a may feel forced to cut its prices too; if not, then firm a may keep its price unchanged. The cross-price elasticities of demand between a firm's product and those of each of its rivals are thus vital pieces of information for a firm when making its production, pricing and marketing plans.

Similarly, a firm will wish to know the cross-price elasticity of demand for its product with any complementary good. Car producers will wish to know the effect of petrol price increases on the sales of their cars.

Price elasticity of supply ($P\varepsilon_S$)

Just as we can measure the responsiveness of demand to a change in one of the determinants of demand, so too we can measure the responsiveness of supply to a change in one of the determinants of supply. The price elasticity of supply refers to the responsiveness of supply to a change in price. We define it as follows:

$$P\varepsilon_s = \frac{\text{proportionate (or percentage) change in quantity supplied}}{\text{proportionate (or percentage) change in price}}$$

Thus if a 15 per cent rise in the price of a product causes a 30 per cent rise in the quantity supplied, the price elasticity of supply will be:

30%/15% = 2

> **Definition**
>
> **Price elasticity of supply**
> The responsiveness of quantity supplied to a change in price: the proportionate change in quantity supplied divided by the proportionate change in price.

Figure 5.7 Price elasticity of supply

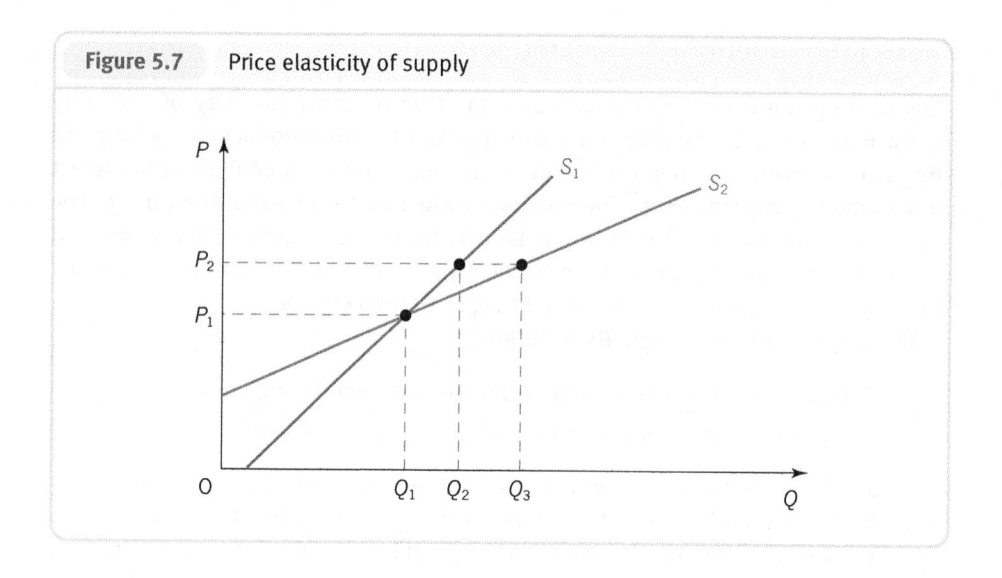

In Figure 5.7, curve S_2 is more elastic between any two prices than curve S_1. Thus, when price rises from P_1 to P_2 there is a larger increase in quantity supplied with S_2 (namely, Q_1 to Q_3) than there is with S_1 (namely, Q_1 to Q_2).

Determinants of price elasticity of supply

The amount that costs rise as output rises. The less the additional costs of producing additional output, the more firms will be encouraged to produce for a given price rise: the more elastic will supply be.

Supply is thus likely to be elastic if firms have plenty of spare capacity, if they can readily get extra supplies of raw materials, if they can easily switch away from producing alternative products and if they can avoid having to introduce overtime working (at higher rates of pay). If all these conditions hold, costs will be little affected by a rise in output, and supply will be relatively elastic. The less these conditions apply, the less elastic will supply be.

Time period (see Figure 5.8)

- Immediate time period. Firms are unlikely to be able to increase supply by much immediately. Supply is virtually fixed, or can vary only according to available stocks. Supply is highly inelastic. In the diagram S_1 is drawn with $Pe_S = 0$. If demand increases to D_2, supply will not be able to respond. Price will rise to P_2. Quantity will remain at Q_1. Equilibrium will move to point b.
- Short run. If a slightly longer time period is allowed to elapse, some inputs can be increased (e.g. raw materials), while others will remain fixed (e.g. heavy machinery). Supply can increase somewhat. This is illustrated by S_S. Equilibrium will move to point c with price falling again, to P_3, and quantity rising to Q_3.
- Long run. In the long run, there will be sufficient time for all inputs to be increased and for new firms to enter the industry. Supply, therefore, is likely to be highly elastic. This is illustrated by curve S_L. Long-run equilibrium will be at point d with price falling back even further, to P_4, and quantity rising all the way to Q_4. In some circumstances the supply curve may even slope downward. (See the section on economies of scale in Chapter 9, pages 180–2.)

Figure 5.8 Supply in different time periods

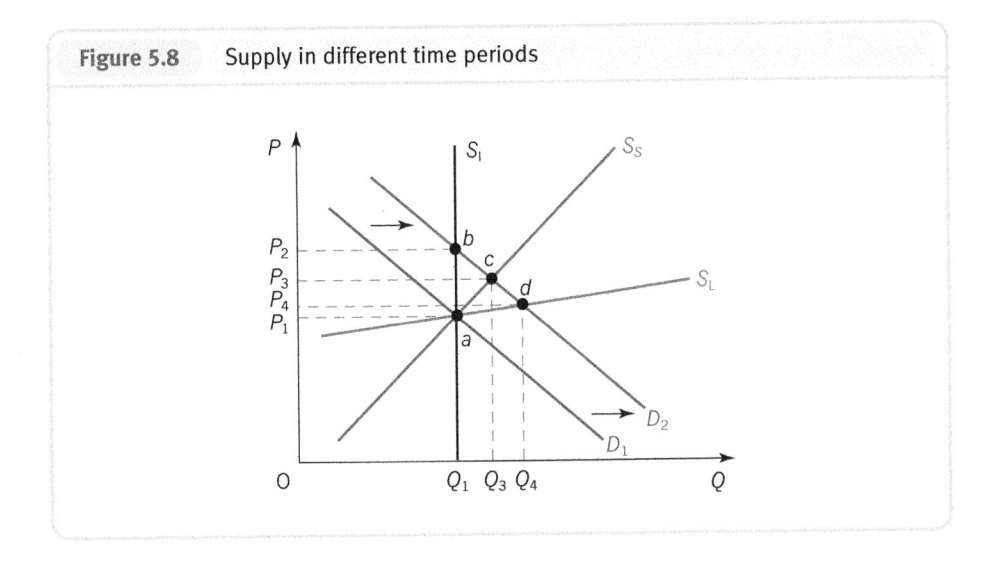

THE TIME DIMENSION OF MARKET ADJUSTMENT

5.4

The full adjustment of price, demand and supply to a situation of disequilibrium will not be instantaneous. It is necessary, therefore, to analyse the time path which supply takes in responding to changes in demand, and which demand takes in responding to changes in supply.

Short-run and long-run adjustment

As we have already seen, elasticity varies with the time period under consideration. The reason is that producers and consumers take time to respond to a change in price. The longer the time period, the bigger the response, and thus the greater the elasticity of supply and demand.

This is illustrated in Figures 5.9 and 5.10. In both cases, as equilibrium moves from points *a* to *b* to *c*, there is a large short-run price change (P_1 to P_2) and a small

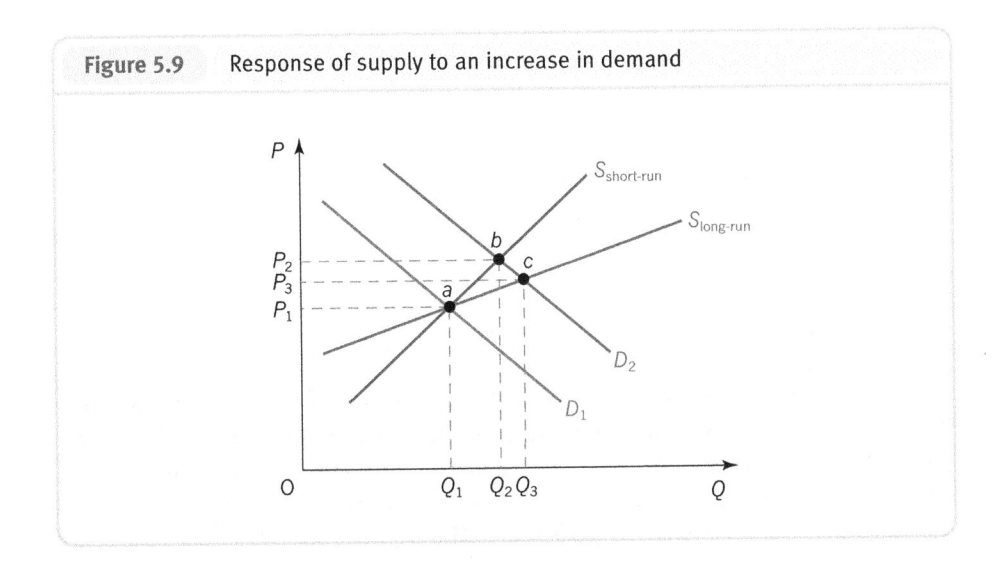

Figure 5.9 Response of supply to an increase in demand

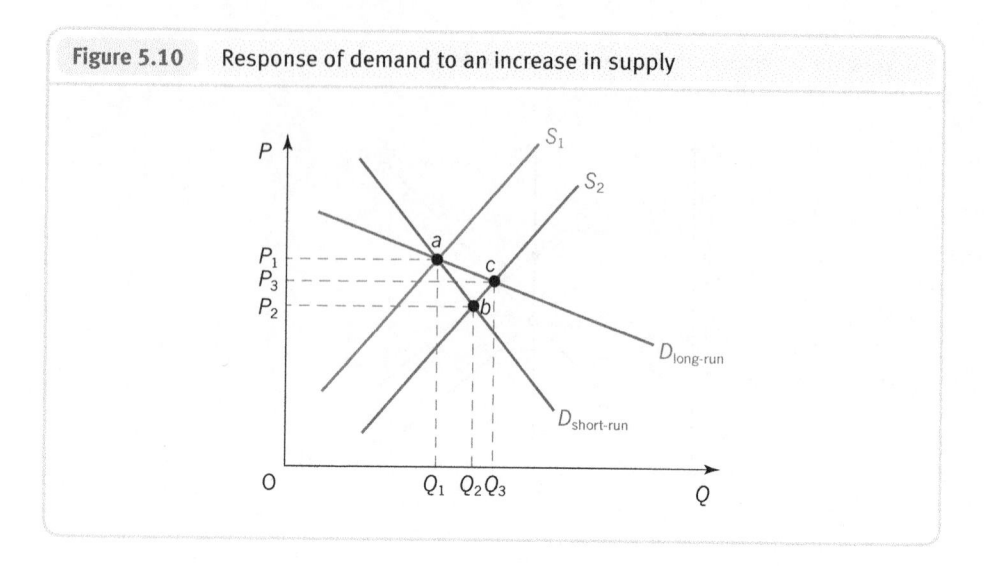

Figure 5.10 Response of demand to an increase in supply

short-run quantity change (Q_1 to Q_2), but a small long-run price change (P_1 to P_3) and a large long-run quantity change (Q_1 to Q_3).

Price expectations and speculation

In a world of shifting demand and supply curves, prices do not stay the same. Sometimes they go up; sometimes they come down. If prices are likely to change in the foreseeable future, this will affect the behaviour of buyers and sellers *now*. If, for example, it is now December and you are thinking of buying a new winter coat, you might decide to wait until the January sales, and in the meantime make do with your old coat. If, on the other hand, when January comes you see a new summer jacket in the sales, you might well buy it now and not wait until the summer, for fear that the price will have gone up by then. Thus a belief that prices will go up will cause people to buy now; a belief that prices will come down will cause them to wait.

The reverse applies to sellers. If you are thinking of selling your house and prices are falling, you will want to sell it as quickly as possible. If, on the other hand, prices are rising sharply, you will wait as long as possible so as to get the highest price. Thus a belief that prices will come down will cause people to sell now; a belief that prices will go up will cause them to wait.

> **KEY IDEA 13**
> *People's actions are influenced by their expectations.* People respond not just to what is happening now (such as a change in price), but to what they anticipate will happen in the future.

Definition

Speculation
This is where people make buying or selling decisions based on their anticipations of future prices.

This behaviour of looking into the future and making buying and selling decisions based on your predictions is called speculation. Speculation is often based on current trends in price behaviour. If prices are currently rising, people may try to decide whether they are about to peak and go back down again, or whether they are likely to go on rising. Having made their prediction, they will then act on it. This speculation will thus affect demand and supply, which in turn will affect price. Speculation is commonplace in many markets: the stock exchange (see Box 4.2), the foreign exchange market and the housing market (see Box 4.1) are

Figure 5.11 Speculation (initial rise in price)

(a) Stabilising speculation

(b) Destabilising speculation

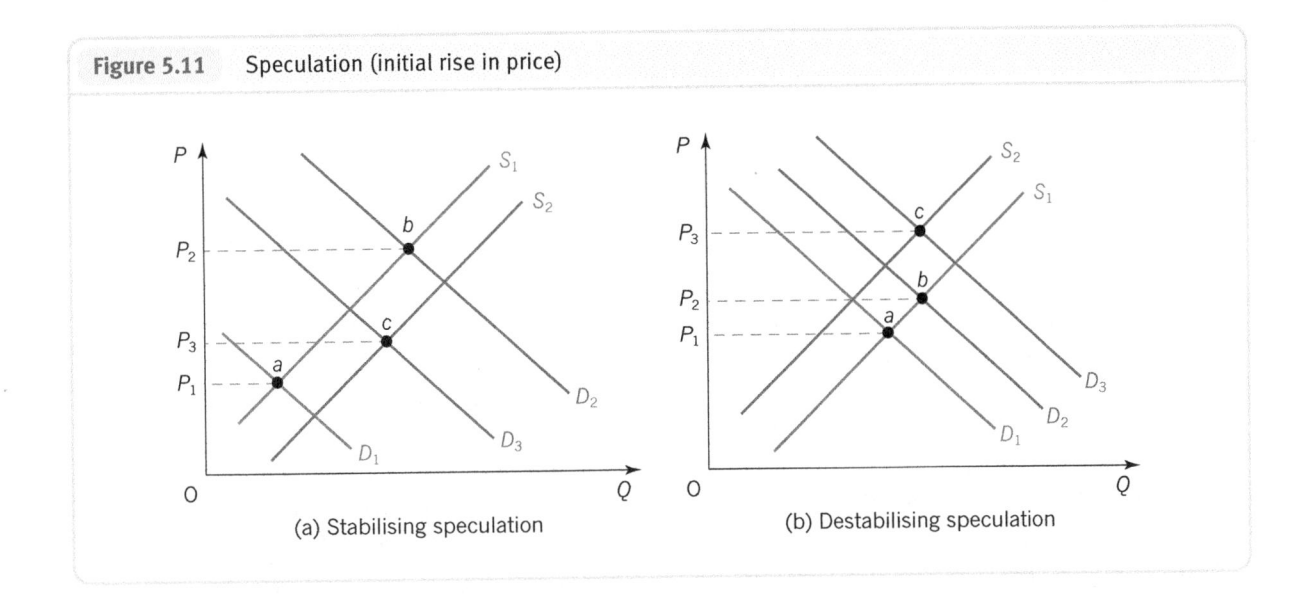

three examples. Large firms often employ specialist buyers who choose the right time to buy inputs, depending on what they anticipate will happen to their price.

Speculation tends to be **self-fulfilling**. In other words, the actions of speculators tend to bring about the very effect on prices that speculators had anticipated. For example, if speculators believe that the price of BP shares is about to rise, they will buy more BP shares. But by doing this they will ensure that the price *will* rise. The prophecy has become self-fulfilling.

Speculation can either help to reduce price fluctuations or aggravate them: it can be stabilising or destabilising.

Stabilising speculation

Speculation will tend to have a **stabilising** effect on price fluctuations when suppliers and/or demanders believe that a change in price is only *temporary*.

Assume, for example, that there has recently been a rise in price, caused, say, by an increase in demand. In Figure 5.11(a) demand has shifted from D_1 to D_2. Equilibrium has moved from point *a* to point *b*, and price has risen from P_1 to P_2. How do people react to this rise in price?

Given that they believe this rise in price to be only temporary, suppliers bring their goods to market now, before price falls again. Supply shifts from S_1 to S_2. Demanders, however, hold back until price does fall. Demand shifts from D_2 to D_3. The equilibrium moves to point *c*, with price falling back towards P_1.

A good example of stabilising speculation is that which occurs in agricultural commodity markets. Take the case of wheat. When it is harvested in the autumn there will be a plentiful supply. If all this wheat were to be put on the market, the price would fall to a very low level. Later in the year, when most of the wheat would have been sold, the price would then rise to a very high level. This is all easily predictable.

So what do farmers do? The answer is that they speculate. When the wheat is harvested they know its price will tend to fall, and so instead of bringing it all to market they put a lot of it into store. The more price falls, the more they will put into store *anticipating that the price will later rise*. But this holding back of supplies prevents prices from falling. In other words, it stabilises prices.

Definitions

Self-fulfilling speculation
The actions of speculators tend to cause the very effect that they had anticipated.

Stabilising speculation
This is where the actions of speculators tend to reduce price fluctuations.

BOX 5.2 ADJUSTING TO OIL PRICE SHOCKS

Short-run and long-run demand and supply responses

Between December 1973 and June 1974, the Organization of Petroleum Exporting Countries (OPEC) put up the price of oil from $3 to $12 per barrel. It was further raised to over $30 in 1979. In the 1980s the price fluctuated, but the trend was downward. Except for a sharp rise at the time of the Gulf War in 1990, the trend continued through most of the 1990s, at times falling as low as $11.

In the early 2000s, oil prices were generally higher, first fluctuating between $19 and $33 per barrel and then, from 2004 to 2006, steadily rising. The price then increased dramatically from January 2007, when it was just over $50 per barrel, to mid-2008 when it reached $147 per barrel. By late 2008, however, the price had fallen back sharply to under $50 per barrel as fears of a world recession cut the demand for oil.

The price movements can be explained using simple demand and supply analysis.

The initial rise in price

In the 1970s OPEC raised the price from P_1 to P_2 (see diagram (a)). To prevent surplus at that price, OPEC members restricted their output by agreed amounts. This had the effect of shifting the supply curve to S_2, with Q_2 being produced. This reduction in output needed to be only relatively small because the short-run demand for oil was highly price inelastic: for most uses there are no substitutes in the short run.

Long-run effects on demand

The long-run demand for oil was more elastic (see diagram (b)). With high oil prices persisting, people tried to find ways of cutting back on consumption. People bought smaller cars. They converted to gas or solid-fuel central heating. Firms switched to other fuels. Less use was made of oil-fired power stations for electricity generation. Energy-saving schemes became widespread both in firms and in the home.

(a) An initial restriction of supply

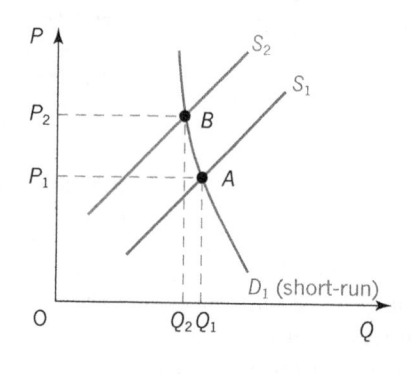

(b) Long-run demand response

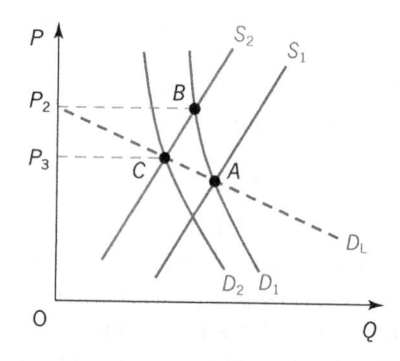

Later in the year, when the price begins to rise, they will gradually release grain on to the market from the stores. The more the price rises, the more will they release on to the market *anticipating that the price will fall again by the time of the next harvest*. But this releasing of supplies will again stabilise prices by preventing them rising so much.

Destabilising speculation

Speculation will tend to have a destabilising effect on price fluctuations when suppliers and/or buyers believe that a change in price heralds similar changes to come.

Assume again that there has recently been a rise in price, caused by an increase in demand. In Figure 5.11(b), demand has shifted from D_1 to D_2 and price has risen from P_1 to P_2. This time, however, believing that the rise in price heralds further rises to come, suppliers wait until the price rises further. Supply shifts from S_1 to S_2.

Definition

Destabilising speculation
This is where the actions of speculators tend to make price movements larger.

This had the effect of shifting the short-run demand curve from D_1 to D_2. Price fell back from P_2 to P_3. This gave a long-run demand curve of D_L: the curve that joins points A and C.

The fall in demand was made bigger by a world recession in the early 1980s.

Long-run effects on supply

With oil production so much more profitable, there was an incentive for non-OPEC oil producers to produce oil. Prospecting went on all over the world and large oil fields were discovered and opened up in the North Sea, Alaska, Mexico, China and elsewhere. In addition, OPEC members were tempted to break their 'quotas' (their allotted output) and sell more oil.

The net effect was an increase in world oil supplies. In terms of the diagrams, the supply curve of oil started to shift to the right from the mid-1980s onwards, causing oil prices to fall through most of the period up to 1998.

Back to square one?

By the late 1990s, with the oil price as low as $10 per barrel, OPEC once more cut back supply. The story had come full circle. This cut-back is once more illustrated in diagram (a).

The trouble this time was that worldwide economic growth was picking up. Demand was shifting to the right. The result was a rise in oil prices to around $33, which then fell back again in 2001 as the world slipped into recession and the demand curve shifted to the left.

There were then some very large price increases, first as a result of OPEC in late 2001 attempting once more to restrict supply (a leftward shift in supply), and then, before the Iraq war of 2003, because of worries about possible adverse effects on oil supplies (a rightward shift in demand as countries stocked up on oil). The worries about long-run security of supply continued after the invasion of Iraq and the continuing political uncertainty in the region.

The rises in the price of oil from 2004 through to mid-2008 were fuelled partly by rapidly expanding demand (a rightward shift in short-run demand), especially in countries such as China and India, and by speculation on the future price of oil. On the supply side, producers could not respond rapidly to meet this demand and there has been further disruption to supply in some oil-producing countries, including Nigeria and Algeria (a leftward shift in short-run supply). However, the dramatic rise in oil prices fuelled inflation across the world. Consumers and industry faced much higher costs and looked at methods to conserve fuel.

In late 2008, the global financial crisis was followed by recession. The price of oil began to fall back as the demand curve for oil shifted leftwards. It fell from a peak of $147 per barrel in July 2008 to a mere $34 per barrel by the end of the year. But then, as the world economy slowly recovered, so oil prices rose again. By late 2010, oil was trading at around $80 per barrel.

With both demand and supply being price *inelastic* in the short run, large fluctuations in price are only to be expected. And these are amplified by speculation.

The problem is made worse by an income *elastic* demand for oil. Demand can rise rapidly in times when the global economy is booming, only to fall back substantially in times of recession.

Give some examples of things that could make the demand for oil more elastic. What specific policies could the government introduce to make demand more elastic?

Demanders buy now before any further rise in price. Demand shifts from D_2 to D_3. As a result the price continues to rise: to P_3.

Box 4.1 examined the housing market. In this market, speculation is frequently destabilising. Assume that people see house prices beginning to move upward. This might be the result of increased demand brought about by a cut in mortgage interest rates or by growth in the economy. People may well believe that the rise in house prices signals a boom in the housing market: that prices will go on rising. Potential buyers will thus try to buy as soon as possible before prices rise any further. This increased demand (as in Figure 5.11(b)) will thus lead to even bigger price rises. This is precisely what happened in the UK housing market in 1999–2007.

Pause for thought

Draw two diagrams like Figures 5.11(a) and (b), only this time assume an initial fall in demand and hence price. The first diagram should show the effects of stabilising speculation and the second the effect of destabilising speculation.

> **Pause for thought**
>
> *What are the advantages and disadvantages of speculation from the point of view of (a) the consumer; (b) firms?*

Conclusion

In some circumstances, then, the action of speculators can help keep price fluctuations to a minimum (stabilising speculation). This is most likely when markets are relatively stable in the first place, with only moderate underlying shifts in demand and supply.

In other circumstances, however, speculation can make price fluctuations much worse. This is most likely in times of uncertainty, when there are significant changes in the determinants of demand and supply. Given this uncertainty, people may see price changes as signifying some trend. They then 'jump on the bandwagon' and do what the rest are doing, further fuelling the rise or fall in price.

5.5 DEALING WITH UNCERTAINTY

Risk and uncertainty

When price changes are likely to occur, buyers and sellers will try to anticipate them. Unfortunately, on many occasions no one can be certain just what these price changes will be. Take the case of stocks and shares. If you anticipate that the price of, say, BP shares is likely to go up substantially in the near future, you may well decide to buy some now and then sell them later after the price has risen. But you cannot be certain that they will go up in price: they may fall instead. If you buy the shares, therefore, you will be taking a gamble.

Now gambles can be of two types. The first is where you know the odds. Let us take the simplest case of a gamble on the toss of a coin. Heads you win; tails you lose. You know that the odds of winning are precisely 50 per cent. If you bet on the toss of a coin, you are said to be operating under conditions of risk. *Risk is when the probability of an outcome is known.* Risk itself is a measure of the *variability* of an outcome. For example, if you bet £1 on the toss of a coin, such that heads you win £1 and tails you lose £1, then the variability is –£1 to +£1.

The second form of gamble is the more usual. This is where the odds are not known or are known only roughly. Gambling on the Stock Exchange is like this. You may have a good idea that a share will go up in price, but is it a 90 per cent chance, an 80 per cent chance or what? You are not certain. Gambling under these sorts of conditions is known as operating under uncertainty. *This is when the probability of an outcome is not known.*

You may well disapprove of gambling and want to dismiss people who engage in it as foolish or morally wrong. But 'gambling' is not just confined to horses, cards, roulette and the like. Risk and uncertainty pervade the whole of economic life and decisions are constantly having to be made whose outcome cannot be known for certain. Even the most morally upright person will still have to decide which career to go into, whether and when to buy a house, or even something as trivial as whether or not to take an umbrella when going out. Each of these decisions and thousands of others are made under conditions of uncertainty (or occasionally risk).

> **Definitions**
>
> **Risk**
> This is when an outcome may or may not occur, but where its probability of occurring is known.
>
> **Uncertainty**
> This is when an outcome may or may not occur and where its probability of occurring is not known.

> **KEY IDEA 14**
>
> *People's actions are influenced by their attitudes towards risk.* Many decisions are taken under conditions of risk or uncertainty. Generally, the lower the probability of (or the more uncertain) the desired outcome of an action, the less likely will people be to undertake the action.

We shall be examining how risk and uncertainty affect economic decisions at several points throughout the book. For example, in the next chapter we will see how it affects people's attitudes and actions as consumers, and how taking out insurance can help to reduce their uncertainty. At this point, however, let us focus on firms' attitudes when supplying goods.

Stock holding as a way of reducing the problem of uncertainty. A simple way that suppliers can reduce risks is by holding stocks. Take the case of the wheat farmers we saw in the previous section. At the time when they are planting the wheat in the spring, they are uncertain as to what the price of wheat will be when they bring it to market. If they keep no stores of wheat, they will just have to accept whatever the market price happens to be at harvest time. If, however, they have storage facilities, they can put the wheat into store if the price is low and then wait until it goes up. Alternatively, if the price of wheat is high at harvest time, they can sell it straight away. In other words, they can wait until the price is right.

> **Pause for thought**
>
> *The demand for pears is more price elastic than the demand for bread and yet the price of pears fluctuates more than that of bread. Why should this be so? If pears could be stored as long and as cheaply as flour, would this affect the relative price fluctuations? If so, how?*

Purchasing information. One way of reducing uncertainty is to buy information. A firm could commission various forms of market research or purchase the information from specialist organisations. It is similar for consumers. You might take advice on shares from a stockbroker, or buy a copy of a consumer magazine, such as *Which?*. The buying and selling of information in this way helps substantially to reduce uncertainty.

Better information can also, under certain circumstances, help to make any speculation more stabilising. With poor information, people are much more likely to be guided by rumour or fear, which could well make speculation destabilising as people 'jump on the bandwagon'. If people generally are better informed, however, this is likely to make prices go more directly to a long-run stable equilibrium.

Dealing in futures markets

Another way of reducing or even eliminating uncertainty is by dealing in futures or forward markets. Let us examine the activities first of sellers and then of buyers.

Sellers

Suppose you are a farmer and want to store grain to sell some time in the future, expecting to get a better price then than now. The trouble is that there is a chance that the price will go down. Given this uncertainty, you may be unwilling to take a gamble.

An answer to your problem is provided by the *commodity futures market*. This is a market where prices are agreed between sellers and buyers *today* for delivery at some specified date in the *future*.

For example, if it is 20 October today, you could be quoted a price *today* for delivery in six months' time (i.e. on 20 April). This is known as the six-month future price. Assume that the six-month future price for wheat is £60 per tonne. If you agree to this price and make a six-month forward contract, you are agreeing to sell a specified amount of wheat at £60 on 20 April. No matter what happens to the spot price (i.e. the current market price) in the meantime, your selling price has been agreed. The spot price could have fallen to £30 (or risen to £100) by April, but your selling price when 20 April arrives is fixed at £60. There is thus *no risk to you whatsoever of the price going down*. You will, of course, lose out if the spot price is *more* than £60 in April.

> **Definitions**
>
> **Futures** or **forward market**
> A market in which contracts are made to buy or sell at some future date at a price agreed today.
>
> **Future price**
> A price agreed today at which an item (e.g. commodities) will be exchanged at some set date in the future.
>
> **Spot price**
> The current market price.

> **BOX 5.3** **DON'T SHOOT THE SPECULATOR**
>
> ### Well not yet, anyway!
>
> In February 2008 the United Nations Food and Agricultural Organisation stated that the price of cereals had risen 83 per cent over the previous 12 months, with dire consequences for developing nations in particular. In July 2008 the price of oil rose to the unprecedented high of over $140 per barrel, with devastating consequences for the millions of users of oil and oil-based products. During October 2008 the FTSE 100 fell almost 11 per cent, a fall that had not been seen since October 1987, offering misery to millions of ordinary investors and those with pensions.
>
> Much of the blame for these dramatic changes is placed on speculators who are seen as exacerbating the problem. They are seen as greedy and acting immorally, and affecting the lives of millions of ordinary people through their actions. Thankfully, no one in power has yet adopted Vladimir Lenin's declaration to a meeting at the Petrograd Soviet in 1918 that 'Speculators who are caught and fully exposed as such shall be shot . . . on the spot.' However, religious leaders, politicians and regulators have been calling for, and getting, stricter controls over their operations.
>
> This commonly held view of the speculator, however, is not held by everyone. Consider the following taken from *The Economist* in regard to the rapid rise in oil prices in 2008.
>
>> Jeffrey Harris, the chief economist of the Commodity Futures Trading Commission (CFTC), which regulates NYMEX and other American commodities exchanges, does not see any evidence that the growth of speculation in oil has caused the price to rise. Rising prices, after all, might have been stimulating the growing investment, rather than the other way around. There is no clear correlation between increased speculation and higher prices in commodities markets in general. Despite a continuing flow of investment in nickel, for example, its price has fallen by half over the past year.
>>
>> By the same token, the prices of several commodities that are not traded on any exchange, and are therefore much harder for speculators to invest in, have risen even faster than that of oil. Deutsche Bank calculates that cadmium, a rare metal, has appreciated twice as much as oil since 2001, for example, and the price of rice has risen fractionally more.
>>
>> Investment can flood into the oil market without driving up prices because speculators are not buying any actual crude. Instead, they buy contracts for future delivery. When those contracts mature, they either settle them with a cash payment or sell them on to genuine consumers. Either way, no oil is hoarded or somehow kept off the market. The contracts are really a bet about which way the price will go and the number of bets does not affect the amount of oil available. As Mr Harris puts it, there is no limit to the number of 'paper barrels' that can be bought and sold.
>>
>> That makes it harder for a bubble to develop in oil than in the shares of internet firms, say, or in housing, where the supply of the asset is finite. Ultimately, . . . there is only one type of customer for crude: refineries. If speculators on the futures markets get carried away, pushing prices so high that refineries run at a loss, they will simply shut down, causing the price to fall again. Moreover, speculators do not always assume that prices will rise.[1]
>
> Thus, speculators are adjusting their decisions in line with changing circumstances. In other words, they are being efficient, although this does not necessarily imply that their decisions are correct!
>
> *How might it be beneficial for the economy if speculators were less efficient?*
>
> ---
>
> [1] 'Double, double, toil and trouble', *The Economist*, 29 May 2008. Copyright © 2008 The Economist Newspapers Limited, London. Reproduced with permission.

Buyers

Now suppose that you are a flour miller. In order to plan your expenditures, you would like to know the price you will have to pay for wheat, not just today, but also at various future dates. In other words, if you want to take delivery of wheat at some time in the future, you would like a price quoted *now*. You would like the risks removed of prices going *up*.

Let us assume that today (20 October) you want to *buy* the same amount of wheat on 20 April that a farmer wishes to sell on that same date. If you agree to the £60 future price, a future contract can be made with the farmer. You are then guaranteed that purchase price, no matter what happens to the spot price in the meantime. There is thus *no risk to you whatsoever of the price going up.* You will, of course, lose out if the spot price is *less* than £60 in April.

The determination of the future price

Prices in the futures market are determined in the same way as in other markets: by demand and supply. For example, the six-month wheat price or the three-month coffee price will be that which equates the demand for those futures with the supply. If the five-month sugar price is currently £200 per tonne and people expect by then, because of an anticipated good beet harvest, that the spot price for sugar will be £150 per tonne, there will be few who will want to buy the futures at £200 (and many who will want to sell). This excess of supply of futures over demand will push the price down.

Speculators

Many people operate in the futures market who never actually handle the commodities themselves. They are neither producers nor users of the commodities. They merely speculate. Such speculators may be individuals, but they are more likely to be financial institutions.

Let us take a simple example. Suppose that the six-month (April) coffee price is £1000 per tonne and that you, as a speculator, believe that the spot price of coffee is likely to rise above that level between now (October) and six months' time. You thus decide to buy 20 tonnes of April coffee futures now.

But you have no intention of taking delivery. After four months, let us say, true to your prediction, the spot price (February) has risen and as a result the April price (and other future prices) have risen too. You thus decide to *sell* 20 tonnes of April (two-month) coffee futures, whose price, let us say, is £1200. You are now 'covered'.

When April comes, what happens? You have agreed to buy 20 tonnes of coffee at £1000 per tonne and to sell 20 tonnes of coffee at £1200 per tonne. All you do is hand the futures contract to buy to the person to whom you agreed to sell. They sort out delivery between them and you make £200 per tonne profit.

If, however, your prediction had been wrong and the price had *fallen*, you would have made a loss. You would have been forced to sell coffee contracts at a lower price than you had bought them.

Speculators in the futures market thus incur risks, unlike the sellers and buyers of the commodities, for whom the futures market eliminates risk. Financial institutions offering futures contracts will charge for the service: for taking on the risks.

SUMMARY

1a Price elasticity of demand measures the responsiveness of demand to a change in price. It is defined as the proportionate (or percentage) change in quantity demanded divided by the proportionate (or percentage) change in price.

1b If quantity demanded changes proportionately more than price, the figure for elasticity will be greater than 1 (ignoring the sign): it is elastic. If the quantity demanded changes proportionately less than price, the figure for elasticity will be less than 1: it is inelastic. If they change by the same proportion, the elasticity has a value of 1: it is unit elastic.

1c Given that demand curves are downward sloping, price elasticity of demand will have a negative value.

1d Demand will be more elastic the greater the number and closeness of substitute goods, the higher the proportion of income spent on the good and the longer the time period that elapses after the change in price.

1e Demand curves normally have different elasticities along their length. We can thus normally refer only to the specific value for elasticity between two points on the curve or at a single point.

2a It is important for firms to know the price elasticity of demand for their product whenever they are considering a price change. The reason is that the effect of the price change on the firm's sales revenue will depend on the product's price elasticity.

2b When the demand for a firm's product is price elastic, a rise in price will lead to a reduction in consumer expenditure on the good and hence to a reduction in the total revenue of the firm.

2c When demand is price inelastic, however, a rise in price will lead to an increase in total revenue for the firm.

3a Income elasticity of demand measures the responsiveness of demand to a change in income. For normal goods it has a positive value. Demand will be more income elastic the more luxurious the good and the less rapidly demand is satisfied as consumption increases.

3b Cross-price elasticity of demand measures the responsiveness of demand for one good to a change in the price of another. For substitute goods the value will be positive; for complements it will be negative. The cross-price elasticity will be greater the closer the two goods are as substitutes or complements.

3c Price elasticity of supply measures the responsiveness of supply to a change in price. It has a positive value. Supply will be more elastic the less costs per unit rise as output rises and the longer the time period.

4a A complete understanding of markets must take into account the time dimension.

4b Given that producers and consumers take a time to respond fully to price changes, we can identify different equilibria after the elapse of different lengths of time. Generally, short-run supply and demand tend to be less price elastic than long-run supply and demand. As a result any shifts in demand or supply curves tend to have a relatively bigger effect on price in the short run and a relatively bigger effect on quantity in the long run.

4c People often anticipate price changes and this will affect the amount they demand or supply. This speculation will tend to stabilise price fluctuations if people believe that the price changes are only temporary. However, speculation will tend to destabilise these fluctuations (i.e. make them more severe) if people believe that prices are likely to continue to move in the same direction as at present (at least for some time).

5a A lot of economic decision making is made under conditions of risk or uncertainty.

5b Risk is when the probability of an outcome occurring is known. Uncertainty is when the probability is not known.

5c One way of reducing risks is to hold stocks. If the price of a firm's product falls unexpectedly, it can build up stocks rather than releasing its product on to the market. If the price later rises, it can then release stocks on to the market. Similarly with inputs: if their price falls unexpectedly, firms can build up their stocks, only to draw on them later if input prices rise.

5d A way of eliminating risk and uncertainty is to deal in the futures markets. When firms are planning to buy or sell at some point in the future, there is the danger that price could rise or fall unexpectedly in the meantime. By agreeing to buy or sell at some particular point in the future at a price agreed today (a 'future' price), this danger can be eliminated. The bank or other institution offering the price (the 'speculator') is taking on the risk, and will charge for this service.

REVIEW QUESTIONS

1. Why does price elasticity of demand have a negative value, whereas price elasticity of supply has a positive value?

2. Rank the following in ascending order of elasticity: jeans, black Levi jeans, black jeans, black Levi 501 jeans, trousers, outer garments, clothes.

3. How might a firm set about making the demand for its brand less elastic?

4. Will a general item of expenditure like food or clothing have a price elastic or inelastic demand?

5. Assuming that a firm faces an inelastic demand and wants to increase its total revenue, how much should it raise its price? Is there any limit?

6. Can you think of any examples of goods which have a totally inelastic demand (a) at all prices; (b) over a particular price range?

7 Which of these two pairs are likely to have the highest cross-price elasticity of demand: two brands of coffee, or coffee and tea?

8 Why are both the price elasticity of demand and the price elasticity of supply likely to be greater in the long run?

9 Redraw Figure 5.11, only this time assume that it was an initial shift in supply that caused price to change in the first place.

10 Give some examples of decisions you have taken recently that were made under conditions of uncertainty. With hindsight do you think you made the right decisions? Explain.

11 What methods can a firm use to reduce risk and uncertainty?

12 If speculators believed that the price of cocoa in six months was going to be below the six-month future price quoted today, how would they act?

Additional Part B case studies on the *Economics for Business* website (www.pearsoned.co.uk/sloman)

B.1 **The interdependence of markets.** A case study of the operation of markets, examining the effects on a local economy of the discovery of a large coal deposit.

B.2 **Adam Smith (1723–1790).** Smith, the founder of modern economics, argued that markets act like an 'invisible hand' guiding production and consumption.

B.3 **Shall we put up our price?** Some examples of firms charging high prices in markets where demand is relatively inelastic.

B.4 **Any more fares?** Pricing on the buses: an illustration of the relationship between price and total revenue.

B.5 **Elasticities of demand for various foodstuffs.** An examination of the evidence about price and income elasticities of demand for food in the UK.

B.6 **Adjusting to oil price shocks.** A case study showing how demand and supply analysis can be used to examine the price changes in the oil market since 1973.

B.7 **Income elasticity of demand and the balance of payments.** This examines how a low income elasticity of demand for the exports of many developing countries can help to explain their chronic balance of payments problems.

B.8 **The cobweb.** An outline of the theory that explains price fluctuations in terms of time lags in supply.

B.9 **The role of the speculator.** This assesses whether the activities of speculators are beneficial or harmful to the rest of society.

B.10 **Rationing.** A case study in the use of rationing as an alternative to the price mechanism. In particular, it looks at the use of rationing in the UK during the Second World War.

B.11 **Rent control.** This shows how setting (low) maximum rents is likely to lead to a shortage of rented accommodation.

B.12 **Agriculture and minimum prices.** This shows how setting (high) minimum prices is likely to lead to surpluses.

B.13 **The fallacy of composition.** An illustration from agricultural markets of the fallacy of composition: 'what applies in one case will not necessarily apply when repeated in all cases'.

Websites relevant to Part B

Numbers and sections refer to websites listed in the Web appendix and hotlinked from this book's website at **www.pearsoned.co.uk/sloman**

- For news articles relevant to Part B, see the *Economics News Articles* link from the book's website.
- For general news on markets, see websites in section A, and particularly A2, 3, 4, 5, 8, 9, 18, 20–26, 35, 36. See also site A42 for links to economics news articles from newspapers worldwide.
- For links to sites on markets, see the relevant sections of I4, 7, 11, 17.
- For data on the housing market (Box 4.1), see sites B7, 8, 11.
- For student resources relevant to Part B, see sites C1–7, 9, 10, 19; D3.
- For sites favouring the free market, see C17 and E34.

Chapter 9

Costs of production

Business issues covered in this chapter

- What do profits consist of?
- How are costs of production measured?
- What is the relationship between inputs and outputs in both the short and long run?
- How do costs vary with output in both the short and long run?
- What are meant by 'economies of scale' and what are the reasons for such economies?
- How can a business combine its inputs in the most efficient way?

9.1 THE MEANING OF COSTS

Opportunity cost

When measuring costs, economists always use the concept of opportunity cost. As we saw in Chapter 2, opportunity cost is the cost of any activity measured in terms of the sacrifice made in doing it: in other words, the cost measured in terms of the opportunities forgone. If a car manufacturer can produce 10 small saloon cars with the same amount of inputs as it takes to produce 6 large saloon cars, then the opportunity cost of producing 1 small car is 0.6 of a large car. If a taxi and car hire firm uses its cars as taxis, then the opportunity cost includes not only the cost of employing taxi drivers and buying fuel, but also the sacrifice of rental income from hiring its vehicles out.

> **Definition**
>
> **Opportunity cost**
> Cost measured in terms of the next best alternative forgone.

Measuring a firm's opportunity costs

Just how do we measure a firm's opportunity cost? First we must discover what factors of production it has used. Then we must measure the sacrifice involved in using them. To do this it is necessary to put factors into two categories.

Factors not owned by the firm: explicit costs

The opportunity cost of those factors not already owned by the firm is simply the price that the firm has to pay for them. Thus if the firm uses £100 worth of electricity, the opportunity cost is £100. The firm has sacrificed £100 which could have been spent on something else.

These costs are called explicit costs because they involve direct payment of money by firms.

Factors already owned by the firm: implicit costs

When the firm already owns factors (e.g. machinery), it does not as a rule have to pay out money to use them. Their opportunity costs are thus implicit costs. They are equal to what the factors *could* earn for the firm in some alternative use, either within the firm or hired out to some other firm.

Here are some examples of implicit costs:

- A firm owns some buildings. The opportunity cost of using them is the rent it could have received by letting them out to another firm.
- A firm draws £100 000 from the bank out of its savings in order to invest in new plant and equipment. The opportunity cost of this investment is not just the £100 000 (an explicit cost), but also the interest it thereby forgoes (an implicit cost).

> **Definitions**
>
> **Explicit costs**
> The payments to outside suppliers of inputs.
>
> **Implicit costs**
> Costs which do not involve a direct payment of money to a third party, but which nevertheless involve a sacrifice of some alternative.

BOX 9.1 THE FALLACY OF USING HISTORIC COSTS

Or there's no point crying over spilt milk

'What's done is done.'
'Write it off to experience.'
'You might as well make the best of a bad job.'

These familiar sayings are all everyday examples of a simple fact of life: once something has happened, you cannot change the past. You have to take things as they are *now*.

If you fall over and break your leg, there is little point in saying, 'If only I hadn't done that I could have gone on that skiing holiday; I could have taken part in that race; I could have done so many other things (sigh).' Wishing things were different won't change history. You have to manage as well as you can *with* your broken leg.

It is the same for a firm. Once it has purchased some inputs, it is no good then wishing it hadn't. It has to accept that it has now got them, and make the best decisions about what to do with them.

Take a simple example. The local convenience store in early December decides to buy 100 Christmas trees for £10 each. At the time of purchase this represents an opportunity cost of £10 each, since the £10 could have been spent on something else. The shopkeeper estimates that there is enough local demand to sell all 100 trees at £20 each, thereby making a reasonable profit (even after allowing for handling costs).

But the estimate turns out to be wrong. On 23 December there are still 50 trees unsold. What should be done? At this stage the £10 that was paid for the trees is irrelevant. It is a historic cost. It cannot be recouped: the trees cannot be sold back to the wholesaler!

In fact the opportunity cost is now zero. It might even be negative if the shopkeeper has to pay to dispose of any unsold trees. It might, therefore, be worth selling the trees at £10, £5 or even £1. Last thing on Christmas Eve it might even be worth giving away any unsold trees.

Why is the correct price to charge (for the unsold trees) the one at which the price elasticity of demand equals −1? (Assume no disposal costs.)

Costs of Production

- The owner of the firm could have earned £15 000 per annum by working for someone else. This £15 000 is the opportunity cost of the owner's time.

If there is no alternative use for a factor of production, as in the case of a machine designed to produce a specific product, and if it has no scrap value, the opportunity cost of using it is *zero*. In such a case, if the output from the machine is worth more than the cost of all the *other* inputs involved, the firm might as well use the machine rather than let it stand idle.

What the firm paid for the machine – its historic cost – is irrelevant. Not using the machine will not bring that money back. It has been spent. These are sometimes referred to as sunk costs.

> **KEY IDEA 18**
> The *'bygones' principle* states that sunk (fixed) costs should be ignored when deciding whether to produce or sell more or less of a product. Only variable costs should be taken into account.

Likewise, the replacement cost is irrelevant. That should be taken into account only when the firm is considering replacing the machine.

> **Pause for thought**
>
> *Assume that a farmer decides to grow wheat on land that could be used for growing barley. Barley sells for £100 per tonne. Wheat sells for £150 per tonne. Seed, fertiliser, labour and other costs of growing crops are £80 per tonne for both wheat and barley. What are the farmer's costs and profit per tonne of growing wheat?*

> **Definitions**
>
> **Historic costs**
> The original amount the firm paid for factors it now owns.
>
> **Sunk costs**
> Costs that cannot be recouped (e.g. by transferring assets to other uses).

PRODUCTION IN THE SHORT RUN 9.2

The cost of producing any level of output will depend on the amount of inputs used and the price that the firm must pay for them. Let us first focus on the quantity of inputs used.

> **KEY IDEA 19**
> *Output depends on the amount of resources and how they are used.* Different amounts and combinations of inputs will lead to different amounts of output. If output is to be produced efficiently, then inputs should be combined in the optimum proportions.

Short-run and long-run changes in production

If a firm wants to increase production, it will take time to acquire a greater quantity of certain inputs. For example, a manufacturer can use more electricity by turning on switches, but it might take a long time to obtain and install more machines, and longer still to build a second or third factory.

If, then, the firm wants to increase output in a hurry, it will only be able to increase the quantity of certain inputs. It can use more raw materials, more fuel, more tools and possibly more labour (by hiring extra workers or offering overtime to its existing workforce). But it will have to make do with its existing buildings and most of its machinery.

The distinction we are making here is between fixed factors and variable factors. A *fixed* factor is an input that cannot be increased within a given time period (e.g. buildings). A *variable* factor is one that can.

> **Definitions**
>
> **Replacement costs**
> What the firm would have to pay to replace factors it currently owns.
>
> **Fixed factor**
> An input that cannot be increased in supply within a given time period.
>
> **Variable factor**
> An input that *can* be increased in supply within a given time period.

> **Definitions**
>
> **Short run**
> The period of time over which at least one factor is fixed.
>
> **Long run**
> The period of time long enough for *all* factors to be varied.

The distinction between fixed and variable factors allows us to distinguish between the short run and the long run.

The short run is a time period during which at least one factor of production is fixed. In the short run, then, output can be increased only by using more variable factors. For example, if a shipping line wanted to carry more passengers in response to a rise in demand, it could accommodate more passengers on existing sailings if there was space. It could increase the number of sailings with its existing fleet, by hiring more crew and using more fuel. But in the short run it could not buy more ships: there would not be time for them to be built.

The long run is a time period long enough for all inputs to be varied. Given long enough, the shipping company can have a new ship built.

The actual length of the short run will differ from firm to firm. It is not a fixed period of time. Thus if it takes a farmer a year to obtain new land, buildings and equipment, the short run is any time period up to a year and the long run is any time period longer than a year. But if it takes a shipping company three years to obtain an extra ship, the short run is any period up to three years and the long run is any period longer than three years.

For this and the next section we will concentrate on *short-run* production and costs. We will look at the long run in sections 9.4 and 9.5.

> **Pause for thought**
>
> *How will the length of the short run for the shipping company depend on the state of the shipbuilding industry?*

Production in the short run: the law of diminishing returns

Production in the short run is subject to *diminishing returns*. You may well have heard of 'the law of diminishing returns': it is one of the most famous of all 'laws' of economics. To illustrate how this law underlies short-run production, let us take the simplest possible case where there are just two factors: one fixed and one variable.

Take the case of a farm. Assume the fixed factor is land and the variable factor is labour. Since the land is fixed in supply, output per period of time can be increased only by increasing the number of workers employed. But imagine what would happen as more and more workers crowded on to a fixed area of land. The land cannot go on yielding more and more output indefinitely. After a point the additions to output from each extra worker will begin to diminish.

We can now state the law of diminishing (marginal) returns.

> **Definitions**
>
> **Law of diminishing (marginal) returns**
> When one or more factors are held fixed, there will come a point beyond which the extra output from additional units of the variable factor will diminish.
>
> **Total physical product**
> The total output of a product per period of time that is obtained from a given amount of inputs.

> **KEY IDEA 20**
>
> *The law of diminishing marginal returns.* When increasing amounts of a variable factor are used with a given amount of a fixed factor, there will come a point when each extra unit of the variable factor will produce less extra output than the previous unit.

A good example of the law of diminishing returns is given in Case D.3 on the book's website (www.pearsoned.co.uk/sloman). The case looks at diminishing returns to the application of nitrogen fertiliser on farmland.

The short-run production function: total product

Let us now see how the law of diminishing returns affects total output or total physical product (*TPP*).

Table 9.1 Wheat production per year from a particular farm (tonnes)

	Number of workers (Lb)	TPP	APP (= TPP/Lb)	MPP (= ΔTPP/ΔLb)
a	0	0	–	
				3
	1	3	3	
				7
	2	10	5	
b				14
	3	24	8	
				12
c	4	36	9	
				4
	5	40	8	
				2
	6	42	7	
d				0
	7	42	6	
				−2
	8	40	5	

The relationship between inputs and output is shown in a production function. In the simple case of the farm with only two factors – namely, a fixed supply of land ($\bar{L}n$) and a variable supply of farm workers (Lb) – the production function would be:

$$TPP = f(\bar{L}n, Lb)$$

This states that total physical product (i.e. the output of the farm) over a given period of time is a function of (i.e. depends on) the quantity of land and labour employed.

The production function can also be expressed in the form of a table or a graph. Table 9.1 and Figure 9.1 show a hypothetical production function for a farm producing wheat. The first two columns of Table 9.1 and the top diagram in Figure 9.1 show how wheat output per year varies as extra workers are employed on a fixed amount of land.

With nobody working on the land, output will be zero (point a). As the first farm workers are taken on, wheat output initially rises more and more rapidly. The assumption behind this is that with only one or two workers efficiency is low, since the workers are spread too thinly. With more workers, however, they can work together – each, perhaps, doing some specialist job – and thus they can use the land more efficiently. In the top diagram of Figure 9.1, output rises more and more rapidly up to the employment of the third worker (point b).

After point b, however, diminishing marginal returns set in: output rises less and less rapidly, and the TPP curve correspondingly becomes less steeply sloped.

When point d is reached, wheat output is at a maximum: the land is yielding as much as it can. Any more workers employed after that are likely to get in each other's way. Thus beyond point d, output is likely to fall again: eight workers produce less than seven workers.

The short-run production function: average and marginal product

In addition to total physical product, two other important concepts are illustrated by a production function: namely, average physical product (*APP*) and marginal physical product (*MPP*).

Average physical product

This is output (*TPP*) per unit of the variable factor (*Qv*). In the case of the farm, it is the output of wheat per worker.

$$APP = TPP/Qv$$

Definitions

Production function
The mathematical relationship between the output of a good and the inputs used to produce it. It shows how output will be affected by changes in the quantity of one or more of the inputs.

Average physical product (APP)
Total output (*TPP*) per unit of the variable factor in question: $APP = TPP/Qv$.

Marginal physical product (MPP)
The extra output gained by the employment of one more unit of the variable factor: $MPP = \Delta TPP/\Delta Qv$.

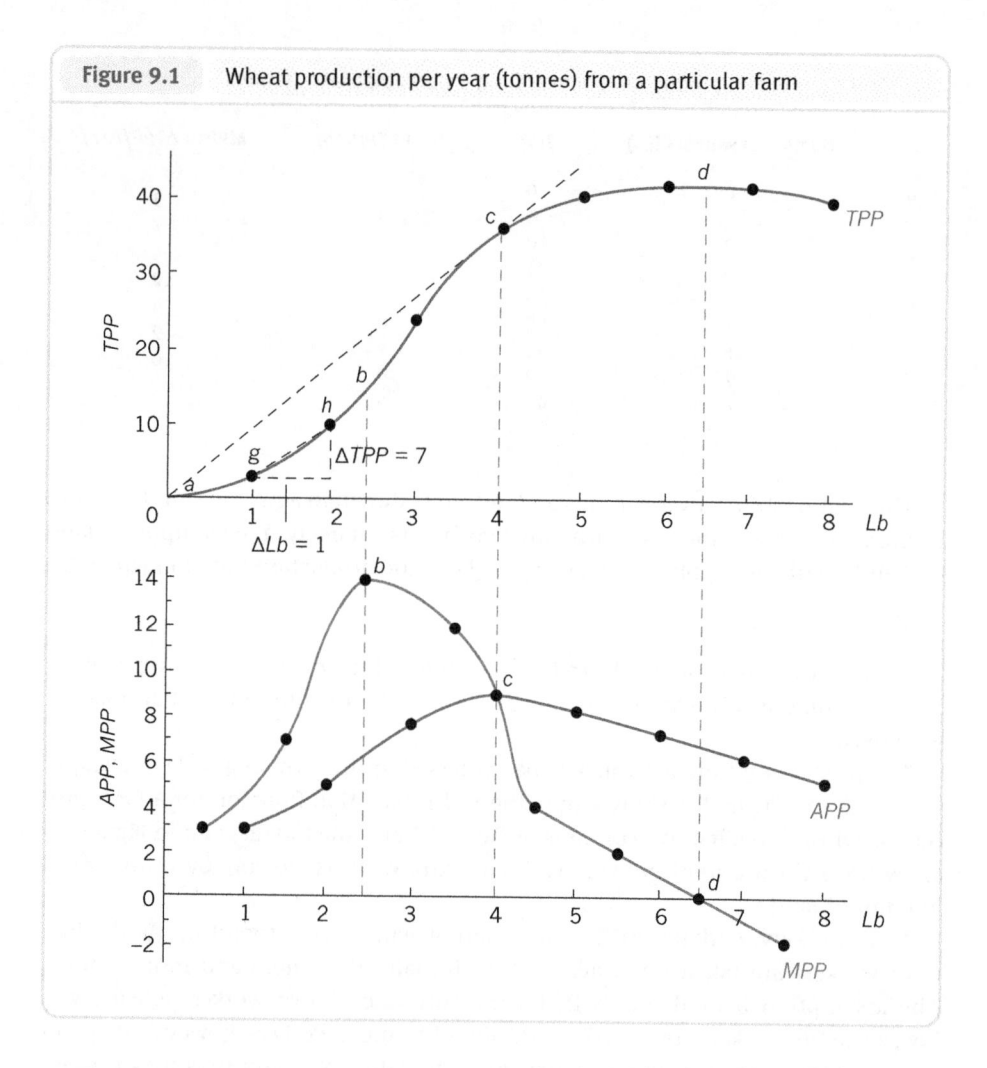

Figure 9.1 Wheat production per year (tonnes) from a particular farm

Thus in Table 9.1, the average physical product of labour when four workers are employed is 36/4 = 9 tonnes per year.

Marginal physical product

This is the *extra* output (ΔTPP) produced by employing *one more* unit of the variable factor.

Thus in Table 9.1 the marginal physical product of the fourth worker is 12 tonnes. The reason is that, by employing the fourth worker, wheat output has risen from 24 tonnes to 36 tonnes: a rise of 12 tonnes.

In symbols, marginal physical product is given by:

$$MPP = \Delta TPP/\Delta Qv$$

Thus in our example:

$$MPP = 12/1 = 12$$

The reason why we divide the increase in output (ΔTPP) by the increase in the quantity of the variable factor (ΔQv) is that some variable factors can be increased only in multiple units. For example, if we wanted to know the *MPP* of fertiliser and we found out how much extra wheat was produced by using an extra 20 kg bag, we would have to divide this output by 20 (ΔQv) to find the *MPP* of *one* more kilogram.

Note that in Table 9.1 the figures for *MPP* are entered in the spaces between the other figures. The reason is that *MPP* can be seen as the *difference* in output *between* one level of input and another. Thus in the table the difference in output between five and six workers is 2 tonnes.

The figures for *APP* and *MPP* are plotted in the lower diagram of Figure 9.1. We can draw a number of conclusions from these two diagrams.

- The *MPP* between two points is equal to the slope of the *TPP* curve between those two points. For example, when the number of workers increases from 1 to 2 ($\Delta Lb = 1$), *TPP* rises from 3 to 10 tonnes ($\Delta TPP = 7$). *MPP* is thus 7: the slope of the line between points *g* and *h*.
- *MPP* rises at first: the slope of the *TPP* curve gets steeper.
- *MPP* reaches a maximum at point *b*. At that point the slope of the *TPP* curve is at its steepest.
- After point *b*, diminishing returns set in. *MPP* falls. *TPP* becomes less steep.
- *APP* rises at first. It continues rising as long as the addition to output from the last worker (*MPP*) is greater than the average output (*APP*): the *MPP* pulls the *APP* up. This continues beyond point *b*. Even though *MPP* is now falling, the *APP* goes on rising as long as the *MPP* is still above the *APP*. Thus *APP* goes on rising to point *c*.
- Beyond point *c*, *MPP* is below *APP*. New workers add less to output than the average. This pulls the average down: *APP* falls.
- As long as *MPP* is greater than zero, *TPP* will go on rising: new workers add to total output.
- At point *d*, *TPP* is at a maximum (its slope is zero). An additional worker will add nothing to output: *MPP* is zero.
- Beyond point *d*, *TPP* falls. *MPP* is negative.

> **Pause for thought**
>
> What is the significance of the slope of the line *ac* in the top part of Figure 9.1?

COSTS IN THE SHORT RUN   9.3

Having looked at the background to costs in the short run, we now turn to examine short-run costs themselves. We will be examining how costs change as a firm changes the amount it produces. Obviously, if it is to decide how much to produce, it will need to know just what the level of costs will be at each level of output.

Costs and inputs

A firm's costs of production will depend on the factors of production it uses. The more factors it uses, the greater will its costs be. More precisely, this relationship depends on two elements.

The productivity of the factors. The greater their physical productivity, the smaller will be the quantity of them that is needed to produce a given level of output, and hence the lower will be the cost of that output. In other words, there is a direct link between *TPP*, *APP* and *MPP* and the costs of production.

The price of the factors. The higher their price, the higher will be the costs of production.

> **Definitions**
>
> **Fixed costs**
> Total costs that do not vary with the amount of output produced.
>
> **Variable costs**
> Total costs that do vary with the amount of output produced.
>
> **Total cost (*TC*)**
> The sum of total fixed costs (*TFC*) and total variable costs (*TVC*): *TC* = *TFC* + *TVC*.

In the short run, some factors are fixed in supply. Their total costs, therefore, are fixed, in the sense that they do not vary with output. Rent on land is a fixed cost. It is the same whether the firm produces a lot or a little.

The cost of variable factors, however, does vary with output. The cost of raw materials is a variable cost. The more that is produced, the more raw materials are used and therefore the higher is their total cost.

Total cost

The total cost (*TC*) of production is the sum of the *total variable costs* (*TVC*) and the *total fixed costs* (*TFC*) of production.

TC = *TVC* + *TFC*

Consider Table 9.2 and Figure 9.2. They show the total costs for an imaginary firm for producing different levels of output (*Q*). Let us examine each of the three cost curves in turn.

Total fixed cost (TFC)

In our example, total fixed cost is assumed to be £12. Since this does not vary with output, it is shown by a horizontal straight line.

Table 9.2 Total costs for firm X

Output (Q)	TFC (£)	TVC (£)	TC (£)
0	12	0	12
1	12	10	22
2	12	16	28
3	12	21	33
4	12	28	40
5	12	40	52
6	12	60	72
7	12	91	103

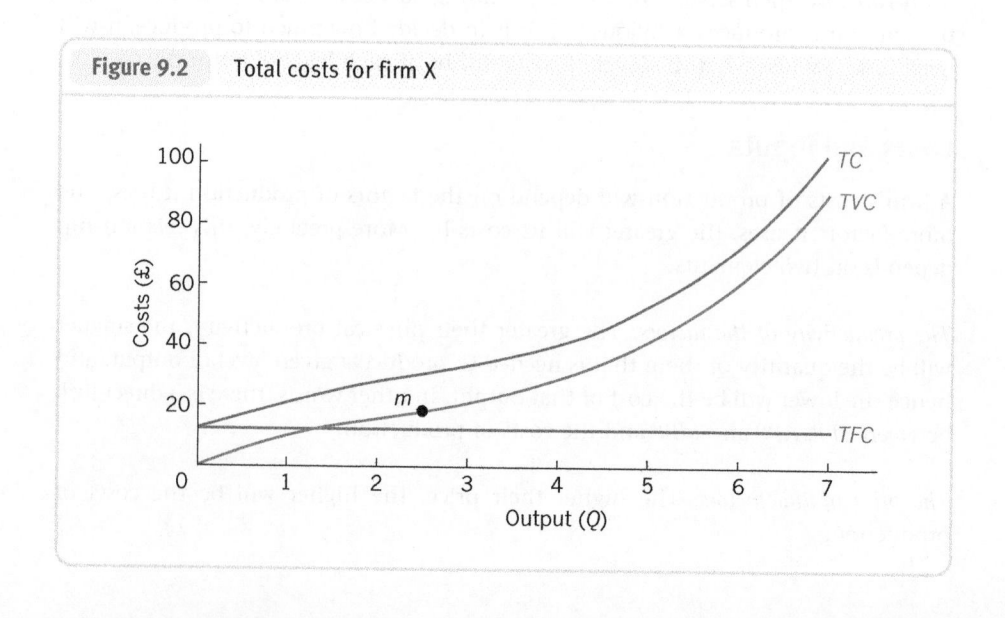

Figure 9.2 Total costs for firm X

Total variable cost (TVC)

With a zero output, no variable factors will be used. Thus $TVC = 0$. The TVC curve, therefore, starts from the origin.

The shape of the TVC curve follows from the law of diminishing returns. Initially, *before* diminishing returns set in, TVC rises less and less rapidly as more variable factors are added. For example, in the case of a factory with a fixed supply of machinery, initially as more workers are taken on the workers can do increasingly specialist tasks and make a fuller use of the capital equipment. This corresponds to the portion of the TPP curve that rises more rapidly (up to point *b* in the top diagram of Figure 9.1).

As output is increased beyond point *m* in Figure 9.2, diminishing returns set in. Given that extra workers (the extra variable factors) are producing less and less extra output, the extra units of output they do produce will be costing more and more in terms of wage costs. Thus TVC rises more and more rapidly. The TVC curve gets steeper. This corresponds to the portion of the TPP curve that rises less rapidly (between points *b* and *d* in Figure 9.1).

Total cost (TC)

Since $TC = TVC + TFC$, the TC curve is simply the TVC curve shifted vertically upwards by £12.

Average and marginal cost

Average cost (AC) is cost per unit of production.

$$AC = TC/Q$$

Thus if it costs a firm £2000 to produce 100 units of a product, the average cost would be £20 for each unit (£2000/100).

Like total cost, average cost can be divided into the two components, fixed and variable. In other words, average cost equals average fixed cost ($AFC = TFC/Q$) plus average variable cost ($AVC = TVC/Q$).

$$AC = AFC + AVC$$

Marginal cost (MC) is the *extra* cost of producing *one more unit*: that is, the rise in total cost per one unit rise in output.

$$MC = \frac{\Delta TC}{\Delta Q}$$

where Δ means 'a rise in'.

For example, assume that a firm is currently producing 1 000 000 boxes of matches a month. It now increases output by 1000 boxes, (another batch): $\Delta Q = 1000$. As a result its total costs rise by £30: $\Delta TC = £30$. What is the cost of producing *one* more box of matches? It is:

$$MC = \frac{\Delta TC}{\Delta Q} = \frac{£30}{1000} = 3p$$

(Note that all marginal costs are variable, since, by definition, there can be no extra fixed costs as output rises.)

Given the TFC, TVC and TC for each output, it is possible to derive the AFC, AVC, AC and MC for each output using the above definitions. For example, using the data of Table 9.2, Table 9.3 can be constructed.

> **Definitions**
>
> **Average (total) cost (AC)**
> Total cost (fixed plus variable) per unit of output:
> $AC = TC/Q = AFC + AVC$.
>
> **Average fixed cost (AFC)**
> Total fixed cost per unit of output: $AFC = TFC/Q$.
>
> **Average variable cost (AVC)**
> Total variable cost per unit of output:
> $AVC = TVC/Q$.
>
> **Marginal cost (MC)**
> The cost of producing one more unit of output:
> $MC = \Delta TC/\Delta Q$.

Table 9.3 Costs

Output (Q) (units)	TFC (£)	AFC (TFC/Q) (£)	TVC (£)	AVC (TVC/Q) (£)	TC (TFC + TVC) (£)	AC (TC/Q) (£)	MC (ΔTC/ΔQ) (£)
0	12	–	0	–	12	–	
1	12	12	10	10	22	22	10
2	12	6	16	8	28	14	6
3	12	4	21	7	33	11	5
4	12	3	28	7	40	10	7
5	12	2.4	40	8	52	10.4	12
6	12	2	60	10	72	12	20
7	12	1.7	91	13	103	14.7	31

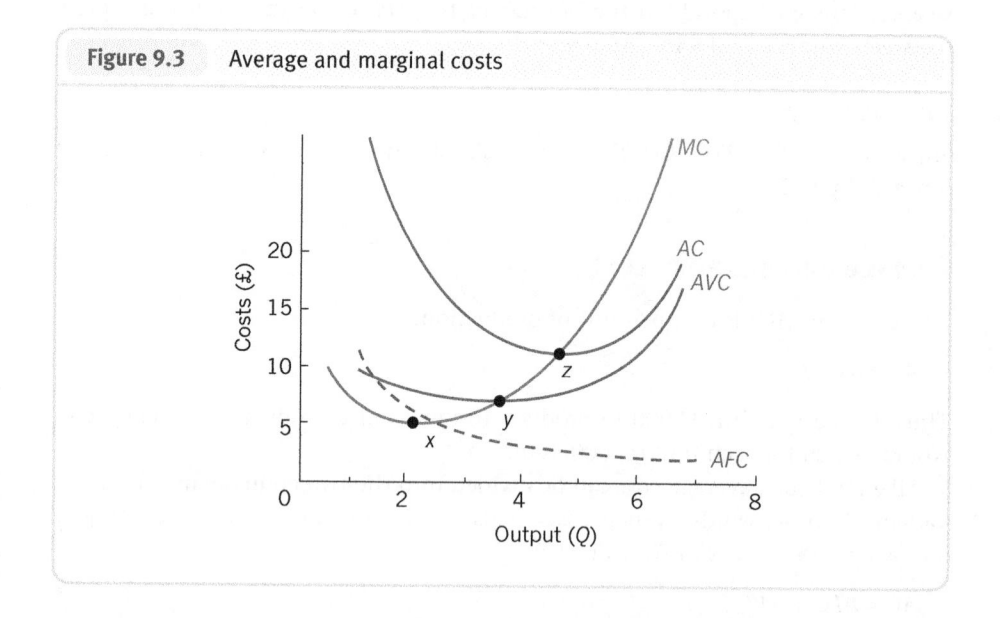

Figure 9.3 Average and marginal costs

What will be the shapes of the *MC*, *AFC*, *AVC* and *AC* curves? These follow from the nature of the *MPP* and *APP* curves that we looked at in section 9.2.

Marginal cost (MC)

The shape of the *MC* curve follows directly from the law of diminishing returns. Initially, in Figure 9.3, as more of the variable factor is used, extra units of output cost less than previous units. *MC* falls. This corresponds to the portion of the *TVC* curve in Figure 9.2 to the left of point *m*.

Beyond a certain level of output, diminishing returns set in. This is shown as point *x* in Figure 9.3 and corresponds to point *m* in Figure 9.2. Thereafter *MC* rises. Additional units of output cost more and more to produce, since they require ever increasing amounts of the variable factor.

Average fixed cost (AFC)

This falls continuously as output rises, since *total* fixed costs are being spread over a greater and greater output.

Average variable cost (AVC)

The shape of the AVC curve depends on the shape of the APP curve. As the average product of workers rises, the average labour cost per unit of output (the AVC) falls: up to point y in Figure 9.3. Thereafter, as APP falls, AVC must rise.

Average (total) cost (AC)

This is simply the vertical sum of the AFC and AVC curves. Note that, as AFC gets less, the gap between AVC and AC narrows.

The relationship between average cost and marginal cost

This is simply another illustration of the relationship that applies between *all* averages and marginals.

As long as new units of output cost less than the average, their production must pull the average cost down. That is, if MC is less than AC, AC must be falling. Likewise, if new units cost more than the average, their production must drive the average up. That is, if MC is greater than AC, AC must be rising. Therefore, the MC crosses the AC at its minimum point (point z in Figure 9.3).

> **Pause for thought**
>
> *Before you read on, can you explain why the marginal cost curve will always cut the average cost curve at its lowest point?*

BOX 9.2 SHORT-RUN COST CURVES IN PRACTICE

When fixed factors are divisible

Are short-run cost curves always the shape depicted in this chapter? The answer is no. Sometimes, rather than being U-shaped, the AVC and MC curves are flat bottomed, like the curves in the diagram. Indeed, they may be constant (and equal to each other) over a *substantial* range of output.

The reason for this is that sometimes fixed factors may not have to be in full use all the time. Take the case of a firm with 100 identical machines, each one requiring one person to operate it. Although the firm cannot use *more* than the 100 machines, it could use fewer: in other words, some of the machines could be left idle. Assume, for example, that instead of using 100 machines, the firm uses only 90. It would need only 90 operatives and 90 per cent of the raw materials. Similarly, if it used only 20 machines, its total variable costs (labour and raw materials) would be only 20 per cent. What we are saying here is that *average* variable cost remains constant – and over a very large range of output: using anything from 1 machine to 100 machines.

The reason for the constant AVC (and MC) is that by varying the amount of fixed capital used, the *proportions* used of capital, labour and raw materials can be kept the same and hence the average and marginal productivity of labour and raw materials will remain constant.

Only when all machines are in use (at Q_1) will AVC start to rise if output is further expanded. Machines may then have to work beyond their optimal speed, using more raw materials per unit of output (diminishing returns to raw materials), or workers may have to work longer shifts with higher (overtime) pay.

1. Assume that a firm has 5 identical machines, each operating independently. Assume that with all 5 machines operating normally, 100 units of output are produced each day. Below what level of output will AVC and MC rise?
2. Manufacturing firms like the one we have been describing will have other fixed costs (such as rent and managerial overheads). Does the existence of these affect the argument that the AVC curve will be flat bottomed?

Since all marginal costs are variable, the same relationship holds between *MC* and *AVC*.

9.4 PRODUCTION IN THE LONG RUN

In the long run *all* factors of production are variable. There is time for the firm to build a new factory (maybe in a different part of the country), to install new machines, to use different techniques of production, and in general to combine its inputs in whatever proportion and in whatever quantities it chooses.

In the long run, then, a firm will have to make a number of decisions: about the scale of its operations, the location of its operations and the techniques of production it will use. These decisions will affect the costs of production. It is important, therefore, to get them right.

The scale of production

If a firm were to double all of its inputs – something it could do in the long run – would it double its output? Or would output more than double or less than double? We can distinguish three possible situations.

- *Constant returns to scale*. This is where a given percentage increase in inputs will lead to the same percentage increase in output.
- *Increasing returns to scale*. This is where a given percentage increase in inputs will lead to a larger percentage increase in output.
- *Decreasing returns to scale*. This is where a given percentage increase in inputs will lead to a smaller percentage increase in output.

Notice the terminology here. The words 'to scale' mean that *all* inputs increase by the same proportion. Decreasing returns to *scale* are therefore quite different from *diminishing* marginal returns (where only the *variable* factor increases). The differences between marginal returns to a variable factor and returns to scale are illustrated in Table 9.4.

In the short run, input 1 is assumed to be fixed in supply (at 3 units). Output can be increased only by using more of the variable factor (input 2). In the long run, however, both input 1 and input 2 are variable.

In the short-run situation, diminishing returns can be seen from the fact that output increases at a decreasing rate (25 to 45 to 60 to 70 to 75) as input 2 is increased. In the long-run situation, the table illustrates increasing returns to scale.

Table 9.4 Short-run and long-run increases in output

Short run			Long run		
Input 1	Input 2	Output	Input 1	Input 2	Output
3	1	25	1	1	15
3	2	45	2	2	35
3	3	60	3	3	60
3	4	70	4	4	90
3	5	75	5	5	125

Output increases at an *increasing* rate (15 to 35 to 60 to 90 to 125) as both inputs are increased.

Economies of scale

The concept of increasing returns to scale is closely linked to that of economies of scale. A firm experiences economies of scale if costs per unit of output fall as the scale of production increases. Clearly, if a firm is getting increasing returns to scale from its factors of production, then as it produces more, it will be using smaller and smaller amounts of factors per unit of output. Other things being equal, this means that it will be producing at a lower unit cost.

There are a number of reasons why firms are likely to experience economies of scale. Some are due to increasing returns to scale; some are not.

Specialisation and division of labour. In large-scale plants, workers can do more simple, repetitive jobs. With this specialisation and division of labour, less training is needed; workers can become highly efficient in their particular job, especially with long production runs; there is less time lost in workers switching from one operation to another; supervision is easier. Workers and managers can be employed who have specific skills in specific areas.

Indivisibilities. Some inputs are of a minimum size. They are indivisible. The most obvious example is machinery. Take the case of a combine harvester. A small-scale farmer could not make full use of one. They only become economical to use, therefore, on farms above a certain size. The problem of indivisibilities is made worse when different machines, each of which is part of the production process, are of a different size. For example, if there are two types of machine, one producing 6 units a day, the other packaging 4 units a day, a minimum of 12 units per day will have to be produced, involving two production machines and three packaging machines, if all machines are to be fully utilised.

The 'container principle'. Any capital equipment that contains things (blast furnaces, oil tankers, pipes, vats, etc.) will tend to cost less per unit of output, the larger its size. The reason has to do with the relationship between a container's volume and its surface area. A container's cost will depend largely on the materials used to build it and hence roughly on its *surface area*. Its output will depend largely on its *volume*. Large containers have a bigger volume relative to surface area than do small containers. For example, a container with a bottom, top and four sides, with each side measuring 1 metre, has a volume of 1 cubic metre and a surface area of 6 square metres (6 surfaces of 1 square metre each). If each side were now to be doubled in length to 2 metres, the volume would be 8 cubic metres and the surface area 24 square metres (6 surfaces of 4 square metres each). Thus an eightfold increase in capacity has been gained at only a fourfold increase in the container's surface area, and hence an approximate fourfold increase in cost.

Greater efficiency of large machines. Large machines may be more efficient, in the sense that more output can be gained for a given amount of inputs. For example, only one worker may be required to operate a machine whether it be large or small. Also, a large machine may make more efficient use of raw materials.

By-products. With production on a large scale, there may be sufficient waste products to enable them to make some by-product.

> **Definitions**
>
> **Economies of scale**
> When increasing the scale of production leads to a lower cost per unit of output.
>
> **Specialisation and division of labour**
> Where production is broken down into a number of simpler, more specialised tasks, thus allowing workers to acquire a high degree of efficiency.
>
> **Indivisibilities**
> The impossibility of dividing a factor into smaller units.

Multistage production. A large factory may be able to take a product through several stages in its manufacture. This saves time and cost moving the semi-finished product from one firm or factory to another. For example, a large cardboard-manufacturing firm may be able to convert trees or waste paper into cardboard and then into cardboard boxes in a continuous sequence.

All the above are examples of plant economies of scale. They are due to an individual factory or workplace or machine being large. There are other economies of scale that are associated with the firm being large – perhaps with many factories.

Organisational. With a large firm, individual plants can specialise in particular functions. There can also be centralised administration of the firms. Often, after a merger between two firms, savings can be made by rationalising their activities in this way.

Spreading overheads. Some expenditures are economic only when the *firm* is large, such as research and development: only a large firm can afford to set up a research laboratory. This is another example of indivisibilities, only this time at the level of the firm rather than the plant. The greater the firm's output, the more these overhead costs are spread.

Financial economies. Large firms may be able to obtain finance at lower interest rates than small firms. They may be able to obtain certain inputs cheaper by buying in bulk.

Economies of scope. Often a firm is large because it produces a range of products. This can result in each individual product being produced more cheaply than if it was produced in a single-product firm. The reason for these economies of scope is that various overhead costs and financial and organisational economies can be shared between the products. For example, a firm that produces a whole range of CD players, DVD players and recorders, games consoles, TVs and so on can benefit from shared marketing and distribution costs and the bulk purchase of electronic components.

Diseconomies of scale

When firms get beyond a certain size, costs per unit of output may start to increase. There are several reasons for such diseconomies of scale:

- Management problems of coordination may increase as the firm becomes larger and more complex, and as lines of communication get longer. There may be a lack of personal involvement by management.
- Workers may feel 'alienated' if their jobs are boring and repetitive, and if they feel an insignificantly small part of a large organisation. Poor motivation may lead to shoddy work.
- Industrial relations may deteriorate as a result of these factors and also as a result of the more complex interrelationships between different categories of worker.
- Production-line processes and the complex interdependencies of mass production can lead to great disruption if there are hold-ups in any one part of the firm.

Whether firms experience economies or diseconomies of scale will depend on the conditions applying in each individual firm.

Definitions

Plant economies of scale
Economies of scale that arise because of the large size of the factory.

Rationalisation
The reorganising of production (often after a merger) so as to cut out waste and duplication and generally to reduce costs.

Overheads
Costs arising from the general running of an organisation, and only indirectly related to the level of output.

Economies of scope
When increasing the range of products produced by a firm reduces the cost of producing each one.

Diseconomies of scale
Where costs per unit of output increase as the scale of production increases.

Location

In the long run, a firm can move to a different location. The location will affect the cost of production, since locations differ in terms of the availability and cost of raw materials, suitable land and power supply, the qualifications, skills and experience of the labour force, wage rates, transport and communications networks, the cost of local services, and banking and financial facilities. In short, locations differ in terms of the availability, suitability and cost of the factors of production.

Transport costs will be an important influence on a firm's location. Ideally, a firm will wish to be as near as possible to both its raw materials and the market for its finished product. When market and raw materials are in different locations, the firm will minimise its transport costs by locating somewhere between the two. In general, if the raw materials are more expensive to transport than the finished product, the firm should locate as near as possible to the raw materials. This will normally apply to firms whose raw materials are heavier or more bulky than the finished product. Thus heavy industry, which uses large quantities of coal and various ores, tends to be concentrated near the coal fields or near the ports. If, on the other hand, the finished product is more expensive to transport (e.g. bread or beer), the firm will probably be located as near as possible to its market.

When raw materials or markets are in many different locations, transport costs will be minimised at the 'centre of gravity'. This location will be nearer to those raw materials and markets whose transport costs are greater per mile.

The size of the whole industry

As an *industry* grows in size, this can lead to external economies of scale for its member firms. This is where a firm, whatever its own individual size, benefits from the *whole industry* being large. For example, the firm may benefit from having access to specialist raw material or component suppliers, labour with specific skills, firms that specialise in marketing the finished product, and banks and other financial institutions with experience of the industry's requirements. What we are referring to here is the industry's infrastructure: the facilities, support services, skills and experience that can be shared by its members.

The member firms of a particular industry might experience external diseconomies of scale. For example, as an industry grows larger, this may create a growing shortage of specific raw materials or skilled labour. This will push up their prices, and hence the firms' costs.

The optimum combination of factors

In the long run, all factors can be varied. The firm can thus choose what techniques of production to use: what design of factory to build, what types of machine to buy, how to organise the factory, and whether to use highly automated processes or more labour-intensive techniques. It must be very careful in making these decisions. Once it has built its factory and installed the machinery, these then become fixed factors of production, maybe for many years: the subsequent 'short-run' time period may in practice last a very long time!

For any given scale, how should the firm decide what technique to use? How should it decide the optimum 'mix' of factors of production?

Definitions

External economies of scale
Where a firm's costs per unit of output decrease as the size of the whole *industry* grows.

Industry's infrastructure
The network of supply agents, communications, skills, training facilities, distribution channels, specialised financial services, etc. that support a particular industry.

External diseconomies of scale
Where a firm's costs per unit of output increase as the size of the whole industry increases.

Pause for thought

Would you expect external economies of scale to be associated with the concentration of an industry in a particular region? Explain.

BOX 9.3 UK COMPETITIVENESS: MOVING TO THE NEXT STAGE

The importance of location

In May 2003 Professor Michael Porter and Christian Ketels of Harvard Business School published a review of the UK's competitiveness on behalf of the UK government. The authors declared that since 1980 the UK had done remarkably well in halting its economic decline on world markets, and had in fact matched and even bettered its main rivals in many industrial sectors. However, they were quick to sound a note of caution.

> The UK currently faces a transition to a new phase of economic development. The old approach to economic development is reaching the limits of its effectiveness, and government, companies, and other institutions need to rethink their policy priorities. This rethinking is not a sign of the past strategy's failure; it is a necessary part of graduating to the new stage.[1]

Porter's view is that economic development is achieved through a series of stages. The factor-driven stage identifies factors of production as the basis of competitive advantage: you have an advantage in those industries where you have a plentiful supply of the relevant factors of production. The investment-driven stage of development focuses upon efficiency and productivity as the key to competitive success. The third stage, into which Porter believes the UK is shifting, is innovation-driven. Here competitive advantage is achieved through the production of innovative products and services.

The importance of industrial clusters

One of the key characteristics of a successful innovation-led development strategy is the existence of industrial clusters.

> Clusters are geographically proximate groups of interconnected companies, suppliers, service providers, and associated institutions in a particular field, linked by commonalties and complementarities.[2]

Porter suggests that clusters are vital for competitiveness in three crucial respects:

- Clusters improve productivity. The close proximity of suppliers and other service providers enhances flexibility.
- Clusters aid innovation. Interaction among business within a cluster stimulates new ideas and aids their dissemination.
- Clusters contribute to new business formation. Clusters are self-reinforcing, in so far as specialist factors such as dedicated venture capital, and labour skills, help reduce costs and lower the risks of new business start-up.

Given that national economies tend to specialise in certain industrial clusters, we can identify where clusters occur and their importance, by considering their share of national output and export earnings. Export earnings in particular are a good indicator of how globally competitive a cluster might be.

The UK's industrial clusters were seen by Porter as being relatively weak, and in fact many traditional clusters, such as steel and car manufacturing, had thinned to the point where they now lacked critical mass and failed to benefit from the clustering effect. Where the UK had strengths were in the areas of services, such as financial services and media, defence, products for personal use, health care and telecommunications.

Porter and Katels concluded that, to improve its competitiveness, the UK must not only support what clusters it has but 'mount a sustained programme of cluster development to create a more conducive environment for productivity growth and innovation through the collective action of companies and other institutions'.[3]

The UK government responded to this report by devolving responsibility for cluster policy to Regional Development Agencies in recognition that they had an important bearing on economic development in localities, cities and regions. Further, cluster development became an integral part of the remit of other policy areas, including science and innovation, export and foreign investment promotion and small and medium-sized enterprise policies.

Recent evidence

The performance of UK clusters has not changed greatly since the earlier report by Porter and Katels, but more information is coming to light. The European Cluster Observatory, an EU project, has identified locations where employment is highly concentrated in particular industrial clusters across Europe.[4] These industrial locations are then scored in terms of their export performance and their ability to innovate.

The table shows the UK position. Information from the Observatory also shows that the UK leads the rest of Europe in their cluster developments in Business Services, Finance and Transportation and Logistical Services,

---

[1] M. E. Porter and C. H. M. Ketels, *UK Competitiveness: moving to the next stage* (DTI and ESRC, May 2003), p. 5.
[2] Ibid., p. 27.
[3] Ibid., p. 46.
[4] See www.clusterobservatory.eu

The Top UK industry clusters ranked by employment, 2006

Region	Cluster category	Employees	Size	Specialsation	Focus	Stars	Innovation	Exports
Inner London	Finance	254 760	3.58%	2.77	10.71%	***	High	Very strong
Inner London	Business Services	186 696	4.32%	3.35	7.85%	***	High	Strong
Outer London	Transportation	117 606	1.91%	2.10	7.03%	***	High	Strong
Outer London	Business Services	105 373	2.44%	2.68	6.30%	***	High	Strong
Berks, Bucks and Oxon	Business Services	73 865	1.71%	2.87	6.73%	***	High	Strong
Surrey and Sussex	Business Services	66 558	1.54%	2.51	5.88%	***	High	Strong
Berks, Bucks and Oxon	Education	61 200	1.72%	2.89	5.57%	***	High	N/A
Greater Manchester	Business Services	54 394	1.26%	2.00	4.69%	***	High	Strong
Beds and Herts	Business Services	53 807	1.25%	3.10	7.26%	***	High	Strong
Hants and Isle of Wight	Business Services	50 972	1.18%	2.62	6.14%	***	High	Strong
Gloucs, Wilts and N Som	Business Services	50 581	1.17%	2.05	4.82%	***	High	Strong
Berks, Bucks and Oxon	IT	45 071	2.19%	3.68	4.10%	***	High	Weak
Leics, Rut and Northants	Business Services	39 895	0.92%	2.31	5.41%	***	High	Strong
E Anglia	Education	38 150	1.07%	2.07	4.00%	***	High	N/A
West Midlands	Automotive	37 913	1.46%	2.26	3.20%	***	High	Weak
East Scotland	Education	35 846	1.01%	2.07	3.99%	***	Medium	N/A
NE Scotland	Oil and Gas	20 382	5.76%	40.23	7.73%	***	Medium	Weak
Highlands and Islands	Fishing	4 694	1.30%	15.16	2.97%	***	Medium	Weak

Source: EU Cluster Observatory, www.clusterobservatory.eu

Notes:
The EU cluster observatory uses three measures to define a cluster, all based on employment. If a location meets each criterion it is awarded a star. Only industries that achieved three stars are included in the table.

The criteria for defining a cluster are as follows:

Size: If a cluster is in the top 10% of similar clusters in Europe in terms of employees it receives a star (Europe is defined as the EU-27, Iceland, Israel, Norway, Switzerland and Turkey)

Specialisation: If a specialisation quotient of 2 or more it is awarded a star. Specialisation is measured by

$$\frac{\text{UK employment in a region in a cluster category/total UK employment}}{\text{European employment in a cluster category/total European employment}}$$

Focus: The 'focus' measure shows the extent to which the regional economy is focused upon the industries comprising the cluster category. This measure relates employment in the cluster to total employment in the region. The top 10% of clusters which account for the largest proportion of their region's total employment receive a star.

The performance of each cluster is determined by their propensity to innovate and their export performance. The ranking for innovation is high, medium and low and is based upon the Regional Innovation Index used in the EU. Export performance is shown to be weak if a country's share in a given cluster is less than its share in overall exports. A 'strong' value was assigned if the country's share in a cluster was greater than its overall export share but less than twice as large as its overall share. A 'very strong' value was assigned if the country's share in a cluster was at least twice as large as its overall share.

with most of these clusters occurring in London and the South East.

The UK has also been very successful relative to the rest of Europe in developing clusters in the provision of Education and Knowledge Creation, notably in Oxford, Cambridge and East Scotland. Outside of these sectors the UK advantage relative to the rest of Europe is very limited, although there are pockets of success. For example, the UK has achieved some success in IT (around Oxford and the south coast of England), oil and gas (around Aberdeen in Scotland), the automotive industry (in the West Midlands) and fishing (around Inverness in Scotland). These locations have achieved the size, specialisation and focus that have enabled them to develop positive spillovers and linkages which create local prosperity. Much more, though, has to be done.

What policies or initiatives might a 'programme of cluster development' involve? Distinguish between policies that government and business might initiate.

The profit-maximising firm will obviously want to use the least costly combination of factors to produce any given output. It will therefore substitute factors, one for another, if by so doing it can reduce the cost of a given output. What, then, is the optimum combination of factors?

The simple two-factor case

Take first the simplest case where a firm uses just two factors: labour (L) and capital (K). The least-cost combination of the two will be where:

$$\frac{MPP_L}{P_L} = \frac{MPP_K}{P_K}$$

In other words, it is where the extra product (MPP) from the last pound spent on each factor is equal. But why should this be so? The easiest way to answer this is to consider what would happen if they were not equal.

If they were not equal, it would be possible to reduce cost per unit of output, by using a different combination of labour and capital. For example, if:

$$\frac{MPP_L}{P_L} > \frac{MPP_K}{P_K}$$

more labour should be used relative to capital, since the firm is getting a greater physical return for its money from extra workers than from extra capital. As more labour is used per unit of capital, however, diminishing returns to labour set in. Thus MPP_L will fall. Likewise, as less capital is used per unit of labour, the MPP_K will rise. This will continue until:

$$\frac{MPP_L}{P_L} = \frac{MPP_K}{P_K}$$

At this point, the firm will stop substituting labour for capital.

Since no further gain can be made by substituting one factor for another, this combination of factors or 'choice of techniques' can be said to be the most efficient. It is the least-cost way of combining factors for any given output. Efficiency in this sense of using the optimum factor proportions is known as **technical or productive efficiency**.

> **Definition**
>
> **Technical or productive efficiency**
> The least-cost combination of factors for a given output.

The multifactor case

Where a firm uses many different factors, the least-cost combination of factors will be where:

$$\frac{MPP_a}{P_a} = \frac{MPP_b}{P_b} = \frac{MPP_c}{P_c} \ldots = \frac{MPP_n}{P_n}$$

where $a \ldots n$ are different factors of production.

The reasons are the same as in the two-factor case. If any inequality exists between the MPP/P ratios, a firm will be able to reduce its costs by using more of those factors with a high MPP/P ratio and less of those with a low MPP/P ratio until the ratios all become equal.

A major problem for a firm in choosing the least-cost technique is in predicting future factor price changes.

If the price of a factor were to change, the MPP/P ratios would cease to be equal. The firm, to minimise costs, would then like to alter its factor combinations until the *MPP/P* ratios once more become equal. The trouble is that, once it has committed itself to a particular technique, it may be several years before it can switch to an alternative one. Thus if a firm invests in labour-intensive methods of production and is then faced with an unexpected wage rise, it may regret not having chosen a more capital-intensive technique.

Postscript: decision making in different time periods

We have distinguished between the short run and the long run. Let us introduce two more time periods to complete the picture. The complete list then reads as follows.

Very short run (immediate run). All factors are fixed. Output is fixed. The supply curve is vertical. On a day-to-day basis, a firm may not be able to vary output at all. For example, a flower seller, once the day's flowers have been purchased from the wholesaler, cannot alter the amount of flowers available for sale on that day. In the very short run, all that may remain for a producer to do is to sell an already-produced good.

Short run. At least one factor is fixed in supply. More can be produced, but the firm will come up against the law of diminishing returns as it tries to do so.

Long run. All factors are variable. The firm may experience constant, increasing or decreasing returns to scale. But although all factors can be increased or decreased, they are of a fixed *quality*.

Very long run. All factors are variable, *and* their quality and hence productivity can change. Labour productivity can increase as a result of education, training, experience and social factors. The productivity of capital can increase as a result of new inventions (new discoveries) and innovation (putting inventions into practice).

Improvements in factor quality will increase the output they produce: *TPP*, *APP* and *MPP* will rise. These curves will shift vertically upward.

Just how long the 'very long run' is will vary from firm to firm. It will depend on how long it takes to develop new techniques, new skills or new work practices.

It is important to realise that decisions *for* all four time periods can be made *at* the same time. Firms do not make short-run decisions *in* the short run and long-run decisions *in* the long run. They can make both short-run and long-run decisions today. For example, assume that a firm experiences an increase in consumer demand and anticipates that it will continue into the foreseeable future. It thus wants to increase output. Consequently, it makes the following four decisions *today*:

> **Pause for thought**
>
> 1 What will the long-run market supply curve for a product look like? How will the shape of the long-run curve depend on returns to scale?
> 2 Why would it be difficult to construct a very-long run supply curve?

- *(Very short run)* It accepts that for a few days it will not be able to increase output. It informs its customers that they will have to wait. It may temporarily raise prices to choke off some of the demand.
- *(Short run)* It negotiates with labour to introduce overtime working as soon as possible, to tide it over the next few weeks. It orders extra raw materials from its suppliers. It launches a recruitment drive for new labour so as to avoid paying overtime longer than is necessary.

- *(Long run)* It starts proceedings to build a new factory. The first step may be to discuss requirements with a firm of consultants.
- *(Very long run)* It institutes a programme of research and development and/or training in an attempt to increase productivity.

Although we distinguish these four time periods, it is the middle two we are primarily concerned with. The reason for this is that there is very little that the firm can do in the very short run. And in the very long run, although the firm will obviously want to increase the productivity of its inputs, it will not be in a position to make precise calculations of how to do it. It will not know precisely what inventions will be made, or just what will be the results of its own research and development.

9.5 COSTS IN THE LONG RUN

When it comes to making long-run production decisions, the firm has much more flexibility. It does not have to operate with plant and equipment of a fixed size. It can expand the whole scale of its operations. All its inputs are variable, and thus the law of diminishing returns does not apply. The firm may experience economies of scale or diseconomies of scale, or its average costs may stay constant as it expands the scale of its operations.

Since there are no fixed factors in the long run, there are no long-run fixed costs. For example, the firm may rent more land in order to expand its operations. Its rent bill therefore goes up as it expands its output.

All costs, then, in the long run are variable costs.

Long-run average costs

Although it is possible to draw long-run total, marginal and average cost curves, we will concentrate on long-run average cost (*LRAC*) curves. These curves can take various shapes, but a typical one is shown in Figure 9.4.

It is often assumed that, as a firm expands, it will initially experience economies of scale and thus face a downward-sloping *LRAC* curve. After a point (Q_1 in Figure 9.4),

> **Definition**
>
> **Long-run average cost (*LRAC*) curve**
> A curve that shows how average cost varies with output on the assumption that *all* factors are variable. (It is assumed that the least-cost method of production will be chosen for each output.)

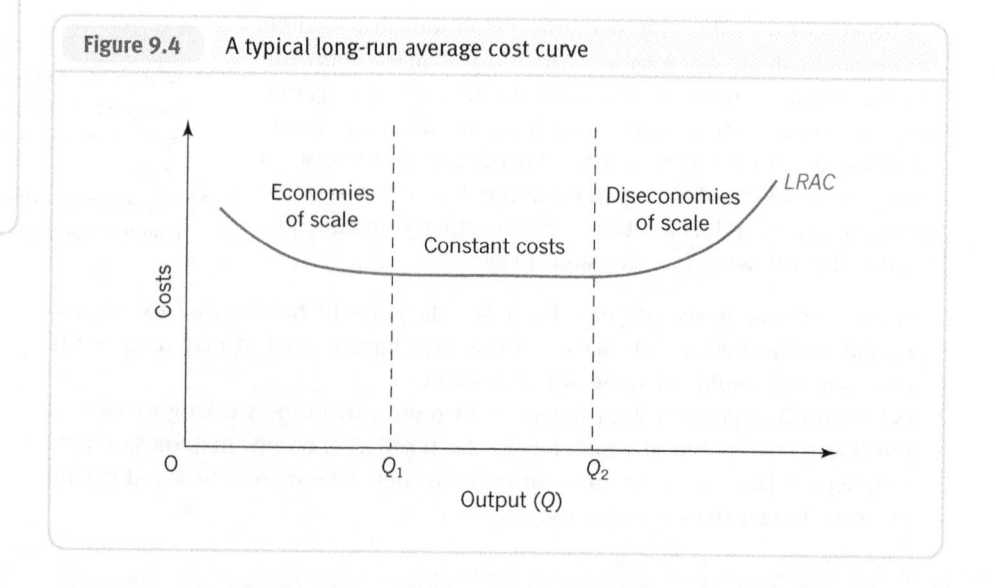

Figure 9.4 A typical long-run average cost curve

however, all such economies will have been achieved and thus the curve will flatten out. Then, possibly after a period of constant *LRAC* (between Q_1 and Q_2), the firm will get so large that it will start experiencing diseconomies of scale and thus a rising *LRAC*. At this stage, production and financial economies begin to be offset by the managerial problems of running a giant organisation. The effect of this, then, is to give a L-shaped or saucer shaped curve.

Assumptions behind the long-run average cost curve

We make three key assumptions when constructing long-run average cost curves.

Factor prices are given. At each output, a firm will be faced with a given set of factor prices. If factor prices *change*, therefore, both short- and long-run cost curves will shift. Thus an increase in wages would shift the curves upwards.

However, factor prices might be different at *different* levels of output. For example, one of the economies of scale that many firms enjoy is the ability to obtain bulk discount on raw materials and other supplies. In such cases the curve does *not* shift. The different factor prices are merely experienced at different points along the curve, and are reflected in the shape of the curve. Factor prices are still given for any particular level of output.

The state of technology and factor quality are given. These are assumed to change only in the very long run. If a firm gains economies of scale, it is because it is being able to exploit *existing* technologies and make better use of the existing availability of factors of production.

Firms choose the least-cost combination of factors for each output. The assumption here is that firms operate efficiently: that they choose the cheapest possible way of producing any level of output. In other words, at every point along the *LRAC* curve the firm will adhere to the cost-minimising formula:

$$\frac{MPP_a}{P_a} = \frac{MPP_b}{P_b} = \frac{MPP_c}{P_c} \ldots = \frac{MPP_n}{P_n}$$

where a ... n are the various factors that the firm uses.

If the firm did not choose the optimum factor combination, it would be producing at a point above the *LRAC* curve.

The relationship between long-run and short-run average cost curves

Take the case of a firm which has just one factory and faces a short-run average cost curve illustrated by $SRAC_1$ in Figure 9.5.

In the long run, it can build more factories. If it thereby experiences economies of scale (due, say, to savings on administration), each successive factory will allow it to produce with a new lower *SRAC* curve. Thus with two factories it will face curve $SRAC_2$; with three factories curve $SRAC_3$, and so on. Each *SRAC* curve corresponds to a particular amount of the factor that is fixed in the short run: in this case, the factory. (There are many more *SRAC* curves that could be drawn between the ones shown, since factories of different sizes could be built or existing ones could be expanded.)

From this succession of short-run average cost curves we can construct a long-run average cost curve. This is shown in Figure 9.5 and is known as the **envelope curve**, since it envelops the short-run curves.

> **Definition**
>
> **Envelope curve**
> A long-run average cost curve drawn as the tangency points of a series of short-run average cost curves.

> **Pause for thought**
>
> *Will the envelope curve be tangential to the bottom of each of the short-run average cost curves? Explain why it should or should not be.*

BOX 9.4 MINIMUM EFFICIENT SCALE

The extent of economies of scale in practice

Two of the most important studies of economies of scale have been those made by C. F. Pratten[1] in the late 1980s and by a group advising the European Commission[2] in 1997. Both studies found strong evidence that many firms, especially in manufacturing, experienced substantial economies of scale.

In a few cases long-run average costs fell continuously as output increased. For most firms, however, they fell up to a certain level of output and then remained constant.

The extent of economies of scale can be measured by looking at a firm's *minimum efficient scale (MES)*. The *MES* is the size beyond which no significant additional economies of scale can be achieved: in other words, the point where the *LRAC* curve flattens off. In Pratten's studies he defined this level as the minimum scale above which any possible doubling in scale would reduce average costs by less than 5 per cent (i.e. virtually the bottom of the *LRAC* curve). In the diagram *MES* is shown at point *a*.

The *MES* can be expressed in terms either of an individual factory or of the whole firm. Where it refers to the minimum efficient scale of an individual factory, the *MES* is known as *the minimum efficient plant size (MEPS)*.

The *MES* can then be expressed as a percentage of the total size of the market or of total domestic production. Table (a), based on the Pratten study, shows *MES* for

---

[1] C. F. Pratten, 'A survey of the economies of scale', in *Research on the 'Costs of Non-Europe'*, vol. 2 (Office for Official Publications of the European Communities, 1988).
[2] European Commission/Economists Advisory Group Ltd, 'Economies of scale', The Single Market Review, Subseries V, Volume 4 (Office for Official Publications of the European Communities, 1997).

Table (a)

Product	MES as % of production		% additional cost at $1/2$ MES
	UK	EU	
Individual plants			
Cellulose fibres	125	16	3
Rolled aluminium semi-manufactures	114	15	15
Refrigerators	85	11	4
Steel	72	10	6
Electric motors	60	6	15
TV sets	40	9	9
Cigarettes	24	6	1.4
Ball-bearings	20	2	6
Beer	12	3	7
Nylon	4	1	12
Bricks	1	0.2	25
Tufted carpets	0.3	0.04	10
Shoes	0.3	0.03	1
Firms			
Cars	200	20	9
Lorries	104	21	7.5
Mainframe computers	>100	n.a.	5
Aircraft	100	n.a.	5
Tractors	98	19	6

Sources: C. F. Pratten (1988), see footnote 1 above; M. Emerson, *The Economics of 1992* (Oxford University Press, 1988).

Long-run cost curves in practice

Firms do experience economies of scale. Some experience continuously falling *LRAC* curves. Others experience economies of scale up to a certain output and thereafter constant returns to scale.

Table (b)

Plants	MES as % of total EU production
Aerospace	12.19
Tractors and agricultural machinery	6.57
Electric lighting	3.76
Steel tubes	2.42
Shipbuilding	1.63
Rubber	1.06
Radio and TV	0.69
Footwear	0.08
Carpets	0.03

Source: see footnote 2 opposite

plants and firms in various industries. The first column shows MES as a percentage of total UK production. The second column shows MES as a percentage of total EU production. Table (b), based on the 1997 study, shows MES for various plants as a percentage of total EU production.

Expressing MES as a percentage of total output gives an indication of how competitive the industry could be. In some industries (such as footwear and carpets), economies of scale were exhausted (i.e. MES was reached) with plants or firms that were still small relative to total UK production and even smaller relative to total EU production. In such industries there would be room for many firms and thus scope for considerable competition.

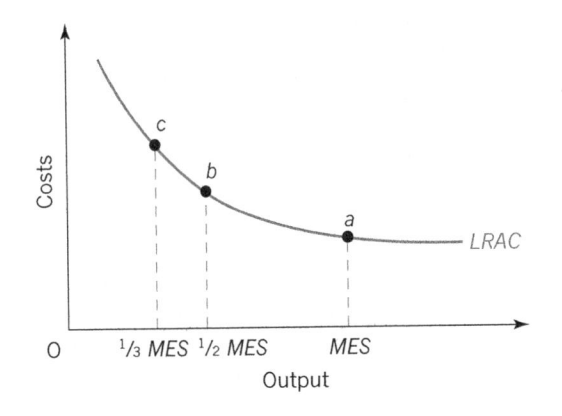

In other industries, however, even if a single plant or firm were large enough to produce the whole output of the industry in the UK, it would still not be large enough to experience the full potential economies of scale: the MES is greater than 100 per cent. Examples from Table (a) include factories producing cellulose fibres, and car manufacturers. In such industries there is no possibility of competition. In fact, as long as the MES exceeds 50 per cent there will not be room for more than one firm large enough to gain full economies of scale. In this case the industry is said to be *a natural monopoly*. As we shall see in the next few chapters, when competition is lacking, consumers may suffer by firms charging prices considerably above costs.

A second way of measuring the extent of economies of scale is to see how much costs would increase if production were reduced to a certain fraction of MES. The normal fractions used are $\frac{1}{2}$ or $\frac{1}{3}$ MES. This is illustrated in the diagram. Point *b* corresponds to $\frac{1}{2}$ MES; point *c* to $\frac{1}{3}$ MES. The greater the percentage by which LRAC at point *b* or *c* is higher than at point *a*, the greater will be the economies of scale to be gained by producing at MES rather than at $\frac{1}{2}$ MES or $\frac{1}{3}$ MES. For example, in the table there are greater economies of scale to be gained from moving from $\frac{1}{2}$ MES to MES in the production of electric motors than in cigarettes.

The main purpose of the studies was to determine whether the single EU market is big enough to allow both economies of scale and competition. The tables suggest that in all cases, other things being equal, the EU market is large enough for firms to gain the full economies of scale *and* for there to be enough firms for the market to be competitive.

The second study also found that 47 of the 53 manufacturing sectors analysed had scope for further exploitation of economies of scale.

?
1. Why might a firm operating with one plant achieve MEPS and yet not be large enough to achieve MES? (Clue: are all economies of scale achieved at plant level?)
2. Why might a firm producing bricks have an MES which is only 0.2 per cent of total EU production and yet face little effective competition from other EU countries?

Evidence is inconclusive on the question of diseconomies of scale. There is little evidence to suggest the existence of technical diseconomies, but the possibility of diseconomies due to managerial and industrial relations problems cannot be ruled out.

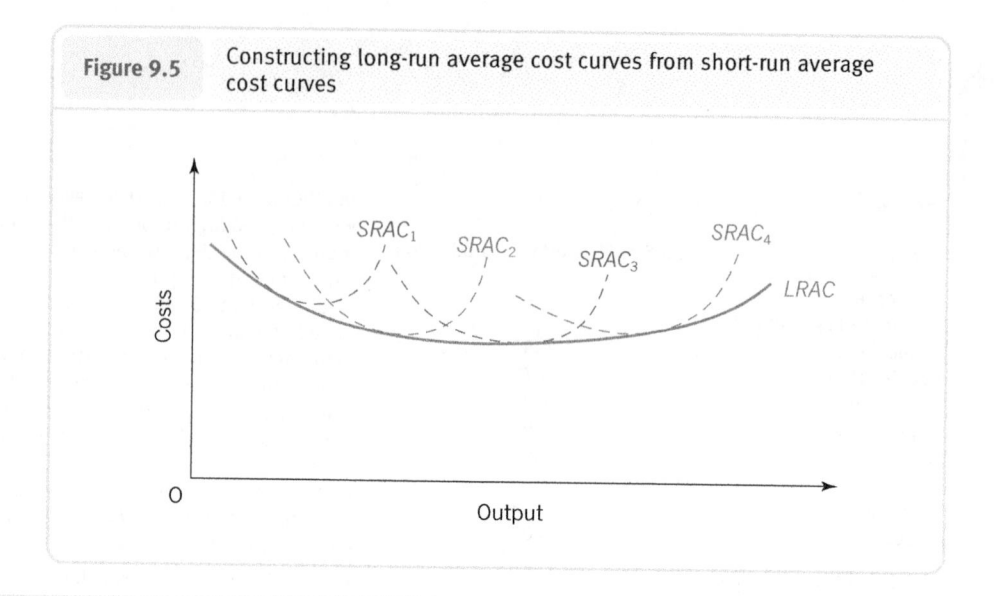

Figure 9.5 Constructing long-run average cost curves from short-run average cost curves

BOX 9.5 FOLLOWERS OF FASHION

For many products, style is a key component to their success. Two such products are clothing and cars. Both markets exhibit 'fashion price cycles'. In recent times, however, whereas seasonal price variations for clothes have become more pronounced, those for cars have diminished. The extract below, taken from *The Economist* of 23 December 1995, explores the factors affecting the price of fashion products, and in particular looks at the role of costs.

> According to standard economic theory, Giorgio Armani, a world-famous Italian fashion designer, runs a simple business. His company combines inputs of labour (seamstresses), capital (dyeing and weaving machines) and raw materials (cloth) to make clothes with the best possible trade-off between cost and quality. He then calculates what the demand is for his designs, and estimates how many units he can make without marginal costs exceeding marginal revenues. He sells these at the market-clearing price, and earns just enough profit to compensate him for his investment of time and money.
>
> The flaw of this stylised view is that it ignores the most important thing that designers such as Mr Armani sell: fashion itself.

The article observes that the prices of fashion-sensitive goods, such as clothing and cars, follow well-established 'fashion cycles'. At the beginning of the season, prices are set at a high level. Then, as the season progresses, prices gradually fall, only to rise again as new styles are introduced for the next season.

> The main reason for this is uncertainty. When producers introduce a new line they do not know how successful it will be. To avoid selling it for less than is necessary, they initially set a high price, then lower it for lines that do not sell well. A good way to measure the importance of fashion, therefore, is to look at the variation in seasonal prices.
>
> Over the past few decades, seasonal price variations for women's clothing have become more pronounced. However, prices in the American car market, which also tend to follow a 'fashion' cycle, have displayed the opposite trend.

Clothing prices, relative to the average

The explanation for these differences, claims the article, is to be found in changes in technology in the two industries.

> Advances in the textile industry, such as the development of sophisticated electronic weaving, have made it cheaper for designers to revamp their lines each season. But in the car industry, it has become more costly to make radical style changes each year. Although new technology has made it easier to change the size and shape of a car's body, the costs of doing so as a share of the total production costs have actually risen.

1. If consumers are aware that unsuccessful lines of clothing will fall in price as the season progresses, why do they buy when prices are set high at the start of the season? What does this tell us about the shape of the demand curve for a given fashion product (a) at the start, and (b) at the end of the season?
2. What has happened to fixed costs as a proportion of total costs in the production of cars? How has this affected car design strategy?
3. How might we account for the changing magnitudes of the fashion price cycles of clothing and cars? What role do fixed costs play in the explanation?

SUMMARY

1a When measuring costs of production, we should be careful to use the concept of opportunity cost.

1b In the case of factors not owned by the firm, the opportunity cost is simply the explicit cost of purchasing or hiring them. It is the price paid for them.

1c In the case of factors already owned by the firm, it is the implicit cost of what the factor could have earned for the firm in its next best alternative use.

2a A production function shows the relationship between the amount of inputs used and the amount of output produced from them (per period of time).

2b In the short run it is assumed that one or more factors (inputs) are fixed in supply. The actual length of the short run will vary from industry to industry.

2c Production in the short run is subject to diminishing returns. As greater quantities of the variable factor(s) are used, so each additional unit of the variable factor will add less to output than previous units: total physical product will rise less and less rapidly.

2d As long as marginal physical product is above average physical product, average physical product will rise. Once *MPP* has fallen below *APP*, however, *APP* will fall.

3a With some factors fixed in supply in the short run, their total costs will be fixed with respect to output. In the case of variable factors, their total cost will increase as more output is produced and hence as more of them are used.

3b Total cost can be divided into total fixed and total variable cost. Total variable cost will tend to increase less rapidly at first as more is produced, but then, when diminishing returns set in, it will increase more and more rapidly.

3c Marginal cost is the cost of producing one more unit of output. It will probably fall at first (corresponding to the part of the *TVC* curve where the slope is getting shallower), but will start to rise as soon as diminishing returns set in.

3d Average cost, like total cost, can be divided into fixed and variable costs. Average fixed cost will decline as more output is produced. The reason is that the total fixed cost is being spread over a greater and greater number of units of output. Average variable cost will tend to decline at first, but once the marginal cost has risen above it, it must then rise.

4a In the long run, a firm is able to vary the quantity it uses of all factors of production. There are no fixed factors.

4b If it increases all factors by the same proportion, it may experience constant, increasing or decreasing returns to scale.

4c Economies of scale occur when costs per unit of output fall as the scale of production increases. This can be due to a number of factors, some of which are directly caused by increasing (physical) returns to scale. These include the benefits of specialisation and division of labour, the use of larger and more efficient machines, and the ability to have a more integrated system of production. Other economies of scale arise from the financial and administrative benefits of large-scale organisations having a range of products (economies of scope).

4d Long-run costs are also influenced by a firm's location. The firm will have to balance the need to be as near as possible both to the supply of its raw materials and to its market. The optimum balance will depend on the relative costs of transporting the inputs and the finished product.

4e To minimise costs per unit of output, a firm should choose that combination of factors which gives an equal marginal product for each factor relative to its price: i.e. $MPP_a/P_a = MPP_b/P_b = MPP_c/P_c$, etc. (where a, b and c are different factors). If the *MPP/P* ratio for any factor is greater than that for another, more of the first should be used relative to the second.

4f Four distinct time periods can be distinguished. In addition to the short- and long-run periods, we can also distinguish the very-short- and very-long-run periods. The very short run is when all factors are fixed. The very long run is where not only the quantity of factors but also their quality is variable (as a result of changing technology, etc.).

5a In the long run, all factors are variable. There are thus no long-run fixed costs.

5b When constructing long-run cost curves, it is assumed that factor prices are given, that the state of technology is given and that firms will choose the least-cost combination of factors for each given output.

5c The *LRAC* curve can be downward sloping, upward sloping or horizontal, depending in turn on whether there are economies of scale, diseconomies of scale or neither. Typically, *LRAC* curves are drawn as saucer-shaped or l-shaped. As output expands, initially there are economies of scale. When these are exhausted, the curve will become flat. When the firm becomes very large, it may begin to experience diseconomies of scale. If this happens, the *LRAC* curve will begin to slope upward again.

5d An envelope curve can be drawn which shows the relationship between short-run and long-run average cost curves. The *LRAC* curve envelops the short-run *AC* curves: it is tangential to them.

REVIEW QUESTIONS

1. Are all explicit costs variable costs? Are all variable costs explicit costs?

2. Up to roughly how long is the short run in the following cases?
   (a) A mobile disco firm.
   (b) Electricity power generation.
   (c) A small grocery retailing business.
   (d) 'Superstore Hypermarkets plc'.
   In each case, specify your assumptions.

3. Given that there is a fixed supply of land in the world, what implications can you draw from Figure 9.1 about the effects of an increase in world population for food output per head?

4. The following are some costs incurred by a shoe manufacturer. Decide whether each one is a fixed cost or a variable cost or has some element of both.
   (a) The cost of leather.
   (b) The fee paid to an advertising agency.
   (c) Wear and tear on machinery.
   (d) Business rates on the factory.
   (e) Electricity for heating and lighting.
   (f) Electricity for running the machines.
   (g) Basic minimum wages agreed with the union.
   (h) Overtime pay.
   (i) Depreciation of machines as a result purely of their age (irrespective of their condition).

5. Assume that you are required to draw a *TVC* curve corresponding to Figure 9.1. What will happen to this *TVC* curve beyond point *d*?

6. Why is the minimum point of the *AVC* curve at a lower level of output than the minimum point of the *AC* curve?

7. Which economies of scale are due to increasing returns to scale and which are due to other factors?

8. What economies of scale is a large department store likely to experience?

9. Why are many firms likely to experience economies of scale up to a certain size and then diseconomies of scale after some point beyond that?

10. Why are bread and beer more expensive to transport per mile than the raw materials used in their manufacture?

11. Name some industries where external economies of scale are gained. What are the specific external economies in each case?

12. How is the opening up of trade and investment between eastern and western Europe likely to affect the location of industries within Europe that have (a) substantial economies of scale; (b) little or no economies of scale?

13. If factor X costs twice as much as factor Y ($P_X/P_Y = 2$), what can be said about the relationship between the *MPP*s of the two factors if the optimum combination of factors is used?

14. Could the long run and the very long run ever be the same length of time?

15. Examine Figure 9.4. What would (a) the firm's long-run total cost curve, and (b) its long-run marginal cost curve look like?

16. Under what circumstances is a firm likely to experience a flat-bottomed *LRAC* curve?

Chapter 10

Revenue and profit

> **Business issues covered in this chapter**
>
> - How does a business's sales revenue vary with output?
> - How does the relationship between output and sales revenue depend on the type of market in which a business is operating?
> - How do we measure profits?
> - At what output will a firm maximise its profits? How much profit will it make at this output?
> - At what point should a business call it a day and shut down?

In this chapter we will identify the output and price at which a firm will maximise its profits, and how much profit will be made at that level. Remember that we defined a firm's total profit ($T\Pi$) as its total revenue minus its total costs of production.

$$T\Pi = TR - TC$$

In the previous chapter we have looked at costs in some detail. We must now turn to the revenue side of the equation. As with costs, we distinguish between three revenue concepts: total revenue (TR), average revenue (AR) and marginal revenue (MR).

10.1 REVENUE

Total, average and marginal revenue

Total revenue (TR)

Total revenue is the firm's total earnings per period of time from the sale of a particular amount of output (Q).

> **Definition**
>
> **Total revenue**
> A firm's total earnings from a specified level of sales within a specified period: $TR = P \times Q$.

> **Definitions**
>
> **Average revenue**
> Total revenue per unit of output. When all output is sold at the same price, average revenue will be the same as price: $AR = TR/Q = P$.
>
> **Marginal revenue**
> The extra revenue gained by selling one or more unit per time period: $MR = \Delta TR/\Delta Q$.
>
> **Price taker**
> A firm that is too small to be able to influence the market price.

For example, if a firm sells 1000 units (Q) per month at a price of £5 each (P), then its monthly total revenue will be £5000: in other words, £5 × 1000 ($P \times Q$). Thus:

$$TR = P \times Q$$

Average revenue (AR)

Average revenue is the amount the firm earns per unit sold. Thus:

$$AR = TR/Q$$

So if the firm earns £5000 (TR) from selling 1000 units (Q), it will earn £5 per unit. But this is simply the price! Thus:

$$AR = P$$

(The only exception to this is when the firm is selling its products at different prices to different consumers. In this case AR is simply the (weighted) average price.)

Marginal revenue (MR)

Marginal revenue is the extra total revenue gained by selling one more unit (per time period). So if a firm sells an extra 20 units this month compared with what it expected to sell, and in the process earns an extra £100, then it is getting an extra £5 for each extra unit sold: $MR = £5$. Thus:

$$MR = \Delta TR/\Delta Q$$

We now need to see how each of these three revenue concepts (TR, AR and MR) varies with output. We can show this relationship graphically in the same way as we did with costs.

The relationship will depend on the market conditions under which a firm operates. A firm which is too small to be able to affect market price will have different-looking revenue curves from a firm which is able to choose the price it charges. Let us examine each of these two situations in turn.

Revenue curves when price is not affected by the firm's output

Average revenue

If a firm is very small relative to the whole market, it is likely to be a price taker. That is, it has to accept the price given by the intersection of demand and supply in the whole market. But, being so small, it can sell as much as it is capable of producing at that price. This is illustrated in Figure 10.1.

Diagram (a) shows market demand and supply. Equilibrium price is £5. Diagram (b) looks at the demand for an individual firm which is tiny relative to the whole market. (Look at the difference in the scale of the horizontal axes in the two diagrams.)

Being so small, any change in the firm's output will be too insignificant to affect the market price. The firm thus faces a horizontal demand 'curve' at this price. It can sell 200 units, 600 units, 1200 units or whatever without affecting this £5 price.

Average revenue is thus constant at £5. The firm's average revenue curve must therefore lie along exactly the same line as its demand curve.

Marginal revenue

In the case of a horizontal demand curve, the marginal revenue curve will be the same as the average revenue curve, since selling one more unit at a constant price

Figure 10.1 Deriving a firm's AR and MR: price-taking firm

(a) The market

(b) The firm

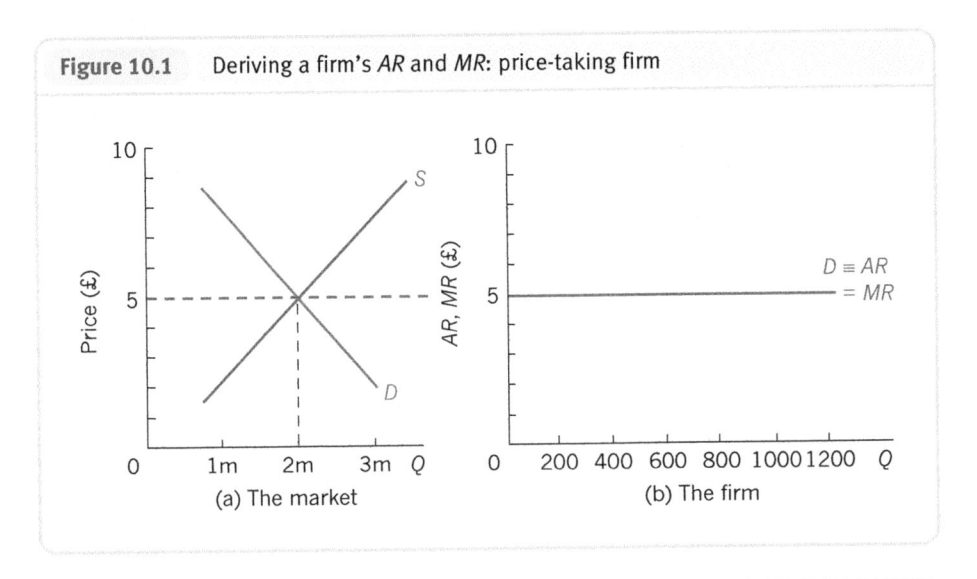

Table 10.1 Deriving total revenue

Quantity (units)	Price = AR = MR (£)	TR (£)
0	5	0
200	5	1000
400	5	2000
600	5	3000
800	5	4000
1000	5	5000
1200	5	6000

(AR) merely adds that amount to total revenue. If an extra unit is sold at a constant price of £5, an extra £5 is earned.

Total revenue

Table 10.1 shows the effect on total revenue of different levels of sales with a constant price of £5 per unit.

As price is constant, total revenue will rise at a constant rate as more is sold. The TR 'curve' will therefore be a straight line through the origin, as in Figure 10.2.

Pause for thought

What would happen to the TR curve if the market price rose to £10? Try drawing it.

Revenue curves when price varies with output

The three curves (TR, AR and MR) will look quite different when price does vary with the firm's output.

If a firm has a relatively large share of the market, it will face a downward-sloping demand curve. This means that if it is to sell more, it must lower the price. But it could also choose to raise its price. If it does so, however, it will have to accept a fall in sales.

Average revenue

Remember that average revenue equals price. If, therefore, the price has to be reduced to sell more output, average revenue will fall as output increases.

Figure 10.2 Total revenue curve for a price-taking firm

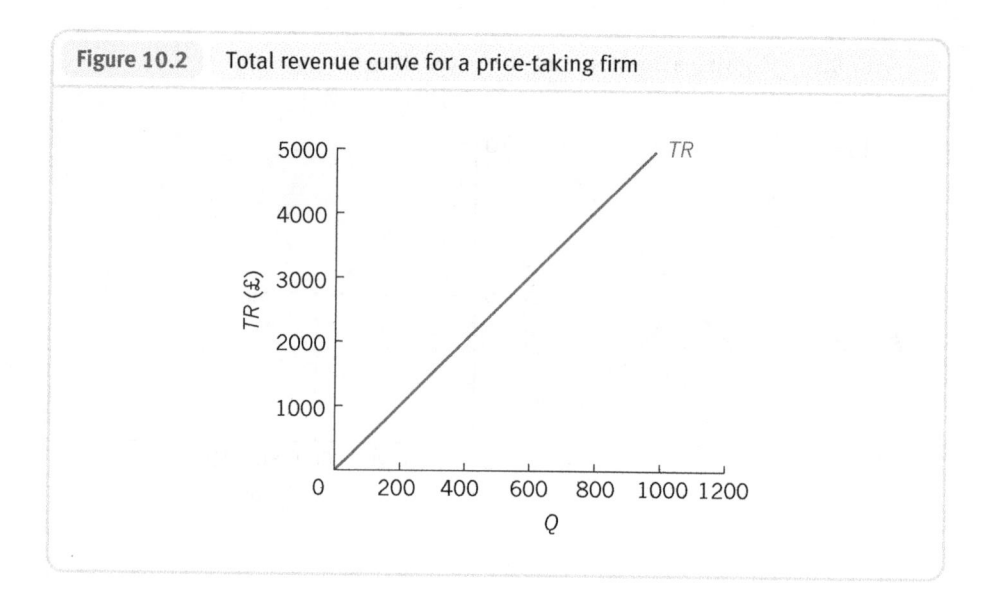

Table 10.2 Revenues for a firm facing a downward-sloping demand curve

Q (units)	P = AR (£)	TR (£)	MR (£)
1	8	8	
2	7	14	6
3	6	18	4
4	5	20	2
5	4	20	0
6	3	18	−2
7	2	14	−4
.	.	.	.

Table 10.2 gives an example of a firm facing a downward-sloping demand curve. The demand curve (which shows how much is sold at each price) is given by the first two columns.

Note that, as in the case of a price-taking firm, the demand curve and the AR curve lie along exactly the same line. The reason for this is simple: $AR = P$, and thus the curve relating price to quantity (the demand curve) must be the same as that relating average revenue to quantity (the AR curve).

Marginal revenue

When a firm faces a downward-sloping demand curve, marginal revenue will be less than average revenue, and may even be negative. But why?

If a firm is to sell more per time period, it must lower its price (assuming it does not advertise). This will mean lowering the price not just for the extra units it hopes to sell, but also for those units it would have sold had it not lowered the price.

Thus the marginal revenue is the price at which it sells the last unit, *minus* the loss in revenue it has incurred by reducing the price on those units it could otherwise have sold at the higher price. This can be illustrated with Table 10.2.

Assume that price is currently £7. Two units are thus sold. The firm now wishes to sell an extra unit. It lowers the price to £6. It thus gains £6 from the sale of the third unit, but loses £2 by having to reduce the price by £1 on the two units it could otherwise have sold at £7. Its net gain is therefore £6 − £2 = £4. This is the marginal

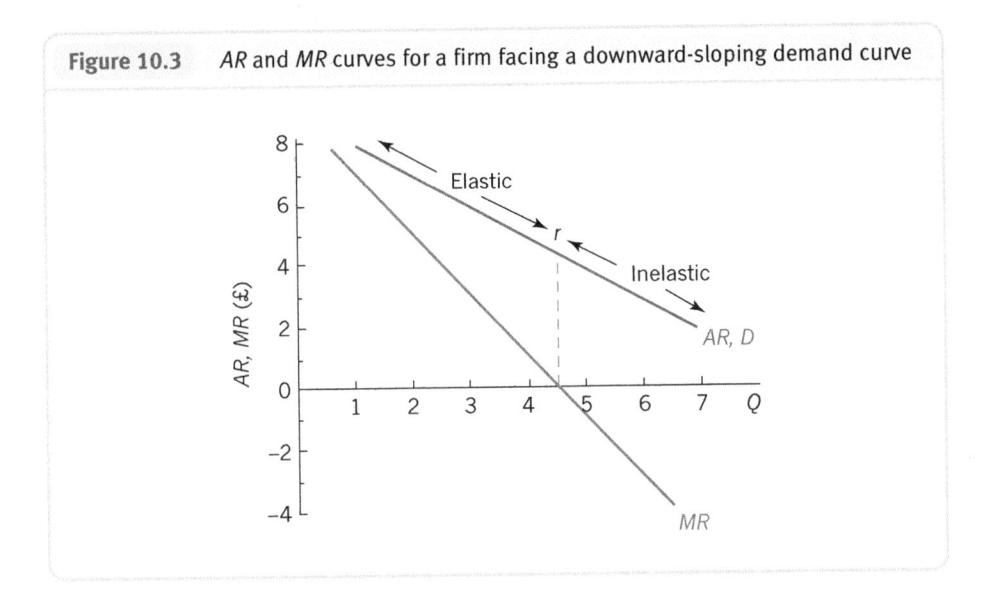

Figure 10.3 AR and MR curves for a firm facing a downward-sloping demand curve

revenue: it is the extra revenue gained by the firm from selling one more unit. Try using this method to check out the remaining figures for *MR* in Table 10.2. (Note that in the table the figures for *MR* are entered in the spaces between the figures for the other three columns.)

There is a simple relationship between marginal revenue and *price elasticity of demand*. Remember from Chapter 5 (see pages 83–4) that if demand is price elastic, a *decrease* in price will lead to a proportionately larger increase in the quantity demanded and hence an *increase* in revenue. Marginal revenue will thus be positive. If, however, demand is inelastic, a decrease in price will lead to a proportionately smaller increase in sales. In this case the price reduction will more than offset the increase in sales and as a result revenue will fall. Marginal revenue will be negative.

If, then, marginal revenue is a positive figure (i.e. if sales per time period are 4 units or less in Figure 10.3), the demand curve will be elastic at that point, since a rise in quantity sold (as a result of a reduction in price) would lead to a rise in total revenue. If, on the other hand, marginal revenue is negative (i.e. at a level of sales of 5 or more units in Figure 10.3), the demand curve will be inelastic at that point, since a rise in quantity sold would lead to a *fall* in total revenue.

Thus the demand (*AR*) curve of Figure 10.3 is elastic to the left of point *r* and inelastic to the right.

Total revenue

Total revenue equals price times quantity. This is illustrated in Table 10.2. The *TR* column from Table 10.2 is plotted in Figure 10.4.

Unlike in the case of a price-taking firm, the *TR* curve is not a straight line. It is a curve that rises at first and then falls. But why? As long as marginal revenue is positive (and hence demand is price elastic), a rise in output will raise total revenue. However, once marginal revenue becomes negative (and hence demand is inelastic), total revenue will fall. The peak of the *TR* curve will be where *MR* = 0. At this point, the price elasticity of demand will be equal to –1.

Shifts in revenue curves

We saw in Chapter 4 that a change in *price* will cause a movement along a demand curve. It is similar with revenue curves, except that here the causal connection is in

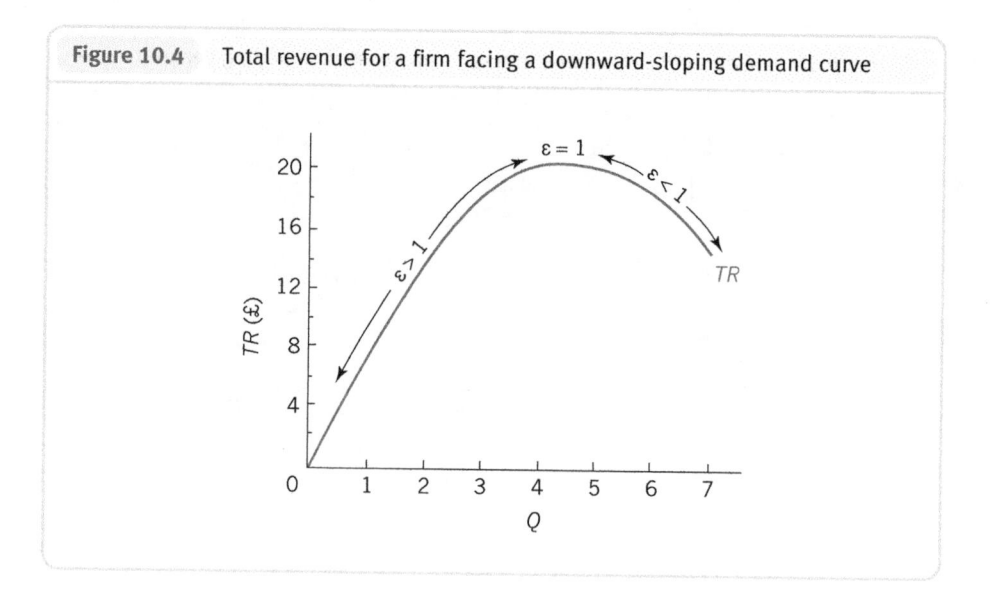

Figure 10.4 Total revenue for a firm facing a downward-sloping demand curve

the other direction. Here we ask what happens to revenue when there is a change in the firm's *output*. Again the effect is shown by a movement along the curves.

A change in any *other* determinant of demand, such as tastes, income or the price of other goods, will shift the demand curve. By affecting the price at which each level of output can be sold, it will cause a shift in all three revenue curves. An increase in revenue is shown by a vertical shift upwards; a decrease by a shift downwards.

10.2 PROFIT MAXIMISATION

We are now in a position to put costs and revenue together to find the output at which profit is maximised, and also to find out how much that profit will be.

There are two ways of doing this. The first and simpler method is to use total cost and total revenue curves. The second method is to use marginal and average cost and marginal and average revenue curves. Although this method is a little more complicated (but only a little!), it is more useful when we come to compare profit maximising under different market conditions (see Chapters 11 and 12).

We will look at each method in turn. In both cases we will concentrate on the short run: namely, that period in which one or more factors are fixed in supply. In both cases we take the case of a firm facing a downward-sloping demand curve.

Short-run profit maximisation: using total curves

Table 10.3 shows the total revenue figures from Table 10.2. It also shows figures for total cost. These figures have been chosen so as to produce a *TC* curve of a typical shape.

Total profit ($T\Pi$) is found by subtracting *TC* from *TR*. Check this out by examining the table. Where $T\Pi$ is negative, the firm is making a loss. Total profit is maximised at an output of 3 units: namely, where there is the greatest gap between total revenue and total costs. At this output, total profit is £4 (£18 − £14).

Table 10.3

Q (units)	TR (£)	TC (£)	TΠ (£)
0	0	6	−6
1	8	10	−2
2	14	12	2
3	18	14	4
4	20	18	2
5	20	25	−5
6	18	36	−18
7	14	56	−42
.	.	.	.

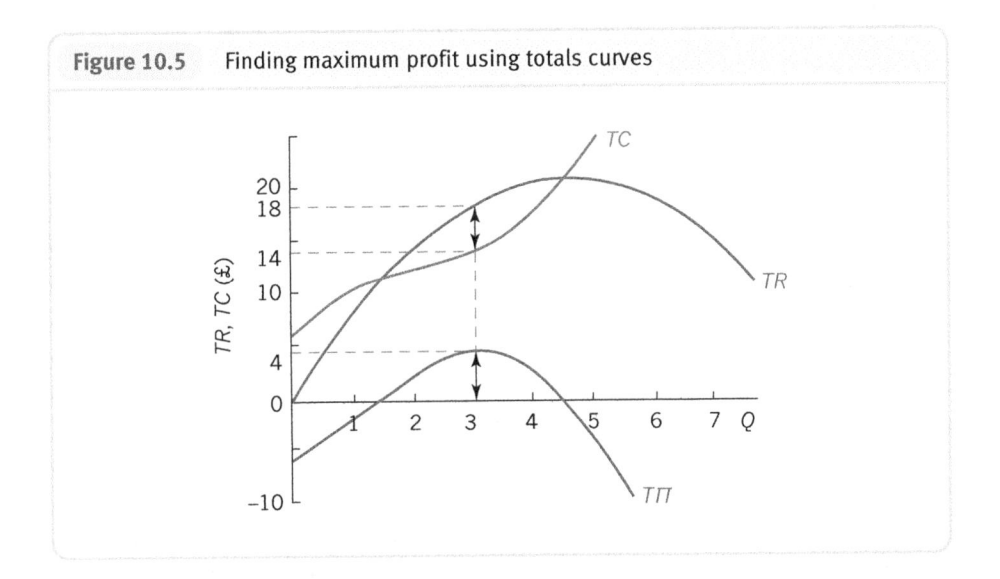

Figure 10.5 Finding maximum profit using totals curves

The TR, TC and TΠ curves are plotted in Figure 10.5. The size of the maximum profit is shown by the arrows.

Short-run profit maximisation: using average and marginal curves

Table 10.4 is based on the figures in Table 10.3.

Finding the maximum profit that a firm can make is a two-stage process. The first stage is to find the profit-maximising output. To do this we use the MC and MR curves. The second stage is to find out just how much profit is at this output. To do this we use the AR and AC curves.

Pause for thought

Why are the figures for MR and MC entered in the spaces between the lines in Table 10.4?

Stage 1: Using marginal curves to arrive at the profit-maximising output

There is a very simple **profit-maximising rule**: if profits are to be maximised, MR must equal MC. From Table 10.4 it can be seen that MR = MC at an output of 3. This is shown as point *e* in Figure 10.6.

But why are profits maximised when MR = MC? The simplest way of answering this is to see what the position would be if MR did not equal MC.

Definition

Profit-maximising rule
Profit is maximised where marginal revenue equals marginal cost.

Table 10.4

Q (units)	P = AR (£)	TR (£)	MR (£)	TC (£)	AC (£)	MC (£)	TP (£)	AΠ (£)
0	9	0		6	–		–6	–
			8			4		
1	8	8		10	10		–2	–2
			6			2		
2	7	14		12	6		2	1
			4			2		
3	6	18		14	$4^{2}/_{3}$		4	$1^{1}/_{3}$
			2			4		
4	5	20		18	$4^{1}/_{2}$		2	$^{1}/_{2}$
			0			7		
5	4	20		25	5		–5	–1
			–2			11		
6	3	18		36	6		–18	–3
			–4			20		
7	2	14		56	8		–42	–6
.	.	.	.	.	.	.	.	.

Figure 10.6 Finding the profit-maximising output using the marginal curves

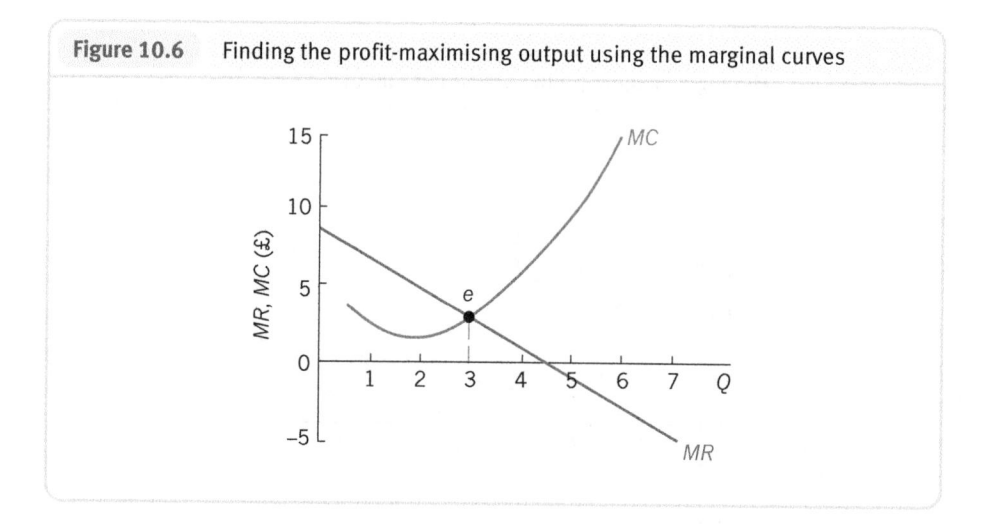

Referring to Figure 10.6, at a level of output below 3, MR exceeds MC. This means that by producing more units there will be a bigger addition to revenue (MR) than to cost (MC). Total profit will *increase*. *As long as MR exceeds MC, profit can be increased by increasing production.*

At a level of output above 3, MC exceeds MR. All levels of output above 3 thus add more to cost than to revenue and hence *reduce* profit. *As long as MC exceeds MR, profit can be increased by cutting back on production.*

Profits are thus maximised where MC = MR: at an output of 3. This can be confirmed by reference to the TΠ column in Table 10.4.

Students worry sometimes about the argument that profits are maximised when MR = MC. Surely, they say, if the last unit is making no profit, how can profit be at a *maximum*? The answer is very simple. If you cannot *add* anything more to a total, the total must be at the maximum. Take the simple analogy of going up a hill. When you cannot go any higher, you must be at the top.

Stage 2: Using average curves to measure the size of the profit

Once the profit-maximising output has been discovered, we now use the average curves to measure the *amount* of profit at the maximum. Both marginal and average curves corresponding to the data in Table 10.4 are plotted in Figure 10.7.

First, average profit (AΠ) is found. This is simply AR – AC. At the profit-maximising output of 3, this gives a figure for AΠ of £6 – £$4^{2}/_{3}$ = £$1^{1}/_{3}$. Then total profit is obtained by multiplying average profit by output:

Figure 10.7 Measuring the maximum profit using average curves

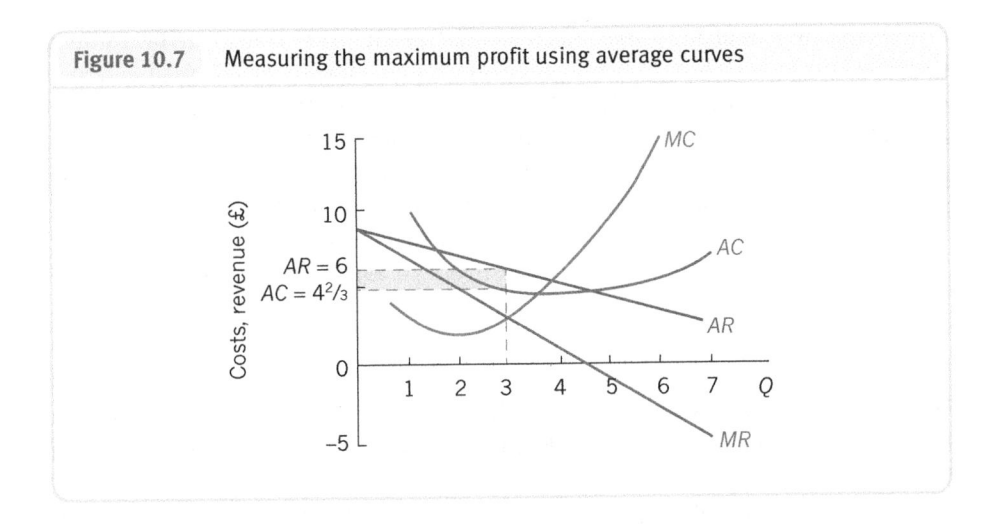

$T\Pi = A\Pi \times Q$

This is shown as the shaded area. It equals £1⅓ × 3 = £4. This can again be confirmed by reference to the $T\Pi$ column in Table 10.4.

> **Pause for thought**
>
> What will be the effect on a firm's profit-maximising output of a rise in fixed costs?

Some qualifications

Long-run profit maximisation

Assuming that the AR and MR curves are the same in the long run as in the short run, long-run profits will be maximised at the output where MR equals the *long-run MC*. The reasoning is the same as with the short-run case.

The meaning of 'profit'

One element of cost is the opportunity cost to the owners of the firm incurred by being in business. This is the minimum return that the owners must make on their capital in order to prevent them from eventually deciding to close down and perhaps move into some alternative business. It is a *cost* since, just as with wages, rent, etc., it has to be covered if the firm is to continue producing. This opportunity cost to the owners is sometimes known as normal profit, and *is included in the cost curves*.

What determines this normal rate of profit? It has two components. First, someone setting up in business invests capital in it. There is thus an opportunity cost. This is the interest that could have been earned by lending it in some riskless form (e.g. by putting it in a savings account in a bank). Nobody would set up a business unless they expected to earn at least this rate of profit. Running a business is far from riskless, however, and hence a second element is a return to compensate for risk. Thus:

normal profit (%) = rate of interest on a riskless loan + a risk premium

The risk premium varies according to the line of business. In those with fairly predictable patterns, such as food retailing, it is relatively low. Where outcomes are very uncertain, such as mineral exploration or the manufacture of fashion garments, it is relatively high.

> **Definition**
>
> **Normal profit**
> The opportunity cost of being in business. It consists of the interest that could be earned on a riskless asset, plus a return for risk-taking in this particular industry. It is counted as a cost of production.

Thus if owners of a business earn normal profit, they will (just) be content to remain in that industry. If they earn more than normal profit, they will also (obviously) prefer to stay in this business. If they earn less than normal profit, then after a time they will consider leaving and using their capital for some other purpose.

Given that normal profits are included in costs, any profit that is shown diagrammatically (e.g. the shaded area in Figure 10.7) must therefore be over and above normal profit. It is known by several alternative names: **supernormal profit**, **pure profit**, **economic profit**, **abnormal profit** or sometimes simply **profit**. They all mean the same thing: the excess of profit over normal profit.

Loss minimising

It may be that there is no output at which the firm can make a profit. Such a situation is illustrated in Figure 10.8: the AC curve is above the AR curve at all levels of output.

In this case, the output where $MR = MC$ will be the loss-minimising output. The amount of loss at the point where $MR = MC$ is shown by the shaded area in Figure 10.8.

Whether or not to produce at all

The short run. Fixed costs have to be paid even if the firm is producing nothing at all. Rent has to be paid, business rates have to be paid, etc. Providing, therefore, that the firm is more than covering its *variable* costs, it can go some way to paying off these fixed costs and therefore will continue to produce.

It will shut down if it cannot cover its variable costs: that is, if the AVC curve is above, or the AR curve is below, that illustrated in Figure 10.9. This situation is known as the **short-run shut-down point**.

> **Definitions**
>
> **Supernormal profit** (also known as **pure profit**, **economic profit**, **abnormal profit** or simply **profit**)
> The excess of total profit above normal profit.
>
> **Short-run shut-down point**
> This is where the AR curve is tangential to the AVC curve. The firm can only just cover its variable costs. Any fall in revenue below this level will cause a profit-maximising firm to shut down immediately.

BOX 10.1 SELLING ICE CREAM WHEN I WAS A STUDENT

John's experience of competition

When I was a student, my parents lived in Exeter in Devon, and at that time, the city's bypass became completely jammed on a summer Saturday as holidaymakers made their way to the coast. Traffic queues were several miles long.

For a summer job, I drove a small ice-cream van. Early on, I had the idea of selling ice cream from a tray to the people queuing in their cars. I made more money on a Saturday than the rest of the week put together. I thought I was on to a good thing.

But news of this lucrative market soon spread, and each week new ice-cream sellers appeared – each one reducing my earnings! By the middle of August there were over 30 ice-cream sellers from five different ice-cream companies. Most tried to get to the beginning of the queue, to get ahead of their rivals.

Imagine the scene. A family driving to the coast rounds a bend and is suddenly met by a traffic jam and several ice-cream sellers all jostling to sell them an ice cream. It was quite surreal. Not surprisingly, many of the potential customers refused to buy, feeling somewhat intimidated by the spectacle. It was not long before most of us realised that it was best to disperse and find a section of the road where there were no other sellers.

But with so many ice-cream sellers, no one made much money. My supernormal earnings had been reduced to a normal level. I made about the same on Saturday to people stuck in queues as I would have done if I had driven my van around the streets.

> *Imagine that you live in a popular and sunny seaside town and that the local council awarded you the only licence to sell ice cream in the town. Would you be earning normal or supernormal profit? Explain your answer.*

Figure 10.8 Loss-minimising output

Figure 10.9 The short-run shut-down point

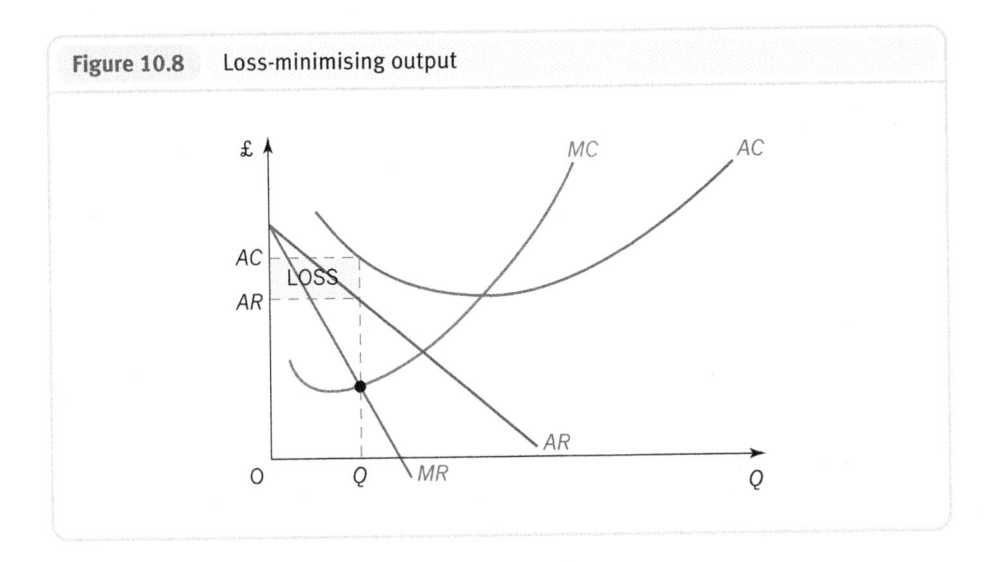

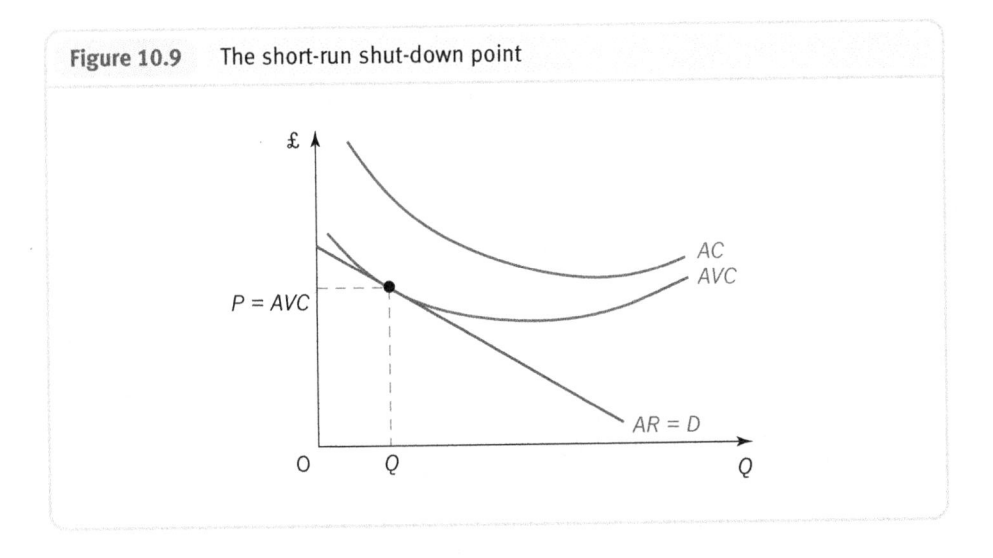

The long run. All costs are variable in the long run. If, therefore, the firm cannot cover its long-run average costs (which include normal profit), it will close down. The **long-run shut-down point** will be where the *AR* curve is tangential to the *LRAC* curve.

Pause for thought

Why might it make sense for a firm which cannot sell its output at a profit to continue in production for the time being?

Definition

Long-run shut-down point
This is where the *AR* curve is tangential to the *LRAC* curve. The firm can just make normal profits. Any fall in revenue below this level will cause a profit-maximising firm to shut down once all costs have become variable.

SUMMARY

1a Just as we could identify total, average and marginal costs, so too we can identify total, average and marginal revenue.

1b Total revenue (*TR*) is the total amount a firm earns from its sales in a given time period. It is simply price times quantity: $TR = P \times Q$.

1c Average revenue (*AR*) is total revenue per unit: $AR = TR/Q$. In other words, $AR = P$.

1d Marginal revenue is the extra revenue earned from the sale of one more unit per time period.

1e The *AR* curve will be the same as the demand curve for the firm's product. In the case of a price taker, the demand curve and hence the *AR* curve will be a horizontal straight line and will also be the same as the *MR* curve. The *TR* curve is an upward-sloping straight line from the origin.

1f A firm that faces a downward-sloping demand curve must obviously also face the same downward-sloping *AR* curve. The *MR* curve will also slope downwards, but will be below the *AR* curve and steeper than it. The *TR* curve will be an arch shape starting from the origin.

1g When demand is price elastic, marginal revenue will be positive and the *TR* curve will be upward sloping. When demand is price inelastic, marginal revenue will be negative and the *TR* curve will be downward sloping.

1h A change in output is represented by a movement along the revenue curves. A change in any other determinant of revenue will shift the curves up or down.

2a Total profit equals total revenue minus total cost. By definition, then, a firm's profits will be maximised at the point where there is the greatest gap between total revenue and total cost.

2b Another way of finding the maximum-profit point is to find the output where marginal revenue equals marginal cost. Having found this output, the level of maximum profit can be found by finding the average profit ($AR - AC$) and then multiplying it by the level of output.

2c Normal profit is the minimum profit that must be made to persuade a firm to stay in business in the long run. It is counted as part of the firm's cost. Supernormal profit is any profit over and above normal profit.

2d For a firm that cannot make a profit at any level of output, the point where $MR = MC$ represents the loss-minimising output.

2e In the short run, a firm will close down if it cannot cover its variable costs. In the long run, it will close down if it cannot make normal profits.

REVIEW QUESTIONS

1 Draw a downward-sloping demand curve. Now put in scales of your own choosing for both axes. Read off various points on the demand curve and use them to construct a table showing price and quantity. Use this table to work out the figures for a marginal revenue column. Now use these figures to draw an *MR* curve.

2 Copy Figures 10.3 and 10.4 (which are based on Table 10.2). Now assume that incomes have risen and that, as a result, two more units per time period can be sold at each price. Draw a new table and plot the resulting new *AR*, *MR* and *TR* curves on your diagrams. Are the new curves parallel to the old ones? Explain.

3 What can we say about the slope of the *TR* and *TC* curves at the maximum-profit point? What does this tell us about marginal revenue and marginal cost?

4 Using the following information, construct a table like Table 10.3.

Q	0	1	2	3	4	5	6	7
P	12	11	10	9	8	7	6	5
TC	2	6	9	12	16	21	28	38

Use your table to draw diagrams like Figures 10.5 and 10.7. Use these two diagrams to show the profit-maximising output and the level of maximum profit. Confirm your findings by reference to the table you have constructed.

5 The following table shows the average cost and average revenue (price) for a firm at each level of output.

(a) Construct a table to show *TC*, *MC*, *TR* and *MR* at each level of output (put the figures for *MC* and *MR* midway between the output figures).

Output	1	2	3	4	5	6	7	8	9	10
AC (£)	7.00	5.00	4.00	3.30	3.00	3.10	3.50	4.20	5.00	6.00
AR (£)	10.00	9.50	9.00	8.50	8.00	7.50	7.00	6.50	6.00	5.50

(b) Using *MC* and *MR* figures, find the profit-maximising output.
(c) Using *TC* and *TR* figures, check your answer to (b).
(d) Plot the *AC*, *MC*, *AR* and *MR* figures on a graph.
(e) Mark the profit-maximising output and the *AR* and *AC* at this output.
(f) Shade in an area to represent the level of profits at this output.

6 Normal profits are regarded as a cost (and are included in the cost curves). Explain why.

7 What determines the size of normal profit? Will it vary with the general state of the economy?

8 A firm will continue producing in the short run even if it is making a loss, providing it can cover its variable costs. Explain why. Just how long will it be willing to continue making such a loss?

9 Would there ever be a point in a firm attempting to continue in production if it could not cover its *long-run* average (total) costs?

10 The price of pocket calculators and digital watches fell significantly in the years after they were first introduced and at the same time demand for them increased substantially. Use cost and revenue diagrams to illustrate these events. Explain the reasoning behind the diagram(s) you have drawn.

11 In February 2000, Unilever, the giant consumer products company, announced that it was to cut 25 000 jobs, close 100 plants and rely more on the Internet to purchase its supplies. It would use part of the money saved to increase promotion of its leading brands, such as Dove skincare products, Lipton tea, Omo detergents and Calvin Klein cosmetics. The hope was to boost sales and increase profits. If it meets these targets, what is likely to have happened to its total costs, total revenue, average costs and average revenue? Give reasons for your answer.

Additional Part D case studies on the *Economics for Business* website (www.pearsoned.co.uk/sloman)

D.1 Malthus and the dismal science of economics. A gloomy warning, made over 200 years ago by Robert Malthus, that diminishing returns to labour would lead to famine for much of the world's population.

D.2 Division of labour in a pin factory. This is the famous example of division of labour given by Adam Smith in his *Wealth of Nations* (1776).

D.3 Diminishing returns to nitrogen fertiliser. This case study provides a good illustration of diminishing returns in practice by showing the effects on grass yields of the application of increasing amounts of nitrogen fertiliser.

D.4 Diminishing returns in the bread shop. An illustration of the law of diminishing returns.

D.5 The relationship between averages and marginals. An examination of the rules showing how an average curve relates to a marginal curve.

D.6 Deriving cost curves from total physical product information. This shows how total, average and marginal costs can be derived from a total product information and the price of inputs.

Websites relevant to Part D

Numbers and sections refer to websites listed in the Web appendix and hotlinked from this book's website at **www.pearsoned.co.uk/sloman**

- For news articles relevant to Part D, see the *Economics News Articles* link from the book's website.
- For student resources relevant to Part D, see sites C1–7, 9, 10, 14, 19, 20.
- For a case study examining costs, see site D2.
- For sites that look at companies, their scale of operation and market share, see B2; E4, 10; G7, 8.
- For links to sites on various aspects of production and costs, see section *Microeconomics* > Production in site I7 and 11.

Chapter 11

Profit maximisation under perfect competition and monopoly

> **Business issues covered in this chapter**
>
> - What determines the degree of market power of a firm?
> - Why does operating under conditions of perfect competition make being in business a constant battle for survival?
> - How do firms get to become monopolies and remain so?
> - At what price and output will a monopolist maximise profits and how much profit will it make?
> - How well or badly do monopolies serve the consumer compared with competitive firms?
> - Why will the size of entry barriers to an industry (the degree of 'contestability' of a market) affect the amount of profit a monopolist can make?

11.1 ALTERNATIVE MARKET STRUCTURES

It is traditional to divide industries into categories according to the degree of competition that exists between the firms within the industry. There are four such categories.

At one extreme is perfect competition, where there are very many firms competing. Each firm is so small relative to the whole industry that it has no power to influence price. It is a price taker. At the other extreme is monopoly, where there

> **Definitions**
>
> **Perfect competition**
> A market structure in which there are many firms; where there is freedom of entry to the industry; where all firms produce an identical product; and where all firms are price takers.
>
> **Monopoly**
> A market structure where there is only one firm in the industry.

> **Definitions**
>
> **Monopolistic competition**
> A market structure where, like perfect competition, there are many firms and freedom of entry into the industry, but where each firm produces a differentiated product and thus has some control over its price.
>
> **Oligopoly**
> A market structure where there are few enough firms to enable barriers to be erected against the entry of new firms.

is just one firm in the industry, and hence no competition from *within* the industry. In the middle comes monopolistic competition, which involves quite a lot of firms competing and where there is freedom for new firms to enter the industry, and oligopoly, where there are only a few firms and where entry of new firms is restricted.

To distinguish more precisely between these four categories, the following must be considered:

- How freely can firms enter the industry: is entry free or restricted? If it is restricted, just how great are the barriers to the entry of new firms?
- The nature of the product. Do all firms produce an identical product, or do firms produce their own particular brand or model or variety?
- The degree of control the firm has over price. Is the firm a price taker or can it choose its price, and if it can, how will changing its price affect its profits? What we are talking about here is the nature of the demand curve it faces. How elastic is it? If it puts up its price, will it lose (a) all its sales (a horizontal demand curve), or (b) a large proportion of its sales (a relatively elastic demand curve), or (c) just a small proportion of its sales (a relatively inelastic demand curve)?

> **KEY IDEA 21**
>
> *Market power benefits the powerful at the expense of others.* When firms have market power over prices, they can use this to raise prices and profits above the perfectly competitive level. Other things being equal, the firm will gain at the expense of the consumer. Similarly, if consumers or workers have market power, they can use this to their own benefit.

Table 11.1 shows the differences between the four categories.

The market structure under which a firm operates will determine its behaviour. Firms under perfect competition behave quite differently from firms that are monopolists, which behave differently again from firms under oligopoly or monopolistic competition.

This behaviour (or 'conduct') will in turn affect the firm's performance: its prices, profits, efficiency, etc. In many cases it will also affect other firms' performance:

Table 11.1 Features of the four market structures

Type of market	Number of firms	Freedom of entry	Nature of product	Examples	Implication for demand curve for firm
Perfect competition	Very many	Unrestricted	Homogeneous (undifferentiated)	Cabbages, carrots (these approximate to perfect competition)	Horizontal. The firm is a price taker
Monopolistic competition	Many/several	Unrestricted	Differentiated	Builders, restaurants	Downward sloping, but relatively elastic. The firm has some control over price
Oligopoly	Few	Restricted	1. Undifferentiated or 2. Differentiated	1. Cement 2. Cars, electrical appliances	Downward sloping, relatively inelastic but depends on reactions of rivals to a price change
Monopoly	One	Restricted or completely blocked	Unique	Local water company, many prescription drugs	Downward sloping, more inelastic than oligopoly. Firm has considerable control over price

BOX 11.1 CONCENTRATION RATIOS

Measuring the degree of competition

We can get some indication of how competitive a market is by observing the number of firms: the more firms, the more competitive the market would seem to be. However, this does not tell us anything about how *concentrated* the market might be. There may be *many* firms (suggesting a situation of perfect competition or monopolistic competition), but the largest two firms might produce 95 per cent of total output. This would make these two firms more like oligopolists.

Thus even though a large number of producers may make the market *seem* highly competitive, this could be deceiving. Another approach, therefore, to measuring the degree of competition is to focus on the level of concentration of firms.

The simplest measure of industrial concentration involves adding together the market share of the largest so many firms: e.g. the largest three, five or fifteen. This would give what is known as the '3-firm', '5-firm' or '15-firm concentration ratio'. There are different ways of estimating market share: by revenue, by output, by profit, etc.

The table shows the 5-firm concentration ratios of selected industries in the UK by output. As you can see, there is an enormous variation in the degree of concentration from one industry to another.

One of the main reasons for this is differences in the percentage of total industry output at which economies of scale are exhausted (see Box 9.4). If this occurs at a low level of output, there will be room for several firms in the industry which are all benefiting from the maximum economies of scale.

The degree of concentration will also depend on the barriers to entry of other firms into the industry (see pages 222–3) and on various factors such as transport costs and historical accident. It will also depend on how varied the products are within any one industrial category. For example, in categories as large as furniture and construction there is room for many firms, each producing a specialised range of products.

So is the degree of concentration a good guide to the degree of competitiveness of the industry? The answer is that it is *some* guide, but on its own it can be misleading. In particular it ignores the degree of competition from abroad, and from other industries within the country.

1. What are the advantages and disadvantages of using a 5-firm concentration ratio rather than a 10-firm, 3-firm or even a 1-firm ratio?
2. Why are some industries like bread baking and brewing relatively concentrated, in that a few firms produce a large proportion of total output (see web case E9), and yet there are also many small producers?

Concentration ratios for business by industry (2004)

Industry	5-firm ratio	15-firm ratio	Industry	5-firm ratio	15-firm ratio
Sugar	99	99	Alcoholic beverages	50	78
Tobacco products	99	99	Soap and toiletries	40	64
Oils and fats	88	95	Accountancy services	36	47
Confectionary	81	91	Motor vehicles	34	54
Gas distribution	82	87	Glass and glass products	26	49
Soft drinks, mineral water	75	93	Fishing	16	19
Postal/courier services	65	75	Advertising	10	20
Telecommunications	61	75	Wholesale distribution	6	11
Inorganic chemicals	57	80	Furniture	5	13

Source: based on data in Table 8.31 of *United Kingdom Input–Output Analyses* 2006 (National Statistics)

their prices, profits, efficiency, etc. The collective conduct of all the firms in the industry will affect the whole industry's performance.

Some economists thus see a causal chain running from market structure to the performance of that industry.

Structure → Conduct → Performance

This does not mean, however, that all firms operating in a particular market structure will behave in exactly the same way.

Pause for thought

Give one more example in each of the four market categories in Table 11.1.

For example, some firms under oligopoly may be highly competitive, whereas others may collude with each other to keep prices high. This conduct may then, in turn, influence the development of the market structure. For example, the interaction between firms may influence the development of new products or new production methods, and may encourage or discourage the entrance of new firms into the industry.

It is for this reason that government policy towards firms – known as 'competition policy' – prefers to focus on the *conduct* of individual firms, rather than simply on the market structure within which they operate. Indeed, competition policy in most countries accepts that market structures evolve naturally (e.g. because of economies of scale or changing consumer preferences) and do not necessarily give rise to competition problems.

Nevertheless, market structure still influences firms' behaviour and the performance of the industry, even though it does not, in the case of oligopoly and monopoly, rigidly determine it. We look at these influences in this chapter and the next. First, we look at the two extreme market structures: perfect competition and monopoly. Then we turn to look at the two intermediate cases of monopolistic competition and oligopoly (Chapter 12).

These two intermediate cases are sometimes referred to collectively as imperfect competition. The vast majority of firms in the real world operate under imperfect competition. It is still worth studying the two extreme cases, however, because they provide a framework within which to understand the real world. Some industries tend more to the competitive extreme, and thus their performance corresponds to some extent to perfect competition. Other industries tend more to the other extreme: for example, when there is one dominant firm and a few much smaller firms. In such cases, their performance corresponds more to monopoly.

> **Definition**
>
> **Imperfect competition**
> The collective name for monopolistic competition and oligopoly.

11.2 PERFECT COMPETITION

The theory of perfect competition illustrates an extreme form of capitalism. In it firms are entirely subject to market forces. They have no power whatsoever to affect the price of the product. The price they face is that determined by the interaction of demand and supply in the whole *market*.

Assumptions

The model of perfect competition is built on four assumptions:

1. Firms are *price takers*. There are so many firms in the industry that each one produces an insignificantly small proportion of total industry supply, and therefore has *no power whatsoever* to affect the price of the product. It faces a horizontal demand 'curve' at the market price: the price determined by the interaction of demand and supply in the whole market.
2. There is complete *freedom of entry* into the industry for new firms. Existing firms are unable to stop new firms setting up in business. Setting up a business takes time, however. Freedom of entry therefore applies in the long run.
3. All firms produce an *identical product*. (The product is 'homogeneous'.) There is therefore no branding or advertising.

4 Producers and consumers have *perfect knowledge* of the market. That is, producers are fully aware of prices, costs and market opportunities. Consumers are fully aware of price, quality and availability of the product.

These assumptions are very strict. Few, if any, industries in the real world meet these conditions. Certain agricultural markets perhaps are closest to perfect competition. The market for fresh vegetables is an example.

> **Pause for thought**
>
> *It is sometimes claimed that the market for various stocks and shares is perfectly competitive, or nearly so. Take the case of the market for shares in a large company, such as BP. Go through each of the four assumptions above and see if they apply in this case. (Don't be misled by the first assumption. The 'firm' in this case is not BP itself, but rather the owners of the shares.)*

The short-run equilibrium of the firm

In the short run, we assume that the number of firms in the industry cannot be increased; there is simply no time for new firms to enter the market.

Figure 11.1 shows a short-run equilibrium for both industry and a firm under perfect competition. Both parts of the diagram have the same scale for the vertical axis. The horizontal axes have totally different scales, however. For example, if the horizontal axis for the firm were measured in, say, thousands of units, the horizontal axis for the whole industry might be measured in millions or tens of millions of units, depending on the number of firms in the industry.

Let us examine the determination of price, output and profit in turn.

> **Definition**
>
> **The short run under perfect competition**
> The period during which there is too little time for new firms to enter the industry.

Price

The price is determined in the industry by the intersection of demand and supply. The firm faces a horizontal demand (or average revenue) 'curve' at this price. It can sell all it can produce at the market price (P_e), but nothing at a price above P_e.

Output

The firm will maximise profit where marginal cost equals marginal revenue ($MR = MC$), at an output of Q_e. Note that, since the price is not affected by the firm's output, marginal revenue will equal price (see pages 196–7 and Figure 10.1). Thus the firm's *MR* 'curve' and *AR* 'curve' (= demand 'curve') are the same horizontal straight line.

Figure 11.1 Short-run equilibrium of industry and firm under perfect competition
(a) Industry
(b) Firm

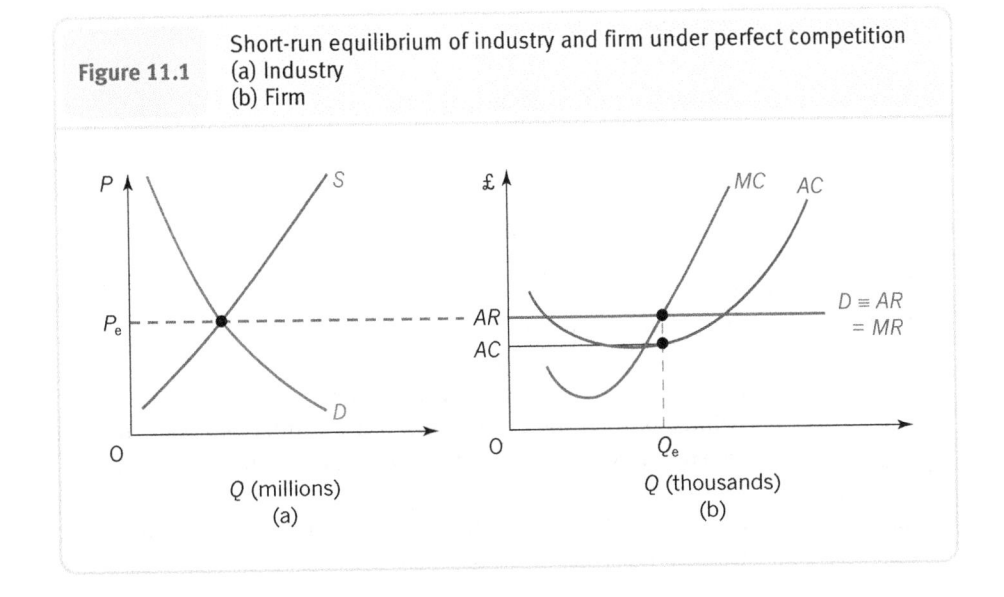

Figure 11.2 Loss minimising under perfect competition

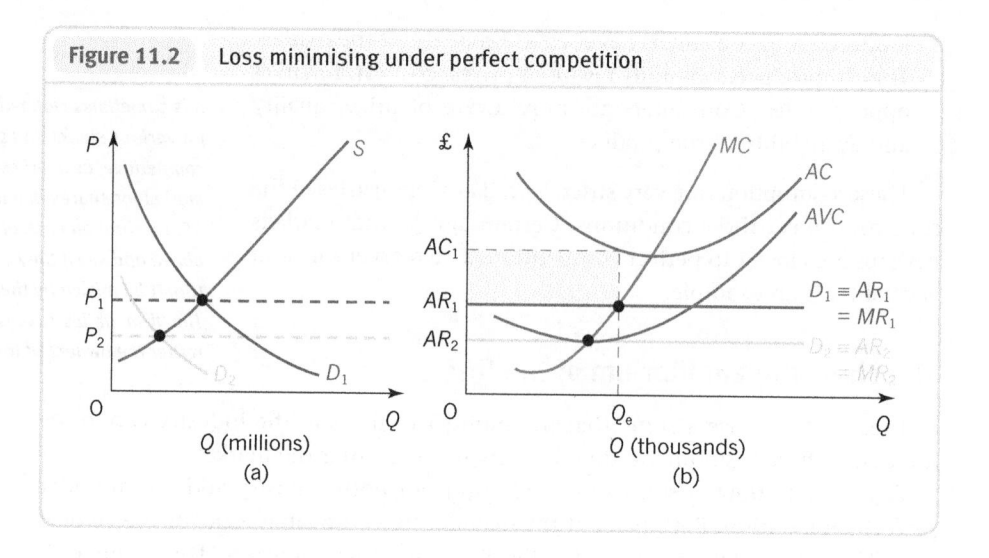

Profit

If the average cost (AC) curve (which includes normal profit) dips below the average revenue (AR) 'curve', the firm will earn supernormal profit. Supernormal profit per unit at Q_e is the vertical difference between AR and AC at Q_e. Total supernormal profit is the shaded rectangle in Figure 11.1 (i.e. profit per unit times quantity sold).

What happens if the firm cannot make a profit at *any* level of output? This situation would occur if the AC curve were above the AR curve at all points. This is illustrated in Figure 11.2 where the market price is P_1. In this case, the point where MC = MR represents the *loss-minimising* point (where loss is defined as anything less than normal profit). This amount of the loss is represented by the shaded rectangle.

As we saw in Chapter 10, whether the firm is prepared to continue making a loss in the short run or whether it will close down immediately depends on whether it can cover its *variable* costs. Provided price is above average variable cost (AVC), the firm will continue producing in the short run: it can pay its variable costs and go some way to paying its fixed costs. It will shut down in the short run only if the market price falls below P_2 in Figure 11.2.

The long-run equilibrium of the firm

In the long run, if typical firms are making supernormal profits, new firms will be attracted into the industry. Likewise, if existing firms can make supernormal profits by increasing the scale of their operations, they will do so, since all factors of production are variable in the long run.

The effect of the entry of new firms and/or the expansion of existing firms is to increase industry supply. This is illustrated in Figure 11.3.

The industry supply curve shifts to the right. This in turn leads to a fall in price. Supply will go on increasing, and price falling, until firms are making only normal profits. This will be when price has fallen to the point where the demand 'curve' for the firm just touches the bottom of its long-run average cost curve. Q_L is thus the long-run equilibrium output of the firm, with P_L the long-run equilibrium price.

> **Definition**
>
> **The long run under perfect competition**
> The period of time which is long enough for new firms to enter the industry.

> **Pause for thought**
>
> *Before you read on, can you explain why perfect competition and substantial economies of scale are likely to be incompatible?*

Figure 11.3 Long-run equilibrium under perfect competition
(a) Industry
(b) Firm

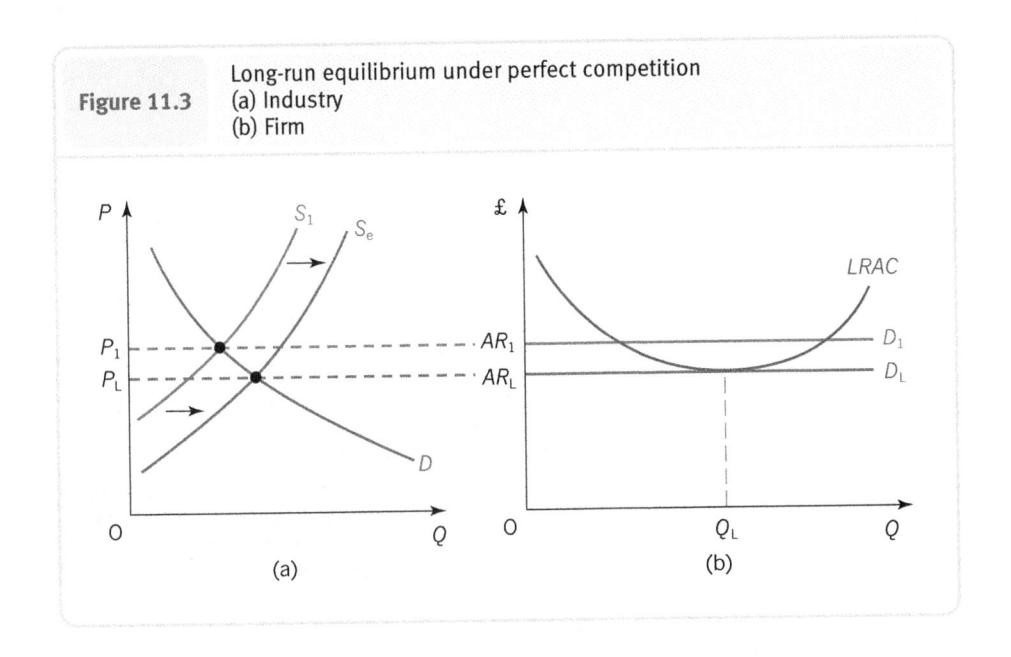

Figure 11.4 Long-run equilibrium of the firm under perfect competition

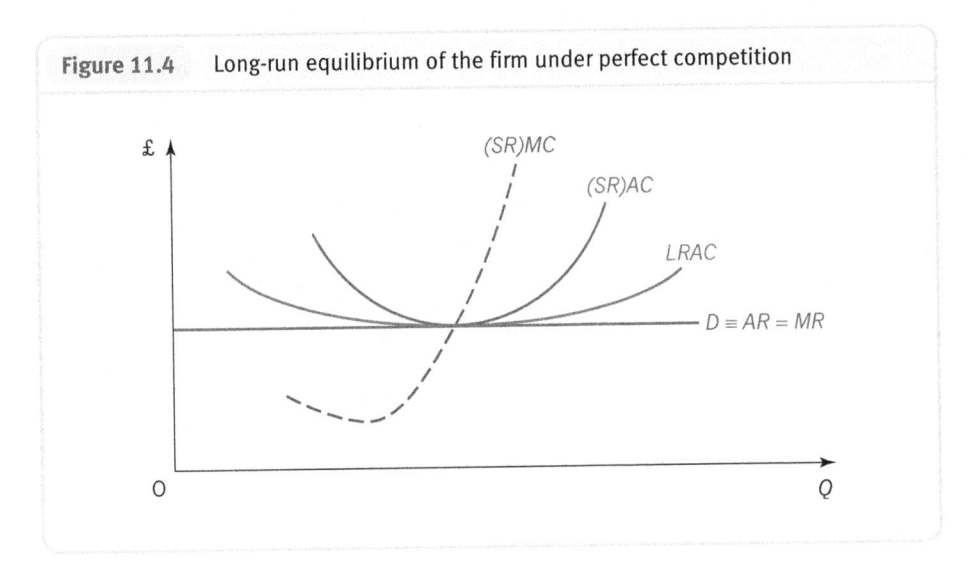

Since the *LRAC* curve is tangential to all possible short-run *AC* curves (see section 9.5), the full long-run equilibrium will be as shown in Figure 11.4 where:

$LRAC = AC = MC = MR = AR$

The incompatibility of perfect competition and substantial economies of scale

Why is perfect competition so rare in the real world – if it even exists at all? One important reason for this has to do with economies of scale.

In many industries, firms may have to be quite large if they are to experience the full potential economies of scale. But perfect competition requires there to be *many* firms. Firms must therefore be small under perfect competition: too small in most cases for economies of scale.

> **BOX 11.2** **E-COMMERCE**
>
> ### A modern form of perfect competition?
>
> The relentless drive towards big business in recent decades has seen many markets become more concentrated and increasingly dominated by large producers. And yet forces are at work that are undermining this dominance and bringing more competition to markets. One of these forces is *e-commerce*.
>
> In this case study, we will consider just how far e-commerce is returning 'power to the people'.
>
> **Moving markets back towards perfect competition?**
>
> To see the extent to which e-commerce is making markets more competitive, let's look at the assumptions of perfect competition.
>
> *Large number of firms.* The growth of e-commerce has led to many new firms starting up in business. It's not just large firms like Amazon.com that are providing increased competition for established firms, but the thousands of small online companies that are being established every day. Many of these firms are selling directly to us as consumers. This is known as 'B2C' (business-to-consumers) e-commerce. But many more are selling to other firms ('B2B'). More and more companies, from the biggest to the smallest, are transferring their purchasing to the Web and are keen to get value for money.
>
> The reach of the Web is global. This means that firms, whether conventional or web-based, have to keep an eye on the prices and products of competitors in the rest of the world, not just in the local neighbourhood. Firms' demand curves are thus becoming very price elastic. This is especially so for goods that are cheap to transport, or for services such as insurance and banking where no transport is required.
>
> *Perfect knowledge.* There are various ways in which e-commerce is adding to the consumer's knowledge. There is greater price transparency, with consumers able to compare prices on-line. Online shopping agents, such as Kelkoo and DealTime, can quickly locate a list of alternative suppliers. There is greater information on product availability and quality and this information is available at very little cost to the consumer. Virtual shopping malls, full of e-retailers, place the high street retailer under intense competitive pressure.
>
> The pressure is even greater in the market for intermediate products. Many firms are constantly searching for cheaper sources of supply, and the Internet provides a cheap and easy means of conducting such searches.
>
> *Freedom of entry.* Internet companies often have lower start-up costs than their conventional rivals. Their premises are generally much smaller, with no 'shop-front' costs and lower levels of stockholding; in fact many of these businesses are initially operated from their owners' homes. Marketing costs can also be relatively low, especially given the ease with which companies can be located with search engines. Internet companies are often smaller and more specialist, relying on Internet 'outsourcing' (buying parts, equipment and other supplies through the Internet), rather than making everything themselves. They are also more likely to use delivery firms rather than having their own transport fleet. All this makes it relatively cheap for new firms to set up and begin trading over the Internet.
>
> One consequence of e-commerce is that the distinction between firms and consumers is becoming increasingly blurred. With the rise of eBay, more and more people are

Once a firm expands sufficiently to achieve economies of scale, it will usually gain market power. It will be able to undercut the prices of smaller firms, which will thus be driven out of business. Perfect competition is destroyed.

Perfect competition could only exist in any industry, therefore, if there were no (or virtually no) economies of scale.

Does the firm benefit from operating under perfect competition?

Under perfect competition the firm faces a constant battle for survival. If it becomes less efficient than other firms, it will make less than normal profits and be driven out of business. If it becomes more efficient, it will earn supernormal profits. But these supernormal profits will not last for long. Soon other firms, in order to survive themselves, will be forced to copy the more efficient methods of the new firm.

finding going into business incredibly easy. Some people are finding a market for all the junk they've collected over the years, while others are selling products they produce at home and yet others specialise in selling on products using the marketing power of eBay. As a consequence there are over 84 million active eBay users worldwide, and hundreds of thousands of people make a full-time living from buying and selling on eBay. Annual sales on eBay are worth over £8 billion.

Not only do these factors make markets more price competitive, they also bring other benefits. Costs are driven down, as firms economise on stockholding, rely more on outsourcing and develop more efficient relationships with suppliers. 'Procurement hubs', online exchanges and trading communities are now well established in many industries. The competition also encourages innovation, which improves quality and the range of products.

What are the limits to e-commerce?

In 20 years, will we be doing all our shopping on the Internet? Will the only shopping malls be virtual ones? Although e-commerce is revolutionising some markets, it is unlikely that things will go anything like that far.

The benefits of 'shop shopping' are that you get to see the good, touch it and use it. You can buy the good there and then, and take instant possession of it: you don't have to wait. Shopping is also an enjoyable experience. Many people like wandering round the shops, meeting friends, seeing what takes their fancy, trying on clothes, browsing through DVDs, and so on. 'Retail therapy' for many is a leisure activity.

Online shopping is limited by current technology; Internet access may be slow and frustrating; 'surfing' may instead become 'wading'; you have to wait for goods to be delivered; and what if deliveries are late or fail completely? (See Box 6.2.) Online shopping requires access to a credit or debit card, which might not be available to everyone, particularly younger consumers and those on low incomes.

Also costs might not be as low as expected. How efficient is it to have many small deliveries of goods? How significant are the lost cost savings from economies of scale that larger producers or retailers are likely to generate?

Nevertheless, e-commerce has made many markets, both retail and B2B, more competitive. This is especially so for services and for goods whose quality is easy to identify online. Many firms are being forced to face up to having their prices determined by the market.

1. Why may the Internet work better for replacement buys than for new purchases?
2. Give three examples of products that are particularly suitable for selling over the Internet and three that are not. Explain your answer.
3. In 2008 eBay sellers called for a boycott of the site, following changes in the fees being charged and the removal of their ability to leave feedback on buyers. Explain how eBay can both increase competition across the economy and simultaneously acquire very substantial monopoly power.

KEY IDEA 22

Economic efficiency is achieved when each good is produced at the minimum cost and where consumers get maximum benefit from their income.

It is the same with the development of new products. If a firm is able to produce a new product that is popular with consumers, it will be able to gain a temporary advantage over its rivals. But again, any supernormal profits will last only as long as it takes other firms to respond. Soon the increase in supply of the new product will drive the price down and eliminate these supernormal profits. Similarly, the firm must be quick to copy new products developed by its rivals. If it does not, it will soon make a loss and be driven out of the market.

Thus being in perfect competition is a constant battle for survival. It might benefit the consumer, but most firms in such an environment would love to be able to gain some market power: power to be able to restrict competition and to retain supernormal profits into the long run.

The extreme case of market power is that of monopoly: a firm that faces no competition – at least not from *within* its industry. Monopoly is the subject of the next section.

11.3 MONOPOLY

What is a monopoly?

This may seem a strange question because the answer seems obvious. A monopoly exists when there is only one firm in the industry.

But whether an industry can be classed as a monopoly is not always clear. It depends how narrowly the industry is defined. For example, a textile company may have a monopoly on certain types of fabric, but it does not have a monopoly on fabrics in general. The consumer can buy fabrics other than those supplied by the company. A rail company may have a monopoly over rail services between two cities, but it does not have a monopoly over public transport between these two cities. People can travel by coach or air. They could also use private transport.

To some extent, the boundaries of an industry are arbitrary. What is more important for a firm is the amount of monopoly *power* it has, and that depends on the closeness of substitutes produced by rival industries. The Post Office, before 2006, had a monopoly over the delivery of letters, but it faces competition in communications from telephone, faxes and e-mail.

Barriers to entry

For a firm to maintain its monopoly position, there must be barriers to the entry of new firms. Barriers also exist under oligopoly, but in the case of monopoly they must be high enough to block the entry of new firms. Barriers can take various forms.

Economies of scale. If the monopolist's costs go on falling significantly up to the output that satisfies the whole market, the industry may not be able to support more than one producer. This case is known as **natural monopoly**. It is particularly likely if the market is small. For example, two bus companies might find it unprofitable to serve the same routes, each running with perhaps only half-full buses, whereas one company with a monopoly of the routes could make a profit. Electricity transmission via a national grid is another example of a natural monopoly.

Even if a market could support more than one firm, a new entrant is unlikely to be able to start up on a very large scale. Thus the monopolist which is already experiencing economies of scale can charge a price below the cost of the new entrant and drive it out of business. If, however, the new entrant is a firm already established in another industry, it may be able to survive this competition.

Economies of scope. A firm that produces a range of products is also likely to experience a lower average cost of production. For example, a large pharmaceutical company producing a range of drugs and toiletries can use shared research, marketing, storage and transport facilities across its range of products. These lower costs make it difficult for a new single-product entrant to the market, since the large firm will be able to undercut its price and drive it out of the market.

> **Definition**
>
> **Natural monopoly**
> A situation where long-run average costs would be lower if an industry were under monopoly than if it were shared between two or more competitors.

Product differentiation and brand loyalty. If a firm produces a clearly differentiated product, where the consumer associates the product with the brand, it will be very difficult for a new firm to break into that market. Rank Xerox invented, and patented, the plain paper photocopier. After this legal monopoly (see below) ran out, people still associated photocopiers with Rank Xerox. It is still not unusual to hear someone say that they are going to 'Xerox the article' or, for that matter, 'Hoover their carpet'. Other examples of strong brand image include Guinness, Kelloggs Cornflakes, Coca-Cola, Nescafé and Sellotape.

Lower costs for an established firm. An established monopoly is likely to have developed specialised production and marketing skills. It is more likely to be aware of the most efficient techniques and the most reliable and/or cheapest suppliers. It is likely to have access to cheaper finance. It is thus operating on a lower cost curve. New firms would therefore find it hard to compete and would be likely to lose any price war.

> **Pause for thought**
>
> *Illustrate the situation described above using AC curves for both a new entrant and an established firm.*

Ownership of, or control over, key inputs or outlets. If a firm governs the supply of vital inputs (say, by owning the sole supplier of some component part), it can deny access to these inputs to potential rivals. On a world scale, the de Beers company has a monopoly in fine diamonds because all diamond producers market their diamonds through de Beers.

Similarly, if a firm controls the outlets through which the product must be sold, it can prevent potential rivals from gaining access to consumers. For example, Birds Eye Walls used to supply freezers free to shops on the condition that they stocked only Wall's ice cream in them.

Legal protection. The firm's monopoly position may be protected by patents on essential processes, by copyright, by various forms of licensing (allowing, say, only one firm to operate in a particular area) and by tariffs (i.e. customs duties) and other trade restrictions to keep out foreign competitors. Examples of monopolies protected by patents include most new medicines developed by pharmaceutical companies (e.g. anti-AIDS drugs), Microsoft's Windows operating systems and agro-chemical companies, such as Monsanto, with various genetically modified plant varieties and pesticides.

Mergers and takeovers. The monopolist can put in a takeover bid for any new entrant. The sheer threat of takeovers may discourage new entrants.

Aggressive tactics. An established monopolist can probably sustain losses for longer than a new entrant. Thus it could start a price war, mount massive advertising campaigns, offer attractive after-sales service, introduce new brands to compete with new entrants, and so on.

Equilibrium price and output

Since there is, by definition, only one firm in the industry, the firm's demand curve is also the industry demand curve.

Compared with other market structures, demand under monopoly will be relatively inelastic at each price. The monopolist can raise its price and consumers have no alternative firm to turn to within the industry. They either pay the higher price, or go without the good altogether.

Figure 11.5 Profit maximising under monopoly

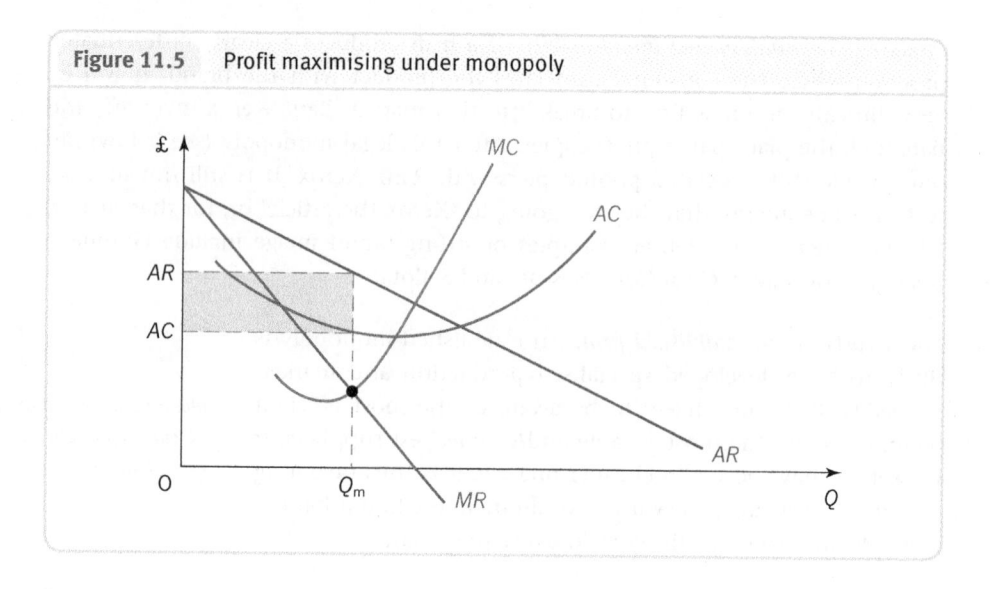

Unlike the firm under perfect competition, the monopoly firm is thus a 'price maker'. It can choose what price to charge. Nevertheless, it is still constrained by its demand curve. A rise in price will reduce the quantity demanded.

As with firms in other market structures, a monopolist will maximise profit where $MR = MC$. In Figure 11.5 profit is maximised at Q_m. The supernormal profit obtained is shown by the shaded area.

These profits will tend to be larger, the less elastic is the demand curve (and hence the steeper is the MR curve), and thus the bigger is the gap between MR and price (AR). The actual elasticity will depend on whether reasonably close substitutes are available in *other* industries. The demand for a rail service will be much less elastic (and the potential for profit greater) if there is no bus service to the same destination.

Since there are barriers to the entry of new firms, a monopolist's supernormal profits will not be competed away in the long run. The only difference, therefore, between short-run and long-run equilibrium is that in the long run the firm will produce where $MR = $ long-run MC.

Comparing monopoly with perfect competition

Because it faces a different type of market environment, the monopolist will produce a quite different output and at a quite different price from a perfectly competitive industry.

Let us compare the two.

The monopolist will produce a lower output at a higher price in the short run. Figure 11.6 compares the profit-maximising position for an industry under monopoly with that under perfect competition. Note that we are comparing the monopoly with the whole *industry* under perfect competition. That way we can assume, for the sake of comparison, that they both face the same demand curve. We also assume for the moment that they both face the same cost curves.

The monopolist will produce Q_1 at a price of P_1. This is where $MC = MR$.

If the same industry were under perfect competition, however, it would produce at Q_2 and P_2 – a higher output and a lower price. But why? The reason for this is that

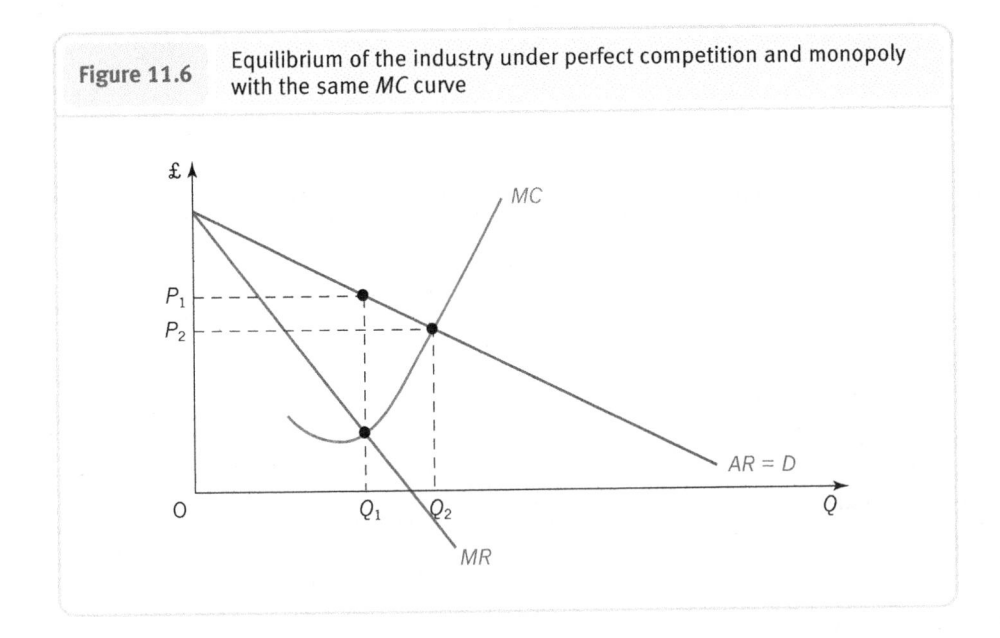

Figure 11.6 Equilibrium of the industry under perfect competition and monopoly with the same MC curve

for each of the firms in the industry – and it is at this level that the decisions are made – marginal revenue is the same as price. Remember that the *firm* under perfect competition faces a perfectly elastic demand (AR) curve, which also equals MR (see Figure 11.1). Thus producing where $MC = MR$ also means producing where $MC = P$. When *all* firms under perfect competition do this, price and quantity in the *industry* will be given by P_2 and Q_2 in Figure 11.6.

The monopolist may also produce a lower output at a higher price in the long run. Under perfect competition, freedom of entry eliminates supernormal profit and forces firms to produce at the bottom of their *LRAC* curve. The effect, therefore, is to keep long-run prices down. Under monopoly, however, barriers to entry allow profits to remain supernormal in the long run. The monopolist is not forced to operate at the bottom of the *AC* curve. Thus, other things being equal, long-run prices will tend to be higher, and hence output lower, under monopoly. (In section 20.2 we examine this in more detail by considering the impact of monopoly on consumer and producer surplus. You might wish to take a preliminary look at pages 418–21 now.)

> **Pause for thought**
>
> *If the shares in a monopoly (such as a water company) were very widely distributed among the population, would the shareholders necessarily want the firm to use its monopoly power to make larger profits?*

Costs under monopoly. The sheer survival of a firm in the long run under perfect competition requires that it uses the most efficient known technique, and develops new techniques wherever possible. The monopolist, however, sheltered by barriers to entry, can still make large profits even if it is not using the most efficient technique. It has less incentive, therefore, to be efficient.

On the other hand, the monopoly may be able to achieve substantial economies of scale due to larger plant, centralised administration and the avoidance of unnecessary duplication (e.g. a monopoly water company would eliminate the need for several sets of rival water mains under each street). If this results in an *MC* curve substantially below that of the same industry under perfect competition, the monopoly may even produce a *higher* output at a *lower* price.

Another reason why a monopolist may operate with lower costs is that it can use part of its supernormal profits for research and development and investment. It

BOX 11.3 WINDOWS CLEANING

The Microsoft Monopoly under challenge?

In March 2004 the European Commission fined Microsoft €497 million for an Abuse of a Dominant Position in the operating system market. It found that Microsoft had harmed competition in the media player market by bundling Windows Media Player with its operating system. Further, Microsoft had refused to supply information about its secret software code to suppliers of alternative network software at reasonable rates. Such code was needed to allow non-Windows network software to be inter-operable with ('talk' to) Windows network software. Without it, firms who had purchased Windows Network servers would be solely tied in to Microsoft server software. This, in turn, would discourage the development of application software products by Microsoft's rivals.

In April 2006, Microsoft launched an appeal against the judgement claiming that the EU's ruling violated international law by forcing the company to share information with rivals. However, the Court of First Instance found in the Commission's favour. Microsoft complied with the first ruling and unbundled Windows Media Player from its operating systems, much to the annoyance of computer suppliers who argued that their customers could easily upload alternative media players from the web.

However, until October 2007 Microsoft continued to charge high royalty rates and fees for inter-operability information that would allow competitors to access secret source code on the Windows Network System. As a result, in February 2008 the Commission penalised Microsoft a further €899 million for non-compliance with its 2004 decision and Microsoft became the first company in fifty years of EU competition policy to be fined for non-compliance with a Commission decision.[1]

Earlier anti-monopoly rulings in other countires

Microsoft is no stranger to anti-monopoly law suits. In 2005 Microsoft was fined 33bn Won ($32 million; £18.4 million) by South Korea's Fair Trade Commission for breaches of anti-monopoly legislation that covered very similar issues to that which had occurred in the EU investigation.

In August 2008, Microsoft was investigated by Taiwan's Fair Trade Commission because of its monopoly position in the operating system market.

Perhaps the most famous investigation began on 18 May 1998, when the US government accused Microsoft of abusing its market power and seeking to crush its rivals. The US Justice Department alleged that Microsoft had committed the following anti-competitive actions:

- In May 1995 Microsoft attempted to collude with Netscape Communications to divide the Internet browser market. Netscape Communications refused.
- Microsoft had forced personal computer manufacturers to install *Internet Explorer* in order to obtain a *Windows 95* operating licence.
- Microsoft insisted that PC manufacturers conformed to a Microsoft front screen for *Windows*. This included specified icons, one of which was Microsoft's *Internet Explorer*.
- It had set up reciprocal advertising arrangements with America's largest Internet service providers, such as America Online. Here Microsoft would promote America Online via *Windows*. In return, America Online would not promote Netscape's browsers.

One solution, posed by Federal Judge Thomas Penfield Jackson in 2000, was that Microsoft be split in two to prevent it operating as a monopoly. One company would produce and market the *Windows* operating system; the other would produce and market the applications software, such as *Microsoft Office* and the web browser, *Internet Explorer*.

This was overturned on appeal in June 2001 and Microsoft agreed to provide technical information about *Windows* to other companies so that potential rivals could write software that would compete with Microsoft's own software. Also Microsoft would not be allowed to retaliate against computer manufacturers that installed rival products or removed icons for Microsoft applications.

Microsoft and the public interest

These lawsuits raise an important issue: is Microsoft acting for or against the public interest?

The classic case against monopoly suppliers is that they charge higher prices and offer lower quantities to consumers than would be the case under perfect competition. In addition, the supernormal profit that monopolies earn may be detrimental to society if it is used to continue to support the monopoly position, say by lobbying or bribing government officials. Further, if no competition prevails then monopoly suppliers may become more inefficient.

However, the competition authorities have never penalised Microsoft simply for possessing monopoly

---

[1] See Antitrust: Commission imposes €899 million penalty on Microsoft for non-compliance with March 2004 Decision, IP/08/318, 27 February 2008.

power. It has been fined when it has *abused* its market power. That is, it is not the monopoly market structure that matters per se to competition authorities; rather, it is the behaviour of the firm when it has monopoly power. Through its actions, Microsoft had raised barriers to entry by restricting the opportunities for potential rival firms to offer alternative products to customers. Choice was thereby restricted.

In its defence, Microsoft has argued that it has continually sought to reinvest its profits in new product development and offered a number of innovative solutions over the past 30 years for individuals and businesses alike. (Can you think of all the versions of *Windows* and the 'free updates' there have been?)

Further, in an environment where technology is changing rapidly, Microsoft's control over standards gives the user a measure of stability, knowing that any new products and applications will be compatible with existing ones. In other words, new software can be incorporated into existing systems. In this respect Microsoft can be viewed as operating in society's interest. Microsoft would argue that it has a right to protect its in-house software code from competitors and receive a fair price for it. Indeed, it is a natural response for a firm to protect its intellectual property rights. Failure to do so could lead to the firm's demise.

Network effects

Microsoft is a vertically integrated firm (see pages 304–5), with a dominant position in the operating system market (e.g. *Windows* and *Vista*) and in certain application software (*Office* and *Windows Media Player*) markets. It has built this position by creating networks of users but this brings benefits and costs to society.

Network effects arise when consumers of a product benefit from it being used by *other* consumers. In the case of Microsoft's products, firms benefit from lower training costs because individuals who have learnt to use Microsoft products elsewhere can be readily absorbed into the firm. Individuals benefit too because they do not have to learn to use new software when they move to another organisation and the learning costs are fairly low as a new version of the software is introduced.

The negative aspect of developing strong networks is that users can get 'locked in' to using the software and they become reluctant to switch to alternative systems. Protecting the network is vital to Microsoft's competitive edge.

Challenges to Microsoft monopoly

Microsoft is facing increasing competitive pressure. The recent challenges from competition authorities have opened up the browser market, for example. Microsoft's *Internet Explorer* is still the dominant browser, but since the mid-2000s its market share has fallen quite significantly as other browsers, notably *Mozilla Firefox*, have grown in usage.[2]

There is also a growing challenge from new Internet firms, such as Google and Facebook. Both Google and Facebook have created enormous networks of users who are then targeted with tailored adverts paid for by firms who want to reach these vast audiences.

This is a very different business model from that of Microsoft and, as part of the desire to create large networks of users, free products are being released that will compete with that of Microsoft. For example, Google's *Google Docs* and *Chrome* compete with Microsoft's *Office* and *Internet Explorer*, respectively. These, however, still have very small market shares at present.

It remains unclear whether Microsoft's dominance in the operating system market will be challenged in the near future. Apple is the only likely rival to Microsoft for operating systems on standalone computers. However, it has a small market share of the operating system market because it wants to concentrate on particular sorts of user – those who appreciate good design. It has also shifted its business emphasis in recent times by developing iPhone and iTunes technologies.

The open-source operating system, Linux, still has less then 5 per cent of the operating system market and is also no threat to Microsoft at the moment. However, things do change rapidly in the technology sector.

You might want to follow subsequent events as the news unfolds (see section A of the Hotlinks section of this book's website for links to newspaper sites).

1. In what respects might Microsoft's behaviour be deemed to have been: (a) against the public interest; (b) in the public interest?
2. Being locked in to a product or technology is only a problem if such a product can be clearly shown to be inferior to an alternative. What difficulties might there be in establishing such a case?

---

[2] For figures on browser usage, see http://en.wikipedia.org/wiki/Usage_share_of_web_browsers

may not have the same *incentive* to become efficient as the perfectly competitive firm which is fighting for survival, but it may have a much greater *ability* to become efficient than has the small firm with limited funds.

Although a monopoly faces no competition in the goods market, it may face an alternative form of competition in financial markets. A monopoly, with potentially low costs, which is currently run inefficiently, is likely to be subject to a takeover bid from another company. This competition for corporate control may thus force the monopoly to be efficient in order to prevent being taken over.

Innovation and new products. The promise of supernormal profits, protected perhaps by patents, may encourage the development of new (monopoly) industries producing new products. It is this chance of making monopoly profits that encourages many people to take the risks of going into business.

> **Definition**
>
> **Competition for corporate control**
> The competition for the control of companies through takeovers.

11.4 POTENTIAL COMPETITION OR POTENTIAL MONOPOLY? THE THEORY OF CONTESTABLE MARKETS

Potential competition

In recent years, economists have developed the theory of contestable markets. This theory argues that what is crucial in determining price and output is not whether an industry is *actually* a monopoly or competitive, but whether there is the real *threat* of competition.

If a monopoly is protected by high barriers to entry – say that it owns all the raw materials – then it will be able to make supernormal profits with no fear of competition.

If, however, another firm *could* take over from it with little difficulty, it will behave much more like a competitive firm. The threat of competition has a similar effect to actual competition.

As an example, consider a catering company that is given permission by a factory to run its canteen. The catering company has a monopoly over the supply of food to the workers in that factory. If, however, it starts charging high prices or providing a poor service, the factory could offer the running of the canteen to an alternative catering company. This threat may force the original catering company to charge 'reasonable' prices and offer a good service.

Perfectly contestable markets

A market is perfectly contestable when the costs of entry and exit by potential rivals are zero, and when such entry can be made very rapidly. In such cases, the moment the possibility of earning supernormal profits occurs, new firms will enter, thus driving profits down to a normal level. The sheer threat of this happening, so the theory goes, will ensure that the firm already in the market will (a) keep its prices down, so that it just makes normal profits, and (b) produce as efficiently as possible, taking advantage of any economies of scale and any new technology. If the existing firm did not do this, entry would take place and potential competition would become actual competition.

> **Definition**
>
> **Perfectly contestable market**
> A market where there is free and costless entry and exit.

Contestable markets and natural monopolies

So why in such cases are the markets not *actually* perfectly competitive? Why do they remain monopolies?

The most likely reason has to do with economies of scale and the size of the market. To operate on a minimum efficient scale, the firm may have to be so large relative to the market that there is only room for one such firm in the industry. If a new firm does come into the market, then one or other of the two firms will not survive the competition. The market is simply not big enough for both of them.

If, however, there are no entry or exit costs, new firms will be perfectly willing to enter even though there is only room for one firm, provided they believe that they are more efficient than the existing firm. The existing firm, knowing this, will be forced to produce as efficiently as possible and with only normal profit.

The importance of costless exit

Setting up in a new business usually involves large expenditures on plant and machinery. Once this money has been spent, it becomes fixed costs. If these fixed costs are no higher than those of the existing firm, then the new firm could win the battle. But, of course, there is always the risk that it might lose.

But does losing the battle really matter? Can the firm not simply move to another market?

It does matter if there are substantial costs of exit. This will be the case if the capital equipment cannot be transferred to other uses. In this case these fixed costs are known as sunk costs. The losing firm is left with capital equipment it cannot use. The firm may therefore be put off entering in the first place. The market is not perfectly contestable, and the established firm can make supernormal profit.

If, however, the capital equipment can be transferred, the exit costs will be zero (or at least very low), and new firms will be more willing to take the risks of entry. For example, a rival coach company may open up a service on a route previously operated by only one company, and where there is still only room for one operator. If the new firm loses the resulting battle, it can still use the coaches it has purchased. It simply uses them for a different route. The cost of the coaches is not a sunk cost.

Costless exit, therefore, encourages firms to enter an industry, knowing that, if unsuccessful, they can always transfer their capital elsewhere.

The lower the exit costs, the more contestable the market. This implies that firms already established in other similar markets may provide more effective competition against monopolists, since they can simply transfer capital from one market to another. For example, studies of airlines in the USA show that entry to a particular route may be much easier for an established airline, which can simply transfer planes from one route to another.

> **Definition**
>
> **Sunk costs**
> Costs that cannot be recouped (e.g. by transferring assets to other uses).

Assessment of the theory

Simple monopoly theory merely focuses on the existing structure of the industry and makes no allowance for potential competition. The theory of contestable markets, however, goes much further and examines the *size* of entry barriers and exit costs. The bigger these are, the less contestable the market and therefore the greater the monopoly power of the existing firm. Various attempts have been made to measure monopoly power in this way.

> **BOX 11.4** **'IT COULD BE YOU'**
>
> ### Bidding for the UK National Lottery
>
> Since its launch in November 1994, the UK National Lottery has struck at the heart of the British psyche because it offers the opportunity to win a fortune and support worthwhile ventures. By the end of 2008 the lottery had created over 2200 millionaires. It had also generated over £22 billion for 'Good Causes' and will contribute £2.175 billion to the London Olympic and Paralympic games in 2012.
>
> Around 70 per cent of UK adults play the lottery, spending on average about £3 per week. Around £26 billion had been paid out in prize money by the end of 2005. On average, for every pound spent on the lottery, 50p is paid to the winners, 28p goes to the Good Causes as set out by Parliament, 12p goes to the government in the form of tax, 5p goes to the retailer and 5p goes to Camelot, the operator, and its shareholders (Cadbury Schweppes plc, De La Rue Holdings, Fujitsu Services Ltd, Royal Mail Enterprises Ltd and Thales Electronics).
>
> Sales of lottery tickets grew dramatically in the early years of operation but waned around the turn of the century. There has been a recovery since then. Sales in the half-year to 27 September 2008 were £2.56 billion – a 7.6 per cent increase on the previous six months. This is the longest period of growth in lottery sales in its 14-year history.
>
> #### The institutional framework
>
> There are a number of institutions involved in providing the lottery. The Department of Culture, Media and Sport oversees the lottery as directed by the National Lottery Act and dictates its strategic direction. It appoints the National Lottery Commission (NLC), which ensures that bids for the lottery licence and the running of the lottery games maximise the returns for 'Good Causes'. There are also a number of distribution bodies that provide lottery funds to thousands of local projects.
>
> The main point of contact for lottery buyers is Camelot, which runs the lotto and scratchcard games via retail outlets, mobile phones, digital television and the Internet. Camelot won the first, second and third licences for the right to run the UK National Lottery from 1994, 2002 and 2009 respectively.
>
> #### The rationale for a monopoly supplier
>
> Camelot is a monopoly supplier of the UK National Lottery, although it need not be so. The legislation currently allows for two licences, one to operate the infrastructure and another to run the games. It is possible for other companies to run games on the computer network owned by Camelot, much in the same way that Network Rail owns the railway tracks, tunnels, etc. and allows competition between firms on particular routes on the network. Indeed, this option was briefly undertaken by Camelot in 1998, when Vernons Pools sold its 'Easy Play' game using the National Lottery retailer network. Its sales, though, were poor and it was scrapped in May 1999.
>
> However, the government has a strong preference for a single owner of the infrastructure and a single supplier of National Lottery games. The rationale for having a single owner of the infrastructure is fairly standard; this is a natural monopoly and it would be pointless having two lottery computer networks, just as it would be having two separately owned rail lines from Edinburgh to London. With one firm controlling the infrastructure, economies of scale can be reaped.
>
> One of the arguments for having a single supplier of games is known, rather bizarrely, as 'peculiar economies of scale'.[1] This is a situation in which a company that offered a portfolio of innovative lottery games would be more likely to induce additional players to participate in games because they can raise the size of the prize to be won. In other words, good game design can lead to more and bigger jackpots and thus more people buying lottery tickets. This reduces the average costs of supplying tickets and raises the money for 'Good Causes'.
>
> Arguably, more than one firm may be able to supply an innovative portfolio of games if the market is large enough. However, the government is concerned about the risks involved in regulating relationships between network owners and network users (a problem that has occurred in regulating the railways – see Box 22.3). For example, there might be a lengthy legal dispute if a supplier of games is
>
> ---
> [1] See, for example, P. Daffern, 'Assessment of the effects of competition on the National Lottery', *Technical Paper No. 6*, Department of Culture, Media and Sport, 2006.

One criticism of the theory, however, is that it does not take sufficient account of the possible reactions of the established firm. There may be no cost barriers to entry or exit (i.e. a perfectly contestable market), but the established firm may let it be known that any firm that dares to enter will face all-out war! This may act as a deterrent to entry. In the meantime, the established firm may charge high prices and make supernormal profits.

accused of unacceptable performance but it, in turn, accuses the network owner of poor service. This would then have a detrimental effect on the money raised for 'Good Causes'. Thus the government has always preferred a single firm framework for running the National Lottery.

Bidding for the National Lottery monopoly

Unlike auctions to run national rail franchises or a local bus route, bidding for the lottery does not involve any payment on the part of the successful bidder. The bid is purely a detailed business plan outlining all aspects of running the lottery, but its main emphasis is on providing likely revenue scenarios from games that would maximise money for 'Good Causes' and safeguard players. It was the uncertainty over future revenue flows that led the government in 1994 to require a paper-based bidding scheme for the first lottery licence. This view did not change when subsequent licences came up for renewal.

The NLC is responsible for evaluating the bids and awarding the licence. There were seven bidders for the first licence but for the second licence there were only two tabled 'bids', one from Camelot and other from Sir Richard Branson's The People's Lottery (and initially the NLC rejected both before settling on the incumbent).

For the third licence, the NLC tried to encourage as many bids as possible to come forward. Only one other bidder, Sugal and Dumani UK Ltd, submitted a bid. Camelot won because the NLC believed that, at a similar level of sales, they would be slightly more generous to Good Causes and that 'there was a higher probability that they would achieve higher sales over the length of the licence'.[2]

Clearly, incumbent firms like Camelot have considerable advantages over potential rivals when contracts have to be renewed and thus the number of new bidders is likely to be low. Two problems, in particular, stand out for rivals.

The 'Winner's Curse'. If a potential entrant outbids the incumbent in an auction to run (say) a local bus service, then it could be that winner has paid too much. After all, the incumbent has more knowledge about running the bus service and the likely revenues that may prevail. This situation is known as the 'Winner's Curse' and a similar scenario may occur in respect of the lottery. Potential bidders may be put off from bidding because they don't have the same knowledge about the UK lottery market.

Arguably, the lottery market might be considered a mature market and more is now known about lottery sales and the gaming market in general. However, there are strong incentives for risk-averse regulators to continue with accepting bids from incumbent firms because they are known to provide a certain level of sales and service.

The handover problem. If Camelot were to lose the lottery licence, there would be some large risks in transferring to the new bidder. Arguably, Camelot could sell its infrastructure to the new lottery provider, but there is a valuation dilemma. In terms of opportunity cost, Camelot would value the infrastructure at scrap value (if it has no alternative use for it), whereas a winner with no alternative source for such infrastructure would value Camelot's assets at close to their replacement value. This could lead to some difficult negotiations.

Because of this difficulty, the NLC did require bidders for the third lottery licence to provide new infrastructure, but recognised that this would take time to have in place (imagine trying to replace 30 000 retail terminals as well as to make online, television and mobile games work well). Given this difficulty, it is not surprising that there was only one rival bidder to Camelot.

Camelot managed to achieve a first-mover advantage (see page 254) by winning the initial lottery licence in 1994. It is now to continue providing the UK National Lottery until 2019 and so will have been sole monopoly provider for 25 years. Removing Camelot after that date could prove to be difficult.

---

[2] NLC press release, 'Preferred bidder announced for the third National Lottery licence', 7/8/2007. Available at www.natlotcomm.gov.uk/CLIENT/news_item.ASP?NewsId=49

1 If Camelot is maximising revenue, what is the price elasticity of demand for lottery tickets?
2 To what extent is the National Lottery market a contestable market?

If a monopoly operates in a perfectly contestable market, it might bring the 'best of both worlds' for the consumer. Not only will it be able to achieve low costs through economies of scale, but also the potential competition will keep profits and hence prices down.

> **Pause for thought**
>
> *Think of two examples of highly contestable monopolies (or oligopolies). How well is the consumer's interest served?*

SUMMARY

1a There are four alternative market structures under which firms operate. In ascending order of firms' market power, they are: perfect competition, monopolistic competition, oligopoly and monopoly.

1b The market structure under which a firm operates will affect its conduct and its performance.

2a The assumptions of perfect competition are: a very large number of firms, complete freedom of entry, a homogeneous product and perfect knowledge of the good and its market by both producers and consumers.

2b In the short run, there is not time for new firms to enter the market, and thus supernormal profits can persist. In the long run, however, any supernormal profits will be competed away by the entry of new firms.

2c The short-run equilibrium for the firm will be where the price, as determined by demand and supply in the market, is equal to marginal cost. At this output the firm will be maximising profit.

2d The long-run equilibrium will be where the market price is just equal to firms' long-run average cost.

2e There are no substantial economies of scale to be gained in a perfectly competitive industry. If there were, the industry would cease to be perfectly competitive as the large, low-cost firms drove the small, high-cost ones out of business.

3a A monopoly is where there is only one firm in an industry. In practice, it is difficult to determine where a monopoly exists because it depends on how narrowly an industry is defined.

3b Barriers to the entry of new firms will normally be necessary to protect a monopoly from competition. Such barriers include economies of scale (making the firm a natural monopoly or at least giving it a cost advantage over new (small) competitors), control over supplies of inputs or over outlets, patents or copyright, and tactics to eliminate competition (such as takeovers or aggressive advertising).

3c Profits for the monopolist (as for other firms) will be maximised where $MC = MR$.

3d If demand and cost curves are the same in a monopoly and a perfectly competitive industry, the monopoly will produce a lower output and at a higher price than the perfectly competitive industry.

3e On the other hand, any economies of scale will in part be passed on to consumers in lower prices, and the monopolist's high profits may be used for research and development and investment, which in turn may lead to better products at possibly lower prices.

4a Potential competition may be as important as actual competition in determining a firm's price and output strategy.

4b The threat of this competition is greater, the lower are the entry and exit costs to and from the industry. If the entry and exit costs are zero, the market is said to be *perfectly* contestable. Under such circumstances, an existing monopolist will be forced to keep its profits down to the normal level if it is to resist entry of new firms. Exit costs will be lower, the lower are the sunk costs of the firm.

4c The theory of contestable markets provides a more realistic analysis of firms' behaviour than theories based simply on the *existing* number of firms in the industry.

REVIEW QUESTIONS

1 Why do economists treat normal profit as a cost of production? What determines (a) the level and (b) the rate of normal profit for a particular firm?

2 Why is perfect competition so rare?

3 Why does the market for fresh vegetables approximate to perfect competition, whereas that for frozen or tinned ones does not?

4 Illustrate on a diagram similar to Figure 11.3 what would happen in the long-run if price were initially below P_L.

5 As an illustration of the difficulty in identifying monopolies, try to decide which of the following are monopolies: a train-operating company; your local evening newspaper; British Gas; the village post office; the Royal Mail; Interflora; the London Underground; ice creams in the cinema; Guinness; food on trains; TippEx; the board game 'Monopoly'.

6 Try this brain teaser. A monopoly would be expected to face an inelastic demand. After all, there are no direct substitutes. And yet, if it produces where $MR = MC$, MR must be positive, demand must therefore be elastic. Therefore the monopolist must face an elastic demand! Can you solve this conundrum?

7 For what reasons would you expect a monopoly to charge (a) a higher price, and (b) a lower price than if the industry were operating under perfect competition?

8 In which of the following industries are exit costs likely to be low: (a) steel production; (b) market gardening; (c) nuclear power generation; (d) specialist financial advisory services; (e) production of fashion dolls; (f) production of a new drug; (g) contract catering; (h) mobile discos; (i) car ferry operators? Are these exit costs dependent on how narrowly the industry is defined?

9 Think of three examples of monopolies (local or national) and consider how contestable their markets are.

Chapter 12

Profit maximisation under imperfect competition

Business issues covered in this chapter

- How will firms behave under monopolistic competition (i.e. where there are many firms competing, but where they produce differentiated products)?

- Why will firms under monopolistic competition make only normal profits in the long run?

- How are firms likely to behave when there are just a few of them competing ('oligopolies')?

- What determines whether oligopolies will engage in all-out competition or instead collude with each other?

- What strategic games are oligopolists likely to play in their attempt to out-do their rivals?

- Why might such games lead to an outcome where all the players are worse off than if they had colluded?

- Does oligopoly serve the consumer's interests?

Very few markets in practice can be classified as perfectly competitive or as a pure monopoly. The vast majority of firms do compete with other firms, often quite aggressively, and yet they are not price takers: they do have some degree of market power. Most markets, therefore, lie between the two extremes of monopoly and perfect competition, in the realm of 'imperfect competition'. As we saw in section 11.1, there are two types of imperfect competition: namely, monopolistic competition and oligopoly.

MONOPOLISTIC COMPETITION 12.1

Monopolistic competition is nearer to the competitive end of the spectrum. It can best be understood as a situation where there are a lot of firms competing, but where each firm does nevertheless have some degree of market power (hence the term 'monopolistic' competition): each firm has some discretion as to what price to charge for its products.

Assumptions of monopolistic competition

- There is *quite a large number of firms*. As a result, each firm has only a small share of the market and, therefore, its actions are unlikely to affect its rivals to any great extent. What this means is that each firm in making its decisions does not have to worry about how its rivals will react. It assumes that what its rivals choose to do will not be influenced by what it does.
  This is known as the assumption of independence. (As we shall see later, this is not the case under oligopoly. There we assume that firms believe that their decisions do affect their rivals, and that their rivals' decisions will affect them. Under oligopoly we assume that firms are interdependent.)
- There is freedom of entry of new firms into the industry. If any firm wants to set up in business in this market, it is free to do so.

In these two respects, therefore, monopolistic competition is like perfect competition.

- Unlike perfect competition, however, each firm produces a product or provides a service that is in some way different from its rivals. As a result, it can raise its price without losing all its customers. Thus its demand curve is downward sloping, albeit relatively elastic given the large number of competitors to whom customers can turn. This is known as the assumption of product differentiation.

Petrol stations, restaurants, hairdressers and builders are all examples of monopolistic competition.

When considering monopolistic competition it is important to take account of the distance consumers are willing to travel to buy a product. In other words, the geographical size of the market matters. For example, McDonald's is a major global and national fast-food restaurant. However, in any one location it experiences intense competition in the 'informal eating-out' market from Indian, Chinese, Italian and other restaurants (see Box 12.1). So in any one local area, there is competition between firms each offering differentiated products.

> **Definitions**
>
> **Independence (of firms in a market)**
> When the decisions of one firm in a market will not have any significant effect on the demand curves of its rivals.
>
> **Product differentiation**
> When one firm's product is sufficiently different from its rivals' to allow it to raise the price of the product without customers all switching to the rivals' products. A situation where a firm faces a downward-sloping demand curve.

Equilibrium of the firm

Short run

As with other market structures, profits are maximised at the output where $MC = MR$. The diagram will be the same as for the monopolist, except that the AR and MR curves will be more elastic. This is illustrated in Figure 12.1(a). As with perfect competition, it is possible for the monopolistically competitive firm to make supernormal profit in the short run. This is shown as the shaded area.

Just how much profit the firm will make in the short run depends on the strength of demand: the position and elasticity of the demand curve. The further to the right the demand curve is relative to the average cost curve, and the less elastic the

> **Pause for thought**
>
> Which of these two items is a petrol station more likely to sell at a discount: (a) oil; (b) sweets? Why?

demand curve is, the greater will be the firm's short-run profit. Thus a firm facing little competition and whose product is considerably differentiated from its rivals may be able to earn considerable short-run profits.

Long run

If typical firms are earning supernormal profit, new firms will enter the industry in the long run. As new firms enter, they will take some of the customers away from established firms. The demand for the established firms' products will therefore fall. Their demand (*AR*) curve will shift to the left, and will continue doing so as long as supernormal profits remain and thus new firms continue entering.

Long-run equilibrium will be reached when only normal profits remain: when there is no further incentive for new firms to enter. This is illustrated in Figure 12.1(b). The firm's demand curve settles at D_L, where it is tangential to (i.e. just touches) the firm's *LRAC* curve. Output will be Q_L: where $AR_L = LRAC$. (At any other output, *LRAC* is greater than *AR* and thus less than normal profit would be made.)

Limitations of the model

There are various problems in applying the model of monopolistic competition to the real world:

- Information may be imperfect. Firms will not enter an industry if they are unaware of the supernormal profits currently being made, or if they underestimate the demand for the particular product they are considering selling.
- Firms are likely to differ from each other, not only in the product they produce or the service they offer, but also in their size and in their cost structure. What is more, entry may not be completely unrestricted. For example, two petrol stations could not set up in exactly the same place – on a busy crossroads, say – because of local authority planning controls. Thus although the typical or 'representative' firm may only earn normal profit in the long run, other firms may be able to earn long-run supernormal profit. They may have some cost advantage or produce a product that is impossible to duplicate perfectly.

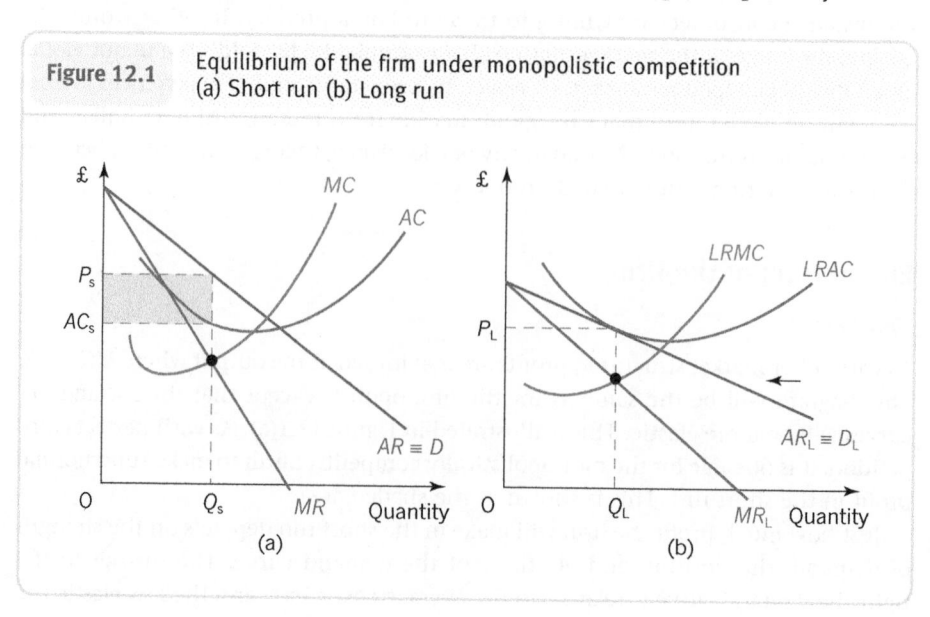

Figure 12.1 Equilibrium of the firm under monopolistic competition (a) Short run (b) Long run

- Existing firms may make supernormal profits, but if a new firm entered, this might reduce everyone's profits below the normal level. Thus a new firm will not enter and supernormal profits will persist into the long run. An example would be a small town with two chemist shops. They may both make more than enough profit to persuade them to stay in business. But if a third set up (say midway between the other two), there would not be enough total sales to allow them all to earn even normal profit. This is a problem of indivisibilities. Given the overheads of a chemist shop, it is not possible to set up one small enough to take away just enough customers to leave the other two with normal profits.
- One of the biggest problems with the simple model outlined above is that it concentrates on price and output decisions. In practice, the profit-maximising firm under monopolistic competition will also need to decide the exact variety of product to produce, and how much to spend on advertising it. This will lead the firm to take part in non-price competition (which we examined in Chapter 8).

Comparing monopolistic competition with perfect competition and monopoly

Comparison with perfect competition

It is often argued that monopolistic competition leads to a less efficient allocation of resources than perfect competition.

Figure 12.2 compares the long-run equilibrium positions for two firms. One firm is under perfect competition and thus faces a horizontal demand curve. It will produce an output of Q_1 at a price of P_1. The other is under monopolistic competition and thus faces a downward-sloping demand curve. It will produce the lower output of Q_2 at the higher price of P_2. A crucial assumption here is that a firm would have the *same* long-run average cost ($LRAC$) curve in both cases. Given this assumption, we can make the following two predictions about monopolistic competition:

- Less will be sold and at a higher price.
- Firms will not be producing at the least-cost point.

By producing more, firms would move to a lower point on their $LRAC$ curve. Thus firms under monopolistic competition are said to have **excess capacity**. In Figure 12.2 this excess capacity is shown as $Q_1 - Q_2$. In other words, monopolistic competition

> **Definition**
>
> **Excess capacity (under monopolistic competition)**
> In the long run, firms under monopolistic competition will produce at an output below their minimum-cost point.

> **Pause for thought**
>
> Which would you rather have: five restaurants to choose from, each with very different menus and each having spare tables so that you could always guarantee getting one; or just two restaurants to choose from, charging a bit less but with less choice and making it necessary to book well in advance?

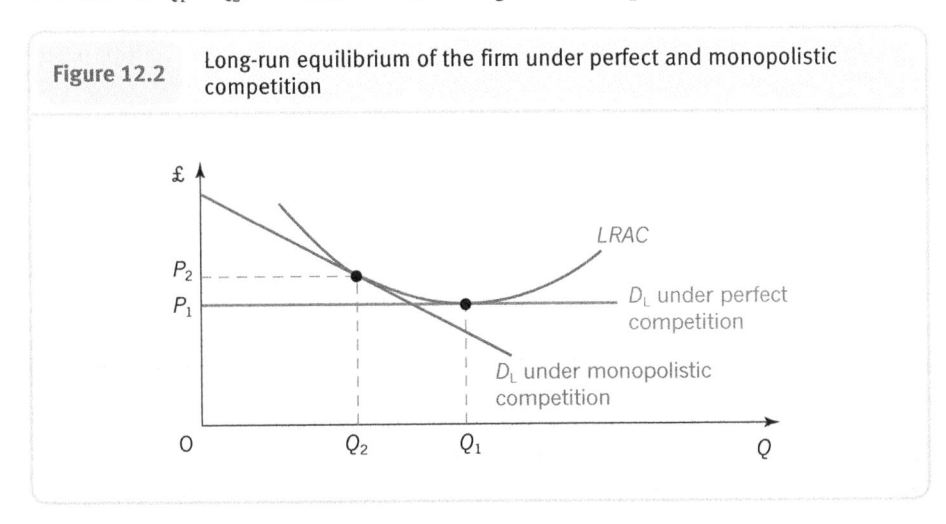

Figure 12.2 Long-run equilibrium of the firm under perfect and monopolistic competition

> **BOX 12.1 EATING OUT IN BRITAIN**
>
> **A monopolistically competitive sector**
>
> The 'eating-out' sector (i.e. takeaways and restaurants) is a vibrant market in the UK, with sales of some £30.5 billion in 2007 according to Mintel.[1] Although the sector has grown less strongly in recent years than in the late 1990s, it has still grown in real terms by around 7 per cent per annum since 2000.
>
> The sector exhibits many of the characteristics of a monopolistically competitive market.
>
> - *Large number of local buyers*. According to the Mintel survey in 2008, around 93 per cent of UK adults had eaten out within the previous three months.
> - *Large number of firms*. In 2007 there were nearly 150 000 hotel, restaurant and pub enterprises in the UK. Other information shows that there were 101 motorway service areas, 10 500 fish and chip shops, over 10 000 Indian restaurants and countless fast-food outlets. Although the sector has some large national and global chains, these are usually competing in local markets.
> - *Competitive prices*. Margins are very tight (around 2 per cent in the hotel business) because firms have to price very competitively to catch local custom. Only around 60 per cent of these businesses survive longer than three years.
> - *Differentiated products*. To attract customers, suppliers must each differentiate their product in various ways, such as food type, ambience, comfort, service, quality, advertising and opening hours. Firms have to cater for the dynamic nature of consumer preferences and constantly adapt or go under.
>
> **Changing consumer tastes**
>
> Most of the growth in the eating-out sector is in the fast-food segment. Consumers value convenience because they lead busy lives. However, they are expressing a growing preference for more healthy food. There has thus been a shift towards buying healthy snacks from retail outlets and away from hamburger bars. For example, McDonald's, which had dramatically increased the number of outlets in the 1990s, suffered a downturn in fortunes because its products were not associated with healthy eating. In 2003 the company fundamentally changed its product menu to accommodate healthier eating options, such as porridge, bagels, fruit and a variety of salads alongside the traditional meals.
>
> In addition, the traditional hamburger bars are facing active competition from the chicken burger bars such as KFC and (the relatively new entrant) Nandos, because of the quality problems associated with beef in recent times (i.e. BSE and Foot and Mouth).
>
> **Ethnic foods**
>
> Ethnic food forms a substantial part of eating out in the UK. Around 62 per cent of those who had eaten out in 2007 had been to an Indian, Chinese or other ethnic restaurant, according to Mintel. However, in terms of *market value*, ethnic takeaways and restaurants accounted for only 5.8 per cent and 6.7 per cent respectively in 2007 – a slight fall from 2003. With the exception of the
>
> ---
> [1] *Ethnic Restaurants and Takeaways*, Mintel (2008).

is typified by quite a large number of firms (e.g. petrol stations), all operating at less than optimum output, and thus being forced to charge a price above that which they could charge if they had a bigger turnover.

So how does this affect the consumer? Although the firm under monopolistic competition may charge a higher price than under perfect competition, the difference may be very small. Although the firm's demand curve is downward sloping, it is still likely to be highly elastic due to the large number of substitutes. Furthermore, the consumer may benefit from monopolistic competition by having a greater variety of products to choose from. Each firm may satisfy some particular requirement of particular consumers.

Comparison with monopoly

The arguments are very similar here to those when comparing perfect competition and monopoly.

On the one hand, freedom of entry for new firms and hence the lack of long-run supernormal profits under monopolistic competition are likely to help keep prices down for the consumer and encourage cost saving. On the other hand, monopolies

medium and premium brand end of the market, there has been limited innovation in the ethnic eating-out sector. Consumers are looking for alternative cuisine when they eat out and have become tired of the traditional format.

Ethnic restaurants are also facing problems on the supply side. The sector has been hit by minimum wage legislation since 1999 (see section 19.6) and global food price inflation during 2007/8, both of which raised costs. Moreover, there has been a tightening up of the immigration laws which makes it difficult to recruit suitably qualified people, and younger members of these largely family-owned businesses are looking to careers outside of the sector because hours are long and rewards low.

The Indian restaurant

The traditional Indian curry house – the institution that made curry the UK's favourite dish – accounted for 24 per cent of meals eaten out by UK adults in 2007. In recent times, however, Indian restaurants have suffered from changing British preferences and supply-side pressures. They are also facing direct competition from ready-to-eat curries sold in local supermarkets and the sale of curry in local pubs.

Competition to attract the discerning local customer is keen *within* the Indian restaurant trade too. In the 1990s 'Curry Wars' developed around the country, with local Indian restaurants undercutting each other's prices. Profits tumbled. Eventually, strong cultural ties among the local Asian communities helped to avert such cut-throat competition. It was realised that, as prices in Indian restaurants were considerably less than in Italian and French ones, fixing minimum curry prices would raise incomes. In effect 'curry cartels' were being proposed.

Such activity – however well intentioned – is illegal in the UK. It is also unlikely to last for long as other segments of the market develop to undercut curry-house prices or attract consumers with a new culinary offering.

The Indian restaurant has to relaunch its appeal. One reported method of attracting customers to Birmingham's 'Balti Belt' in the early 2000s was for rival Indian restaurants to have the most visible Las Vegas-style neon sign. This, however, has not been a common response and the lower end of the market is still stagnating.

Innovation is starting to develop in the premium end of the market where returns are greatest. Mintel reports, for example, that some of the high-end Indian restaurants in London have achieved Michelin stars. There is growth in this market segment but there is some debate about the sustainability of these high-end ventures, given the nature of international competition for high-quality chefs.

It will be interesting to see how the market develops over the next 10 years.

1. *What has happened to the price elasticity of demand for Indian restaurant curries over time? What can be said about cross-price elasticity of demand for pub meals?*
2. *Collusion between restaurants would suggest that they are operating under oligopoly, not monopolistic competition. Do you agree?*

are likely to achieve greater economies of scale and have more funds for investment and research and development.

OLIGOPOLY

Oligopoly occurs when just a few firms between them share a large proportion of the industry. Some of the best-known companies are oligopolists, including Ford, Coca-Cola, BP and Nintendo.

There are, however, significant differences in the structure of industries under oligopoly, and similarly significant differences in the behaviour of firms. The firms may produce a virtually identical product (e.g. metals, chemicals, sugar, petrol). Most oligopolists, however, produce differentiated products (e.g. cars, soap powder, soft drinks, electrical appliances). Much of the competition between such oligopolists is in terms of the marketing of their particular brand. Marketing practices may differ considerably from one industry to another.

The two key features of oligopoly

Despite the differences between oligopolies, there are two crucial features that distinguish oligopoly from other market structures.

Barriers to entry

Unlike firms under monopolistic competition, there are various barriers to the entry of new firms. These are similar to those under monopoly (see pages 222–3). The size of the barriers, however, will vary from industry to industry. In some cases entry is relatively easy, whereas in others it is virtually impossible.

Interdependence of the firms

Because there are only a few firms under oligopoly, each firm will have to take account of the others. This means that they are mutually dependent: they are *interdependent*. Each firm is affected by its rivals' actions. If a firm changes the price or specification of its product, for example, or the amount of its advertising, the sales of its rivals will be affected. The rivals may then respond by changing their price, specification or advertising. No firm can therefore afford to ignore the actions and reactions of other firms in the industry.

> **KEY IDEA 23**
>
> *People often think and behave strategically.* How you think others will respond to your actions is likely to influence your own behaviour. Firms, for example, when considering a price or product change will often take into account the likely reactions of their rivals.

It is impossible, therefore, to predict the effect on a firm's sales of, say, a change in its price without first making some assumption about the reactions of other firms. Different assumptions will yield different predictions. For this reason there is no single, generally accepted theory of oligopoly. Firms may react differently and unpredictably.

Competition and collusion

Oligopolists are pulled in two different directions:

- The interdependence of firms may make them wish to *collude* with each other. If they can club together and act as if they were a monopoly, they could jointly maximise industry profits.
- On the other hand, they will be tempted to *compete* with their rivals to gain a bigger share of industry profits for themselves.

These two policies are incompatible. The more fiercely firms compete to gain a bigger share of industry profits, the smaller these industry profits will become! For example, price competition drives down the average industry price, while competition through advertising raises industry costs. Either way, industry profits fall.

Sometimes firms will collude. Sometimes they will not. The following sections examine first *collusive oligopoly* (both open and tacit), and then *non-collusive oligopoly*.

Collusive oligopoly

When firms under oligopoly engage in collusion, they may agree on prices, market share, advertising expenditure, etc. Such collusion reduces the uncertainty they

---

Definitions

Interdependence (under oligopoly)
One of the two key features of oligopoly. Each firm will be affected by its rivals' decisions. Likewise its decisions will affect its rivals. Firms recognise this interdependence. This recognition will affect their decisions.

Collusive oligopoly
When oligopolists agree (formally or informally) to limit competition between themselves. They may set output quotas, fix prices, limit product promotion or development, or agree not to 'poach' each other's markets.

Non-collusive oligopoly
When oligopolists have no agreement between themselves – formal, informal or tacit.

Figure 12.3 Profit-maximising cartel

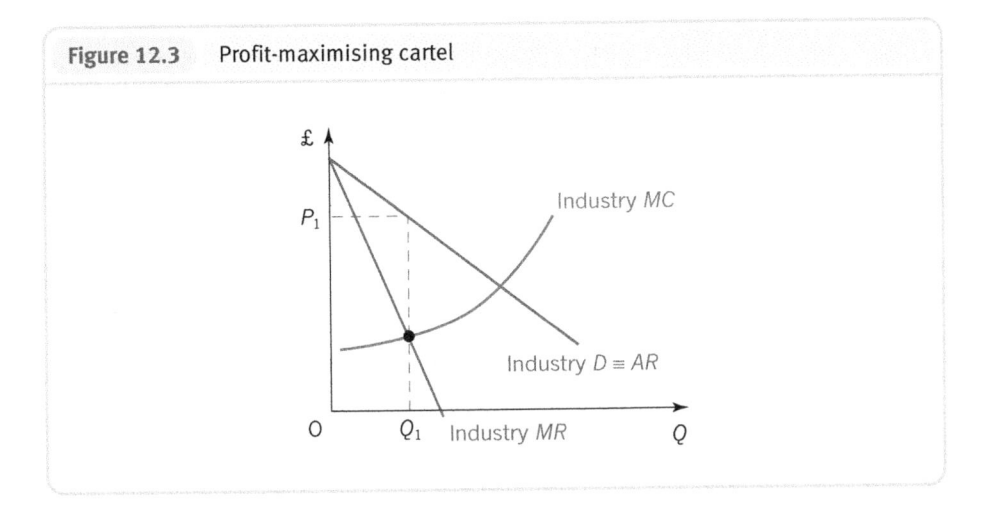

face. It reduces the fear of engaging in competitive price cutting or retaliatory advertising, both of which could reduce total industry profits.

Cartels

A formal collusive agreement is called a **cartel**. The cartel will maximise profits if it acts like a monopoly: if the members behave as if they were a single firm. This is illustrated in Figure 12.3.

The total market demand curve is shown with the corresponding market MR curve. The cartel's MC curve is the *horizontal* sum of the MC curves of its members (since we are adding the *output* of each of the cartel members at each level of marginal cost). Profits are maximised at Q_1 where $MC = MR$. The cartel must therefore set a price of P_1 (at which Q_1 will be demanded).

Having agreed on the cartel price, the members may then compete against each other using *non-price competition*, to gain as big a share of resulting sales (Q_1) as they can.

Alternatively, the cartel members may somehow agree to divide the market between them. Each member would be given a **quota**. The sum of all the quotas must add up to Q_1. If the quotas exceeded Q_1, either there would be output unsold if price remained fixed at P_1, or the price would fall.

But if quotas are to be set by the cartel, how will it decide the level of each individual member's quota? The most likely method is for the cartel to divide the market between the members according to their current market share. That is the solution most likely to be accepted as 'fair'.

In many countries cartels are illegal, being seen by the government as a means of driving up prices and profits and thereby as being against the public interest. Government policy towards cartels is examined in Chapter 21.

Where open collusion is illegal, firms may simply break the law, or get round it. Alternatively, firms may stay within the law, but still *tacitly* collude by watching each other's prices and keeping theirs similar. Firms may tacitly 'agree' to avoid price wars or aggressive advertising campaigns.

Tacit collusion

One form of **tacit collusion** is where firms keep to the price that is set by an established leader. The leader may be the largest firm: the firm which dominates the

> **Definitions**
>
> **Cartel**
> A formal collusive agreement.
>
> **Quota (set by a cartel)**
> The output that a given member of a cartel is allowed to produce (production quota) or sell (sales quota).
>
> **Tacit collusion**
> When oligopolists take care not to engage in price cutting, excessive advertising or other forms of competition. There may be unwritten 'rules' of collusive behaviour such as price leadership.

> **Pause for thought**
>
> If this 'fair' solution were adopted, what effect would it have on the industry MC curve in Figure 12.3?

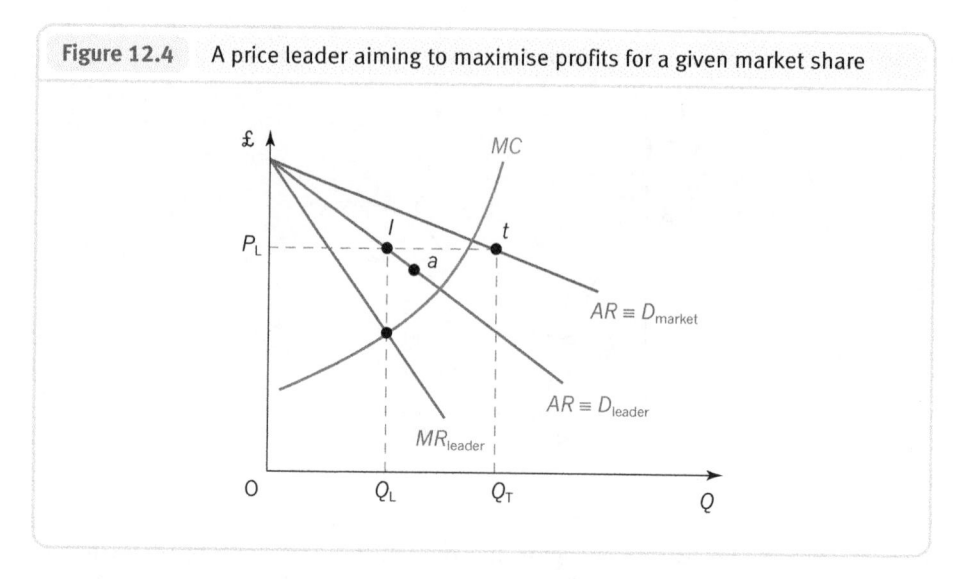

Figure 12.4 A price leader aiming to maximise profits for a given market share

industry. This is known as **dominant firm price leadership**. Alternatively, the price leader may simply be the one that has proved to be the most reliable one to follow: the one that is the best barometer of market conditions. This is known as **barometric firm price leadership**. Let us examine each of these two types of price leadership in turn.

Dominant firm price leadership. How does the leader set the price? This depends on the assumptions it makes about its rivals' reactions to its price changes. If it assumes that rivals will simply follow it by making exactly the same percentage price changes up or down, then a simple model can be constructed. This is illustrated in Figure 12.4. The leader assumes that it will maintain a constant market share (say 50 per cent).

The leader will maximise profits where its marginal revenue is equal to its marginal cost. It knows its current position on its demand curve (say, point *a*). It then estimates how responsive its demand will be to industry-wide price changes and thus constructs its demand and *MR* curves on that basis. It then chooses to produce Q_L at a price of P_L: at point *l* on its demand curve (where *MC* = *MR*). Other firms then follow that price. Total market demand will be Q_T, with followers supplying that portion of the market not supplied by the leader: namely, $Q_T - Q_L$.

There is one problem with this model. That is the assumption that the followers will want to maintain a constant market share. It is possible that, if the leader raises its price, the followers may want to supply more, given that the new price (= *MR* for a price-taking follower) may well be above their marginal cost. On the other hand, the followers may decide merely to maintain their market share for fear of invoking retaliation from the leader, in the form of price cuts or an aggressive advertising campaign.

Barometric firm price leadership. A similar exercise can be conducted by a barometric firm. Although the firm is not dominating the industry, its price will be followed by the others. It merely tries to estimate its demand and *MR* curves – assuming, again, a constant market share – and then produces where *MR* = *MC* and sets price accordingly.

In practice, which firm is taken as the barometer may frequently change. Whether we are talking about oil companies, car producers or banks, any firm may take the initiative in raising prices. If the other firms are merely waiting for someone to take

Definitions

Dominant firm price leadership
When firms (the followers) choose the same price as that set by a dominant firm in the industry (the leader).

Barometric firm price leadership
Where the price leader is the one whose prices are believed to reflect market conditions in the most satisfactory way.

the lead – say, because costs have risen – they will all quickly follow suit. For example, if one of the bigger building societies or banks raises its mortgage rates by 1 per cent, this is likely to stimulate the others to follow suit.

Other forms of tacit collusion. An alternative to having an established leader is for there to be an established set of simple 'rules of thumb' that everyone follows.

One such example is average cost pricing. Here producers, instead of equating *MC* and *MR*, simply add a certain percentage for profit on top of average costs. Thus, if average costs rise by 10 per cent, prices will automatically be raised by 10 per cent. This is a particularly useful rule of thumb in times of inflation, when all firms will be experiencing similar cost increases.

Another rule of thumb is to have certain price benchmarks. Thus clothes may sell for £9.95, £14.95 or £39.95 (but not £12.31 or £36.42). If costs rise, then firms simply raise their price to the next benchmark, knowing that other firms will do the same. Average cost pricing and other pricing strategies are considered in more detail in Chapter 17.

Rules of thumb can also be applied to advertising (e.g. you do not criticise other firms' products, only praise your own); or to the design of the product (e.g. lighting manufacturers tacitly agreeing not to bring out an everlasting light bulb).

> **Definitions**
>
> **Average cost pricing**
> Where a firm sets its price by adding a certain percentage for (average) profit on top of average cost.
>
> **Price benchmark**
> This is a price which is typically used. Firms, when raising prices, will usually raise it from one benchmark to another.

> **Pause for thought**
>
> *If a firm has a typical shaped average cost curve and sets prices 10 per cent above average cost, what will its supply curve look like?*

Factors favouring collusion

Collusion between firms, whether formal or tacit, is more likely when firms can clearly identify with each other or some leader and when they trust each other not to break agreements. It will be easier for firms to collude if the following conditions apply:

- There are only very few firms, all well known to each other.
- They are open with each other about costs and production methods.
- They have similar production methods and average costs, and are thus likely to want to change prices at the same time and by the same percentage.
- They produce similar products and can thus more easily reach agreements on price.
- There is a dominant firm.
- There are significant barriers to entry and thus there is little fear of disruption by new firms.
- The market is stable. If industry demand or production costs fluctuate wildly, it will be difficult to make agreements, partly due to difficulties in predicting and partly because agreements may frequently have to be amended. There is a particular problem in a declining market where firms may be tempted to undercut each other's price in order to maintain their sales.
- There are no government measures to curb collusion.

Non-collusive oligopoly: the breakdown of collusion

In some oligopolies, there may be only a few (if any) factors favouring collusion. In such cases, the likelihood of price competition is greater.

Even if there is collusion, there will always be the temptation for individual oligopolists to 'cheat', by cutting prices or by selling more than their allotted quota. The danger, of course, is that this would invite retaliation from the other members of the cartel, with a resulting price war. Price would then fall and the cartel could well break up in disarray.

When considering whether to break a collusive agreement, even if only a tacit one, a firm will ask: (1) 'How much can we get away with without inviting retaliation?' and (2) 'If a price war does result, will we be the winners? Will we succeed in driving some or all of our rivals out of business and yet survive ourselves, and thereby gain greater market power?'

The position of rival firms, therefore, is rather like that of generals of opposing armies or the players in a game. It is a question of choosing the appropriate *strategy*: the strategy that will best succeed in outwitting your opponents. The strategy that a firm adopts will, of course, be concerned not just with price, but also with advertising and product development.

Non-collusive oligopoly: assumptions about rivals' behaviour

Even though oligopolists might not collude, they will still need to take account of rivals' likely behaviour when deciding their own strategy. In doing so they will probably look at rivals' past behaviour and make assumptions based on it. There are three well-known models, each based on a different set of assumptions.

Assumption that rivals produce a given quantity: the Cournot model

One assumption is that rivals will produce a particular *quantity*. This is most likely when the market is stable and the rivals have been producing a relatively constant quantity for some time. The task, then, for the individual oligopolist is to decide its own price and quantity given the presumed output of its competitors.

The earliest model based on this assumption was developed by the French economist Augustin Cournot[1] in 1838. The Cournot model (which is developed in Web Appendix 4.2) takes the simple case of just two firms (a duopoly) producing an identical product: for example, two electricity generating companies supplying the whole country.

This is illustrated in Figure 12.5, which shows the profit-maximising price and output for firm A. The total market demand curve is shown as D_M. Assume that firm A believes that its rival, firm B, will produce Q_{B1} units. Thus firm A perceives its own

> **Definitions**
>
> **Cournot model**
> A model of duopoly where each firm makes its price and output decisions on the assumption that its rival will produce a particular quantity.
>
> **Duopoly**
> An oligopoly where there are just two firms in the market.

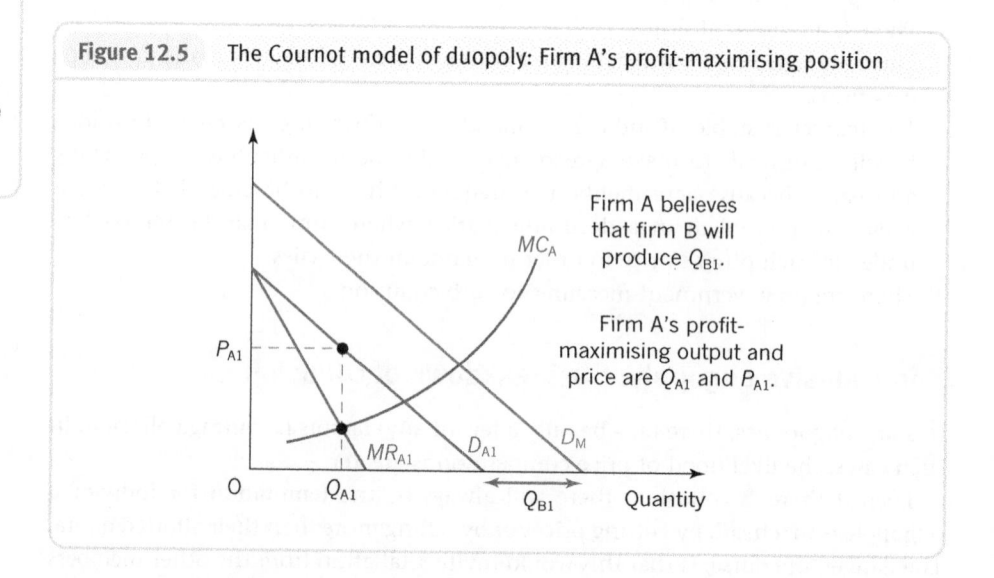

Figure 12.5 The Cournot model of duopoly: Firm A's profit-maximising position

---

[1] See http://cepa.newschool.edu/het/profiles/cournot.htm for a profile of Cournot and his work.

demand curve (D_{A1}) to be Q_{B1} units less than total market demand. In other words, the horizontal gap between D_M and D_{A1} is Q_{B1} units. Given its perceived demand curve of D_{A1}, its marginal revenue curve will be MR_{A1} and the profit-maximising output will be Q_{A1}, where $MR_{A1} = MC_A$. The profit-maximising price will be P_{A1}.

If firm A believed that firm B would produce *more* than Q_{B1}, its perceived demand and *MR* curves would be further to the left and the profit-maximising quantity and price would both be lower.

Profits in the Cournot model. Industry profits will be *less* than under a monopoly or a cartel. The reason is that price will be lower than the monopoly price. This can be seen from Figure 12.5. If this were a monopoly, then to find the profit-maximising output, we would need to construct an *MR* curve corresponding to the market demand curve (D_M). This would intersect with the *MC* curve at a higher output than Q_{A1} and a *higher* price (given by D_M).

Nevertheless, profits in the Cournot model will be higher than under perfect competition, since price is still above marginal cost.

Assumption that rivals set a particular price: the Bertrand model

An alternative assumption is that rival firms set a particular price and stick to it. This scenario is more realistic when firms do not want to upset customers by frequent price changes or want to produce catalogues which specify prices. The task, then, for a given oligopolist is to choose its own price and quantity in the light of the prices set by rivals.

The most famous model based on this assumption was developed by another French economist, Joseph Bertrand, in 1883. Bertrand again took the simple case of a duopoly, but its conclusions apply equally to oligopolies with three or more firms.

The outcome is one of price cutting until all supernormal profits are competed away. The reason is simple. If firm A assumes that its rival, firm B, will hold price constant, then firm A should undercut this price by a small amount and as a result gain a large share of the market. At this point, firm B will be forced to respond by cutting its price. What we end up with is a price war until price is forced down to the level of average cost, with only normal profits remaining.

Nash equilibrium. The equilibrium outcome in either the Cournot or Bertrand models is not in the *joint* interests of the firms. In each case, total profits are less than under a monopoly or cartel. But, in the absence of collusion, the outcome is the result of each firm doing the best it can, given its assumptions about what its rivals are doing. The resulting equilibrium is known as a Nash equilibrium, after John Nash, a US mathematician (and subject of the film *A Beautiful Mind*) who introduced the concept in 1951.

In practice, when competition is intense, as in the Bertrand model, the firms may seek to collude long before profits have been reduced to a normal level. Alternatively, firms may put in a takeover bid for their rival(s).

The kinked demand-curve assumption

In 1939 a theory of non-collusive oligopoly was developed simultaneously on both sides of the Atlantic: in the USA by Paul Sweezy and in Britain by R. L. Hall and C. J. Hitch. This kinked demand theory has since become perhaps the most famous of all theories of oligopoly. The model seeks to explain how it is that, even

Definitions

Nash equilibrium
The position resulting from everyone making their optimal decision based on their assumptions about their rivals' decisions.

Takeover bid
Where one firm attempts to purchase another by offering to buy the shares of that company from its shareholders.

Kinked demand theory
The theory that oligopolists face a demand curve that is kinked at the current price: demand being significantly more elastic above the current price than below. The effect of this is to create a situation of price stability.

BOX 12.2 REINING IN BIG BUSINESS

Market power in oligopolistic industries

In recent years the car industry, the large supermarket chains and the banks have all been charged with 'ripping off' the consumer. Such has been the level of concern, that all three industries were referred to the UK Competition Commission (see section 20.1). In this box we consider developments in each sector in turn.

Car industry

The Competition Commission report, published in April 2000, found that car buyers in Britain were paying on average some 10 to 12 per cent more than those in France, Germany and Italy for the same models.[1] The price discrepancies between Britain and mainland Europe were maintained by car manufacturers blocking cheaper European cars coming into the UK. This was achieved by threatening mainland European car dealers with losing their dealership if they sold to British buyers, and delaying the delivery date of right-hand drive models to European dealers in the hope that British buyers would change their minds and go back to a British dealership.

As the problem involved more than one EU country, the European Commission (EC) also examined the issue. It concluded that the motor vehicle manufacturers had agreements with distributors that were too restrictive. In 2002, the EC changed the 'Block Exemption' regulations governing the sector to allow distributors to set up in different countries and to sell multiple brands of car within their showrooms. Furthermore, distributors which are offered an exclusive 'sales territory' distribution agreement by car manufacturers are now allowed to resell cars to other distributors which are not part of the manufacturer's network. This has helped to develop other sales outlets such as car supermarkets and Internet retailers. In addition, the regulation has opened up the repair and spare parts sector to more firms.

Changes in the regulations, and the addition of ten new EU member states in 2004 and another two in 2007, have made the car market more competitive by increasing the sources of supply. Slowly, prices of new car prices have been converging across the EU towards the lower-price markets.[2]

But what about the UK? Since 2003 new car prices have, on average, fallen. In the year to January 2008 new car prices fell by 1.1 per cent, while general price inflation over the same period was 2.2 per cent. This is in contrast to the rest of the EU where car prices rose by 0.2 per cent and headline inflation was 3.4 per cent. Nevertheless there is still scope for shopping around outside of the UK – 27 out of 83 models listed by the EU in January 2008 were at least 10 per cent higher than the lowest EU price.

With the recession of 2008/9, the demand for new cars plummeted. Competition became intense and new cars were heavily discounted. Some dealers went out of business and there were mergers of car manufacturers, such as Fiat and Chrysler. Many car factories went on to short-time working. It will be interesting to see whether these events will make the car market less competitive when the world economy expands again.

Supermarkets

Consumers, suppliers and regulators have commented upon the use (or abuse) of market power in the supermarket sector during recent times. Three major areas of concern have arisen.

Barriers to entry. The most important barrier to entry is the difficulty in getting planning permission to open a new supermarket thus restricting consumer choice. Furthermore, supermarkets own covenants on land ('land banks') suitable for siting new stores and by not releasing them to competitors they thereby restrict competition.

Another barrier are the large economies of scale and the huge buying power of the established supermarkets, which make it virtually impossible for a new player or for the smaller convenience stores to match their low costs. Indeed, the big supermarkets have used their scale to enter the convenience sector with considerable effect. Thus brands like 'Tesco Metro' and 'Sainsbury's Local' have been successful in driving out many small stores from the market.

Relationships with suppliers. One of the most contentious issues concerns the major supermarket chains' huge buying power. They have been able to drive costs down by forcing suppliers to offer discounts. Many suppliers, such as growers, have found their profit margins cut to the bone. However, in many cases these cost savings to the supermarkets have not been passed on to shoppers.

Price competition. National advertising campaigns tell us that supermarkets are concerned about keeping prices lower than their competitors on a number of items. However, this can often mask certain pricing concerns. For some goods the supermarkets have, on occasion, adopted a system of 'shadow pricing', a form of tacit collusion whereby they all observe each other's prices and ensure that they remain at similar levels – often similarly high levels rather than similarly low levels! This has limited the extent of true price competition, and the resulting high prices have seen profits grow as costs have been driven ever downwards.

---

[1] Competition Commission (2000) 'New cars: a report on the supply of new motor cars within the UK' (Cm 4660). Available at www.competition-commission.org.uk/rep_pub/reports/2000/439cars.htm

[2] http://ec.europa.eu/competition/sectors/motor_vehicles/prices/report.html

Moreover, the supermarkets have been observed charging high prices where there is little or no competition, notably in rural locations, and charging lower prices on some items, often below cost, where competition is more intense.

But intense price competition tends to be only over basic items, such as the own-brand 'value' products. To get to the basic items, you normally have to pass the more luxurious ones, which are much more highly priced! Supermarkets rely on shoppers making impulse buys of the more expensive lines: lines that have much higher profit margins.

In response to these claims, the Competition Commission reported in 2008 that it found little evidence of tacit collusion.[3] Further, the nature of below-cost selling on grocery items by the supermarkets did not mislead consumers in relation to the overall cost of shopping at a particular store. Indeed, temporary promotions on some products, including fuel, may represent effective competition between supermarkets and lower the average price of a basket of goods for customers.

However, the Commission did have some concerns in relation to the existence of a number of stores owned by the same supermarket chain in a particular location (e.g. Tesco Metro and Tesco Superstore) and the covenants on land owned by supermarkets that restrict entry by competitors. To this end it proposed a 'competition test' in planning decisions and action to prevent land agreements, both of which would lessen the market power of supermarkets in local areas.

The Commission also found that the supermarkets had substantial buying power and that the drive to lower supply prices may have had an inhibiting effect on innovation. It therefore proposed the creation of a new strengthened and extended Groceries Supply Code of Practice that would be enforced by an independent ombudsman and incorporated the bigger firms.

The government broadly welcomed the recommendations and is looking to consult further. Tesco, however, launched an appeal to the Competition Appeal Tribunal in July 2008 seeking to have the 'competition test' quashed. We await the outcome of this with interest.

Banks

In 2002, the Competition Commission reported that the then 'Big Four' UK banks (Barclays, HSBC, Lloyds-TSB, RBS Group) charged excessive prices to small and medium-sized enterprises (SMEs) in England and Wales.[4] This resulted in excessive profits of some £725 million per year.

It found that each of the four banks pursued similar pricing practices. These included no interest on current accounts; free banking offered only to some categories of SMEs, usually start-ups; the use of negotiation to reduce charges for those considering switching to other banks; lower charges or free banking to those switching from other banks. Switching to another bank, however, requires considerable time and effort for most SMEs. They are therefore locked into a particular bank for a long time. The result is very little competition between the Big Four for the majority of small business customers.

The Competition Commission also found significant barriers to entry to the banking market, and especially to the market for 'liquidity management' services (i.e. the management of current accounts and overdraft facilities) and for general-purpose business loans.

It recommended a reduction in barriers to entry to permit more competition within the industry. This could best be achieved by requiring banks to permit fast and error-free switching by SMEs to other banks (to enable SMEs to shop around for the best value in banking services) and either to pay interest on current account holdings or to offer free banking services.

In May 2005 the OFT referred the supply of current account banking services in Northern Ireland to the Competition Commission. This market is tightly concentrated and the Competition Commission found that the banks impose a number of charges when customers are overdrawn, or in credit, that are not found in the rest of the UK.[5] Furthermore, it found that there is limited switching by customers to other accounts and that firms do not actively compete on price. The Commission proposed a number of changes to unravel the complexities of personal current account banking and these have been implemented.

1. Identify the main barriers to entry in each of the three sectors.
2. Update each of the cases and consider the economic implications for consumers.

---

[3] Competition Commission (2008) 'Market investigation into the supply of groceries in the UK'. Available at www.competition-commission.org.uk/inquiries/ref2006/grocery/index.htm

[4] Competition Commission (2002) 'The supply of banking services by clearing banks to small and medium-sized enterprises: a report on the supply of banking services by clearing banks to small and medium-sized enterprises within the UK' (Cm 5319, March). Available at www.competition-commission.org.uk/rep_pub/reports/2002/462banks.htm

[5] Competition Commission (2007) 'Northern Irish personal banking'. Available at www.competition-commission.org.uk/inquiries/ref2005/banking/index.htm

when there is no collusion at all between oligopolists, prices can nevertheless remain stable.

The theory is based on two asymmetrical assumptions:

- If an oligopolist cuts its price, its rivals will feel forced to follow suit and cut theirs, to prevent losing customers to the first firm.
- If an oligopolist raises its price, however, its rivals will *not* follow suit since, by keeping their prices the same, they will thereby gain customers from the first firm.

On these assumptions, each oligopolist will face a demand curve that is *kinked* at the current price and output (see Figure 12.6(a)). A rise in price will lead to a large fall in sales as customers switch to the now relatively lower-priced rivals. The firm will thus be reluctant to raise its price. Demand is relatively elastic above the kink. On the other hand, a fall in price will bring only a modest increase in sales, since rivals lower their prices too and therefore customers do not switch. The firm will thus also be reluctant to lower its price. Demand is relatively inelastic below the kink. Thus oligopolists will be reluctant to change prices at all.

This price stability can be shown formally by drawing in the firm's marginal revenue curve, as in Figure 12.6(b).

To see how this is done, imagine dividing the diagram into two parts either side of Q_1. At quantities less than Q_1 (the left-hand part of the diagram), the *MR* curve will correspond to the shallow part of the *AR* curve. At quantities greater than Q_1 (the right-hand part), the *MR* curve will correspond to the steep part of the *AR* curve. To see how this part of the *MR* curve is constructed, imagine extending the steep part of the *AR* curve back to the vertical axis. This and the corresponding *MR* curve are shown by the dotted lines in Figure 12.6(b).

As you can see, there will be a gap between points *a* and *b*. In other words, there is a vertical section of the *MR* curve between these two points.

Profits are maximised where *MC* = *MR*. Thus, if the *MC* curve lies anywhere between MC_1 and MC_2 (i.e. between points *a* and *b*), the profit-maximising price and output will be P_1 and Q_1. Thus prices will remain stable *even with a considerable change in costs*.

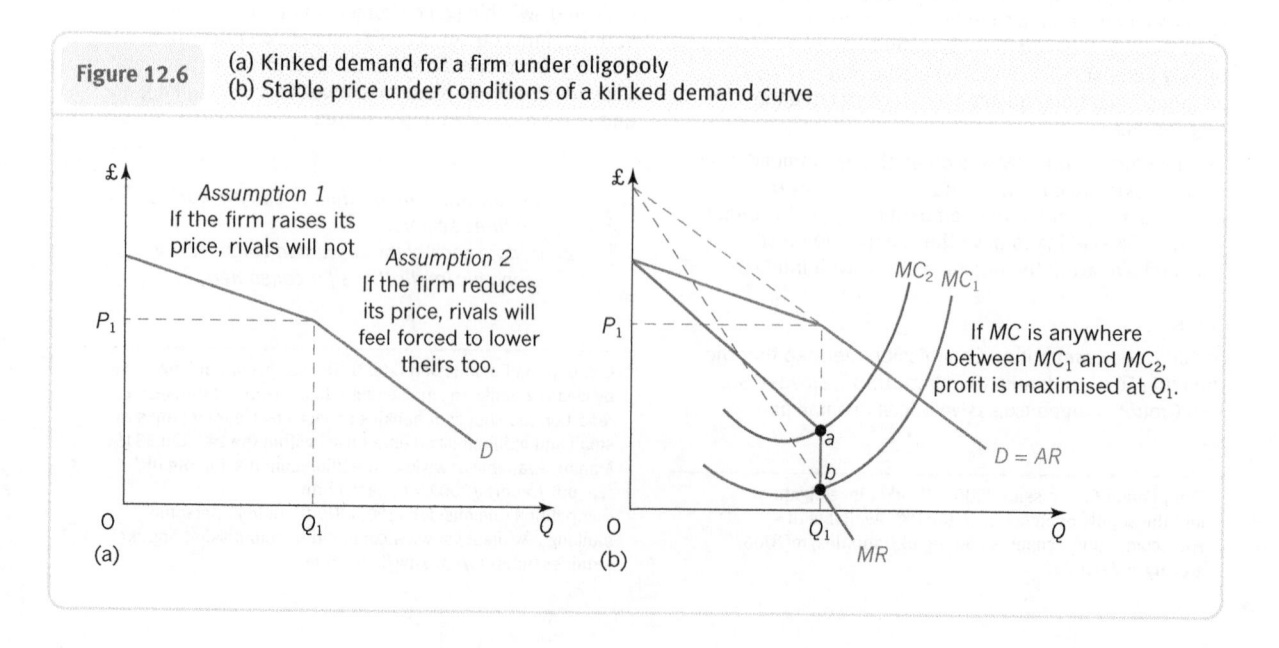

Figure 12.6 (a) Kinked demand for a firm under oligopoly
(b) Stable price under conditions of a kinked demand curve

Oligopoly and the consumer

If oligopolists act collusively and jointly maximise industry profits, they will in effect be acting together as a monopoly. In such cases, prices may be very high. This is clearly not in the best interests of consumers.

Furthermore, in two respects, oligopoly may be more disadvantageous than monopoly:

- Depending on the size of the individual oligopolists, there may be less scope for economies of scale to mitigate the effects of market power.
- Oligopolists are likely to engage in much more extensive advertising than a monopolist.

These problems will be less severe, however, if oligopolists do not collude, if there is some degree of price competition and if barriers to entry are weak.

Moreover, the power of oligopolists in certain markets may to some extent be offset if they sell their product to other powerful firms. Thus oligopolistic producers of baked beans or soap powder sell a large proportion of their output to giant supermarket chains, which can use their market power to keep down the price at which they purchase these products. This phenomenon is known as **countervailing power**.

In some respects, oligopoly may be more beneficial to the consumer than other market structures:

> **Definition**
>
> **Countervailing power**
> When the power of a monopolistic/oligopolistic seller is offset by powerful buyers who can prevent the price from being pushed up.

> **Pause for thought**
>
> *Assume that two brewers announce that they are about to merge. What information would you need to help you decide whether the merger would be in the consumer's interests?*

- Oligopolists, like monopolists, can use part of their supernormal profit for research and development. Unlike monopolists, however, oligopolists will have a considerable *incentive* to do so. If the product design is improved, this may allow the firm to capture a larger share of the market, and it may be some time before rivals can respond with a similarly improved product. If, in addition, costs are reduced by technological improvement, the resulting higher profits will improve the firm's capacity to withstand a price war.
- Non-price competition through product differentiation may result in greater choice for the consumer. Take the case of stereo equipment. Non-price competition has led to a huge range of different products of many different specifications, each meeting the specific requirements of different consumers.

It is difficult to draw any general conclusions, since oligopolies differ so much in their performance.

Oligopoly and contestable markets

The theory of contestable markets has been applied to oligopoly as well as to monopoly, and similar conclusions are drawn.

The lower the entry and exit costs for new firms, the more difficult it will be for oligopolists to collude and make supernormal profits. If oligopolists do form a cartel (whether legal or illegal), this will be difficult to maintain if it very soon faces competition from new entrants. What a cartel has to do in such a situation is to erect entry barriers, thereby making the 'contest' more difficult. For example, the cartel could form a common research laboratory, denied to outsiders. It might attempt to control the distribution of the finished product by buying up wholesale or retail outlets. Or it might simply let it be known to potential entrants that they will face all-out price, advertising and product competition from all the members if they should dare to set up in competition.

> **Pause for thought**
>
> *Which of the following markets do you think are contestable: (a) credit cards; (b) brewing; (c) petrol retailing; (d) insurance services; (e) compact discs?*

The industry is thus likely to behave competitively if entry and exit costs are low, with all the benefits and costs to the consumer of such competition – even if the new firms do not actually enter. However, if entry and/or exit costs are high, the degree of competition will simply depend on the relations between existing members of the industry.

12.3 GAME THEORY

As we have seen, the behaviour of a firm under non-collusive oligopoly depends on how it thinks its rivals will react to its decisions. When considering whether to cut prices in order to gain a larger market share, a firm will ask itself two key questions: first, how much it can get away with, without inciting retaliation; second, if its rivals do retaliate and a price-war ensues, whether it will be able to 'see off' some or all of its rivals, while surviving itself.

Economists use game theory to examine the best strategy a firm can adopt for each assumption about its rivals' behaviour.

> **Definition**
>
> **Game theory (or the theory of games)**
> The study of alternative strategies that oligopolists may choose to adopt, depending on their assumptions about their rivals' behaviour.

Single-move games

The simplest type of 'game' is a single-move or single-period game, sometimes known as a normal-form game. This involves just one 'move' by each firm in the game. For example two or more firms are bidding for a contract which will be awarded to the lowest bidder. When the bids are all made, the contract will be awarded to the lowest bidder; the 'game' is over.

Simple dominant strategy games

Many single-period games have predictable outcomes, no matter what assumptions each firm makes about its rivals' behaviour. Such games are known as dominant strategy games. The simplest case is where there are just two firms with identical costs, products and demand. They are both considering which of two alternative prices to charge. Table 12.1 shows typical profits they could each make.

Table 12.1 Profits for firms A and B at different prices

		X's price £2	X's price £1.80
Y's price	**£2**	A: £10 m each	B: £5 m for Y, £12 m for X
	£1.80	C: £12 m for Y, £5 m for X	D: £8 m each

Let us assume that at present both firms (X and Y) are charging a price of £2 and that they are each making a profit of £10 million, giving a total industry profit of £20 million. This is shown in the top left-hand cell (A).

Now assume they are both (independently) considering reducing their price to £1.80. In making this decision, they will need to take into account what their rival might do, and how this will affect them. Let us consider X's position. In our simple example there are just two things that its rival, firm Y, might do. Either Y could cut its price to £1.80, or it could leave its price at £2. What should X do?

One alternative is to go for the *cautious* approach and think of the worst thing that its rival could do. If X kept its price at £2, the worst thing for X would be if its rival Y cut its price. This is shown by cell C: X's profit falls to £5 million. If, however, X cut its price to £1.80, the worst outcome would again be for Y to cut its price, but this time X's profit only falls to £8 million. In this case, then, if X is cautious, it will *cut its price to £1.80*. Note that Y will argue along similar lines, and if it is cautious, it too will cut its price to £1.80. This policy of adopting the safer approach is known as maximin. Following a maximin approach, the firm will opt for the alternative that will *max*imise its *min*imum possible profit.

An alternative is to go for the *optimistic* approach and assume that your rivals react in the way most favourable to you. Here the firm will go for the strategy that yields the highest possible profit. In X's case this will be again to cut price, only this time on the optimistic assumption that firm Y will leave its price unchanged. If firm X is correct in its assumption, it will move to cell B and achieve the maximum possible profit of £12 million. This approach of going for the maximum possible profit is known as maximax. Note that again the same argument applies to Y. Its maximax strategy will be to cut price and hopefully end up in cell C.

Given that in this 'game' *both* approaches, maximin and maximax, lead to the *same* strategy (namely, cutting price), this is known as a dominant strategy game. The result is that the firms will end up in cell D, earning a lower profit (£8 million each) than if they had charged the higher price (£10 million each in cell A).

As we saw, the equilibrium outcome of a game where there is no collusion between the players is known as a *Nash equilibrium*. The Nash equilibrium in this game is cell D.

> **KEY IDEA 24**
>
> *Nash equilibrium.* The position resulting from everyone making their optimal decision based on their assumptions about their rivals' decisions. Without collusion, there is no incentive for any firm to move from this position.

In our example, collusion rather than a price war would have benefited both firms. Yet, even if they did collude, both would be tempted to cheat and cut prices. This is known as the prisoners' dilemma (see Box 12.3).

More complex games with no dominant strategy

More complex 'games' can be devised with more than two firms, many alternative prices, differentiated products and various forms of non-price competition (e.g. advertising). In such cases, the cautious (maximin) strategy may suggest a different policy (e.g. do nothing) from the high-risk (maximax) strategy (e.g. cut prices substantially).

In many situations, firms will have a number of different options open to them and a number of possible reactions by rivals. In such cases, the choices facing firms may be many. They may opt for a compromise strategy between maximax and

---

Definitions

Maximin
The strategy of choosing the policy whose worst possible outcome is the least bad.

Maximax
The strategy of choosing the policy which has the best possible outcome.

Dominant strategy game
Where different assumptions about rivals' behaviour lead to the adoption of the same strategy.

Prisoners' dilemma
Where two or more firms (or people), by attempting independently to choose the best strategy for whatever the other(s) are likely to do, end up in a worse position than if they had cooperated in the first place.

maximin. This could be a strategy that is more risky than the maximin one, but with the chance of a higher profit; but not as risky as the maximax one, but where the maximum profit possible is not so high.

Multiple-move games

In many situations, firms will *react* to what their rivals do; their rivals, in turn, will react to what they do. In other words, the game moves back and forth from one 'player' to the other like a game of chess or cards. Firms will still have to think strategically (as you do in chess), considering the likely responses of their rivals to their own actions. These multiple-move games are known as *repeated games* or *extensive-form games*.

One of the simplest repeated games is the tit-for-tat. This is where a firm will cut prices, or make some other aggressive move, *only* if the rival does so first. To illustrate this in a multiple-move situation let us look again at the example we considered in Table 12.1, but this time we will extend it beyond one time period.

Assume that firm X is adopting the tit-for-tat strategy. If firm Y cuts its price from £2.00 to £1.80, then firm X will respond in round 2 by also cutting its price. The two firms will end up in cell D – worse off than if neither had cut their price. If, however, firm Y had left its price at £2.00 then firm X would respond by leaving its price unchanged too. Both firms would remain in cell A with a higher profit than cell D.

As long as firm Y knows that firm X will respond in this way, it has an incentive not to cut its price. Thus it is in X's interests to make sure that Y clearly 'understands' how X will react to any price cut. In other words, X will make a threat.

The importance of threats and promises

In many situations, an oligopolist will make a threat or promise that it will act in a certain way. As long as the threat or promise is credible (i.e. its competitors believe it), the firm can gain and it will influence its rivals' behaviour.

Take the simple situation where a large oil company, such as Esso, states that it will match the price charged by any competitor within a given radius. Assume that competitors believe this 'price promise' but also that Esso will not try to *undercut* their price. In the simple situation where there is only one other filling station in the area, what price should it charge? Clearly it should charge the price which would maximise its profits, assuming that Esso will charge the *same* price. In the absence of other filling stations in the area, this is likely to be a relatively high price.

Now assume that there are several filling stations in the area. What should the company do now? Its best bet is probably to charge the same price as Esso and hope that no other company charges a lower price and forces Esso to cut its price. Assuming that Esso's threat is credible, other companies are likely to reason in a similar way.

The importance of timing

Most decisions by oligopolists are made by one firm at a time rather than simultaneously by all firms. Sometimes a firm will take the initiative. At other times it will respond to decisions taken by other firms.

Take the case of a new generation of large passenger aircraft which can fly further without refuelling. Assume that there is a

> **Definition**
>
> **Tit-for-tat**
> Where a firm will cut prices, or make some other aggressive move, *only* if the rival does so first. If the rival knows this, it will be less likely to make an initial aggressive move.

> **Definition**
>
> **Credible threat (or promise)**
> One that is believable to rivals because it is in the threatener's interests to carry it out.

> **Pause for thought**
>
> *Assume that there are two major oil companies operating filling stations in an area. The first promises to match the other's prices. The other promises to sell at 1p per litre cheaper than the first. Describe the likely sequence of events in this 'game' and the likely eventual outcome. Could the promise of the second company be seen as credible?*

BOX 12.3 THE PRISONERS' DILEMMA

Game theory is relevant not just to economics. A famous non-economic example is the prisoners' dilemma.

Nigel and Amanda have been arrested for a joint crime of serious fraud. Each is interviewed separately and given the following alternatives:

- First, if they say nothing, the court has enough evidence to sentence both to a year's imprisonment.
- Second, if either Nigel or Amanda *alone* confesses, he or she is likely to get only a three-month sentence but the partner could get up to ten years.
- Third, if both confess, they are likely to get three years each.

What should Nigel and Amanda do?

Let us consider Nigel's dilemma. Should he confess in order to get the short sentence (the maximax strategy)? This is better than the year he would get for not confessing. There is, however, an even better reason for confessing. Suppose Nigel doesn't confess but, unknown to him, Amanda does confess. Then Nigel ends up with the long sentence. Better than this is to confess and to get no more than three years: this is the safest (maximin) strategy.

Amanda is in the same dilemma. The result is simple. When both prisoners act selfishly by confessing, they both end up in position D with relatively long prison terms. Only when they collude will they end up in position A with relatively short prison terms, the best combined solution.

Of course the police know this and will do their best to prevent any collusion. They will keep Nigel and Amanda in separate cells and try to persuade each of them that the other is bound to confess.

Thus the choice of strategy depends on:

- Nigel's and Amanda's risk attitudes: i.e. are they 'risk lovers' or 'risk averse'?
- Nigel's and Amanda's estimates of how likely the other is to own up.

?
1 Why is this a dominant strategy game?
2 How would Nigel's choice of strategy be affected if he had instead been involved in a joint crime with Adam, Ashok, Diana and Rikki, and they had all been caught?

Let us now look at two real-world examples of the prisoners' dilemma.

Standing at concerts

When people go to some public event, such as a concert or a match, they often stand in order to get a better view. But once people start standing, everyone is likely to do so: after all, if they stayed sitting, they would not see at all. In this Nash equilibrium, most people are worse off, since, except for tall people, their view is likely to be worse and they lose the comfort of sitting down.

Too much advertising

Why do firms spend so much on advertising? If they are aggressive, they do so to get ahead of their rivals (the maximax approach). If they are cautious, they do so in case their rivals increase their advertising (the maximin approach). Although in both cases it may be in the individual firm's best interests to increase advertising, the resulting Nash equilibrium is likely to be one of excessive advertising: the total spent on advertising (by all firms) is not recouped in additional sales.

? *Give one or two other examples (economic or non-economic) of the prisoners' dilemma.*

	Amanda's alternatives	
Nigel's alternatives	Not confess	Confess
Not confess	A Each gets 1 year	B Nigel gets 10 years Amanda gets 3 months
Confess	C Nigel gets 3 months Amanda gets 10 years	D Each gets 3 years

market for a 500-seater version of this type of aircraft and a 400-seater version, but that the market for each sized aircraft is not big enough for the two manufacturers, Boeing and Airbus, to share it profitably. Let us also assume that the 400-seater market would give an annual profit of £50 million to a single manufacturer and the 500-seater would give an annual profit of £30 million, but that if both manufacturers produced the same version, they would each make an annual loss of £10 million.

Assume that Boeing announces that it is building the 400-seater plane. What should Airbus do? The choice is illustrated in Figure 12.7. This diagram is called a

Figure 12.7 A decision tree

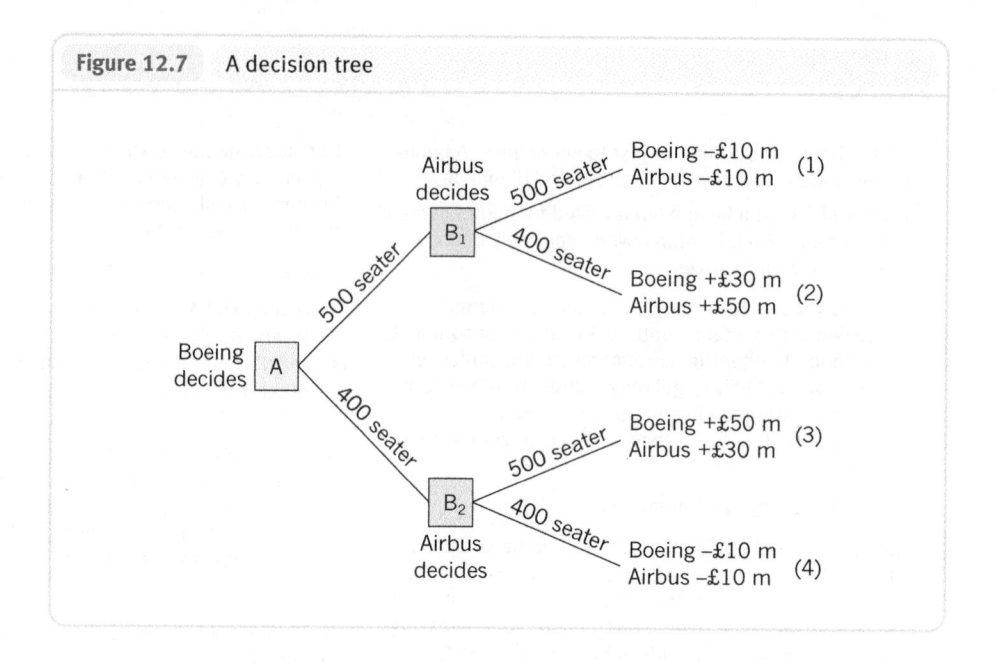

```
                          500 seater    Boeing −£10 m
              Airbus     ──────────     Airbus −£10 m    (1)
              decides
               [B₁]
          500           400 seater      Boeing +£30 m
         seater         ──────────      Airbus +£50 m    (2)
Boeing
decides
 [A]
         400           500 seater       Boeing +£50 m
         seater        ──────────       Airbus +£30 m    (3)
               [B₂]
              Airbus     400 seater     Boeing −£10 m
              decides    ──────────     Airbus −£10 m    (4)
```

Definitions

Decision tree (or game tree)
A diagram showing the sequence of possible decisions by competitor firms and the outcome of each combination of decisions.

First-mover advantage
When a firm gains from being the first one to take action.

decision tree and shows the sequence of events. The small square at the left of the diagram is Boeing's decision point (point A). If it had decided to build the 500-seater plane, we would move up the top branch. Airbus would now have to make a decision (point B_1). If it too built the 500-seater plane, we would move to outcome 1: a loss of £10 million for both manufacturers. Clearly, with Boeing building a 500-seater plane, Airbus would choose the 400-seater plane: we would move to outcome 2, with Boeing making a profit of £30 million and Airbus a profit £50 million. Airbus would be very pleased!

Boeing's best strategy at point A, however, would be to build the 400-seater plane. We would then move to Airbus's decision point B_2. In this case, it is in Airbus's interests to build the 500-seater plane. Its profit would be only £30 million (outcome 3), but this is better than a £10 million loss if it too built the 400-seater plane (outcome 4). With Boeing deciding first, the Nash equilibrium will thus be outcome 3.

There is clearly a **first-mover advantage** here. Once Boeing has decided to build the more profitable version of the plane, Airbus is forced to build the less profitable one. Naturally, Airbus would like to build the more profitable one and be the first mover. Which company succeeds in going first depends on how advanced they are in their research and development and in their production capacity.

Pause for thought

Give an example of decisions that two firms could make in sequence, each one affecting the other's next decision.

More complex decision trees. The aircraft example is the simplest version of a decision tree, with just two companies and each one making only one key decision. In many business situations, much more complex trees could be constructed. The 'game' would be more like one of chess, with many moves and several options on each move. If there were more than two companies, the decision tree would be more complex still.

The usefulness of game theory

The advantage of the game-theory approach is that the firm does not need to know which response its rivals will make. It does, however, need to be able to measure the effect of each possible response. This will be virtually impossible to do when there are many firms competing and many different responses that could be made. The approach is only useful, therefore, in relatively simple cases, and even here the estimates of profit from each outcome may amount to no more than a rough guess.

It is thus difficult for an economist to predict with any accuracy what price, output and level of advertising the firm will choose. This problem is compounded by the difficulty of predicting the type of strategy – safe, high risk, compromise – that the firm will adopt.

In some cases, firms may compete hard for a time (in price or non-price terms) and then realise that maybe no one is winning. Firms may then jointly raise prices and reduce advertising. Later, after a period of tacit collusion, competition may break out again. This may be sparked off by the entry of a new firm, by the development of a new product design, by a change in market demand, or simply by one or more firms no longer being able to resist the temptation to 'cheat'. In short, the behaviour of particular oligopolists may change quite radically over time.

SUMMARY

1a Monopolistic competition occurs where there is free entry to the industry and quite a large number of firms operating independently of each other, but where each firm has some market power as a result of producing differentiated products or services.

1b In the short run, firms can make supernormal profits. In the long run, however, freedom of entry will drive profits down to the normal level. The long-run equilibrium of the firm is where the (downward-sloping) demand curve is tangential to the long-run average cost curve.

1c The long-run equilibrium is one of excess capacity. Given that the demand curve is downward sloping, its tangency point with the *LRAC* curve will not be at the bottom of the *LRAC* curve. Increased production would thus be possible at *lower* average cost.

1d In practice, supernormal profits may persist into the long run: firms have imperfect information; entry may not be completely unrestricted; there may be a problem of indivisibilities; firms may use non-price competition to maintain an advantage over their rivals.

1e Monopolistically competitive firms, because of excess capacity, may have higher costs, and thus higher prices, than perfectly competitive firms, but consumers may gain from a greater diversity of products.

1f Monopolistically competitive firms may have less economies of scale than monopolies and conduct less research and development, but the competition may keep prices lower than under monopoly. Whether there will be more or less choice for the consumer is debatable.

2a An oligopoly is where there are just a few firms in the industry with barriers to the entry of new firms. Firms recognise their mutual dependence.

2b Oligopolists will want to maximise their joint profits. This will tend to make them collude to keep prices high. On the other hand, they will want the biggest share of industry profits for themselves. This will tend to make them compete.

2c They are more likely to collude: if there are few of them; if they are open with each other; if they have similar products and cost structures; if there is a dominant firm; if there are significant entry barriers; if the market is stable; and if there is no government legislation to prevent collusion.

2d Collusion can be open or tacit.

2e A formal collusive agreement is called a 'cartel'. A cartel aims to act as a monopoly. It can set price and leave the members to compete for market share, or it can assign quotas. There is always a temptation for cartel members to 'cheat' by undercutting the cartel price if they think they can get away with it and not trigger a price war.

2f Tacit collusion can take the form of price leadership. This is where firms follow the price set by either a dominant firm in the industry or one seen as a reliable 'barometer' of market conditions. Alternatively, tacit collusion can simply involve following various rules of thumb such as average cost pricing and benchmark pricing.

2g Even when firms do not collude they will still have to take into account their rivals' behaviour. In the Cournot model, firms assume that their rivals' output is given and then choose the profit-maximising price and output in the light of this assumption. The resulting price and profit are lower than under monopoly, but still higher than under perfect competition. In the Bertrand model, firms assume that their rivals' price is given. This will result in prices being competed down until only normal profits remain.

2h In the kinked-demand curve model, firms are likely to keep their prices stable unless there is a large shift in costs or demand.

2i Non-collusive oligopolists will have to work out a price strategy. This will depend on their attitudes towards risk and on the assumptions they make about the behaviour of their rivals.

2j Whether consumers benefit from oligopoly depends on: the particular oligopoly and how competitive it is; whether there is any countervailing power; whether the firms engage in extensive advertising and of what type; whether product differentiation results in a wide range of choice for the consumer; how much of the profits are ploughed back into research and development; and how contestable the market is. Since these conditions vary substantially from oligopoly to oligopoly, it is impossible to state just how well or how badly oligopoly in general serves the consumer's interest.

3a Game theory is a way of modelling behaviour in strategic situations where the outcome for an individual or firm depends on the choices made by others. Thus game theory examines various strategies that firms can adopt when the outcome of each is not certain.

3b The simplest type of 'game' is a single-move or single-period game, sometimes known as a normal-form game. Many single-period games have predictable outcomes, no matter what assumptions each firm makes about its rivals' behaviour. Such games are known dominant strategy games.

3c Non-collusive oligopolists will have to work out a price strategy. They can adopt a low-risk 'maximin' strategy of choosing the policy that has the least-bad worst outcome, or a high-risk 'maximax' strategy of choosing the policy with the best possible outcome, or some compromise. Either way, a 'Nash' equilibrium is likely to be reached which is not in the best interests of the firms collectively. It will entail a lower level of profit than if they had colluded.

3d In multiple-move games, play is passed from one 'player' to the other sequentially. Firms will respond not only to what firms do, but also to what they say they will do. To this end, a firm's threats or promises must be credible if they are to influence rivals' decisions.

3e A firm may gain a strategic advantage over its rivals by being the first one to take action (e.g. launch a new product). A decision tree can be constructed to show the possible sequence of moves in a multiple-move game.

REVIEW QUESTIONS

1 Think of ten different products or services and estimate roughly how many firms there are in the market. You will need to decide whether 'the market' is a local one, a national one or an international one. In what ways do the firms compete in each of the cases you have identified?

2 Imagine there are two types of potential customer for jam sold by a small food shop. One is the person who has just run out and wants some now. The other is the person who looks in the cupboard, sees that the pot of jam is less than half full and thinks, 'I will soon need some more.' How will the price elasticity of demand differ between these two customers?

3 Why may a food shop charge higher prices than supermarkets for 'essential items' and yet very similar prices for delicatessen items?

4 How will the position and shape of a firm's short-run demand curve depend on the prices that rivals charge?

5 Assuming that a firm under monopolistic competition can make supernormal profits in the short run, will there be any difference in the long-run and short-run elasticity of demand? Explain.

6 Firms under monopolistic competition generally have spare capacity. Does this imply that if, say, half of the petrol stations were closed down, the consumer would benefit? Explain.

7 Will competition between oligopolists always reduce total industry profits?

8 In which of the following industries is collusion likely to occur: bricks, beer, margarine, cement, crisps, washing powder, blank audio or video cassettes, carpets?

9 Draw a diagram like Figure 12.4. Illustrate what would happen if there were a rise in market demand.

10 Devise a box diagram like that in Table 12.1, only this time assume that there are three firms,

each considering the two strategies of keeping price the same or reducing it by a set amount. Is the game still a 'dominant strategy game'?

11 What are the limitations of game theory in predicting oligopoly behaviour?

12 Which of the following are examples of effective countervailing power?

(a) A power station buying coal from a large local coal mine.
(b) A large factory hiring a photocopier from Rank Xerox.
(c) Marks and Spencer buying clothes from a garment manufacturer.
(d) A small village store (but the only one for miles around) buying food from a wholesaler.

Is it the size of the purchasing firm that is important in determining its power to keep down the prices charged by its suppliers?

Additional Part E case studies on the *Economics for Business* website (www.pearsoned.co.uk/sloman)

E.1 **Is perfect best?** An examination of the meaning of the word 'perfect' in perfect competition.

E.2 **B2B electronic marketplaces.** This case study examines the growth of firms trading with each other over the Internet (business to business or 'B2B') and considers the effects on competition.

E.3 **Measuring monopoly power.** An examination of how the degree of monopoly power possessed by a firm can be measured.

E.4 **X-inefficiency.** A type of inefficiency suffered by many large firms, resulting in a wasteful use of resources.

E.5 **Competition in the pipeline.** An examination of attempts to introduce competition into the gas industry in the UK.

E.6 **Airline deregulation in the USA and Europe.** Whether the deregulation of various routes has led to more competition and lower prices.

E.7 **The motor vehicle repair and servicing industry.** A case study of monopolistic competition.

E.8 **Bakeries: oligopoly or monopolistic competition.** A case study on the bread industry, showing that small-scale local bakeries can exist alongside giant national bakeries.

E.9 **Oligopoly in the brewing industry.** A case study showing how the UK brewing industry is becoming more concentrated.

E.10 **OPEC.** A case study examining OPEC's influence over oil prices from the early 1970s to the current day.

Websites relevant to Part E

Numbers and sections refer to websites listed in the Web appendix and hotlinked from this book's website at **www.pearsoned.co.uk/sloman**

- For news articles relevant to Part E, see the *Economics News Articles* link from the book's website.

- For general news on companies and markets, see websites in section A, and particularly A1, 2, 3, 4, 5, 8, 9, 18, 23, 24, 25, 26, 35, 36. See also A38, 39 and 43 for links to newspapers worldwide; and A42 for links to economics news articles from newspapers worldwide.

- For sites that look at competition and market power, see B2; E4, 10, 18; G7, 8. See also links in I7, 11, 14 and 17. In particular see the following links in sites I7: *Microeconomics > Competition and Monopoly*.

- For a site on game theory, see A40 including its home page. See also D4; C20; I17 and 4 (in the EconDirectory section).

Chapter 14

Alternative theories of the firm

> **Business issues covered in this chapter**
>
> - Why is it often difficult for a firm to identify its profit-maximising price and output?
> - Why may managers pursue goals other than maximising profit?
> - What other goals might they pursue?
> - What will be the effect of alternative business objectives on price and output?
> - Why might businesses have multiple objectives and, if they do, how do they reconcile conflicts between them?

14.1 PROBLEMS WITH TRADITIONAL THEORY

The traditional profit-maximising theories of the firm have been criticised for being unrealistic. The criticisms are mainly of two sorts: (a) that firms wish to maximise profits, but for some reason or other are unable to do so; or (b) that firms have aims other than profit maximisation. Let us examine each in turn.

Difficulties in maximising profit

One criticism of traditional theory sometimes put forward is that firms do not use MR and MC concepts. This may be true, but firms could still arrive at maximum profit by trial and error adjustments of price, or by finding the output where TR and TC are furthest apart. Provided they end up maximising profits, they will be equating MC and MR, even if they do not know it! In this case, traditional models will still be useful in predicting price and output.

Lack of information

The main difficulty in trying to maximise profits is a lack of information.

Firms may well use accountants' cost concepts not based on opportunity cost (see section 9.1). If it is thereby impossible to measure true profit, a firm will not be able to maximise profit except by chance.

More importantly, firms are unlikely to know precisely (or even approximately) their demand curves and hence their *MR* curves. Even though (presumably) they will know how much they are selling at the moment, this only gives them one point on their demand curve and no point at all on their *MR* curve. In order to make even an informed guess about marginal revenue, they must have some idea of how responsive demand will be to a change in price. But how are they to estimate this price elasticity? Market research may help. But even this is frequently very unreliable.

The biggest problem in estimating the firm's demand curve is in estimating the actions and reactions of *other* firms and their effects. Collusion between oligopolists or price leadership would help, but there will still be a considerable area of uncertainty, especially if the firm faces competition from abroad or from other industries.

Game theory may help a firm decide its price and output strategy: it may choose to sacrifice the chance of getting the absolute maximum profit (the high-risk, maximax option), and instead go for the safe strategy of getting probably at least reasonable profits (maximin). But even this assumes that it knows the consequences for its profits of each of the possible reactions of its rivals. In reality, it will not even have this information to any degree of certainty, because it simply will not be able to predict just how consumers will respond to each of its rivals' alternative reactions.

> **Pause for thought**
>
> *What cost concepts are there other than those based on opportunity cost? Would the use of these concepts be likely to lead to an output greater or less than the profit-maximising one?*

Time period

Finally, there is the problem in deciding the *time period* over which the firm should be seeking to maximise profits. Firms operate in a changing environment. Demand curves shift; supply curves shift. Some of these shifts occur as a result of factors outside the firm's control, such as changes in competitors' prices and products, or changes in technology. Some, however, change as a direct result of a firm's policies, such as an advertising campaign, the development of a new improved product, or the installation of new equipment. The firm is not, therefore, faced with static cost and revenue curves from which it can read off its profit-maximising price and output. Instead it is faced with a changing (and often highly unpredictable) set of curves. If it chooses a price and an output that maximise profits this year, it may as a result jeopardise profits in the future.

Take a simple example. The firm may be considering whether to invest in new expensive equipment. If it does, its costs will rise in the short run and thus short-run profits will fall. On the other hand, if the quality of the product thereby increases, demand is likely to increase over the longer run. Also variable costs are likely to decrease if the new equipment is more efficient. In other words, long-run profit is likely to increase, but probably by a highly uncertain amount.

Given these extreme problems in deciding profit-maximising price and output, firms may adopt simple rules of thumb for pricing. These are examined in Chapter 17.

Alternative aims

An even more fundamental attack on the traditional theory of the firm is that firms do not even *aim* to maximise profits (even if they could).

The traditional theory of the firm assumes that it is the *owners* of the firm that make price and output decisions. It is reasonable to assume that owners *will* want to maximise profits: this much most of the critics of the traditional theory accept. The question is, however, whether the owners do in fact make the decisions.

Alternative Theories of the Firm

In Chapter 3 we saw that in public limited companies there is generally a separation of ownership and control. The shareholders are the owners and presumably will want the firm to maximise profits so as to increase their dividends and the value of their shares. Shareholders elect directors. Directors in turn employ professional managers, who are often given considerable discretion in making decisions. But what are the objectives of managers? Will *they* want to maximise profits, or will they have some other aim?

Managers may be assumed to want to *maximise their own utility*. This may well involve pursuits that conflict with profit maximisation. They may, for example, pursue higher salaries, greater power or prestige, better working conditions, greater sales, etc. Different managers in the same firm may well pursue different aims.

Managers will still have to ensure that *sufficient* profits are made to keep shareholders happy, but that may be very different from *maximising* profits.

Alternative theories of the firm to those of profit maximisation, therefore, tend to assume that large firms are profit satisficers. That is, managers strive hard for a minimum target level of profit, but are less interested in profits above this level.

Such theories fall into two categories: first those theories that assume that firms attempt to maximise some other aim, provided that sufficient profits are achieved (these are examined in section 14.2); and second, those theories that assume that firms pursue a number of potentially conflicting aims, of which sufficient profit is merely one (these theories are examined in section 14.3).

> **Definitions**
>
> **Profit satisficing**
> Where decision-makers in a firm aim for a target level of profit rather than the absolute maximum level.
>
> **Long-run profit maximisation**
> An alternative theory which assumes that managers aim to shift cost and revenue curves so as to maximise profits over some longer time period.

ALTERNATIVE MAXIMISING THEORIES 14.2

Long-run profit maximisation

The traditional theory of the firm is based on the assumption of *short-run* profit maximisation. Many actions of firms may be seen to conflict with this aim and yet could be consistent with the aim of long-run profit maximisation. For example, policies to increase the size of the firm or the firm's share of the market may involve heavy advertising or low prices to the detriment of short-run profits. But if this results in the firm becoming larger, with a larger share of the market, the resulting economic power may enable the firm to make larger profits in the long run.

At first sight, a theory of long-run profit maximisation would seem to be a realistic alternative to the traditional short-run profit-maximisation theory. In practice, however, the theory is not a very useful predictor of firms' behaviour and is very difficult to test.

A claim by managers that they were attempting to maximise long-run profits could be an excuse for virtually any policy. When challenged as to why the firm had, say, undertaken expensive research, or high-cost investment, or engaged in a damaging price war, the managers could reply, 'Ah, yes, but in the long run it will pay off.' This is very difficult to refute (until it is too late!).

Even if long-run profit maximisation *is* the prime aim, the means of achieving it are extremely complex. The firm will need a plan of action for prices, output, investment, etc., stretching from now into the future. But today's prices and marketing decisions affect tomorrow's demand. Therefore, future demand curves cannot be taken as given. Similarly, today's investment decisions will affect tomorrow's costs. Therefore, future cost curves cannot be taken as given. These shifts in demand and cost curves will be very difficult to estimate with any precision. Quite apart from

> **BOX 14.1 IN SEARCH OF LONG-RUN PROFITS**
>
> ### The video games war
>
> Traditional economic theory argues that firms will seek to maximise their short-run profits, and therefore adopt a range of strategies to achieve this goal. There are, however, plenty of examples from the world of business to suggest that firms often take a longer-term perspective. One example is the long-running video games war between Sony, Nintendo and Microsoft.
>
> #### The static games console market
>
> The static console games market is now dominated by Nintendo and its Wii with estimated global sales by the end of 2008 of 44.5 million units, followed by Microsoft's Xbox 360 with sales of 27.7 million units and Sony's PlayStation 3 with sales of 24.2 million units.[1]
>
> It wasn't always this way. New console developments, which occur every few years, have a dramatic impact on the shape of the industry. For example, Nintendo was the industry leader with its GameCube until the mid-1990s when Sony launched its PlayStation 1. Sony managed to increase its sales from 2000 when it launched PlayStation 2 but it suffered a set back in 2005 when, because of technical difficulties, it failed to deliver PlayStation 3 on schedule.
>
> Microsoft launched Xbox 360 in November 2005 at prices between £209 and £279.99, depending on whether a basic or premium model was purchased, and it quickly became the market leader. However, when Nintendo launched the Wii in 2006 at a price of £179, targeting a much wider audience than the traditional male gamer aged 16 to 24, it was catapulted into first place in the market. In response, Microsoft has slashed prices below that of Nintendo, but this has had a limited impact on market shares to date.
>
> #### The market for mobile gaming hardware
>
> The other strand of the gaming market is the mobile gaming sector, but Microsoft is notably absent from this segment thus far. Mobile gaming is also dominated today by Nintendo, primarily because of its main product, the DS, which had cumulative global sales of 77.5 million units by the end of 2008.[2] Sony successfully entered the market in 2004 with its own mobile gaming handset, the PSP, and had sold 41 million units by the end of 2008.
>
> However, both are facing new competitive pressure from firms such as Apple, which manufactures the iPhone and iPod Touch. These two devices have gaming capability because users can upload games software from the online 'App Store'. Some 100 days after Apple launched its online App Store in late 2008, there were 200 million downloads from the store and six out of the top ten downloads were games.
>
> It is difficult to say what impact Apple or other potential entrants will have on the mobile gaming market – the primary function of the iPhone and the iPod Touch is not
>
> ---
>
> [1] 'Microsoft will cut Xbox prices in the US', *Business Week*, 3 September 2008.
>
> [2] 'Apple gets in touch with the console market', *Guardian*, 15 January 2009.

this, the actions of competitors, suppliers, unions and so on are difficult to predict. Thus the picture of firms making precise calculations of long-run profit-maximising prices and outputs is a false one.

It may be useful, however, simply to observe that firms, when making current price, output and investment decisions, try to judge the approximate effect on new entrants, consumer demand, future costs, etc., and try to avoid decisions that would appear to conflict with long-run profits. Often this will simply involve avoiding making decisions (e.g. cutting price) that may stimulate an unfavourable reaction from rivals (e.g. rivals cutting their price).

> **Definition**
>
> **Managerial utility maximisation**
> An alternative theory which assumes that managers are motivated by self-interest. They will adopt whatever policies are perceived to maximise their own utility.

Managerial utility maximisation

One of the most influential of the alternative theories of the firm, managerial utility maximisation, was developed by O.E. Williamson[1] in the 1960s. Williamson argued that, provided satisfactory levels of profit are achieved, managers often have the discretion to choose what policies to pursue. In other words, they are free

---

[1] *The Economics of Discretionary Behaviour* (Prentice Hall, 1964), p. 3.

gaming – but clearly technologies such as phones, cameras, media players, office organisers and games machines can be converged on to one handheld device because that is what many consumers like.

The secret of success

The gaming market is a rich source of income and grown rapidly in recent times. Mintel[3] reports that the number of Internet users in the UK over 16 years old who consider themselves avid gamers has increased by over 7 per cent from 22 to 29 per cent over the period 2006 to 2008. Higher income groups are the largest users of computer games and women are no longer peripheral users of games. The report also shows that the number of handheld and static consoles owned by consumers increased from 2005 to 2007. It seems therefore that consumers like dedicated games machines too.

Static and mobile console sales are only successful if they play games and have other features that are attractive to consumers. Strong vertical relationships with gaming software companies are essential. Only technologically sophisticated games that appeal to particular audiences are chosen by console manufacturers. Console manufacturers reportedly earn a royalty of approximately $10 per sale from the licence they grant to the software developer, and so getting the right games is essential. This helps lower the substantial set-up costs in console development but, more importantly, good games generate greater software sales and create a network of loyal users.

Another important feature of these best-selling static and mobile gaming machines is online gaming capability and global connectivity. Console owners can play a favourite game online against a stranger in another part of the world. Moreover, connection to the Internet has facilitated a move towards the use of consoles as 'digital entertainment centres', in which users can download content, including TV channels, films and music. These developments will continue as long as broadband Internet connectivity improves and remains fairly cheap to use.

All three companies – Nintendo, Sony and Microsoft – know how to be successful in the gaming industry: technological excellence and innovation, appropriate pricing strategies and visionary marketing. There are high costs, but high rewards if the business is a long-term venture.

1. What can you say about the price and income elasticity of demand for new technologies such as the Nintendo Wii?
2. How does the maximisation of long-run profits conflict with the maximisation of short-run profits?
3. What factors might favour collusion in the video games market? What factors might make collusion unlikely?

---

[3] *Video and Computer Games*, Mintel, August 2008.

---

to pursue their own interests. And what are the managers' interests? To maximise their own utility, argued Williamson.

Williamson identified a number of factors that affect a manager's utility. The four main ones were salary, job security, dominance (including status, power and prestige) and professional excellence.

Of these only salary is *directly* measurable. The rest have to be measured indirectly. One way of doing this is to examine managers' expenditure on various items, and in particular on *staff*, on *perks* (such as a company car and a plush office) and on *discretionary investment*. The greater the level of expenditure by managers on these items, the greater is likely to be their status, power, prestige, professional excellence and job security, and hence utility.

Having identified the factors that influence a manager's utility, Williamson developed several models in which managers seek to maximise their utility. He used these models to predict managerial behaviour under various conditions and argued that they performed better than traditional profit-maximising theory.

One important conclusion was that average costs are likely to be higher when managers have the discretion to pursue their own utility. For example, perks and unnecessarily high staffing levels add to costs. On the other hand, the resulting 'slack' allows managers to rein in these costs in times of low demand (see page 293). This enables them to maintain their profit levels. To support these claims he conducted a number of case studies. These did indeed show that staff and perks were cut during recessions and expanded during booms, and that new managers were frequently able to reduce staff levels without influencing the productivity of firms.

Sales revenue maximisation (short run)

Perhaps the most famous of all alternative theories of the firm is that developed by William Baumol in the late 1950s. This is the theory of sales revenue maximisation. Unlike the theories of long-run profit maximisation and managerial utility maximisation, it is easy to identify the price and output that meet this aim – at least in the short run.

So why should managers want to maximise their firm's sales revenue? The answer is that the success of managers, and especially sales managers, may be judged according to the level of the firm's sales. Sales figures are an obvious barometer of the firm's health. Managers' salaries, power and prestige may depend directly on sales revenue. The firm's sales representatives may be paid commission on their sales. Thus sales revenue maximisation may be a more dominant aim in the firm than profit maximisation, particularly if it has a dominant sales department.

Sales revenue will be maximised at the top of the TR curve at output Q_1 in Figure 14.1. Profits, by contrast, would be maximised at Q_2. Thus, for given total revenue and total cost curves, sales revenue maximisation will tend to lead to a higher output and a lower price than profit maximisation.

The firm will still have to make sufficient profits, however, to keep the shareholders happy. Thus firms can be seen to be operating with a profit constraint. They are *profit satisficers*.

The effect of this profit constraint is illustrated in Figure 14.2. The diagram shows a total profit curve. (This is found by simply taking the difference between TR and TC at each output.) Assume that the minimum acceptable profit is Π (whatever the output). Any output greater than Q_3 will give a profit less than Π. Thus the sales revenue maximiser who is also a profit satisficer will produce Q_3 not Q_1. Note, however, that this output is still greater than the profit-maximising output Q_2.

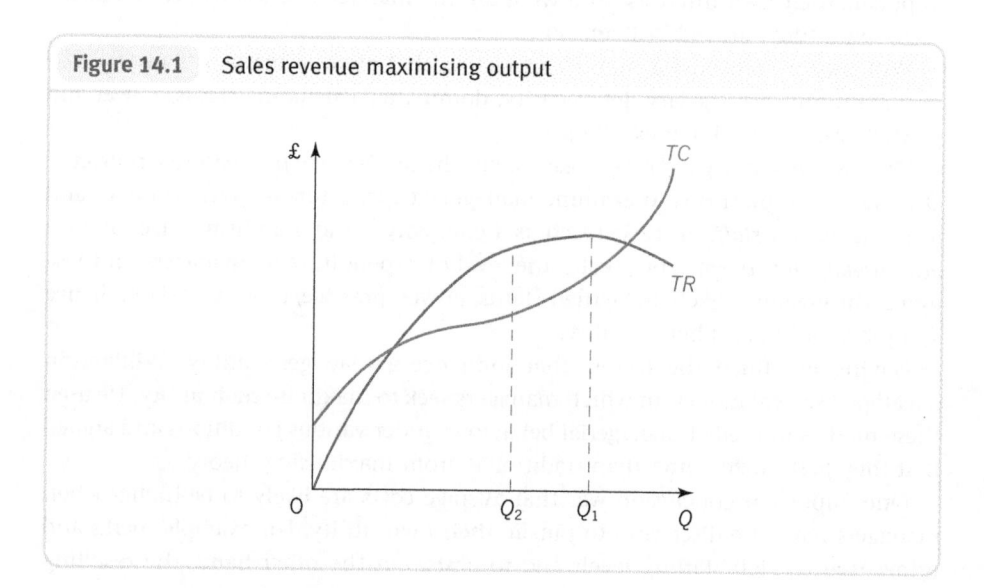

> **Definition**
>
> **Sales revenue maximisation**
> An alternative theory of the firm which assumes that managers aim to maximise the firm's short-run total revenue.

Figure 14.1 Sales revenue maximising output

Figure 14.2 Sales revenue maximising with a profit constraint

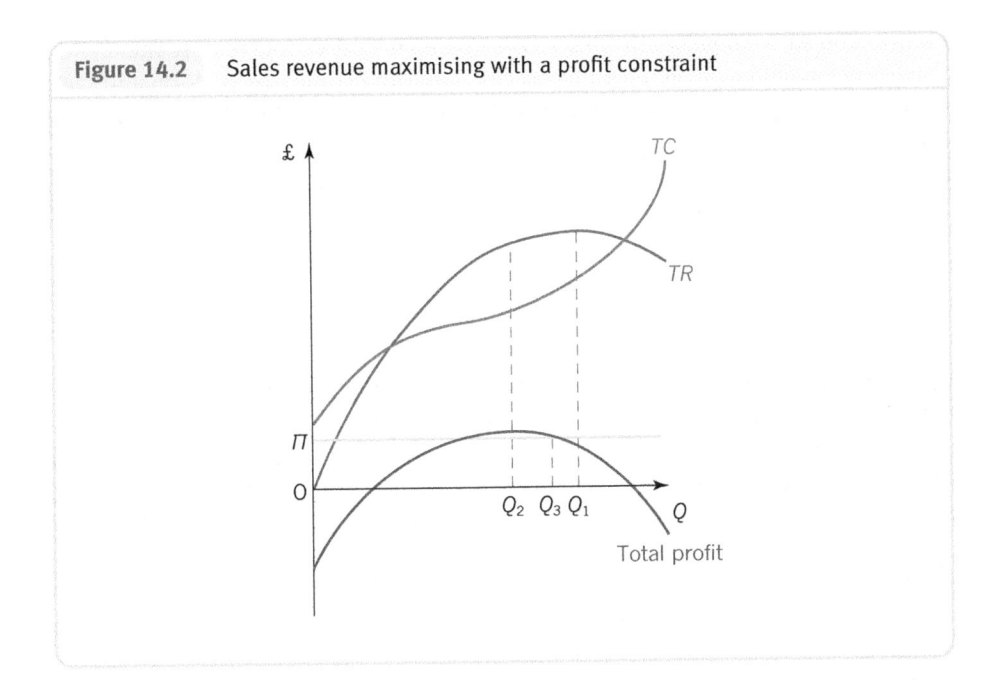

If the firm could maximise sales revenue and still make more than the minimum acceptable profit, it would probably spend this surplus profit on advertising to increase revenue further. This would have the effect of shifting the *TR* curve upward and also the *TC* curve (since advertising costs money).

Sales revenue maximisation will tend to involve more advertising than profit maximisation. Ideally the profit-maximising firm will advertise up to the point where the marginal revenue of advertising equals the marginal cost of advertising (assuming diminishing returns to advertising). The firm aiming to maximise sales revenue will go beyond this, since further advertising, although costing more than it earns the firm, will still add to total revenue. The firm will continue advertising until surplus profits above the minimum have been used up.

Growth maximisation

Rather than aiming to maximise *short-run* revenue, managers may take a longer-term perspective and aim for growth maximisation in the size of the firm. They may gain utility directly from being part of a rapidly growing 'dynamic' organisation; promotion prospects are greater in an expanding organisation, since new posts tend to be created; large firms may pay higher salaries; managers may obtain greater power in a large firm.

Growth is probably best measured in terms of a growth in sales revenue, since sales revenue (or 'turnover') is the simplest way of measuring the size of a business. An alternative would be to measure the capital value of a firm, but this will depend on the ups and downs of the stock market and is thus a rather unreliable method.

If a firm is to maximise growth, it needs to be clear about the time period over which it is setting itself this objective. For example, maximum growth over the next two or three years might be obtained by running factories to absolute maximum capacity, cramming in as many machines and workers as possible, and backing this up with massive advertising campaigns and price cuts. Such policies, however, may not be sustainable in the longer run. The firm may simply not be able to finance

> **Definition**
>
> **Growth maximisation**
> An alternative theory which assumes that managers seek to maximise the growth in sales revenue (or the capital value of the firm) over time.

them. A longer-term perspective (say, 5–10 years) may therefore require the firm to 'pace' itself, and perhaps to direct resources away from current production and sales into the development of new products that have a potentially high and growing long-term demand.

Equilibrium for a growth-maximising firm

What will a growth-maximising firm's price and output be? Unfortunately, there is no simple formula for predicting this.

In the short run, the firm may choose the profit-maximising price and output – so as to provide the greatest funds for investment. On the other hand, it may be prepared to sacrifice some short-term profits in order to mount an advertising campaign. It all depends on the strategy it considers most suitable to achieve growth.

In the long run, prediction is more difficult still. The policies that a firm adopts will depend crucially on the assessments of market opportunities made by managers. But this involves judgement, not fine calculation. Different managers will judge a situation differently.

One prediction can be made. Growth-maximising firms are likely to diversify into different products, especially as they approach the limits to expansion in existing markets.

Alternative growth strategies are considered in Chapter 15.

Alternative maximising theories and the consumer

It is difficult to draw firm conclusions about how the behaviour of firms in these alternative maximising theories will affect the consumer's interest.

In the case of sales revenue maximisation, a higher output will be produced than under profit maximisation, but the consumer will not necessarily benefit from lower prices, since more will be spent on advertising – costs that will be passed on to the consumer.

In the case of growth and long-run profit maximisation, there are many possible policies that a firm could pursue. To the extent that a concern for the long run encourages firms to look to improved products, new products and new techniques, the consumer may benefit from such a concern. To the extent, however, that growth encourages a greater level of industrial concentration through merger, the consumer may lose from the resulting greater level of monopoly power.

As with the traditional theory of the firm, the degree of competition that a firm faces is a crucial factor in determining just how responsive it will be to the wishes of the consumer.

> **Pause for thought**
>
> *How will competition between growth-maximising firms benefit the consumer?*

14.3 MULTIPLE AIMS

Satisficing and the setting of targets

Firms may have more than one aim. For example, they may try to achieve increased sales revenue *and* increased profit. The problem with this is that, if two aims conflict, it will not be possible to maximise both of them. For example, sales revenue will probably be maximised at a different price and output from that at which profits are maximised. Where firms have two or more aims, a compromise may be for targets to be set for individual aims which are low enough to achieve simultaneously, and yet which are sufficient to satisfy the interested parties. This is known as 'satisficing' (as opposed to maximising) behaviour.

Such target setting is also likely when the maximum value of a particular aim is unknown. If, for example, the maximum achievable profit is unknown, the firm may well set a target for profit which it feels is both satisfactory and achievable.

Behavioural theories of the firm: the setting of targets

A major advance in alternative theories of the firm has been the development of behavioural theories.[2] Rather than setting up a model to show how various objectives could in theory be achieved, behavioural theories of the firm are based on observations of how firms *actually* behave.

Large firms are often complex institutions with several departments (sales, production, design, purchasing, personnel, finance, etc.). Each department is likely to have its own specific set of aims and objectives, which may possibly come into conflict with those of other departments. These aims in turn will be constrained by the interests of shareholders, workers, customers and creditors (collectively known as stakeholders), who will need to be kept sufficiently happy.

Behavioural theories do not lay down rules of how to *achieve* these aims, but rather examine what these aims are, the motivations underlying them, the conflicts that can arise between aims, and how these conflicts are resolved.

In many firms, targets are set for production, sales, profit, stockholding, etc. If, in practice, target levels are not achieved, a 'search' procedure will be started to find what went wrong and how to rectify it. If the problem cannot be rectified, managers will probably adjust the target downwards. If, on the other hand, targets are easily achieved, managers may adjust them upwards. Thus the targets to which managers aspire depend to a large extent on the success in achieving *previous* targets. Targets are also influenced by expectations of demand and costs, by the achievements of competitors and by expectations of competitors' future behaviour. For example, if it is expected that the economy is likely to move into recession, sales and profit targets may be adjusted downwards.

If targets conflict, the conflict will be settled by a bargaining process between managers. The outcome of the bargaining, however, will depend on the power and ability of the individual managers concerned. Thus a similar set of conflicting targets may be resolved differently in different firms.

Behavioural theories of the firm: organisational slack

Since changing targets often involves search procedures and bargaining processes and is therefore time consuming, and since many managers prefer to avoid conflict, targets tend to be changed fairly infrequently. Business conditions, however, often change rapidly. To avoid the need to change targets, therefore, managers will tend to be fairly conservative in their aspirations. This leads to the phenomenon known as organisational slack.

When the firm does better than planned, it will allow slack to develop. This slack can then be taken up if the firm does worse than planned. For example, if the firm produces more than it planned, it will build up stocks of finished goods and draw

> **Definitions**
>
> **Behavioural theories of the firm**
> Theories that attempt to predict the actions of firms by studying the behaviour of various groups of people within the firm and their interactions under conditions of potentially conflicting interests.
>
> **Stakeholders (in a company)**
> People who are affected by a company's activities and/or performance (customers, employees, owners, creditors, people living in the neighbourhood, etc.). They may or may not be in a position to take decisions, or influence decision taking, in the firm.
>
> **Organisational slack**
> When managers allow spare capacity to exist, thereby enabling them to respond more easily to changed circumstances.

---

[2] See in particular: R. M. Cyert and J. G. March, *A Behavioural Theory of the Firm* (Prentice Hall, 1963).

BOX 14.2 STAKEHOLDER POWER

Who governs the firm?

The concept of the 'stakeholder economy' became fashionable in the late 1990s. Rather than the economy being governed by big business, and rather than businesses being governed in the interests of shareholders (many of whom are big institutions, such as insurance companies and pension funds), the economy should serve the interests of everyone. But what does this mean for the governance of firms?

The stakeholders of a firm include customers, employees (from senior managers to the lowest-paid workers), shareholders, suppliers, lenders and the local and national communities.

The supporters of a stakeholding economy argue that *all* these interest groups ought to have a say in the decisions of the firm. Trade unions or workers' councils ought to be included in decisions affecting the workforce, or indeed all company decisions. They could be represented on decision-making bodies and perhaps have seats on the board of directors. Alternatively, the workforce might be given the power to elect managers.

Banks or other institutions lending to firms ought to be included in investment decisions. In Germany, where banks finance a large proportion of investment, banks are represented on the boards of most large companies.

Local communities ought to have a say in any projects (such as new buildings or the discharge of effluent) that affect the local environment. Customers ought to have more say in the quality of products being produced, for example by being given legal protection against the production of shoddy or unsafe goods. Where interest groups cannot be directly represented in decision making, then companies ought to be regulated by the government in order to protect the interests of the various groups. For example, if farmers and other suppliers to supermarkets are paid very low prices, then the purchasing behaviour of the supermarkets could be regulated by some government agency.

But is this vision of a stakeholder economy likely to become reality? Trends in the international economy suggest that the opposite might be occurring. The growth of multinational corporations, with their ability to move finance and production to wherever it is most profitable, has weakened the power of employees, local interest groups and even national governments.

Employees in one part of the multinational may have little in the way of common interests with employees in another. In fact, they may vie with each other, for example over which plant should be expanded or closed down. What is more, many firms are employing a larger and larger proportion of casual, part-time, temporary or agency workers. With these new 'flexible labour markets' such employees have far less say in the company than permanent members of staff: they are 'outsiders' to decision making within the firm (see section 18.7).

Also, the widespread introduction of share incentive schemes for managers (whereby managers are rewarded with shares) has increasingly made profits their driving goal. Finally, the policies of opening up markets and deregulation, policies that were adopted by many governments round the world up to the mid-1990s, have again weakened the power of many stakeholders.

Are customers' interests best served by profit-maximising firms, answerable primarily to shareholders, or by firms where various stakeholder groups are represented in decision taking?

---

on them if production subsequently falls. It would not, in the meantime, increase its sales target or reduce its production target. If it did, and production then fell below target, the production department might not be able to supply the sales department with its full requirement.

Thus keeping targets fairly low and allowing slack to develop allows all targets to be met with minimum conflict.

Organisational slack, however, adds to a firm's costs. If firms are operating in a competitive environment, they may be forced to cut slack in order to survive. In the 1970s, many Japanese firms succeeded in cutting slack by using **just-in-time** methods of production. These involve keeping stocks to a minimum and ensuring that inputs are delivered as required. Clearly, this requires that production is tightly controlled and that suppliers are reliable. Many firms today have successfully cut their warehouse costs by using such methods. These methods are examined in section 18.7.

Definition

Just-in-time methods
Where a firm purchases supplies and produces both components and finished products as they are required. This minimises stockholding and its associated costs.

Multiple goals: some predictions of behaviour

Conservatism

Some firms may be wary of unnecessary change. Change is risky. They may prefer to stick with tried and tested practices. 'If it works, stick with it.' This could apply to pricing policies, marketing techniques, product design and range, internal organisation of the firm, etc.

If something does not work, however, managers will probably change it, but again they may be conservative and only try a cautious change: perhaps imitating successful competitors.

This safe, satisficing approach makes prediction of any given firm's behaviour relatively easy. You simply examine its past behaviour. Making generalisations about all such cautious firms, however, is more difficult. Different firms are likely to have established different rules of behaviour depending on their own particular experiences of their market.

Comparison with other firms

Managers may judge their success by comparing their firm's performance with that of rival firms. For example, growing market share may be seen as a more important indicator of 'success' than simple growth in sales. Similarly, they may compare their profits, their product design, their technology or their industrial relations with those of rivals. To many managers it is *relative* performance that matters, rather than absolute performance.

What predictions can be made if this is how managers behave? The answer is that it depends on the nature of competition in the industry. The more profitable, innovative and efficient are the competitors, the more profitable, innovative and efficient will managers try to make their particular firm.

The further ahead of their rivals that firms try to stay, the more likely it is that there will be a 'snowballing' effect: each firm trying to outdo the other.

> **Pause for thought**
>
> *Will this type of behaviour tend to lead to profit maximisation?*

Satisficing and the consumer's interest

Firms with multiple goals will be satisficers. The greater the number of goals of the different managers, the greater is the chance of conflict and the more likely it is that organisational slack will develop. Satisficing firms are therefore likely to be less responsive to changes in consumer demand and changes in costs than profit-maximising firms. They may thus be less efficient.

On the other hand, such firms may be less eager to exploit their economic power by charging high prices, or to use aggressive advertising, or to pay low wages.

The extent to which satisficing firms do act in the public interest will, as in the case of other types of firm, depend to a large extent on the amount and type of competition they face, and their attitudes towards this competition. Firms that compare their performance with that of their rivals are more likely to be responsive to consumer wishes than firms that prefer to stick to well-established practices. On the other hand, they may be more concerned to 'manipulate' consumer tastes than the more traditional firm.

SUMMARY

1a There are two major types of criticism of the traditional profit-maximising theory: (a) firms may not have the information to maximise profits; (b) they may not even want to maximise profits.

1b Lack of information on demand and costs and on the actions and reactions of rivals, and a lack of use of opportunity cost concepts may mean that firms adopt simple 'rules of thumb' for pricing.

1c In large companies there is likely to be a divorce between ownership and control. The shareholders (the owners) may want maximum profits, but it is the managers who make the decisions, and managers are likely to aim to maximise their own utility rather than that of the shareholders. This leads to profit 'satisficing'. This is where managers aim to achieve sufficient profits to keep shareholders happy, but this is a secondary aim to one or more alternative aims.

1d Some alternative theories assume that there is a single alternative aim that firms seek to maximise. Others assume that managers have a series of (possibly conflicting) aims.

2a Rather than seeking to maximise short-run profits, a firm may take a longer-term perspective. It is very difficult, however, to predict the behaviour of a long-run profit-maximising firm, since (a) different managers are likely to make different judgements about how to achieve maximum profits, and (b) demand and cost curves may shift unpredictably both in response to the firm's own policies and as a result of external factors.

2b Managers may seek to maximise their own utility, which, in turn, will depend on factors such as salary, job security, power within the organisation and the achievement of professional excellence. Given, however, that managerial utility depends on a range of variables, it is difficult to use the theory to make general predictions of firms' behaviour.

2c Managers may gain utility from maximising sales revenue. However, they will still have to ensure that a satisfactory level of profit is achieved. The output of a firm which seeks to maximise sales revenue will be higher than that for a profit-maximising firm. Its level of advertising will also tend to be higher. Whether price will be higher or lower depends on the relative effects on demand and the cost of the additional advertising.

2d Many managers aim for maximum growth of their organisation, believing that this will help their salaries, power, prestige, etc.

2e As with long-run profit-maximising theories, it is difficult to predict the price and output strategies of a growth-maximising firm. Much depends on the judgements of particular managers about growth opportunities.

3a In large firms, decisions are taken by, or influenced by, a number of different people, including various managers, shareholders, workers, customers, suppliers and creditors. If these different people have different aims, then a conflict between them is likely to arise. A firm cannot maximise more than one of these conflicting aims. The alternative is to seek to achieve a satisfactory target level of a number of aims.

3b Behavioural theories of the firm examine how managers and other interest groups actually behave, rather than merely identifying various equilibrium positions for output, price, investment, etc.

3c If targets were easily achieved last year, they are likely to be made more ambitious next year. If they were not achieved, a search procedure will be conducted to identify how to rectify the problem. This may mean adjusting targets downwards, in which case there will be some form of bargaining process between managers.

3d Life is made easier for managers if conflict can be avoided. This will be possible if slack is allowed to develop in various parts of the firm. If targets are not being met, the slack can then be taken up without requiring adjustments in other targets.

3e Satisficing firms may be less innovative, less aggressive and less willing to initiate change. If they do change, it is more likely to be in response to changes made by their competitors. Managers may judge their performance by comparing it with that of rivals.

3f Satisficing firms may be less aggressive in exploiting a position of market power. On the other hand, they may suffer from greater inefficiency.

REVIEW QUESTIONS

1. In the traditional theory of the firm, decision-makers are often assumed to have perfect knowledge and to be able to act, therefore, with complete certainty. It is now widely accepted that in practice firms will be certain about very few things. Of the following: (a) production costs; (b) demand; (c) elasticity; (d) supply; (e) consumer tastes; (f) technology; (g) government policy, which might they be certain of? Which might they be uncertain of?

2. Make a list of six aims that a manager of a high street department store might have. Identify some conflicts that might arise between these aims.

3. When are increased profits in a manager's personal interest?

4. Draw a diagram with *MC* and *MR* curves. Mark the output (a) at which profits are maximised; (b) at which sales revenue is maximised.

5. Since advertising increases a firm's costs, will prices necessarily be lower with sales revenue maximisation than with profit maximisation?

6. We have seen that a firm aiming to maximise sales revenue will tend to produce more than a profit-maximising firm. This conclusion certainly applies under monopoly and oligopoly. Will it also apply under (a) perfect competition and (b) monopolistic competition, where in both cases there is freedom of entry?

7. A frequent complaint of junior and some senior managers is that they are frequently faced with new targets from above, and that this makes their life difficult. If their complaint is true, does this conflict with the hypothesis that managers will try to build in slack?

8. What evidence about firms' behaviour could be used to refute the argument that firms will tend to build in organisational slack and as a result be inherently conservative?

Chapter 20

Reasons for government intervention in the market

Business issues covered in this chapter

- To what extent does business meet the interests of consumers and society in general?
- In what sense are perfect markets 'socially efficient' and why do most markets fail to achieve social efficiency?
- In what ways do governments intervene in markets and attempt to influence business behaviour?
- Can taxation be used to correct the shortcomings of markets, or is it better to use the law?
- What are the drawbacks of government intervention?
- What is meant by 'corporate social responsibility' and what determines firms' attitudes towards society and the environment?
- What is the relationship between business ethics and business performance?

20.1 MARKETS AND THE ROLE OF GOVERNMENT

Government intervention and social objectives

In order to decide the optimum amount of government intervention, it is first necessary to identify the various social goals that intervention is designed to meet. Two of the major objectives of government intervention identified by economists are social efficiency and equity.

Definitions

Social efficiency
Production and consumption at the point where $MSB = MSC$.

Equity
The fair distribution of a society's resources.

Social efficiency. If the marginal benefits to society – or 'marginal social benefits' (*MSB*) – of producing any given good or service exceed the marginal costs to society or 'marginal social costs' (*MSC*) – then it is said to be socially efficient to produce more. For example, if people's gains from having additional motorways exceed *all* the additional costs to society (both financial and non-financial) then it is socially efficient to construct more motorways.

If, however, the marginal social costs of producing any good or service exceed the marginal social benefits, then it is socially efficient to produce less.

It follows that if the marginal social benefits of any activity are equal to the marginal social costs, then the current level is the optimum. To summarise: for social efficiency in the production of any good or service:

$MSB > MSC \rightarrow$ produce more

$MSC > MSB \rightarrow$ produce less

$MSB = MSC \rightarrow$ keep production at its current level

Similar rules apply to consumption. For example, if the marginal social benefits of consuming more of any good or service exceed the marginal social costs, then society would benefit from more of the good being consumed.

Social efficiency is an example of 'allocative efficiency': in other words, the best allocation of resources between alternative uses.

> **KEY IDEA 30**
>
> **Allocative efficiency in any activity is achieved where any reallocation would lead to a decline in net benefit.** It is achieved where marginal benefit equals marginal cost. Private efficiency is achieved where marginal private benefit equals marginal private cost ($MB = MC$). Social efficiency is achieved where marginal social benefit equals marginal social cost ($MSB = MSC$).

In the real world, the market rarely leads to social efficiency: the marginal social benefits of most goods and services do not equal the marginal social costs. In this chapter we examine why the free market fails to lead to social efficiency and what the government can do to rectify the situation. We also examine why the government itself may fail to achieve social efficiency.

> **KEY IDEA 31**
>
> **Markets generally fail to achieve social efficiency.** There are various types of market failure. Market failures provide one of the major justifications for government intervention in the economy.

Equity. Most people would argue that the free market fails to lead to a *fair* distribution of resources, if it results in some people living in great affluence while others live in dire poverty. Clearly what constitutes 'fairness' is a highly contentious issue: those on the political right generally have a quite different view from those on the political left. Nevertheless, most people would argue that the government does have some duty to redistribute incomes from the rich to the poor through the tax and benefit system, and perhaps to provide various forms of legal protection for the poor (such as a minimum wage rate).

> **KEY IDEA 32**
> *Equity* is where income is distributed in a way that is considered to be fair or just. Note that an equitable distribution is not the same as a totally equal distribution and that different people have different views on what is equitable.

Although our prime concern in this chapter is the question of social efficiency, we will be touching on questions of distribution too.

TYPES OF MARKET FAILURE 20.2

Externalities

The market will not lead to social efficiency if the actions of producers or consumers affect people *other than themselves*. These effects on other people are known as **externalities**: they are the side-effects, or 'third-party' effects, of production or consumption. Externalities can be either desirable or undesirable. Whenever other people are affected beneficially, there are said to be **external benefits**. Whenever other people are affected adversely, there are said to be **external costs**.

> **KEY IDEA 33**
> *Externalities are spillover costs or benefits.* Where these exist, even an otherwise perfect market will fail to achieve social efficiency.

Definitions

Externalities
Costs or benefits of production or consumption experienced by society but not by the producers or consumers themselves. Sometimes referred to as 'spillover' or 'third-party' costs or benefits.

External benefits
Benefits from production (or consumption) experienced by people *other* than the producer (or consumer).

External costs
Costs of production (or consumption) borne by people *other* than the producer (or consumer).

Social cost
Private cost plus externalities in production.

Social benefit
Private benefit plus externalities in consumption.

Thus the full cost to society (the *social cost*) of the production of any good or service is the private cost faced by firms plus any externalities of production (positive or negative). Likewise the full benefit to society (the *social benefit*) from the consumption of any good is the private benefit enjoyed by consumers plus any externalities of consumption (positive or negative).

There are four major types of externality.

External costs of production (MSC > MC)

When a chemical firm dumps waste in a river or pollutes the air, the community bears costs additional to those borne by the firm. The marginal *social* cost (MSC) of chemical production exceeds the marginal private cost (MC). Diagrammatically, the MSC curve is above the MC curve. This is shown in Figure 20.1(a), which assumes that the firm in other respects is operating in a perfect market, and is therefore a price taker (i.e. faces a horizontal demand curve).

The firm maximises profits at Q_1: the output where marginal cost equals price (see section 11.2). The price is what people buying the good are prepared to pay for one more unit (if it wasn't, they wouldn't buy it) and therefore reflects their marginal benefit. We assume no externalities from consumption, and therefore the marginal benefit to consumers is the same as the marginal *social* benefit (MSB).

The socially optimum output would be Q_2, where P (i.e. MSB) = MSC. The firm, however, produces Q_1, which is more than the optimum. Thus external costs lead to overproduction from society's point of view.

The problem of external costs arises in a free-market economy because no one has legal ownership of the air or rivers and no one, therefore, can prevent or charge

Figure 20.1 Externalities in production (a) External costs from production (b) External benefits from production

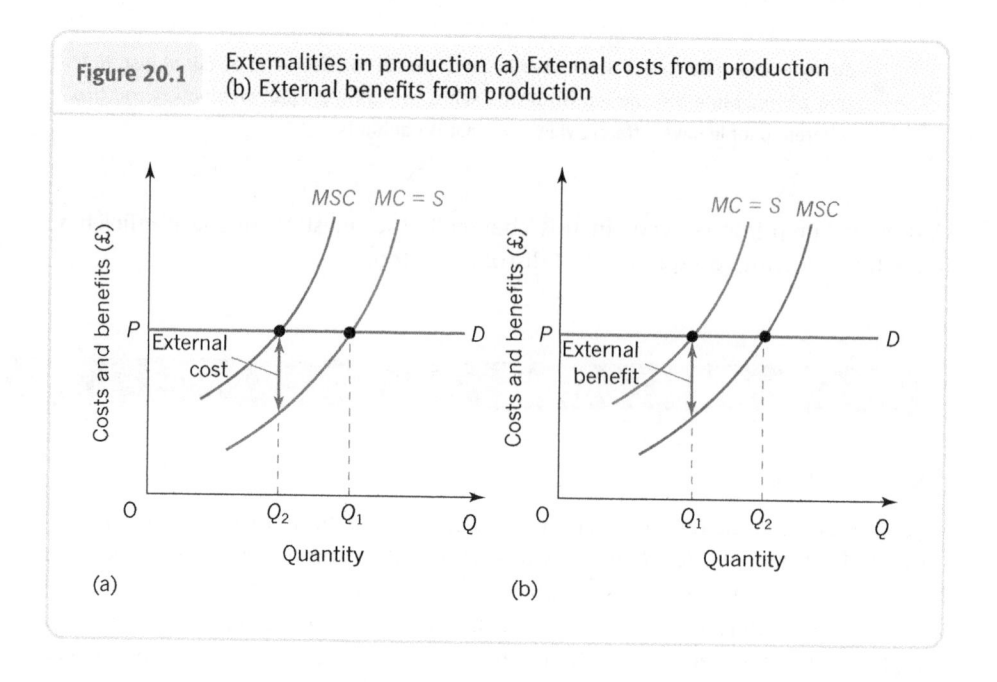

for their use as a dump for waste. Such a 'market' is missing. Control must, therefore, be left to the government or local authorities.

Other examples include extensive farming that destroys hedgerows and wildlife, and global warming caused by CO_2 emissions from power stations.

External benefits of production (MSC < MC)

If a forestry company plants new woodlands, there is a benefit not only to the company itself, but also to the world through a reduction of CO_2 in the atmosphere (forests are a carbon sink). The marginal *social* cost of providing timber, therefore, is less than the marginal *private* cost to the company.

In Figure 20.1(b), the *MSC* curve is *below* the *MC* curve. The level of output provided by a forestry company is Q_1, where $P = MC$, a *lower* level than the social optimum, Q_2, where $P = MSC$.

Another example of external benefits in production is that of research and development. If other firms have access to the results of the research, then clearly the benefits extend beyond the firm which finances it. Since the firm only receives the private benefits, it will conduct a less than optimal amount of research.

External costs of consumption (MSB < MB)

When people use their cars, other people suffer from their exhaust, the added congestion, the noise, etc. These 'negative externalities' make the marginal social benefit of using cars less than the marginal private benefit (i.e. marginal utility to the car user).

Figure 20.2(a) shows the marginal utility and price to a motorist (i.e. the consumer) of using a car. The optimal distance travelled for this motorist will be Q_1 miles: i.e. where $MU = P$ (where price is the cost of petrol, oil, wear and tear, etc. per mile). The *social* optimum, however, would be less than this, namely Q_2, where $MSB = P$.

Other examples of negative externalities of consumption include noisy radios in public places, the smoke from cigarettes, and litter.

Reasons for Government Intervention in the Market **167**

Figure 20.2 Externalities in consumption (a) External cost from consumption (b) External benefit from consumption

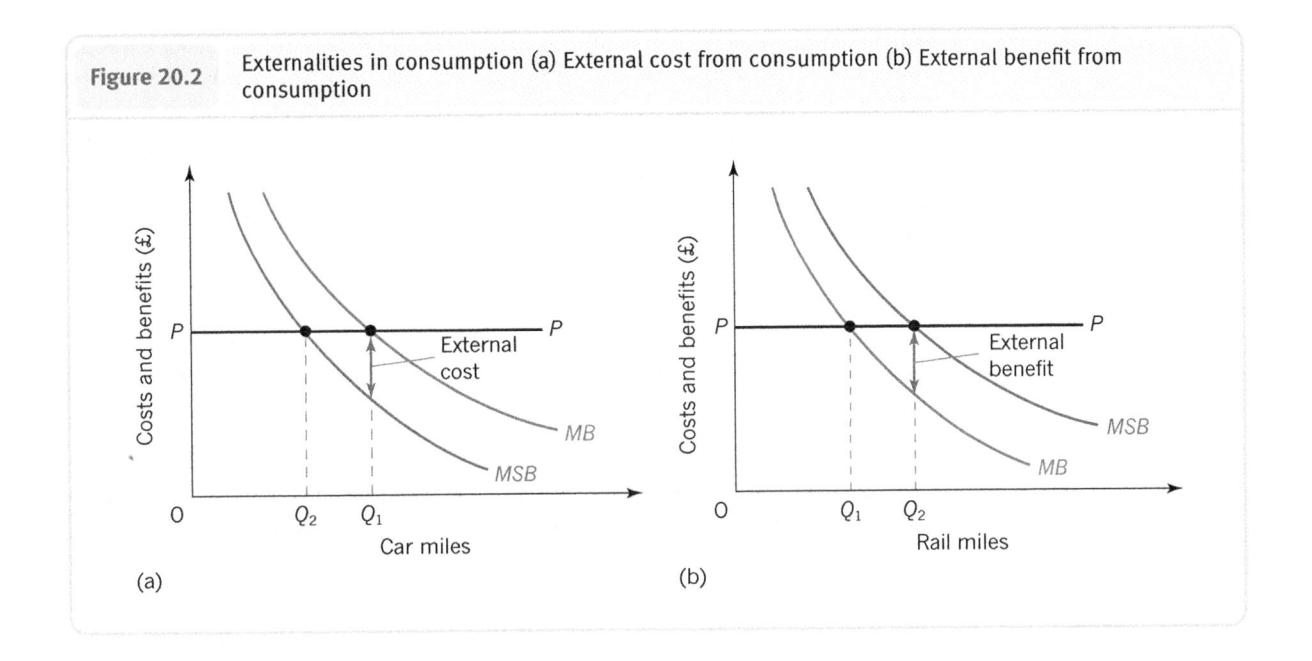

(a) Graph with Costs and benefits (£) on vertical axis, Car miles on horizontal axis. Horizontal line at P. Two downward-sloping curves labelled MB (outer) and MSB (inner). External cost shown between them. Quantities $Q_2 < Q_1$ marked.

(b) Graph with Costs and benefits (£) on vertical axis, Rail miles on horizontal axis. Horizontal line at P. Two downward-sloping curves labelled MSB (outer) and MB (inner). External benefit shown between them. Quantities $Q_1 < Q_2$ marked.

External benefits of consumption (MSB > MB)

When people travel by train rather than by car, other people benefit by there being less congestion and exhaust and fewer accidents on the roads. Thus the marginal social benefit of rail travel is *greater* than the marginal private benefit (i.e. the marginal utility to the rail passenger). There are external benefits from rail travel. In Figure 20.2(b), the *MSB* curve is *above* the private *MB* curve. The actual level of consumption (Q_1) is thus below the socially optimal level of consumption (Q_2).

Other examples include the beneficial effects for other people of deodorants, vaccinations and attractive clothing.

> **Definition**
>
> **Public good**
> A good or service which has the features of non-rivalry and non-excludability and as a result would not be provided by the free market.

To summarise: whenever there are external benefits, there will be too little produced or consumed. Whenever there are external costs, there will be too much produced or consumed. The market will not equate *MSB* and *MSC*.

The above arguments have been developed in the context of perfect competition with prices given to the producer or consumer by the market. Externalities also occur in all other types of market.

> **Pause for thought**
>
> *Give other examples of each of the four types of externality.*

Public goods

There is a category of goods where the positive externalities are so great that the free market, whether perfect or imperfect, may not produce at all. They are called public goods. Examples include lighthouses, pavements, flood control dams, public drainage, public services such as the police and even government itself.

Public goods have two important characteristics: *non-rivalry* and *non-excludability*:

- If I consume a bar of chocolate, it cannot then be consumed by someone else. If, however, I enjoy the benefits of street lighting, it does not prevent you or anyone else doing the

> **Pause for thought**
>
> *Which of the following have the property of non-rivalry: (a) a can of drink; (b) public transport; (c) a commercial radio broadcast; (d) the sight of flowers in a public park?*

> **Definitions**
>
> **Non-rivalry**
> Where the consumption of a good or service by one person will not prevent others from enjoying it.
>
> **Non-excludability**
> Where it is not possible to provide a good or service to one person without it thereby being available for others to enjoy.
>
> **Free-rider problem**
> When it is not possible to exclude other people from consuming a good that someone has bought.

same. There is thus what we call **non-rivalry** in the consumption of such goods. These goods tend to have large external benefits relative to private benefits. This makes them socially desirable, but privately unprofitable. No one person on their own would pay to have a pavement built along his or her street. The private benefit would be too small relative to the cost. And yet the social benefit to all the other people using the pavement may far outweigh the cost.

If I spend money erecting a flood control dam to protect my house, my neighbours will also be protected by the dam. I cannot prevent them enjoying the benefits of my expenditure. This feature of **non-excludability** means that they would get the benefits free, and would therefore have no incentive to pay themselves. This is known as the **free-rider problem**.

> **KEY IDEA 34**
>
> *The free-rider problem.* People are often unwilling to pay for things if they can make use of things other people have bought. This problem can lead to people not purchasing things which would be to the benefit of them and other members of society to have.

When goods have these two features, the free market will simply not provide them. Thus these public goods can only be provided by the government or by the government subsidising private firms. (Note that not all goods and services produced by the public sector come into the category of public goods and services: thus education and health are publicly provided, but they *can* be, and indeed are, privately provided.)

Market power

Whenever markets are imperfect, whether as pure monopoly or monopsony or whether as some form of imperfect competition, the market will fail to equate MSB and MSC, even if there are no externalities.

Take the case of monopoly. A monopoly will produce less than the socially efficient output. This is illustrated in Figure 20.3. A monopoly faces a downward-sloping demand curve, and therefore marginal revenue is below average revenue ($= P = MSB$). Profits are maximised at an output of Q_1, where marginal revenue equals marginal cost (see Figure 11.6 on page 225). If there are no externalities, the socially efficient output will be at the higher level of Q_2, where $MSB = MSC$.

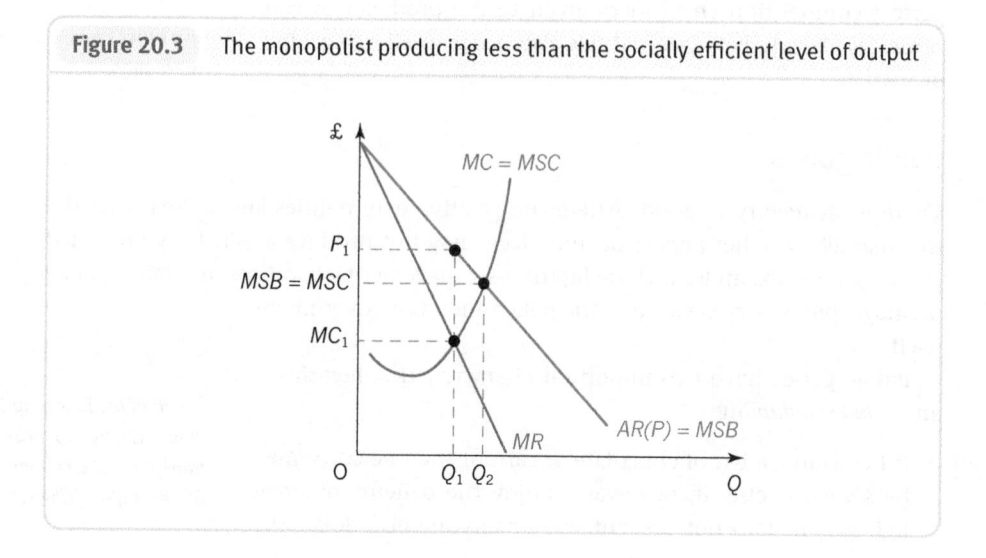

Figure 20.3 The monopolist producing less than the socially efficient level of output

Figure 20.4 Deadweight loss from monopoly

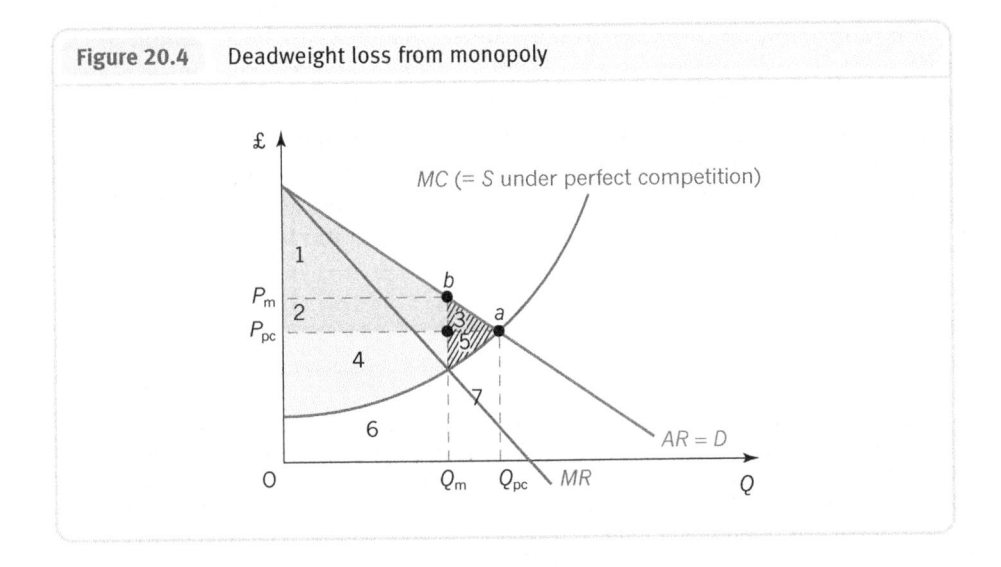

Deadweight loss under monopoly

One way of analysing the welfare loss that occurs under monopoly is to use the concepts of *consumer* and *producer surplus*. The two concepts are illustrated in Figure 20.4. The diagram shows an industry which is initially under perfect competition and then becomes a monopoly (but faces the same revenue and cost curves).

Consumer surplus. As we saw on page 109, consumer surplus from a good is the difference between the total utility received by consumers and their total expenditure on the good. Under *perfect competition* the industry will produce an output of Q_{pc} at a price of P_{pc}, where $MC(=S) = P(=AR)$: i.e. at point *a*. Consumers' total utility is given by the area under the demand (MU) curve (the sum of all the areas 1–7). Consumers' total expenditure is $P_{pc} \times Q_{pc}$ (areas 4 + 5 + 6 + 7). Consumers' surplus is thus the area between the price and the demand curve (areas 1 + 2 + 3).

Producer surplus. Producer surplus is similar to profit. It is the difference between total revenue and total variable cost. (It will be more than profit if there are any fixed costs.) Total revenue is $P_{pc} \times Q_{pc}$ (areas 4 + 5 + 6 + 7). Total cost is the area under the MC curve (areas 6 + 7). The reason for this is that each point on the marginal cost curve shows what the last unit costs to produce. The area under the MC curve thus gives all the marginal costs starting from an output of zero to the current output: i.e. it gives total costs. Producer surplus is thus the area between the price and the MC curve (areas 4 + 5).

Total (private) surplus. Total consumer plus producer surplus is therefore the area between the demand and MC curves. This is shown by the total shaded area (areas 1 + 2 + 3 + 4 + 5).

The effect of monopoly on total surplus

What happens when the industry is under *monopoly*? The firm will produce where $MC = MR$, at an output of Q_m and a price of P_m (at point *b* on the demand curve). Total revenue is $P_m \times Q_m$ (areas 2 + 4 + 6). Total cost is the area under the MC curve (area 6). Thus the producer surplus is areas 2 + 4. This is clearly a *larger* surplus than under perfect competition (since area 2 is larger than area 5): monopoly profits are larger than profits under perfect competition.

> **Definitions**
>
> **Consumer surplus**
> The excess of what a person would have been prepared to pay for a good (i.e. the utility measured in money terms) over what that person actually pays. Total consumer surplus equals total utility minus total expenditure.
>
> **Producer surplus**
> The excess of a firm's total revenue over its total (variable) cost.

Consumer surplus, however, will be much smaller. With consumption at Q_m, total utility is given by areas 1 + 2 + 4 + 6, whereas consumer expenditure is given by areas 2 + 4 + 6. Consumer surplus, then, is simply area 1. (Note that area 2 has been transformed from consumer surplus to producer surplus.)

Total surplus under monopoly is therefore areas 1 + 2 + 4: a smaller surplus than under perfect competition. 'Monopolisation' of the industry has resulted in a loss of total surplus of areas 3 + 5. The producer's gain has been more than offset

---

BOX 20.1 CAN THE MARKET PROVIDE ADEQUATE PROTECTION FOR THE ENVIRONMENT?

In recent years people have become acutely aware of the damage being done to the environment by pollution. But if the tipping of chemicals and sewage into the rivers and seas and the spewing of toxic gases into the atmosphere cause so much damage, why does it continue? If we all suffer from these activities, both consumers and producers alike, then why will a pure market system not deal with the problem? After all, a market should respond to people's interests.

The reason is that the costs of pollution are largely *external* costs. They are borne by society at large and only very slightly (if at all) by the polluter. If, for example, 10 000 people suffer from the smoke from a factory (including the factory owner) then that owner will only bear approximately 1/10 000 of the suffering. That personal cost may be quite insignificant when the owner is deciding whether the factory is profitable. And if the owner lives far away, the personal cost of the pollution will be zero.

Thus the *social* costs of polluting activities exceed the *private* costs. If people behave selfishly and only take into account the effect their actions have on themselves, there will be an *overproduction* of polluting activities.

Thus it is argued that governments must intervene to prevent or regulate pollution, or alternatively to tax the polluting activities or subsidise measures to reduce the pollution (see section 22.1).

But if people are purely selfish, why do they buy 'green' products? Why do they buy, for example, 'ozone-friendly' aerosols? After all, the amount of damage done to the ozone layer from their own personal use of 'non-friendly' aerosols would be absolutely minute. The answer is that many people have a social conscience. They *do* sometimes take into account the effect their actions have on other people. They are not totally selfish. They like to do their own little bit, however small, towards protecting the environment.

Nevertheless to rely on people's consciences may be a very unsatisfactory method of controlling pollution. In a market environment where people are all the time being encouraged to consume more and more goods and where materialism is the religion of the age, there would have to be a massive shift towards 'green thinking' if the market were to be a sufficient answer to the problem of pollution.

Certain types of environmental problem may get high priority in the media, such as global warming or toxic waste. However, the sheer range of polluting activities makes reliance on people's awareness of the problems and their social consciences far too arbitrary.

> The table gives the costs and benefits of an imaginary firm operating under perfect competition whose activities create a certain amount of pollution. (It is assumed that the costs of this pollution to society can be accurately measured.)
> (a) What is the profit-maximising level of output for this firm?
> (b) What is the socially efficient level of output?
> (c) Why might the marginal pollution costs increase in the way illustrated in this example?

Output (units)	Price per unit (MSB) (£)	Marginal (private) costs to the firm (MC) (£)	Marginal external (pollution) costs (MEC) (£)	Marginal social costs (MSC = MC + MEC) (£)
1	100	30	20	50
2	100	30	22	52
3	100	35	25	60
4	100	45	30	75
5	100	60	40	100
6	100	78	55	133
7	100	100	77	177
8	100	130	110	240

by the consumers' loss. This loss of surplus is known as deadweight welfare loss of monopoly.

Ignorance and uncertainty

Perfect competition assumes that consumers, firms and factor suppliers have perfect knowledge of costs and benefits. In the real world there is often a great deal of ignorance and uncertainty. Thus people are unable to equate marginal benefit with marginal cost.

Consumers purchase many goods only once or a few times in a lifetime. Cars, washing machines, televisions and other consumer durables fall into this category. Consumers may not be aware of the quality of such goods until they have purchased them, by which time it is too late. Advertising may contribute to people's ignorance by misleading them as to the benefits of a good.

Firms are often ignorant of market opportunities, prices, costs, the productivity of workers (especially white-collar workers), the activity of rivals, etc.

Many economic decisions are based on expected future conditions. Since the future can never be known for certain, many decisions may turn out to be wrong.

Immobility of factors and time-lags in response

Even under conditions of perfect competition, factors may be very slow to respond to changes in demand or supply. Labour, for example, may be highly immobile both occupationally and geographically. This can lead to large price changes and hence to large supernormal profits and high wages for those in the sectors of rising demand or falling costs. The long run may be a very long time coming!

In the meantime, there will be further changes in the conditions of demand and supply. Thus the economy is in a constant state of disequilibrium and the long run never comes. As firms and consumers respond to market signals and move towards equilibrium, so the equilibrium position moves and the social optimum is never achieved.

> **KEY IDEA 35**
> *The problem of time lags.* Many economic actions can take a long time to take effect. This can cause problems of instability and an inability of the economy to achieve social efficiency.

Whenever monopoly/monopsony power exists, the problem is made worse as firms or unions put up barriers to the entry of new firms or factors of production.

Protecting people's interests

The government may feel that people need protecting from poor economic decisions that they make on their *own* behalf. It may feel that in a free market people will consume too many harmful things. Thus if the government wants to discourage smoking and drinking, it can put taxes on tobacco and alcohol. In more extreme cases it could make various activities illegal: activities such as prostitution, certain types of gambling, and the sale and consumption of drugs.

On the other hand, the government may feel that people consume too little of things that are good for them: things such as education, health care and sports facilities. Such goods are known as merit goods. The government could either provide them free or subsidise their production.

> **Definitions**
>
> **Deadweight welfare loss**
> The loss of consumer plus producer surplus in imperfect markets (when compared with perfect competition).
>
> **Merit goods**
> Goods which the government feels that people will underconsume and which therefore ought to be subsidised or provided free.

20.3 GOVERNMENT INTERVENTION IN THE MARKET

Faced with all the problems of the free market, what is a government to do?

There are several policy instruments that the government can use. At one extreme, it can totally replace the market by providing goods and services itself. At the other extreme, it can merely seek to persuade producers, consumers or workers to act differently. Between the two extremes the government has a number of instruments it can use to change the way markets operate. These include taxes, subsidies, laws and regulatory bodies. In this section we examine these different forms of government intervention.

> **KEY IDEA 36**
>
> *Government intervention may be able to rectify various failings of the market.* Government intervention in the market can be used to achieve various economic objectives which may not be best achieved by the market. Governments, however, are not perfect, and their actions may bring adverse as well as beneficial consequences.

Taxes and subsidies

When there are imperfections in the market, social efficiency will not be achieved. Marginal social benefit (*MSB*) will not equal marginal social cost (*MSC*). A different level of output would be more desirable.

Taxes and subsidies can be used to correct these imperfections. Essentially the approach is to tax those goods or activities where the market produces too much, and subsidise those where the market produces too little.

Taxes and subsidies to correct externalities. The rule here is simple: the government should impose a tax equal to the marginal external cost (or grant a subsidy equal to the marginal external benefit).

Assume, for example, that a chemical works emits smoke from a chimney and thus pollutes the atmosphere. This creates external costs for the people who breathe in the smoke. The marginal social cost of producing the chemicals thus exceeds the marginal private cost to the firm: $MSC > MC$.

This is illustrated in Figure 20.5. The marginal pollution cost (the externality) is shown by the vertical distance between the *MC* and *MSC* curves. For simplicity, it is assumed that the firm is a price taker. It produces Q_1 where $P = MC$ (its profit-maximising output), but in doing so takes no account of the external pollution costs it imposes on society.

If the government now imposes a tax on production equal to the marginal pollution cost, it will effectively 'internalise' the externality. The firm will have to pay an amount equal to the external cost it creates. It will therefore now maximise profits at Q_2, which is the socially optimum output where $MSB = MSC$.

Taxes and subsidies to correct for monopoly. If the problem of monopoly that the government wishes to tackle is that of *excessive profits*, it can impose a lump-sum tax on the monopolist: that is, a tax of a fixed absolute amount irrespective of how much the monopolist produces, or the price it charges. Since a lump-sum tax is an additional *fixed* cost to the firm, and hence will not affect the firm's marginal cost, it will not reduce the amount that the monopolist produces (which *would* be

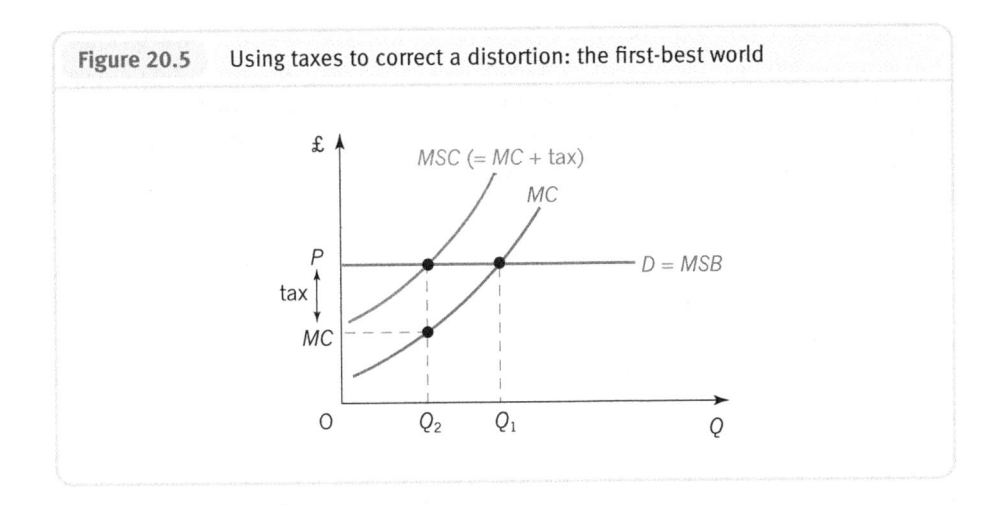

Figure 20.5 Using taxes to correct a distortion: the first-best world

[Figure: Graph showing MSC (= MC + tax) curve above MC curve, with horizontal D = MSB line at price P. Tax is the vertical distance between MC and MSC at quantity Q_2. Q_2 is the socially efficient output, Q_1 is the market output.]

the case with a per-unit tax). Two examples of such taxes are the 'windfall taxes' imposed by the UK Labour government. The first, in 1997, was on the profits of various privatised utilities. The second, in 2005, was on the 'excess' profits of oil companies operating in the North Sea. These had been the result of large increases in world oil prices.

If the government is concerned that the monopolist produces *less* than the socially efficient output, it could give the monopolist a per-unit *subsidy* (which would encourage the monopolist to produce more). But would this not *increase* the monopolist's profit? The answer to this is to impose a harsh lump-sum tax in addition to the subsidy. The tax would not undo the subsidy's benefit of encouraging the monopolist to produce more, but it could be used to reduce the monopolist's profits below the original (i.e. pre-subsidy) level.

Advantages of taxes and subsidies

Many economists favour the tax/subsidy solution to market imperfections (especially the problem of externalities) because it still allows the market to operate. It forces firms to take on board the full social costs and benefits of their actions. It is also adjustable according to the magnitude of the problem.

What is more, by taxing firms for polluting, say, they are encouraged to find cleaner ways of producing. The tax thus acts as an incentive over the longer run to reduce pollution: the more a firm can reduce its pollution, the more taxes it can save.

Likewise, when *good* practices are subsidised, firms are given the incentive to adopt more good practices.

Disadvantages of taxes and subsidies

Infeasible to use different tax and subsidy rates. Each firm produces different levels and types of externality and operates under different degrees of imperfect competition. It would be expensive and administratively very difficult, if not impossible, to charge every offending firm its own particular tax rate (or grant every relevant firm its own particular rate of subsidy).

> **Pause for thought**
>
> Why is it easier to use taxes and subsidies to tackle the problem of car exhaust pollution than to tackle the problem of peak-time traffic congestion in cities?

Lack of knowledge. Even if a government did decide to charge a tax equal to each offending firm's marginal external costs, it would still have the problem of measuring that cost and apportioning blame. The damage to lakes and forests from acid rain has been a major concern since the beginning of the 1980s. But just how serious is that damage? What is its current monetary cost? How long lasting is the damage? What will be the position in 20 years? Just what and who are to blame? These are questions that cannot be answered precisely. It is thus impossible to fix the 'correct' pollution tax on, say, a particular coal-fired power station.

Despite these problems, it is nevertheless possible to charge firms by the amount of a particular emission. For example, firms could be charged for chimney smoke by so many parts per million of a given pollutant. Although it is difficult to 'fine-tune' such a system so that the charge reflects the precise number of people affected by the pollutant and by how much, it does go some way to internalising the externality.

Changes in property rights

One cause of market failure is the limited nature of property rights. If someone dumps a load of rubble in your garden, you can insist that it is removed. If, however, someone dumps a load of rubble in his or her *own* garden, which is next door to yours, what can you do? You can still see it from your window. It is still an eyesore. But you have no property rights over the next-door garden.

Property rights define who owns property, to what uses it can be put, the rights other people have over it and how it may be transferred. By *extending* these rights, individuals may be able to prevent other people imposing costs on them, or charge them for doing so.

The socially efficient level of charge would be one that was equal to the marginal external cost (and would have the same effect as the government charging a tax on the firm of that amount (see Figure 20.5). The Coase theorem[1] states that in an otherwise perfectly competitive market, the socially efficient charge *will* be levied. But why?

Let us take the case of river pollution by a chemical works that imposes a cost on people fishing in the river. If property rights to the river were now given to the fishing community, they could impose a charge on the chemical works per unit of output. If they charged *less* than the marginal external cost, they would suffer more from the last unit (in terms of lost fish) than they were being compensated. If they charged *more*, and thereby caused the firm to cut back its output below the socially efficient level, they would be sacrificing receiving charges that would be greater than the marginal suffering. It will be in the sufferers' best interests, therefore, to charge an amount *equal* to the marginal externality.

In most instances, however, this type of solution is totally impractical. It is impractical when *many* people are *slightly* inconvenienced, especially if there are many culprits imposing the costs. For example, if I were disturbed by noisy lorries outside my home, it would not be practical to negotiate with every haulage company involved. What if I wanted to ban the lorries from the street, but my next-door neighbour wanted to charge them 10p per journey? Who gets their way?

The extension of private property rights becomes a more practical solution where the culprits are few in number, are easily identifiable and impose clearly defined costs. Thus a noise abatement act could be passed which allowed me to prevent

> **Pause for thought**
>
> *If the sufferers had no property rights, show how it would still be in their interests to 'bribe' the firm to produce the socially efficient level of output.*

> **Definition**
>
> **Coase theorem**
> When sufferers from externalities do deals with perpetrators (by levying charges or offering bribes), the externality will be 'internalised' and the socially efficient level of output will be achieved.

---

[1] Named after Ronald Coase, who developed the theory. See his article, 'The problem of social cost', *Journal of Law and Economics* (1960).

Reasons for Government Intervention in the Market

BOX 20.2 DEADWEIGHT LOSS FROM TAXES ON GOODS AND SERVICES

The excess burden of taxes

Taxation can be used to correct market failures, but taxes can have adverse effects themselves. One such effect is the deadweight loss that results when taxes are imposed on goods and services.

The diagram shows the demand and supply of a particular good. Equilibrium is initially at a price of P_1 and a level of sales of Q_1 (i.e. where $D = S$). Now an excise tax is imposed on the good. The supply curve shifts upwards by the amount of the tax, to S + tax. Equilibrium price rises to P_2 and equilibrium quantity falls to Q_2. Producers receive an after-tax price of P_2 − tax.

Consumer surplus falls from areas 1 + 2 + 3, to area 1 (the upper grey area). Producer surplus falls from areas 4 + 5 + 6 to area 6 (the lower grey area). Does this mean, therefore, that total surplus falls by areas 2 + 3 + 4 + 5? The answer is no, because there is a gain to the government from the tax revenue (and hence a gain to the population from the resulting government expenditure). The revenue from the tax is known as the government surplus. It is given by areas 2 + 4 (the blue area).

But, even after including government surplus, there is still a fall in total surplus of areas 3 + 5 (the pink area). This is the deadweight loss of the tax. It is sometimes known as the excess burden of the tax.

Does this loss of total surplus from taxation imply that taxes on goods are always a 'bad thing'? The answer is no. This conclusion would only follow in a 'first-best' world where there were no market failures: where competition was perfect, where there were no externalities and where income distribution was optimum. In such a world, the loss of surplus from imposing a tax on a good would represent a reduction in welfare.

In the real world of imperfect markets and inequality, taxes can do more good than harm. As we have shown in this section, they can help to correct for externalities. They can also be used as a means of redistributing incomes. Nevertheless, the excess burden of taxes is something that ideally ought to be considered when weighing up the desirability of imposing taxes on goods and services, or of increasing their rate.

Deadweight loss from an indirect tax

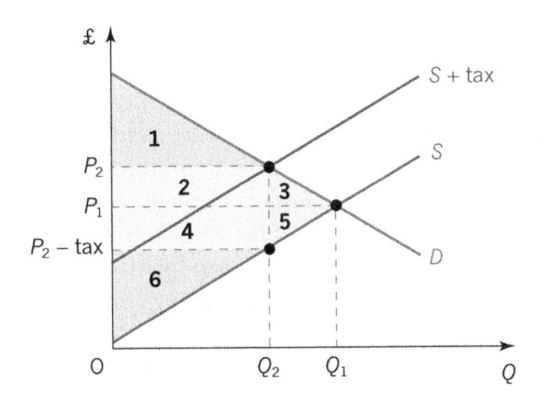

1. How would the burden of taxation change if (a) demand was more inelastic and (b) supply was more inelastic?
2. How far can an economist contribute to this highly political debate over the desirability of an excise tax?

my neighbours playing noisy radios, having noisy parties or otherwise disturbing the peace in my home. The onus would be on me to report them. Or I could agree not to report them if they paid me adequate compensation.

But even in cases where only a few people are involved, there may still be the problem of litigation. I may have to incur the time and expense of taking people to court. Justice may not be free, and there is thus a conflict with equity. The rich can afford 'better' justice. They can employ top lawyers. Thus even if I have a right to sue a large company for dumping toxic waste near me, I may not have the legal muscle to win.

Definitions

Government surplus (from a tax on a good)
The total tax revenue earned by the government from sales of a good.

Excess burden (of a tax on a good)
The amount by which the loss in consumer plus producer surplus exceeds the government surplus.

Finally, there is the broader question of *equity*. The extension of private property rights may favour the rich (who tend to have more property) at the expense of the poor. Ramblers may get great pleasure from strolling across a great country estate, along public rights of way. This may annoy the owner. If the owner's property rights were now extended to exclude the ramblers, is this a social gain?

Of course, equity considerations can also be dealt with by altering property rights, but in a different way. *Public* property like parks, open spaces, libraries and historic buildings could be extended. Also the property of the rich could be redistributed to the poor. Here it is less a question of the rights that ownership confers, and more a question of altering the ownership itself.

> **Pause for thought**
>
> *Would it be a good idea to extend countries' territorial waters in order to bring key open seas fishing grounds within countries' territory? Could it help to solve the problem of overfishing?*

Laws prohibiting or regulating undesirable structures or behaviour

Laws are frequently used to correct market imperfections. Laws can be of three main types: those that prohibit or regulate behaviour that imposes external costs, those that prevent firms providing false or misleading information, and those that prevent or regulate monopolies and oligopolies (see Chapter 21).

Advantages of legal restrictions

- They are usually simple and clear to understand and are often relatively easy to administer. For example, various polluting activities could be banned or restricted.
- When the danger is very great, it might be much safer to ban various practices altogether (e.g. the use of various toxic chemicals) rather than to rely on taxes or on individuals attempting to assert their property rights through the civil courts.
- When a decision needs to be taken quickly, it might be possible to invoke emergency action. For example, in a city like Athens it has been found to be simpler to ban or restrict the use of private cars during a chemical smog emergency than to tax their use.
- Because consumers suffer from imperfect information, consumer protection laws can make it illegal for firms to sell shoddy or unsafe goods, or to make false or misleading claims about their products.

Disadvantages of legal restrictions

The main problem is that legal restrictions tend to be a rather blunt weapon. If, for example, a firm were required to reduce the effluent of a toxic chemical to 20 tonnes per week, there would be no incentive for the firm to reduce it further. With a tax on the effluent, however, the more the firm reduced the effluent, the less tax it would pay. Thus with a system of taxes there is a *continuing* incentive to cut pollution, to improve safety, or whatever.

Regulatory bodies

Rather than using the blunt weapon of general legislation to ban or restrict various activities, a more 'subtle' approach can be adopted. This involves the use of various regulatory bodies. Having identified possible cases where action might be required (e.g. potential cases of pollution, misleading information or the abuse of monopoly power), the regulatory body would probably conduct an investigation and then prepare a report containing its findings and recommendations. It might also have the power to enforce its decisions.

In the UK there are regulatory bodies for each of the major privatised utilities (see section 22.3). Another example is the Office of Fair Trading (OFT), which investigates and reports on suspected cases of anti-competitive practices. The OFT can order such firms to cease or modify these practices. Alternatively it can refer them to the Competition Commission (CC), which then conducts an investigation, and makes a ruling (see section 21.1).

The advantage of such bodies is that a case-by-case approach can be adopted and, as a result, the most appropriate solution adopted. However, investigations may be expensive and time consuming; only a few cases may be examined; and offending firms may make various promises of good behaviour which may not in fact be carried out owing to a lack of follow-up by the regulatory body.

> **Pause for thought**
>
> *What other forms of intervention are likely to be necessary to back up the work of regulatory bodies?*

Price controls

Price controls can be used either to raise prices above, or to reduce them below, the free-market level.

Prices could be raised above the market equilibrium to support the incomes of certain suppliers. For example, until recently, under the Common Agricultural Policy of the European Union, high prices for food were set so as to raise farmers' incomes above the free-market level.

Prices could be lowered in order to protect consumers' interests. For example, the government, or another body, may prevent a monopoly or oligopoly from charging excessive prices. This is one of the major roles of the regulatory bodies for the privatised utilities. Here the industry is not allowed to raise its prices by more than a certain amount below the rate of inflation.

Provision of information

When ignorance is a reason for market failure, the direct provision of information by the government or one of its agencies may help to correct that failure. An example is the information on jobs provided by job centres to those looking for work. They thus help the labour market to work better and increase the elasticity of supply of labour. Another example is the provision of consumer information: for example, on the effects of smoking, or of eating certain foodstuffs. Another is the provision of government statistics on prices, costs, employment, sales trends, etc. This enables firms to plan with greater certainty.

The direct provision of goods and services

In the case of public goods and services, such as streets, pavements, seaside illumination and national defence, the market may completely fail to provide. In this case the government must take over the role of provision. Central government, local government or some other public agency could provide these goods and services directly. Alternatively, they could pay private firms to do so. The public would pay through central and local taxation.

The government could also provide goods and services directly which are *not* public goods. Examples include health and education. There are four reasons why such things are provided free or at well below cost.

Social justice. Society may feel that these things should not be provided according to ability to pay. Rather they should be provided as of right: an equal right based on need.

Large positive externalities. People other than the consumer may benefit substantially. If a person decides to get treatment for an infectious disease, other people benefit by not being infected. A free health service thus helps to combat the spread of disease.

Dependants. If education were not free, and if the quality of education depended on the amount spent, and if parents could choose how much or little to buy, then the quality of children's education would depend not just on their parents' income, but also on how much they cared. A government may choose to provide such things free in order to protect children from 'bad' parents. A similar argument is used for providing free prescriptions and dental treatment for all children.

Ignorance. Consumers may not realise how much they will benefit. If they have to pay, they may choose (unwisely) to go without. Providing health care free may persuade people to consult their doctors before a complaint becomes serious.

20.4 THE CASE FOR LESS GOVERNMENT INTERVENTION

Government intervention in the market can itself lead to problems. The case for less government intervention is not that the market is the *perfect* means of achieving given social goals, but rather that the problems created by intervention are greater than the problems overcome by that intervention.

Drawbacks of government intervention

Shortages and surpluses. If the government intervenes by fixing prices at levels other than the equilibrium, this will create either shortages or surpluses.

If the price is fixed *below* the equilibrium, there will be a shortage. For example, if the rent of council houses is fixed below the equilibrium in order to provide cheap housing for poor people, demand will exceed supply. In the case of such shortages the government will have to adopt a system of waiting lists, or rationing, or giving certain people preferential treatment. Alternatively it will have to allow allocation to be on a first-come, first-served basis or allow queues to develop. Underground markets are likely to occur.

If the price is fixed *above* the equilibrium price, there will be a surplus. For example, if the price of food is fixed above the equilibrium in order to support farmers' incomes, supply will exceed demand. Either government will have to purchase such surpluses and then perhaps store them, throw them away or sell them cheaply in another market, or it will have to ration suppliers by allowing them to produce only a certain quota, or allow them to sell to whom they can.

Poor information. The government may not know the full costs and benefits of its policies. It may genuinely wish to pursue the interests of consumers or any other group and yet may be unaware of people's wishes or misinterpret their behaviour.

Bureaucracy and inefficiency. Government intervention involves administrative costs. The more wide reaching and detailed the intervention, the greater the number of people and material resources that will be involved. These resources may be used wastefully.

Lack of market incentives. If government intervention removes market forces or cushions their effect (by the use of subsidies, welfare provisions, guaranteed prices or wages, etc.), it may remove certain useful incentives. Subsidies may allow inefficient firms to survive. Welfare payments may discourage effort. The market may be imperfect, but it does tend to encourage efficiency by allowing the efficient to receive greater rewards.

Shifts in government policy. The economic efficiency of industry may suffer if government intervention changes too frequently. It makes it difficult for firms to plan if they cannot predict tax rates, subsidies, price and wage controls, etc.

Lack of freedom for the individual. Government intervention involves a loss of freedom for individuals to make economic choices. The argument is not just that the pursuit of individual gain is seen to lead to the social good, but that it is desirable in itself that individuals should be as free as possible to pursue their own interests with the minimum of government interference: that minimum being largely confined to the maintenance of laws consistent with the protection of life, liberty and property.

Advantages of the free market

Although markets in the real world are not perfect, even imperfect markets can be argued to have positive advantages over government provision or even government regulation. These might include the following.

Automatic adjustments. Government intervention requires administration. A free-market economy, on the other hand, leads to the automatic, albeit imperfect, adjustment to demand and supply changes.

Dynamic advantages of capitalism. The chances of making high monopoly/oligopoly profits will encourage entrepreneurs to invest in new products and new techniques. Prices may be high initially, but consumers will gain from the extra choice of products. Furthermore, if profits are high, new firms will sooner or later break into the market and competition will ensue.

> **Pause for thought**
>
> *Are there any features of the free market that would discourage innovation?*

A high degree of competition even under monopoly/oligopoly. Even though an industry at first sight may seem to be highly monopolistic, competitive forces may still work as a result of the following:

- A fear that excessively high profits might encourage firms to attempt to break into the industry (assuming that the market is contestable).
- Competition from closely related industries (e.g. coach services for rail services, or electricity for gas).
- The threat of foreign competition.

- Countervailing powers (see page 249). Large powerful producers often sell to large powerful buyers. For example, the power of detergent manufacturers to drive up the price of washing powder is countered by the power of supermarket chains to drive down the price at which they purchase it. Thus power is to some extent neutralised.
- The competition for corporate control (see page 228).

20.5 FIRMS AND SOCIAL RESPONSIBILITY

Definition

Social responsibility Where a firm takes into account the interests and concerns of a community rather than just its shareholders.

It is often assumed that firms are simply concerned to maximise profits: that they are not concerned with broader issues of social responsibility. What this assumption means is that firms are only concerned with the interests of shareholders (or managers) and are not concerned for the well-being of the community at large.

It is then argued, however, that competitive forces could result in society *benefiting* from the self-interested behaviour of firms: i.e. that profit maximisation will lead to social efficiency under conditions of perfect competition and the absence of externalities. But, as we have seen, in the real world markets are not perfect and there are often considerable externalities. In such cases, a lack of social responsibility on the part of firms can have profoundly adverse effects on society. Indeed, many forms of market failure can be attributed directly to business practices that could not be classified as 'socially responsible': advertising campaigns that seek to misinform, or in some way deceive the consumer; monopoly producers exploiting their monopoly position through charging excessively high prices; the conscious decision to ignore water and air pollution limits, knowing that the chances of being caught are slim.

So should businesses be simply concerned with profit, or should they take broader social issues into account? If they do behave in an anti-social way, is the only answer to rely on government intervention, or are there any social pressures that can be brought to bear to persuade businesses to modify their behaviour?

Two views of social responsibility

The classical view. According to this view, business managers are responsible only to their shareholders, and as such should be concerned solely with profit maximisation. If managers in their business decisions take into account a wider set of social responsibilities, not only will they tend to undermine the market mechanism, but they will be making social policy decisions in fields where they may have little skill or expertise. If being socially responsible ultimately reduces profits, then the shareholder loses and managers have failed to discharge their duty. By diluting their purpose in pursuit of *social* goals, businesses extend their influence over society as a whole, which cannot be good given the lack of public accountability to which business leaders are subject.

The socioeconomic view. This view argues that the role of modern business has changed, and that society expects business to adhere to certain moral and social responsibilities. Modern businesses are seen as more than economic institutions, as they are actively involved in society's social, political and legal environments. As such, all businesses are responsible not only to their shareholders but to all stakeholders. Stakeholders are all those affected by the business's operations: not only shareholders, but workers, customers, suppliers, creditors and people living in the neighbourhood. Given the far-reaching environmental effects of many businesses, stakeholding might extend to the whole of society.

In this view of corporate social responsibility, it is not just a moral argument that managers should take into account broader social and environmental issues, but also a financial one. It is argued that a business will maximise profits over the *long term* only if its various social responsibilities are taken into account. If a business is seen as ignoring the interests of the wider community and failing to protect society's welfare, then this will be 'bad for business': the firm's reputation and image will suffer.

In many top corporations, environmental scanning is now an integral part of the planning process. This involves the business surveying changing political, economic, social, technological, environmental and legal trends in the external environment in order to remain in tune with consumer concerns (see section 1.1). For example, the general public's growing concern over 'green' issues has significantly influenced many businesses' product development programmes and R&D strategies (see Box 20.3 later). The more successful a business is in being able to associate the image of 'environmentally friendly' to a particular product or brand, the more likely it is to enhance its sales or establish a measure of brand loyalty, and thereby to strengthen its competitive position.

Many businesses today thus feel that it is not enough to be seen merely *complying* with laws on the environment, product standards or workplace conditions: i.e. just to be doing the legal minimum. There is now a growing philosophy of 'compliance plus', with many businesses competing against each other in terms of their social image.

But does social responsibility not impose costs on firms, which might more than offset any increase in revenue from increased sales? In fact, the opposite can occur. Socially responsible business can reduce the need for government regulation, and the subsequent costs and restrictions that such intervention places upon managerial decision making. Many industries prefer to be self-regulating, not just to avoid government interference and restrictions, but because they can achieve any given social goal at lower costs: after all, a firm is likely to be better placed than government to know how given standards can be met in its own specific case. It is nevertheless the case that there are still many firms that care little about the environment. They may prefer 'self-regulation' because it makes it easier for them to avoid their social responsibilities!

> **Definitions**
>
> **Stakeholder**
> An individual affected by the operations of a business.
>
> **Environmental scanning**
> Where a business surveys political, economic, social, technological, environmental and legal trends in the external environment to aid its decision-making process.

The virtue matrix: generating corporate social responsibility

In an article in the *Harvard Business Review*,[2] Roger L. Martin developed a framework for analysing corporate social responsibility and the factors that influence it. The framework is the 'virtue matrix' and an adaptation of it is illustrated in Figure 20.6.

The matrix is divided into four cells, each of which shows types of action taken by a firm that have social effects.

---

[2] Roger L. Martin 'The virtue matrix: calculating the return on corporate responsibility', *Harvard Business Review*, March 2002.

Figure 20.6 The 'virtue matrix': generating corporate social responsibility

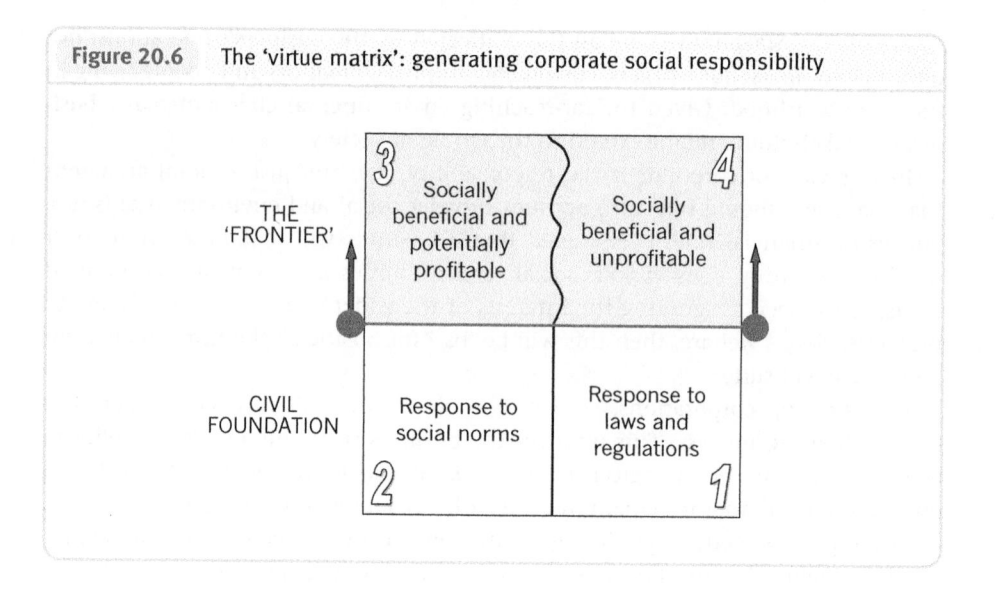

THE 'FRONTIER'	3. Socially beneficial and potentially profitable	4. Socially beneficial and unprofitable
CIVIL FOUNDATION	2. Response to social norms	1. Response to laws and regulations

The civil foundation

The bottom two cells are in what is termed the 'civil foundation'. They refer to socially responsible actions that society expects firms to take and firms will normally do so.

Cell 1 refers to actions in response to laws and regulations. For example, firms may control the emissions of toxic waste because they are obliged to do so by law. Similarly, they may provide a clean and safe environment for their workers because of health and safety legislation.

Cell 2 refers to the types of behaviour expected of firms by society and where firms would come in for criticism, or even condemnation, if they did not abide by these social norms. For example, employers may operate flexible working hours or set up nursery facilities to help workers with small children; manufacturers may landscape the surroundings to their factories or build factories of a pleasant design so as to make them more attractive to local residents and visitors. They are not obliged to take such actions by law, but feel that it is expected of them.

A key point about actions in the civil foundation is that they are likely to be consistent with the aim of profit maximisation or maximising shareholder value. In other words, shareholders' and society's interests are likely to coincide. This is obvious in the case of abiding by the law. Except in cases where breaking the law can go undetected, firms must abide by the law if they are to avoid prosecution with all the risks to profits that this entails. But abiding by social norms (cell 2) is also likely to contribute towards profit. The extra costs associated with such actions will probably be recouped from extra sales associated with achieving a good public image or extra productivity from a contented workforce.

The frontier

The top two cells represent 'the frontier'. These refer to activities that are not directly in the interests of shareholders, but have a moral or social motivation.

Cell 3 represents those actions that are not immediately profitable, but could possibly become so in the future because of positive reactions from consumers, employees, competitors or government. To quote from Martin, 'When Prudential allowed people with AIDS to tap the death benefits in their life assurance policies to pay for medical expenses, the move generated so much goodwill that competing insurers soon offered [such] settlements as well. Very quickly, corporate behavior that had seemed radical became business as usual throughout the insurance industry.'[3] Generally activities in cell 3 are risky and the willingness of firms to engage in them depends on their attitudes towards risk.

Cell 4 represents the most radical departure from shareholders' interests. Here managers take action that benefits society but at the *expense* of profit. As we saw in Chapter 14, managers are not always ruthless profit maximisers. They can be motivated by a range of objectives. One of these is 'to do the right thing' by employees, customers or society generally. For example, improving working conditions for employees is seen not just as a way of improving productivity, but as a moral duty towards the workforce. Likewise managers may control toxic emissions beyond the legal minimum requirement because of their genuine concern for the environment.

The development of corporate social responsibility over time

Pressures from various stakeholders are likely to increase corporate social responsibility over time. These pressures are summarised in Figure 20.7. They come from

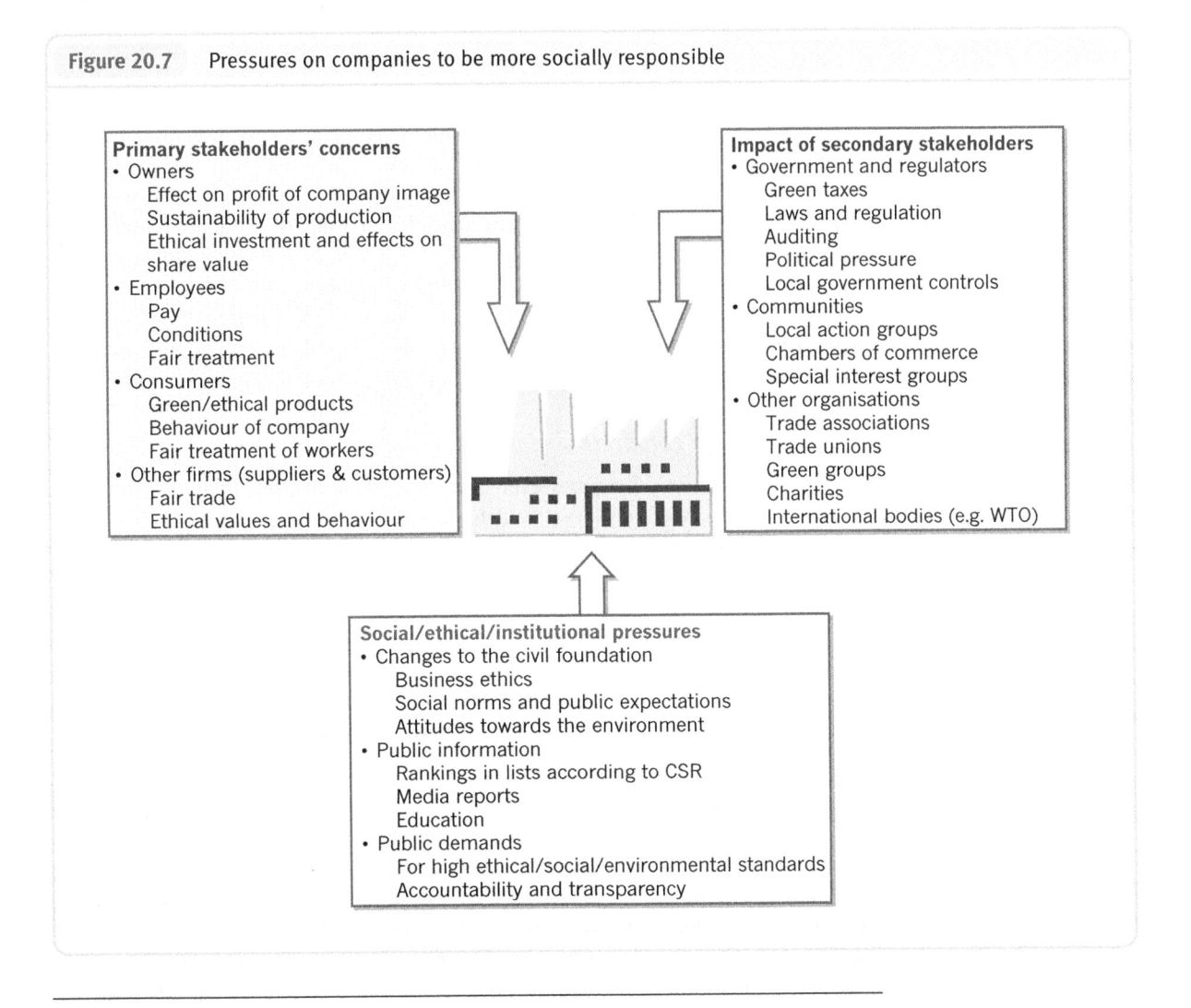

Figure 20.7 Pressures on companies to be more socially responsible

Primary stakeholders' concerns
- Owners
    - Effect on profit of company image
    - Sustainability of production
    - Ethical investment and effects on share value
- Employees
    - Pay
    - Conditions
    - Fair treatment
- Consumers
    - Green/ethical products
    - Behaviour of company
    - Fair treatment of workers
- Other firms (suppliers & customers)
    - Fair trade
    - Ethical values and behaviour

Impact of secondary stakeholders
- Government and regulators
    - Green taxes
    - Laws and regulation
    - Auditing
    - Political pressure
    - Local government controls
- Communities
    - Local action groups
    - Chambers of commerce
    - Special interest groups
- Other organisations
    - Trade associations
    - Trade unions
    - Green groups
    - Charities
    - International bodies (e.g. WTO)

Social/ethical/institutional pressures
- Changes to the civil foundation
    - Business ethics
    - Social norms and public expectations
    - Attitudes towards the environment
- Public information
    - Rankings in lists according to CSR
    - Media reports
    - Education
- Public demands
    - For high ethical/social/environmental standards
    - Accountability and transparency

---

[3] Ibid., page 8.

three sources: from the primary stakeholders, such as shareholders, employees, customers and suppliers; from secondary stakeholders, such as the government and other local, national and international organisations; and from changes to the whole civil foundation, with its norms and values and what is regarded as 'acceptable' corporate behaviour.

These pressures have tended to grow over time. This has resulted in the boundary between the civil foundation and the frontier moving upwards as activities that start in the frontier and then are copied by competitor firms become the norm. The norms of corporate behaviour in Victorian Britain would seem totally unacceptable in Britain today. The long hours, child labour, appalling working conditions, lack of redress for grievances, the filthy conditions of the workplace, the smoke and other pollution pouring from factories are not only illegal nowadays, but totally alien to the norms of society.

Although the boundary tends to move upwards, this is not necessarily the case. Martin gives the example of Russia in the immediate post-communist period, where a collapse of the old order and the development of 'cowboy' capitalism led to a decline in standards and the non-enforcement of many regulations governing things such as working conditions and child labour. Many developing countries have a very much lower boundary, which is constantly in danger of being pushed lower by ruthless forces of globalisation and non-representative governments conniving in the process.

Another factor leading to the development of corporate social responsibility is the movement of activities from cell 4 to cell 3. Activities that start as socially desirable but unprofitable tend to become profitable as consumers come to expect firms to behave in socially responsible ways and punish firms that do not by boycotting their products. Thus companies such as Nestlé, McDonald's and Nike have been very concerned to 'clean up' their corporate image because of adverse publicity. Of course, part of the reaction of companies to social pressure may be simply to improve their public relations, but part may be a genuine improvement in their behaviour.

Globalisation and corporate social responsibility

As the world economy becomes ever more intertwined, many companies in rich countries, with a relatively deep civil foundation, are outsourcing much of their production to developing countries, which have a relatively shallow and less secure civil foundation. This can have the effect of either levelling up or levelling down. Nike and Gap, which produce much of their footwear and clothing in south-east Asia, have been accused of operating sweatshops in these countries, with low wages and poor working conditions – a case of levelling down to the civil foundation of these developing countries. Nike and Gap reply that, compared with other factories in these countries, pay and conditions are better – a case of levelling up.

Economic performance and social responsibility

If corporate social responsibility has grown as a business objective, has this in any way impinged upon business performance? Studies, empirical and otherwise, suggest that rather than detracting from business performance and harming shareholder value, in fact the opposite appears to be the case. Corporate social responsibility appears to offer a positive contribution to business performance, especially over the longer term.

The following factors have been identified as some of the positive economic benefits that firms have gained from adopting a more socially responsible position.

Improved economic performance

A large number of studies have attempted to identify and evaluate the economic returns from social responsibility. Factors that have been considered include business growth rates, stock prices and sales and revenue. A survey by van Beurden and Gössling[4] evaluated the findings of 34 studies that considered the link between business ethics and enhanced profits. They concluded that 23 studies showed a positive link, 9 suggested neutral effects or were inconclusive, and the remaining 2 suggested that there was a negative relationship.

Although this evidence would on balance favour an argument that corporate social responsibility is good business practice, the whole area of linking ethics and responsibility to profit is a contentious one. When considering ethics and social responsibility, what are we including within this definition? Is the business merely complying with a business code, developed either within the business or by a third party? Such codes essentially state 'what is not acceptable business behaviour', such as taking bribes or pursuing anti-competitive behaviour. They can be seen as lying in the civil foundation. Or does the understanding of an 'ethical business' go further and entail positive social actions, ranging from giving money to good causes, to contributing to particular programmes in which the business has competency? For example, a pharmaceutical company might develop a drug that benefits the populations of the world's poorest countries, with no possibility of profit. Such actions lie in the frontier.

So at what level do we identify an ethical business, and to what degree might this level of responsibility influence profitability?

The concept of profitability is also contentious, most crucially in respect to the time frame over which the assessment takes place. Linking long-run profitability with an ethical or socially responsible programme is fraught with difficulties. How are all the other factors that influence business performance over the longer term accounted for? How do you attribute a given percentage or contribution to profit to the adoption of a more socially responsible business position? Can it ever be this precise, or are we merely left with intimating that a link exists, and is this good enough?

Enhancing the brand

Related to profitability is the issue of how far corporate social responsibility enhances brand image and the firm's reputation. This would not only strengthen consumer loyalty but also aid the firm in raising finance and attracting trading partners.

Surveys have identified that the ethical dimension of the firm is becoming increasingly important in consumer buying decisions. For example, the annual Cooperative Bank Ethical Consumerism Report shows that the proportion of people who purchased a product at least once a year for ethical reasons rose from 29 per cent in 1999 to 51 per cent in 2008.[5] The report also shows that, in

---

[4] P. van Beurden and T. Gössling, 'The worth of values – a literature review on the relation between corporate social and financial performance', *Journal of Business Ethics*, vol. 82, no. 2, October 2008, pp. 407–24.
[5] Cooperative Bank, *The Ethical Consumerism Report* (2008). Available at www.goodwithmoney.co.uk

BOX 20.3 THE BODY SHOP

Is it 'worth it'?

The Body Shop shot to fame in the 1980s. It stood for environmental awareness and an ethical approach to business. But its success had as much to do with what it sold as what it stood for. It sold natural cosmetics, Raspberry Ripple Bathing Bubbles and Camomile Shampoo, products that were immensely popular with consumers.

Its profits increased from a little over €1.7 million in 1985 to nearly €64 million in 2007. Sales, meanwhile, grew even more dramatically, from €8.4 million to €756 million in 2008. By the end of 2008, The Body Shop had 2550 stores worldwide, opening 124 stores in the year.

What makes this success so remarkable is that The Body Shop did virtually no advertising. Its promotion has largely stemmed from the activities and environmental campaigning of its founder, Anita Roddick, and the company's uncompromising claims that it sold only 'green' products and conducted its business operations with high ethical standards. It actively supported green causes, such as saving whales and protecting rainforests, and it refused to allow its products to be tested on animals. Perhaps most surprising in the world of big business was its high-profile initiative 'trade not aid', whereby it claimed to pay 'fair' prices for its ingredients, especially those supplied from people in developing countries, who were open to exploitation by large companies.

The growth strategy of The Body Shop, since its founding in 1976, has focused upon developing a distinctive and highly innovative product range, and at the same time identifying such products with major social issues of the day such as the environment and animal rights.

Its initial expansion was based on a process of franchising.

> . . . franchising. We didn't know what it was, but all these women came to us and said, 'if you can do this and you can't even read a balance sheet, then we can do it'. I had a cabal of female friends all around Brighton, Hove and Chichester, and they started opening little units, all called the Body Shop. I just supplied them with gallons of products – we only had 19 different products, but we made it look like more as we sold them in five different sizes![1]

In 1984 the company went public. In the 1990s, however, sales growth was less rapid and in 1998 Anita Roddick stepped down as chief executive, but for a while she and her husband remained as co-chairmen. In 2003 she was awarded a knighthood and became Dame Anita Roddick. Sales began to grow rapidly from 2004 to 2006 from €553 million to €709 million.

Acquisition of the Body Shop by L'Oréal

A dramatic strategic event occurred in 2006 when The Body Shop was sold to the French cosmetics giant L'Oréal, which was 26 per cent owned by Nestlé. The event resulted in the magazine, *Ethical Consumer*, downgrading The Body Shop's ethical rating from 11 out of 20 to a mere 2.5 and calling for a boycott of the company.

There were a number of reasons for this. L'Oréal's animal-testing policies conflict with that of The Body Shop and L'Oréal has been accused of being involved in price fixing with other French perfume houses. L'Oréal's part-owner, Nestlé, has also been subject to various criticisms for ethical misconduct, including promoting formula milk to mothers with babies in poor countries rather than breast milk and using slave labour in cocoa farms in West Africa.

Anita Roddick, however, believed that, by taking over The Body Shop, L'Oréal would develop a more ethical approach to business. L'Oréal has publicly recognised that it would have to develop its ethical policies.

Sadly, Anita Roddick died in 2007 and so has not been able to witness changes. L'Oréal though has begun to address its ethical approach. It adopted a new Code of Business Ethics in 2007 and it is gaining some external accreditation for its approach to sustainability and ethics. Notably, L'Oréal was ranked as one of the world's 100 most ethical companies by Ethisphere in 2007. It has also allowed The Body Shop to continue with its ethical policies.

L'Oréal has, however, looked to inject greater finance into the company aimed at improving the marketing of products. In autumn 2006 a transactional website was launched and there have been greater press marketing campaigns. Profits continued to rise in 2006 and 2007, but fell back quite dramatically from €64 million in 2007 to €36 million in 2008 as recession hit the high streets.

So, it is probably too early to answer the question of 'why did L'Oréal acquire the Body Shop?' with the answer from its own advertising slogan, 'Because they're worth it' – but time will tell.

1. What assumptions has The Body Shop made about the 'rational consumer'?
2. How has The Body Shop's economic performance been affected by its attitudes towards ethical issues? (You could do an Internet search to find further evidence about its performance and the effects of its sale to L'Oréal.)

---
[1] Anita Roddick interview, Startups.co.uk

2008, 57 per cent of people surveyed avoided buying a product or service from a company because of its reputation; the comparable figure in 1999 was 44 per cent. Moreover, 26 per cent of people had actively campaigned on a social or environmental issue in 2008 compared to 15 per cent in 1999.

Thus, environmental responsibility and active participation in the community are the social factors most likely to influence consumers' purchasing behaviour.

Firms may be further encouraged to develop the social image of their brand with the increasing number of awards given to recognise and promote corporate social responsibility. 'Most admired companies' lists, such as those presented by *Management Today* in the UK and *Fortune* in America, are based on criteria such as reputation for ethics and honesty, use of corporate assets, and community and environmental responsibility. The public relations and marketing potential that can be gained from such awards help firms to strengthen further their socially responsible image.

Attracting and retaining employees

It increasingly appears to be the case that companies with clear ethical and social positions find it easier not only to recruit, but to hold on to their employees. In a number of surveys of graduate employment intentions, students have claimed that they would be prepared to take a lower salary in order to work for a business with high ethical standards and a commitment to socially responsible business practices.

An international survey in 2005 in 15 European, Middle Eastern and African countries[6] showed that 28 per cent of job seekers considered the ethical conduct and values of an employer to be an important factor in deciding whether to apply for work there. (Top of the list was security and stability (47%), followed by pay (42%).)

Access to capital

Investment in ethically screened investment funds has grown rapidly in recent years. This has been driven not only by the demands of shareholders for ethical funds, but also by a realisation from investors generally that socially responsible business has the potential to be hugely profitable.

The Ethical Investment Research Service estimates that the total number of holders of ethically screened funds increased from 137 000 in 1997 to 720 312 in December 2007, a rise of 426 per cent[7] – bringing the value of these funds to nearly £9 billion.

The likelihood of returns being lower in ethically screened funds has been questioned by a number of papers.[8] Indeed, evidence shows that investing in ethical funds in the UK, USA, Germany and Canada does not lead to returns that are significantly different from those obtained from conventional funds.[9] It is difficult to ascertain precisely why this is. However, it could be that environmental performance is a good indicator of general management quality, which is the main determinant of stock price.

---

[6] *What Makes a Great Employer?* (MORI survey for Manpower, October 2005).
[7] Ethical Investment Research Service. Available at www.eiris.org
[8] See, for example, MISTRA, The Foundation for Strategic Environmental Research, *Screening of Screening Companies* (2001) and P. Rivoli, 'Making a difference or making a statement? Finance research and socially responsible investment', *Business Ethics Quarterly* 13(3), 2003, pp. 271–87.
[9] See R. Bauer, J. Derwall and R. Otten, 'The ethical mutual fund performance debate: new evidence from Canada', *Journal of Business Ethics*, 70, 2007, pp. 111–124; and R. Bauer, K. Koedijk and R. Otten, 'International evidence on ethical mutual fund performance and investment style', *Journal of Banking and Finance* 29, 2005, pp. 1751–67.

Social responsibility appears not only to bring a range of benefits to business and society, but also to be generally profitable. It is likely to enhance business performance, strengthen brand image, reduce employee turnover and increase access to stock market funds. Box 20.3 gives an example of a company that built its reputation on being socially and environmentally responsible – The Body Shop. See also Box 16.2 on page 330.

SUMMARY

1. Government intervention in the market sets out to attain two goals: social efficiency and equity. Social efficiency is achieved at the point where the marginal benefits to society for either production or consumption are equal to the marginal costs of either production or consumption. Issues of equity are difficult to judge due to the subjective assessment of what is, and what is not, a fair distribution of resources.

2a. Externalities are spillover costs or benefits. Whenever there are external costs, the market will (other things being equal) lead to a level of production and consumption above the socially efficient level. Whenever there are external benefits, the market will (other things being equal) lead to a level of production and consumption below the socially efficient level.

2b. Public goods will be underprovided by the market. The problem is that they have large external benefits relative to private benefits, and without government intervention it would not be possible to prevent people having a 'free ride' and thereby escaping contributing to their cost of production.

2c. Monopoly power will (other things being equal) lead to a level of output below the socially efficient level. It will lead to a deadweight welfare loss: a loss of consumer plus producer surplus.

2d. Ignorance and uncertainty may prevent people from consuming or producing at the levels they would otherwise choose. Information may sometimes be provided (at a price) by the market, but it may be imperfect; in some cases it may not be available at all.

2e. Markets may respond sluggishly to changes in demand and supply. The time lags in adjustment can lead to a permanent state of disequilibrium and to problems of instability.

2f. In a free market there may be inadequate provision for dependants and an inadequate output of merit goods.

3a. Taxes and subsidies are one means of correcting market distortions. Externalities can be corrected by imposing tax rates equal to the size of the marginal external cost, and granting rates of subsidy equal to marginal external benefits.

3b. Taxes and subsidies can also be used to affect monopoly price, output and profit. Subsidies can be used to persuade a monopolist to increase output to the competitive level. Lump-sum taxes can be used to reduce monopoly profits without affecting price or output.

3c. Taxes and subsidies have the advantages of 'internalising' externalities and of providing incentives to reduce external costs. On the other hand, they may be impractical to use when different rates are required for each case, or when it is impossible to know the full effects of the activities that the taxes or subsidies are being used to correct.

3d. An extension of property rights may allow individuals to prevent others from imposing costs on them. This is not practical, however, when many people are affected to a small degree, or where several people are affected but differ in their attitudes towards what they want doing about the 'problem'.

3e. Laws can be used to regulate activities that impose external costs, to regulate monopolies and oligopolies, and to provide consumer protection. Legal controls are often simpler and easier to operate than taxes, and are safer when the danger is potentially great. However, they tend to be rather a blunt weapon.

3f. Regulatory bodies can be set up to monitor and control activities that are against the public interest (e.g. anti-competitive behaviour of oligopolists). They can conduct investigations of specific cases, but these may be expensive and time consuming, and may not be acted on by the authorities.

3g. The government may provide information in cases where the private sector fails to provide an adequate level. It may also provide goods and services directly. These could be either public goods or other goods where the government feels that provision by the market is inadequate. The government could also influence production in publicly owned industries.

4a. Government intervention in the market may lead to shortages or surpluses; it may be based on poor information; it may be costly in terms of administration; it may stifle incentives; it may be disruptive if government policies change too frequently; it may not represent the majority of voters' interests if the government is elected by a minority, or if voters did not fully understand the issues at election time, or if the policies were not in the government's manifesto; it may remove certain liberties.

4b By contrast, a free market leads to automatic adjustments to changes in economic conditions; the prospect of monopoly/oligopoly profits may stimulate risk taking and hence research and development and innovation, and this advantage may outweigh any problems of resource misallocation; there may still be a high degree of actual or potential competition under monopoly and oligopoly.

5a There are two views of social responsibility. The first states that it should be of no concern to business, which would do best for society by serving the interests of its shareholders. Social policy should be left to politicians. The alternative view is that business needs to consider the impact of its actions upon society, and to take changing social and political considerations into account when making decisions. This, anyway, is generally good business.

5b The virtue matrix is a means of illustrating the drivers of corporate social responsibility. Firms will take socially responsible actions if they are required to by law or if social norms dictate. These pressures on firms represent the 'civil foundation'. Some firms will take corporate social responsibility further and thus move into the 'frontier'. Here they may do things that are socially beneficial and may only possibly lead to higher profits, or may even clearly reduce profits. As firms become more socially responsible over time and as social pressures on business increase, so the civil foundation is likely to grow.

5c Evidence suggests that economic performance is likely to be enhanced as the corporate responsibility of firms grows.

REVIEW QUESTIONS

1 Assume that a firm discharges waste into a river. As a result, the marginal social costs (*MSC*) are greater than the firm's marginal (private) costs (*MC*). The following table shows how *MC*, *MSC*, *AR* and *MR* vary with output.

Output	1	2	3	4	5	6	7	8
MC(£)	23	21	23	25	27	30	35	42
MSC(£)	35	34	38	42	46	52	60	72
TR(£)	60	102	138	168	195	219	238	252
AR(£)	60	51	46	42	39	36.5	34	31.5
MR(£)	60	42	36	30	27	24	19	14

(a) How much will the firm produce if it seeks to maximise profits?
(b) What is the socially efficient level of output (assuming no externalities on the demand side)?
(c) How much is the marginal external cost at this level of output?
(d) What size tax would be necessary for the firm to reduce its output to the socially efficient level?
(e) Why is the tax less than the marginal externality?
(f) Why might it be equitable to impose a lump-sum tax on this firm?
(g) Why will a lump-sum tax not affect the firm's output (assuming that in the long run the firm can still make at least normal profit)?

2 Distinguish between publicly provided goods, public goods and merit goods.

3 Name some goods or services provided by the government or local authorities that are not public goods.

4 Some roads could be regarded as a public good, but some could be provided by the market. Which types of road could be provided by the market? Why? Would it be a good idea?

5 Assume that you wanted the information given in (a)–(h) below. In which cases could you (i) buy perfect information; (ii) buy imperfect information; (iii) be able to obtain information without paying for it; (iv) not be able to obtain information?

(a) Which washing machine is the most reliable?
(b) Which of two jobs that are vacant is the most satisfying?
(c) Which builder will repair my roof most cheaply?
(d) Which builder will make the best job of repairing my roof?
(e) Which builder is best value for money?
(f) How big a mortgage would it be wise for me to take out?
(g) What course of higher education should I follow?
(h) What brand of washing powder washes whiter?

In which cases are there non-monetary costs to you of finding out the information? How can you know whether the information you acquire is accurate or not?

6. Make a list of pieces of information a firm might want to know and consider whether it could buy the information and how reliable that information might be.

7. Why might it be better to ban certain activities that cause environmental damage rather than to tax them?

8. Consider the advantages and disadvantages of extending property rights so that everyone would have the right to prevent people imposing any costs on them whatsoever (or charging them to do so).

9. How suitable are legal restrictions in the following cases?

   (a) Ensuring adequate vehicle safety (e.g. that tyres have sufficient tread or that the vehicle is roadworthy).
   (b) Reducing traffic congestion.
   (c) Preventing the use of monopoly power.
   (d) Ensuring that mergers are in the public interest.
   (e) Ensuring that firms charge a price equal to marginal cost.

10. Evaluate the following statement: 'Despite the weaknesses of a free market, the replacing of the market by the government generally makes the problem worse.'

11. In what ways might business be socially responsible?

12. What economic costs and benefits might a business experience if it decided to adopt a more socially responsible position? How might such costs and benefits change over the longer term?

Chapter 21

Government and the firm

Business issues covered in this chapter

- How do governments attempt to prevent both the abuse of monopoly power and collusion by oligopolists ('competition policy')?
- How effective is competition policy?
- Why does a free market fail to achieve the optimal amount of research and development?
- What can the government do to encourage technological development and innovation?
- Why is training so important for a country's economic performance?
- Why do governments pursue a training policy and not just leave it to employers?
- How do training policies differ between countries?

In this chapter we shall consider the relationship between government and the individual firm. This relationship is not simply one of regulation and control, but can involve the active intervention of government in attempting to improve the economic performance of business. We shall consider government attitudes and policy towards enhancing research and technology development, and training, as well as the more punitive area of business regulation through the use of monopolies and mergers legislation.

21.1 COMPETITION POLICY

Competition, monopoly and the public interest

Most markets in the real world are imperfect, with firms having varying degrees of market power. But will this power be against the public interest? This question has been addressed by successive governments in framing legislation to deal with monopolies and oligopolies.

It might be thought that market power is always 'a bad thing', certainly as far as the consumer is concerned. After all, it enables firms to make supernormal profit, thereby 'exploiting' the consumer. The greater the firm's power, the higher prices will be relative to the costs of production. Also, a lack of competition removes the incentive to become more efficient.

But market power is not necessarily a bad thing. Firms may not fully exploit their position of power – perhaps for fear that very high profits would eventually lead to other firms overcoming entry barriers, or perhaps because they are not aggressive profit maximisers. Even if they do make large supernormal profits, they may still charge a lower price than more competitive sectors of the industry because of their economies of scale. Finally, they may use their profits for research and development and for capital investment. The consumer might then benefit from improved products at lower prices.

Competition policy could seek to ban various structures. For example, it could ban mergers leading to market share of more than a certain amount. Most countries, however, prefer to focus on whether the *practices* of particular monopolists or oligopolists are anti-competitive. Some of these practices may be made illegal, such as price fixing by oligopolists; others may be assessed on a case-by-case approach to determine whether or not they should be permitted. Such an approach does not presume that the mere possession of power is against the public interest, but rather that certain uses of that power may be.

There are three possible targets of competition policy:

- the abuse of the existing power of monopolies and oligopolies – monopoly policy;
- the growth of power through mergers and acquisitions – merger policy;
- oligopolistic collusion – restrictive practices policy.

Competition policy in the European Union

EU competition legislation is contained in Articles 101 and 102 of the Treaty of Lisbon (formerly Articles 81 and 82 of the Treaty of Amsterdam) and in additional regulations covering mergers, which came into force in 1990 and were amended in 2004.

Article 101 is concerned with restrictive practices and Article 102 with the abuse of market power. The Articles are largely confined to firms trading between EU members and thus do not cover monopolies or oligopolies operating solely within a member country. The policy is implemented by the European Commission. If any firm appears to be breaking the provisions of either of the Articles, the Commission can refer it to the European Court of Justice.

EU restrictive practices policy

Article 101 covers *agreements* between firms, *joint decisions*, and concerted *practices* which prevent, restrict or distort competition. In other words it covers all types of oligopolistic collusion that are against the interests of consumers.

Article 101 is not designed to prevent oligopolistic *structures* (i.e. the simple existence of cooperation between firms), but rather collusive *behaviour*. No matter what form collusion takes, if the European Commission finds that firms are committing anti-competitive *practices*, they will be banned from doing so and possibly fined (up to 10 per cent of annual turnover), although firms do have the right of appeal to the European Court of Justice.

Practices considered anti-competitive include firms colluding to do any of the following:

- fix prices (i.e. above competitive levels);
- limit production, markets, technical development or investment;
- share out markets or sources of supply;
- charge discriminatory prices or operate discriminatory trading conditions, such as to benefit the colluding parties and disadvantage others;
- make other firms who sign contracts with any of the colluding firms accept unfavourable obligations which, by their nature, have no connection with the subject of such contracts.

In recent years the Commission has adopted a tough stance and has fined many firms (see Box 21.1 in which a number of European cartel cases are discussed).

EU monopoly policy

Article 102 relates to the abuse of market power and has also been extended to cover mergers. As with Article 101, it is the *behaviour* of firms that is the target of the legislation. The following are cited as examples of abuse of market power:

- charging unfairly high prices to consumers, or paying unfairly low prices to suppliers;
- limiting production, markets or technical developments to the detriment of consumers;
- using price discrimination or other discriminatory practices to the detriment of certain parties;
- making other firms that sign contracts with it accept unfavourable obligations which, by their nature, have no connection with the subject of such contracts.

As you can see, these abuses are very similar to those in Article 101.

Under Article 102, such practices can be banned and firms can be fined where they are found to have abused a dominant position (see Box 11.3 for an example in relation to Microsoft). A firm does not need to have some specified minimum market share before Article 102 can be invoked. Instead, if firms are able to conduct anti-competitive practices, it is simply assumed that they must be in a position of market power. This approach is sensible, given the difficulties of identifying the boundaries of a market, either in terms of geography or in terms of type of product.

EU merger policy

The 1990 merger control measures tightened up the legislation in Article 102. They cover mergers where combined worldwide annual sales exceed €5 billion; where EU sales of at least two of the companies exceed €250 million; and where at least one of the companies conducts no more than two-thirds of its EU-wide business in a single member state. (Less than 4 per cent of mergers involving European companies meet these conditions.)

Relevant mergers must be notified to the Commission, which must then conduct preliminary investigations (Phase 1). A decision must then be made, normally within 25 working days, whether to conduct a formal investigation (Phase 2) or to let the merger proceed. A formal investigation must normally be completed within a further 90 working days (or 110 days in complex cases).

The process of EU merger control is thus very rapid and administratively inexpensive. The regulations are also potentially quite tough. Mergers are disallowed if they result in 'a concentration which would significantly impede effective competition, in particular by the creation or strengthening of a dominant position'. But the regulations are also flexible, since they recognise that mergers *may* be in the interests of consumers if they result in cost reductions. In such cases they are permitted.

The merger investigation process is now overseen by a Chief Competition Economist and a panel to scrutinise the investigating team's conclusions. One concern of this panel is that the Commission, in being willing to show flexibility, must not be too easily persuaded by firms, and impose conditions on them which are too lax and rely too much on the firms' cooperation. Indeed, from 1990 to the end of 2009 4274 mergers were notified to the Commission, but only 191 proceeded to Phase 2 and only 20 were prohibited. In many cases (too many, claim critics), the Commission accepted the undertakings of firms.

In May 2004, the European Commission introduced a number of changes to the administration of competition law to accommodate the accession of ten new EU member states (and two more in 2007). These changes included:

- A further decentralisation of *enforcement* powers to national jurisdictions with respect to Articles 101 and 102. The European Commission is overseeing the process and is encouraging the further development of the 'European Competition Network', whereby national competition authorities exchange information on competition cases that have cross-border implications.
- The establishment of clearer rules on agreements between firms. One type of agreement that is now permitted concerns the transfer of technology between firms.
- The introduction of a new merger regulation, EC139/2004, which simplifies the merger control process. It also clarifies the law in relation to post-merger scenarios that create or strengthen oligopolistic dominance.
- The regulation of air transport between EU and non-EU airports. This gave the Commission clear and effective powers to review the impact on consumers of alliances between airlines (see pages 312–3) based inside and outside the EU.

> **Pause for thought**
>
> *To what extent is Article 102 consistent with both these points of view?*

There has been considerable disagreement in the EU between those who want to encourage competition *within* the EU and those who want to see European companies being world leaders. For them, the ability to compete in *world* markets normally requires that companies are large, which may well imply having monopoly power within the EU.

UK competition policy

There have been substantial changes to UK competition policy since the first legislation was introduced in 1948 (see Table 21.1). The current approach is based on the 1998 Competition Act and the 2002 Enterprise Act.

The Competition Act brought UK policy in line with EU policy, detailed above. The Act has two key sets (or 'chapters') of prohibitions. Chapter I prohibits various restrictive practices, and mirrors Article 101. Chapter II prohibits various abuses of monopoly power, and mirrors Article 102.

The Enterprise Act strengthened the Competition Act and introduced new measures for the control of mergers.

Under the two Acts, the body charged with ensuring that the prohibitions are carried out is the Office of Fair Trading (OFT). The OFT can investigate any firms suspected of engaging in one or more of the prohibited practices. Its officers have the power to enter and search premises and can require the production and explanation of documents. Where the OFT decides that an infringement of one of the prohibitions has occurred, it can direct the offending firms to modify their behaviour or

Table 21.1 UK competition legislation

Year	Act	Provisions
1948	Monopolies and Restrictive Practices Act	Set up Monopolies and Restrictive Practices Commission (MRC) to investigate suspected cases of abuse by a firm or group of firms of a dominant market position.
1956, 1968, 1976	Restrictive Trade Practices Acts	Set up Restrictive Practices Court (RPC). All restrictive practices had to be registered. These would then have to be justified to the RPC. MRC renamed Monopolies Commission.
1964, 1976	Resale Prices Acts	Resale price maintenance banned unless firm could demonstrate to the RPC that it was in the public interest.
1965	Monopolies and Mergers Act	Role of Monopolies Commission now extended to examine mergers that would lead to a dominant market position.
1973	Fair Trading Act	Office of Fair Trading established. Its Director-General (DGFT) is responsible for referrals to the RPC or the renamed Monopolies and Mergers Commission (MMC).
1980	Competition Act	Various types of anti-competitive practice were specified. OFT would investigate alleged cases of such practices and possibly refer to MMC.
1989	Companies Act	Simplified and speeded up mergers investigation procedures.
1998	Competition Act	Brought UK legislation in line with EU legislation. Chapter I prohibition applies to restrictive practices. Chapter II prohibition applies to the abuse of a dominant position. MMC replaced by Competition Commission (CC).
2002	Enterprise Act	Made OFT and CC independent of government. Made various cartel agreements a criminal offence. Mergers investigated by OFT and referred, if necessary, to CC for ruling.

cease their practices altogether. Companies in breach of a prohibition are liable to fines of up to 10 per cent of their annual UK turnover. Third parties adversely affected by such breaches can seek compensation through the courts.

The Competition Act also set up a Competition Commission (CC) to which the OFT can refer cases for further investigation. The CC is charged with determining whether the structure of an industry or the practices of firms within it are detrimental to competition.

The Enterprise Act made the OFT and CC independent of government. It also set up a Markets and Policy Initiatives Division (MPI) of the OFT. This carries out investigations into particular markets suspected of not working in the best interests of consumers. The MPI's investigations could lead to the OFT enforcing its findings if anti-competitive practices were taking place (see below). Alternatively, the MPI could refer the case to the CC or make proposals to the government for changes in the law.

If a case is referred to the Competition Commission, it will carry out an investigation to establish whether competition is adversely affected. If it finds that it is, it will decide on the appropriate remedies, such as prohibiting various practices.

Firms affected by an OFT or CC ruling have the right of appeal to the Competition Appeal Tribunal (CAT), which can uphold or quash the original decision. The CAT is entirely independent of the CC and OFT.

UK restrictive practices policy

Under the 2002 Enterprise Act it is a *criminal* offence to engage in cartel agreements (i.e. horizontal, rather than vertical, collusive agreements between firms), irrespective of whether there are appreciable effects on competition. Convicted offenders may receive a prison sentence of up to five years and/or an unlimited fine. Prosecutions may be brought by the Serious Fraud Office or the OFT. The Act strengthened the OFT's power to enter premises, seize documents and require people to answer questions or provide information. In 2008, three British citizens were jailed under the Enterprise Act for organising a cartel: the first such prosecutions in the UK (see Box 21.1).

But what practices constitute 'cartel agreements'? These involve one or more of the following: price fixing, limiting supply, sharing out markets, limiting supply or bid-rigging. In more detail these include:

- Horizontal price-fixing agreements. These are agreements between competitors to set one or more of the following: fixed prices, minimum prices, the amount or percentage by which prices may be increased, or a range outside which prices may not move. The object is to restrict price competition and thus to keep prices higher than they would otherwise be.
- Agreements to share out markets. These may be by geographical area, type or size of customer, or nature of outlet. By limiting or even eliminating competition within each part of the market, such agreements can be an effective means of keeping prices high (or quality low).
- Agreements to limit production. This may involve output quotas or a looser agreement not to increase output wherever this would drive down prices.
- Agreements to limit or coordinate investment. By restraining capacity, this will help firms to keep output down and prices up.
- Collusive tendering. This is where two or more firms put in a tender for a contract at secretly agreed (high) prices. A well-known case throughout most of the 1980s and 1990s was that of firms supplying ready-mixed concrete agreeing on prices they would tender to local authorities (see Web Case H.5 and Box 21.1).
- Agreements between purchasers. These could be to reduce prices paid to suppliers. For example, large supermarkets could collude to keep prices low to farmers. An alternative form of agreement would be to deal with certain suppliers only.
- Agreements to boycott suppliers or distributors that deal with competitors to the colluding firms.

> **Definitions**
>
> **Collusive tendering**
> Where two or more firms secretly agree on the prices they will tender for a contract. These prices will be above those which would be put in under a genuinely competitive tendering process.
>
> **Resale price maintenance**
> Where the manufacturer of a product (legally) insists that the product should be sold at a specified retail price.

In the case of other types of agreement, the OFT has the discretion to decide, on a case-by-case basis, whether or not competition is appreciably restricted, and whether, therefore, they should be terminated or the firms should be exempted. Such cases include the following:

> **Pause for thought**
>
> *Are all such agreements necessarily against the interests of consumers?*

- Vertical price-fixing agreements. These are price agreements between purchasing firms and their suppliers. An example of this is resale price maintenance. This is where a manufacturer or distributor sets the price for retailers to charge. It may well distribute a price list to retailers (e.g. a car manufacturer may distribute a price list to car showrooms). Resale price maintenance is a way of preventing

competition between retailers driving down retail prices and ultimately the price they pay to the manufacturer. Both manufacturers and retailers, therefore, are likely to gain from resale price maintenance.
- Agreements to exchange information that could have the effect of reducing competition. For example, if producers exchange information on their price intentions, it is a way of allowing price leadership, a form of tacit collusion, to continue.

UK monopoly policy

Under the Chapter II prohibition of the 1998 Competition Act, it is illegal for a dominant firm to exercise its market power in such a way as to reduce competition. Any suspected case is investigated by the OFT, which uses a two-stage process in deciding whether an abuse has taken place.

The first stage is to establish whether a firm has a position of dominance. The firm does not literally have to be a monopoly. Rather 'dominance' normally involves the firm having at least a 40 per cent share of the market (national or local, whichever is appropriate), although this figure will vary from industry to industry. Also dominance depends on the barriers to entry to new competitors. The higher the barriers to the entry of new firms, the less contestable will be the market (see pages 228–9), and the more dominant a firm is likely to be for any given current market share.

If the firm *is* deemed to be dominant, the second stage involves the OFT then deciding whether the firm's practices constitute an abuse of its position. As with restrictive practices, Chapter II follows EU legislation. It specifies the same four types of market abuse as does Article 102 (see above). Within these four categories, the OFT identifies the following practices as being overtly anti-competitive:

- *Charging excessively high prices*. These are prices above those the firm would charge if it faced effective competition. One sign of excessively high prices is abnormally high rates of profit.
- *Price discrimination*. This is regarded as an abuse only to the extent that the higher prices are excessive or the lower prices are used to exclude competitors.
- *Predatory pricing*. This is where prices are set at loss-making levels, so as to drive competitors out of business (see page 350). The test is to look at the dominant firm's price in relation to its average costs. If its price is below average variable cost, predation would be assumed. If its price is above average variable cost, but below average total cost, then the Director General would need to establish whether the reason was to eliminate a competitor.

In November 2008 the OFT decided that Cardiff Bus engaged in predatory conduct intended to eliminate a competitor, 2 Travel, during the period April 2004 to February 2005. Before 2 Travel's entry into the market, Cardiff Bus had a substantial market share, carrying 80 000 passengers per day. However, 'Cardiff Bus responded to the introduction of a new no-frills bus service by another bus company, 2 Travel, by introducing its own no-frills bus services which ran on the same routes, at similar times as 2 Travel's services and made a loss for Cardiff Bus. Shortly after 2 Travel's exit from the market Cardiff Bus withdrew its own no-frills services.'[1]

---

[1] *'Cardiff Bus engaged in predatory conduct against competitor, OFT decides'* (OFT press release, 133/08. 18 November 2008). In this instance, the OFT decided not to fine Cardiff Bus because its turnover did not exceed £50 million at the time of the infringement of Chapter II of the Competition Act 1998.

BOX 21.1 THE UMPIRES STRIKE BACK

The price of cartel behaviour

Back in 1776, Adam Smith had noted the sinister nature of collusive behaviour when he famously wrote in *The Wealth of Nations* that:

> People of the same trade seldom meet together, even for merriment and diversion, but the conversation ends in a conspiracy against the public, or in some contrivance to raise prices.

As we saw in Chapter 12, cartels have detrimental effects on economic efficiency. They lead to higher prices and lower output than under competitive situations, thereby transferring wealth away from consumers to cartel members. In addition, cartel members have a reduced incentive to control costs and innovate.

An OECD report in 2005[1] noted that cartel prices were, on average, between 20 and 30 per cent higher than competitive levels. There were, however, significant variations between countries. In Japan, prices were some 16 per cent higher, while 'hard core' cartels in the USA could overprice by between 60 and 70 per cent – although the US Sentencing Commission assumes a figure of only 10 per cent! The report also noted that EU domestic cartels overcharged by between 13 and 19 per cent during the period 1990 to 2004.

Attempts to estimate their overall economic effects are subject to numerous assumptions, but the OECD estimated that the impact on commerce of 16 significant cases was a massive $55 billion.

Types of cartel

Cartels take various forms. A cursory glance around the press releases from competition authority websites shows they can be domestic or international in character, and they take on a vertical as well as a horizontal form, although the latter dominate. We identify three recent cases below.

Bid-rigging cartels: the case of collusive tendering for flat roof and car park surfacing contracts in England and Scotland.[2] In 2006, 13 roofing contractors were fined a total of £2.3 million. This was for a series of separate collusive agreements in tendering for contracts to install, maintain, service and repair flat roofs or car park surfaces in London, Doncaster, Glasgow, Edinburgh, the Midlands and the south-east. The offences took place over the period 2000 to 2002. They involved actions such as paying potential bidders compensation to deter them from bidding and putting in high bids in the knowledge that they would lose a particular bid this time but win on another occasion.

Vertical restraints: Peugeot restricting new car exports from the Netherlands.[3] In late 2005, the European Commission fined Peugeot €49.5 million for obstructing the export of new cars by Dutch dealers to customers in other member states. (Prices in the Netherlands were considerably lower than in other EU countries, such as France and Germany.) This vertical restraint of a manufacturer on dealers lasted from January 1997 to September 2003 and was in direct violation of Article 101. Peugeot's strategy included refusing to pay performance bonuses to dealers selling to non-Dutch consumers and threatening to cut the number of cars supplied to such dealers.

The international cartel in marine hoses.[4] Marine hoses are used to transport crude oil to and from ships for transportation from production sites. However, a number of firms in this global industry had been involved in fixing prices for marine hoses, allocating bids and markets and exchanging commercially sensitive information over the period 1986 to 2007.

In January 2009, the EU fined five groups (Bridgestone, Dunlop Oil & Marine/Continental, Trelleborg, Parker ITR and Manuli) €131.5 million for participating in a cartel in contravention of Article 101. Yokohama, a Japanese firm, was also involved in the cartel but received immunity from prosecution under the EU's leniency policy for cartel whistle blowers. The EC estimated the European market value of the activity at around €32 million per annum between 2004 and 2006.

The international tentacles of this cartel also brought them into contact with competition authorities in the UK, USA and Japan. In May 2007 officers of the US Antitrust Division and the FBI arrested eight foreign executives from the United Kingdom, France, Italy and Japan in Houston and San Francisco for their roles in the marine hose conspiracy. Offices were raided simultaneously in the USA, UK and Europe. The Japan Fair Trade Commission later searched offices in Japan.

---

[1] *Hard Core Cartels: Third Report on the Implementation of the 1998 Recommendation* (OECD, 2005).

[2] *'OFT fines roofing contractors in England and Scotland'* (OFT press release, 23 February 2006).

[3] *'Commission imposes €49.5 million fine on Peugeot for obstructing new car exports from the Netherlands'* (EU press release, 5 October 2005).

[4] Information for this section came from *'Three imprisoned in first OFT criminal prosecution for bid rigging'* (OFT press release 72/08,11 June 2008); *'Commission fines 4 marine hose producers €131 million for market sharing and price-fixing cartel'* (EU press release, 29 January 2009.); Scott D. Hammond, *'Recent developments, trends, and milestones in the Antitrust Division's criminal enforcement program'*, Department of Justice, 26 March 2008.

The arrests in the USA led to three British citizens being given the longest jail sentences ever imposed by US courts on foreign nationals in December 2007 (30, 24, and 20 months). However, as the UK Office of Fair Trading wanted to prosecute the three under the Enterprise Act, they were allowed to trade one day in a US jail for each day of any imprisonment imposed by the British courts.

In May 2008, they were convicted at Southwark Crown Court in London for 'dishonestly participating in a cartel to allocate markets and customers, restrict supplies, fix prices and rig bids for the supply of marine hose and ancillary equipment'. They became the first British citizens to be sent to prison under the Enterprise Act since it came into force in 2003, receiving the same sentences as the US court imposed.

A tougher approach from competition authorities

As the case of the marine hose cartel illustrates, competition authorities around the world have taken a much tougher approach to cartels in recent years.

- There is greater international cooperation in tackling cartels. The International Competition Network exchanges information in respect of cross-border cartels and the European Competition Network provides the same service at the EU level.
- There are greater resources devoted to cartel detection and methods of enforcement have been widened. For example, in Brazil the government has created a new cartel investigation centre and is working with prosecutors to introduce dawn raids and wire tapping. Since 2003 EU inspectors have had the power to enter and seal any business premises and seize books or recordings. They can also enter non-business premises, such as the family home, and take oral statements in leniency applications.
- The level of fines has been increased and leniency programmes introduced for those cooperating (or, where criminal sanctions are relevant, immunity from prosecution). Nearly all OECD nations have adopted this twin approach to encourage 'whistle blowing' on the whole cartel. The size of the fines can be large. For example, in the EU over the period 2004 to 2008, 33 cartels were uncovered with fines totalling over €8.5 billion. The top three fines were handed out to the car glass cartel in 2008 (€1.38 billion), the lifts and escalators cartel in 2007 (€992 million) and the vitamin cartel in 2001 (€791 million) (see Web Case H.6). Collected fines are put into the EU budget.[5]
- Some firms, as we have seen, escape fines (or have their fine reduced) because of their willingness to come forward. However, in South Korea individuals are reluctant to engage in whistle blowing – it is not part of their culture. Thus, the South Korean Federal Trade Commission has taken to offering large rewards for good-quality information that leads to prosecution.
- Criminal sanctions, including jail sentences, for participants in cartels (e.g. the USA and the UK) are becoming more commonplace. This is meant to send a strong message of punishment to would-be colluders. In the USA over the period 1999 to 2007, more than 150 individuals have spent time in prison for participating in cartels, including 31 foreign nationals from 9 different countries. The view taken is that fines are almost never paid by the individuals involved.
- Finally, some nations (e.g. UK, EU and USA) are offering victims of cartels the opportunity for compensation against miscreant firms, although the main successes in this regard thus far have been in the USA.

The policy mix used by countries to deter cartels depends on the legislative framework and tradition. However, the prospect of larger fines and jail sentences is having an effect. The number of cartels and restrictive practices in the UK, for example, has fallen since the passing of the 1998 Competition Act.

There has been some impact on prices too. Following a major investigation into fixing the price of replica football kits in the UK, in which ten suppliers were fined £18.6 million in 2003, prices dropped by 30 per cent or more and remained at these lower levels. Similarly, prices fell in the Swedish and Finnish asphalt industry by around 20 to 25 per cent following an investigation by competition authorities. In Israel, prices of envelopes fell by between 40 and 60 per cent following action against suppliers.

As the umpires strike back it may suggest that cartels are becoming a creature of the past. However, the OECD reckons that, despite these improvements, around one in six or seven cartels goes undetected. Clearly, for many firms the benefits from successful collusion still outweigh the penalties of detection.

---

[5] Commission cartel statistics (http://ec.europa.eu/competition/cartels/statistics/statistics.pdf).

Why might global cartels be harder to identify and eradicate than cartels solely located within the domestic economy? What problems does this raise for competition policy?

> **Definitions**
>
> **Vertical restraints**
> Conditions imposed by one firm on another which is either its supplier or its customer.
>
> **Tie-in-sales**
> Where a firm is only prepared to sell a first product on the condition that its customers buy a second product from it.

- *Vertical restraints.* This is where a supplying firm imposes conditions on a purchasing firm (or vice versa). For example, a manufacturer may impose rules on retailers about displaying the product or the provision of after-sales service, or it may refuse to supply certain outlets (e.g. perfume manufacturers refusing to supply discount chains, such as Superdrug). Another example is tie-in sales. This is where a firm controlling the supply of a first product insists that its customers buy a second product from it rather than from its rivals.

The simple *existence* of any of these practices may not constitute an abuse. The OFT has to decide whether their *effect* is to restrict competition.

If the case is not straightforward, the OFT can refer it to the Competition Commission (CC). The CC will then carry out a detailed investigation to establish whether competition is restricted or distorted. If it is, the CC will rule what actions must be taken to remedy the situation.

UK merger policy

Merger policy is covered by the 2002 Enterprise Act. It seeks to prevent mergers that are likely to result in a substantial lessening of competition.

A merger or takeover will be investigated by the OFT if the target company has a turnover of £70 million or more, or if the merger results in the new company having a market share of 25 per cent or more. The OFT conducts a preliminary investigation to see whether competition is likely to be threatened. If it is, and if there are unlikely to be any substantial compensating benefits to consumers, the OFT refers the case to the Competition Commission.

If reference is made to the CC, it conducts a detailed investigation to establish whether the merger is likely to lead to a significant reduction in competition. If so, it can prohibit the merger. Alternatively, it can require the merged firm to behave in certain ways in order to protect consumers' interests. In such cases, the OFT then monitors the firm to ensure that it is abiding by the CC's conditions. CC investigations must normally be completed within 24 weeks.

The 2002 Act tightened up merger legislation. In the past, the vast majority of mergers were not referred to the CC (or its predecessor, the Monopolies and Mergers Commission). Yet studies had shown that mergers were generally *not* in the public interest. Mergers had contributed to a growing degree of market concentration in the UK. The 2002 Act sought to rectify this problem.

Assessment of EU and UK competition policy

With UK competition legislation having been brought in line with EU legislation, it is possible to consider the two together.

It is generally agreed by commentators that the policy is correct to concentrate on anti-competitive *practices* and their *effects* rather than simply on the existence of agreements or on the size of a firm's market share. After all, economic power is only a problem when it is abused. When, by contrast, it enables firms to achieve economies of scale, or more finance for investment, the result can be to the benefit of consumers. In other words, the assumption that structure determines conduct and performance (see pages 15 and 215) is not necessarily true, and certainly it is not necessarily true that market power is always bad or competitive industries are always good.

Secondly, most commentators favour the system of certain practices being *prohibited*, with fines applicable to the first offence. This acts as an important deterrent to anti-competitive behaviour.

Similar conclusions have been reached in the USA, where the application of competition law has undergone changes in recent years. In the past, the focus was on the structure of an industry. Under the Sherman Act of 1890, oligopolistic collusion in the 'restraint of trade' was made illegal, as was any attempt to establish a monopoly. Although, under the Clayton Act of 1914, various potentially anti-competitive practices (such as price discrimination) were only illegal when they substantially lessened competition, the application of these two 'anti-trust' laws was largely directed to breaking up large firms. Today, the approach is to focus on efficiency, rather than on market share; and on the effects on consumers of any collusion or cooperation between firms, rather than on the simple collusion itself.

A problem with any policy to deal with collusion is the difficulty in rooting it out. When firms do all their deals 'behind closed doors' and are careful not to keep records or give clues, then collusion can be very hard to spot. The cases that have come to light, such as that of collusive tendering between firms supplying ready-mixed concrete, may be just the tip of an iceberg.

POLICIES TOWARDS RESEARCH AND DEVELOPMENT (R&D) 21.2

The impact of technology not only on the practice of business, but on the economy in general is vividly illustrated by the development and use of the Internet. In 1997, worldwide some 40 million people and 25 000 firms used the Internet. By 2009, there were 1.6 billion users. By 2015 the figure is forecast to be over 2 billion – though if Internet access rates improve in countries such as China and India, this figure may be exceeded sooner.

The commercial possibilities of the Internet range from the selling of information and services, to global forms of catalogue shopping where you can browse through a business's product range (or surf the net) and use your credit card number to pay. The Internet is just one example of how technology and technological change are shaping the whole structure and organisation of business (see Chapter 3 on the flat organisation), the experience of work for the worker, and the productivity of business and hence the competitive performance of national economies.

If a business fails to embrace new technology, its productivity and profitability will almost certainly lag behind those businesses that do. It is the same for countries. Unless they embrace new technology, the productivity gap between them and those that do is likely to widen. Once such a gap has been opened, it will prove very difficult to close. Those countries ahead in the technological race will tend to get further ahead as the dynamic forces of technology enhance their competitiveness, improve their profits, and provide yet greater potential for technological advance. How then might countries set about preventing such technological gaps opening, or, once they have become established, set about closing them?

Technology policy refers to a series of government initiatives to affect the process of technological change and its rate of adoption. The nature of the policy will depend on which stage of the introduction of new technology it is designed to affect. Three stages can be identified:

- *Invention*. In this initial stage, research leads to new ideas and new products. Sometimes the ideas arise from general research; sometimes the research is directed towards a particular goal, such as the development of a new type of car engine or computer chip.

> **Definition**
>
> **Technology policy**
> Involves government initiatives to affect the process and rate of technological change.

- *Innovation.* In this stage, the new ideas are put into practice. A firm will introduce the new technology, and will hopefully gain a commercial advantage from so doing.
- *Diffusion.* In the final stage, the new products and processes are copied, and possibly adapted, by competitor firms. The effects of the new technology thus spread throughout the economy, affecting general productivity levels and competitiveness.

Technology policy can be focused on any or all of these stages of technological change.

Technological change and market failure

Why is a technology policy needed in the first place? The main reason is that the market system might fail to provide those factors vital to initiate technological change, and there are a number of reasons for this, including the following.

R&D free riders. If an individual business can benefit from the results of *other* businesses conducting R&D, with all its associated costs and risks, then it is less likely to conduct R&D itself. It will simply 'free ride' on such activity. As a consequence, it would be in the interest of the firm conducting R&D to keep its findings secret or under some kind of property right, such as a patent, so as to gain as much competitive advantage as possible from its investment.

Although it is desirable to encourage firms to conduct R&D, and for this purpose it may be necessary to have a strict patent system in force, it is also desirable that there is the maximum *social* benefit from such R&D. This would occur only if such findings were widely disseminated. It is thus important that technology policy finds the optimum balance between the two objectives of (a) encouraging individual firms to conduct research and (b) disseminating the results.

Monopolistic and oligopolistic market structures. The more a market is dominated by a few large producers, the less incentive they will have to conduct R&D and innovate as a means of reducing costs. The problem is most acute under monopoly. Nevertheless, despite a lower incentive to innovate, the higher profits of firms with monopoly power will at least put them in a position of being more able to afford to conduct research.

Duplication. Not only is it likely that there is too little R&D being conducted, there is also the danger that resources may be wasted in duplicating research. The more firms there are conducting R&D, the greater the likelihood of some form of duplication. Given the scarcity of R&D resources, any duplication would be a highly inefficient way to organise production.

Risk and uncertainty. Because the payoffs from R&D activity are so uncertain, there will tend to be a natural caution on the part of both the business conducting R&D and (if different) the financier. Only R&D activity which has a clear market potential, or is of low risk, is likely to be considered. It has been found that financial markets in particular will tend to adopt a risk-averting strategy and fail to provide an adequate pool of long-term funds. This is another manifestation of the 'short-termism' we considered in section 19.4.

Forms of intervention

Attempts to correct the above market failures and develop a technology policy might include the use of the following.

The patent system. The strengthening of legal rights over the development of new products will encourage businesses to conduct R&D, as they will be able to reap greater rewards from successful R&D investment.

> **Pause for thought**
>
> Before you read on, can you identify the main forms of intervention the government might use in order to encourage and support R&D?

Public provision. In an attempt to overcome the free-rider problem and the inefficiency of R&D duplication, government might provide R&D itself, either through its own research institutions or via funding to university and other research councils. This is of particular importance in the case of basic research, where the potential outcomes are far less certain than those of applied research.

R&D subsidies. If the government provided subsidies to businesses conducting R&D activity, it not only would reduce the cost and hence the risk for business, but could ensure that the outcome from the R&D activity is more rapidly diffused throughout the economy than might otherwise be expected. This would help improve general levels of technological innovation.

Cooperative R&D. Given that the benefits of technological developments are of widespread use, the government could encourage cooperative R&D. The government could take various roles here, from being actively involved in the R&D process, to acting as a facilitator, bringing private-sector businesses together. The key advantages of this policy are that it will not only reduce the potential for duplication, but also encourage the pooling of scarce R&D resources.

Diffusion policies. Such policies tend to be of two types: the provision of information concerning new technology, and the use of subsidies to encourage businesses to adopt new technology.

Other policies. A wide range of other policies, primarily adopted for other purposes, might also influence R&D. These might include: education and training policy; competition policy; national defence policies and initiatives; and policies on standards and compatibility.

Technology policy in the UK and EU

The UK's poor technological performance since 1945 can be attributed to many factors, from a lack of entrepreneurial vision on the part of business, to the excessive short-termism of the UK's financial institutions. Equally there appears to have been a failure on the part of government to initiate suitable strategies to overcome such problems.

In the UK, the current attitude towards technology policy is one in which the role of government is kept to a minimum, and support is given only when 'a worthwhile and viable project is at risk through the failure of the market mechanism'. Actively interventionist strategies, such as the use of R&D subsidies, are kept to a

BOX 21.2 THE R&D SCOREBOARD

For many years it has been suggested that the UK's poor international competitive record has been in no small part due to its failure to invest in research and development. The UK's R&D intensity – that is, the ratio of R&D spending to sales – has been considerably lower than that of its main economic rivals.

Each year the Department for Innovation, Universities and Skills publishes the R&D Scoreboard. This gives details of the R&D expenditures of the top R&D spending companies in the UK and worldwide. It also investigates emerging trends and patterns in R&D spending. The 2008 Scoreboard is composed of the 850 leading R&D spending UK companies (UK850) and the 1400 leading global R&D spenders (G1400). Of the world's leading 1400 companies 88 UK companies made the list.

The following extracts are taken from the 2008 R&D Scoreboard.[1]

R&D: the global picture in 2008
Global R&D spending by the G1400 rose by 9.5 per cent to £274 billion [from 2007 to 2008]. It continues to be dominated by companies registered in just five countries – the USA, Japan, Germany, France and the UK – which contributed around 85 per cent of R&D by the G1400 (see the chart). Globally, average R&D intensity remains broadly similar at 3.3 per cent of sales.

R&D investment in the global pharmaceuticals sector grew by 12 per cent in the last year; it has remained as the largest global R&D sector. Other rapidly growing sectors amongst the ten largest investors were the software and technology and hardware sectors which both grew at more than 12 per cent.

The global leaders in R&D
[The table shows the 25 leading global investors in R&D in 2007.] Microsoft invested the most of any company having been fourth in the list in the previous year. The biggest climber in the Top 25 was Nokia, which increased investment in R&D by 42 per cent over the last year. The firm which dropped the most places in the Top 25 was Siemens, which fell from eighth place to twenty-second. Other significant rises were General Motors (to second), Roche (to eighth) and Volkswagen (to ninth). The global list is dominated by firms from the automobiles and parts and pharmaceuticals and biotechnology sectors.

The UK's top R & D companies
R&D is a key expenditure in many sectors. UK aerospace, automobiles, pharmaceuticals and software and technology firms invested substantially more in R&D than they earned as profits.

. . . Overall; the UK850 companies . . . increased their R&D expenditure more quickly [in 2007] than their global peers in the aerospace, fixed line communications, oil and gas producing and software sectors. In many sectors, however, UK firms increased their R&D more slowly than their global peers – such as in banking, electronic and technology sectors.

---

[1] Extracts from *R&D Scorecard 2008* (DIUS, 2008) www.innovation.gov.uk/rd_scoreboard/?p=68 © Crown Copyright 2008. Crown copyright material is reproduced with permission of the Controller of Her Majesty's Stationery Office (HMSO).

The R&D of the global top 1400 companies by country

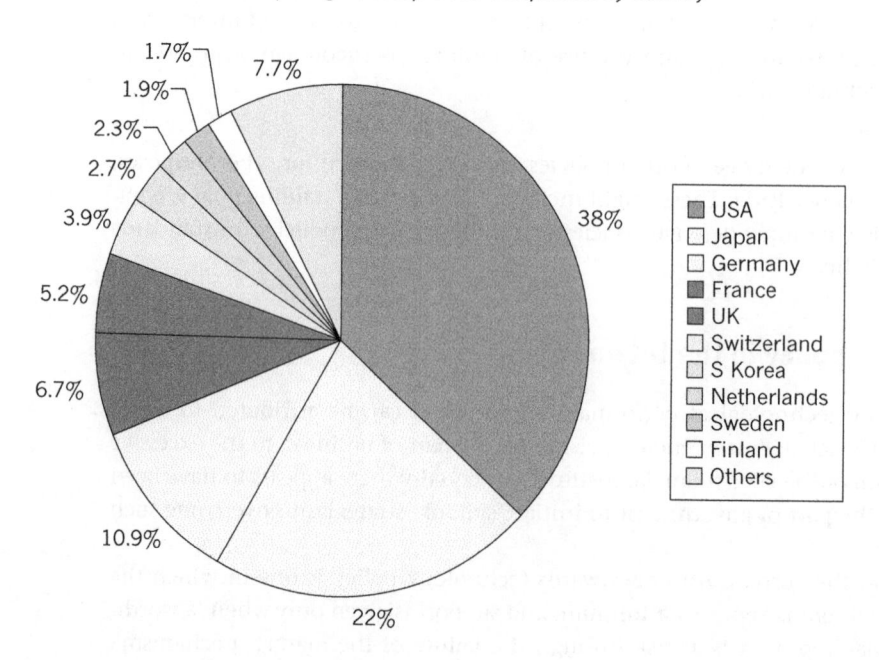

- USA: 38%
- Japan: 22%
- Germany: 10.9%
- France: 6.7%
- UK: 5.2%
- Switzerland: 3.9%
- S Korea: 2.7%
- Netherlands: 2.3%
- Sweden: 1.9%
- Finland: 1.7%
- Others: 7.7%

Source: *2008 R&D Scoreboard* (based on company data) (DIUS, 2008)

Top 25 global companies by R&D investment

Rank	Company	Industry	2007/08 R&D investment £m	Growth over last year %	R&D as % of sales %	Rank in 2006
1	Microsoft, USA	Software and Computer Services	4101.28	15	13.5	4
2	General Motors, USA	Automobiles and parts	4069.13	23	4.4	9
3	Pfizer, USA	Pharmaceuticals and biotechnology	4063.60	6	16.7	1
4	Toyota Motor, Japan	Automobiles and parts	4005.68	10	3.9	6
5	Nokia, Finland	Technology hardware & equipment	3878.81	42	10.3	17
6	Johnson & Johnson, USA	Pharmaceuticals and biotechnology	3858.13	8	12.6	3
7	Ford Motor, USA	Automobiles and parts	3767.71	4	4.3	2
8	Roche, Switzerland	Pharmaceuticals and biotechnology	3679.89	26	18.0	15
9	Volkswagen, Germany	Automobiles and parts	3615.87	16	4.5	14
10	Daimler, Germany	Automobiles and parts	3590.16	−7	3.8	5
11	Sanofi-Aventis, France	Pharmaceuticals and biotechnology	3351.45	4	16.3	12
12	Samsung Electronics, South Korea	Electronic and electrical equipment	3259.79	6	6.2	10
13	GlaxoSmithKline, UK	Pharmaceuticals and biotechnology	3246.00	−6	14.3	7
14	Novartis, Switzerland	Pharmaceuticals and biotechnology	3222.14	21	16.1	16
15	Intel, USA	Technology hardware & equipment	2891.09	−2	15.0	11
16	IBM, USA	Software and Computer Services	2887.07	1	5.8	13
17	Robert Bosch, Germany	Automobiles and parts	2614.76	5	7.7	20
18	Matsushita Electric, Japan	Leisure goods	2599.55	2	6.3	19
19	AstraZeneca, UK	Pharmaceuticals and biotechnology	2532.91	30	17.1	n.a.
20	Honda Motor, Japan	Automobiles and parts	2481.55	8	5.0	22
21	Alcatel-Lucent, France	Technology hardware & equipment	2473.74	69	18.7	n.a.
22	Siemens, Germany	Electronic and electrical equipment	2472.27	2	3.7	8
23	Merck, USA	Pharmaceuticals and biotechnology	2452.93	2	20.2	18
24	Sony, Japan	Leisure goods	2445.98	2	7.0	21
25	BMW, Germany	Automobiles and parts	2309.22	−2	5.6	23
	All companies		273 850.6	9.1	3.4	

The UK's 88 biggest R&D investors – which also form part of the 'G1400' largest R&D spenders worldwide – conducted two thirds of the UK850's R&D. They grew their R&D by 10.3 per cent over the previous year whereas their global peers averaged a 9.5 per cent increase.

Business performance and R&D expenditure

As part of the preparation for this R&D Scoreboard, an econometric/statistical analysis has been undertaken using the Scoreboard dataset to examine whether there is evidence of a statistical relationship between investment in R&D and business performance.

The analysis focused on considering whether changes in business performance over the last five years – as measured by sales growth, profitability and stock market capitalisation – could be explained in terms of changes in investment in R&D over the same period, and other factors captured in this year's Scoreboard database.

Despite extensive analysis, no statistically significant relationships were found. To some extent this is not surprising because:

- there may be long lags between changes in investment in R&D and subsequent company performance;
- there are effects on work at levels within companies that cannot be isolated at whole firm level; and
- there are important omitted variables in the data set available.

Our current conclusion here is that the relationship between R&D and firm performance is complex rather than non-existent. Certainly, the firms in the FTSE100 with higher R&D as a proportion of sales have been judged by the market to be more successful over the recent past than the index as a whole. [Thus,] the value of a portfolio [of FTSE100 firms spending at least 4% of their sales on R&D] has risen by 51% since 2001 [while] the FTSE100 index rose by 27% over the same period.

1. What are the economic costs and benefits of R&D spending to the national economy? Distinguish between the short and long run.
2. R&D is only one indicator, albeit an important one, of innovation potential. What other factors are likely to affect innovation?
3. What is the economic case for and against government intervention in the field of R&D?

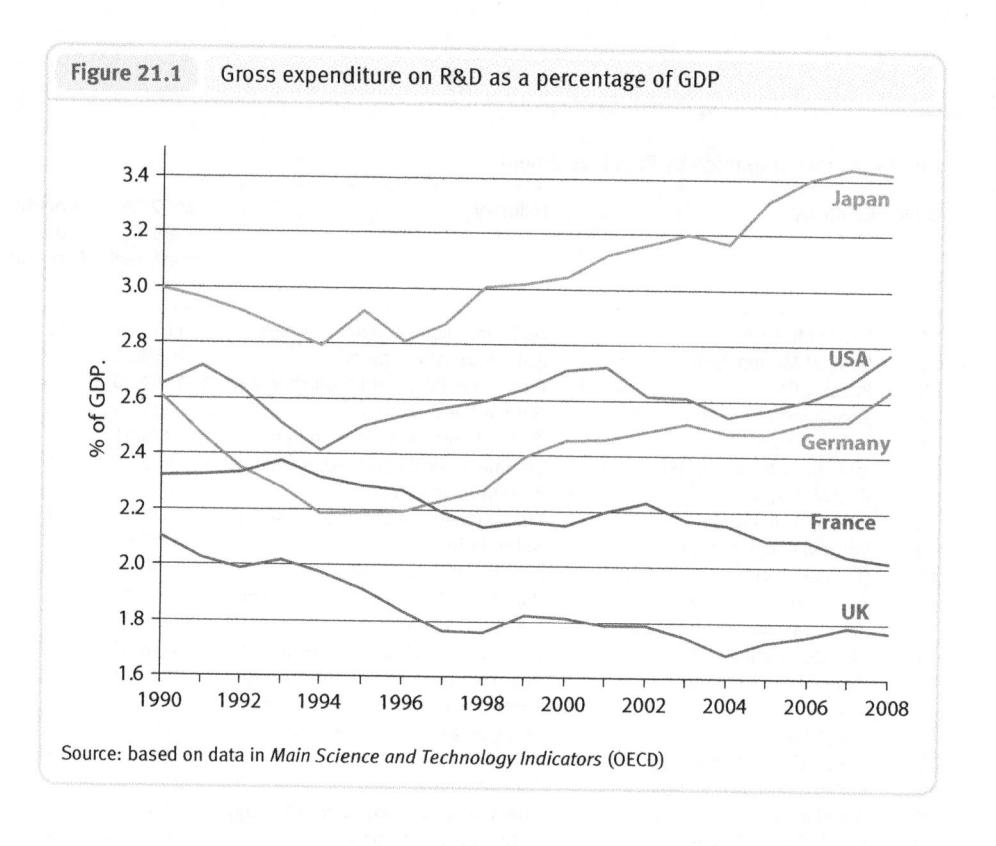

Figure 21.1 Gross expenditure on R&D as a percentage of GDP

Source: based on data in *Main Science and Technology Indicators* (OECD)

minimum, and the emphasis of policy is to encourage greater collaboration between companies within the private sector.

This strategy does not appear to have been very successful. Since 1990, UK gross expenditure on research and development as a percentage of GDP has been lower than that of its main economic rivals (see Figure 21.1).

In contrast to the UK's approach to R&D, the EU is more interventionist, and attempts to provide a unified strategy of R&D subsidies and collaborative R&D research programmes. EU initiatives range from general programmes such as the European Strategic Programme for Research in Information Technology (ESPRIT), to specific research fields such as medicine and health (BIOMED) and communications technology and services (ACTS), to name but two from a wide range of such initiatives.

The main source of funding is from the Research and Technology Programme. In 2005, spending on research represented 4.83 per cent of the total EU budget. The Seventh Framework Programme, which runs from 2007 to 2013, is set to double the EU's research budget to €67.8 billion. The Barcelona Summit of the Council of Ministers in 2002 set the EU a target of achieving an R&D to GDP ratio of 3 per cent by 2010. The Seventh Framework Programme was thus established to improve radically the EU's competitive stance relative to the USA and Japan through investment in capacity building and new scientific research.

In principle, the move toward greater R&D intensity is to be welcomed, but there is some scepticism whether the EU's 3 per cent R&D to GDP target can be achieved, or even if there is a commitment to it. The UK, for example, set a ten-year target of only 2.5 per cent to be achieved by 2014.

21.3 POLICIES TOWARDS TRAINING

It is generally recognised by economists and politicians alike that improvements in training and education can yield significant supply-side gains. Indeed, the UK's failure to invest as much in training as many of its major competitors is seen as a key explanation for the country's poor economic performance since the early 1970s. In the UK about 35 per cent of workers are classified as low skilled. This compares with only 17 per cent in Germany.

Training and economic performance

Training and economic performance are linked in three main ways.

Labour productivity. In various studies comparing the productivity of UK and German industry, education and training was seen as the principal reason for the productivity gap between the two countries (see Box 21.3).

Innovation and change. A key factor in shaping a firm's willingness to introduce new products or processes will be the adaptability and skills of its workforce. If the firm has to spend a lot of money on retraining, or on attracting skilled workers away from other firms, the costs may prove prohibitive.

Costs of production. A shortage of skilled workers will quickly create labour bottlenecks and cause production costs to increase. This will stifle economic growth.

Training policy

If training is left to the employer, the benefits will become an externality if the workers leave to work elsewhere. Society has benefited from the training, but the firm has not. The free market, therefore, will provide a less than optimal amount of training. The more mobile the labour force, and the more 'transferable' the skills acquired from training, the more likely it is that workers will leave, and the less willing will firms be to invest in training.

In the UK, there is a high level of labour turnover. What is more, wage differentials between skilled and unskilled workers are narrower than in many other countries, and so there is less incentive for workers to train.

How can increased training be achieved? There are three broad approaches:

- Workers could be encouraged to stay with their employer so that employers would be more willing to invest in training. Externalities would be reduced.
- The government could provide subsidies for training. Alternatively, the government or some other agency could provide education and training directly.
- Firms could cooperate to prevent 'poaching' and set up industry-wide training programmes, perhaps in partnership with the government and unions.

Training policy in various countries

As far as the first approach is concerned, most countries have seen a movement towards *greater* labour mobility. The rise in the 'flexible firm' has involved the employment of fewer permanent workers and more part-time and temporary workers.

Some countries, such as Japan and Germany, however, have a generally lower rate of labour turnover than most. In Japan, in particular, it is common for workers to stay with one employer throughout their career. There the relationship between employer and employee extends well beyond a simple short-term economic arrangement. Workers give loyalty and commitment to their employer, which in return virtually guarantees long-term employment and provides various fringe benefits (such as housing, child care, holiday schemes and health care). It is not surprising that Japanese firms invest highly in training.

In the USA, labour turnover is very high and yet there is little in the way of industry-wide training. Instead, by having a high percentage of young people in further and higher education, the US government hopes that sufficient numbers and quality of workers are available for industry. Approximately 39 per cent of the US population aged 25 to 34 has a first degree or higher but less than 0.6 per cent of GDP is spent on training and labour market programmes.

In Germany the proportion entering higher education is considerably lower (some 22 per cent aged 25 to 34), but expenditure on training and labour market programmes accounts for nearly 3.8 per cent of GDP. Most young people who do not enter higher education embark on some form of apprenticeship. They attend school for part of the week, and receive work-based training for the rest. The state, unions and employers' associations work closely in determining training provision, and they have developed a set of vocational qualifications based around the apprenticeship system. Given that virtually all firms are involved in training, the 'free-rider' problem of firms poaching labour without themselves paying for training is virtually eliminated. The result is that the German workforce is highly skilled. Many of the skills, however, are highly specific. This is a problem when the demand for particular skills declines.

The UK approach

> **Pause for thought**
>
> *What advantages and drawbacks are there in leaving training provision to employers? Clue: think about how training provision might be influenced by the business cycle (the cycle of booms and recessions in the economy).*

In the UK, the former Conservative government's attitude toward training was initially influenced by its free-market approach to supply-side policy. Training was to be left largely to employers. However, with growing worries over the UK's 'productivity gap', the government set up Training and Enterprise Councils (TECs) in 1988. The TECs identified regional skills needs, organised training and financed work-based training schemes.

The TECs were replaced in 2001 by the Learning and Skills Council (LSC). For 2008/09 the LSC has an investment budget of some £11.3 billion and is responsible for planning and funding sixth forms, further education colleges, work-based training for young people aged 16 to 24 ('Apprenticeships' and 'Advanced Apprenticeships'), adult and community learning, the provision of information, advice and guidance for adults, and developing links between education and business. Through its 'Connexions service', it offers training and employment advice and support for young people between the ages of 13 and 19.

The National Vocational Qualification (NVQ) was launched in 1991 specifically to support workplace learning for young people. A young person works for an employer and receives on-the-job training. They also attend college on an occasional basis. The NVQ is awarded when they have achieved sufficient competence. In addition, the government launched General National Vocational Qualifications (GNVQs). These further-education qualifications were aimed to bridge the gap between education and work, by ensuring that education was more work relevant.

The GNVQ system was modelled on that in France, where a clear vocational educational route is seen as the key to reducing skills shortages. At the age of fourteen, French students can choose to pursue academic or vocational education routes. The vocational route provides high-level, broad-based skills (unlike in Germany, where skills tend to be more job specific).

However, GNVQs were competing alongside other well-established vocational qualifications such as City and Guilds and BTEC certificates and diplomas. Such competition led to the withdrawal of the GNVQ by October 2007. The NVQ survives largely because it complements other vocational qualifications, for example on apprenticeship schemes.

Education and training policy in the UK aims to encourage 'lifelong learning' and so support business. Other measures of note in this regard include:

- A University for Industry, which through its 'Learndirect' brand offers online courses in basic English and maths as well as courses in business and management and IT. There are almost 700 Learndirect centres across England and Wales in 2008.
- Work-based Learning for Adults in England and Wales and Training for Work in Scotland: two schemes to provide work-based training for people aged 25 and over who have been out of work for six months or more, with grants paid to employers.
- The introduction of two-year Foundation Degrees. These are offered by universities or higher education colleges. They are designed in conjunction with employers to meet various skill shortages. They are taken at a university or college, normally on a part-time basis, and often include work-based study with local employers. In 2001–2, when they were introduced, there 4320 students enrolled on these courses. In 2007–8, the corresponding number was 71 915.

Critics of the UK skills strategy have argued that employers still face the threat of having newly trained labour poached; that the regional activities of the LSC fail to account for national, long-term training issues; and that the vocational qualifications framework lacks any coherence.

In 2004 the government appointed Lord Leitch to consider what the UK's long-term ambition should be for developing skills in order to maximise economic prosperity and productivity, and to improve social justice. The assessment was rather gloomy; the Leitch Committee stated in its interim report that the UK had to 'raise its game' (see Box 21.3).

There has been considerable concern in the UK with respect to training and skilling the workforce to levels appropriate for future national prosperity.

The final report of the Leitch Committee was launched in December 2006 and reaffirmed the need for substantial investment and reform for the UK to become a world leader in skills. It suggested actions that amounted to a dramatic improvement in the skills profile of the UK working population, including ensuring that all young people remain in full- or part-time education or workplace training up until the age of 18. The new reforms and substantial investment required should build on existing partnerships between learners, industry, training providers and government but offer a more flexible 'demand-led' service, rather than the centrally planned system that had existed in the past.

Perhaps pre-empting the Leitch reports, the government produced two White Papers covering skills and further education in 2005 and 2006, respectively. These were accepted and developed by the Command paper, *World-class Skills: Implementing the Leitch Review of Skills in England* in July 2007.

BOX 21.3 THE UK NEEDS TO 'RAISE ITS GAME'

The Leitch review of future skill needs

In his pre-Budget speech in November 2005, the Chancellor of the Exchequer announced the publication of an interim review of the UK's future skill needs by Lord Leitch, Chairman of the National Employment Panel. The report noted that the UK had to 'raise its game' if it was to be successful in the increasingly competitive global economy. The following extracts are taken from the executive summary of the *Leitch Review*.[1]

Skills in the UK in 2005

The UK starts from a strong economic position. It is the fourth largest economy in the world and has the highest employment rate in the G7 group of industrialised nations. Despite this strong performance, the UK today faces important economic challenges. In particular, despite some recent improvements, the UK continues to have relatively poor productivity performance which still trails some of the UK's main comparator nations. Output per hour worked is almost 30 per cent higher in France and more than 10 per cent higher in Germany and the USA than it is in the UK.

Evidence shows that a significant contributory factor to the UK's relatively poor productivity performance is its low overall level of skills. For example, one fifth of the gap with France and Germany is a result of the UK's comparatively poor skills. Low levels of skills in the UK constrain growth and innovation in firms . . .

---

[1] HM Treasury (2005) *Skills in the UK: The Long-term Challenge* (Leitch Committee interim report, December 2005) (HMSO, December 2005). © Crown Copyright 2005. Crown copyright material is reproduced with permission of the Controller of Her Majesty's Stationery Office (HMSO).

Today, the UK's human capital is poor in relation to key comparator nations:

- the proportion of adults in the UK without a basic school-leaving qualification is double that of Canada and Germany;
- over 5 million people of working age in the UK have no qualification at all; and
- one in six adults do not have the literacy skills expected of an 11-year-old. Almost half do not have these levels of functional numeracy; only half of adults who lack these functional skills are in work.

Although the position in higher-level skills is better, with over one quarter of adults in the UK holding a degree-level qualification, other countries such as USA, Japan and Canada are still in a superior position (see the chart).

Skill deficiencies are reflected in employers' experiences. In survey evidence from across the UK, employers report significant skills shortages within their own workforce and in the pool of labour from which they recruit. Recent evidence shows persistent recruitment difficulties across the skills spectrum, in low skilled service jobs as well as in skilled craft jobs. This affects the ability of firms to grow and become more productive and profitable. Almost one third of firms who report skills gaps in their workforce say that these gaps prevent them from modernising their business to move into higher value added – and more productive – economic activity.

Skill levels have an important impact on employment and social welfare. For example, only half of those

International comparisons of qualifications profiles

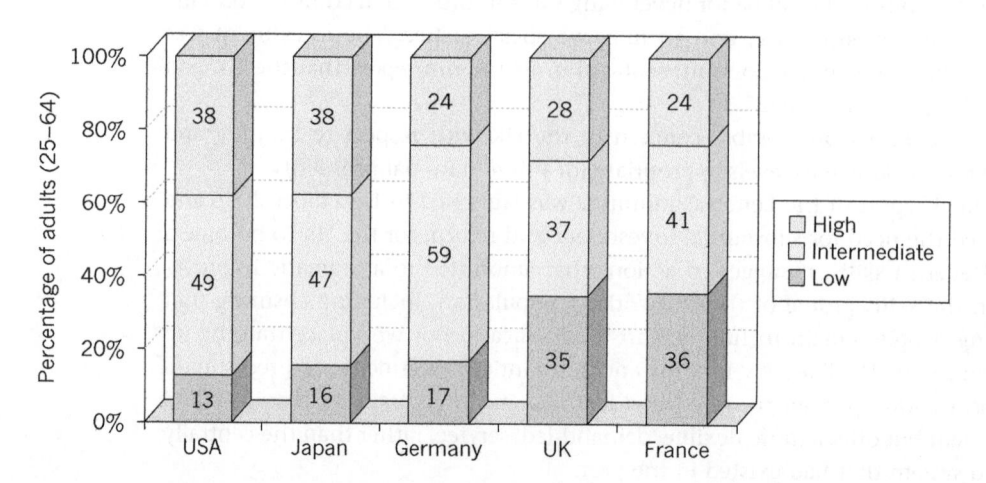

Country	Low	Intermediate	High
USA	13	49	38
Japan	16	47	38
Germany	17	59	24
UK	35	37	28
France	36	41	24

(Percentage of adults 25–64)

Source: H. M. Treasury, *Skills in the UK: The Long-term Challenge* (Leitch Committee interim report, December 2005), Chart 3 (based on data in *Education at a glance*, OECD, 2005). © Crown Copyright 2005. Crown copyright material is reproduced with permission of the Controller of Her Majesty's Stationery Office (HMSO)

people with no qualifications are in work compared to 90 per cent of adults qualified to at least degree level. Low skills levels are particularly pronounced in certain groups. For example, over 40 per cent of people with a disability have no qualifications at all. The unequal distribution of skills has adverse affects on income equality and constrains social mobility, which has deteriorated in the UK over the past two decades. Evidence suggests that skills gaps exacerbate social deprivation including poverty, poor health and crime . . .

Over the last decade, the UK has made real improvements to its skills profile. The proportion of the working age population with a degree has increased from one fifth to over one quarter. The proportion of adults who hold no qualifications has fallen by one third, from one fifth of the working age population to 14 per cent.

These changes are primarily due to younger, better-qualified people flowing into the workforce, while older and less well-qualified people retire. One in ten 25–34-year-olds has no qualifications compared to one in four 55–64-year-olds. Over the last decade, there has been a significant decrease in the proportion of people who lack a qualification at the equivalent level to five good GCSEs, falling by almost one half from 43 per cent to 23 per cent.

The Government has set ambitious targets to further improve the skills profile of the UK. These include addressing the stock of adults who lack basic literacy and numeracy skills; reducing the stock of adults without the equivalent of a good school-leaving qualification; and increasing the numbers of young people with a degree. Meeting these targets will bring significant improvements to the stock of skills in the UK. However, the Review believes that, on current trends, achieving these targets will be extremely challenging.

Looking forward to 2020
[F]urther improvements [in] the skills of young people alone will not [raise] the UK's overall skills profile significantly enough by 2020 because:

- 70 per cent of the working age population in 2020 have already completed their compulsory school education; and
- half of the working age population in 2020 is already over 25 years old. This is beyond the age when people are likely to participate in the traditional education route from school through to university.

By 2020, there will be about 3.5 million more people in the working age population and the population will have aged significantly. Adults aged 50–65 years will account for 60 per cent of the growth in the working age population. The contribution of older people to the labour market will become increasingly important. By 2020, 30 per cent of the working age population will be over 50, compared with 25 per cent today. These demographic changes make it essential to improve the skills of older groups in the workforce.

The Review has undertaken new analysis to assess the UK's current trajectory in developing its skills profile and the likely stock of skills in 2020 if all current targets are met. The most marked changes over the next 15 years will occur at each end of the skills spectrum:

- by 2020, the proportion of working age adults without any qualifications will fall to 4 per cent;
- the proportion without qualifications at the equivalent level to five good GCSEs will halve from 31 per cent today to 16 per cent in 2020; and
- the proportion holding a degree or better would increase from 27 per cent to 38 per cent of the working age population.

The Review's analysis suggests that the economic benefits from meeting these current ambitions would be substantial. Productivity could be 3 per cent higher compared to what it would otherwise be and the employment rate could increase by 0.75 per cent. This is a net benefit to the economy of an average £3 billion each year – equivalent to 0.3 per cent of gross domestic product (GDP). One fifth of this benefit is due to increased employment; the rest is due to adults who are already in work improving their skills further and becoming more productive.

However, even if the Government's current ambitious targets were met, significant problems would remain with the UK's skills base in 2020. At least 4 million adults will still not have literacy skills expected of an 11-year-old, at least 12 million will be without numeracy skills at this level (equivalent to three in ten adults) and 6.5 million adults will not have qualifications at the equivalent level to five good GCSEs. In comparative terms, the UK will continue to be an 'average performer' – positioned at best, in the middle of the OECD ranking. It will continue to have smaller proportions of intermediate and higher-level skills than key comparator countries such as France and the USA.

1. What other factors help to raise long-term productivity in the UK?
2. To what extent is the UK on target to achieve the ambitions set out in the Leitch Committee reports? Explore the UK government websites and other sources to help you come to a view.

The skills strategy for the UK continues to reinforce the role of business in shaping vocational qualifications and training. The government wants to develop its flagship project, 'Train to Gain', a work-based national training framework established in 2006 in which firms undergo a training needs analysis and are offered part funding to raise skill levels. There is also provision for Skills Accounts in which employees are offered grants for those who want to achieve level 3 (e.g. post A-level qualifications). In other words, a demand-led training system has been adopted by the government.

Further there is an acceptance that all young people should continue in learning until they are 18. GCSEs and A-levels are retained but 14 new diplomas are to be developed by 2015. Five of these (Construction and the Built Environment; ICT; Engineering; Society, Health and Development; Creative and Media) were launched in September 2008 and eight more are planned to follow by 2010. Apprenticeships, which will form a major plank of the new work-based training for young people, are to be aligned with the new diplomas.

As part of its further education reforms, the government is also to provide free education for 19- to 25-year-olds who want to take level 3 qualifications (i.e. A-levels or their equivalents) and embark on an ambitious capital and revenue expenditure plan to improve the quality of further education provision.

Thus, the government has taken on the challenge offered in the Leitch Review. We await with interest the extent to which the UK will have 'raised its game' by 2020.

SUMMARY

1a Competition policy in most countries recognises that monopolies, mergers and restrictive practices can bring both costs and benefits to the consumer. Generally, though, restrictive practices tend to be more damaging to consumers' interests than simple monopoly power or mergers.

1b European Union legislation applies to firms trading between EU countries. Article 101 applies to restrictive practices. Article 102 applies to dominant firms. There are also separate merger control provisions.

1c UK legislation is largely covered by the 1998 Competition Act and 2002 Enterprise Act. The Chapter I prohibition of the 1998 Act applies to restrictive practices and is similar to Article 101. The Chapter II prohibition applies to dominant firms and is similar to Article 102. The 2002 Act made certain cartel agreements a criminal offence and required mergers over a certain size to be investigated by the Office of Fair Trading with possible reference to the Competition Commission. Both the OFT and CC were made independent of government.

1d The focus of both EU and UK legislation is on anti-competitive practices rather than on the simple existence of agreements between firms or market dominance. Practices that are found after investigation to be detrimental to competition are prohibited and heavy fines can be imposed, even for a first offence.

2a The importance of technology in determining national economic success is growing. There is now a need for government to formulate a technology policy to ensure that the national economy has every chance to remain competitive.

2b Technological change, when left to the market, is unlikely to proceed rapidly enough or to a socially desirable level. Reasons for this include R&D free riders, monopolistic market structures, duplication of R&D activities, and risk and uncertainty.

2c Government technology policy might involve intervention at different levels of the technology process (invention, innovation and diffusion). Such intervention might involve extending ownership rights over new products, providing R&D directly or using subsidies to encourage third parties. Government might also act in an advisory/coordinating capacity.

2d Technology policy in the UK has tended to emphasise the market as the principal provider of technological change. Where possible, government's role has been kept to a minimum. Within the EU, policy has been more interventionist and a wide range of initiatives have been launched to encourage greater levels of R&D.

3a A well-trained workforce contributes to economic performance by enhancing productivity, encouraging and enabling change, and, in respect to supplying scarce skills to the workplace, helps to reduce wage costs.

3b Training policy in the UK has largely been the responsibility of industry. The result has been a less than optimum amount of training. In other countries, such as Germany, the state plays a far greater role in training provision. Since 1979 training and education policy in the UK has become increasingly vocational.

REVIEW QUESTIONS

1. Try to formulate a definition of the public interest.

2. What are the advantages and disadvantages of the current system of controlling restrictive practices?

3. What problems are likely to arise in identifying which firms' practices are anti-competitive? Should the OFT take firms' assurances into account when deciding whether to grant an exemption?

4. If anti-monopoly legislation is effective enough, is there ever any need to prevent mergers from going ahead?

5. If two or more firms were charging similar prices, what types of evidence would you look for to prove that this was collusion rather than mere coincidence?

6. Should governments or regulators always attempt to eliminate the supernormal profits of monopolists/oligopolists?

7. We can distinguish three clear stages in the development and application of technology: invention, innovation and diffusion. How might forms of technology policy intervention change at each stage of this process?

8. Governments and educationalists generally regard it as desirable that trainees acquire transferable skills. Why may many employers disagree?

9. There are externalities (benefits) when employers provide training. What externalities are there from the undergoing of training by the individual? Do they imply that individuals will choose to receive more or less than the socially optimal amount of training?

Chapter 22

Government and the market

Business issues covered in this chapter

- Why is a free market unlikely to lead to environmentally sustainable development?
- What policies can governments pursue to protect the environment and what are their impacts on business?
- What determines the allocation of road space?
- What are the best policies for reducing traffic congestion?
- What forms has privatisation taken and has it been beneficial?
- How are privatised industries regulated and how has competition been increased in these industries?

In the previous chapter we considered examples of the relationship between the government and the individual firm. In this chapter we turn to examine government policy at the level of the whole market. Although such policies are generally directed at a whole industry or sector, they nevertheless still affect individual businesses, and indeed the effects may well vary from one firm to another.

22.1 ENVIRONMENTAL POLICY

Growing concerns over global warming, industrial and domestic waste, traffic fumes and other forms of pollution have made the protection of the environment a major political and economic issue. The subject of environmental degradation lies clearly within the realm of economics, since it is a direct consequence of production and consumption decisions. So how can economic analysis help us to understand the nature of the problem and design effective policies for sustainable development? What will be the impact of such policies on business?

The environment and production

In section 20.2 we considered how pollution could be classified as a 'negative externality' of production or consumption. In the case of production, this means that the marginal social costs (*MSC*) are greater than the marginal private costs (*MC*) to the polluter. The failure of the market system to equate *MSC* and marginal social benefit (*MSB*) is due to the lack of property rights of those suffering the pollution. The fact that no charge is levied on the producer for use of the air or rivers means that the environment is effectively a free good, and as such is overused.

In order to ensure that the environment is taken sufficiently into account by both firms and consumers, the government must intervene. It must devise an appropriate environmental policy. Such a policy will involve measures to ensure that at least a specified minimum level of environmental quality is achieved. Ideally, however, the policy would ensure that all externalities are fully 'internalised'. This means that firms and consumers are forced to pay the *full* costs of production or consumption: i.e. their marginal private costs *plus* any external costs.

> **Definition**
>
> **Environmental policy**
> Initiatives by government to ensure a specified minimum level of environmental quality.

Problems with policy intervention

Valuing the environment

The principal difficulty facing government in constructing its environmental policy is that of *valuing* the environment and hence of estimating the costs of its pollution. If policy is based upon the principle that the polluter pays, then an accurate assessment of pollution costs is vital if the policy is to establish a socially efficient level of production.

Three common methods used for valuing environmental damage are: the financial costs to *other* users; revealed preferences; and 'contingent valuation' (or stated preference).

The financial costs to other users. In this method, environmental costs are calculated by considering the financial costs imposed on other businesses or individuals by polluting activities. For example, if firm A feeds chemical waste into a local stream, then firm B, which is downstream and requires a clean water supply, may have to introduce a water purification process. The expense of this to firm B can be seen as an external cost of firm A.

The main problem with this method is that not all external costs entail a direct financial cost for the sufferers. Many external costs may therefore be overlooked.

Revealed preferences. If the direct financial costs of pollution are difficult to identify, let alone calculate, then an alternative approach to valuing the environment might be to consider how individuals or businesses change their *behaviour* in response to environmental changes. Such changes in behaviour frequently carry a financial cost, which makes calculation easier. For example, the building of a new superstore on a greenfield site overlooked by your house might cause you to move. Moving house entails a financial cost, including the loss in value of your property resulting from the opening of the store. Clearly, in such a case, by choosing to move you would be regarding the cost of moving to be less than the cost to you of the deterioration in your environment.

Contingency valuation. In this method, people likely to be affected are asked to evaluate the effect on them of any proposed change to their environment. In the case of the superstore, local residents might be asked how much they would be willing to pay in order for the development not to take place, or alternatively, how much they would need to be compensated if it were to take place.

The principal concern with this method is how reliable the answers are to the questionnaires. There are two major problems:

- *Ignorance.* People will not know just how much they will suffer *until* the project goes ahead.
- *Dishonesty.* People will tend to exaggerate the compensation they would need. After all, if compensation is actually going to be paid, people will want to get as much as possible. But even if it is not, the more people exaggerate the costs to them, the more likely it is that they can get the project stopped.

These problems can be lessened if people are questioned who have already experienced a similar project elsewhere. They are more knowledgeable and have less to gain from being dishonest.

Research on contingency valuation has focused heavily on the questioning process and how monetary values of costs and benefits might be accurately established. Of all the methods, contingency valuation has grown most in popularity over recent years, despite its limitations.

Other problems

As well as the problems of value, other aspects of environmental damage make policy making particularly difficult. These include the following:

- *Spatial issues.* The place where pollution is produced and the places where it is deposited may be geographically very far apart. Pollution crosses borders (e.g. acid rain) or can be global (e.g. greenhouse gases). In both cases, national policies might be of little value, especially if you are a receiver of others' pollution! In such circumstances, international agreements would be needed, and these can be very difficult to reach.
- *Temporal issues.* Environmental problems such as acid rain and the depletion of the ozone layer have been occurring over many decades. Thus the full effect of pollution on the environment may be identifiable only in the long term. As a consequence, policy initiatives are required to be forward looking and proactive, if the cumulative effects of pollution are to be avoided. Most policy tends to be reactive, however, dealing only with problems as they arise. In such cases, damage to the environment may have already been done.
- *Irreversibility issues.* Much environmental damage might be irreversible: once a species is extinct, for example, it cannot normally be reintroduced.

Environmental policy options

Environmental policy can take many forms. However, it is useful to put the different types of policy into three broad categories: market based, non-market based, and mixed. The most important market-based solution is to use taxes and subsidies. Non-market-based solutions usually involve imposing regulations and controls. The most important mixed system is that of tradable permits. Let us examine each of these three categories in turn.

Market-based environmental policy: taxation

Market-based solutions attempt to internalise the costs of the externality, and ensure that the polluter pays. The most common market-based approach to environmental

Table 22.1 Types of environmental taxes and charges

Motor fuels	Other goods	Air transport
Leaded/unleaded	Batteries	Noise charges
Diesel (quality differential)	Plastic carrier bags	Aviation fuels
Carbon/energy taxation	Glass containers	**Water**
Sulphur tax	Drink cans	Water charges
Other energy products	Tyres	Sewage charges
Carbon/energy tax	CFCs/halons	Water effluent charges
Sulphur tax or charge	Disposable razors/cameras	Manure charges
NO_2 charge	Lubricant oil charge	**Direct tax provisions**
Methane charge	Oil pollutant charge	Tax relief on green investment
Agricultural inputs	Solvents	Taxation on free company cars
Fertilisers	**Waste disposal**	Employer-paid commuting expenses taxable
Pesticides	Municipal waste charges	Employer-paid parking expenses taxable
Manure	Waste-disposal charges	Commuter use of public transport tax deductible
Vehicle-related taxation	Hazardous waste charges	
Sales tax depends on car size	Landfill tax or charges	
Road tax depends on car size	Duties on waste water	

policy is to impose indirect taxes on specific types of polluting activity, such as the use of carbon-based fuels. To achieve a socially efficient output, the rate of tax should be equal to the marginal external cost (see Figure 20.5 on page 423).

Taxes have the advantage of relating the size of the penalty to the amount of pollution. This means that there is continuous pressure to cut down on production or consumption of polluting products or activities in order to save tax.

One approach is to modify *existing* taxes. In most developed countries there are now higher taxes on high-emission cars.

Increasingly, however, countries are introducing *new* 'green' taxes in order to discourage pollution as goods are produced, consumed or disposed of. Table 22.1 shows the wide range of green taxes and charges used around the world and Figure 22.1 shows green tax revenues as a percentage of GDP in various countries. As you can see, they are higher than average in the Netherlands and the Scandinavian nations, reflecting the strength of their environmental concerns. They are lowest in the USA. By far the largest green tax revenues come from fuel taxes. Fuel taxes are relatively high in the UK and so, therefore, are green tax revenues.

There are various problems with using the tax weapon in the fight against pollution.

Identifying the socially efficient tax rate. It will be difficult to identify the marginal pollution cost of each firm, given that each one is likely to produce different amounts of pollutants for any given level of output. Even if two firms produce identical amounts of pollutants, the environmental damage might be quite different, because the ability of the environment to cope with it will differ between the two locations. Also, the number of people suffering will differ (a factor that is very important when considering the *human* impact of pollution). What is more, the harmful effects are likely to build up over time, and predicting these effects is fraught with difficulty.

Problems of demand inelasticity. The less elastic the demand for the product, the less effective will a tax be in cutting production and hence in cutting pollution. Thus taxes on petrol would have to be very high indeed to make significant reductions

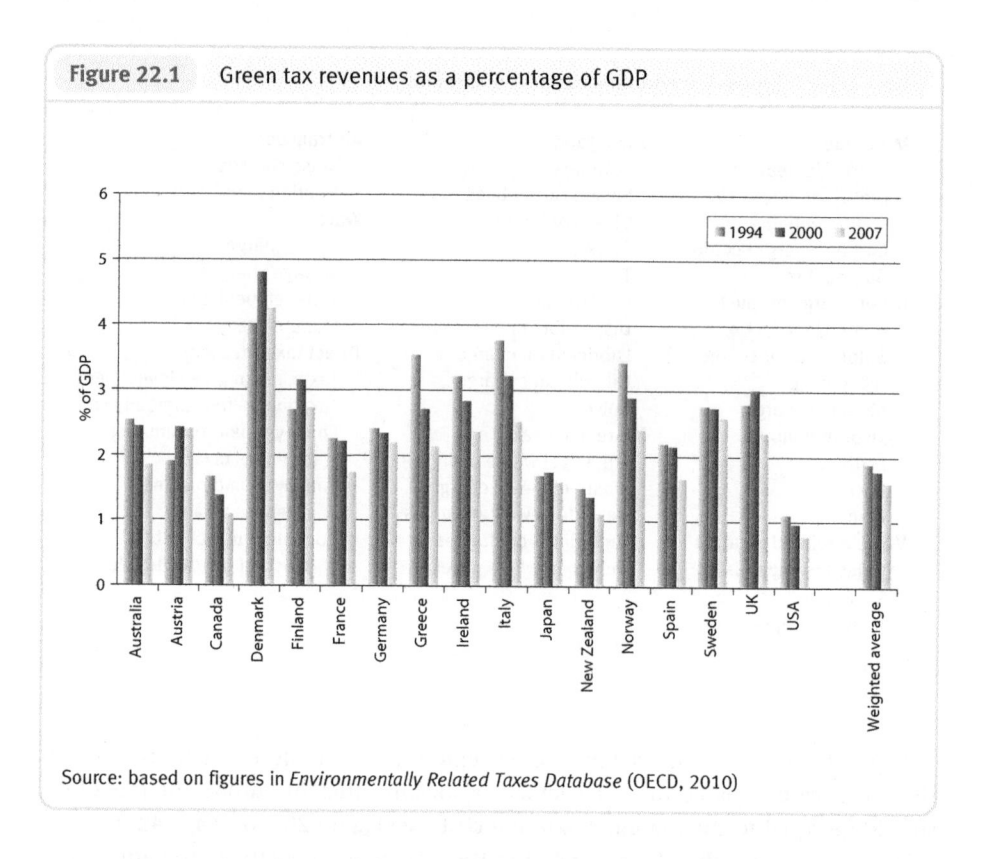

Figure 22.1 Green tax revenues as a percentage of GDP

Source: based on figures in Environmentally Related Taxes Database (OECD, 2010)

in the consumption of petrol and hence significant reductions in the exhaust gases that contribute towards global warming and acid rain.

Redistributive effects. The poor spend a higher proportion of their income on domestic fuel than the rich. A 'carbon tax' on such fuel will, therefore, have the effect of redistributing incomes away from the poor. The poor also spend a larger proportion of their income on food than do the rich. Taxes on agriculture, designed to reduce intensive use of fertilisers and pesticides, will again tend to hit the poor proportionately more than the rich.

However, not all green taxes hit the poor more than the rich. The rich spend a higher proportion of their income on motoring than the poor. Thus petrol and other motoring taxes could help to reduce inequality.

Problems with international trade. If a country imposes pollution taxes on its industries, its products will become less competitive in world trade. To compensate for this, the industries may need to be given tax rebates for exports. Also taxes would need to be imposed on imports of competitors' products from countries where there is no equivalent green tax.

Evidence on the adverse effect of environmental taxes on a country's exports is inconclusive, however. Over the long term, in countries with high environmental taxes (or other tough environmental measures), firms will be stimulated to invest in low-pollution processes and products. This will later give such countries a competitive advantage if *other* countries then impose tougher environmental standards.

Effects on employment. Reduced output in the industries affected by green taxes will lead to a reduction in employment. If, however, the effect was to encourage investment in new cleaner technology, employment might not fall. Furthermore, employment opportunities could be generated elsewhere if the extra revenues from the green taxes were spent on alternative products, such as buses and trains rather than cars.

Non-market-based environmental policy: command-and-control systems (laws and regulations)

The traditional way of tackling pollution has been to set maximum permitted levels of emission or resource use, or minimum acceptable levels of environmental quality, and then to fine firms contravening these limits. Measures of this type are known as **command-and-control (CAC) systems**. Clearly, there have to be inspectors to monitor the amount of pollution, and the fines have to be large enough to deter firms from exceeding the limit.

Virtually all countries have environmental regulations of one sort or another. For example, the EU has over 200 items of legislation covering areas such as air and water pollution, noise, the marketing and use of dangerous chemicals, waste management, the environmental impacts of new projects (such as power stations, roads and quarries), recycling, depletion of the ozone layer and global warming.

Typically there are three approaches to devising CAC systems.[1]

- **Technology-based standards.** The focus could be on the amount of pollution generated, irrespective of its environmental impact. As technology for reducing pollutants improves, so tougher standards could be imposed, based on the 'best available technology' (as long as the cost was not excessive). Thus car manufacturers could be required to ensure that new car engines meet lower CO_2 emission levels as the technology enabled them to do so.
- **Ambient-based standards.** Here the focus is on the environmental impact. For example, standards could be set for air or water purity. Depending on the location and the number of polluters in that area, a given standard would be achieved with different levels of discharge. If the object is a cleaner environment, then this approach is more efficient than technology-based standards.
- **Social-impact standards.** Here the focus is on the effect on people. Thus tougher standards would be imposed in densely populated areas. Whether this approach is more efficient than that of ambient-based standards depends on the approach to sustainability. If the objective is to achieve social efficiency, then human-impact standards are preferable. If the objective is to protect the environment for its own sake (a 'deeper green' approach), then ambient standards would be preferable.

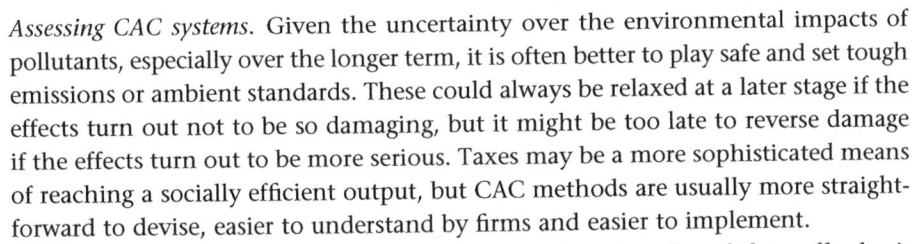

Assessing CAC systems. Given the uncertainty over the environmental impacts of pollutants, especially over the longer term, it is often better to play safe and set tough emissions or ambient standards. These could always be relaxed at a later stage if the effects turn out not to be so damaging, but it might be too late to reverse damage if the effects turn out to be more serious. Taxes may be a more sophisticated means of reaching a socially efficient output, but CAC methods are usually more straightforward to devise, easier to understand by firms and easier to implement.

Where command-and-control systems are weak is that they fail to offer business any incentive to do better than the legally specified level. By contrast, with a pollution tax, the lower the pollution level, the less tax there will be to pay. There

> **Definitions**
>
> **Command-and-control (CAC) systems**
> The use of laws or regulations backed up by inspections and penalties (such as fines) for non-compliance.
>
> **Technology-based standards**
> Pollution control that requires firms' emissions to reflect the levels that could be achieved from using the best available pollution control technology.
>
> **Ambient-based standards**
> Pollution control that requires firms to meet minimum standards for the environment (e.g. air or water quality).
>
> **Social-impact standards**
> Pollution control that focuses on the effects on people (e.g. on health or happiness).

---

[1] See R. K. Turner, D. Pearce and I. Bateman, *Environmental Economics* (Harvester Wheatsheaf, 1994), p. 198.

> **Definitions**
>
> **Tradable permits**
> Each firm is given a permit to produce a given level of pollution. If less than the permitted amount is produced, the firm is given a credit. This can then be sold to another firm, allowing it to exceed its original limit.
>
> **Grandfathering**
> Where each firm's emission permit is based on its *current* levels of emission (e.g. permitted levels for all firms could be 80 per cent of their current levels).

is thus a continuing incentive for businesses progressively to cut pollution levels and introduce cleaner technology.

Tradable permits

A policy measure that has grown in popularity in recent years is that of **tradable permits**. This is a combination of command-and-control and market-based systems. A maximum permitted level of emission is set for a given pollutant for a given factory, and the firm is given a permit to emit up to this amount. If it emits less than this amount, it is given a credit for the difference, which it can then use in another of its factories. Alternatively it can sell the credits. The firms buying them are then allowed to emit that amount *over* their permitted level. Thus the overall level of emissions is set by CAC methods, whereas their distribution is determined by the market.

Take the example of firms A and B, which are currently producing 12 units of a pollutant each. Now assume that a standard is set permitting them to produce only 10 units each. If firm A managed to reduce the pollutant to 8 units, it would be given a credit for 2 units. It could then sell this to firm B, enabling B to continue emitting 12 units. The effect would still be a total reduction of 4 units between the two firms. However, the trade in pollution allows pollution reduction to be concentrated where it can be achieved at lowest cost. In our example, if it cost firm B more to reduce its pollution than firm A, then the permits could be sold from A to B at a price that was profitable to both (i.e. at a price above the cost of emission reduction to A, but below the cost of emission reduction to B).

> **Pause for thought**
>
> *To what extent will the introduction of tradable permits lead to a lower level of total pollution (as opposed to its redistribution)?*

The principle of tradable permits can be used as the basis of international agreements on pollution reduction. Each country could be required to achieve a certain percentage reduction in a pollutant (e.g. CO_2 or SO_2), but any country exceeding its reduction could sell its right to these emissions to other (presumably richer) countries (see Box 22.1).

A similar principle can be adopted for using natural resources. Thus fish quotas could be assigned to fishing boats or fleets or countries. Any parts of these quotas not used could then be sold.

How are the permitted pollution levels (or fish quotas) to be decided? The way that seems to be the most acceptable is to base them on firms' *current* levels, with any subsequent reduction in total permitted pollution being achieved by requiring firms to reduce their emissions by the *same* percentage. This approach is known as **grandfathering**. The main problem with this approach is that it could be seen as unfair by those firms that are already using cleaner technology. Why should they be required to make the same reductions as firms using dirty technology?

The EU carbon trading system. In the EU, a carbon Emissions Trading Scheme (ETS) has been in place since January 2005 as part of the EU's approach to meeting its targets under the Kyoto Treaty (see Box 22.1). This is known as a 'cap and trade' scheme. Some 11 500 industrial plants have been allocated CO_2 emissions allowances, or credits, by their respective governments. Companies that exceed their limits must purchase credits to cover the difference, while those that reduce their emissions can sell their surplus credits for a profit. Companies can trade directly with each other or through brokers operating throughout Europe.

Assessing the system of tradable permits. The main advantage of tradable permits is that they combine the simplicity of CAC methods with the benefits of achieving

BOX 22.1 A STERN REBUKE ABOUT CLIMATE CHANGE INACTION

Who can 'save the planet'?

Martin Wolf points out that business on its own cannot 'save the planet'.[1] Firms respond to incentives. Unfortunately, in a free market, profit-maximising firms have no incentive to internalise the externality caused by greenhouse gas emissions. The costs of doing so are too high if competitors do not similarly reduce emissions. This is a classic market failure and governments must take action to ensure that firms engage in environmentally friendly production.

Problems do not come much bigger than climate change. Carbon dioxide emissions, one of the major greenhouse gases, have increased dramatically over the past 60 years (see figure (a)). A review led by economist Lord Stern, published in 2006 for the UK government, argued that the annual costs of stabilising CO_2 emissions in the atmosphere below 550 ppm would be around 1 per cent of global GDP by 2050.[2] Failure to deal with this would increase global temperatures by between 2 and 5 per cent, and the related environmental catastrophes would lead to falls in GDP of between 5 and 20 per cent.

Critics of Stern pointed out that such a large fall in GDP requires that consumers have a low time preference: i.e. they put too much emphasis on consumption today rather than tomorrow – a feature not found in other studies. However, there has been considerable support for the Stern Review from economists and politicians.

Indeed, there were strong indications that Stern may have underestimated the costs of climate change. Thus, a report in 2007 from the Intergovernmental Panel on Climate Change (a UN-appointed panel of 2500 of the world's leading scientists) and the Garnaut Climate Change Review for the Australian Government in 2008 broadly supported the Stern method but cited new scientific evidence that global warming was occurring even more rapidly than Stern assumed.[3]

In a reassessment of his report in 2008, Lord Stern argued that he had underestimated the risks, that CO_2 emissions should be reduced to 500 ppm in the next 10 to 20 years and that this would cost around 2 per cent of global GDP per annum.[4]

---

[1] M. Wolf, 'Clarity is crucial', *Financial Times*, 1 December 2008.
[2] N. Stern, *Stern Review on the Economics of Climate Change* (HMSO, 2006). Available at www.hm-treasury.gov.uk/sternreview_index.htm
[3] IPCC, *Fourth Assessment Report: Climate Change 2007*. Available at www.ipcc.ch/ipccreports/assessments-reports.htm; and R. Garnaut, *The Garnaut Climate Change Review* (Commonwealth of Australia, 2008). Available at www.garnautreview.org.au/index.htm
[4] W. R. Cline, 'Meeting the challenge of global warming', Copenhagen Consensus Challenge Paper, 2004. Available at www.copenhagenconsensus.com/Admin/Public/DWSDownload.aspx?File=Files%2fFiler%2fCC%2fPapers%2fClimate_Change_300404.pdf.

(a) Global CO_2 emissions, 1850–2005

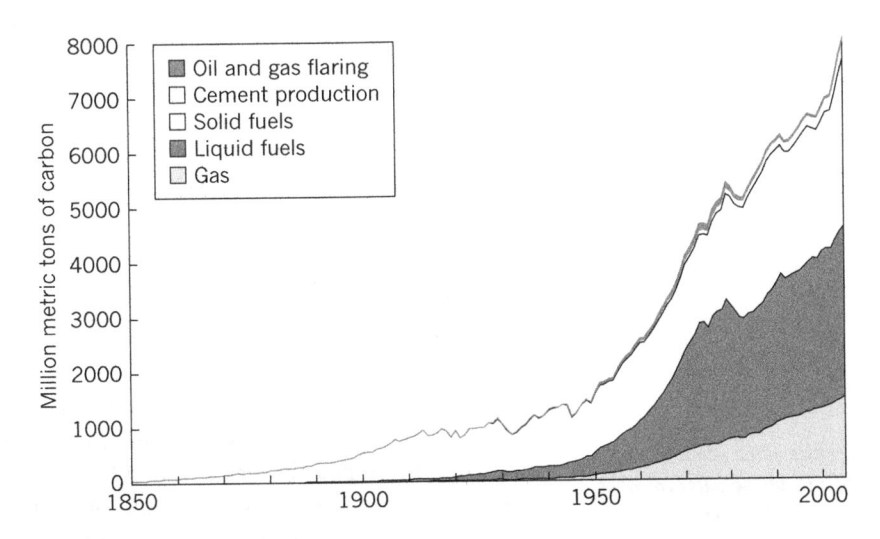

Source: Carbon Dioxide Information Analysis Centre (2009) http://cdiac.ornl.gov/

The Kyoto Protocol: a market-based system

The scale of the problem has led to governments looking for international agreements on climate change. The 'Kyoto Protocol' which originated in 1997 is such an agreement. The signatories set out to reduce greenhouse gas emissions by an average of 5.2 per cent (based on 1990 levels) by the year 2012.

Although 141 nations signed the Kyoto Protocol by 2005, when the agreement became legally binding, the reductions in emissions fell on 39 leading industrialised nations. The UK's target reduction is 12.5 per cent, Germany's is 21 per cent, the EU's as a whole is 8 per cent and Japan's and Canada's 6 per cent each. The USA signed the protocol in 1998, but it was never enacted through Federal Government, and the Bush administration withdrew from it in 2001. The Obama administration, however, has stated that it is committed to joining a successor to the Kyoto Protocol.

The Protocol has led to three distinct market-based mechanisms to counter the costs of climate change:

1. *Emissions trading*. The countries that have ratified the Kyoto Protocol are allowed to trade amongst themselves the rights to emit six greenhouse gases. If a country reduces emissions below its agreed limit, it will be able to sell the additional reduction as a credit. So if a country is finding it difficult to cut emissions, it will be able to buy these credits within some kind of marketplace. (As we saw on page 470, CO_2 trading began within the EU in January 2005.)
2. *Joint implementation*. Under Article 6 of the Protocol, an industrialised country can earn credits by investing in projects that reduce emissions in other industrialised countries (primarily former Soviet countries). These credits then reduce its own requirement to cut emissions.
3. *Clean Development Mechanism*. This is similar to the joint implementation process above, but involves a country or company from the industrialised world earning credit by investing in emissions reduction schemes in *developing* countries. For example, a typical CDM or JI project might involve installing solar panels, planting forests or investing in a factory producing energy-efficient light bulbs.

Assessing the Kyoto Protocol

Critics of Kyoto have argued that the reductions in emission levels are insufficient to meet climate change needs. The Intergovernmental Panel on Climate Change (a UN-appointed panel of 2500 of the world's leading scientists) estimates that a 60 to 80 per cent cut in greenhouse gas emissions from 1990 levels will ultimately be needed to avert serious climate disruption. In the light of this, a 5.2 per cent reduction, which will probably not be met anyway, seems minuscule.

There is also the danger that businesses, rather than cutting greenhouse gas emissions, will simply buy credits offered for sale on the open market, many of which will not be earned from reducing current emissions. For example, Russia has CO_2 emissions considerably below its 1990 level and as such has a massive emissions credit for sale. However, such credit is not the result of Russian environmental policy, but rather the consequence of the collapse and closure of large sections of Russian industry and the replacing of old dirty factories with much more profitable ones. In other words, the reductions would have taken place anyway. The EU has consistently argued that, to ensure some real gains are made, no more than 50 per cent of the emissions reduction should be achieved through these market-based mechanisms.

Probably the biggest problem with the Kyoto Protocol is that there is considerable disagreement among the big polluting nations about how to deal with climate change.

Moving forward

Developing nations such as China do not have to reduce emissions under the Kyoto Protocol. China though is now the world's biggest polluter in absolute terms (see figure (b)), followed by the USA, Russia and India. China's CO_2 emissions per unit of GDP are the highest of all nations; they are almost twice as large as the USA and nearly three times greater than the UK, suggesting that their production techniques are not as environmentally friendly as other nations. Clearly though, much of recent GDP growth in China has been fuelled by demand from the industrialised nations and, cumulatively, industrialised nations have contributed more to greenhouse gas emissions than developing countries. Thus, while developing nations will have to embrace reductions if the planet is to avoid the concerns set out by Lord Stern, the industrialised nations will still have to bear most of the burden of emission reductions.

At the 'Washington Declaration' in February 2007 the heads of government from the major industrialised and BRIC (Brazil, Russia, India and China) nations, agreed in

> **Pause for thought**
>
> *What determines the size of the administrative costs of a system of tradable permits? For what reasons might green taxes be cheaper to administer than a system of tradable permits?*

pollution reduction in the most efficient way. There is also the advantage that firms have a financial incentive to cut pollution. This might then make it easier for governments to impose tougher standards (i.e. impose lower permitted levels of emission).

There are, however, various general problems with tradable permits. One is how to distribute the permissions in a way that all firms regard as fair. Another is the possibility that trade will lead to pollution being concentrated in certain geographical

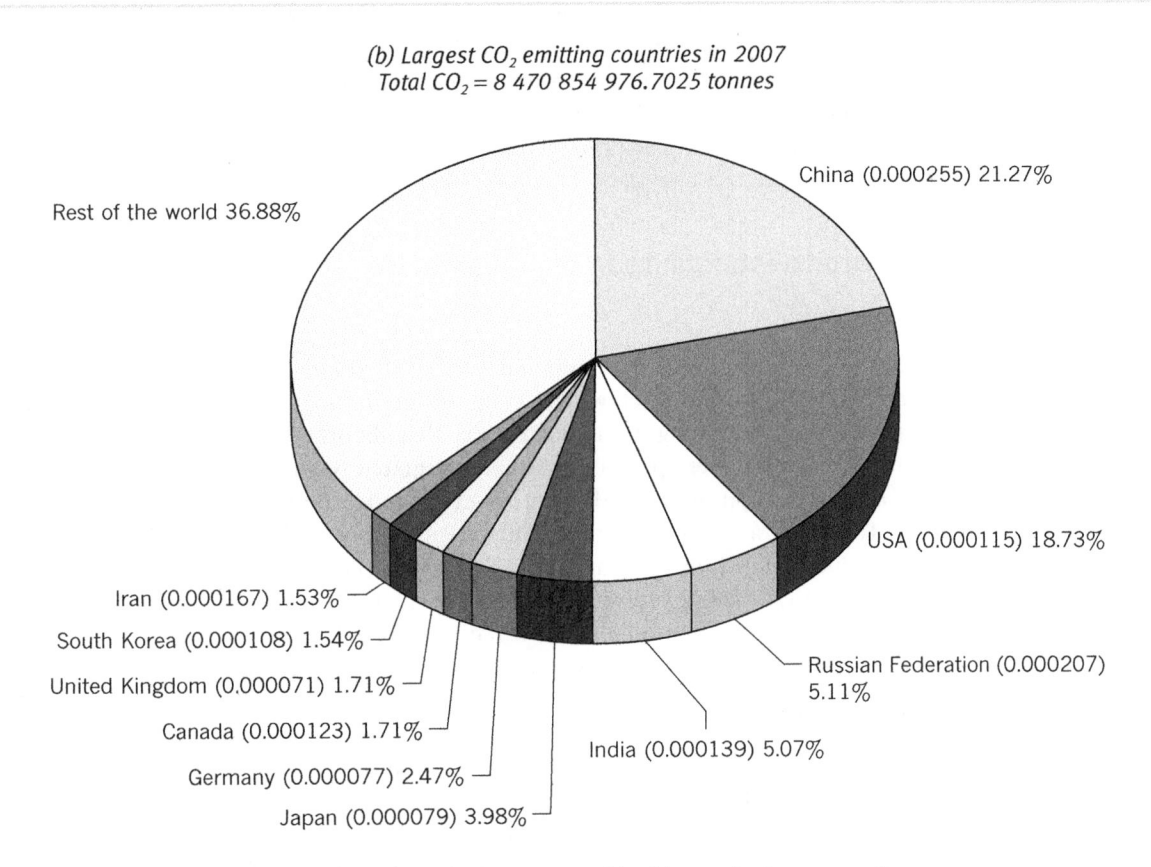

(b) Largest CO_2 emitting countries in 2007
Total CO_2 = 8 470 854 976.7025 tonnes

- Rest of the world 36.88%
- China (0.000255) 21.27%
- USA (0.000115) 18.73%
- Russian Federation (0.000207) 5.11%
- India (0.000139) 5.07%
- Japan (0.000079) 3.98%
- Germany (0.000077) 2.47%
- Canada (0.000123) 1.71%
- United Kingdom (0.000071) 1.71%
- South Korea (0.000108) 1.54%
- Iran (0.000167) 1.53%

Notes: Figures in parentheses = CO_2 emissions per unit of GDP measured in US$ at purchasing power parity.
Based on preliminary data for 2007.
Source: Carbon Dioxide Information Analysis Centre, 2009 (http://cdiac.ornl.gov/) and *World Economic Outlook*

principle to a successor to the Kyoto Protocol. This envisaged a global cap and trade scheme that would apply to both developed and developing nations, the details of which would be specified in time for the Copenhagen Conference in December 2009.

In December 2008, the EU independently offered legally binding targets for 2020: to cut greenhouse gas emissions by 20 per cent; to establish a 20 per cent share for renewable energy; and to improve energy efficiency by 20 per cent. It offered a 30 per cent reduction in emissions provided there was international agreement for a post-Kyoto Protocol initiative.

We await the outcome of intergovernmental talks with interest. If Lord Stern is correct in his assessment of climate change, we still have a long way to go to save the planet and the economic prosperity of future generations.

? *Explain who are likely to be the 'winners' and 'losers' as a result of recent talks on carbon dioxide emissions. Use the concepts of game theory to illustrate your argument.*

areas. Another is that it may reduce the pressure on dirtier factories (or countries) to cut their emissions.

Finally, the system will lead to significant cuts in pollution only if the permitted levels are low. Once the system is in place, the government might then feel that the pressure is off to *reduce* the permitted levels. This was a major criticism of the first trading period of the EU's ETS from 2005 to 2007. Emissions allowances were relatively generous. As a result many firms found it easy to produce surplus credits, which pushed their price to a low level, reaching a minuscule €0.02 per tonne by the end of 2007. This, in turn, made it cheap for 'dirty' firms to buy credits and thus reduced the pressure on them to cut pollution. In answer to this, the allowances were somewhat tighter in the second trading period (2008–12). By mid-2008, carbon was trading at around €28 per tonne. With the recession of 2008/9, however, the price fell as firms cut back production. By early 2009, the price was around €8 per tonne, although it rose again to about €14 by mid-2009.

Environmental policy in the UK and EU

UK policy

In the UK, current policy is embodied in the 1990 Environmental Protection Act, the 1995 Environment Act (which set up the Environment Agency), the 2003 Waste and Emissions Trading Act and the 2005 Neighbourhoods and Environment Act. The Acts are an attempt to establish an integrated pollution control strategy. This has been the approach in other European countries, notably Holland.

Following a number of energy White Papers and Reviews, the UK government introduced the Climate Change and Sustainable Energy Act and Climate Change Programme in 2006. This obliged government to report to Parliament on greenhouse gas emissions and measures taken to reduce these emissions.

In 2008 the Climate Change Act established legally binding targets on the UK to achieve reductions in greenhouse gases of at least 80 per cent by 2050 on 1990 levels, and a 26 per cent reduction in carbon dioxide emissions by 2020. This will be achieved through carbon budgets which will set caps on emissions affecting all businesses, including shipping and aviation. There is also scope within the Act for the government to introduce local emission trading schemes if required and powers to provide financial incentives to reduce household waste in England. The UK is the first country to establish a long-range carbon reduction target in law.

EU policy

In addition to offering a 30 per cent reduction in greenhouse gases if there is an agreement for a post-Kyoto Protocol initiative (see Box 22.1) and initiating a carbon trading scheme (see above), the EU has developed environmental strategies covering seven areas: air pollution; prevention and recycling of waste; protection and conservation of the marine environment; soil; sustainable use of pesticides; sustainable use of resources; and urban environment. Each of these strategies has involved a review of research, consultation with business and other stakeholders, the simplification and clarification of existing legislation and proposals for new legislation. The aim is to identify the most appropriate instruments to deliver sustainable development in the least burdensome and most cost-effective way possible.

These seven strategies are part of the EU's *Sixth Environment Action Programme* (2002–12). It provides the environmental component of the EU's strategy for sustainable development. The programme identifies four main areas to which policy should be directed: climate change; nature and biodiversity; environment and health and quality of life; and sustainable use and management of natural resources and waste.

The programme advocates the use of various policy instruments, such as legislation, inspection, taxation and information. The choice of instrument should be one that tackles the problem at source and is both efficient and effective. The programme identified 156 areas where action was needed and these were delivered by 2007. However, while the policy framework is in place, the 2007 Environmental Policy Review revealed that implementation by member states was often slow and incomplete.

TRANSPORT POLICY

22.2

Traffic congestion is a challenge for all nations, particularly in the large cities and at certain peak times. This problem has become more acute as our lives have become increasingly dominated by the motor car. Sitting in a traffic jam is both time wasting and frustrating. It adds considerably to the costs and stress of modern living.

And it is not only the motorist that suffers. Congested streets make life less pleasant for the pedestrian, and increased traffic leads to increased accidents. What is more, the inexorable growth of traffic has led to significant problems of pollution. Traffic is noisy and car fumes are unpleasant and lead to substantial environmental damage.

Between 1970 and 2007 road traffic in Great Britain rose by 156 per cent, whereas the length of public roads rose by only 23 per cent (albeit some roads were widened). Most passenger and freight transport is by road. In 2007, 92 per cent of passenger kilometres and 68 per cent of domestic freight tonnage kilometres in Great Britain were by road, whereas rail accounted for a mere 7 per cent of passenger traffic and 8 per cent of freight tonnage. Of road passenger kilometres, 92 per cent was by car in 2007, and, as Table 22.2 shows, this proportion has been growing. Motoring costs now amount to some 12 per cent of average weekly household expenditure.

But should the government do anything about the problem? Is traffic congestion a price worth paying for the benefits we gain from using cars? Or are there things that can be done to ease the problem without greatly inconveniencing the traveller?

The existing system of allocating road space

The allocation of road space depends on both demand and supply. Demand is by individuals who base their decisions on largely private considerations. Supply, by contrast, is usually by the central government or local authorities. Let us examine each in turn.

Demand for road space (by car users)

The demand for road space can be seen largely as a *derived* demand. What people want is not the car journey for its own sake, but to get to their destination. The greater the benefit they gain at their destination, the greater the benefit they gain from using their car to get there.

Table 22.2 Passenger transport in Great Britain: percentage of passenger kilometres by mode of transport

Year	Cars	Motor cycles	Buses and coaches	Bicycles	Rail	Air
1957	38	4	34	7	17	0.2
1967	70	2	17	2	9	0.5
1977	77	1	13	1	7	0.5
1987	83	1	8	1	6	0.7
1997	86	1	6	1	6	0.9
2007	84	1	6	1	7	1.2

Source: *Transport Statistics Great Britain 2008* (Department for Transport, National Statistics 2008). © Crown Copyright 2008. Crown copyright material is reproduced with permission of the Controller of Her Majesty's Stationery Office (HMSO)

The demand for road space, like the demand for other goods and services, has a number of determinants. If congestion is to be reduced, it is important to know how responsive demand is to a change in any of these: it is important to consider the various elasticities of demand.

Price. This is the *marginal cost* to the motorist of a journey. It includes petrol, oil, maintenance, depreciation and any toll charges.

The price elasticity of demand for motoring tends to be relatively low. There can thus be a substantial rise in the price of petrol and there will be only a modest fall in traffic.

Recent estimates of the short-run price elasticity of demand for road fuel in industrialised countries typically range from −0.15 to −0.28. Long-run elasticities are somewhat higher, but are still generally inelastic.[2] The low price elasticity of demand suggests that any schemes to tackle traffic congestion that merely involve raising the costs of motoring will have only limited success.

Income. The demand for road space also depends on people's income. As incomes rise, so car ownership and hence car usage increase substantially. Demand is elastic with respect to income. Figure 22.2 shows the increase in car ownership in various countries.

Price of substitutes. If bus and train fares came down, people might switch from travelling by car. The cross-price elasticity is likely to be relatively low, however, given that most people regard these alternatives as a poor substitute for travelling in their own car. Cars are seen as more comfortable and convenient.

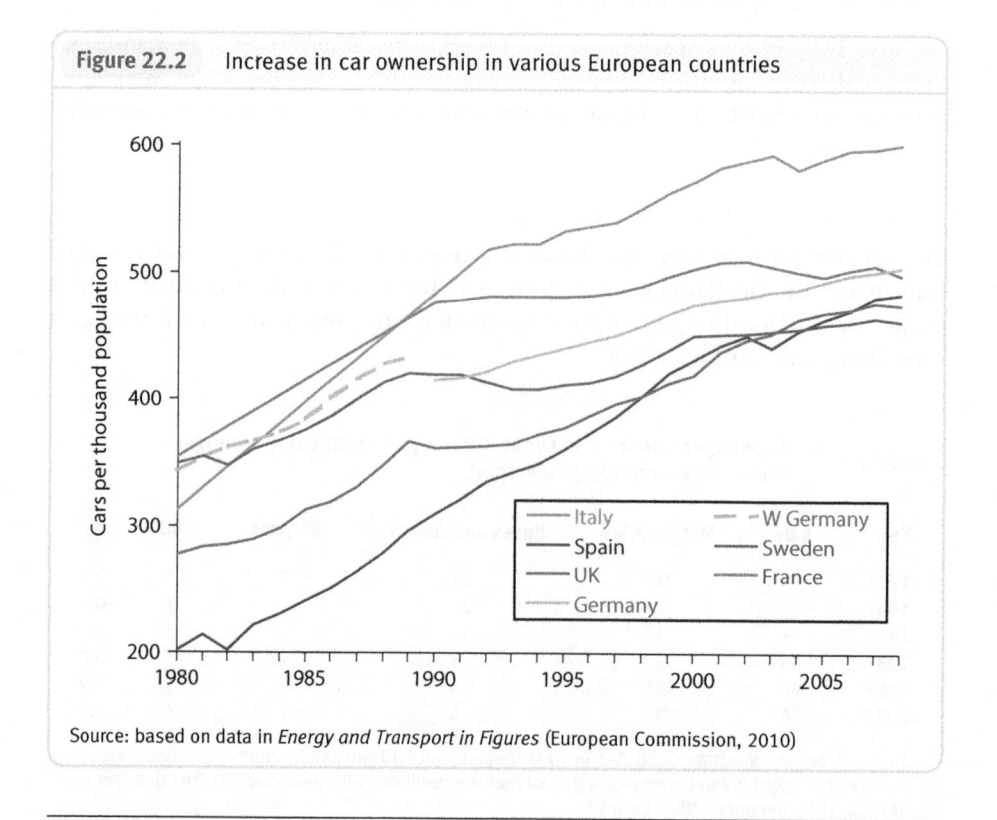

Figure 22.2 Increase in car ownership in various European countries

Source: based on data in *Energy and Transport in Figures* (European Commission, 2010)

---

[2] See *Environmentally Related Taxes in OECD Countries: Issues and Strategies* (OECD, 2001), pp. 99–103.

Price of complements. Demand for road space will depend on the price of cars. The higher the price of cars, the fewer people will own cars and thus the fewer will be the cars on the road.

Demand will also depend on the price of complementary services, such as parking. A rise in car parking charges will reduce the demand for car journeys. But here again the cross elasticity is likely to be relatively low. In most cases, the motorist will either pay the higher charge or park elsewhere, such as in side streets.

> **Pause for thought**
>
> *Go through each of the determinants we have identified so far and show how the respective elasticity of demand makes the problem of traffic congestion difficult to tackle.*

Tastes/utility. Another factor explaining the preference of many people for travelling by car is the pleasure they gain from it compared with alternative modes of transport. Car ownership is regarded by many people as highly desirable, and once accustomed to travelling in their own car, most people are highly reluctant to give it up.

One important feature of the demand for road space is that it fluctuates. There will be periods of peak demand, such as during the rush hour or at holiday weekends. At such times, roads can get totally jammed. At other times, however, the same roads may be virtually empty.

Supply of road space

The supply of road space can be examined in two contexts: the short run and the long run.

The short run. In the short run, the supply of road space is constant. When there is no congestion, supply is more than enough to satisfy demand. There is spare road capacity. At times of congestion, however, there is pressure on this fixed supply. Maximum supply for any given road is reached at the point where there is the maximum flow of vehicles per minute along the road.

The long run. In the long run, the authorities can build new roads or improve existing ones. This will require an assessment of the costs and benefits of such schemes.

Identifying a socially efficient level of road usage (short run)

The existing system of *government* provision of roads and *private* ownership of cars is unlikely to lead to an optimum allocation of road space. So how do we set about identifying just what the social optimum is?

In the short run, the supply of road space is fixed. The question of the short-run optimum allocation of road space, therefore, is one of the optimum usage of existing road space. It is a question of *consumption* rather than supply. For this reason we must focus on the road user, rather than on road provision.

A socially efficient level of consumption occurs where the marginal social benefit of consumption equals its marginal social cost ($MSB = MSC$). So what are the marginal social benefits and costs of using a car?

Marginal social benefit of road usage

Marginal social benefit equals marginal private benefit plus externalities.

Marginal private benefit is the direct benefit to the car user and is reflected in the demand for car journeys, the determinants of which we examined above. External benefits are few. The one major exception occurs when drivers give lifts to other people.

Marginal social cost of road usage

Marginal social cost equals marginal private cost plus externalities.

Marginal private costs to the motorist were identified when we looked at demand. They include the costs of petrol, wear and tear, and tolls. They also include the time costs of travel.

There may also be substantial external costs. These include the following.

Congestion costs: time. When a person uses a car on a congested road, it will add to the congestion. This will therefore slow down the traffic even more and increase the journey time of *other* car users.

Congestion costs: monetary. Congestion increases fuel consumption, and the stopping and starting increases the costs of wear and tear. So when a motorist adds to congestion, there will be additional monetary costs imposed on other motorists.

Environmental costs. When motorists use a road, they reduce the quality of the environment for others. Cars emit fumes and create noise. This is bad enough for pedestrians and other car users, but can be particularly distressing for people living along the road. Driving can cause accidents, a problem that increases as drivers become more impatient as a result of delays.

The socially efficient level of road usage

The optimum level of road use is where the marginal social benefit is equal to the marginal social cost. In Figure 22.3 costs and benefits are shown on the vertical axis and are measured in money terms. Thus any non-monetary costs or benefits (such as time costs) must be given a monetary value. The horizontal axis measures road usage in terms of cars per minute passing a specified point on the road.

For simplicity it is assumed that there are no external benefits from car use and that therefore marginal private and marginal social benefits are the same. The *MSB* curve is shown as downward sloping. The reason for this is that different road users put a different value on this particular journey. If the marginal (private) cost of making the journey were high, only those for whom the journey had a high marginal benefit would travel along the road. If the marginal cost of making the

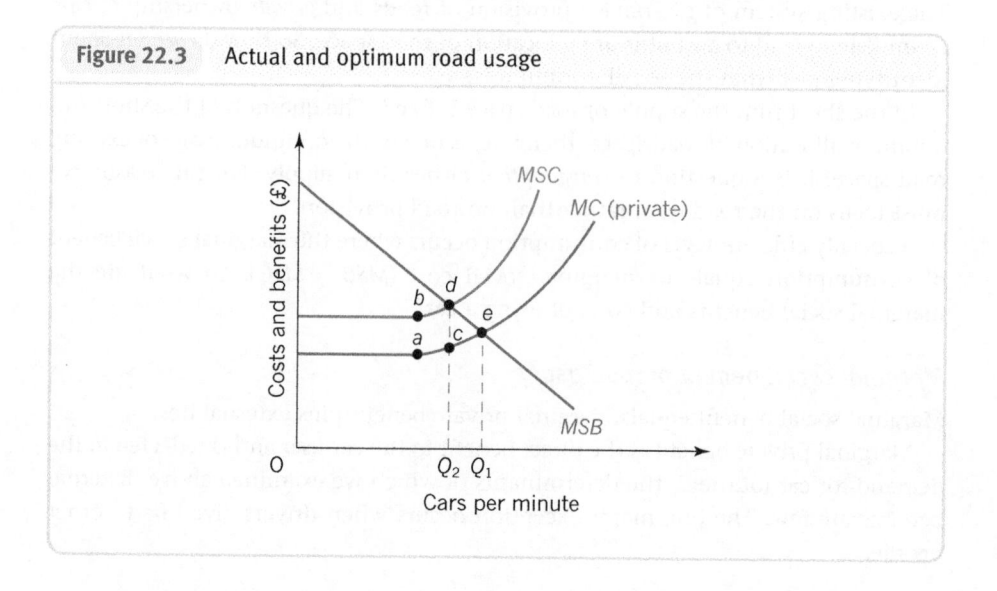

Figure 22.3 Actual and optimum road usage

journey fell, more people would make the journey: people would choose to make the journey at the point at which the marginal cost of using their car had fallen to the level of their marginal benefit. Thus, the greater the number of cars, the lower the marginal benefit.

The marginal (private) cost curve (MC) is likely to be constant up to the level of traffic flow at which congestion begins to occur. This is shown as point *a* in Figure 22.3. Beyond this point, marginal cost is likely to rise as time costs increase and as fuel consumption rises.

The marginal *social* cost curve (MSC) is drawn above the marginal private cost curve. The vertical difference between the two represents the external costs. Up to point *b*, external costs are simply the environmental costs. Beyond point *b*, there are also external congestion costs, since additional road users slow down the journey of *other* road users. These external costs get progressively greater as the level of traffic increases.

The actual level of traffic flow will be at Q_1, where marginal private costs and benefits are equal (point *e*). The socially efficient level of traffic flow, however, will be at the lower level of Q_2, where marginal social costs and benefits are equal (point *d*). In other words, the existing system of allocating road space is likely to lead to an excessive level of road usage.

Identifying a socially optimum level of road space (long run)

In the long run, the supply of road space is not fixed. The authorities must therefore assess what new road schemes (if any) to adopt. This will involve the use of some form of cost–benefit analysis.

The socially efficient level of construction will be where the marginal social benefit from construction is equal to the marginal social cost. This means that schemes should be adopted as long as their marginal social benefit exceeds their marginal social cost. But how are these costs and benefits assessed in practice? Case study H.15 on the book's website examines the procedure used in the UK.

> **Definition**
>
> **Cost–benefit analysis**
> The identification, measurement and weighing-up of the costs and benefits of a project in order to decide whether or not it should go ahead.

We now turn to look at different solutions to traffic congestion. These can be grouped into three broad types.

Solution 1: direct provision (supply-side solutions)

The road solution

One obvious solution to traffic congestion is to build more roads. At first sight this may seem an optimum strategy, provided the costs and benefits of road-building schemes are carefully assessed and only those schemes are adopted where the benefits exceed the costs.

However, there are serious problems with this approach.

The objective of equity. The first problem concerns that of *equity*. After all, social efficiency is not the only possible economic objective. For example, when an urban motorway is built, those living beside it will suffer from noise and fumes. Motorway users gain, but the local residents lose. The question is whether this is fair.

The more the government tries to appeal to the car user by building more and better roads, the fewer will be the people who use public transport, and thus the more will public transport decline. Those without cars lose, and these tend to be from the most vulnerable groups – the poor, the elderly, children and the disabled.

Congestion may not be solved. Increasing the amount of road space may encourage more people to use cars. A good example is the London orbital motorway, the M25. In planning the motorway, not only did the government underestimate the general rate of traffic growth, but it also underestimated the direct effect it would have on encouraging people to use the motorway rather than some alternative route, or some alternative means of transport, or even not to make the journey at all. It also underestimated the effect it would have on encouraging people to live further from their place of work and to commute along the motorway. The result is that there is now serious congestion on the M25.

Thus new roads may simply generate extra traffic, with little overall effect on congestion.

The environmental impact of new roads. New roads lead to loss of agricultural land, the destruction of many natural habitats, noise, the splitting of communities and disruption to local residents. To the extent that they encourage a growth in traffic, they add to atmospheric pollution and a depletion of oil reserves.

Government or local authority provision of public transport

An alternative supply-side solution is to increase the provision of public transport. If, for example, a local authority ran a local bus service and decided to invest in additional buses, open up new routes, including park-and-ride, and operate a low-fare policy, these services might encourage people to switch from using their cars.

To be effective, this would have to be an attractive alternative. Many people would switch only if the buses were frequent, cheap, comfortable and reliable, and if there were enough routes to take people close to where they wanted to go.

Solution 2: regulation and legislation

An alternative strategy is to restrict car use by various forms of regulation and legislation.

Restricting car access

One approach involves reducing car access to areas that are subject to high levels of congestion. The following measures are widely used: bus and cycle lanes, no entry to side streets, 'high-occupancy vehicle lanes' (confined to cars with one or more passengers) and pedestrian-only areas.

However, there is a serious problem with these measures. They tend not to solve the problem of congestion, but merely to divert it. Bus lanes tend to make the car lanes more congested; no entry to side streets tends to make the main roads more congested; and pedestrian-only areas often make the roads round these areas more congested.

Parking restrictions

An alternative to restricting road access is to restrict parking. If cars are not allowed to park along congested streets, this will improve the traffic flow. Also, if parking is difficult, this will discourage people from using their cars to come into city centres. The problems with this solution include:

- possibly increased congestion as people drive round and round looking for parking spaces;
- illegal parking;
- parking down side streets, causing a nuisance for local residents.

Solution 3: changing market signals

The solution favoured by many economists is to use the price mechanism. As we have seen, one of the causes of traffic congestion is that road users do not pay the full marginal social costs of using the roads. If they could be forced to do so, a social optimum usage of road space could be achieved.

In Figure 22.3 (page 478) this would involve imposing a charge on motorists of $d - c$. By 'internalising' the congestion and environmental externalities in this way, traffic flow will be reduced to the social optimum of Q_2.

So how can these external costs be charged to the motorist? There are several possible ways.

Extending existing taxes

Three major types of tax are levied on the motorist: fuel tax, taxes on new cars and car licences. Could increasing these taxes lead to the optimum level of road use being achieved?

Increasing the rates of new car tax and car licences may have some effect on reducing the total level of car ownership, but will probably have little effect on car use. The problem is that these taxes do not increase the marginal cost of car use. They are fixed costs. Once you have paid these taxes, there is no extra to pay for each extra journey you make. They do not discourage you from using your car.

Unlike the other two, fuel taxes are a marginal cost of car use. The more you use your car, the more fuel you use and the more fuel tax you pay. They are also mildly related to the level of congestion, since fuel consumption tends to increase as congestion increases. Nevertheless, they are not ideal. The problem is that all motorists would pay an increase in fuel tax, even those travelling on uncongested roads. To have a significant effect on congestion, there would have to be a very large increase in fuel taxes and this would be very unfair on those who are not causing congestion, especially those who have to travel long distances. There is also a political problem. Most motorists regard fuel taxes as too high and would resent paying higher rates.

> **Pause for thought**
>
> *Would a tax on car tyres be a good way of restricting car usage?*

Road pricing

Charging people for using roads is a direct means of achieving an efficient use of road space. The higher the congestion, the higher should be the charge.

Area charges. One simple and practical means of charging people to use congested streets is the area charge. People would have to pay (normally by the day) for using their car in a city centre. Earlier versions of this scheme involved people having to purchase and display a ticket on their car, rather like a 'pay-and-display' parking system.

More recently, electronic versions have been developed. The London Congestion Charge is an example. Originally covering the Inner London area, it was extended to cover parts of west London in 2007. Car drivers must pay £8 per day to enter the 'congestion zone' any time between 7.00 and 18.00, Monday to Friday. Payment can be made by various means, including post, Internet, telephone, mobile phone SMS text message, and at various shops and petrol stations. Payment can be in advance or up to midnight on the day of travel, or up to midnight the next day for an extra £2. Cars entering the congestion zone have their number plate recorded by camera and a computer check then leads to a fine of £120 being sent to those who have not paid.

BOX 22.2 ROAD PRICING IN SINGAPORE

Part of an integrated transport policy

It takes only one hour to drive from one end of Singapore to the other. Yet the average Singaporean driver travels an estimated 20 800 km per year, more than the average US driver, and over 50 per cent more than the average Japanese driver. But despite very high levels of traffic density, Singapore suffers much less than many of its neighbours from traffic congestion. Part of the reason is that it has an integrated transport policy. This includes the following:

- Restricting the number of new car licences, and allowing their price to rise to the corresponding equilibrium. This makes cars in Singapore among the most expensive in the world.
- A 111-kilometre-long mass rail transit (MRT) system with subsidised fares. Trains are comfortable, clean and frequent. Stations are air-conditioned.
- A programme of building new estates near MRT stations.
- Cheap, frequent buses, serving all parts of the island.

But it is in respect to road usage that the Singaporean authorities have been most innovative.

The first innovation came in 1975. The city centre was made a restricted zone. Motorists who wished to enter this zone had to buy a ticket (an 'area licence') at any one of 33 entry points. Police were stationed at these entry points to check that cars had paid and displayed.

Then in 1990 a quota system for new cars was established. The government decides the total number of cars the country should have, and issues just enough licences each month to maintain that total. These licences (or 'Certificates of Entitlement') are for ten years and are offered at auction. Their market price varies from around £10 000 to £30 000.

A problem with the licences is that they are a once-and-for-all payment, which does not vary with the amount people use their car. In other words, their marginal cost (for additional miles driven) is zero. Many people feel that, having paid such a high price for their licence, they ought to use their car as much as possible in order to get value for money!

With traffic congestion steadily worsening, it was recognised that something more had to be done. Either the Area Licensing Scheme had to be widened, or some other form of charging had to be adopted. The decision was taken to introduce electronic road pricing (ERP). This alternative would not only save on police labour costs, but enable charge rates to be varied according to levels of congestion, times of the day, and locality.

What, then, would be the optimum charge? If the objective is to reduce traffic from Q_1 to Q_2 in Figure 22.3 on page 478, then a charge of $d - c$ should be levied.

Since 1998 all vehicles in Singapore have been fitted with an in-vehicle unit (IU). Every journey made requires the driver to insert a smart card into the IU. On specified roads, overhead gantries read the IU and deduct the appropriate charge from the card. If a car does not have sufficient funds on its smart card, the car's details are relayed to a control centre and a fine is imposed. The system has the benefit of operating on three-lane highways and does not require traffic to slow down.

The ERP system operates on Mondays to Fridays from 8 a.m. to 8.00 p.m. in the central area and from 7.30 a.m. to 9.30 a.m. on the expressways and outer ring roads, with charges varying every 5, 20 or 30 minutes within these times. Rates are published in advance but are reviewed every three months. The system is thus very flexible to allow traffic to be kept at the desired level.

The system was expensive to set up, however. Cheaper schemes have been adopted elsewhere, such as Norway and parts of the USA. These operate by funnelling traffic into a single lane in order to register the car, but they have the disadvantage of slowing the traffic down.

One message is clear from the Singapore solution. Road pricing alone is not enough. Unless there are fast, comfortable and affordable public transport alternatives, the demand for cars will be highly price inelastic. People have to get to work!

Explain how, by varying the charge debited from the smart card according to the time of day or level of congestion, a socially optimal level of road use can be achieved.

The London congestion charging system has reduced traffic in the zone by nearly 20 per cent and has significantly increased the rate of traffic flow. The charge is not a marginal one, however, in the sense that it does not vary with the degree of congestion or the amount of time spent or distance travelled by a motorist within the zone. This is an intrinsic problem of area charges. Nevertheless, their simplicity makes the system easy to understand and relatively cheap to operate.

Variable electronic road pricing. The scheme most favoured by many economists and traffic planners is that of variable electronic road pricing. It is the scheme that can most directly relate the price that the motorist is charged to the specific level of marginal social cost. The greater the congestion, the greater the charge imposed on the motorist. Ideally, the charge would be equal to the marginal congestion cost plus any marginal environmental costs additional to those created on non-charged roads.

Various systems have been adopted in various parts of the world, or are under consideration. One involves devices in the road which record the number plates of cars as they pass; alternatively cars must be fitted with sensors. A charge is registered to that car on a central computer. The car owner then receives a bill at periodic intervals, in much the same way as a telephone bill. Several cities around the world are already operating such schemes, including Barcelona, Dallas, Orlando, Lisbon, Oklahoma City and Oslo.

Another involves having a device installed in the car into which a 'smart card' (like a telephone or photocopying card) is inserted. The cards have to be purchased and contain a certain number of units. Beacons or overhead gantries automatically deduct units from the smart cards at times of congestion. If the card is empty, the number of the car is recorded and the driver fined. Such a system was introduced in 1997 on Stockholm's ring road, and in 1998 in Singapore (see Box 22.2).

With both these types, the rate can easily be varied electronically according to the level of congestion (and pollution too). The rates could be in bands and the current bands displayed by the roadside and/or broadcast on local radio so that motorists knew what they were being charged.

The most sophisticated scheme, still under development, involves equipping all vehicles with a receiver. Their position is located by satellites, which then send this information to a dashboard unit that deducts charges according to location, distance travelled, time of day and type of vehicle. The charges can operate through either smart cards or central computerised billing. It is likely that such schemes would initially be confined to lorries.

Despite the enthusiasm for such schemes amongst economists, there are nevertheless various problems associated with them:

- Estimates of the level of external costs are difficult to make.
- Motorists will have to be informed in advance what the charges will be, so that they can plan the timing of their journeys.
- There may be political resistance. Politicians may therefore be reluctant to introduce road pricing for fear of losing popular support.
- If demand is relatively inelastic, the charges might have to be very high to have a significant effect on congestion.
- The costs of installing road-pricing equipment could be very high.
- If road pricing were introduced only in certain areas, shoppers and businesses would tend to move to areas without the charge.
- A new industry in electronic evasion may spring up!

Subsidising alternative means of transport

An alternative to charging for the use of cars is to subsidise the price of alternatives, such as buses and trains. But cheaper fares alone may not be enough. The government may also have to invest directly in or subsidise an *improved* public transport service: more frequent services, more routes, more comfortable buses and trains.

Subsidising public transport need not be seen as an alternative to road pricing: it can be seen as complementary. If road pricing is to persuade people not to travel by car, the alternatives must be attractive. Unless public transport can be made to be seen by the traveller as a close substitute for cars, the elasticity of demand for car use is likely to remain low.

Subsidising public transport can also be justified on grounds of equity. It benefits poorer members of society who cannot afford to travel by car.

It is unlikely that any one policy can provide the complete solution. Certain policies or combinations of policies are better suited to some situations than others. It is important for governments to learn from experiences both within their own country and in others, in order to find the optimum solution to each specific problem.

22.3 PRIVATISATION AND REGULATION

One solution to market failure, advocated by some on the political left, is nationalisation. If industries are not being run in the public interest by the private sector, then bring them into public ownership. This way, so the argument goes, the market failures can be corrected. Problems of monopoly power, externalities, inequality, etc. can be dealt with directly if these industries are run with the public interest, rather than private gain, at heart.

In the late 1940s and early 1950s the Labour government of the time nationalised many of the key transport, communications and power industries, such as the railways, freight transport, airlines, coal, gas, electricity and steel.

From the early 1980s, however, the Conservative governments under Margaret Thatcher and John Major engaged in an extensive programme of 'privatisation', returning most of the nationalised industries in the UK to the private sector. Other countries have followed similar programmes of privatisation in what has become a worldwide phenomenon. Privatisation has been seen as a means of revitalising ailing industries and as a golden opportunity to raise revenues to ease budgetary problems.

> **Definition**
>
> **Nationalised industries**
> State-owned industries that produce goods or services that are sold in the market.

The arguments for and against privatisation

The following are the major arguments that have been used for and against privatisation.

Arguments for privatisation

Market forces. The first argument is that privatisation will expose these industries to market forces, from which will flow the benefits of greater efficiency, faster growth and greater responsiveness to the wishes of the consumer.

If privatisation involved splitting an industry into competing companies, this greater competition in the goods market would force the companies to keep their costs as low as possible in order to stay in business.

Privatised companies do not have direct access to government finance. To finance investment they must now go to the market: they must issue shares or borrow from banks or other financial institutions. In doing so, they will be competing for funds with other companies, and thus must be seen as capable of using these funds profitably.

Market discipline will also be enforced by shareholders. Shareholders want a good return on their shares and will thus put pressure on the privatised company to perform well. If the company does not make sufficient profits, shareholders will sell their shares. The share price will fall, and the company will be in danger of being taken over. The market for corporate control (see page 228) thus provides incentives for firms to be efficient.

Reduced government interference. In nationalised industries, managers may frequently be required to adjust their targets for political reasons. At one time they may have to keep prices low as part of a government drive against inflation. At another they may have to raise their prices substantially in order to raise extra revenue for the government and help finance tax cuts. Privatisation frees the company from these constraints and allows it to make more rational economic decisions and plan future investments with greater certainty.

Financing tax cuts. The privatisation issue of shares directly earns money for the government and thus reduces the amount it needs to borrow. Effectively, then, the government can use the proceeds of privatisation to finance tax cuts. There is a danger here, however, that in order to raise the maximum revenue the government will want to make the industries as potentially profitable as possible. This may involve selling them as monopolies. But this, of course, would probably be against the interests of the consumer.

Arguments against privatisation

Natural monopolies. The market forces argument for privatisation largely breaks down if a public monopoly is simply replaced by a private monopoly, as in the case of the water companies, each of which has a monopoly in its own area. Critics of privatisation argue that at least a public-sector monopoly is not out to maximise profits and thereby exploit the consumer.

The public interest. Will the questions of externalities and social justice not be ignored after privatisation? Critics of privatisation argue that only the most glaring examples of externalities and injustice can be taken into account, given that the whole ethos of a private company is different from that of a nationalised one: private profit is the goal rather than public service. Externalities, they argue, are extremely widespread and need to be taken into account by the industry itself and not just by an occasionally intervening government. A railway or an underground line, for example, may considerably ease congestion on the roads, thus benefiting road as well as rail users. Other industries may cause substantial external costs. Nuclear power stations may produce nuclear waste that is costly to dispose of safely, and/or provides hazards for future generations. Coal-fired power stations may pollute the atmosphere and cause acid rain.

> **Pause for thought**
>
> *To what extent can the problems with privatisation be seen as arguments in favour of nationalisation?*

In assessing these arguments, a lot depends on the toughness of government legislation and the attitudes and powers of regulatory agencies after privatisation.

Regulation

Identifying the short-run optimum price and output

Privatised industries, if left free to operate in the market, will have monopoly power; they will create externalities; and they will be unlikely to take into account questions of fairness. An answer to these problems is for the government or some independent agency to regulate their behaviour so that they produce at the socially

BOX 22.3 THE RIGHT TRACK TO REFORM?

Reorganising the railways in the UK

Few train routes across Europe are profitable and thus they have to be subsidised by governments. Such has been the strain placed upon public finances that European governments in recent years have been looking for ways of reforming their railways. The most radical approach has been adopted in the UK, which involved dividing up the rail system and privatising its various parts.

Privatisation of the rail system in the UK

The UK Conservative government in 1993 stated that the aim of rail privatisation was to 'improve the quality of rail services for the travelling public and for freight customers'. The 1993 Railways Act detailed the privatisation programme. The management of rail infrastructure, such as track, signalling and stations, was to be separated from the responsibility for running trains. There would be 25 passenger train operating companies (TOCs), each having a franchise lasting between seven and fifteen years. These companies would have few assets, being forced to rent track and lease stations from the infrastructure owner (Railtrack), and to lease trains and rolling stock from three new rolling-stock companies. There would be three freight companies, which would also pay Railtrack for the use of track and signalling. In practice, the 25 franchises were operated by just 11 companies (with one, National Express, having nine of the franchises).

Railtrack would be responsible for maintaining and improving the rail infrastructure, but rather than providing this itself, it would be required to purchase the necessary services from private contractors.

To oversee the new rail network, two new posts were created. The first was a rail franchising director, who would be responsible for specifying the length and cost of franchises, as well as for outlining passenger service requirements, including minimum train frequency, stations served and weekend provision. The second post created was that of the rail regulator, who would be responsible both for promoting competition and for protecting consumer interests, which might include specifying maximum permitted fares.

Although the individual train operators generally have a monopoly over a given route, many saw themselves directly competing with coaches and private cars. Several began replacing or refurbishing rolling stock and running additional services.

Developments in the UK since privatisation

Crisis in the early 2000s. Following the Hatfield rail disaster in October 2000, when lives were lost as a result of a faulty rail, the UK rail network was reduced to a virtual state of crisis. Trains were unreliable; fares were rising by more than the rate of inflation; services were being reduced; and passenger complaints were increasing. There seemed to be few, if any, benefits from privatisation. Six of the train operating companies were operating under short-term management contracts, and seven were given government subsidies totalling some £100 million to prevent them going bust.

In fact, part of the industry was 'semi' renationalised, when Railtrack, the privatised track owner, was placed into receivership in 2002. It was replaced by Network Rail, which is a not-for-profit company, wholly dependent upon the UK Treasury for any shortfall in its funds. Any profits are reinvested in the rail infrastructure.

---

optimum price and output. This has been the approach adopted for the major privatisations in the UK.

Regulation in practice

The behaviour of privatised industries is generally governed by the Competition and Enterprise Acts (see section 21.1) and overseen by a separate regulatory office and the Office of Fair Trading. Currently, the privatised utility regulators are as follows: the Office for Gas and Electricity Markets (Ofgem), the Office of Communications (Ofcom), the Office of Rail Regulation (ORR) and the Office of Water Services (Ofwat).

As well as supervising the competitive behaviour of the privatised utility, they set terms under which the industries have to operate. For example, the ORR sets the terms under which rail companies have access to track and stations. The terms set by the regulator can be reviewed by negotiation between the regulator and the industry. If agreement cannot be reached, the Competition Commission acts as an appeal court and its decision is binding.

In June 2003 the Strategic Rail Authority (SRA) decided to withdraw the operating licence of the French company Connex South Eastern. Not only was one in every five of its trains running late but, following the receipt of £58 million of public money, the company had failed to turn around its failing financial position. In fact, Connex was asking for a further £200 million in state aid.

Many critics claimed that running the privatised rail network was becoming increasingly difficult, with Connex's failure signalling that yet more public money might be required to keep the network afloat.

Turning the railways around? The structure of the industry has changed in recent times. As new franchises came up for renewal, so some contracts were merged, so that by 2007, the 25 franchises had been reduced to 20, with the number of TOCs reduced to nine (six held by National Express and four by the First Group). The benefits of economies of scale and coordinated services within a region exceeded any reduction in competition from having fewer franchises and fewer operators.

Since 2005 the government has taken more strategic control of the railways. It wound up the SRA and passed most of its functions, including the construction and awarding of franchise agreements, to the Department of Transport. It has also continued to pump considerable sums of money into the rail system to improve track and signalling.

Looking forward, the government committed to £15 billion of investment until 2013, including £10 billion investment to increase capacity.

Fares have increased since privatisation (by 6 to 7 per cent per year on average) to contribute toward investment costs.

The government's aim is to shift the balance of paying for the railway to the customer and the TOCs. Indeed, subsidies to the TOCs are to be reduced, so that by 2012 they will not only receive a zero subsidy but collectively pay the government a premium of £300 million.

With improvements in the infrastructure, investment by the TOCs in new rolling stock and building more slack into timetables, rail punctuality improved and passenger numbers and freight tonnage increased. By 2008/9, just over 90 per cent of trains were arriving on time, compared with 79 per cent in 2002/3. Between 2002 and 2008, passenger kilometres increased by some 23 per cent and freight kilometre tonnage increased by over 14 per cent.

Has the model been adopted elsewhere?

Other countries, such as Japan and Germany, have rejected the UK model in favour of maintaining a vertically integrated rail network, where rail infrastructure and train services are managed by the same company. It is suggested that a single management would be far more capable of successfully coordinating infrastructure and train service activities than two.

Nevertheless, some aspects of the UK model have been adopted under EC Directive 91/440, which allows European train operators access to the rail networks of other companies. This means that several companies (say, from different EU countries) can offer competing services on the same international route.

Why are subsidies more likely to be needed for commuter and regional services than for medium-to-long-distance passenger services?

The regulator for each industry also sets limits to the prices that certain parts of the industry can charge. These parts are those where there is little or no competition: for example, the charges made to electricity and gas retailers by National Grid, the owner of the electricity grid and major gas pipelines.

The price-setting formulae are essentially of the '*RPI* minus *X*' variety. What this means is that the industries can raise their prices by the rate of increase in the retail price index (i.e. by the rate of inflation) *minus* a certain percentage (X) to take account of expected increases in efficiency. Thus if the rate of inflation were 6 per cent, and if the regulator considered that the industry (or firm) could be expected to reduce its costs by 2 per cent ($X = 2\%$), then price rises would be capped at 4 per cent. The *RPI* − *X* system is thus an example of price-cap regulation. The idea of this system of regulation is that it forces the industry to pass cost savings on to the consumer.

Definition

Price-cap regulation
Where the regulator puts a ceiling on the amount by which a firm can raise its price.

Pause for thought

If an industry regulator adopts an RPI − X formula for price regulation, is it desirable that the value of X should be adjusted as soon as cost conditions change?

Assessing the system of regulation in the UK

The system that has evolved in the UK has various advantages over that employed in the USA and elsewhere, where regulation often focuses on the level of *profits* (see Web Case H.17).

- It is a discretionary system, with the regulator able to judge individual examples of the behaviour of the industry on their own merits. The regulator has a detailed knowledge of the industry which would not be available to government ministers or other bodies such as the Office of Fair Trading. The regulator could thus be argued to be the best person to decide on whether the industry is acting in the public interest.
- The system is flexible, since it allows for the licence and price formula to be changed as circumstances change.
- The '*RPI* minus X' formula provides an incentive for the privatised firms to be as efficient as possible. If they can lower their costs by more than X, they will, in theory, be able to make larger profits and keep them. If, on the other hand, they do not succeed in reducing costs sufficiently, they will make a loss. There is thus a continuing pressure on them to cut costs. (In the US system, where *profits* rather than *prices* are regulated, there is little incentive to increase efficiency, since any cost reductions must be passed on to the consumer in lower prices, and do not, therefore, result in higher profits.)

There are, however, some inherent problems with the way in which regulation operates in the UK:

- The '*RPI* minus X' formula was designed to provide an incentive for the firms to cut costs. But if X is too low, the firm might make excessive profits. Frequently, regulators have underestimated the scope for cost reductions resulting from new technology and reorganisation, and have thus initially set X too low. As a result, instead of X remaining constant for a number of years, as intended, new higher values for X have been set after only one or two years. Alternatively, one-off price cuts have been ordered, as happened when the water companies were required by Ofwat to cut prices by an average of 10 per cent in 2000. In either case, the incentive for the industry to cut costs is reduced. What is the point of being more efficient if the regulator is merely going to insist on a higher value for X and thus take away the extra profits?
- Regulation is becoming increasingly complex. This makes it difficult for the industries to plan and may lead to a growth of 'short-termism'. One of the claimed advantages of privatisation was to give greater independence to the industries from short-term government interference, and allow them to plan for the longer term. In practice, one type of interference may have been replaced by another.
- As regulation becomes more detailed and complex and as the regulator becomes more and more involved in the detailed running of the industry, so managers and regulators will become increasingly involved in a game of strategy: each trying to outwit the other. Information will become distorted and time and energy will be wasted in playing this game of cat and mouse.
- There may also be the danger of regulatory capture. As regulators become more and more involved in their industry and get to know the senior managers at a personal level, so they are increasingly likely to see the managers' point of view and become less and less tough. Commentators do not believe that this has happened yet: the regulators are generally independently minded. But it remains a potential danger.

Definition

Regulatory capture
Where the regulator is persuaded to operate in the industry's interests rather than those of the consumer.

- Alternatively, regulators could be captured by government. Instead of being totally independent, there to serve the interests of the consumer, they might bend to pressures from the government to do things which might help the government win the next election.

One way in which the dangers of ineffective or over-intrusive regulation can be avoided is to replace regulation with competition wherever this is possible. Indeed, one of the major concerns of the regulators has been to do just this. (See Web Case H.16 for ways in which competition has been increased in the electricity industry.)

Increasing competition in the privatised industries

Where natural monopoly exists (see page 222), competition is impossible in a free market. Of course, the industry *could* be broken up by the government, with firms prohibited from owning more than a certain percentage of the industry. But this would lead to higher costs of production. Firms would be operating further back up a downward-sloping long-run average cost curve.

But many parts of the privatised industries are not natural monopolies. Generally it is only the *grid* that is a natural monopoly. In the case of gas and water, it is the pipelines. It would be wasteful to duplicate these. In the case of electricity, it is the power lines: the national grid and the local power lines. In the case of the railways, it is the track.

Other parts of these industries, however, have generally been opened up to competition (with the exception of water). Thus there are now many producers and sellers of electricity and gas. This is possible because they are given access, by law, to the national and local electricity grids and gas pipelines.

To help the opening up of competition, regulators have sometimes restricted the behaviour of the established firms (like BT or British Gas), to prevent them using their dominance in the market as a barrier to entry of new firms. For example, British Gas since 1995 has had to limit its share of the industrial gas market to 40 per cent.

As competition has been introduced into these industries, so price-cap regulation has been progressively abandoned. For example, in 2006 Ofcom abandoned price control of BT and other phone companies over line rentals and phone charges. This was in response to the growth in competition from cable operators, mobile phones and free Internet calls from companies such as Skype via VoiP (voice internet protocol).

Even for the parts of industry where there is a natural monopoly, they could be made contestable monopolies. One way of doing this is by granting operators a licence for a specific period of time. This is known as **franchising**. This has been the approach used for the railways (see Box 22.3). Once a company has been granted a franchise, it has the monopoly of passenger rail services over specific routes. But the awarding of the franchise can be highly competitive, with rival companies putting in competitive bids, in terms of both price (or, in the case of railways, the level of government subsidy required) and the quality of service.

Another approach is to give all companies equal access to the relevant grid. For example, regional electricity companies have to charge the same price for using their local power lines to both rival companies and themselves.

But despite attempts to introduce competition into the privatised industries, they are still dominated by giant companies. Even if they are no longer strictly monopolies,

Definition

Franchising
Where a firm is granted the licence to operate a given part of an industry for a specified length of time.

they still have considerable market power and the scope for price leadership or other forms of oligopolistic collusion is great. Thus although regulation through the price formula has been progressively abandoned as elements of competition have been introduced, the regulators have retained a role similar to that of the OFT: namely, to prevent cases of collusion and the abuse of monopoly power. The companies, however, do have the right of appeal to the Competition Commission.

SUMMARY

1a Pollution is a negative externality, and due to the lack of property rights over the environment, it will be treated as a free good and hence overused. Environmental policy attempts to ensure that the full costs of production or consumption are paid for by those who produce and consume.

1b The environment is difficult to value, so it is difficult to estimate the costs of environmental pollution. This is a major problem in being able to devise an efficient environmental policy.

1c Environmental policy can be either market based or non-market based, or a mixture of the two. Market-based solutions focus upon the use of taxes and subsidies to correct market signals. Non-market-based solutions involve the use of regulations and controls over polluting activities.

1d The problem with using taxes and subsidies is in identifying the appropriate rates, since these will vary according to the environmental impact.

1e Command-and-control systems, such as making certain practices illegal or putting limits on discharges, are a less sophisticated alternative to taxes or subsidies. However, they may be preferable when the environmental costs of certain actions are unknown and it is wise to play safe.

1f Tradable permits are a mix of command-and-control and market-based systems. Firms are given permits to emit a certain level of pollution and then these can be traded. A firm that can relatively cheaply reduce its pollution below its permitted level can sell this credit to another firm which finds it more costly to do so. The system is an efficient and administratively cheap way of limiting pollution to a designated level. It can, however, lead to pollution being concentrated in certain areas and can reduce the pressure on firms to find cleaner methods of production.

2a The allocation of road space depends on demand and supply. Demand depends on the price to motorists of using their cars, incomes, the cost of alternative means of transport, the price of cars and complementary services (such as parking), and the comfort and convenience of car transport. The price and cross-price elasticities of demand for car usage tend to be low: many people are unwilling to switch to alternative modes of transport. The income elasticity, on the other hand, is high. The demand for cars and car usage grows rapidly as incomes grow.

2b With road space fixed (at least in the short term), allocation depends on the private decisions of motorists. The problem is that motorists create two types of external cost: pollution costs and congestion costs. Thus $MSC > MC$. Because of these externalities, the actual use of road space (where $MB = MC$) is likely to be greater than the optimum (where $MSB = MSC$).

2c There are various types of solution to traffic congestion. These include direct provision by the government or local authorities (of additional road space or better public transport); regulation and legislation (such as restricting car access – by the use of bus and cycle lanes, no entry to side streets and pedestrian-only areas – and various forms of parking restrictions); and changing market signals (by the use of taxes, by road pricing, and by subsidising alternative means of transport).

2d Problems associated with building additional roads include the decline of public transport, attracting additional traffic on to the roads and environmental costs.

2e The main problem with restricting car access is that it tends merely to divert congestion elsewhere. The main problem with parking restrictions is that they may actually increase congestion.

2f Increasing taxes is effective in reducing congestion only if it increases the *marginal* cost of motoring. Even when it does, as in the case of additional fuel tax, the additional cost is only indirectly related to congestion costs, since it applies to all motorists and not just those causing congestion.

2g Road pricing is the preferred solution of many economists. By the use of electronic devices, motorists can be charged whenever they add to congestion. This should encourage less essential road users to travel at off-peak times or to use alternative modes of transport, while those who gain a high utility from car transport can still use their cars, but at a price. Variable tolls and area charges are alternative forms of congestion pricing, but are generally less effective than the use of variable electronic road pricing.

2h If road pricing is to be effective, there must be attractive substitutes available. A comprehensive policy, therefore, should include subsidising efficient public transport. The revenues required for this could be obtained from road pricing.

3a From around 1983 the Conservative government in the UK embarked on a large programme of privatisation. Many other countries followed suit.

3b The economic arguments for privatisation include: greater competition, not only in the goods market but in the market for finance and for corporate control; reduced government interference; and raising revenue to finance tax cuts.

3c The economic arguments against privatisation are largely the market failure arguments that were used to justify nationalisation. In reply the advocates of privatisation argue that these problems can be overcome through appropriate regulation and increasing the amount of competition.

3d Regulation in the UK has involved setting up regulatory offices for the major privatised utilities. These generally operate informally, using negotiation and bargaining to persuade the industries to behave in the public interest. They also set the terms under which the firms can operate (e.g. access rights to the respective grid).

3e As far as prices are concerned, the industries are required to abide by an '*RPI* minus *X*' formula. This forces them to pass potential cost reductions on to the consumer. At the same time they are allowed to retain any additional profits gained from cost reductions greater than *X*. This provides them with an incentive to achieve even greater increases in efficiency.

3f Many parts of the privatised industries are not natural monopolies. In these parts, competition may be a more effective means of pursuing the public interest. Various attempts have been made to make the privatised industries more competitive, often at the instigation of the regulator. Nevertheless, considerable market power remains in the hands of many privatised firms, and thus the need for regulation will continue.

REVIEW QUESTIONS

1 Why is it so difficult to value the environment? What are the implications of this for government policy on the environment?

2 Is it a good idea to use the revenues from green taxes to subsidise green alternatives (e.g. using petrol taxes for subsidising rail transport)?

3 Compare the relative merits of increased road fuel taxes, electronic road pricing and tolls as means of reducing urban traffic congestion. Why is the price inelasticity of demand for private car transport a problem here, whichever of the three policies is adopted? What could be done to increase the price elasticity of demand?

4 How would you set about measuring the external costs of road transport?

5 Consider the argument that whether an industry is in the public sector or private sector has far less bearing on its performance than the degree of competition it faces.

6 To what extent do the various goals of privatisation conflict?

7 Is it desirable after an industry has been privatised for profitable parts of the industry to cross-subsidise unprofitable parts if they are of public benefit (e.g. profitable railway lines cross-subsidising unprofitable ones)?

8 Should regulators of utilities that have been privatised into several separate companies permit (a) horizontal mergers (within the industry); (b) vertical mergers; (c) mergers with firms in other related industries (e.g. gas and electricity suppliers)?

> **Additional Part H case studies on the *Economics for Business* website (www.pearsoned.co.uk/sloman)**

H.1 **The police as a public service.** The extent to which policing can be classified as a public good.

H.2 **Should health care provision be left to the market?** An examination of the market failures that would occur if health care provision were left to the free market.

H.3 **Corporate social responsibility.** An examination of social responsibility as a goal of firms and its effect on business performance.

H.4 **Public choice theory.** This examines how economists have attempted to extend their analysis of markets to the field of political decision making.

H.5 **Cartels set in concrete, steel and cardboard.** This examines some of the best-known Europe-wide cartels of recent years.

H.6 **Taking your vitamins – at a price.** A case study of a global vitamins cartel.

H.7 **Productivity performance and the UK economy.** A detailed examination of how the UK's productivity compares with that in other countries.

H.8 **Technology and economic change.** How to get the benefits from technological advance.

H.9 **The economics of non-renewable resources.** An examination of how the price of non-renewable resources rises as stocks become depleted, and of how the current price reflects this.

H.10 **A deeper shade of green.** This looks at different perspectives on how we should treat the environment.

H.11 **Perverse subsidies.** An examination of the use of subsidies around the world that are harmful to the environment.

H.12 **Can the market provide adequate protection for the environment?** This explains why markets generally fail to take into account environmental externalities.

H.13 **Environmental auditing.** Are businesses becoming greener? A growing number of firms are subjecting themselves to an 'environmental audit' to judge just how 'green' they are.

H.14 **Restricting car access to Athens.** A case study that examines how the Greeks have attempted to reduce local atmospheric pollution from road traffic.

H.15 **Evaluating new road schemes.** The system used in the UK of assessing the costs and benefits of proposed new roads.

H.16 **Selling power to the people.** Attempts to introduce competition into the UK electricity industry.

H.17 **Regulation US-style.** This examines rate-of-return regulation: an alternative to price-cap regulation.

H.18 **Price-cap regulation in the UK.** How $RPI - X$ regulation has applied to the various privatised industries.

Websites relevant to Part H

Numbers and sections refer to websites listed in the Web appendix and hotlinked from this book's website at **www.pearsoned.co.uk/sloman**

- For news articles relevant to Part H, see the Economics News Articles link from the book's website.

- For general news on market failures and government intervention, see websites in section A, and particularly A1–5, 18, 19, 24, 31. See also links to newspapers in A38, 39 and 43; and see A42 for links to economics news articles from newspapers worldwide.

- Sites I7 and 11 contain links to Competition and monopoly, Policy and regulation and Transport in the Microeconomics section; they also have an Industry and commerce section. Site I4 has links to Environmental and Environmental Economics in the EconDirectory section. Site I17 has several sections of links in the Issues in Society section.

- Sites I7 and 11 also contain links to sites related to corporate social responsibility: see Industry and Commerce > Fair Trade > Corporate Social Responsibility.

- For information on taxes and subsidies, see E30, 36; G13. For use of green taxes, see H5; G11; E2, 14, 30.

- For information on health and the economics of health care (Web Case H.2: see above), see E8; H9. See also links in I8 and 17.

- For sites favouring the free market, see C17; D34. See also C18 for the development of ideas on the market and government intervention.

- For information on training, see E5; G14; H3.

- For the economics of the environment, see links in I4, 7, 11, 17. For policy on the environment and transport, see E2, 7, 11, 14, 29; G10, 11. See also H11.

- UK and EU departments relevant to competition policy can be found at sites E10; G7, 8.

- UK regulatory bodies can be found at sites E4, 11, 15, 16, 18, 19, 21, 22, 25, 29.

- For student resources relevant to this chapter, see sites C1–7, 9, 10, 19.

26.1 MACROECONOMIC OBJECTIVES

There are several macroeconomic variables that governments seek to control, but these can be grouped under four main headings.

Economic growth. Governments try to achieve high rates of economic growth over the long term: in other words, growth that is sustained over the years and is not just a temporary phenomenon. To this end, governments also try to achieve stable growth, avoiding both recessions and excessive short-term growth that cannot be sustained (albeit, governments are sometimes happy to give the economy an excessive boost as an election draws near!).

> **KEY IDEA 38**
>
> ***Economies suffer from inherent instability.*** As a result, economic growth and other macroeconomic indicators tend to fluctuate.

Unemployment. Reducing unemployment is another major macroeconomic aim of governments not only for the sake of the unemployed themselves, but also because it represents a waste of human resources and because unemployment benefits are a drain on government revenues.

Inflation. By inflation we mean a general rise in prices throughout the economy. Government policy here is to keep inflation both low and stable. One of the most important reasons for this is that it will aid the process of economic decision making. For example, businesses will be able to set prices and wage rates, and make investment decisions, with far more confidence. Today we are used to inflation rates of around 2 or 3 per cent per year, but it was not long ago that inflation in most developed countries was in double figures. In 1991, UK inflation reached 11 per cent; in 1975 it had reached 24 per cent!

In most developed countries, governments have a particular target for the rate of inflation. In the UK the target is 2 per cent. The Bank of England then adjusts interest rates to try to keep inflation on target (we see how this works in section 30.3).

The balance of payments. Governments aim to provide an environment in which exports can grow without an excessive growth in imports. They also aim to make the economy attractive to inward investment. In other words, they seek to create a climate in which the country's earnings of foreign currency at least match, or preferably exceed, the country's demand for foreign currency: they seek to achieve a favourable balance of payments.

In order to achieve these goals, the government may seek to control several 'intermediate' variables. These include interest rates, the supply of money, taxes, government expenditure and exchange rates. For example, the achievement of a favourable balance of payments depends, in part, on whether changes in exchange rates allow the country's goods and services to remain price competitive on international markets. A lower exchange rate (i.e. fewer dollars, yen, euros, etc. to the pound) will make UK goods cheaper to overseas buyers, and thus help to boost UK exports. The government may thus seek to manipulate exchange rates to make them 'more favourable'.

In later chapters we will be looking at the various types of macroeconomic policy that governments can adopt. First we will look at the four macroeconomic objectives and identify their main determinants. In this chapter we will examine economic growth, unemployment and inflation. In Chapter 27 we will focus on the balance of payments and its relation to the exchange rate.

Definitions

Rate of economic growth
The percentage increase in output over a twelve-month period.

Rate of inflation
The percentage increase in prices over a twelve-month period.

Balance of payments account
A record of the country's transactions with the rest of the world. It shows the country's payments to or deposits in other countries (debits) and its receipts or deposits from other countries (credits). It also shows the balance between these debits and credits under various headings.

Exchange rate
The rate at which one national currency exchanges for another. The rate is expressed as the amount of one currency that is necessary to purchase one unit of another currency (e.g. £1 = €1.20).

ECONOMIC GROWTH 26.2

The distinction between actual and potential growth

Before examining the causes of economic growth, it is essential to distinguish between *actual* and *potential* economic growth.

Actual growth is the percentage annual increase in national output or 'GDP' (gross domestic product): in other words, the rate of growth in actual output produced. When statistics on GDP growth rates are published, it is actual growth they are referring to. (We examine the measurement of GDP in the appendix to this chapter.)

Potential growth is the speed at which the economy *could* grow. It is the percentage annual increase in the economy's *capacity* to produce: the rate of growth in potential output.

> **KEY IDEA 39**
> ***Living standards are limited by a country's ability to produce.*** Potential national output depends on the country's resources, technology and productivity.

Potential output (i.e. potential GDP) is the level of output when the economy is operating at 'normal capacity utilisation'. This allows for firms having a planned degree of spare capacity to meet unexpected demand or for hold-ups in supply. It also allows for some unemployment as people move from job to job. Potential output is thus somewhat below full-capacity output, which is the absolute maximum that could be produced with firms working flat-out.

The difference between actual and potential output is known as the output gap. Thus if actual output exceeds potential output, the output gap is positive: the economy is operating above normal capacity utilisation. If actual output is below potential output, the output gap is negative: the economy is operating below normal capacity utilisation. Box 26.1 looks at the output gap for the UK and France since 1965.

If the potential growth rate exceeds the actual growth rate, there will be an increase in spare capacity and an increase in unemployment: there will be a growing gap between potential and actual output. To close this gap, the actual growth rate would temporarily have to exceed the potential growth rate. In the long run, however, the actual growth rate will be limited to the potential growth rate.

There are thus two major issues concerned with economic growth: the short-run issue of ensuring that actual growth is such as to keep actual output as close as possible to potential output; and the long-run issue of what determines the rate of potential economic growth.

Actual economic growth and the business cycle

Although growth in potential output varies to some extent over the years – depending on the rate of advance of technology, the level of investment and the discovery of new raw materials – it nevertheless tends to be much more steady than the growth in actual output.

Definitions

Actual growth
The percentage annual increase in national output actually produced.

Potential growth
The percentage annual increase in the capacity of the economy to produce.

Potential output
The output that could be produced in the economy if all firms were operating at their normal level of capacity utilisation.

Output gap
Actual output minus potential output.

Figure 26.1 The business cycle

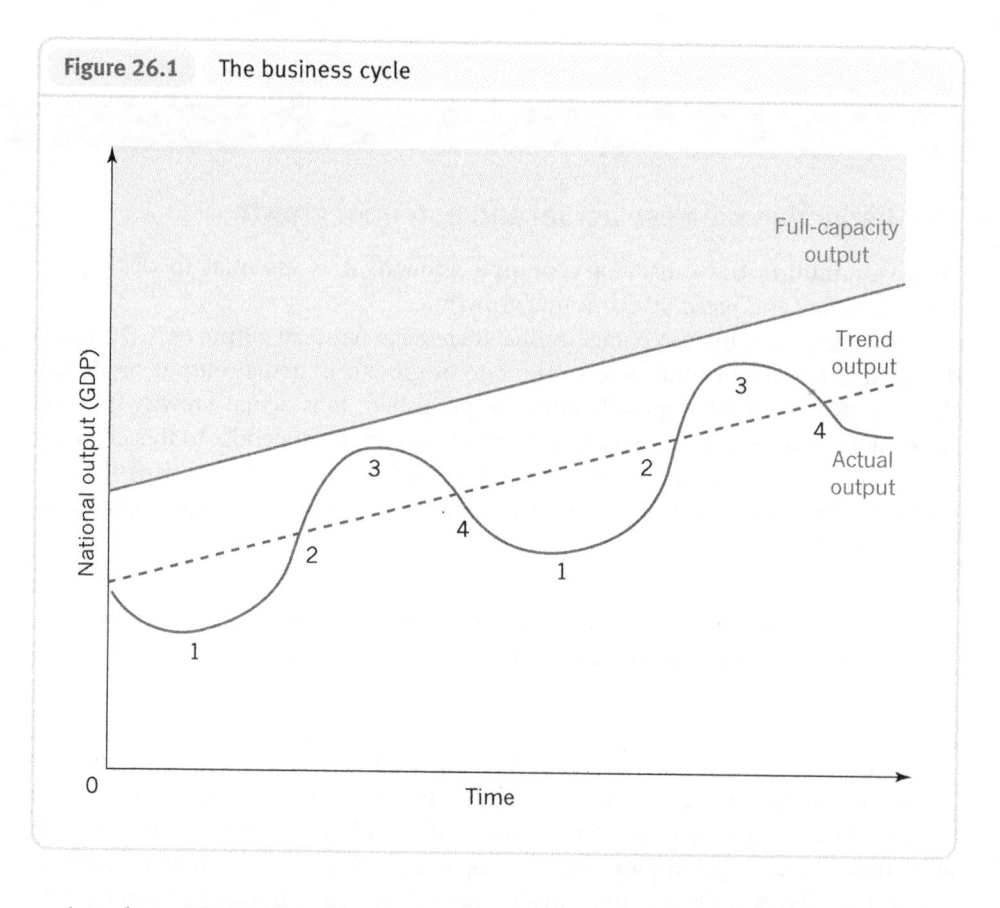

Actual growth tends to fluctuate. In some years there is a high rate of economic growth: the country experiences a boom. In other years, economic growth is low or even negative: the country experiences a recession.[1] This cycle of booms and recessions is known as the **business cycle** or **trade cycle**.

There are four 'phases' of the business cycle. They are illustrated in Figure 26.1.

1 *The upturn*. In this phase, a stagnant economy begins to recover and growth in actual output resumes.
2 *The rapid expansion*. During this phase, there is rapid economic growth: the economy is booming. A fuller use is made of resources and the gap between actual and full-capacity output narrows.
3 *The peaking out*. During this phase, growth slows down or even ceases.
4 *The slowdown, recession or slump*. During this phase, there is little or no growth or even a decline in output. Increasing slack develops in the economy.

Long-term output trend. A line can be drawn showing the trend of national output over time (i.e. ignoring the cyclical fluctuations around the trend). This is shown as the dashed line in Figure 26.1. If, over time, firms on average operate with a 'normal' degree of capacity utilisation, the trend output line will be the same as the potential output line. If the average level of capacity that is unutilised stays constant from one cycle to another, the trend line will have the same slope as the full-capacity output line. In other words, the trend (or potential) rate of growth will be the same as the rate of growth of capacity.

> **Definition**
>
> **Business cycle** or **trade cycle**
> The periodic fluctuations of national output round its long-term trend.

---

[1] In official statistics, a recession is defined as when an economy experiences falling national output (negative growth) for two or more quarters.

If, however, the level of unutilised capacity changes from one cycle to another, then the trend line will have a different slope from the full-capacity output line. For example, if unemployment and unused industrial capacity *rise* from one peak to another, or from one trough to another, then the trend line will move further away from the full-capacity output line (i.e. it will be less steep).

> **Pause for thought**
>
> *If the average percentage (as opposed to the average level) of full-capacity output that was unutilised remained constant, would the trend line have the same slope as the potential output line?*

The business cycle in practice

The business cycle illustrated in Figure 26.1 is a 'stylised' cycle. It is nice and smooth and regular. Drawing it this way allows us to make a clear distinction between each of the four phases. In practice, however, business cycles are highly irregular. They are irregular in two ways.

The length of the phases. Some booms are short lived, lasting only a few months or so. Others are much longer, lasting perhaps three or four years. Likewise some recessions are short, while others are long.

The magnitude of the phases. Sometimes in phase 2 there is a very high rate of economic growth, perhaps 5 per cent per annum or more. On other occasions in phase 2 growth is much gentler. Sometimes in phase 4 there is a recession, with an actual decline in output (e.g. in the early 1980s and early 1990s). On other occasions, phase 4 is merely a 'pause', with growth simply being low.

Nevertheless, despite the irregularity of the fluctuations, cycles are still clearly discernible, especially if we plot *growth* on the vertical axis rather than the *level* of output. This is done in Figure 26.2, which shows the business cycles in selected industrial countries from 1970 to 2011.

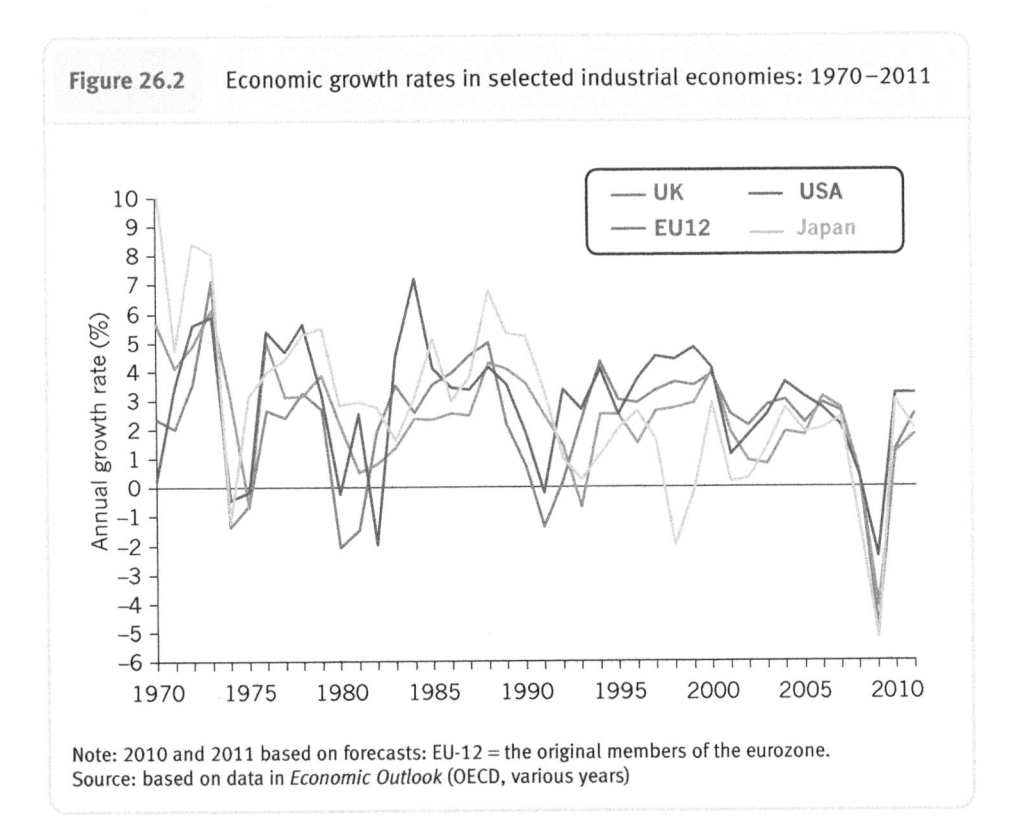

Figure 26.2 Economic growth rates in selected industrial economies: 1970–2011

Note: 2010 and 2011 based on forecasts: EU-12 = the original members of the eurozone.
Source: based on data in *Economic Outlook* (OECD, various years)

BOX 26.1 OUTPUT GAPS

An alternative measure of excess or deficient demand

If the economy grows, how fast and for how long can it grow before it runs into inflationary problems? On the other hand, what minimum rate must be achieved to avoid rising unemployment?

To answer these questions, economists have developed the concept of 'output gaps'.[1] The output gap is the difference between actual output and potential output.

If actual output is below potential output (the gap is negative), there will be a higher than normal level of unemployment as firms are operating below their normal level of capacity utilisation. There will, however, be a downward pressure on inflation, resulting from a lower than normal level of demand for labour and other resources. If actual output is above potential output (the gap is positive), there will be excess demand and a rise in inflation.

Generally, the gap will be negative in a recession and positive in a boom. In other words, output gaps follow the course of the business cycle.

Of course, to measure the output gap we first need to measure potential output. There are two main approaches to producing statistical estimates of potential output.

De-trending techniques. This approach is a purely mechanical exercise which involves smoothing the actual GDP figures. In doing this, it attempts to fit a trend growth path along the lines of the dashed line in Figure 26.1. The main disadvantage of this approach is that it is not grounded in economic theory and therefore does not take into consideration those factors that economists consider to be important in determining output levels over time.

Production function approach. Many institutions, such as the European Union, use an approach which borrows ideas from economic theory. Specifically, it uses the idea of a production function which relates output to a set of inputs. Estimates of potential output are generated by using statistics on the size of a country's capital stock, the potential available labour input and, finally, the productivity or effectiveness of these inputs in producing output.

The table shows the ratio of potential output in 2009 to that in 1965 for both France and the UK, and what this equates to in terms of an annual rate of growth for potential output. We can see that the rate of growth in France's potential output is over $1/2$ a percentage point higher each year than that in the UK. Over the long term, the actual rate of economic growth in both countries is approximately the same as the potential rate. In other words, over the years, the average output gap tends towards zero.

---

[1] See C. Giorno et al., 'Potential output, output gaps and structural budget balances', *OECD Economic Studies*, no. 24, 1995, p. 1.

Table 1 Potential and actual output in France and the UK

	Potential output in 2009/ potential output in 1965	Equivalent annual rate of growth in potential output (%)	Actual output in 2009/ actual output in 1965	Equivalent annual rate of growth in actual output (%)
France	3.34	2.78	3.33	2.77
UK	2.81	2.38	2.76	2.34

Source: Based on data in the annual macro-economic database (AMECO) of the European Commission's Directorate General for Economic and Financial Affairs.
Note: 2009 figures based on forecasts

Output gaps in UK and France

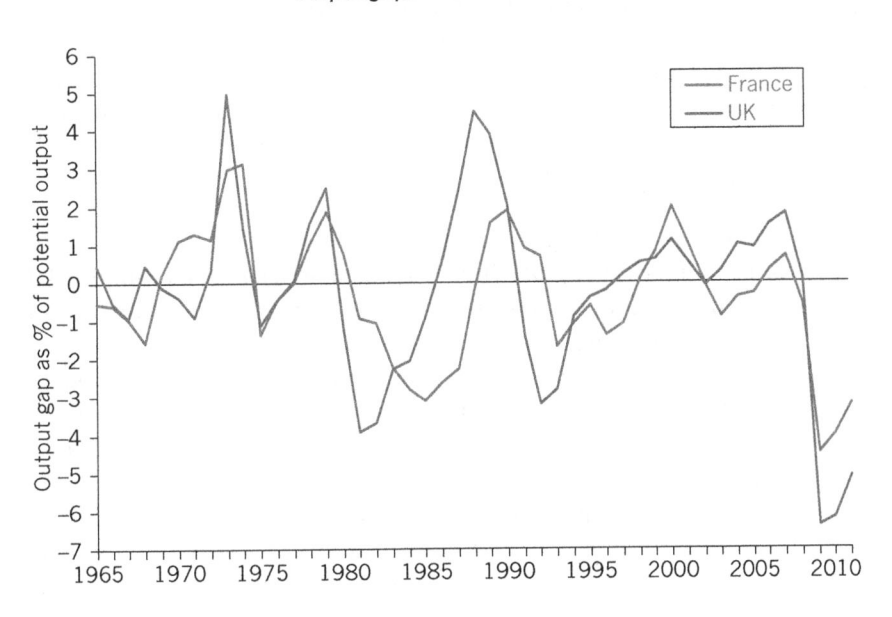

Source: based on data in the annual macro-economic database [AMECO] of the European Commission's Directorate General for Economic and Financial Affairs

The chart shows that the output gaps have tended to fluctuate more in the UK than in France. This is particularly true during the 1980s and early 1990s. Interestingly, during this period the two economies appear to be out of synch. For instance, in 1988 when the UK was experiencing a positive output gap, with actual output estimated to be 4½ per cent above the potential output, in France actual output was below its potential level.

We can use the information on output gaps to identify the length of a particular business cycle, its degree of economic volatility and the growth in potential output during the cycle. The trend growth rate in the UK was about 2½ per cent per year over the full economic cycle to 2008 (i.e. from 1991: the equivalent point in the previous cycle).

Until the recession of the late 2000s, growth rates in the UK had been relatively stable since 1992 compared with previous cycles. In fact, Gordon Brown was claiming in the early 2000s that 'boom and bust' were things of the past. During this period, therefore, output gaps, both positive and negative, were smaller than in the 1980s (or the 1970s for that matter).

Until the recession of 2008/9, it was argued that the greater stability in the UK economy created a climate that encouraged a long-term increase in investment and hence a long-term increase in potential growth. Whether that climate will be resumed in the future will have to be seen.

How might the behaviour of firms differ during periods of negative and positive output gaps?

> **Definition**
>
> **Aggregate demand**
> Total spending on goods and services made in the economy. It consists of four elements: consumer spending (C), investment (I), government spending (G) and the expenditure on exports (X), less any expenditure on foreign goods and services (M): $AD = C + I + G + X - M$.

Causes of fluctuations in actual growth

The major determinants of variations in the rate of actual growth in the *short run* are variations in the growth of 'aggregate demand'.

Aggregate demand (AD) is the total spending on goods and services made within the country. This spending consists of four elements: consumer spending (C), investment expenditure by firms (I), government spending (G) and the expenditure by foreign residents on the country's goods and services (i.e. their purchases of its exports and their new investments in the country) (X). From these four must be subtracted any expenditure that goes on imports (M), since this is expenditure that 'leaks' abroad and is not spent on domestic goods and services. Thus:

$$AD = C + I + G + X - M$$

A rapid rise in aggregate demand will create shortages. This will tend to stimulate firms to increase output, thereby reducing slack in the economy. Likewise, a reduction in aggregate demand will leave firms with increased stocks of unsold goods. They will therefore tend to reduce output.

Aggregate demand and actual output therefore fluctuate together in the short run. A boom is associated with a rapid rise in aggregate demand: the faster the rise in aggregate demand, the higher the short-run growth rate. A recession, by contrast, is associated with a reduction in aggregate demand.

A rapid rise in aggregate demand, however, is not enough to ensure a continuing high level of growth over a *number* of years. Without an expansion of potential output too, rises in actual output must eventually come to an end as spare capacity is used up.

In the long run, therefore, there are two determinants of actual growth:

- the growth in aggregate demand, which determines whether potential output will be realised;
- the growth in potential output.

Potential economic growth

We now turn to the *supply* question. Here we are concerned with the capacity of the economy to produce. There are two main determinants of potential output: (a) the amount of resources available and (b) their productivity.

Increases in the quantity of resources

Capital. The nation's output depends on its stock of capital (K). An increase in this stock (through investment) will increase output. If we ignore the problem of machines wearing out or becoming obsolete and needing replacing, then the stock of capital will increase by the amount of investment. The rise in output that results will depend on the productivity of capital.

As we saw in section 23.7 (page 518), the rate of growth depends on the marginal capital/output ratio (k). This is the amount of extra capital (ΔK) divided by the amount of extra annual output that it produces (ΔY). The lower the value of k, the higher is the productivity of capital (i.e. the less extra capital you need to produce extra output). The rate of growth in potential output also depends on the proportion of national income that is invested (i), which, assuming that all saving is invested, will equal the proportion of national income that is saved (s). The formula for growth becomes:

$$g = i/k \text{ (or } g = s/k\text{)}$$

Thus if 20 per cent of national income went in new investment ($i = 20\%$), and if each £1 of new investment yielded 25p of extra income per year ($k = 4$), then the growth rate would be 5 per cent. A simple example will demonstrate this. If national income is £100 billion, then £20 billion will be invested ($i = 20\%$). This will lead to extra annual output of £5 billion ($k = 4$). Thus national income grows to £105 billion: a growth of 5 per cent.

But what determines the rate of investment? There are a number of determinants. These include the confidence of business people about the future demand for their products, the profitability of business, the tax regime, the rate of growth in the economy and the rate of interest.

Over the long term, if investment is to increase, then *saving* must increase in order to finance that investment. Put another way, people must be prepared to forgo a certain amount of consumption in order to allow resources to be diverted into producing more capital goods: factories, machines, etc.

Note that if investment is to increase, there may also need to be a steady increase in *aggregate demand*. In other words, if firms are to be encouraged to increase their capacity by installing new machines or building new factories, they may need first to see the *demand* for their products growing. Here a growth in *potential* output is the result of a growth in aggregate demand and hence *actual* output.

Labour. If there is an increase in the working population, there will be an increase in potential output. This increase in working population may result from a larger 'participation rate': a larger proportion of the total population in work or seeking work. For example, if a greater proportion of women with children decide to join the labour market, the working population will rise.

Alternatively, a rise in the working population may be the result of an increase in total population. There is a problem here. If a rise in total population does not result in a greater *proportion* of the population working, output *per head of the population* may not rise at all. In practice, many developed countries are faced with a growing proportion of their population above retirement age, and thus a potential *fall* in output per head of the population.

Land and raw materials. The scope for generating growth here is usually very limited. Land is virtually fixed in quantity. Land reclamation schemes and the opening up of marginal land can add only tiny amounts to GDP. Even if new raw materials are discovered (e.g. oil), this will only result in *short-term* growth: i.e. while the rate of extraction is building up. Once the rate of extraction is at a maximum, economic growth will cease. Output will simply remain at the new higher level, until eventually the raw materials begin to run out. Output will then fall back again.

The problem of diminishing returns. If a single factor of production increases in supply while others remain fixed, diminishing returns will set in. For example, if the quantity of capital increases with no increase in other factors of production, then diminishing returns to capital will set in. The rate of return on capital will fall. Unless *all* factors of production increase, therefore, the rate of growth is likely to slow down.

Then there is the problem of the environment. If a rise in labour and capital leads to a more *intensive* use of land and natural resources, the resulting growth in output may be environmentally unsustainable. The solution to the problem of diminishing returns is for there to be an increase in the *productivity* of resources.

Increases in the productivity of resources

Technological improvements can increase the marginal productivity of capital. Much of the investment in new machines is not just in extra machines, but in superior machines producing a higher rate of return. Consider the microchip revolution of recent years. Modern computers can do the work of many people and have replaced many machines which were cumbersome and expensive to build. Improved methods of transport have reduced the costs of moving goods and materials. Improved communications (such as the Internet) have reduced the costs of transmitting information. The high-tech world of today would seem a wonderland to a person of 100 years ago.

As a result of technical progress, the productivity of capital has tended to increase over time. Similarly, as a result of new skills, improved education and training, and better health, the productivity of labour has also tended to increase over time.

> **Pause for thought**
>
> *Will the rate of actual growth have any effect on the rate of potential growth?*

But technical progress on its own is not enough. There must also be the institutions and attitudes that encourage *innovation*. In other words, the inventions must be exploited.

Policies to achieve growth

How can governments increase a country's growth rate? Policies differ in two ways.

First, they may focus on the demand side or the supply side of the economy. In other words, they may attempt to create sufficient *aggregate demand* to ensure that firms wish to invest and that potential output is realised. Or alternatively, they may seek to increase *aggregate supply* by concentrating on measures to increase potential output: measures to encourage research and development, innovation and training. Chapter 30 looks at demand-side policies, while Chapter 31 looks at supply-side ones.

Second, they may be market-orientated or interventionist policies. Many economists and politicians, especially those on the political right, believe that the best environment for encouraging economic growth is one where private enterprise is allowed to flourish: where entrepreneurs are able to reap substantial rewards from investment in new techniques and new products. Such economists therefore advocate policies designed to free up the market. Others, however, argue that a free market will be subject to considerable cyclical fluctuations. The resulting uncertainty will discourage investment. Such economists, therefore, tend to advocate intervention by the government to reduce these fluctuations.

15.1 UNEMPLOYMENT

Unemployment fluctuates with the business cycle. In recessions, such as those experienced by most countries in the early 1980s, the early 1990s and the early and late 2000s, unemployment tends to rise. In boom years, such as the late 1980s, late 1990s and mid 2000s, it tends to fall. Figure 15.1 shows these cyclical movements in unemployment for selected countries.

As well as experiencing fluctuations in unemployment, most countries have experienced long-term changes in average unemployment rates. This is illustrated in Table 15.1, which shows average unemployment in a selection of industrialised countries. Average unemployment rates in the 1980s and 1990s were higher than in the 1970s, and average rates in the 1970s were, in turn, higher than in the 1950s and 1960s. In certain countries, such as the UK and the USA, the late 1990s and early 2000s saw a long-term fall in unemployment.

This section gives an overview of the problem of unemployment: how it is measured and what its costs are. Then we look at the range of possible causes of unemployment. We explore these causes and the policies for tackling unemployment in more detail as the book progresses.

The meaning of 'unemployment'

Unemployment can be expressed either as a number (e.g. 1.6 million) or as a percentage (e.g. 6 per cent). But just who should be included in the statistics? Should it be everyone without a job? The answer is clearly no, since we would not want to include children and pensioners. We would probably also want to exclude those who were not looking for work, such as parents choosing to stay at home to look after children.

The most usual definition that economists use for the **number unemployed** is: *those of working age who are without*

Table 15.1 Average unemployment rates by decade (%)

	1960s	1970s	1980s	1990s	2000s
Australia	1.7	3.8	7.6	9.0	5.5
Canada	5.0	6.7	9.4	9.7	6.8
France	4.9	5.9	8.4	10.4	7.9
Germany	0.7	2.0	5.8	7.6	8.6
Greece	5.1	2.3	6.1	9.3	9.7
Ireland	5.3	7.5	14.2	11.9	5.3
Japan	1.3	1.7	2.5	3.2	4.7
Spain	2.4	4.5	15.4	16.2	11.0
UK	1.6	3.5	9.5	8.1	5.4
USA	4.8	6.2	7.3	5.7	5.6
EU-15	2.2	3.7	8.3	9.2	7.8

Notes: (i) EU-15 = 15 members of the European Union prior to 1 May 2004; (ii) German figures relate to West Germany only up to 1991.
Source: AMECO database, European Commission, DGECFIN.

Definition

Number unemployed (economist's definition) Those of working age who are without work, but who are available for work at current wage rates.

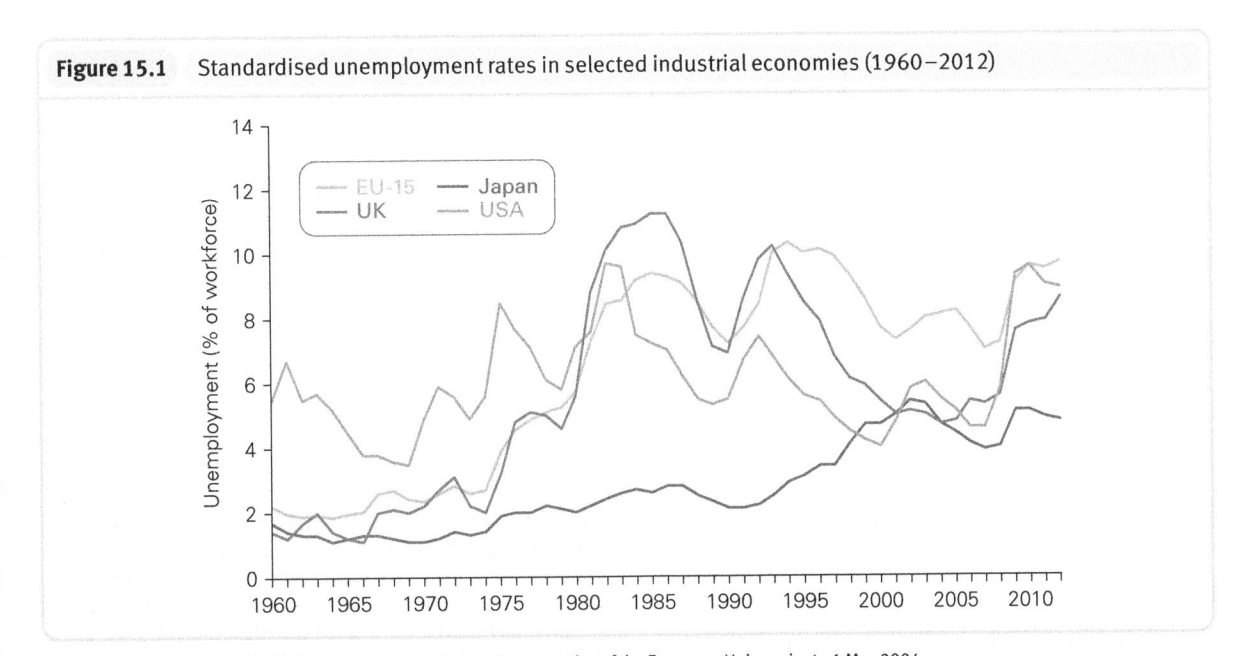

Figure 15.1 Standardised unemployment rates in selected industrial economies (1960–2012)

Notes: 2011 and 2012 based on forecasts; EU-15 = the member countries of the European Union prior to 1 May 2004.
Source: Based on data in AMECO Database, European Commission, DGECFIN.

work, but who are available for work at current wage rates. If the figure is to be expressed as a percentage, then it is a percentage of the total **labour force**. The labour force is defined as *those in employment plus those unemployed*. Thus if 28 million people were employed and 2.5 million people were unemployed, the **unemployment rate** would be

$$\frac{2.5}{28 + 2.5} \times 100 = 8.2\%$$

Official measures of unemployment

Claimant unemployment

Two common measures of unemployment are used in official statistics. The first is *claimant unemployment*. This is simply a measure of all those in receipt of unemployment-related benefits. In the UK claimants receive the 'jobseeker's allowance (JSA)'.

Claimant statistics have the advantage of being very easy to collect. However, they exclude all those of working age who are available for work at current wage rates, but who are *not* eligible for benefits. If the government changes the eligibility conditions so that fewer people are eligible, this will reduce the number of claimants and hence the official number unemployed, even if there has been no change in the numbers with or without work.

The following categories of people in the UK are ineligible for JSA and are thus not included in claimant unemployment:

- People returning to the workforce (e.g. after raising children).
- Those who are on government training schemes (e.g. school leavers without jobs).
- Those whose income (e.g. from property) or savings are too high.
- Those whose spouse or partner earns above a certain level or works more than 24 hours per week.
- Those over the state retirement age.
- Those aged 16 and 17.
- Those in receipt of 'employment and support allowance' (previously called incapacity benefit) but who nevertheless would be available for work of certain types.
- People seeking part-time work, rather than full-time work, for example students.
- Those choosing not to claim.

The claimant statistics in the UK thus understate the true level of unemployment.

Standardised unemployment rates

Recognising the weaknesses of the claimant statistics, the UK government since 1998 has used the *standardised unemployment rate* as the main measure of unemployment. In this measure, the unemployed are defined as people of working age who are without work, available to start work within two weeks and *actively seeking employment* or waiting to take up an appointment.

This is the measure used by the International Labour Organization (ILO) and the Organisation for Economic Co-operation and Development (OECD), two international organisations that publish unemployment statistics for many countries. The figures are compiled from the results of national labour force *surveys*. A representative cross-section of the population is asked whether they are employed, unemployed (using the above definition) or economically inactive. From their replies, national rates of unemployment can be extrapolated. In the UK, the Labour Force Survey is conducted quarterly.

But is the standardised unemployment rate likely to be higher or lower than the claimant unemployment rate? The standardised rate is likely to be higher to the extent that it includes people seeking work who are nevertheless not entitled to claim benefits, but lower to the extent that it excludes those who are claiming benefits and yet who are not actively seeking work. Clearly, the tougher the benefit regulations, the lower the claimant rate will be relative to the standardised rate. In the second quarter of 2011, claimant unemployment in the UK was 1.50 million (4.7 per cent), while standardised unemployment was 2.49 million (7.9 per cent).

> ? *How does the ILO/OECD definition differ from the economist's definition? What is the significance of the phrase 'available for work at current wage rates' in the economist's definition?*

The duration of unemployment

A few of the unemployed may never have had a job and maybe never will. For most, however, unemployment lasts only a certain period. For some it may be just a few days while they are between jobs. For others it may be a few months. For others – the long-term unemployed – it could

---

Definitions

Labour force The number employed plus the number unemployed.

Unemployment rate The number unemployed expressed as a percentage of the labour force.

Claimant unemployment Those in receipt of unemployment-related benefits.

Standardised unemployment rate The measure of the unemployment rate used by the ILO and the OECD. The unemployed are defined as persons of working age who are without work, are available to start work within two weeks and either have actively looked for work in the last four weeks or are waiting to take up an appointment.

Figure 15.2 UK unemployment by duration

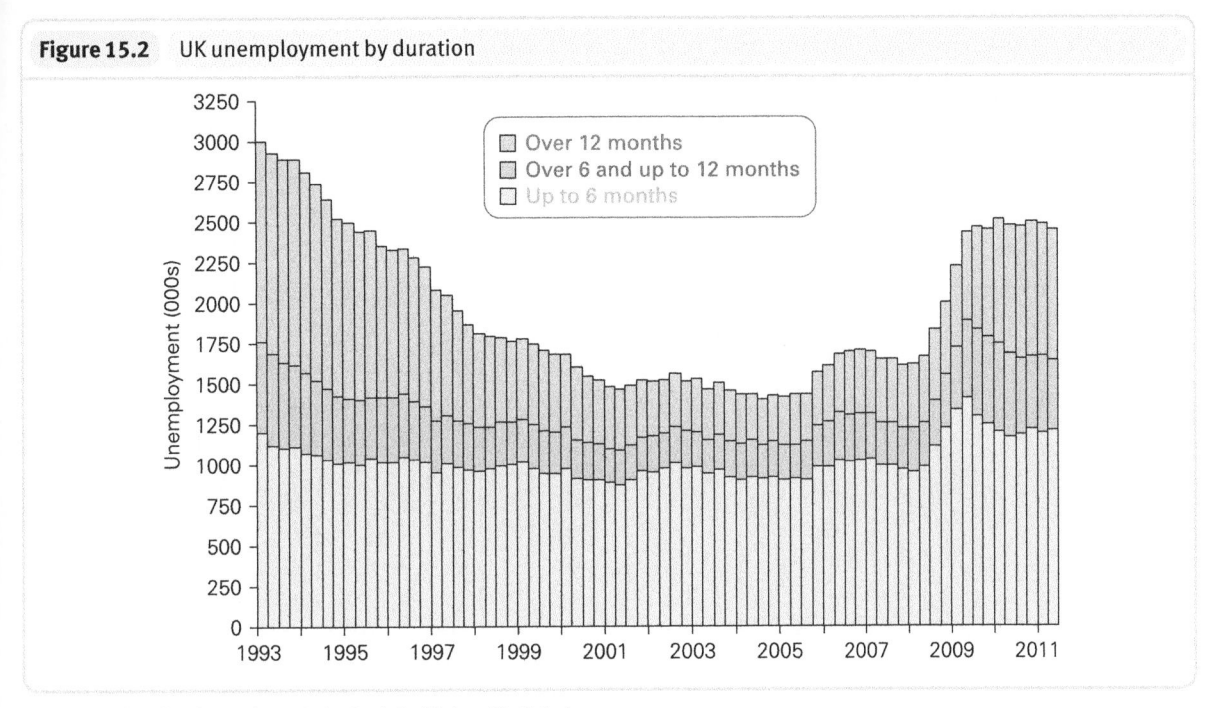

Source: Based on data from *Labour Market Statistics* (National Statistics).

be several years. Figure 15.2 shows the composition of standardised unemployment in the UK by duration.

What determines the average duration of unemployment? There are three important factors here.

The number unemployed (the size of the stock of unemployment). Unemployment is a 'stock' concept (see Box 9.9). It measures a *quantity* (i.e. the number unemployed) at a particular *point in time*. The higher the stock of unemployment, the longer will tend to be the duration of unemployment. There will be more people competing for vacant jobs.

The rate of inflow and outflow from the stock of unemployment. The people making up the unemployment total are constantly changing. Each week some people are made redundant or quit their jobs. They represent an inflow to the stock of unemployment. Other people find jobs and thus represent an outflow from the stock of unemployment. The various inflows and outflows are shown in Figure 15.3.

Unemployment is often referred to as 'the pool of unemployment'. This is quite a good analogy. If the water flowing into a pool exceeds the water flowing out, the

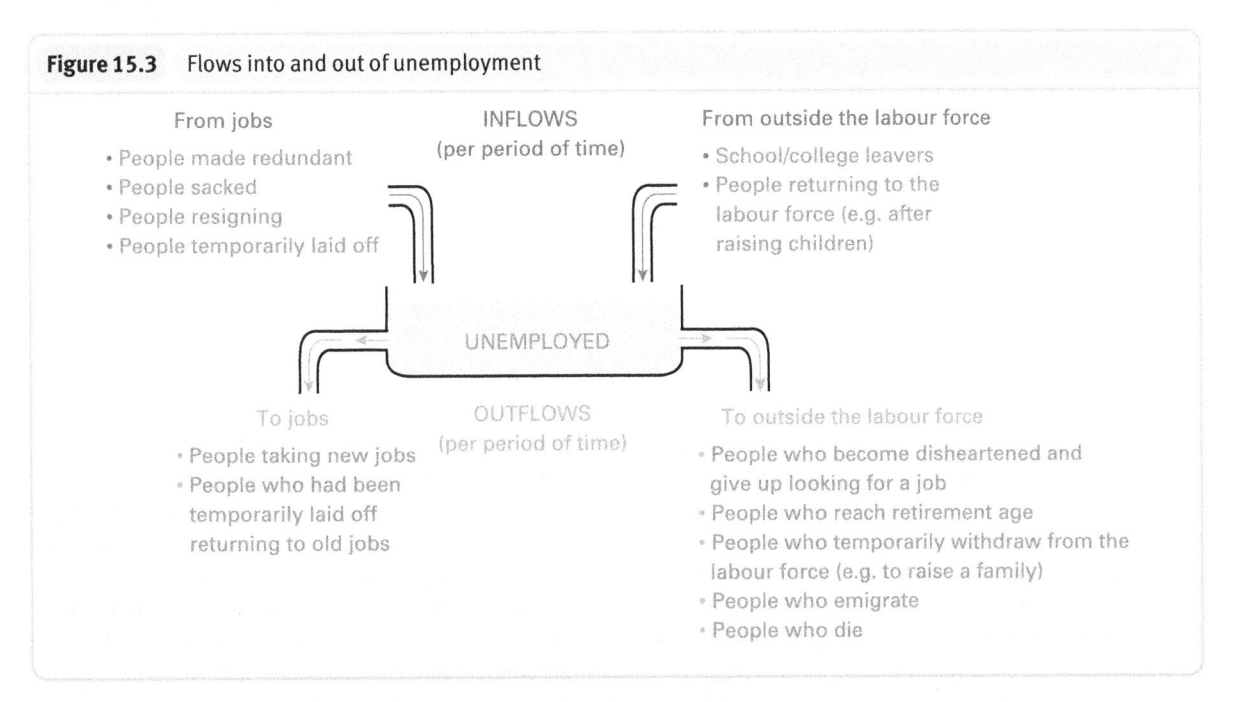

Figure 15.3 Flows into and out of unemployment

INFLOWS (per period of time)

From jobs
- People made redundant
- People sacked
- People resigning
- People temporarily laid off

From outside the labour force
- School/college leavers
- People returning to the labour force (e.g. after raising children)

UNEMPLOYED

OUTFLOWS (per period of time)

To jobs
- People taking new jobs
- People who had been temporarily laid off returning to old jobs

To outside the labour force
- People who become disheartened and give up looking for a job
- People who reach retirement age
- People who temporarily withdraw from the labour force (e.g. to raise a family)
- People who emigrate
- People who die

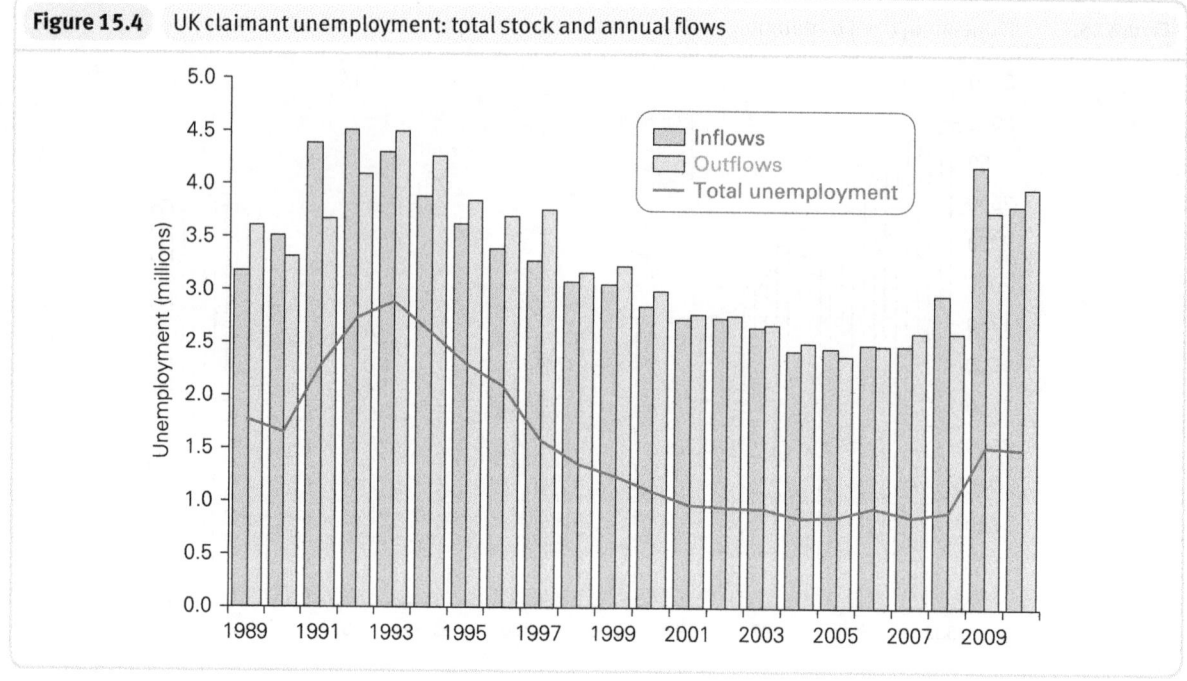

Figure 15.4 UK claimant unemployment: total stock and annual flows

Source: Based on data from *Economic and Labour Market Review* (National Statistics).

level of water in the pool will rise. Similarly, if the inflow of people into unemployment exceeds the outflow, the level of unemployment will rise.

The duration of unemployment will depend on the *rate* of inflow and outflow. The rate is expressed as the number of people per period of time. Figure 15.4 shows the inflows and outflows in the UK since 1989.

Note the magnitude of the flows. In each of the years, the outflows (and inflows) exceed the total number unemployed. The bigger the flows are relative to the total number unemployed, the less will be the average duration of unemployment. This is because people move into and out of the pool more quickly, and hence their average stay will be shorter.

1. If the number unemployed exceeded the total annual outflow, what could we conclude about the average duration of unemployment?
2. Make a list of the various inflows to and outflows from employment from and to (a) unemployment; (b) outside the workforce.

The phase of the business cycle. The duration of unemployment will also depend on the phase of the business cycle. At the onset of a recession, unemployment will rise, but as yet the average length of unemployment is likely to have been relatively short. Once a recession has lasted for a period of time, however, people will on average have been out of work longer, and this long-term unemployment is likely to persist even when the economy is pulling out of recession.

*LOOKING AT THE MATHS

The duration of unemployment (D_u) will equal the stock of unemployment (U) as a proportion of the outflow (F) from unemployment:

$$D_u = \frac{U}{F}$$

Thus the bigger the stock of unemployment relative to the outflow from it, the longer will unemployment last. Taking the figures for 1992:

$$D_u = \frac{2.74}{4.09} = 0.67$$

Thus the average duration of unemployment was 0.67 years or 245 days. By contrast, in 2010, the average duration was 1.50/3.96 = 0.38 years or 138 days.

The composition of unemployment

Unemployment rates vary enormously between countries and between different groups within countries.

Geographical differences. Table 15.2 illustrates the considerable differences in unemployment rates between countries. Compare the unemployment rates in Ireland and Spain! Countries have very different labour markets, very different policies on unemployment, training schemes, redundancy, etc., and very different attitudes of firms towards their workers. Also, countries may not be at precisely the same phase of their respective business cycles.

Table 15.2 Standardised unemployment rates in different sections of the labour market: December 2010

	All ages			Under 25		
	Total	Male	Female	Total	Male	Female
Belgium	8.1	8.1	8.1	20.3	20.6	20.3
Germany	6.6	7.1	6.0	8.5	9.5	7.5
Ireland	13.7	16.6	10.2	28.9	32.7	25.2
Spain	20.4	20.0	20.8	43.0	44.5	41.2
France	9.7	9.5	9.9	24.2	24.2	24.2
Netherlands	4.3	4.2	4.4	8.2	7.9	8.5
Portugal	11.2	10.3	12.3	21.5	19.0	24.4
United Kingdom	7.9	8.5	7.1	20.2	21.7	18.6
United States	9.4	10.1	8.7	18.1	19.9	16.1
EU-15	9.5	9.5	9.5	20.0	20.7	19.1

Source: Statistics Database, Eurostat, European Commission.

Unemployment also varies substantially within a country from one area to another. Most countries have some regions that are more prosperous than others. In the UK, unemployment in the north of England, Scotland and Northern Ireland is higher than in the south of England. For example, in the three months to January 2011, standardised unemployment was 10.2 per cent in the north-east of England and only 6.2 per cent in the east of England.

But geographical differences in unemployment are not just a regional problem. In many countries, inner-city unemployment is very much higher than suburban or rural unemployment, and, as a result, most developed countries have schemes to attract employment to the inner cities. In June 2010, claimant unemployment in Tottenham in London was 7.5 per cent, whereas in West Oxfordshire it was 1.6 per cent.

Differences in unemployment rates between women and men. In many countries, female unemployment has traditionally been higher than male unemployment. Causes have included differences in education and training, discrimination by employers, more casual or seasonally related employment among women and other social factors. In many countries, however, the position has changed in recent years. As you can see, in four of the countries in Table 15.2 male unemployment rates are higher than female rates. The main reason is the decline in many of the older industries, such as coal and steel, which employed mainly men.

BOX 15.1 THE COSTS OF UNEMPLOYMENT

EXPLORING ECONOMICS

Who loses and by how much?

The most obvious cost of unemployment is to the unemployed themselves. There is the direct financial cost of the loss in their earnings. Then there are the personal costs of being unemployed. The longer people are unemployed, the more dispirited they may become. Their self-esteem is likely to fall, and they are more likely to succumb to stress-related illness.

Beyond the unemployed themselves, there are the costs to their family and friends. Personal relations can become strained, and there may be an increase in domestic violence and the number of families splitting up.

Then there are the broader costs to the economy. Unemployment represents a loss of output. In other words, actual output is below potential output. Apart from the loss of disposable income to the unemployed themselves, this underutilisation of resources leads to lower incomes for other people too:

- The government loses tax revenues, since the unemployed pay no income tax and national insurance, and, given that the unemployed spend less, they pay less VAT and excise duties. The government also incurs administrative costs associated with the running of benefit offices. It may also have to spend extra on health care, the social services and the police.
- Firms lose the profits that could have been made if there had been full employment.
- Other workers lose any additional wages they could have earned from higher national output.

What is more, the longer people remain unemployed, the more deskilled they tend to become, thereby reducing potential as well as actual income.

? *Why have the costs to the government of unemployment benefits not been included as a cost to the economy?*

Finally, there is some evidence that higher unemployment leads to increased crime and vandalism. This obviously imposes a cost on the sufferers.

The costs of unemployment are to some extent offset by benefits. If workers voluntarily quit their jobs to look for better ones, then they must reckon that the benefits of a better job more than compensate for their temporary loss of income. From the nation's point of view, a workforce that is prepared to quit jobs and spend a short time unemployed will be a more adaptable, more mobile workforce – one that is responsive to changing economic circumstances. Such a workforce will lead to greater allocative efficiency in the short run and more rapid economic growth over the longer run.

Long-term involuntary unemployment is quite another matter. The costs clearly outweigh any benefits, both for the individuals involved and for the economy as a whole. A demotivated, deskilled pool of long-term unemployed is a serious economic and social problem.

? *Which of the above costs would be recorded as a reduction in GDP?*

Differences in unemployment rates between different age groups. Table 15.2 also shows that unemployment rates in the under-25 age group are higher than the average, and substantially so in many countries. There are various explanations for this, including the suitability (or unsuitability) of the qualifications of school leavers, the attitudes of employers to young people, and the greater willingness of young people to spend time unemployed looking for a better job or waiting to start a further or higher education course. The difference in rates is less in Germany, which has a well-established apprenticeship system.

Differences in unemployment rates between different ethnic groups. In many countries, members of ethnic minorities suffer from higher unemployment rates than the average. In the UK, the unemployment rate for Afro-Caribbeans is 2.5 times greater than that for whites. For those of Pakistani and Bangladeshi origin, it is three times greater. Explanations are complex, but include differences in educational opportunities, a higher proportion of younger people, a greater sense of alienation among the unemployed, and the attitudes and prejudices of employers.

Unemployment and the labour market

We now turn to the causes of unemployment. These causes fall into two broad categories: *equilibrium* unemployment and *disequilibrium* unemployment. To make clear the distinction between the two, it is necessary to look at how the labour market works.

Figure 15.5 shows the **aggregate demand** for labour and **aggregate supply** of labour: that is, the total demand and supply of labour in the whole economy. The *real* average wage rate is plotted on the vertical axis. This is the average wage rate expressed in terms of its purchasing power: in other words, after taking prices into account.

The aggregate supply of labour curve (AS_L) shows the number of workers *willing to accept jobs* at each wage rate. This curve is relatively inelastic, since the size of the labour force at any one time cannot change significantly. Nevertheless, it is not totally inelastic because (a) a higher wage rate will encourage some people to enter the labour market (e.g. parents raising children), and (b) the unemployed will be more willing to accept job offers rather than continuing to search for a better-paid job.

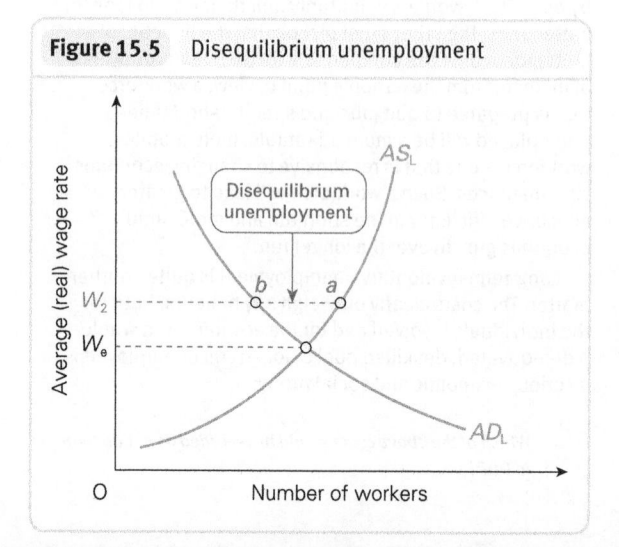

The aggregate demand for labour curve (AD_L) slopes downwards. The higher the wage rate, the more will firms attempt to economise on labour and to substitute other factors of production for labour.

The labour market is in equilibrium at a wage of W_e – where the demand for labour equals the supply.

If the wage rate were above W_e, the labour market would be in a state of disequilibrium. At a wage rate of W_1, there is an excess supply of labour of $a - b$. This is called **disequilibrium unemployment**.

For disequilibrium unemployment to occur, two conditions must hold:

- The aggregate supply of labour must exceed the aggregate demand.
- There must be a 'stickiness' in wages. In other words, the wage rate must not immediately fall to W_e, the market-clearing wage.

Even when the labour market *is* in equilibrium, however, not everyone looking for work will be employed. Some people will hold out, hoping to find a better job. This is illustrated in Figure 15.6.

The curve N shows the total number in the labour force. The horizontal difference between it and the aggregate supply of labour curve (AS_L) represents the excess of people looking for work over those actually willing to accept jobs. Q_e represents the equilibrium level of employment and the distance $d - e$ represents the **equilibrium level of unemployment**. This is sometimes known as the **natural level of unemployment**.

Note that the AS_L curve gets closer to the N curve at higher wages. The reason for this is that the unemployed will be more willing to accept jobs, the higher the wages they are offered.

Figure 15.5 Disequilibrium unemployment

Definitions

Aggregate demand for labour curve A curve showing the total demand for labour in the economy at different average real wage rates.

Aggregate supply of labour curve A curve showing the total number of people willing and able to work at different average real wage rates.

Disequilibrium unemployment Unemployment resulting from real wage rates in the economy being above the equilibrium level.

Equilibrium ('natural') unemployment The difference between those who would like employment at the current wage rate and those willing and able to take a job.

Real-wage unemployment

Real-wage unemployment occurs when trade unions use their monopoly power to drive wages above the market-clearing level. It could also be caused by the government setting the national minimum wage too high. In Figure 15.5, the wage rate is driven up above W_e.

Excessive real wage rates were blamed by the Conservative governments under Thatcher and Major for the high unemployment of the 1980s and 1990s. The possibility of higher real-wage unemployment was also one of the reasons for their rejection of a national minimum wage.

One effect of high real wage rates, however, may help to reduce real-wage unemployment. The extra wages paid to those who are still employed could lead to extra *consumer* expenditure. This addition to aggregate demand would in turn lead to firms demanding more labour, as they attempted to increase output to meet the extra demand. In Figure 15.5, the AD_L curve will shift to the right, thereby reducing the gap $a - b$.

> ? If the higher consumer expenditure and higher wages subsequently led to higher prices, what would happen to (a) real wages; (b) unemployment (assuming no further response from unions)?

Demand-deficient or cyclical unemployment

Demand-deficient or ***cyclical unemployment*** is associated with economic recessions. As the economy moves into recession, consumer demand falls. Firms find that they are unable to sell their current level of output. For a time they may be prepared to build up stocks of unsold goods, but sooner or later they will start to cut back on production and cut back on the amount of labour they employ. The deeper the recession becomes and the longer it lasts, the higher will demand-deficient unemployment become.

As the economy recovers and begins to grow again, so demand-deficient unemployment will start to fall again. Because demand-deficient unemployment fluctuates with the business cycle, it is sometimes referred to as 'cyclical unemployment'. Figure 15.1 (on page 434) showed the fluctuations in unemployment in various industrial countries. If you compare this figure with Figure 14.5 (on page 418), you can see how unemployment tends to rise in recessions and fall in booms.

Demand-deficient unemployment is also referred to as 'Keynesian unemployment', after John Maynard Keynes (see Person Profile in MyEconLab), who saw a deficiency of aggregate demand as the cause of the high unemployment between the two world wars. Today, many economists are

Figure 15.6 Equilibrium unemployment

Figure 15.7 Equilibrium and disequilibrium unemployment

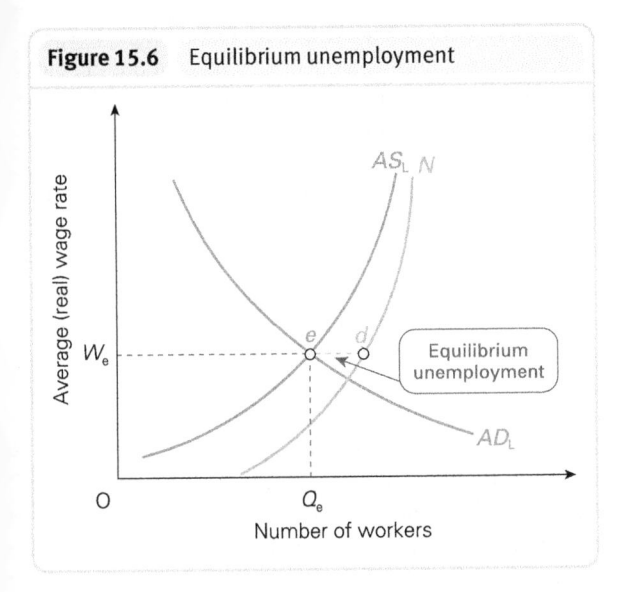

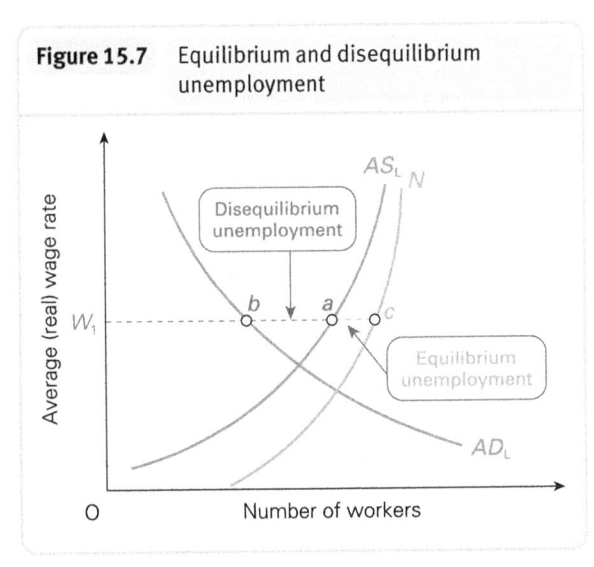

Figure 15.7 shows both equilibrium *and* disequilibrium unemployment. At a wage of W_1, disequilibrium unemployment is $a - b$; equilibrium unemployment is $c - a$; thus total unemployment is $c - b$.

But what are the causes of disequilibrium unemployment? What are the causes of equilibrium unemployment? We will examine each in turn.

Disequilibrium unemployment

There are three possible causes of disequilibrium unemployment.

Definitions

Real-wage unemployment Disequilibrium unemployment caused by real wages being driven up above the market-clearing level.

Demand-deficient or cyclical unemployment Disequilibrium unemployment caused by a fall in aggregate demand with no corresponding fall in the real wage rate.

Figure 15.8 Demand-deficient unemployment

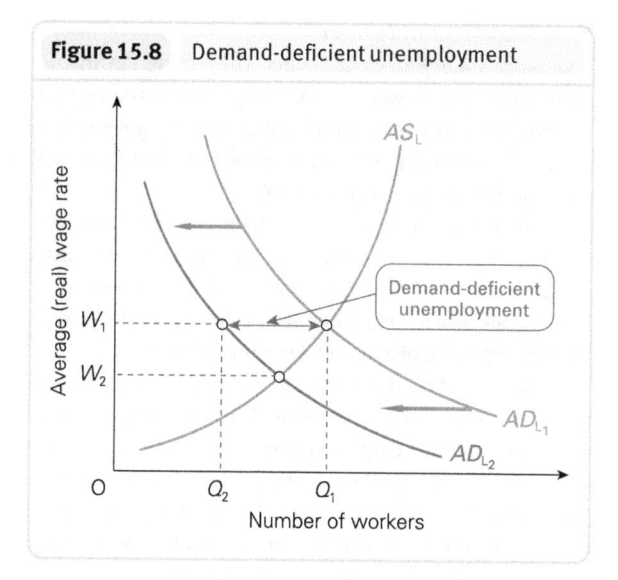

[Graph showing AS_L curve and AD_L1 shifting left to AD_L2, with wage rates W_1 and W_2, and quantities Q_2 and Q_1. Demand-deficient unemployment marked between Q_2 and Q_1 at W_1.]

known as 'Keynesian'. Although there are many strands of Keynesian thinking, these economists all see aggregate demand as important in determining a nation's output and employment.

Demand-deficient unemployment is illustrated in Figure 15.8. Assume initially that the economy is at the peak of the business cycle. The aggregate demand for and supply of labour are equal at the current wage rate of W_1. There is no disequilibrium unemployment. Now assume that the economy moves into recession. Consumer demand falls and as a result firms demand less labour. The demand for labour shifts to AD_{L_2}. If there is a resistance to wage cuts, such that the real wage rate remains fixed at W_1, there will now be disequilibrium unemployment of $Q_1 - Q_2$.

Some Keynesians specifically focus on the reluctance of real wage rates to fall from W_1 to W_2. This downward 'stickiness' in real wage rates may be the result of unions seeking to protect the living standards of their members (even though there are non-members out of work), or of firms worried about the demotivating effects of cutting the real wages of their workers. Sometimes it is simply that wage rates have been agreed through a process of collective bargaining for the following year or more, where the agreement includes an inflation-proofing element to ensure that they are *real* wage rates. For such economists, the problem of demand-deficient unemployment would be solved if there could somehow be a fall in real wage rates.

For other Keynesian economists, however, the problem is much more fundamental than a downward stickiness in real wages. For them the problem is that the low level of aggregate demand causes an *equilibrium* in the *goods* market at an output that is too low to generate full employment. Firms' supply is low (below the full-employment level of supply) because aggregate demand is low.

This low-level equilibrium in the goods market, and the corresponding disequilibrium in the labour market, may *persist*. This is the result of a lack of confidence on the part of firms. After all, why should firms produce more and take on more workers if they believe that the recession will persist and that they will therefore not sell any more? The economy remains trapped in a low-output equilibrium.

In such cases, a fall in real wages would not cure the unemployment. In fact, it might even make the problem worse. In Figure 15.8, even if the average wage rate were to fall to W_2, demand-deficient unemployment would still persist. The reason is that this general cut in wages throughout the economy would reduce workers' incomes and hence reduce their *consumption of goods*. As the aggregate demand for goods fell, there would be a further reduction in demand for labour: the aggregate demand for labour curve would shift to the left again – to the left of AD_{L_2}. By the time the wage had fallen to W_2, W_2 would no longer be the equilibrium wage. There would still be demand-deficient unemployment.

> ? *If this analysis is correct, that is, if a reduction in wages will reduce the aggregate demand for goods, what assumption must we make about the relative proportions of wages and profits that are spent (given that a reduction in real wage rates will lead to a corresponding increase in rates of profit)?*

Growth in the labour supply

If labour supply rises with no corresponding increase in the demand for labour, the equilibrium real wage rate will fall. If the real wage rate is 'sticky' downwards, disequilibrium unemployment will occur.

> ? *On a diagram similar to Figure 15.8, illustrate how a growth in labour supply can cause disequilibrium unemployment.*

This tends not to be such a serious cause of unemployment as demand deficiency, since the supply of labour changes relatively slowly. Nevertheless there is a problem of providing jobs for school leavers each year with the sudden influx of new workers onto the labour market.

> ? *From 2004, with the accession of eastern European countries to the EU, there were significant flows of migrants from eastern to western Europe. Does such immigration create disequilibrium unemployment?*

Equilibrium unemployment (or natural unemployment)

Although there may be overall *macro*economic equilibrium, with the *aggregate* demand for labour equal to the *aggregate* supply, and thus no disequilibrium unemployment, at a *micro*economic level supply and demand may not match. There may be excess demand for labour (vacancies) in some markets and excess supply (unemployment) in others. There may be vacancies for computer technicians and unemployment in the steel industry, but unemployed steel workers cannot immediately become computer technicians. This is when equilibrium unemployment will occur.

There are various types of equilibrium unemployment.

Frictional (search) unemployment

Frictional (search) unemployment occurs when people leave their jobs, either voluntarily or because they are sacked or made redundant, and are unemployed for a period of time while they are looking for a new job. They may not get the first job they apply for, despite a vacancy existing and despite their being suitably qualified.

The problem is that information is imperfect. Employers are not fully informed about what labour is available; workers are not fully informed about what jobs are available and what they entail. Both employers and workers, therefore, have to search: employers searching for the right labour and workers searching for the right jobs.

The longer people search for a job, the better the wage offers they are likely to be made. This is illustrated in Figure 15.9 by the curve W_o. It shows the highest wage offer that the typical worker will have received since being unemployed.

When they first start looking for a job, people may have high expectations of getting a good wage. The longer they are unemployed, however, the more anxious they are likely to be to get a job, and therefore the lower will be the wage they are prepared to accept. The curve W_a shows the wage that is acceptable to the typical worker.

Figure 15.9 Average duration of unemployment

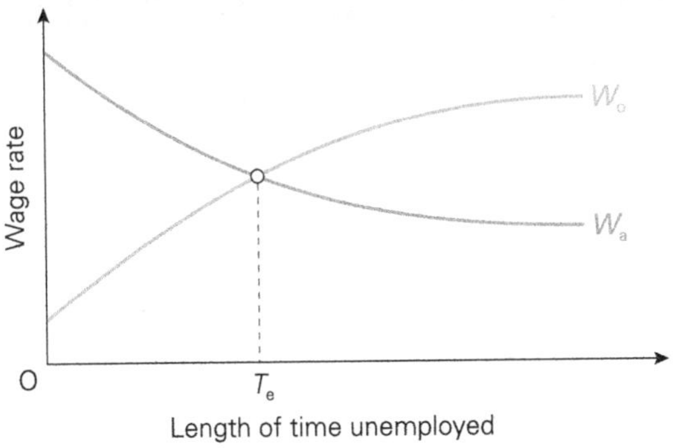

Why are W_o and W_a drawn as curves rather than straight lines?

The average duration of unemployment will be T_e. That is, workers will remain unemployed until they find a job at an acceptable wage.

One obvious remedy for frictional unemployment is to provide better job information through government job centres, private employment agencies, or local and national newspapers. This would have the effect of making the curve W_o reach its peak earlier, and thus of shifting the intersection of W_o and W_a to the left.

Another much more controversial remedy is for the government to reduce the level of unemployment benefit. This will make the unemployed more desperate to get a job and thus prepared to accept a lower wage. It will therefore have the effect of shifting the W_a curve downwards and again of shifting the intersection of W_o and W_a to the left.

Structural unemployment

Structural unemployment occurs where the structure of the economy changes. Employment in some industries may expand while in others it contracts. There are two main reasons for this.

A change in the pattern of demand. Some industries experience declining demand. This may be due to a change in consumer tastes as certain goods go out of fashion; or it may be due to competition from other industries. For example, consumer demand may shift away from coal and to other fuels. This will lead to structural unemployment in mining areas.

A change in the methods of production (technological unemployment). New techniques of production often allow the same level of output to be produced with fewer workers (see Case Study 15.2 in MyEconLab). This is known as 'labour-saving technical progress'. Unless output expands sufficiently to absorb the surplus labour, people will be made redundant. This creates ***technological unemployment***. An example is the loss of jobs in the banking industry caused by the increase in the number of cash machines and by the development of telephone and Internet banking.

Definitions

Frictional (search) unemployment Unemployment that occurs as a result of imperfect information in the labour market. It often takes time for workers to find jobs (even though there are vacancies) and in the meantime they are unemployed.

Structural unemployment Unemployment that arises from changes in the pattern of demand or supply in the economy. People made redundant in one part of the economy cannot immediately take up jobs in other parts (even though there are vacancies).

Technological unemployment Structural unemployment that occurs as a result of the introduction of labour-saving technology.

Structural unemployment often occurs in particular regions of the country. When it does, it is referred to as *regional unemployment*. Regional unemployment is due to the concentration of particular industries in particular areas. For example, the collapse in the South Wales coal-mining industry led to high unemployment in the Welsh valleys.

The level of structural unemployment will depend on three factors:

- The degree of regional concentration of industry. The more that industries are concentrated in particular regions, the greater will be the level of structural unemployment if particular industries decline.
- The speed of change of demand and supply in the economy. The more rapid the rate of technological change or the shift in consumer tastes, the more rapid will be the rate of redundancies.
- The immobility of labour. The less able or willing workers are to move to a new job, the higher will be the level of structural unemployment. Remember from Chapter 9 the distinction we made between geographical and occupational immobility. Geographical immobility is a particular problem with regional unemployment. Occupational immobility is a particular problem with technological unemployment where old skills are no longer required.

There are two broad approaches to tackling structural unemployment: *market-orientated* and *interventionist*.

A market-orientated approach involves encouraging people to look more actively for jobs, if necessary in other parts of the country. It involves encouraging people to adopt a more willing attitude towards retraining, and if necessary to accept some reduction in wages.

An interventionist approach involves direct government action to match jobs to the unemployed. Two examples are providing grants to firms to set up in areas of high unemployment (regional policy), and government-funded training schemes.

Policies to tackle structural unemployment are examined in detail in sections 23.2 and 23.3.

Seasonal unemployment

Seasonal unemployment occurs when the demand for certain types of labour fluctuates with the seasons of the year. This problem is particularly severe in holiday areas, such as Cornwall, where unemployment can reach very high levels in the winter months. Policies for tackling seasonal unemployment are similar to those for structural unemployment.

Definitions

Regional unemployment Structural unemployment occurring in specific regions of the country.

Seasonal unemployment Unemployment associated with industries or regions where the demand for labour is lower at certain times of the year.

Section summary

1. Who should be counted as 'unemployed' is a matter for some disagreement. The two most common measures of unemployment are claimant unemployment (those claiming unemployment-related benefits) and ILO/OECD standardised unemployment (those available for work and actively seeking work or waiting to take up an appointment).

2. The 'stock' of unemployment will grow if the inflow of people into unemployment exceeds the outflow (to jobs or out of the labour market altogether). The more rapid these flows, the shorter the average duration of unemployment.

3. In most countries, unemployment is unevenly distributed across geographical regions, between women and men, between age groups and between different ethnic groups.

4. The costs of unemployment include the financial and other personal costs to the unemployed person, the costs to relatives and friends, and the costs to society at large in terms of lost tax revenues, lost profits and lost wages to other workers, and in terms of social disruption.

5. Unemployment can be divided into disequilibrium and equilibrium unemployment.

6. Disequilibrium unemployment occurs when real wage rates are above the level that will equate the aggregate demand and supply of labour. It can be caused by unions or government pushing up wages (real-wage unemployment), by a fall in aggregate demand but a downward 'stickiness' in real wages (demand-deficient unemployment), or by an increase in the supply of labour with again a downward stickiness in wages.

7. In the case of demand-deficient unemployment, the disequilibrium in the labour market may correspond to a low-output equilibrium in the goods market. A fall in real wage rates may be insufficient to remove the deficiency of demand in the labour market.

8. Equilibrium unemployment occurs when there are people unable or unwilling to fill job vacancies. This may be due to poor information in the labour market and hence a time lag before people find suitable jobs (frictional unemployment), to a changing pattern of demand or supply in the economy and hence a mismatching of labour with jobs (structural unemployment – specific types being technological and regional unemployment), or to seasonal fluctuations in the demand for labour.

26.4 INFLATION

The rate of inflation measures the annual percentage increase in prices. The most usual measure is that of *consumer* prices. The government publishes a 'consumer prices index' (CPI) each month, and the rate of inflation is the percentage increase in that index over the previous 12 months. Figure 26.6 shows the rates of inflation for the USA, Japan, the UK and the EU. As you can see, inflation was particularly severe between 1973 and 1983, and relatively low in the mid-1980s and in recent years. Indeed, Japan experienced a protracted period of deflation – falling prices – during the 2000s. Several other countries also experienced deflation in the recession of 2009.

It is also possible to give the rates of inflation for other prices. For example, indices are published for commodity prices, food prices, house prices, import prices, prices after taking taxes into account and so on. Their respective rates of inflation are simply their annual percentage increase. Likewise it is possible to give the rate of inflation of wage rates ('wage inflation').

When there is inflation, we have to be careful in assessing how much national output, consumption, wages, etc. are increasing. Take the case of GDP. GDP in year 2 may seem higher than in year 1, but this may be partly (or even wholly) the result of higher prices. Thus GDP in money terms may have risen by 5 per cent, but if inflation is 3 per cent, real growth in GDP will be only 2 per cent. In other words, the volume of output will be only 2 per cent higher.

Definitions

Real growth values Values of the rate of growth of GDP or any other variable after taking inflation into account. The real value of the growth in a variable equals its growth in money (or 'nominal') value minus the rate of inflation.

Menu costs of inflation The costs associated with having to adjust price lists or labels.

> **KEY IDEA 40**
> **The distinction between nominal and real figures.** Nominal figures are those using current prices, interest rates, etc. Real figures are figures corrected for inflation.

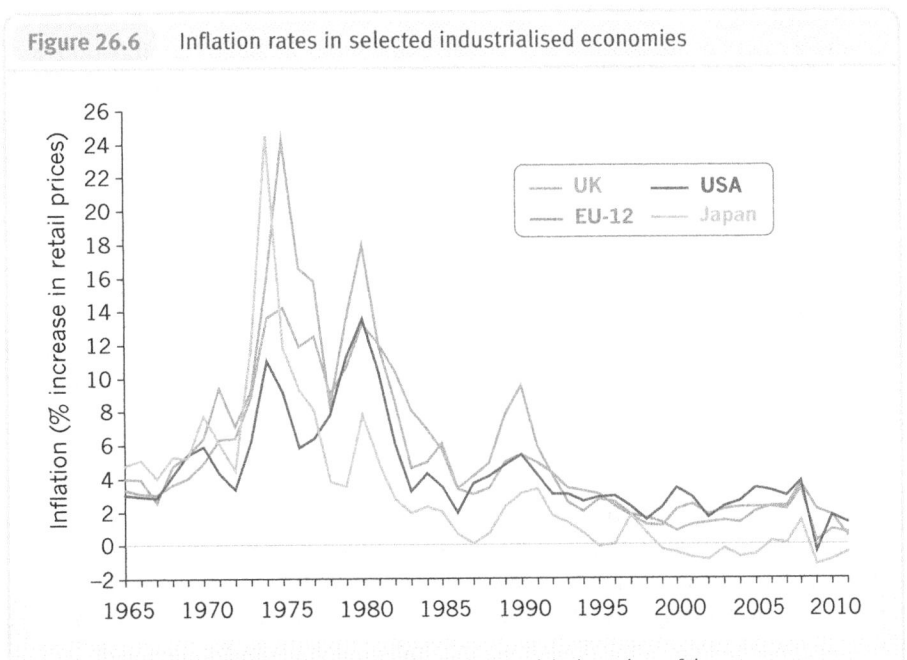

Figure 26.6 Inflation rates in selected industrialised economies

Notes: 2010 and 2011 based on forecasts; EU-12 = the 12 original members of the eurozone.
Source: based on data in *Economic Outlook* (OECD, various years)

Before we proceed, a word of caution: be careful not to confuse a rise or fall in *inflation* with a rise or fall in *prices*. A rise in inflation means a *faster* increase in prices. A fall in inflation means a *slower* increase in prices (but still an increase as long as inflation is positive).

The costs of inflation

A lack of growth is obviously a problem if people want higher living standards. Unemployment is obviously a problem, both for the unemployed themselves and also for society, which suffers a loss in output and has to support the unemployed. But why is inflation a problem? If firms are faced with rising costs, does it really matter if they can simply pass them on in higher prices? Similarly for workers, if their wages keep up with prices, there will not be a cut in their living standards.

If people could correctly anticipate the rate of inflation and fully adjust prices and incomes to take account of it, then the costs of inflation would indeed be relatively small. For us as consumers, they would simply be the relatively minor inconvenience of having to adjust our notions of what a 'fair' price is for each item when we go shopping. For firms, they would again be the relatively minor costs of having to change price labels, or prices in catalogues or on menus, or to adjust slot machines. These are known as menu costs.

In reality, people frequently make mistakes when predicting the rate of inflation and are not able to adapt fully to it. This leads to the following problems, which are likely to be more serious the higher the rate of inflation becomes and the more the rate fluctuates.

Redistribution. Inflation redistributes income away from those on fixed incomes and those in a weak bargaining position, to those who can use their economic power to gain large pay, rent or profit increases. It redistributes wealth to those with assets (e.g. property) that rise in value particularly rapidly during periods of inflation, and away from those with savings that pay rates of interest below the rate of inflation and hence whose value is eroded by inflation. Pensioners may be particularly badly hit by rapid inflation.

Uncertainty and lack of investment. Inflation tends to cause uncertainty in the business community, especially when the rate of inflation fluctuates. (Generally, the higher the rate of inflation, the more it fluctuates.) If it is difficult for firms to predict their costs and revenues, they may be discouraged from investing. This will reduce the rate of economic growth. On the other hand, as will be explained below, policies to reduce the rate of inflation may themselves reduce the rate of economic growth, especially in the short run. This may then provide the government with a policy dilemma.

Balance of payments. Inflation is likely to worsen the balance of payments. If a country suffers from relatively high inflation, its exports will become less competitive in world markets. At the same time, imports will become relatively cheaper than home-produced goods. Thus exports will fall and imports will rise. As a result the balance of payments will deteriorate and/or the exchange rate will fall, or interest rates will have to rise. Each of these effects can cause problems. This is examined in more detail in the next chapter.

Resources. Extra resources are likely to be used to cope with the effects of inflation. Accountants and other financial experts may have to be employed by companies to help them cope with the uncertainties caused by inflation.

The costs of inflation may be relatively mild if inflation is kept to single figures. They can be very serious, however, if inflation gets out of hand. If inflation develops into 'hyperinflation', with prices rising perhaps by several hundred or even thousand per cent per year, the whole basis of the market economy will be undermined. Firms constantly raise prices in an attempt to cover their rocketing costs. Workers demand huge pay increases in an attempt to stay ahead of the rocketing cost of living. Thus prices and wages chase each other in an ever-rising inflationary spiral. People will no longer want to save money. Instead they will spend it as quickly as possible before its value falls any further. People may even resort to barter in an attempt to avoid using money altogether.

> **Pause for thought**
>
> *Do you personally gain or lose from inflation? Why?*

Aggregate demand and supply and the level of prices

The level of prices in the economy is determined by the interaction of aggregate demand and aggregate supply. The analysis is similar to that of demand and supply in individual markets, but there are some crucial differences. Figure 26.7 shows aggregate demand and supply curves. Let us examine each in turn.

Aggregate demand curve

Remember what we said about aggregate demand earlier in the chapter. It is the total level of spending on the country's products: that is, by consumers, by the government, by firms on investment, and by people residing abroad. The aggregate demand curve shows how much national output (GDP) will be demanded at each level of prices. But why does the *AD* curve slope downwards: why do people demand fewer products as prices rise? There are three main reasons:

- If prices rise, people will be encouraged to buy fewer of the country's products and more imports instead (which are now relatively cheaper); also the country will sell fewer exports. Thus aggregate demand will be lower.

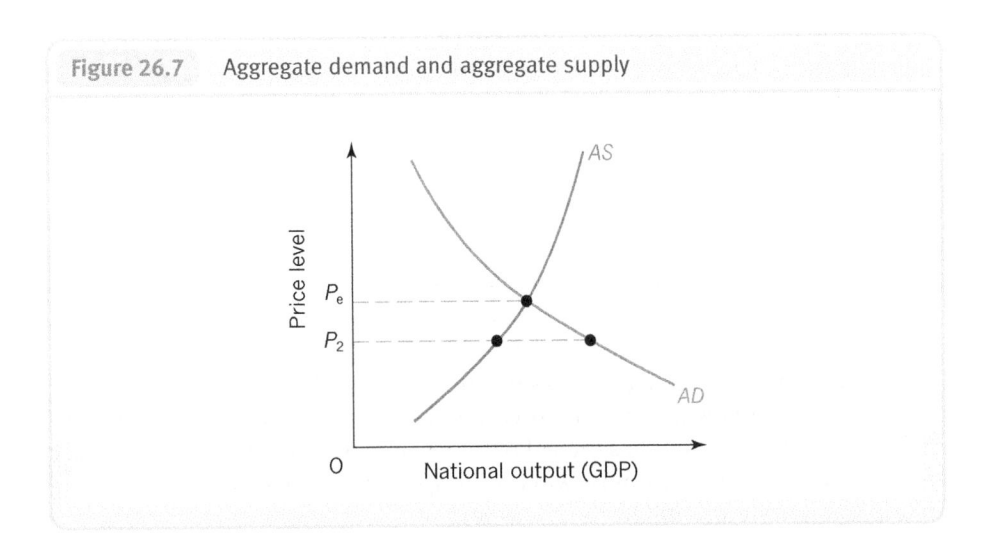

Figure 26.7 Aggregate demand and aggregate supply

- As prices rise, people will need more money to pay for their purchases. With a given supply of money in the economy, this will have the effect of driving up interest rates (we will explore this in Chapter 28). The effect of higher interest rates will be to discourage borrowing and encourage saving. Both will have the effect of reducing spending and hence reducing aggregate demand.
- If prices rise, the value of people's savings will be eroded. They may thus save more (and spend less) to compensate.

Aggregate supply curve

The aggregate supply curve slopes upwards – at least in the short run. In other words, the higher the level of prices, the more will be produced. The reason is simple: provided that factor prices (and, in particular, wage rates) do not rise as rapidly as product prices, firms' profitability at each level of output will be higher than before. This will encourage them to produce more.

Equilibrium

The equilibrium price level will be where aggregate demand equals aggregate supply. To demonstrate this, consider what would happen if aggregate demand exceeded aggregate supply: for example, at P_2 in Figure 26.7. The resulting shortages throughout the economy would drive up prices. This would cause a movement up along both the AD and AS curves until $AD = AS$ (at P_e).

Shifts in the AD or AS curves

If there is a change in the price level there will be a movement *along* the AD and AS curves. If any other determinant of AD or AS changes, the respective curve will shift. The analysis here is very similar to shifts and movements along demand and supply curves in individual markets (see pages 65 and 69).

The aggregate demand curve will shift if there is a change in any of its components: consumption, investment, government expenditure or exports minus imports. Thus if the government decides to spend more, or if consumers spend more as a result of lower taxes, or if business confidence increases so that firms decide to invest more, the AD curve will shift to the right.

Similarly, the aggregate supply curve will shift to the right if there is a rise in labour productivity or in the stock of capital: in other words, if there is a rise in potential output.

> **Pause for thought**
>
> Give some examples of events that could shift (a) the AD curve to the left; (b) the AS curve to the left.

Causes of inflation

Demand-pull inflation

Demand-pull inflation is caused by continuing rises in aggregate demand. In Figure 26.7, the AD curve shifts to the right, and continues doing so. Firms will respond to the rise in aggregate demand partly by raising prices and partly by increasing output (there is a move up along the AS curve). Just how much they raise prices depends on how much their costs rise as a result of increasing output. This in turn depends upon how close actual output is to potential output. The less slack there is in the economy, the more will firms respond to a rise in demand by raising their prices (the steeper will be the AS curve).

> **Definitions**
>
> **Demand-pull inflation**
> Inflation caused by persistent rises in aggregate demand.
>
> **Cost-push inflation**
> Inflation caused by persistent rises in costs of production (independently of demand).

Demand-pull inflation is typically associated with a booming economy. Many economists therefore argue that it is the counterpart of demand-deficient unemployment. When the economy is in recession, demand-deficient unemployment will be high, but demand-pull inflation will be low. When, on the other hand, the economy is near the peak of the business cycle, demand-pull inflation will be high, but demand-deficient unemployment will be low.

Cost-push inflation

Cost-push inflation is associated with continuing rises in costs and hence continuing leftward (upward) shifts in the *AS* curve. Such shifts occur when costs of production rise *independently* of aggregate demand. If firms face a rise in costs, they will respond partly by raising prices and passing the costs on to the consumer, and partly by cutting back on production (there is a movement back along the *AD* curve).

Just how much firms raise prices and cut back on production depends on the shape of the aggregate demand curve. The less elastic the *AD* curve, the less sales will fall as a result of any price rise, and hence the more will firms be able to pass on the rise in their costs to consumers as higher prices.

Note that the effect on output and employment is the opposite of demand-pull inflation. With demand-pull inflation, output and hence employment tend to rise. With cost-push inflation, however, output and employment tend to fall.

It is important to distinguish between *single* shifts in the aggregate supply curve (known as 'supply shocks') and *continuing* shifts. If there is a single leftward shift in aggregate supply, there will be a single rise in the price level. For example, if the government raises the excise duty on oil, there will be a single rise in oil prices and hence in industry's fuel costs. This will cause *temporary* inflation while the price rise is passed on through the economy. Once this has occurred, prices will stabilise at the new level and the rate of inflation will fall back to zero again. If cost-push inflation is to continue over a number of years, therefore, the aggregate supply curve must *continually* shift to the left. If cost-push inflation is to *rise*, these shifts must get more rapid.

Rises in costs may originate from a number of different sources, such as trade unions pushing up wages, firms with monopoly power raising prices in order to increase their profits, or increases in international commodity prices. With the process of globalisation and increased international competition, cost-push pressures have tended to decrease in recent years. The one major exception is the oil shocks that have occurred from time to time. For example, the near tripling of oil prices from $51 per barrel in January 2007 to $147 per barrel in July 2008 put upward pressure on costs and prices around the world.

Demand-pull and cost-push inflation can occur together, since wage and price rises can be caused both by increases in aggregate demand and by independent causes pushing up costs. Even when an inflationary process *starts* as either demand-pull or cost-push, it is often difficult to separate the two. An initial cost-push inflation may encourage the government to expand aggregate demand to offset rises in unemployment. Alternatively, an initial demand-pull inflation may strengthen the power of certain groups, who then use this power to drive up costs. Either way, the result is likely to be continuing rightward shifts in the *AD* curve and leftward shifts in the *AS* curve. Prices will carry on rising.

Expectations and inflation

Workers and firms take account of the *expected* rate of inflation when making decisions.

Imagine that a union and an employer are negotiating a wage increase. Let us assume that both sides expect a rate of inflation of 5 per cent. The union will be happy to receive a wage rise somewhat above 5 per cent. That way the members would be getting a *real* rise in incomes. The employers will be happy to pay a wage rise somewhat below 5 per cent. After all, they can put their price up by 5 per cent, knowing that their rivals will do approximately the same. The actual wage rise that the two sides agree on will thus be somewhere around 5 per cent.

Now let us assume that the expected rate of inflation is 10 per cent. Both sides will now negotiate around this benchmark, with the outcome being somewhere round about 10 per cent.

Thus the higher the expected rate of inflation, the higher will be the level of pay settlements and price rises, and hence the higher will be the resulting actual rate of inflation.

In recent years the importance of expectations in explaining the actual rate of inflation has been increasingly recognised by economists. We examine this in Chapter 29.

BOX 26.3 COPING WITH A LOW-INFLATION ENVIRONMENT

When no inflation seems like a bad thing too!

Figure 26.6 shows how Japan has experienced a protracted period of deflation: a period where the average price level fell. But, we also see that other countries too have become accustomed to historically low inflation rates. In section 26.4 we considered some of the costs of inflation. But, can businesses also be adversely affected by either deflation or very low positive rates of inflation? In this box we consider some of the potential economic effects of what we refer to as a 'low-inflation environment'.

A squeeze on profits. Falling prices (or very slowly rising prices) are a problem for business if costs, such as labour costs, rise more quickly. This adversely impacts on profits. To some extent firms may be able to offset price pressures by looking for productivity improvements or re-evaluating all aspects of their organisation, including relationships with suppliers and purchasers. But, there may be limits to productivity increases and to any cost savings by being leaner or 'doing things better'. Ultimately, profits suffer and this may result in job losses. If this is typical across the economy, job losses and falling household incomes result in further falls in sales.

A deflationary spiral. As consumers we tend to think of falling prices as a good thing. But falling prices can generate a downward spiral. When prices fall – or perhaps even increase very slowly – people may be tempted to defer purchases, believing that prices will be lower in the future. In other words, people respond to an expectation of lower prices by postponing consumption. The expectation of lower prices in the future weakens demand today. This, of course, puts further downward pressure on prices! We end up with a 'deflationary spiral' and a contraction of the economy.

Debts. Low rates of inflation mean that the real value of debt erodes more slowly. One way of thinking about this is to consider the proportion of incomes which firms and households need to devote to debt repayments when rates of inflation are low or even negative. If income streams also grow slowly or, worse still begin to decline, then the proportion of incomes spent servicing debts is likely to increase. Economists refer to such a phenomenon as an increase in income gearing. It becomes harder for firms and households alike to meet their debt commitments. There is, however, one mitigating factor. In a period of deflation, central banks, such as the Bank of England in the UK, are likely to reduce interest rates.

It is perhaps worth noting that central banks that target inflation rates – like the Bank of England and the European Central Bank – do not target zero inflation. The Bank of England, for instance, is charged by the government to meet a central target inflation rate of 2 per cent, but with leeway of 1 percentage point either side of this. So policy-makers also behave as if both too low and too high a rate of inflation is a bad thing!

1 Describe the impact of deflation on the practice of business.
2 Is there an ideal inflation rate for businesses?

26.5 THE BUSINESS CYCLE AND MACROECONOMIC OBJECTIVES

In the short term (up to about two years), the four objectives of faster growth in output, lower unemployment, lower inflation and achieving a favourable balance of payments are all related. They all depend on aggregate demand and vary with the course of the business cycle. This is illustrated in Figure 26.8.

In the expansionary phase of the business cycle (phase 2), aggregate demand grows rapidly. There will be relatively rapid growth in output, with a positive output gap emerging, and (demand-deficient) unemployment will fall. Thus two of the problems are getting better. On the other hand, the other two problems will be getting worse. The growing shortages lead to higher (demand-pull) inflation and a deteriorating balance of payments as the extra demand 'sucks in' more imports and as higher prices make domestic goods less competitive internationally.

At the peak of the cycle (phase 3), unemployment is probably at its lowest and output at its highest (for the time being). But growth has already ceased or at least slowed down. Inflation and balance of payments problems are probably acute.

As the economy moves into phase 4 (let us assume that this is an actual recession with falling output), the reverse will happen to that of phase 2. Falling aggregate demand will make growth negative and demand-deficient unemployment higher, but inflation is likely to slow down and the balance of payments will improve. These two improvements may take some time to occur, however.

Governments are thus faced with a dilemma. If they reflate the economy, they will make two of the objectives better (growth and unemployment), but the other two worse (inflation and balance of payments). If they deflate the economy, it is the other way round: inflation and the balance of payments will improve, but unemployment will rise and growth, or even output, will fall.

> **KEY IDEA 41**
>
> **Societies face trade-offs between economic objectives.** For example, the goal of faster growth may conflict with that of greater equality; the goal of lower unemployment may conflict with that of lower inflation (at least in the short run). This is an example of opportunity cost: the cost of achieving more of one objective may be achieving less of another. The existence of trade-offs means that policy-makers must make choices.

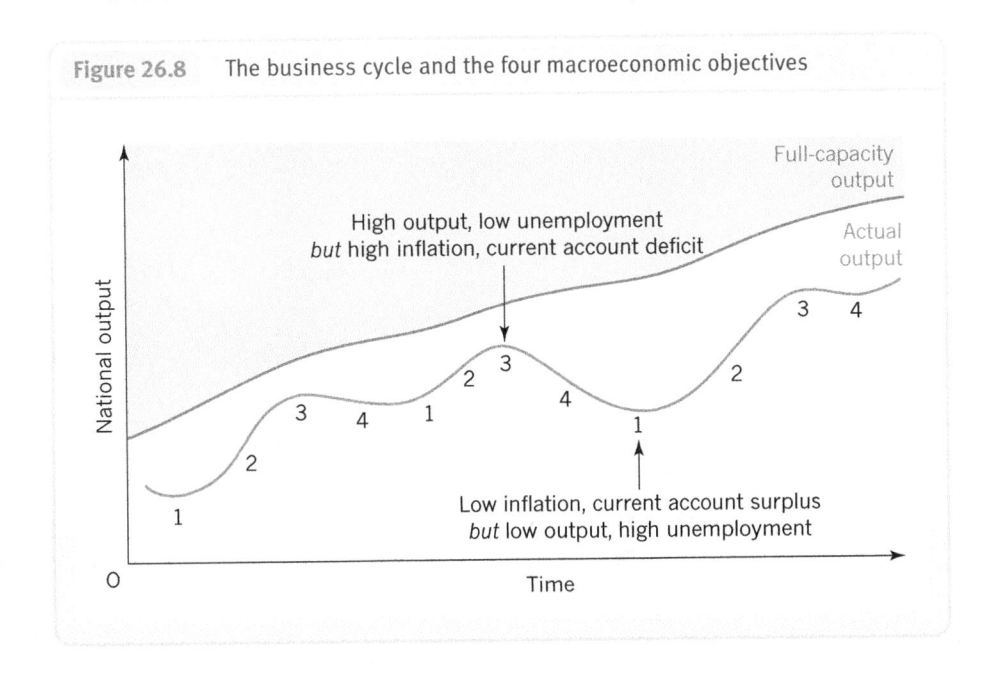

Figure 26.8 The business cycle and the four macroeconomic objectives

THE CIRCULAR FLOW OF INCOME

26.6

Another way of understanding the relationship between the four objectives is to use a simple model of the economy. This is the circular flow of income, which is shown in Figure 26.9. In the diagram, the economy is divided into two major groups: *firms* and *households*. Each group has two roles. Firms are producers of goods and services; they are also the employers of labour and other factors of production. Households (which is the word we use for individuals) are the consumers of goods and services; they are also the suppliers of labour and various other factors of production. In the diagram there is an inner flow and various outer flows of income between these two groups.

Before we look at the various parts of the diagram, a word of warning. Do not confuse *money* and *income*. Money is a stock concept. At any given time, there is a certain quantity of money in the economy (e.g. £1 billion). But that does not tell us the level of national *income*. Income is a flow concept (as is expenditure). It is measured as so much *per period of time*. The relationship between money and income depends on how rapidly the money *circulates*: its 'velocity of circulation'. (We will examine this concept in detail later on.) If there is £1 billion of money in the economy and each £1 on average is paid out as income five times per year, then annual national income will be £5 billion.

The inner flow, withdrawals and injections

The inner flow

Firms pay money to households in the form of wages and salaries, dividends on shares, interest and rent. These payments are in return for the services of the factors of production – labour, capital and land – that are supplied by households. Thus on the left-hand side of the diagram money flows directly from firms to households as 'factor payments'.

Households, in turn, pay money to domestic firms when they consume domestically produced goods and services (C_d). This is shown on the right-hand side of the

> **Definitions**
>
> **The consumption of domestically produced goods and services (C_d)** The direct flow of money payments from households to firms.
>
> **Withdrawals (*W*) (or leakages)** Incomes of households or firms that are not passed on round the inner flow. Withdrawals equal net saving (S) plus net taxes (T) plus import expenditure (M): $W = S + T + M$.

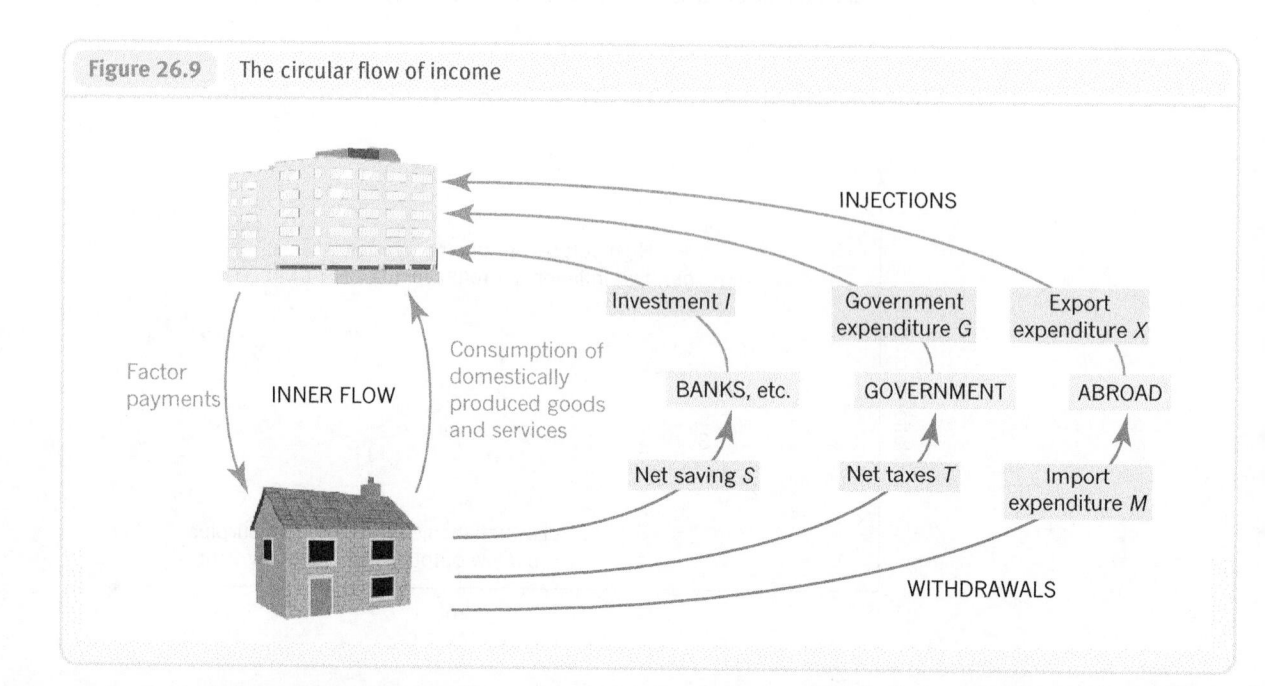

Figure 26.9 The circular flow of income

inner flow. There is thus a circular flow of payments from firms to households to firms and so on.

If households spend *all* their incomes on buying domestic goods and services, and if firms pay out *all* this income they receive as factor payments to domestic households, and if the velocity of circulation does not change, the flow will continue at the same level indefinitely. The money just goes round and round at the same speed and incomes remain unchanged.

In the real world, of course, it is not as simple as this. Not all income gets passed on round the inner flow; some is *withdrawn*. At the same time, incomes are injected into the flow from outside. Let us examine these withdrawals and injections.

> **Pause for thought**
>
> *Would this argument still hold if prices rose?*

Withdrawals

Only part of the incomes received by households will be spent on the goods and services of domestic firms. The remainder will be withdrawn from the inner flow. Likewise, only part of the incomes generated by firms will be paid to domestic households. The remainder of this will also be withdrawn. There are three forms of withdrawals (W) (or 'leakages' as they are sometimes called).

Net saving (S). Saving is income that households choose not to spend but to put aside for the future. Savings are normally deposited in financial institutions such as banks and building societies. This is shown in the bottom right of the diagram. Money flows from households to 'banks, etc'. What we are seeking to measure here, however, is the net flow from households to the banking sector. We therefore have to subtract from saving any borrowing or drawing on past savings by households in order to get the *net* saving flow. Of course, if household borrowing exceeded saving, the net flow would be in the other direction: it would be negative.

Net taxes (T). When people pay taxes (to either central or local government), this represents a withdrawal of money from the inner flow in much the same way as saving: only in this case people have no choice. Some taxes, such as income tax and employees' national insurance contributions, are paid out of household incomes. Others, such as VAT and excise duties, are paid out of consumer expenditure. Others, such as corporation tax, are paid out of firms' incomes before being received by households as dividends on shares. (For simplicity, however, we show taxes being withdrawn at just one point. It does not affect the argument.)

When, however, people receive *benefits* from the government, such as working tax credit, child benefit and pensions, the money flows the other way. Benefits are thus equivalent to a 'negative tax'. These benefits are known as transfer payments. They transfer money from one group of people (taxpayers) to others (the recipients).

In the model, 'net taxes' (T) represent the *net* flow to the government from households and firms. It consists of total taxes minus benefits.

Import expenditure (M). Not all consumption is of totally home-produced goods. Households spend some of their incomes on imported goods and services, or on goods and services using imported components. Although the money that consumers spend on such goods initially flows to domestic retailers, it will eventually find its way abroad, either when the retailers or wholesalers themselves import them, or when domestic manufacturers purchase imported inputs to make their products. This expenditure on imports constitutes the third withdrawal from the inner flow. This money flows abroad.

> **Definitions**
>
> **Transfer payments**
> Moneys transferred from one person or group to another (e.g. from the government to individuals) without production taking place.
>
> **Injections (J)**
> Expenditure on the production of domestic firms coming from outside the inner flow of the circular flow of income. Injections equal investment (I) plus government expenditure (G) plus expenditure on exports (X).

Total withdrawals are simply the sum of net saving, net taxes and the expenditure on imports:

$$W = S + T + M$$

Injections

Only part of the demand for firms' output arises from consumers' expenditure. The remainder comes from other sources outside the inner flow. These additional components of aggregate demand are known as injections (J). There are three types of injection.

Investment (I). This consists of investment in plant and equipment. It also includes the building up of stocks of inputs, semi-finished or finished goods. When firms invest, they obtain the money from various financial institutions, either from past savings or from loans, or through a new issues of shares.

Government expenditure (G). When the government spends money on goods and services produced by firms, this counts as an injection. Examples of such government expenditure are spending on roads, hospitals and schools. (Note that government expenditure in this model does not include state benefits. These transfer payments, as we saw above, are the equivalent of negative taxes and have the effect of reducing the T component of withdrawals.)

Export expenditure (X). Money flows into the circular flow from abroad when residents abroad buy our exports of goods and services.

Total injections are thus the sum of investment, government expenditure and exports:

$$J = I + G + X$$

Aggregate demand, which is the total spending on output, is thus $C_d + J$.

The relationship between withdrawals and injections

There are indirect links between saving and investment via financial institutions, between taxation and government expenditure via the government (central and local), and between imports and exports via foreign countries. These links, however, do not guarantee that $S = I$ or $G = T$ or $M = X$.

Take investment and saving. The point here is that the decisions to save and invest are made by different people, and thus they plan to save and invest different amounts. Likewise the demand for imports may not equal the demand for exports. As far as the government is concerned, it may choose not to make $T = G$. It may choose not to spend all its tax revenues: to run a 'budget surplus' ($T > G$); or it may choose to spend more than it receives in taxes: to run a 'budget deficit' ($G > T$), by borrowing or printing money to make up the difference.

Thus planned injections (J) may not equal planned withdrawals (W).

The circular flow of income and the four macroeconomic objectives

If planned injections are not equal to planned withdrawals, what will be the consequences? If injections exceed withdrawals, the level of expenditure will rise. The extra aggregate demand will generate extra incomes. In other words, *actual* national income will rise. If this rise in actual income exceeds any rise there may have been in potential income, there will be the following effects upon the four macroeconomic objectives:

- There will be economic growth. The greater the initial excess of injections over withdrawals, the bigger will be the rise in national income.
- Unemployment will fall as firms take on more workers in order to meet the extra demand for output.
- Inflation will tend to rise. The more the gap is closed between actual and potential income, the more difficult will firms find it to meet extra demand, and the more likely they will be to raise prices.
- The exports and imports part of the balance of payments will tend to deteriorate. The higher demand sucks more imports into the country, and higher domestic inflation makes exports less competitive and imports relatively cheaper compared with home-produced goods. Thus imports will tend to rise and exports will tend to fall.

Changes in injections and withdrawals thus have a crucial effect on the whole macroeconomic environment in which businesses operate. We will examine some of these effects in more detail in the following chapters.

> **Pause for thought**
>
> *What will be the effect on each of the four objectives if planned injections are less than planned withdrawals?*

Chapter 29

Business activity, employment and inflation

Business issues covered in this chapter

- If there is an increase in investment, how will this affect the economy?
- Why does an increase in aggregate demand of £x lead to a rise in GDP of more than £x?
- To what extent does a rise in the money supply lead to a rise in the economy's output (real GDP) rather than merely a rise in prices?
- What is the relationship between unemployment and inflation? Is the relationship a stable one?
- How do business and consumer expectations affect the relationship between inflation and unemployment? How are such expectations formed?
- How does a policy of targeting the rate of inflation affect the relationship between inflation and unemployment?
- What determines the course of a business cycle and its turning points? Is the business cycle caused by changes in aggregate demand, changes in aggregate supply or both?

In this chapter we examine what determines the level of business activity and why it fluctuates. We also look at the effects of business activity on employment and inflation.

We start, in section 29.1, by looking at the determinants of GDP and, in particular, the role of aggregate demand. After all, the higher the level of aggregate demand, the more will business produce in response to that demand.

In the first section we ignore the role of money and interest rates. In section 29.2, however, we show that changes in money and interest rates can have important, but possibly uncertain, effects on aggregate demand and business activity.

In sections 29.3 and 29.4, we turn to the problems of unemployment and inflation and the relationship between the two. An important influence on both of them is what people *expect* to happen. Generally, if people are optimistic and believe that the economy will grow and unemployment will fall, this will happen. Similarly, if people expect inflation to stay low, it will do. In other words, people's expectations tend to be self-fulfilling. Getting people to expect low rates of inflation is something that can lead central banks to adopt inflation rate targets (the subject of section 29.4).

Finally, in section 29.5, we examine why GDP and business activity fluctuate. In other words, we examine possible causes of the business cycle.

29.1 THE DETERMINATION OF BUSINESS ACTIVITY

How much will business as a whole produce? How many people will be employed? The analysis of output and employment, at least in the short run (one or two years), can be explained most simply in terms of the circular flow of income diagram that we examined on page 584. Figure 29.1 shows a simplified version of the circular flow with injections entering at just one point, and likewise withdrawals leaving at just one point (this simplification does not affect the argument).

If injections (J) do not equal withdrawals (W), a state of disequilibrium exists. What will bring them back into equilibrium is a change in national income (GDP) and employment.

Start with a state of equilibrium, where injections equal withdrawals. If there is now a rise in injections – say, firms decide to invest more – aggregate demand (i.e. the consumption of domestic products (C_d) plus injections (J)) will be higher. Firms will respond to this increased demand by using more labour and other resources and thus paying out more incomes (Y) to households. Household consumption will rise and so firms will sell more.

Firms will respond by producing more, and thus using more labour and other resources. Household incomes will rise again. Consumption and hence production will rise again, and so on. There will thus be a multiplied rise in incomes and employment. This is known as the **multiplier effect**.

> **Definition**
>
> **Multiplier effect**
> An initial increase in aggregate demand of £xm leads to an eventual rise in national income that is greater than £xm.

> **KEY IDEA 42**
> *The principle of cumulative causation.* An initial event can cause an ultimate effect which is much larger.

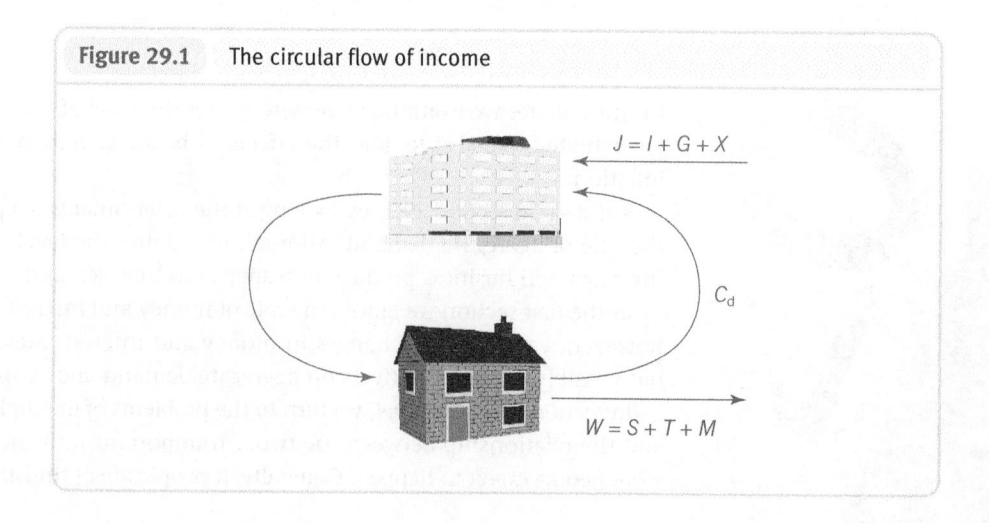

Figure 29.1 The circular flow of income

$$J = I + G + X$$
$$C_d$$
$$W = S + T + M$$

The process, however, does not go on for ever. Each time household incomes rise, households save more, pay more taxes and buy more imports. In other words, withdrawals rise. When withdrawals have risen to match the increase in injections, equilibrium will be restored and national income (GDP) and employment will stop rising. The process can be summarised as follows:

$$J > W \rightarrow Y\uparrow \rightarrow W\uparrow \text{ until } J = W$$

Similarly, an initial fall in injections (or rise in withdrawals) will lead to a multiplied fall in GDP and employment:

$$J < W \rightarrow Y\downarrow \rightarrow W\downarrow, \text{ until } J = W$$

Thus equilibrium in the circular flow of income can be at *any* level of GDP and employment.

Identifying the equilibrium level of GDP

Equilibrium can be shown on a 'Keynesian 45° line diagram'. This is named after the great economist, John Maynard Keynes (1883–1946). Keynes argued that GDP is determined by aggregate demand. A rise in aggregate demand will cause GDP to rise; a fall in aggregate demand will cause GDP to fall.

Equilibrium GDP can be at any level of capacity. If aggregate demand is buoyant, equilibrium GDP can be where businesses are operating at full capacity with full employment. If aggregate demand is low, however, equilibrium GDP can be at well below full capacity with high unemployment (i.e. a recession). Keynes argued that it is important, therefore, for governments to manage the level of aggregate demand to avoid recessions.

The 45° line diagram plots various elements of the circular flow of income, such as consumption, withdrawals, injections and aggregate demand, against GDP (national income).

In Figure 29.2 two continuous lines are shown. The 45° line out from the origin plots $C_d + W$ against GDP. It is a 45° line because, by definition, GDP = $C_d + W$. To understand this, consider what can happen to the income earned from GDP: either it must be spent on domestically produced goods (C_d) or it must be withdrawn from the circular flow – there is nothing else that can happen to it. Thus if GDP were £100 billion, then $C_d + W$ must also be £100 billion. If you draw a line such that whatever value is plotted on the horizontal axis (GDP) is also plotted on the vertical axis ($C_d + W$), the line will be at 45° (assuming that the axes are drawn to the same scale).

The other continuous line plots aggregate demand. In this diagram it is known as the *aggregate expenditure line* (*E*). It consists of $C_d + J$: in other words, the total spending on domestic firms.

To show how this line is constructed, consider the dashed line. This shows C_d. It is flatter than the 45° line. The reason is that for any given rise in GDP and hence people's incomes, only *part* will be spent on domestic products, while the remainder will be withdrawn: i.e. C_d rises less quickly than GDP. The *E* line consists of $C_d + J$. But we have assumed that J is constant with respect to changes in GDP. Thus the *E* line is simply the C_d line shifted upward by the amount of J.

If aggregate expenditure exceeded GDP, at say GDP_1, there would be excess demand in the economy (of $a - b$). In other words, people would be buying more than was currently being produced. Firms would thus find their stocks dwindling and would therefore increase their level of production. In doing so, they would

Figure 29.2 Equilibrium GDP

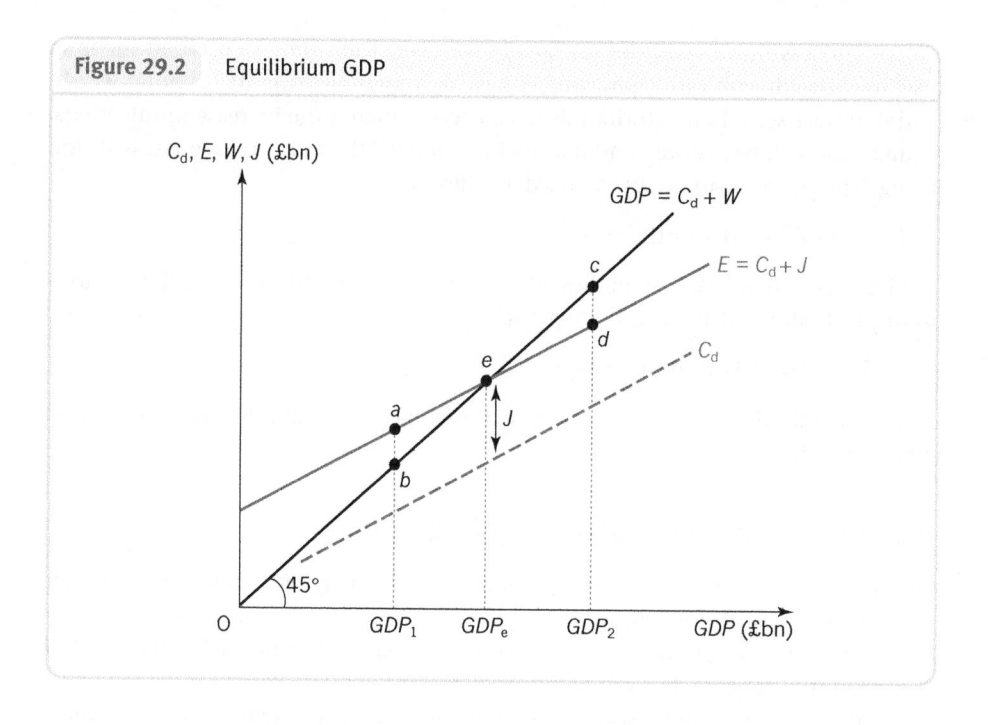

employ more factors of production. GDP would thus rise. As it did so, C_d and hence E would rise. There would be a movement up along the E line. But because not all the extra incomes earned from the rise in GDP would be consumed (i.e. some would be withdrawn), expenditure would rise less quickly than income: the E line is flatter than the GDP line. As income rises towards GDP_e, the gap between the GDP and E lines gets smaller. Once point e is reached, $GDP = E$. There is then no further tendency for GDP to rise.

If GDP exceeded aggregate expenditure, at say GDP_2, there would be insufficient demand for the goods and services currently being produced ($c - d$). Firms would find their stocks of unsold goods building up. They would thus respond by producing less and employing less factors of production. GDP would thus fall and go on falling until GDP_e was reached.

The multiplier

When aggregate expenditure rises, this will cause GDP to rise. But by how much? The answer is that there will be a *multiplied* rise in GDP: i.e. it will rise by more than the rise in aggregate expenditure. The size of the **multiplier** is given by the letter k, where:

$$k = \Delta GDP / \Delta E$$

Thus, if aggregate expenditure rose by £10 million (ΔE) and as a result GDP rose by £30 million (ΔGDP), the multiplier would be 3. Figure 29.3 is drawn on the assumption that the multiplier is 3.

Assume in Figure 29.3 that aggregate expenditure rises by £20 billion, from E_1 to E_2. This could be caused by a rise in injections, or by a fall in withdrawals (and hence a rise in consumption of domestically produced goods) or by some combination of the two. Equilibrium GDP rises by £60 billion, from £100 billion to £160 billion (where the E_2 line crosses the GDP line).

Definition

The multiplier
The number of times a rise in GDP (ΔGDP) is bigger than the initial rise in aggregate expenditure (ΔE) that caused it. Using the letter k to stand for the multiplier, the multiplier is defined as $k = \Delta GDP/\Delta E$.

Figure 29.3 The multiplier: a rise in aggregate expenditure

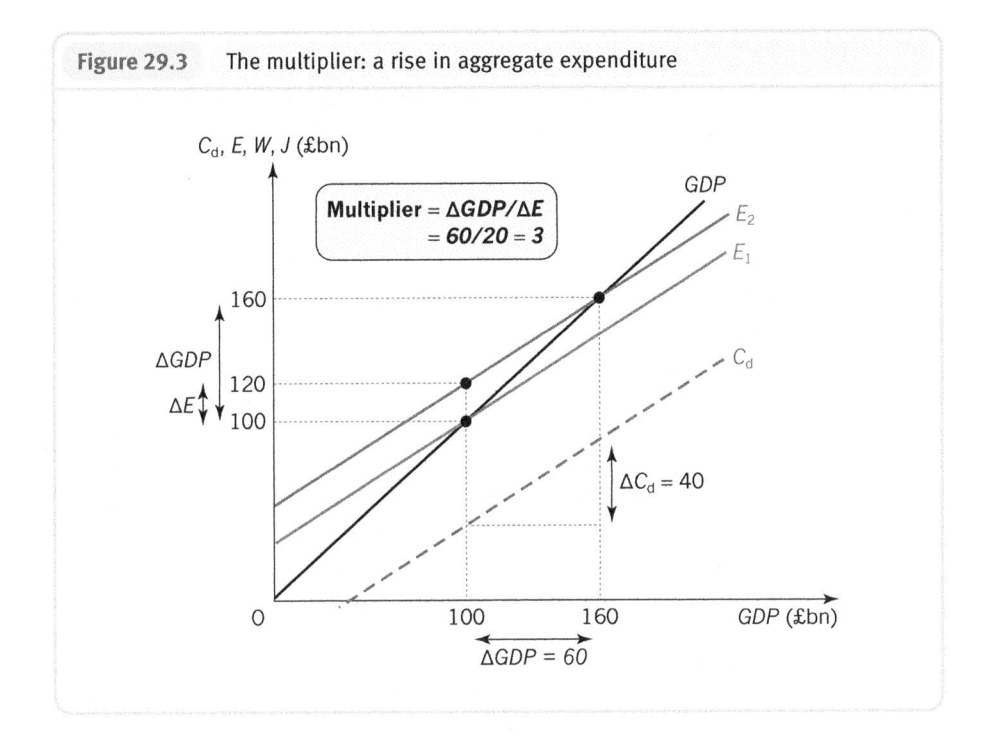

What determines the size of the multiplier? The answer is that it depends on the 'marginal propensity to consume domestically produced goods' (mpc_d). The mpc_d is the proportion of any rise in GDP that gets spent on domestically produced goods (in other words the proportion that is not withdrawn).

$$mpc_d = \Delta C_d / \Delta GDP$$

In Figure 29.3, $mpc_d = \Delta C_d / \Delta GDP = £40\text{bn}/£60\text{bn} = 2/3$ (i.e. the slope of the C_d line). The higher the mpc_d the greater the proportion of income generated from GDP that recirculates around the circular flow of income and thus generates extra output.

The **multiplier formula** is given by:

$$k = \frac{1}{1 - mpc_d}$$

In our example, with $mpc_d = 2/3$

$$k = \frac{1}{1 - 2/3} = \frac{1}{1/3} = 3$$

If the mpc_d were $3/4$, the multiplier would be 4. Thus the higher the mpc_d, the higher the multiplier.

Definition

Multiplier formula
The formula for the multiplier is $k = 1/(1 - mpc_d)$.

Pause for thought

Think of two reasons why a country might have a steep E line, and hence a high value for the multiplier.

THE RELATIONSHIP BETWEEN MONEY AND GDP 29.2

In this section we examine how changes in the money supply affect GDP. One of the simplest ways of understanding this relationship is in terms of the 'equation of exchange'.

The equation of exchange

The **equation of exchange** shows the relationship between the money value of spending and the money value of output (nominal GDP). This identity may be expressed as follows:

$$MV = PY$$

M is the supply of money in the economy (e.g. M4). V is its **velocity of circulation**. This is the number of times per year that money is spent on buying goods and services that have been produced in the economy that year (real GDP). P is the level of prices of domestically produced goods and services, expressed as an index, where the index is 1 in a chosen base year (e.g. 1990). Thus if prices today are double those in the base year, P is 2. Y is *real* national income (real GDP): in other words, the quantity of national output produced in that year measured in base-year prices.

PY is thus *nominal* GDP: i.e. GDP measured at current prices. For example, if GDP at base-year prices (Y) is £1 trillion and the price index is 2, then GDP at current prices (PY) is £2 trillion.

MV is the total spending on the goods and services that make up GDP – in other words, (nominal) aggregate demand. For example, if money supply is £500 billion, and money, as it passes from one person to another, is spent on average four times a year on national output, then total spending (MV) is £2 trillion a year. But this too *must* equal GDP at current prices. The reason is that what is spent on output (by consumers, by firms on investment, by the government or by people abroad on exports) must equal the value of goods produced (PY).

The equation of exchange (or 'quantity equation') is true by definition. MV is *necessarily* equal to PY because of the way the terms are defined. Thus a rise in MV must be accompanied by a rise in PY. What a change in M does to P, however, is a matter of debate. The controversy centres on the impact of changes in the money supply on aggregate demand and then on the impact of changes in aggregate demand on output.

Money supply and aggregate demand

The short run

Chapter 28 identified two ways in which changes in the money supply could affect aggregate demand: the interest-rate and exchange-rate transmission mechanisms. Taken together, the impact of an increase in the money supply can be summarised as follows:

1. A rise in money supply will lead to a fall in the rate of interest.
2. The fall in the rate of interest will lead to a rise in investment and other forms of borrowing. It will also lead to a fall in the exchange rate and hence a rise in exports and a fall in imports.
3. The rise in investment, and the rise in exports and fall in imports, will mean a rise in aggregate demand.

However, there is considerable debate over how these transmission mechanisms function.

How interest-rate sensitive is money demand? The demand for money as a means of storing wealth (the assets motive) can be large and highly responsive to changes in interest rates on alternative assets. Indeed, large sums of money move around the money market as firms and financial institutions respond to and anticipate changes

---

Definitions

Equation of exchange
$MV = PY$. The total level of spending on GDP (MV) equals the total value of goods and services produced (PY) that go to make up GDP.

Velocity of circulation
The number of times annually that money on average is spent on goods and services that made up GDP.

Pause for thought

If the money supply is cut by 10 per cent, what must happen to the velocity of circulation if there is no change in GDP at current prices?

in interest rates. Thus, with an increase in money supply, only a relatively small fall in interest rates on bonds and other assets may be necessary to persuade people to hold all the extra money in bank accounts, thereby greatly slowing down the average speed at which money circulates. The fall in V may virtually offset the rise in M.

In other words, the more sensitive is the demand for money to changes in the rate of interest, the less impact changes in money supply have on aggregate demand.

How stable is the money demand function? Another criticism is that the demand for money is unstable. People hold speculative balances of money when they anticipate that the prices of other assets, such as shares, bonds and bills, will fall (and hence the rate of return or interest on these assets will rise).

There are many factors that could affect such expectations, such as changes in foreign interest rates, changes in exchange rates, statements of government intentions on economic policy, good or bad industrial news, or newly published figures on inflation or money supply. With an unstable demand for money, it is difficult to predict the effect of a change in money supply on interest rates and so aggregate demand.

It is largely for this reason that most central banks usually prefer to control interest rates directly, rather than indirectly by controlling the money supply. We examine the conduct of monetary policy in section 30.2.

How interest-rate sensitive is spending? The problem here is that investment may be insensitive to changes in interest rates. Businesses are more likely to be influenced in their decision to invest by predictions of the future buoyancy of markets. Interest rates do have *some* effect on businesses' investment decisions, but the effect is unpredictable, depending on the confidence of investors.

Where interest rates are likely to have a stronger effect on spending is via mortgages. If interest rates go up, and mortgage rates follow suit, people will suddenly be faced with higher monthly repayments (debt servicing costs) and will therefore have to cut down their expenditure on goods and services.

How interest-rate sensitive is the exchange rate? Also the amount that the exchange rate will depreciate is uncertain, since exchange rate movements, as we saw in Chapter 27, depend crucially on expectations about trade prospects and about future world interest rate movements. Thus the effects on imports and exports are also uncertain.

To summarise: the effects on total spending of a change in the money supply *might* be quite strong, but they could be weak. In other words, the effects are highly unpredictable. Therefore, the control of the money supply can be an unreliable means of controlling aggregate demand – at least in the short run.

And yet, as we shall see in Chapter 30, at the end of the 2000s central banks around the world, including the Bank of England, embarked on a process of increasing the money supply. As national economies shrank, the hope was that financial institutions would ease the very tight credit conditions that had resulted from the global financial crisis and so help to boost aggregate demand. Its impact was to depend, in part, on the willingness of banks to provide additional credit and the willingness of households and businesses to accept this credit and to increase their spending.

The long run

In the long run, there is a stronger link between money supply and aggregate demand. In fact, 'monetarists' claim that in the long run V is determined *totally independently* of the money supply (M). Thus an increase in M will leave V unaffected and hence will directly increase expenditure (MV). But why do they claim this?

If money supply increases over the longer term, people will have more money than they require to hold. They will spend this surplus. Much of this spending will go on goods and services, thereby directly increasing aggregate demand.

The theoretical underpinning for this is given by the *theory of portfolio balance*. People have a number of ways of holding their wealth. They can hold it as money, or as financial assets such as bills, bonds and shares, or as physical assets such as houses, cars and televisions. In other words, people hold a whole portfolio of assets of varying degrees of liquidity – from cash to central heating.

If money supply expands, people will find themselves holding more money than they require: their portfolios are 'unnecessarily liquid'. Some of this money will be used to purchase financial assets and some, possibly after a period of time, to purchase *goods and services*. As more assets are purchased, this will drive up their price. This will effectively reduce their 'yield'. For bonds and other *financial* assets, this means a reduction in their rate of interest. For goods and services, it means an increase in their price relative to their usefulness.

The process will stop when a balance has been restored in people's portfolios. In the meantime, there will have been extra consumption and hence an increase in aggregate demand.

How will a change in aggregate demand affect output and prices?

So if changes in the money supply were to affect aggregate demand – though our discussion above shows that this cannot be taken as given – how would this then affect the economy's output? What effect would it have on prices?

Many economists argue that aggregate supply (GDP) is relatively responsive in the short run to increases in aggregate demand, provided there is slack in the economy. Similarly, reductions in aggregate demand are likely to lead to reductions in GDP. Many also argue, however, that aggregate supply is inelastic in the long run. They see GDP being determined largely or wholly independently of aggregate demand. In the long run, therefore, any rise in MV will be mainly or totally reflected in a rise in prices (P).

In the long run, according to this view, the stock of money therefore determines the price level, and the rate of increase in money supply determines the rate of inflation. It is thus important to ensure that money supply is kept under control if inflation is to be avoided.

We examine monetary policy in section 30.3.

29.3 UNEMPLOYMENT AND INFLATION

We turn now to examine the relationship between aggregate demand and both inflation and unemployment. You might find it useful first to revise sections 26.3 to 26.5.

Unemployment and inflation in the simple Keynesian model

'Full-employment' GDP

In the simple 'Keynesian' theory that we outlined in section 29.1, it is assumed that there is a maximum level of GDP that can be obtained at any one time. If equilibrium GDP is at this level, there will be no deficiency of aggregate demand and hence no disequilibrium unemployment. This level of GDP is referred to as the **full-employment level of GDP** (GDP_F). (In practice, there would still be some unemployment at this level because of the existence of equilibrium unemployment – structural, frictional and seasonal.)

The deflationary gap

If the equilibrium level of GDP (GDP_e) is below the full-employment level (GDP_F), there will be excess capacity in the economy and hence demand-deficient unemployment. This situation is illustrated in Figure 29.4(a). If GDP is to be raised from GDP_e to GDP_F, aggregate expenditure (E) will have to be raised, either by increasing injections or by reducing withdrawals, so as to close the gap $a - b$. This gap is known as the **recessionary or deflationary gap**.

> **Definitions**
>
> **Full-employment level of GDP**
> The level of GDP at which there is no deficiency of demand.
>
> **Recessionary or deflationary gap**
> The shortfall of aggregate expenditure below GDP at the full-employment level of GDP.

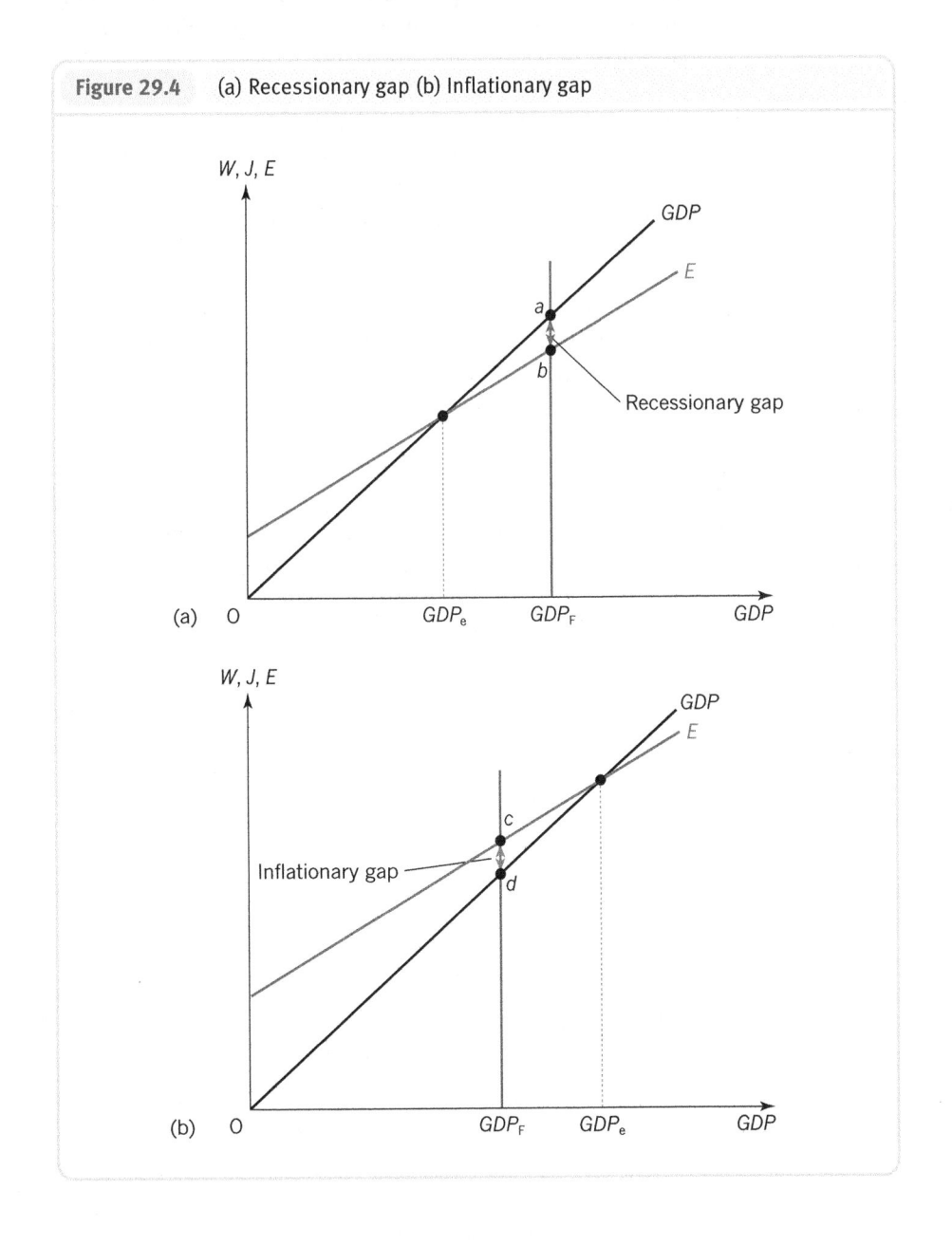

Figure 29.4 (a) Recessionary gap (b) Inflationary gap

Note that the size of the recessionary gap is *less* than the amount by which GDP_e falls short of GDP_F. This is another illustration of the multiplier. If aggregate expenditure is raised by $a - b$, GDP will rise by $GDP_F - GDP_e$. The multiplier is thus given by:

$$\frac{GDP_F - GDP_e}{a - b}$$

> **Definition**
>
> **Inflationary gap**
> The excess of aggregate expenditure over GDP at the full-employment level of GDP.

The inflationary gap

If, at the full-employment level of GDP, aggregate expenditure *exceeds* GDP, there will be a problem of excess demand. GDP_e will be above GDP_F. The problem is that GDP_F represents an effective limit to output, other than in the very short term. GDP can only expand beyond this point by firms operating at above normal capacity levels – by employing people overtime or taking other temporary measures to boost output. The result will be demand-pull inflation.

> **Pause for thought**
>
> Assume that full-employment GDP is £500 billion and that current GDP is £450 billion. Assume also that the mpc_d is $^4/_5$. (a) Is there an inflationary or deflationary gap? (b) What is the size of this gap?

This situation involves an inflationary gap. This is the amount by which aggregate expenditure exceeds national income at the full-employment level of national income. It is illustrated by the gap $c - d$ in Figure 29.4(b). To eliminate this inflation, the inflationary gap must be closed, either by raising withdrawals or by lowering injections.

Many economists thus advocate an active policy of 'demand management': raising aggregate demand (for example, by raising government expenditure or lowering taxes) to close a deflationary gap, and reducing aggregate demand to close an inflationary gap. We explore these 'demand-side' policies in the next chapter).

Unemployment and inflation at the same time

The simple analysis of recessionary and inflationary gaps implies that the aggregate supply curve looks like AS_1 in Figure 29.5. (See pages 579–80 to remind yourself about aggregate demand and supply analysis.) Up to GDP_F, output and employment can rise with no rise in prices at all. The deflationary gap is being closed. At GDP_F no further rises in output are possible. Any further rise in aggregate demand is entirely

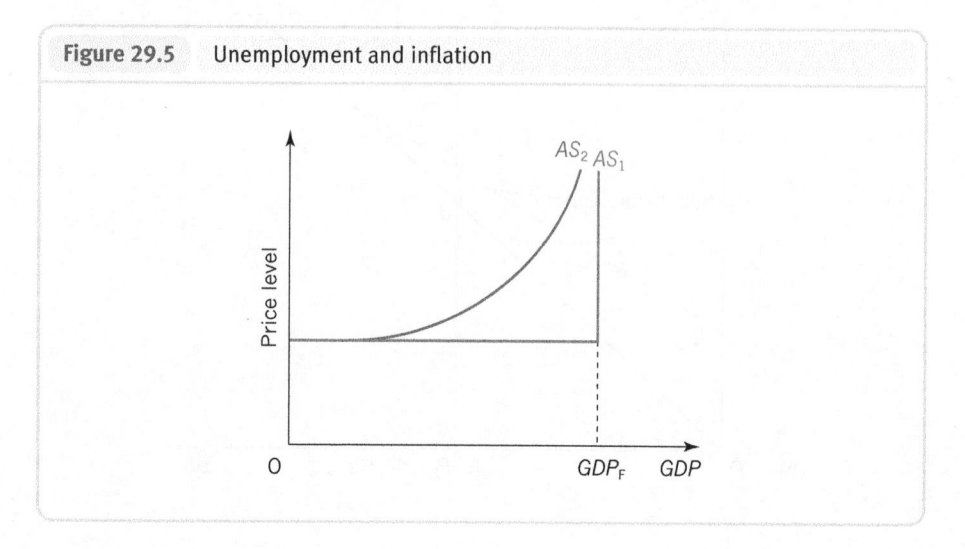

Figure 29.5 Unemployment and inflation

reflected in higher prices. An inflationary gap opens. In other words, this implies that either inflation *or* unemployment can occur, but not both simultaneously.

Two important qualifications need to be made to this analysis to explain the occurrence of both unemployment *and* inflation at the same time.

First, as highlighted in Box 29.1, there are *other* types of inflation and unemployment not caused by an excess or deficiency of aggregate demand: for example, cost-push and expectations-generated inflation; frictional and structural unemployment.

Thus, even if a government could manipulate GDP so as to get GDP_e and GDP_F to coincide, this would not eliminate all inflation and unemployment – only demand-pull inflation and demand-deficient unemployment. For this reason governments may choose to use a whole package of policies, each tailored to the specific type of problem.

Second, not all firms operate with the same degree of slack. A rise in aggregate demand can lead to *both* a reduction in unemployment *and* a rise in prices: some firms responding to the rise in demand by taking up slack and hence increasing output; other firms, having little or no slack, responding by raising prices; others doing both. Similarly, labour markets have different degrees of slack and therefore the rise in demand will lead to various mixes of higher wages and lower unemployment.

Thus the *AS* curve will look like AS_2 in Figure 29.5.

The Phillips curve

The relationship between inflation and unemployment was examined by A. W. Phillips in 1958. He showed the statistical relationship between wage inflation and unemployment in the UK from 1861 to 1957. With wage inflation (W) on the vertical axis and the unemployment rate (U) on the horizontal axis, a scatter of points was obtained. Each point represented the observation for a particular year. The curve that best fitted the scatter has become known as the **Phillips curve**. It is illustrated in Figure 29.6 and shows an inverse relationship between inflation and unemployment.

Given that wage increases over the period were approximately 2 per cent above price increases (made possible by increases in labour productivity), a similar-shaped, but lower curve could be plotted showing the relationship between *price* inflation and unemployment.

> **Definition**
>
> **Phillips curve**
> A curve showing the relationship between (price) inflation and unemployment. The original Phillips curve plotted *wage* inflation against unemployment for the years 1861–1957.

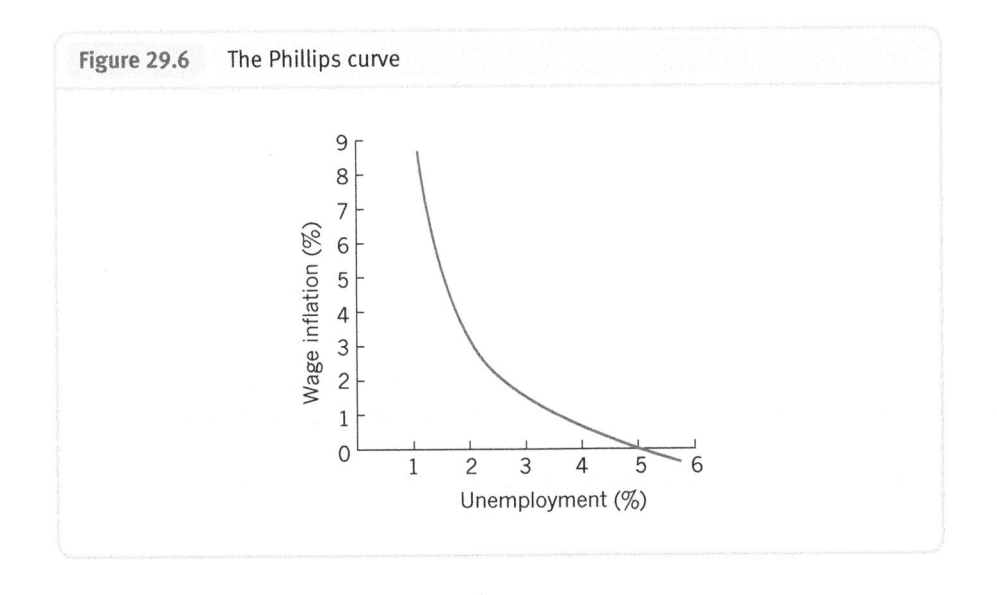

Figure 29.6 The Phillips curve

BOX 29.1 MIND THE GAP

Do output gaps explain inflation?

Chapter 26 introduced the concept of output gaps. An output gap measures the difference between an economy's actual level of output and its potential output (the output level when the economy is operating at 'normal capacity utilisation'). A positive output gap shows that the level of actual output is *greater* than the potential level, while a negative output gap shows that the level of output is *below* the potential level.

The magnitude of the output gap, which is usually expressed as a percentage of potential output, enables us to assess the extent of any demand-deficiency (negative output gap) or the extent of excess demand (positive output gap).

In Chapter 26 we also introduced the aggregate supply curve: the relationship between the economy's general price level and the total output by firms. The slope of the short-run aggregate supply is thought to be affected by the amount of slack in the economy. As the economy approaches or exceeds its potential output, the aggregate supply curve is likely to get steeper as firms' marginal costs rise faster. Consequently, increases in demand at output levels close to or in excess of an economy's potential output will exert more upward pressure on prices than if the economy has a more significant amount of slack. This suggests that the rate of price inflation is positively related to the size of the output gap.

Charts (a) and (b) plot the output gap (as a percentage of potential output) and the annual rate of economy-wide inflation (rate of increase of the GDP deflator) for the UK and France respectively.

It would appear that for the period from 1965 to the end of the 1980s there was a positive correlation between output gaps and inflation rates, albeit that turning points in the rates of inflation lag those in the size of output gaps – in other words, it took time for price pressure to fully work through the economy. This reflects, in part, the fact that some prices, such as wage rates, are adjusted relatively infrequently.

Since the 1990s, however, the relationship between output gaps and inflation rates is less clear. Indeed in both the UK and France there is a general reduction in inflation rates regardless of the size of output gaps. This demonstrates that there are several potential influences on rates of inflation.

One explanation is a reduction in cost-push pressures as labour markets became more competitive and flexible, and as firms faced greater competition from the EU, China and many other countries in an increasingly globalised market.

Another explanation is a growing recognition amongst economists and policy-makers of the importance of inflation rate expectations. It is argued that if policy-makers are perceived as making credible (i.e. trusted) low inflation rate announcements by those that enter into discussions on prices, such as unions and firms when negotiating wage rates, then inflation rates will be lower. A good example of this is the adoption of clear inflation targets by the Bank of England and the ECB.

What factors may have resulted in the lower inflation rates experienced by the UK and France from the 1990s?

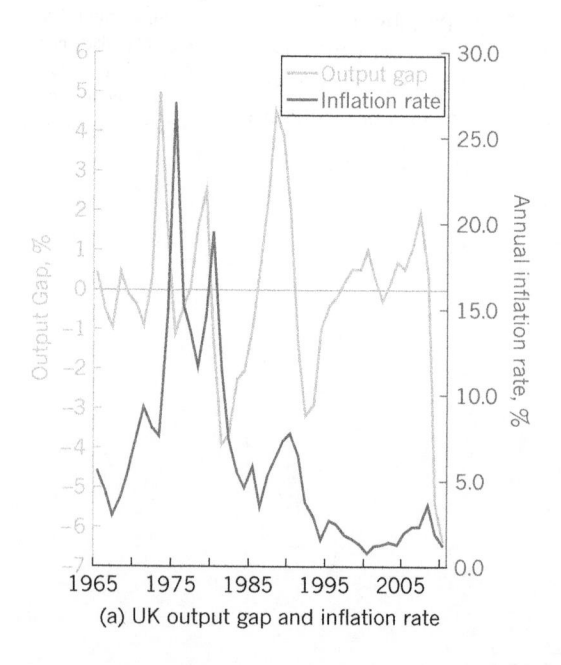

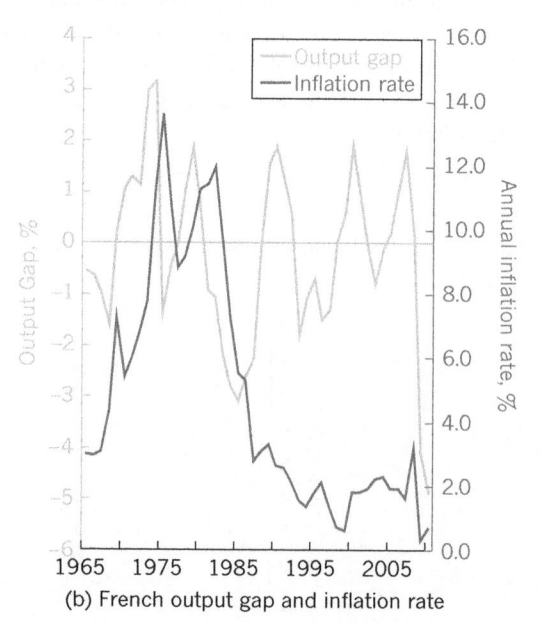

(a) UK output gap and inflation rate

(b) French output gap and inflation rate

Source: based on data in the Annual Macro-economic Database [AMECO] of the European Commission's Directorate General for Economic and Financial Affairs

The curve was often used to illustrate the short-run effects of changes in (real) aggregate demand. When aggregate demand rose (relative to potential output), inflation rose and unemployment fell: there was an upward movement along the curve. When aggregate demand fell, there was a downward movement along the curve.

The Phillips curve was bowed in to the origin. The usual explanation for this is that as aggregate demand expanded, at first there would be plenty of surplus labour, which could be employed to meet the extra demand without the need to raise wage rates very much. But as labour became increasingly scarce, firms would find that they had to offer increasingly higher wage rates to obtain the labour they required, and the position of trade unions would be increasingly strengthened.

The *position* of the Phillips curve depended on *non*-demand factors causing inflation and unemployment: frictional and structural unemployment; and cost-push, and expectations-generated inflation. If any of these non-demand factors changed so as to raise inflation or unemployment, the curve would shift outward to the right.

The Phillips curve seemed to present governments with a simple policy choice. They could trade off inflation against unemployment. Lower unemployment could be bought at the cost of higher inflation, and vice versa. Unfortunately, the experience since the late 1960s has suggested that no such simple relationship exists beyond the short run.

From about 1966 the Phillips curve relationship seemed to break down. The UK, along with many other countries in the Western world, began to experience growing unemployment *and* higher rates of inflation as well.

Figure 29.7 overleaf shows price inflation and unemployment in the UK from 1960 to 2011. From 1960 to 1966 a curve similar to the Phillips curve can be fitted through the data. From 1967 to the early 1990s, however, no simple picture emerges. Certainly the original Phillips curve could no longer fit the data; but whether the curve shifted to the right and then back again somewhat (the broken lines), or whether the relationship broke down completely, or whether there was some quite different relationship between inflation and unemployment, is not clear by simply looking at the data. In fact, in recent years, as inflation has been targeted by central banks, the 'curve' would seem to have become a virtually horizontal straight line!

To explain this apparent breakdown of the Phillips curve, various theories of inflation and unemployment were developed in the 1960s and 1970s that incorporated expectations into the analysis. What was developed was an 'expectations-augmented' version of the Phillips curve.

The effect of expectations

In its simplest form, the **expectations-augmented Phillips curve** is given by the following:

$$\pi = f(1/U) + \pi^e$$

What this states is that inflation (π) depends on two things:

- The inverse of unemployment ($1/U$). This is simply the normal Phillips curve relationship. The higher the rate of (demand-deficient) unemployment, the lower the rate of inflation.
- The expected rate of inflation (π^e). The higher the rate of inflation that people expect, the higher will be the level of wage demands and the more willing will firms be to raise prices. Thus the higher will be the actual rate of inflation and thus the vertically higher will be the whole Phillips curve.

Definition

Expectations-augmented Phillips curve
A (short-run) Phillips curve whose position depends on the expected rate of inflation.

Figure 29.7 The breakdown of the Phillips curve

Possible Phillips curves?

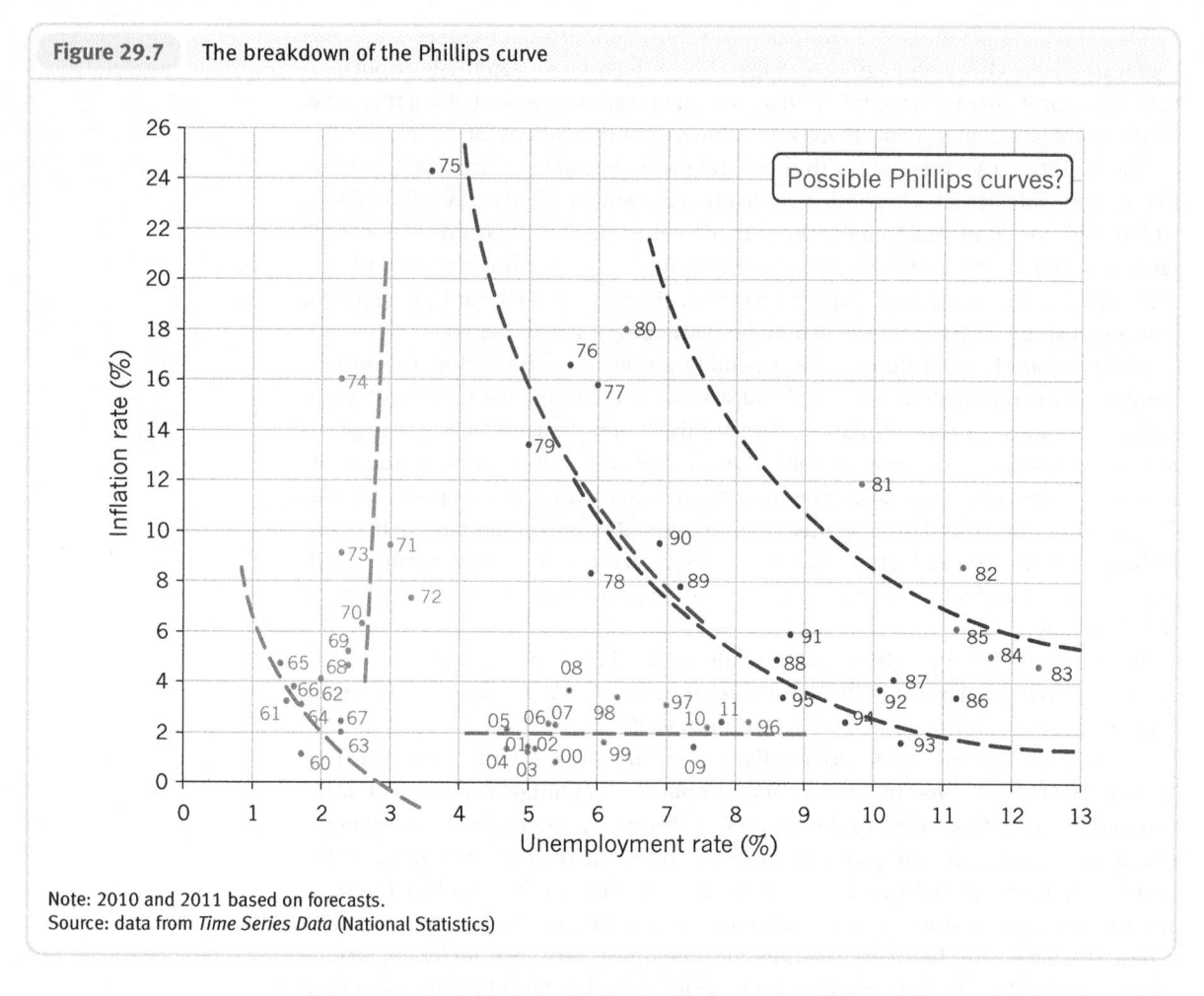

Note: 2010 and 2011 based on forecasts.
Source: data from *Time Series Data* (National Statistics)

Let us assume for simplicity that the rate of inflation people expect this year (π_t^e) (where t represents the current time period: i.e. this year) is the same rate that inflation actually was last year (π_{t-1}).

$$\pi_t^e = \pi_{t-1}$$

Thus if unemployment is such as to push up prices by 4 per cent ($f(1/U) = 4\%$) and if last year's inflation was 6 per cent, then inflation this year will be 4 per cent + 6 per cent = 10 per cent.

The accelerationist theory of inflation

Let us trace the course of inflation and expectations over a number of years in an imaginary economy. To keep the analysis simple, assume there is no growth in the economy.

Year 1. Assume that at the outset, in year 1, there is no inflation at all; that none is expected; that $AD = AS$; and that equilibrium unemployment is 8 per cent. The economy will be at point *a* in Figure 29.8 and Table 29.1.

Year 2. Now assume that the government expands aggregate demand in order to reduce unemployment. Unemployment falls to 6 per cent. The economy moves to point *b* along curve I. Inflation has risen to 4 per cent, but people, basing their

Figure 29.8 The accelerationist theory of inflation and inflationary expectations

[Graph showing Phillips curves with π (%) on vertical axis and U (%) on horizontal axis. Three short-run Phillips curves labelled I ($\pi^e = 0$), II ($\pi^e = 4\%$), and III ($\pi^e = 8\%$), plus a vertical Long-run Phillips curve at $U = 8\%$. Points a (8, 0), b (6, 4), c (8, 4), d (6, 8), e (6, 12) are marked.]

Assume that the government wants to reduce unemployment to 6% and thus expands aggregate demand.

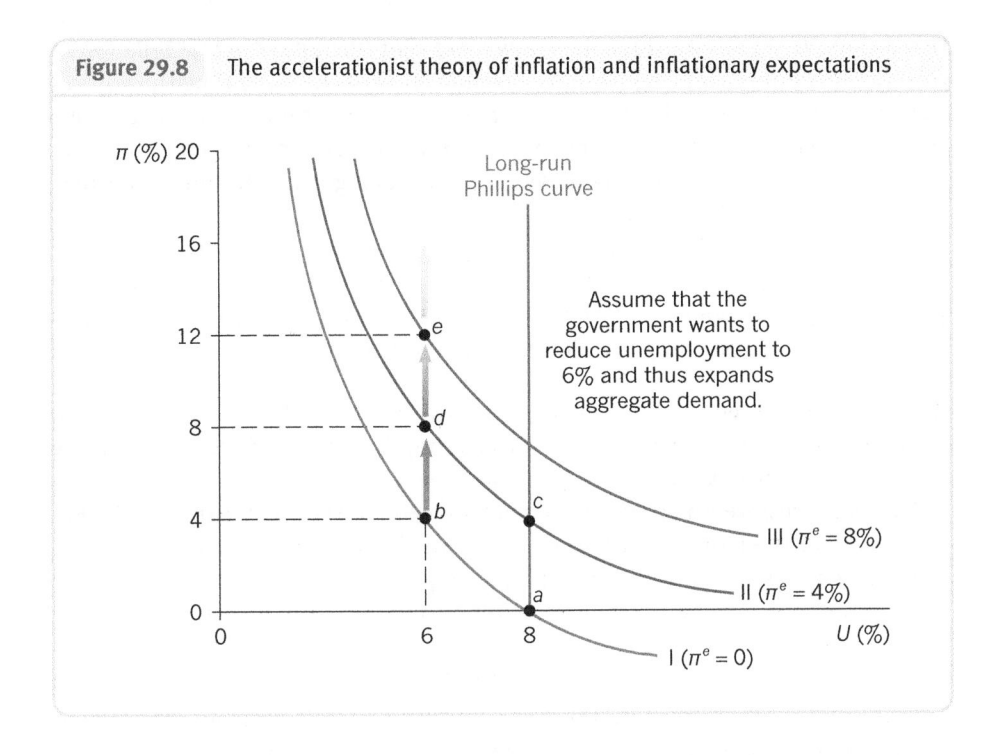

Table 29.1 The accelerationist theory of inflation and inflationary expectations

Year	Point on graph	π	=	$f(1/U)$	+	π^e
1	a	0	=	0	+	0
2	b	4	=	4	+	0
3	c	4	=	0	+	4
4	d	8	=	4	+	4
5	e	12	=	4	+	8

expectations of inflation on year 1, still expect zero inflation. There is therefore no shift as yet in the Phillips curve. Curve I corresponds to an expected rate of inflation of zero.

Year 3. People now revise their expectations of inflation to the level of year 2. The Phillips curve shifts up by 4 percentage points to position II. If nominal aggregate demand (i.e. demand purely in money terms, irrespective of the level of prices) continues to rise at the same rate, the whole of the increase will now be absorbed in higher prices. *Real* aggregate demand will fall back to its previous level and the economy will move to point *c*. Unemployment will return to 8 per cent. There is no *demand-pull* inflation now, ($f(1/U) = 0$), but inflation is still 4 per cent due to expectations, ($\pi^e = 4\%$).

Year 4. Assume now that the government expands *real* aggregate demand again so as to reduce unemployment once more to 6 per cent. This time it must expand nominal aggregate demand *more* than it did in year 2, because this time, as well as reducing unemployment, it also has to validate the 4 per cent expected inflation. The economy moves to point *d* along curve II. Inflation is now 8 per cent.

Year 5 onwards. Expected inflation is now 8 per cent (the rate of actual inflation in year 4). The Phillips curve shifts up to position III. If at the same time the government tries to keep unemployment at 6 per cent, it must expand nominal aggregate demand 4 per cent faster in order to validate the 8 per cent expected inflation. The economy moves to point *e* along curve III. Inflation is now 12 per cent.

To keep unemployment at 6 per cent, the government must continue to increase nominal aggregate demand by 4 per cent more than the previous year. As the expected inflation rate goes on rising, the Phillips curve will go on shifting up each year.

Thus in order to keep unemployment below the initial equilibrium rate, inflation must go on *accelerating* each year. For this reason, this theory of the Phillips curve is sometimes known as the **accelerationist theory**.

The more the government reduces unemployment, the greater the rise in inflation that year, and the more the rise in expectations the following year and each subsequent year; and hence the more rapidly will price rises accelerate. Thus the true longer-term trade-off is between unemployment and the rate of increase in inflation.

The long-run Phillips curve and the natural rate of unemployment

As long as there are demand-pull pressures ($f(1/U) > 0$), inflation will accelerate as the expected rate of inflation (π^e) rises. In the long run, therefore, the Phillips curve will be vertical at the rate of unemployment where *real* aggregate demand equals *real* aggregate supply. This is the *equilibrium* rate of unemployment. It is also known as the **natural rate** or the **non-accelerating-inflation rate of unemployment (NAIRU)**. In Figure 29.8 the equilibrium rate of unemployment is 8 per cent.

The implication for government policy is that expanding aggregate demand can reduce unemployment below the equilibrium rate only in the *short* run. In the long run, the effect will be purely inflationary. On the other hand, a policy of restraining aggregate demand, for example by restraining the growth in the money supply, will *not* in the long run lead to higher unemployment: it will simply lead to lower inflation at the equilibrium rate of unemployment. The implication is that governments should make it a priority to control money supply and thereby nominal aggregate demand and inflation.

Rational expectations

One group, known as 'new classical' economists, go further than the theory described above. They argue that even the short-run Phillips curve is vertical: that there is *no* trade-off between unemployment and inflation, even in the short run. They base their arguments on two key assumptions:

- Prices and wage rates are flexible and thus markets clear very rapidly. This means that there will be no disequilibrium unemployment, even in the short run. All unemployment will be equilibrium unemployment – or 'voluntary unemployment' as new classical economists prefer to call it.
- Expectations are 'rational', but are based on imperfect information.

In the accelerationist theory, expectations are based on *past* information and thus take time to catch up with changes in aggregate demand. Thus for a short time a rise in nominal aggregate demand will raise output and reduce unemployment below the equilibrium rate, while prices and wages are still relatively low.

Pause for thought

What determines how rapidly the short-run Phillips curves in Figure 29.8 shift upwards?

Definitions

Accelerationist theory
The theory that unemployment can only be reduced below the natural rate at the cost of accelerating inflation.

Natural rate of unemployment or **non-accelerating-inflation rate of unemployment (NAIRU)**
The rate of unemployment consistent with a constant rate of inflation: the rate of unemployment at which the vertical long-run Phillips curve cuts the horizontal axis.

The new classical analysis is based on rational expectations. Rational expectations are not based on past rates of inflation. Instead they are based on the current state of the economy and the current policies being pursued by the government. Workers and firms look at the information available to them – at the various forecasts that are published, at various economic indicators and the assessments of them by various commentators, at government pronouncements, and so on. From this information they predict the rate of inflation as well as they can. It is in this sense that the expectations are 'rational': people use their reason to assess the future on the basis of current information.

But forecasters frequently get it wrong, and so do economic commentators! And the government does not always do what it says it will. Thus workers and firms will be basing expectations on *imperfect information*. The crucial point about the rational expectations theory, however, is that these errors in prediction are *random*. People's predictions of inflation are just as likely to be too high as too low.

If the government raises aggregate demand in an attempt to reduce unemployment, people will anticipate that this will lead to higher prices and wages, and that there will be *no* effect on output and employment. If their expectations of higher inflation are correct, this will thus *fully* absorb the increase in nominal aggregate demand such that there will have been no increase in *real* aggregate demand at all. Firms will not produce any more output or employ any more people: after all, why should they? If they anticipate that people will spend 10 per cent more money but that prices will rise by 10 per cent, their *volume* of sales will remain the same.

Output and employment will only rise, therefore, if people make an error in their predictions (i.e. if they underpredict the rate of inflation and interpret an increase in money spent as an increase in *real* demand). But they are as likely to *over*predict the rate of inflation, in which case output and employment will fall! Thus there is no systematic trade-off between inflation and unemployment, even in the short run.

> **Definition**
>
> **Rational expectations**
> Expectations based on the *current* situation. These expectations are based on the information people have to hand. While this information may be imperfect and therefore people will make errors, these errors will be random.

> **Pause for thought**
>
> *For what reasons would a new classical economist support the policy of the Bank of England publishing its inflation forecasts and the minutes of the deliberations of the Monetary Policy Committee?*

Expectations of output and employment

Many economists, especially those who would describe themselves as 'Keynesian', criticise the approach of focusing exclusively on price expectations. Expectations, they argue, influence *output* and *employment* decisions, not just pricing decisions.

If there is a gradual but sustained expansion of aggregate demand, firms, seeing the economy expanding and seeing their orders growing, will start to invest more and make longer-term plans for expanding their labour force. Business and consumers will generally *expect* a higher level of output, and this optimism will cause that higher level of output to be produced. In other words, expectations will affect output and employment as well as prices.

Graphically, the increased output and employment from the recovery in investment will shift the Phillips curve to the left, offsetting (partially, wholly or more than wholly) the upward shift from higher inflationary expectations.

The lesson here for governments is that a sustained, but moderate, increase in aggregate demand can lead to a sustained growth in aggregate supply. What should be avoided is an excessive and unsustainable expansion of aggregate demand. In turn, this raises questions about the role that governments should play in managing aggregate demand in order to achieve economic stability. This has become especially relevant in light of the financial crisis of the late 2000s. Chapter 30 looks at government policy in more detail.

29.4 INFLATION TARGETING AND UNEMPLOYMENT

The Phillips curve appeared to have shifted to the right in the 1970s and 1980s and then back to the left in the 1990s. It also seems to have changed its shape. Far from being vertical in the long run, it appears now to have become horizontal. Figure 29.9 traces out the path of inflation and unemployment from 1967 to 2010.

What explains the shape of this path? Part of the explanation lies in long-term changes in unemployment. Part lies in the policy of inflation targeting, pursued in the UK since 1992.

Changes in equilibrium unemployment

Why was there a substantial rise in unemployment from the early 1970s to the mid-1980s? Why, as a result, was there an apparent rightward shift in the Phillips curve? Why was there then a substantial fall in unemployment from the mid-1990s? To answer this, we need to look at the labour market and the determinants of the equilibrium level of unemployment (i.e. the natural rate of unemployment or NAIRU).

Structural unemployment. The 1970s and 1980s was a period of rapid industrial change. The changes included the following:

- Dramatic changes in technology. The microchip revolution, for example, has led to many traditional jobs becoming obsolete.
- Competition from abroad. The introduction of new products from abroad, often of superior quality to domestic goods, or produced at lower costs, has led to the decline of many older industries: e.g. the textile industry.

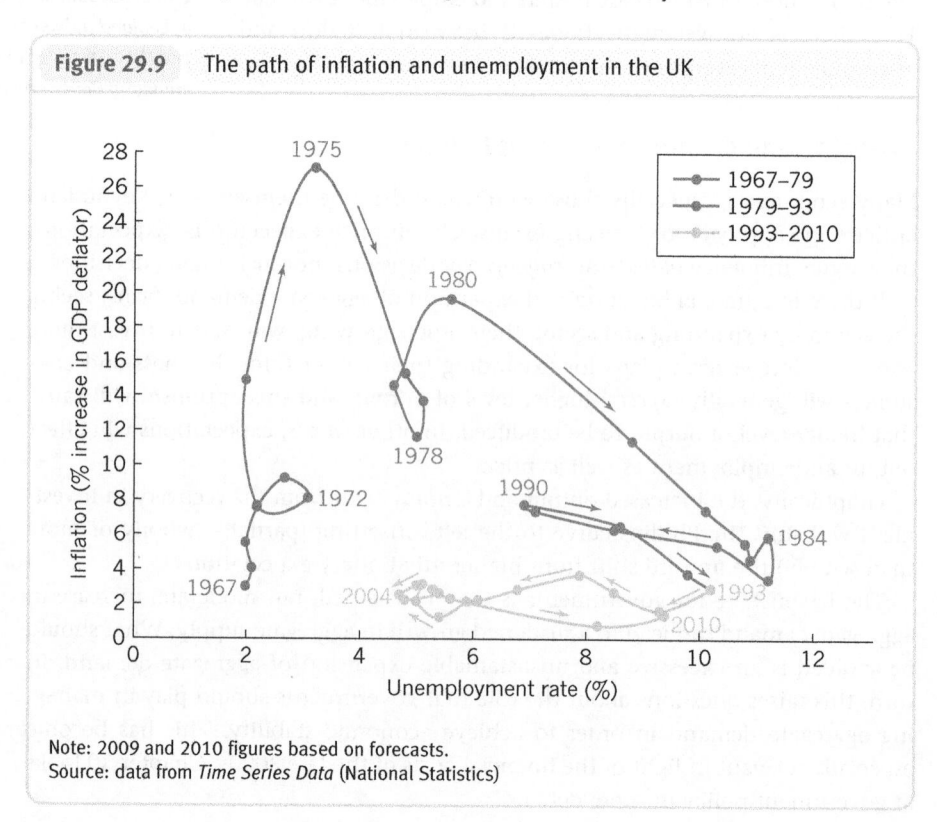

Figure 29.9 The path of inflation and unemployment in the UK

Note: 2009 and 2010 figures based on forecasts.
Source: data from *Time Series Data* (National Statistics)

- Shifts in demand away from the products of older labour-intensive industries to new capital-intensive products.

The free market seemed unable to cope with these changes without a large rise in structural/technological unemployment. Labour was not sufficiently mobile – either geographically or occupationally – to move to industries where there are labour shortages or into jobs where there are skill shortages. A particular problem here was the lack of investment in education and training, with the result that the labour force was not sufficiently flexible to respond to changes in demand for labour.

From the mid-1980s, however, there were increasing signs that the labour market was becoming more flexible (see section 18.7). People seemed more willing to accept that they would have to move from job to job throughout their career. At the same time, policies were introduced to improve training (see section 31.3).

Another explanation for first the rise of equilibrium unemployment and later the fall is the phenomenon of 'hysteresis'.

Hysteresis. If a recession causes a rise in unemployment which is not then fully reversed when the economy recovers, then there is a problem of hysteresis. This term, used in physics, refers to the lagging or persistence of an effect, even when the initial cause has been removed. In our context it refers to the persistence of unemployment even when the initial demand deficiency no longer exists.

The recessions of the early 1980s and early 1990s created a growing number of long-term unemployed who were both deskilled and demotivated. What is more, many firms, in an attempt to cut costs, cut down on training programmes. In these circumstances, a rise in aggregate demand would not simply have enabled the long-term unemployed to be employed again.

The recessions also caused a lack of investment and a reduction in firms' capacity. When demand recovered, many firms were unable to increase output and instead raised prices. Unemployment thus only fell modestly and inflation rose. The NAIRU had increased: the Phillips curve had shifted to the right.

After 1992, however, the economy achieved sustained expansion, with no recession. Equilibrium unemployment began to fall. In other words, the hysteresis was not permanent. As firms increased their investment, the capital stock expanded; firms engaged in more training; the number of long-term unemployed fell.

Whether hysteresis will become a problem again after the recession of 2008/9 remains to be seen. A lot will depend on the opportunities and incentives for retraining.

> **Definition**
>
> **Hysteresis**
> The persistence of an effect even when the initial cause has ceased to operate. In economics it refers to the persistence of unemployment even when the demand deficiency that caused it no longer exists.

Inflation targeting

As we have seen, a major determinant of the actual rate of inflation is the rate of inflation that people expect. Since 1992, a policy of inflation targeting has been adopted, and in 1997 the Bank of England was given independence in setting interest rates to achieve the target rate of inflation.

The target was initially set in October 1992 as a range from 1 to 4 per cent for RPIX inflation.[1] With the election of the Labour government in 1997, a single point

---

[1] RPIX is the retail prices index, excluding mortgage interest payments. CPI is the consumer prices index. Differences in how CPI is compiled means that CPI inflation is typically about 0.5 percentage points below RPIX inflation. Thus the current target of 2 per cent CPI inflation is approximately equivalent to 2.5 per cent RPIX inflation that was used as the target prior to December 2003.

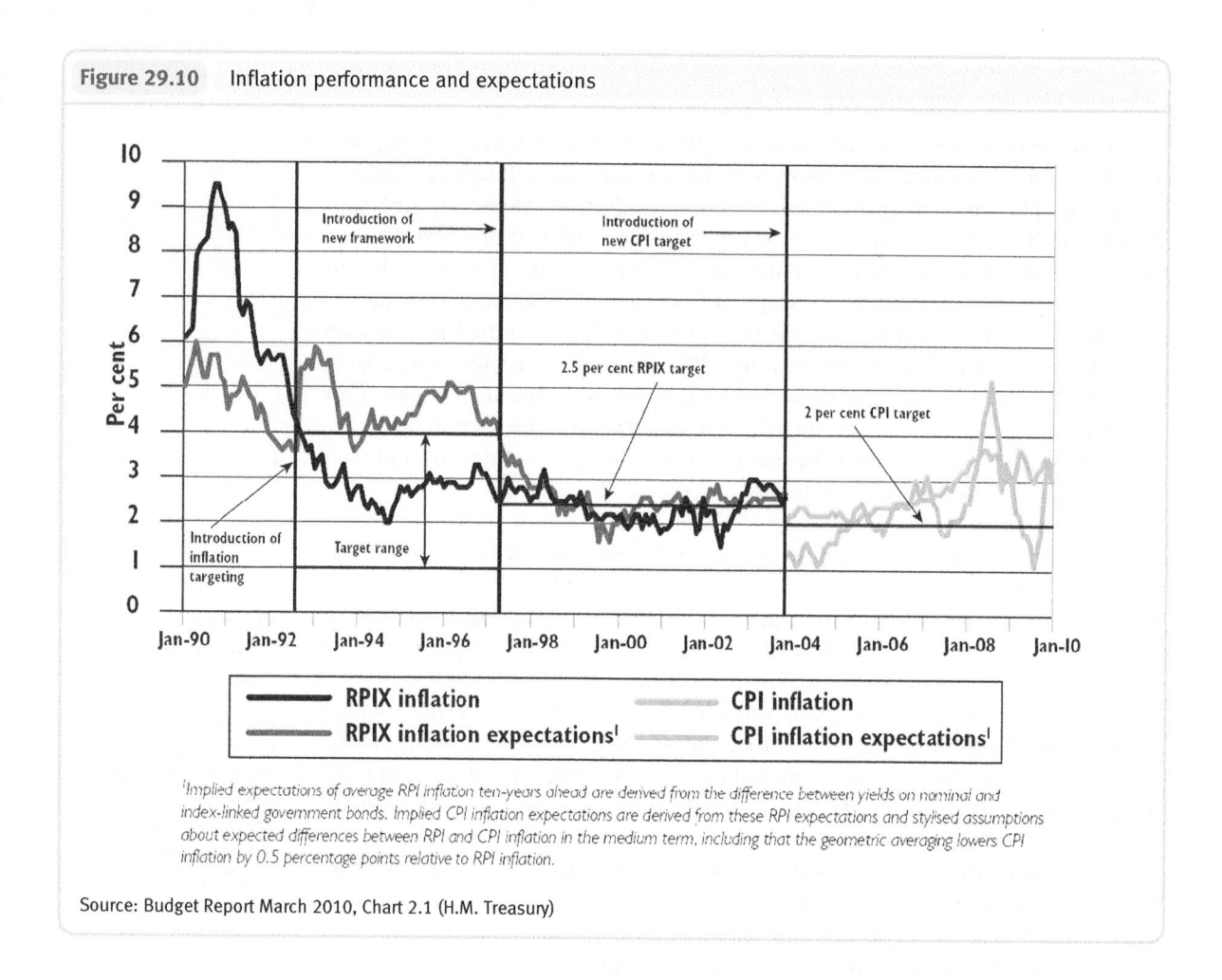

Figure 29.10 Inflation performance and expectations

*Implied expectations of average RPI inflation ten-years ahead are derived from the difference between yields on nominal and index-linked government bonds. Implied CPI inflation expectations are derived from these RPI expectations and stylised assumptions about expected differences between RPI and CPI inflation in the medium term, including that the geometric averaging lowers CPI inflation by 0.5 percentage points relative to RPI inflation.

Source: Budget Report March 2010, Chart 2.1 (H.M. Treasury)

target of 2.5 per cent was adopted. This was changed to a 2 per cent target for CPI inflation in December 2003.

Hitting the target is the central aim of monetary policy and people have grown to believe that the target will be achieved. Figure 29.10 shows expected inflation and actual inflation from 1990 to 2010. As you can see, for the first few years, expected inflation was between 1 and 2 percentage points above actual inflation, but since 1998 expectations have turned out to be pretty well correct.

So, does this mean that the Phillips curve has now become horizontal, as Figure 29.10 would seem to imply? The answer is that it depends on policy. As long as inflation is successfully kept on target, the path of inflation and unemployment will be a horizontal straight line. Movements left and right along the line will depend on what happens to unemployment.

If, however, shocks to the world economy, such as the rapid rises in food, oil and other commodity prices in 2007/8, cause a rise in inflation, then confidence in the central bank's ability to maintain inflation at the target rate may be shaken. Both inflation and unemployment may rise.

Even if the central bank does succeed in achieving the target rate of inflation, in the short term unemployment will fluctuate with the business cycle. Thus there may be movements left or right from one year to the next depending on the level of economic activity. Such fluctuations in unemployment are consistent with stable inflation, provided that the fluctuations are mild and are not enough to alter people's expectations of inflation. Thus there was a very slight rise in unemployment, from 5.1 to 5.2 per cent, from 2001 to 2002 as economic growth slowed slightly and a fall again to 4.8 per cent in 2004 as growth picked up somewhat.

Over the medium term (3 to 6 years), there may be a leftward movement if the economy starts in recession and then the output gap is gradually closed through a process of steady economic growth (growth that avoids 'boom and bust'). Demand-deficient unemployment will be gradually eliminated. Thus between 1992 (the trough of the recession) and 2000, the output gap was closed from −3.2 to +1.3 (see chart (a) in Box 29.1 on page 658). From 2001 to 2006 it stayed between +0.2 and +0.9. Provided the process is gradual, inflation can stay on target.

Over the longer term, movements left (or right) will depend on what happens to equilibrium unemployment. A reduction in equilibrium unemployment will result in a leftward movement. Evidence suggests that since the mid-1980s, there has been a significant reduction in equilibrium unemployment from around 11 per cent to around 5 per cent. The precise amount, however, is not certain as it is subject to measurement errors.

What if inflation targeting were abandoned?

If inflation targeting were abandoned and aggregate demand was expanded rapidly, perhaps through tax cuts or a cut in interest rates, the short-run Phillips curve could re-emerge. A rapid expansion of aggregate demand would both reduce unemployment below the equilibrium rate and raise inflation. There would be a positive output gap.

This position could not be sustained, however, as inflationary expectations would rise and the short-run Phillips curve would begin shifting upwards (as in Figure 29.8 on page 661). A long-run vertical Phillips curve would once more become apparent at the natural (equilibrium) rate of unemployment.

BUSINESS CYCLES 29.5

Business cycles and aggregate demand

Many economists, particularly Keynesian, blame fluctuations in output and employment on fluctuations in aggregate demand. Theirs is therefore a 'demand-side' explanation of the business cycle. In the upturn (phase 1), aggregate demand starts to rise (see Figure 26.1 on page 564). It rises rapidly in the expansionary phase (phase 2). It then slows down and may start to fall in the peaking-out phase (phase 3). It then falls or remains relatively stagnant in the recession (phase 4).

Instability of investment: the accelerator

Investment is typically the most volatile component of aggregate demand (see Box 29.2 on page 670). Therefore, investment is an important factor contributing to the ups and downs of the business cycle.

In a recession, investment in new plant and equipment can all but disappear. After all, what is the point of investing in additional capacity if you cannot even sell what you are currently producing? When an economy begins to recover from a recession, however, and confidence returns, investment can rise very rapidly.

> **Definition**
>
> **Accelerator theory**
> The *level* of investment depends on the *rate of change* of national income, and the result tends to be subject to substantial fluctuations.

In percentage terms the rise in investment may be *several times that of the rise in income*. When the growth of the economy slows down, however, investment can fall dramatically.

The point is that investment depends not so much on the *level* of GDP and consumer demand, as on their *rate of change*. The reason is that investment (except for replacement investment) is to provide *additional* capacity, and thus depends on how much demand has risen, not on its level. But growth rates change by much more than the level of output. For example, if economic growth is 1 per cent in 2010 and 2 per cent in 2011, then in 2011 output has gone up by 2 per cent, but growth has gone up by 100 per cent! (i.e. it has doubled). Thus percentage changes in investment tend to be much more dramatic than percentage changes in GDP. This is known as the accelerator theory.

> **Pause for thought**
>
> *Under what circumstances would you expect a rise in GDP to cause a large accelerator effect?*

These fluctuations in investment, being injections into the circular flow of income, then have a multiplied effect on GDP, thereby magnifying the upswings and downswings of the business cycle.

Fluctuations in stocks

Firms hold stocks of finished goods. These stocks tend to fluctuate with the course of the business cycle, and these fluctuations in stocks themselves contribute to fluctuations in output.

Imagine an economy that is recovering from a recession. At first, firms may be cautious about increasing production. Doing so may involve taking on more labour or making additional investment. Firms may not want to make these commitments if the recovery could soon peter out. They may therefore run down their stocks rather than increase output. Initially, the recovery from recession will be slow.

If the recovery continues, however, firms will start to gain more confidence and will increase their production. Also they will find that their stocks have got rather low and will need building up. This gives a further boost to production, and for a time the growth in output will exceed the growth in demand. This extra growth in output will then, via the multiplier, lead to a further increase in demand.

Once stocks have been built up again, the growth in output will slow down to match the growth in demand. This slowing down in output will, via the accelerator and multiplier, contribute to the ending of the expansionary phase of the business cycle.

As the economy slows down, firms may for a time be prepared to carry on producing and build up stocks. The increase in stocks thus cushions the effect of falling demand on output and employment.

If the recession continues, firms will be unwilling to go on building up stocks. But as firms attempt to reduce their stocks back to the desired level, production will fall *below* the level of sales, despite the fact that sales themselves are lower. This could therefore lead to a dramatic fall in output and, via the multiplier, to an even bigger fall in sales.

Eventually, once stocks have been run down to the minimum, production will have to rise again to match the level of sales. This will contribute to a recovery and the whole cycle will start again.

Aggregate demand and the course of the business cycle

Why do booms and recessions last for several months or even years, and why do they eventually come to an end? Let us examine each in turn.

Why do booms and recessions persist for a period of time?

Time lags. It takes time for changes in injections and withdrawals to be fully reflected in changes in GDP, output and employment. The multiplier process takes time. Moreover, consumers, firms and government may not all respond immediately to new situations. Their responses are spread out over a period of time.

'Bandwagon' effects. Once the economy starts expanding, expectations become buoyant. People think ahead and adjust their expenditure behaviour: they consume and invest more *now*. Likewise in a recession, a mood of pessimism may set in. The effect is cumulative.

The multiplier and accelerator interact: they feed on each other. A rise in GDP causes a rise in investment (the accelerator). This, being an injection into the circular flow, causes a multiplied rise in income. This then causes a further accelerator effect, a further multiplier effect, and so on.

Why do booms and recessions come to an end? What determines the turning points?

Ceilings and floors. Actual output can go on growing more rapidly than potential output only as long as there is slack in the economy. As full employment is approached and as more and more firms reach full capacity, so a ceiling to output is reached.

At the other extreme, there is a basic minimum level of consumption that people tend to maintain. During a recession, people may not buy much in the way of luxury and durable goods, but they will continue to buy food and other basic goods. There is thus a floor to consumption.

The industries supplying these basic goods will need to maintain their level of replacement investment. Also there will always be some minimum investment demand as firms, in order to survive competition, need to install the latest equipment. There is thus a floor to investment too.

Echo effects. Durable consumer goods and capital equipment may last several years, but eventually they will need replacing. The replacement of goods and capital purchased in a previous boom may help to bring a recession to an end.

The accelerator. For investment to continue rising, consumer demand must rise at a *faster and faster* rate. If this does not happen, investment will fall back and the boom will break.

Random shocks. National or international political, social or natural events can affect the mood and attitudes of firms, governments and consumers, and thus affect aggregate demand.

Changes in government policy. In a boom, a government may become most worried by inflation and balance of trade deficits and thus pursue contractionary policies. In a recession, it may become most worried by unemployment and lack of growth and thus pursue expansionary policies. These government policies, if successful, will bring about a turning point in the cycle.

> **Pause for thought**
>
> *Why is it difficult to predict precisely when a recession will come to an end and the economy will start growing rapidly?*

Some economists argue that governments should attempt to reduce cyclical fluctuations by the use of active demand-management policies. These could be either fiscal or monetary policies, or both (see Chapter 30). A more stable economy will provide a better climate for long-term investment, which will lead to faster growth in both potential and actual output.

BOX 29.2 HAS THERE BEEN AN ACCELERATOR EFFECT OVER THE PAST 60 YEARS?

Since 1950, the sum of public and private investment expenditure in the UK has averaged around 15 per cent of gross domestic product. But the level of this investment expenditure has one very notable characteristic: it is highly volatile. We can see from the chart that it is subject to far more violent swings than national income. If we look at the period from 1950 to 2010, the maximum annual rise in GDP was 7.2 per cent and the maximum fall was around 4.7 per cent. By contrast, the maximum annual rise in investment was 25.0 per cent and the maximum fall was 15.0 per cent.

These figures are consistent with the accelerator theory, which argues that the *level* of investment depends on the *rate of change* of national income. A relatively small percentage change in national income can give a much bigger percentage change in investment.

The ups and downs in GDP and investment do not completely match because there are additional factors that determine investment other than simple changes in national income. For starters, capital expenditure by the public sector is determined in a political arena and can also be sensitive to the state of the nation's public finances (see Chapter 30). So far as private sector investment expenditure is concerned, it will be influenced by a variety of factors including: the availability of credit, interest rates, exchange rates, sentiment and business expectations of future demand.

1. Can you identify any time lags in the graph? Why might there be time lags?
2. In what particular industries might we expect investment expenditure to be particularly volatile?

Annual growth in UK real GDP and investment

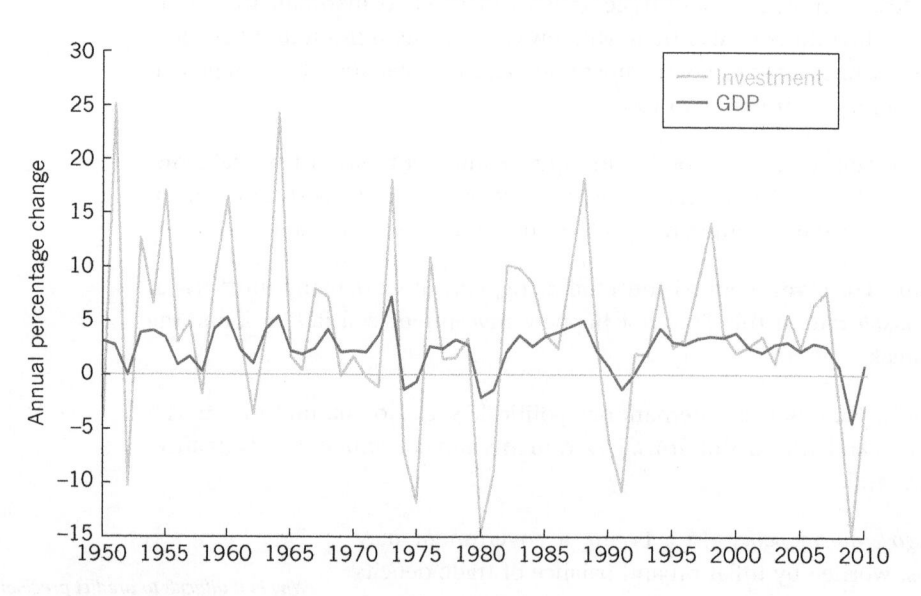

Note: 2010 figures based on forecasts
Source: based on *Time Series Data* (National Statistics) and *World Economic Outlook* (IMF)

Aggregate supply and 'real business cycles'

New classical economists argue that the causes of cyclical fluctuations in business activity lie not on the demand side, but on the *supply* side. A recession is caused by an initial fall in aggregate supply, not aggregate demand. Equilibrium unemployment rises and the vertical Phillips curve shifts to the right. The reverse happens in a boom. Aggregate supply rises and equilibrium unemployment falls. Since the new classical theory of cyclical fluctuations focuses on supply, it is known as real business cycle theory (i.e. concerned with *real* GDP).

But what causes aggregate supply to change in the first place, and why, once there has been an initial change, will the aggregate supply curve *go on* changing, causing a recession or boom to continue?

The initial change in aggregate supply could come from a structural change, such as a shift in demand from older manufacturing industries to new service industries. Because of the immobility of labour, not all those laid off in the older industries will find work in the new industries. Structural unemployment (part of equilibrium unemployment) rises and output falls. *Aggregate* demand may be the same, but because of a change in its pattern, aggregate supply falls and the Phillips curve shifts to the right.

Alternatively, the initial shift in aggregate supply could come from a change in technology. For example, a technological breakthrough in telecommunications could increase aggregate supply. Or it could come from an oil price increase, reducing aggregate supply.

The persistence of supply-side effects

But why, when a change in aggregate supply occurs, does the effect persist? Why is there not a single rise or fall? There are two main reasons. The first is that several changes may take months to complete. For example, a decline in demand for certain older industries, perhaps caused by growing competition from abroad, does not take place overnight. Likewise, a technological breakthrough does not affect all industries simultaneously.

The second reason is that these changes will affect the profitability of investment. If investment rises, this will increase firms' capacity and aggregate supply will increase. If investment falls (as a result, say, of the election of a government less sympathetic to industry), aggregate supply will fall. In other words, investment is causing changes in output not through its effect on aggregate *demand* (through the multiplier), but rather through its effect on aggregate *supply*.

Turning points

So far we have seen how the theory of real business cycles explains persistent rises or falls in aggregate supply. But how does it explain *turning points*? Why do recessions and booms come to an end? The most likely explanation is that, once a shock has worked its way through, aggregate supply will stop shifting. If there is then any shock in the other direction, aggregate supply will start moving back again. For example, after a period of recession, an eventual rise in business confidence will cause investment to rise and hence aggregate supply to shift back to the right. Since these 'reverse shocks' are likely to occur at irregular intervals, they can help to explain why real-world business cycles are themselves irregular.

> **Definition**
>
> **Real business cycle theory**
> The new classical theory which explains cyclical fluctuations in terms of shifts in aggregate supply, rather than aggregate demand.

SUMMARY

1a In the simple circular flow of income model, equilibrium national income (GDP) is where withdrawals equal injections: where $W = J$.

1b Equilibrium can be shown on a Keynesian 45° line diagram. Equilibrium is where GDP (shown by the 45° line) is equal to aggregate expenditure (E).

1c If there is an initial increase in aggregate expenditure (ΔE), which could result from an increase in injections or a reduction in withdrawals, there will be a multiplied rise in GDP. The multiplier is defined as $\Delta GDP/\Delta E$.

1d The size of the multiplier depends on the marginal propensity to consume domestically produced goods (mpc_d). The larger the mpc_d, the more will be spent each time incomes are generated round the circular flow, and thus the more will go round again as *additional* demand for domestic product. The multiplier formula is $1/1 - mpc_d$.

2a The quantity equation $MV = PY$ can be used to analyse the possible relationship between money and prices.

2b In the short run, V tends to vary inversely, but unpredictably, with M. Thus the effect of a change in money supply on nominal GDP (PY) is uncertain.

2c The reason is that the interest-rate transmission mechanism between changes in money and changes in GDP is unreliable and possibly weak. The reasons are (a) an unstable and possibly elastic demand for money and (b) an unstable and possibly inelastic investment demand.

2d The exchange-rate transmission mechanism is stronger but still very unpredictable.

2e In the long run, the transmission mechanisms are stronger and relatively stable. If people have an increase in money in their portfolios, they will attempt to restore portfolio balance by purchasing assets, including goods. Thus an increase in money supply is transmitted directly into an increase in aggregate demand. The interest rate and exchange rate mechanisms are also argued to be strong. The demand for money is seen to be more stable in the long run. This leads to a long-run stability in V (unless it changes as a result of other factors, such as institutional arrangements for the handling of money).

2f The short-run effect of a change in money supply on *real* GDP (Y) depends on the degree of slack in the economy. In the long run, Y is determined largely independently of the money supply. A faster growth in the money supply over a long period is likely to result merely in higher inflation.

3a If equilibrium GDP (GDP_e) is below the full-employment level of GDP (GDP_F), there will be a recessionary gap. This gap is equal to $GDP - E$ at GDP_F. This gap can be closed by expansionary fiscal or monetary policy, which will then cause a multiplied rise in GDP (up to a level of GDP_F) and will eliminate demand-deficient unemployment.

3b If equilibrium GDP exceeds the full-employment level of income, the excess demand gives an inflationary gap, which is equal to $E - GDP$ at GDP_F. This gap can be closed by contractionary policies.

3c This simple analysis tends to imply that the AS curve is horizontal up to GDP_F and then vertical. If allowance is made for other types of inflation and unemployment, however, the AS curve will be upward sloping but getting steeper as full employment is approached and as bottlenecks increasingly occur.

3d The Phillips curve showed the apparent trade-off between inflation and unemployment for more than 100 years prior to 1958. However, after the mid-1960s, the relationship appeared to break down as both inflation and unemployment rose.

3e An explanation for this is given by the adaptive expectations hypothesis. In its simplest form the hypothesis states that the expected rate of inflation this year is what it actually was last year: $\pi_t^e = \pi_{t-1}$.

3f If there is excess demand in the economy, producing upward pressure on wages and prices, initially unemployment will fall. The reason is that workers and firms will believe that wage and price increases represent *real* wage and price increases. Thus workers are prepared to take jobs more readily and firms choose to produce more. But as people's expectations adapt upwards to these higher wages and prices, so ever increasing rises in nominal aggregate demand will be necessary to maintain unemployment below the equilibrium rate. Price and wage rises will accelerate: i.e. inflation will rise.

3g According to this analysis, the Phillips curve is thus vertical at the natural rate of unemployment.

3h The new classical theory assumes flexible prices and wages in the short run as well as in the long run. It also assumes that people base their expectations of inflation on a rational assessment of the *current* situation. People may predict wrongly, but they are equally likely to underpredict or to overpredict. On average over the years they will predict correctly.

3i The rational expectations theory implies that not only the long-run but also the short-run Phillips curve will be vertical. If people correctly predict the rate of inflation, they will correctly predict that any increase in *nominal* aggregate demand will simply be reflected in higher prices. Total output and employment will remain the same: at the equilibrium level.

3k Expectations can also impact upon output and employment. If business is confident that demand will expand and that order books will be healthy, then firms are likely to gear up production and take on extra labour.

4a The Phillips curve shifted to the right in the 1970s and 1980s. Reasons include a growth in equilibrium unemployment caused by rapid technological changes and a persistence of unemployment beyond the recessions of the early 1980s and early 1990s (hysteresis).

4b More recently, equilibrium unemployment has fallen as labour markets have become more flexible and as the lagged effects of the recessions of the early 1980s and early 1990s have faded.

4c Inflation targeting has successfully kept inflation very close to the target level. Expected inflation is close to the target too.

4d The Phillips curve has effectively become horizontal. If inflation targeting were abandoned, however, a negatively sloped short-run Phillips curve would be likely to re-emerge, along with a vertical long-run curve.

5a Many economists, particularly those in the Keynesian tradition, explain cyclical fluctuations in the economy by examining the causes of fluctuations in the level of *demand*.

5b A major part of this explanation of the business cycle is the instability of investment. The accelerator theory explains this instability. It relates the level of investment to *changes* in GDP and consumer demand. An initial increase in consumer demand can result in a very large percentage increase in investment; but as soon as the rise in consumer demand begins to level off, investment will fall; and even a slight fall in consumer demand can reduce investment to virtually zero.

5c Investment in stocks is also unstable and tends to amplify the business cycle.

5d Booms and recessions can persist because of time lags, 'bandwagon' effects and the *interaction* of the multiplier and accelerator. Turning points are explained by ceilings and floors to output, echo effects, the accelerator, swings in government policy and random shocks.

5e Real business cycle theory focuses on aggregate supply shocks, which then persist for a period of time. Eventually their effect will peter out, and supply shocks in the other direction can lead to turning points in the cycle.

REVIEW QUESTIONS

1. Assume that the multiplier has a value of 3. Now assume that the government decides to increase aggregate demand in an attempt to reduce unemployment. It raises government expenditure by £100 million with no increase in taxes. Firms, anticipating a rise in their sales, increase investment by £200 million, of which £50 million consists of purchases of foreign machinery. How much will GDP rise? (Assume *ceteris paribus*.)

2. What factors could explain why some countries have a higher multiplier than others?

3. What are the implications of the relationship between the money supply (M) and the V and Y terms in the quantity equation $MV = PY$ for the effectiveness of controlling the amount of money in the economy as a means of controlling inflation?

4. In the adaptive expectations model of the Phillips curve, if the government tries to maintain unemployment below the equilibrium rate, what will determine the speed at which inflation accelerates?

5. For what reasons might the equilibrium rate of unemployment increase?

6. How can adaptive expectations of inflation result in clockwise Phillips loops? Why would these loops not be completely regular?

7. What implications would a vertical short-run aggregate supply curve have for the effectiveness of demand management policy?

8. Explain the persistence of high levels of unemployment after the 1980s recession. What policies would you advocate to reduce unemployment?

9. How can the interaction of the multiplier and accelerator explain cyclical fluctuations in GDP?

10. What is meant by 'real business cycle' theory? How can such theory account for (a) the persistence of periods of rapid or slow growth; (b) turning points in the cycle?

Additional Part J case studies on the *Economics for Business* website (www.pearsoned.co.uk/sloman)

J.1 **Theories of economic growth.** An overview of classical and more modern theories of growth.

J.2 **The costs of economic growth.** Why economic growth may not be an unmixed blessing.

J.3 **Technology and unemployment.** Does technological progress destroy jobs?

J.4 **The GDP deflator.** An examination of how GDP figures are corrected to take inflation into account.

J.5 **Comparing national income statistics.** The importance of taking the purchasing power of local currencies into account.

J.6 **The UK's balance of payments deficit.** An examination of the UK's persistent trade and current account deficits.

J.7 **Making sense of the financial balances on the balance of payments.** An examination of the three main components of the financial account.

J.8 **A high exchange rate.** This case looks at whether a high exchange rate is necessarily bad news for exporters.

J.9 **The Gold Standard.** A historical example of fixed exchange rates.

J.10 **The importance of international financial movements.** How a current account deficit can coincide with an appreciating exchange rate.

J.11 **Argentina in crisis.** An examination of the collapse of the Argentinean economy in 2001/2.

J.12 **Currency turmoil in the 1990s.** Two examples of speculative attacks on currencies: first on the Mexican peso in 1995; then on the Thai baht in 1997.

J.13 **The attributes of money.** What makes something, such as metal, paper or electronic records, suitable as money?

J.14 **Secondary marketing.** This looks at one of the ways of increasing liquidity without sacrificing profitability. It involves selling an asset to someone else before the asset matures.

J.15 **John Maynard Keynes (1883–1946).** Profile of the great economist.

J.16 **Has there been an accelerator effect since 1978?** An examination of the evidence for an accelerator effect in the UK.

J.17 **The rational expectations revolution.** A profile of two of the most famous economists of the new classical rational expectations school.

J.18 **The phases of the business cycle.** A demand-side analysis of the factors contributing to each of the four phases.

J.19 **How does consumption behave?** The case looks at evidence on the relationship between consumption and disposable income from the 1950s to the current day.

Websites relevant to Part J

Numbers and sections refer to websites listed in the Web appendix and hotlinked from this book's website at **www.pearsoned.co.uk/sloman**

- For news articles relevant to Part J, see the *Economics News Articles* link from the book's website.

- For general news on macroeconomic issues, both national and international, see websites in section A, and particularly A1–5, 7–9. For general news on money, banking and interest rates, see again A1–5, 7–9 and also 20–22, 25, 26, 31, 35, 36. For all of Part J, see also links to macroeconomic and financial news in A42. See also links to newspapers worldwide in A38, 39 and 43, and the news search feature in Google at A41.

- For macroeconomic data, see links in B1 or 2; also see B4 and 12. For UK data, see B3 and 34. For EU data, see G1 > *The Statistical Annex*. For US data, see *Current economic indicators* in B5 and the *Data* section of B17. For international data, see B15, 21, 24, 31, 33. For links to data sets, see B28; I14.

- For national income statistics for the UK (Appendix), see B1, *1. National Statistics* > the fourth link > *Economy* > *United Kingdom Economic Accounts* and *United Kingdom National Accounts – The Blue Book*.

- For the Human Development Index (Box 7.2), see site H17.

- For data on UK unemployment, see B1, *1. National Statistics* > the fourth link > *Labour Market* > *Labour Market Trends*. For International data on unemployment, see G1; H3 and 5.

- For international data on balance of payments and exchange rates, see *World Economic Outlook* in H4 and *OECD Economic Outlook* in B21 (also in section 6 of B1). See also the trade topic in I14.

- For details of individual countries' balance of payments, see B32.

- For UK data on balance of payments, see B1, *1. National Statistics* > the fourth link > *Economy* > *United Kingdom Balance of Payments – the Pink Book*. See also B3, 34; F2. For EU data, see G1 > *The Statistical Annex* > *Foreign trade and current balance*.

- For exchange rates, see A3; B34; F2, 6, 8.

- For discussion papers on balance of payments and exchange rates, see H4 and 7.

- Sites I7 and 11 contain links to *Balance of payments and exchange rates* in *International economics*.

- For monetary and financial data (including data for money supply and interest rates), see section F and particularly F2. Note that you can link to central banks worldwide from site F17. See also the links in B1 or 2.

- For links to sites on money and monetary policy, see the *Financial Economics* sections in I4, 7, 11, 17.

- For information on the development of ideas, see C12, 18; also see links under *Methodology and History of Economic Thought* in C14; links to economists in I4 and 17. See also sites I7 and 11 > *Economic Systems and Theories* > *History of Economic Thought*.

- For student resources relevant to this chapter, see sites C1–7, 9, 10, 12, 13, 19.

Chapter 30

Demand-side policy

Business issues covered in this chapter

- What sorts of government macroeconomic policy are likely to impact on business and in what way?
- What will be the impact on the economy and business of various fiscal policy measures?
- What determines the effectiveness of fiscal policy in smoothing out fluctuations in the economy?
- What fiscal rules are adopted by the government and is following them a good idea?
- How does monetary policy work in the UK and the eurozone, and what are the roles of the Bank of England and the European Central Bank?
- How does targeting inflation influence interest rates and hence business activity?
- Are there better rules for determining interest rates than sticking to a simple inflation target?

There are two major types of demand-side policy: fiscal and monetary. In each case we shall first describe how the policy operates and then examine its effectiveness. We shall also consider the more general question of whether the government and central bank ought to intervene actively to manage the level of aggregate demand, or whether they ought merely to set targets or rules for various indicators – such as money supply, inflation or government budget deficits – and then stick to them.

30.1 FISCAL POLICY

Fiscal policy involves the government manipulating the level of government expenditure and/or rates of tax so as to affect the level of aggregate demand. An

Definition

Fiscal policy
Policy to affect aggregate demand by altering government expenditure and/or taxation.

expansionary fiscal policy will involve raising government expenditure (an injection into the circular flow of income) or reducing taxes (a withdrawal from the circular flow). This will increase aggregate demand and lead to a *multiplied* rise in national income. A *deflationary* (i.e. a contractionary) fiscal policy will involve cutting government expenditure and/or raising taxes.

By changing its fiscal stance, government can affect the *level* of aggregate demand. Why might it wish to do this?

First, it can try to remove any severe deflationary or inflationary gaps. For instance, an expansionary fiscal policy could be used to try to prevent an economy experiencing a severe or prolonged recession. This was the approach taken around the world from 2008 when substantial tax cuts and increases in government expenditure were undertaken. Likewise, deflationary fiscal policy could be used to prevent rampant inflation, such as that experienced in the 1970s.

Second, it can try to smooth out the fluctuations in the economy associated with the business cycle by **fine tuning**. Stabilisation policies involve the government adjusting the level of aggregate demand so as to prevent the economy's actual output level deviating too far from its potential output level – to keep output gaps to a minimum.

Fiscal policy can also be used to influence aggregate *supply*. For example, government can increase its expenditure on infrastructure, or give tax incentives for investment.

Deficits and surpluses

Central government deficits and surpluses

Since an expansionary fiscal policy involves raising government expenditure and/or lowering taxes, this has the effect of either increasing the **budget deficit** or reducing the **budget surplus**. A budget deficit in any one year is where central government's expenditure exceeds its revenue from taxation. A budget surplus is where tax revenues exceed central government expenditure.

For most of the past 50 years, governments around the world have run budget deficits. In recent years, however, many countries, the UK included, made substantial efforts to reduce their budget deficits, and some achieved budget surpluses for periods of time. The position changed dramatically in 2008–9, however, as governments around the world increased their expenditure and cut taxes in an attempt to stave off recession.

General government

'General government' includes central and local government. Table 30.1 shows general government deficits/surpluses and debt for selected countries averaged over three recent periods. They are expressed as a proportion of GDP. Deficits refer to the debt that a government incurs in one year when its spending exceeds its receipts. If the government runs persistent deficits over many years, these debts will accumulate.

As you can see, all of the countries in Table 30.1 experienced deficits in the first period. But, with the exception of Japan, all experienced a reduction of these deficits in the second period and two countries experienced a surplus. All of the countries, however, with the exception of Sweden, experienced an increase in deficits or a reduction in surpluses in the latest period. This was largely the result of measures taken to tackle the deep recession of 2008/9. In order to finance the extra spending and/or tax cuts, governments had to borrow more.

Definitions

Fine tuning
The use of demand management policy (fiscal or monetary) to smooth out cyclical fluctuations in the economy.

Budget deficit
The excess of central government's spending over its tax receipts.

Budget surplus
The excess of central government's tax receipts over its spending.

Table 30.1 General government deficits/surpluses and debt as percentage of GDP

Country	General government deficits (−) or surpluses (+)			General government debt		
	Average 1991–5	Average 1996–2000	Average 2001–10	Average 1991–5	Average 1996–2000	Average 2001–10
Belgium	−6.5	−1.3	−1.5	139.2	125.2	106.1
France	−4.7	−2.6	−4.1	51.2	68.3	72.3
Germany	−2.9	−1.7	−2.6	46.6	61.6	72.7
Greece	−11.2	−4.0	−7.1	99.3	108.9	113.8
Ireland	−2.5	+2.1	−2.1	90.8	55.8	42.9
Italy	−9.9	−3.1	−3.6	127.6	131.0	118.8
Japan	−1.6	−5.8	−6.2	75.0	113.2	192.5
Netherlands	−3.5	−0.2	−1.6	91.6	79.6	59.0
Sweden	−7.4	+1.1	+1.3	74.9	76.9	52.5
UK	−6.0	−0.3	−4.2	44.7	50.9	52.5
USA	−4.5	0.0	−4.8	73.8	66.9	72.4
Euro area	−5.2	−2.1	−3.0	70.9	80.8	78.5

Source: Based on data in *European Economy Statistical Annex* (European Commission)

The whole public sector

To get a more complete view of public finances, we would need to look at the spending and receipts of the entire public sector: namely, central government, local government and public corporations.

Total public expenditure. First we need to distinguish between current and capital expenditures. Current expenditures include items such as wages and salaries of public-sector staff, administration and the payments of welfare benefits. Capital expenditures give rise to a stream of benefits *over time*. Examples include expenditure on roads, hospitals and schools.

Second we must distinguish between final expenditure on goods and services, and transfers. This distinction recognises that the public sector directly adds to the economy's aggregate demand through its spending on goods and services, including the wages of public sector workers, but also that its redistributes incomes between individuals and firms. Transfers include subsidies and benefit payments, such as payments to the unemployed.

Between 2000 and 2008, the UK's public expenditure was typically split 94 to 6 per cent between current and capital expenditure, and 58 to 42 per cent between final expenditure and transfers.

Public sector deficits. If the public sector spends more than it earns (through taxes and the revenues of public corporations, etc.), it runs a deficit. In the UK the principal measure of this deficit is known as the public-sector net cash requirement (PSNCR). It is defined as public-sector expenditure minus public-sector receipts and minus its net lending (financial transactions) to other sectors. The reason for the name 'public-sector net cash requirement' is simple. If the public sector runs a deficit in the current year of, say, £1 billion, then it will have to borrow £1 billion in money this year in order to finance it.

If the public sector runs a surplus (a negative PSNCR), it will be able to repay some of the public-sector debts that have accumulated from previous years.

Definitions

Current expenditure
Recurrent spending on goods and factor payments.

Capital expenditure
Investment expenditure; expenditure on assets.

Final expenditure
Expenditure on goods and services. This is included in GDP and is part of aggregate demand.

Transfers
Transfers of money from taxpayers to recipients of benefits and subsidies. They are not an injection into the circular flow but are the equivalent of a negative tax (i.e. a negative withdrawal).

Public-sector net cash requirement (PSNCR)
The (annual) deficit of the public sector, and thus the amount that the public sector must borrow.

Figure 30.1 UK public-sector net cash requirement, 1965–2010

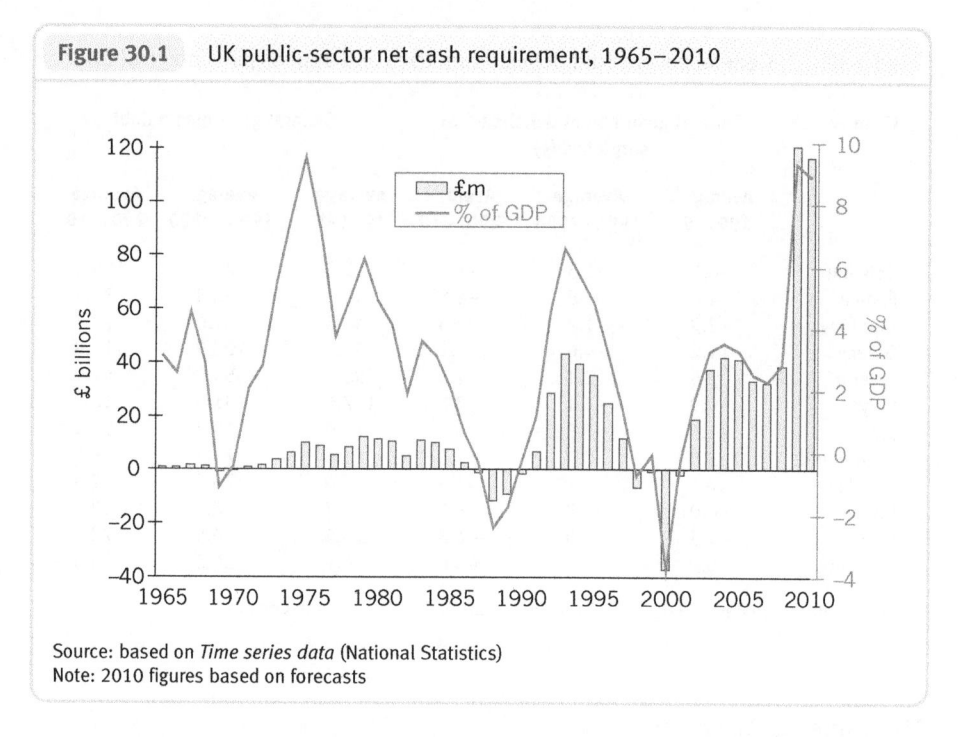

Source: based on *Time series data* (National Statistics)
Note: 2010 figures based on forecasts

Figure 30.1 shows the UK's PSNCR from 1965 to 2010 expressed in money terms and as a percentage of GDP. It shows that public-sector deficits are the norm: in only 10 of these years did the UK experience public-sector surpluses.

The use of fiscal policy

Automatic fiscal stabilisers

To some extent, government expenditure and taxation will have the effect of *automatically* stabilising the economy. For example, as national income rises, the amount of tax people pay automatically rises. This rise in withdrawals from the circular flow of income will help to damp down the rise in national income. This effect will be bigger if taxes are *progressive* (i.e. rise by a bigger percentage than national income). Some government expenditure will have a similar effect. For example, total government expenditure on unemployment benefits will fall, if rises in national income cause a fall in unemployment. This again will have the effect of dampening the rise in national income.

Discretionary fiscal policy

Automatic stabilisers cannot *prevent* fluctuations; they merely reduce their magnitude. If there is a fundamental disequilibrium in the economy or substantial fluctuations in national income, these automatic stabilisers will not be enough. The government may thus choose to *alter* the level of government expenditure or the rates of taxation. This is known as discretionary fiscal policy. Web Case K.4 looks at an example of discretionary fiscal policy in the USA. Web Case K.5 examines the use of discretionary fiscal policy in Japan from 1991 to the present day.

If government expenditure on goods and services (roads, health care, education, etc.) is raised, this will create a full multiplied rise in national income. The reason is that all the money gets spent and thus all of it goes to boosting aggregate demand.

> **Definition**
>
> **Discretionary fiscal policy**
> Deliberate changes in tax rates or the level of government expenditure in order to influence the level of aggregate demand.

Cutting taxes (or increasing benefits), however, will have a smaller effect on national income than raising government expenditure on goods and services by the same amount. The reason is that cutting taxes increases people's *disposable* incomes, of which only part will be spent. Part will be withdrawn into extra saving, imports and other taxes. In other words, not all the tax cuts will be passed on round the circular flow of income as extra expenditure. Thus if one-fifth of a cut in taxes is withdrawn and only four-fifths is spent, the tax multiplier will only be four-fifths as big as the government expenditure multiplier.

> **Pause for thought**
>
> *Why will the multiplier effect of government transfer payments, such as child benefit, pensions and social security benefits be less than the full multiplier effect from government expenditure on goods and services?*

The effectiveness of fiscal policy

How successful will fiscal policy be? Will it be able to 'fine tune' demand? Will it be able to achieve the level of GDP that the government would like it to achieve?

There are various problems with using fiscal policy to manage the economy. These can be grouped under two broad headings: problems of magnitude and problems of timing.

Problems of magnitude

Before changing government expenditure or taxation, the government will need to calculate the effect of any such change on national income, employment and inflation. Predicting these effects, however, is often very unreliable for a number of reasons.

Predicting the effect of changes in government expenditure

A rise in government expenditure of £x may lead to a rise in total injections (relative to withdrawals) that is smaller than £x. This will occur if the rise in government expenditure *replaces* a certain amount of private expenditure. For example, a rise in expenditure on state education may dissuade some parents from sending their children to private schools. Similarly, an improvement in the National Health Service may lead to fewer people paying for private treatment.

Crowding out. Another reason for the total rise in injections being smaller than the rise in government expenditure is a phenomenon known as crowding out. If the government relies on pure fiscal policy – that is, if it does not finance an increase in the budget deficit by increasing the money supply – it will have to borrow the money from the non-bank private sector. It will thus be competing with the private sector for finance and will have to offer higher interest rates. This will force the private sector also to offer higher interest rates, which may discourage firms from investing and individuals from buying on credit. Thus government borrowing *crowds out* private borrowing. In the extreme case, the fall in consumption and investment may completely offset the rise in government expenditure, with the result that aggregate demand does not rise at all.

> **Definitions**
>
> **Crowding out**
> Where increased public expenditure diverts money or resources away from the private sector.
>
> **Pure fiscal policy**
> Fiscal policy which does not involve any change in money supply.

Predicting the effect of changes in taxes

A cut in taxes, by increasing people's real disposable income, increases not only the amount they spend, but also the amount they save. The problem is that it is not easy to predict the relative size of these two increases. In part it will depend on whether people feel that the cut in tax is only temporary, in which case they may simply save the extra disposable income, or permanent, in which case they may adjust their consumption upwards.

Predicting the resulting multiplied effect on national income

Even if the government *could* predict the net initial effect on injections and withdrawals, the extent to which national income will change is still hard to predict for the following reasons:

- The size of the *multiplier* may be difficult to predict, since it is difficult to predict how much of any rise in income will be withdrawn. For example, the amount of a rise in income that households save or consume will depend on their expectations about future price and income changes. The amount of a rise in income spent on imports will depend on the exchange rate, which may fluctuate considerably.
- Induced investment through the *accelerator* is also extremely difficult to predict. It may be that a relatively small fiscal stimulus will be all that is necessary to restore business confidence, and that induced investment will rise substantially. In such a case, fiscal policy can be seen as a 'pump primer'. It is used to *start* the process of recovery, and then the *continuation* of the recovery is left to the market. But for pump priming to work, businesspeople must *believe* that it will work. Business confidence can change very rapidly and in ways that could not have been foreseen a few months earlier.

Random shocks

> **Pause for thought**
>
> *Gives some other examples of 'random shocks' that could undermine the government's fiscal policy.*

Forecasts cannot take into account the unpredictable. For that you would have to consult astrologers or fortune tellers! Unfortunately unpredictable events, such as the attack on the World Trade Center in New York in September 2001, do occur and may seriously undermine the government's fiscal policy.

Problems of timing

Fiscal policy can involve considerable time lags. It may take time to recognise the nature of the problem before the government is willing to take action; tax or government expenditure changes take time to plan and implement – changes will have to wait until the next Budget to be announced and may come into effect some time later; the effects of such changes take time to work their way through the economy via the multiplier and accelerator.

If these time lags are long enough, fiscal policy could even be *de*stabilising. Expansionary policies taken to cure a recession may not come into effect until the economy has *already* recovered and is experiencing a boom. Under these circumstances, expansionary policies are quite inappropriate: they simply worsen the problems of overheating. Similarly, deflationary policies taken to prevent excessive expansion may not take effect until the economy has already peaked and is plunging into recession. The deflationary policies only deepen the recession.

This problem is illustrated in Figure 30.2. Path (a) shows the course of the business cycle without government intervention. Ideally, with no time lags, the economy should be dampened in stage 2 and stimulated in stage 4. This would make the resulting course of the business cycle more like path (b), or even, if the policy were perfectly stabilising, a straight line. With the presence of time lags, however, deflationary policies taken in stage 2 may not come into effect until stage 4,

Figure 30.2 Fiscal policy: stabilising or destabilising?

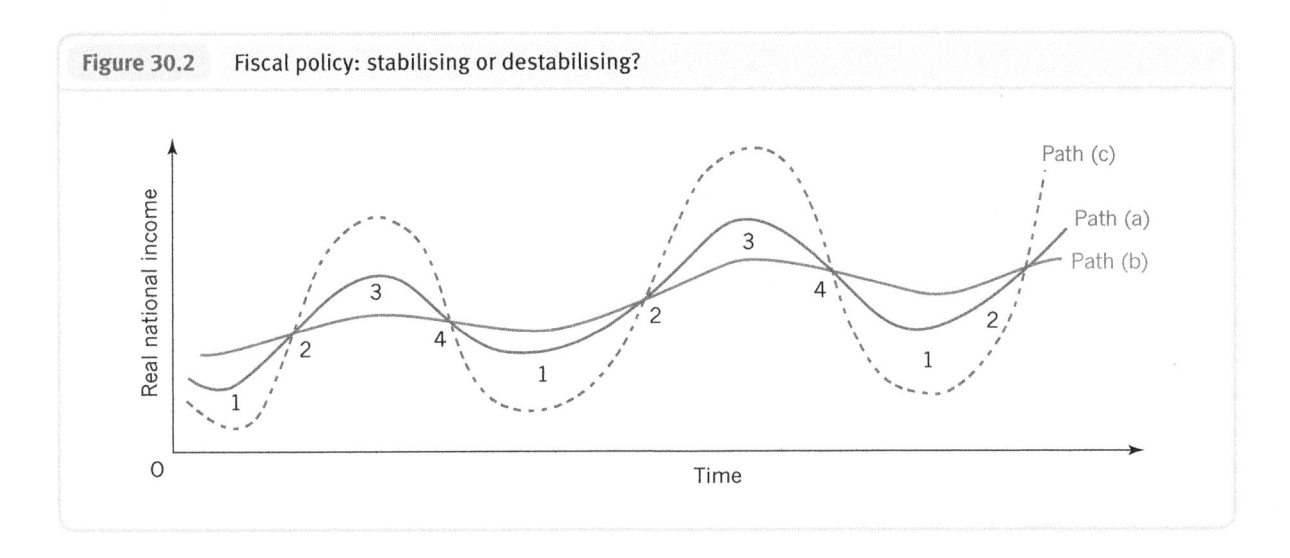

and reflationary policies taken in stage 4 may not come into effect until stage 2. In this case the resulting course of the business cycle will be more like path (c). Quite obviously, in these circumstances 'stabilising' fiscal policy actually makes the economy *less* stable.

If the fluctuations in aggregate demand can be forecast, and if the lengths of the time lags are known, then all is not lost. At least the fiscal measures can be taken early and their delayed effects can be taken into account.

Fiscal rules

Given the problems of pursuing active fiscal policy, many governments today take a much more passive approach. Instead of changing the policy as the economy

BOX 30.1 FROM GOLDEN TO TEMPORARY RULES

Putting the discretion back into fiscal policy

If the government persistently runs a budget deficit, the national debt will rise. If it rises faster than GDP, it will account for a growing proportion of GDP. There is then likely to be an increasing problem of 'servicing' this debt: i.e. paying the interest on it. The government could find itself having to borrow more and more to meet the interest payments, and so the national debt could rise faster still. As the government borrows more and more, so it has to pay higher interest rates to attract finances. If it is successful in this, borrowing and hence investment by the private sector could be crowded out.

Recognising these problems, many governments in recent years have attempted to reduce their debts.

Preparing for the euro

In signing the Maastricht Treaty in 1992, the EU countries agreed that to be eligible to join the single currency (i.e. the euro), they should have sustainable deficits and debts. This was interpreted as follows: the general government deficit should be no more than 3 per cent of GDP and general government debt should be no more than 60 per cent of GDP, or should at least be falling towards that level at a satisfactory pace.

But in the mid-1990s, several of the countries that were subsequently to join the euro had deficits and debts substantially above these levels (see Table 30.1). Getting them down proved a painful business. Government expenditure had to be cut and taxes increased. These fiscal measures, unfortunately, proved to be powerful! Unemployment rose and growth remained low.

The EU Stability and Growth Pact (SGP)

In June 1997, at the European Council in Amsterdam, the EU countries agreed that governments adopting the euro should seek to balance their budgets (or even aim for a

(a) Keeping budget deficits within the 3% ceiling?

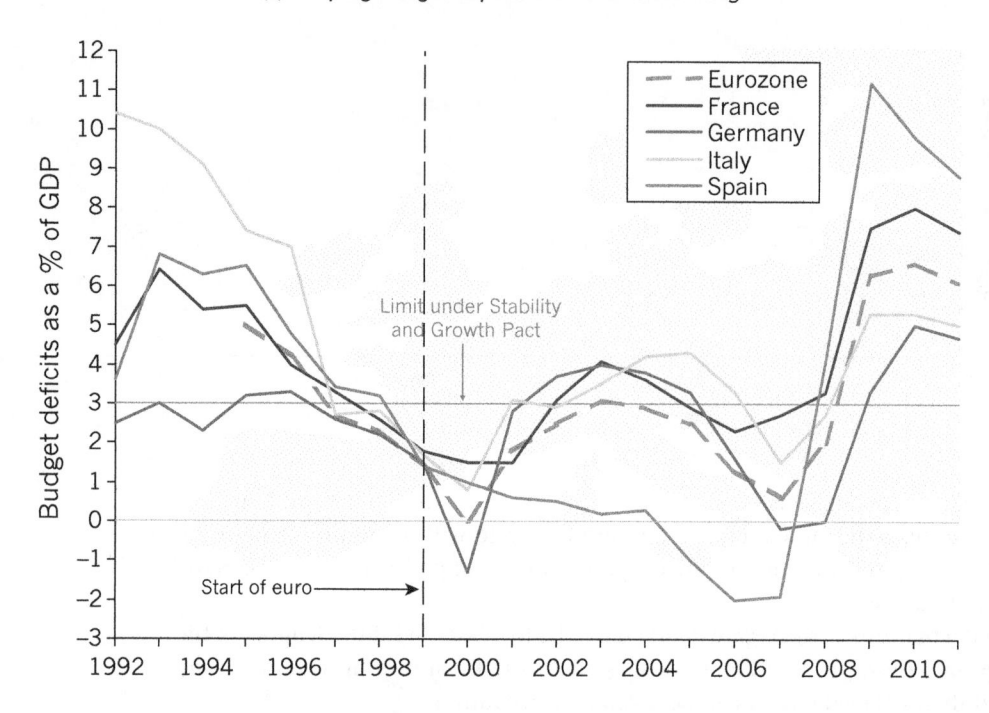

Source: based on data in *European Economy* (European Commission).
Note: 2010 and 2011 based on forecasts.

surplus) averaged over the course of the business cycle, and that deficits should not exceed 3 per cent of GDP in any one year. A country's deficit is permitted to exceed 3 per cent only if its GDP has declined by at least 2 per cent (or 0.75 per cent with special permission from the Council of Ministers). Otherwise, countries with deficits exceeding 3 per cent are required to make deposits of money with the European Central Bank. These then become fines if the excessive budget deficit is not eliminated within two years.

There are two main aims of targeting a zero budget deficit over the business cycle. The first is to allow automatic stabilisers to work without 'bumping into' the 3 per cent deficit ceiling in years when economies are slowing. The second is to allow a reduction in government debts as a proportion of GDP (assuming that GDP grows on average at around 2–3 per cent per year).

From 2002, with slowing growth, both Germany, France and Italy breached the 3 per cent ceiling. By 2007, however, after two years of relatively strong growth, deficits had been reduced well below the ceiling.

But then the credit crunch hit. As the EU economies slowed, so deficits rose. To combat the recession, in November 2008 the European Commission announced a €200 billion fiscal stimulus plan, mainly in the form of increased public expenditure. €170 billion of the money would come from member governments and €30 billion from the EU, amounting to a total of 1.2 per cent of EU GDP. The money would be for a range of projects, such as job training, help to small businesses, developing green energy technologies and energy efficiency. Most member governments quickly followed by announcing how their specific plans would accord with the overall plan.

The combination of the recession and the fiscal measures would push most eurozone countries' budget deficits well above the 3 per cent ceiling (see Figure (a)). But since the recession in EU countries was predicted to deepen markedly in 2009, with GDP forecast to decline by 4.0 per cent in the eurozone as a whole, and by 5.4 per cent in Germany, 4.4 per cent in Italy and 3.0 per cent in France, this was not seen to breach SGP rules.

As the European economy began to recover in 2010, there was tremendous pressure on member countries to begin reining in their deficits. The average eurozone deficit had risen to 6.6 per cent of GDP, and some countries' deficit was much higher. Indeed, with the Greek, Spanish and Irish deficits being 9.3, 9.8 and 11.7 per cent respectively, it would be an especially painful road back to the 3 per cent ceiling under SGP for some countries. In Greece there were riots, with people protesting against cuts in government expenditure and tax rises.

The UK Labour government's golden rule

On being elected in 1997, the Labour government in the UK adopted a similar approach to that of the SGP. It introduced two fiscal rules.

First, under its 'golden rule', the government pledged that over the economic cycle, it would borrow only to invest

(b) Output gap and the cyclically adjusted surplus on UK current budget (% of GDP)

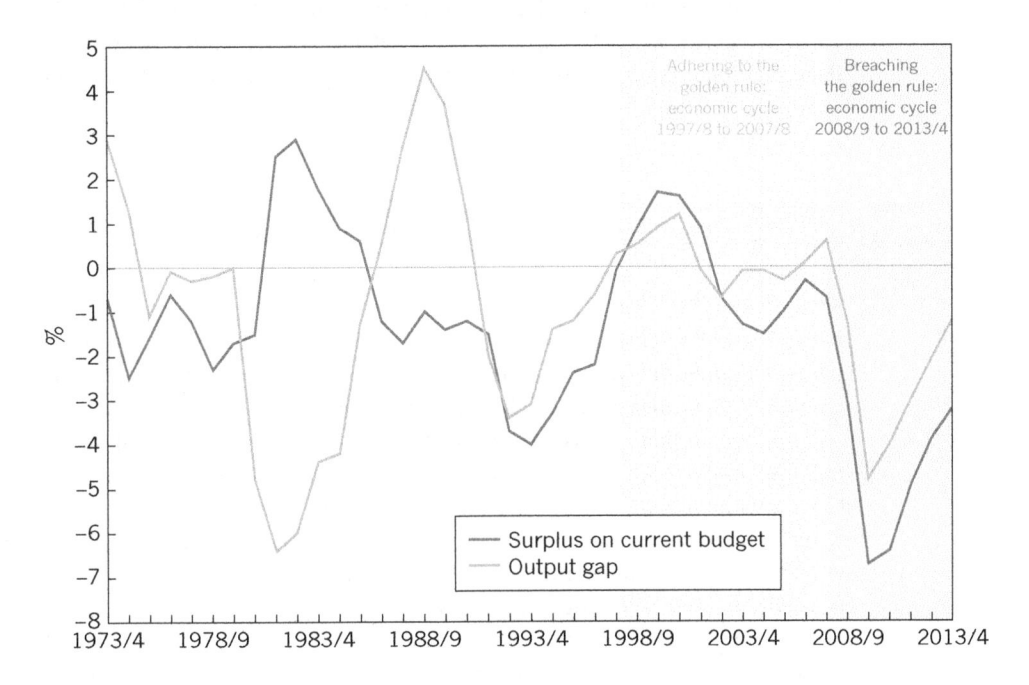

Adhering to the golden rule: economic cycle 1997/8 to 2007/8

Breaching the golden rule: economic cycle 2008/9 to 2013/4

— Surplus on current budget
— Output gap

Note: 2009/10 onwards based on forecasts.
Source: *2009 Budget Report* (HM Treasury) and HM Treasury Public Finances Databank

(e.g. in roads, hospitals and schools) and not to fund current spending (e.g. on wages, administration and benefits). Investment was exempted from the zero borrowing rule because it contributes towards the growth of GDP.

Second, under its 'sustainable investment rule', the government also set itself the target of maintaining a stable public-sector debt/GDP ratio below 40 per cent.

As with the Stability and Growth Pact, the argument for the golden rule was that by using an averaging rule over the cycle, automatic stabilisers would be allowed to work. Deficits of receipts over current spending could occur when the economy is in recession or when growth is sluggish (as in 2001–3), helping to stimulate the economy.

In cyclically adjusting government balances we remove the estimated effects of the economic cycle. For example, during economic downturns we remove the effect of increased welfare payments and lower tax receipts. The government's current budget is the difference between its total receipts and its current expenditures (excluding capital expenditures). Figure (b), shows that the cyclically adjusted current budget balanced across the economic cycle from 1997/8 to 2006/7.

However, in the Pre-Budget Report of November 2008, the government argued that its 'immediate priority' was to support the economy by using discretionary fiscal policy. It therefore suspended its golden rule and the sustainable investment rule.

Amongst other measures the government introduced a 13-month cut in VAT from 17.5 per cent to 15 percent. It also brought forward from 2010/11 £3 billion of capital spending on projects such as motorways, new social housing, schools and energy efficiency. The hope, however, was that, as the economy recovered and the government was able to raise taxes again, the golden rule could be resumed once more.

The approach of the Coalition government

The fiscal priority of the incoming Coalition government in 2010 was to get the deficit down, which by 2010 had reached 11.4 per cent of GDP, one of the highest percentages in the developed world. The government was determined to reduce the structural deficit (i.e. that part that would not disappear with economic recovery) to zero in six years. This would then become the new fiscal rule – very similar to the Stability and Growth Pact.

But to get the structural deficit to zero would mean sharp government expenditure cuts and/or tax rises in the meantime, amounting to a total of £86 billion per year. On its own, the much tighter fiscal policy would substantially dampen aggregate demand. The question was whether the recovery in exports, investment and consumer demand would be sufficient to offset it and prevent a slide back into recession. That, in turn, depended on confidence – of consumers, business and international financiers – and on the effectiveness of expansionary monetary policy (see section 30.2).

What effects will an increase in government investment expenditure have on public-sector debt (a) in the short run; (b) in the long run?

changes, a rule is set for the level of public finances. This rule is then applied year after year, with taxes and government expenditure being planned to meet that rule. For example, a target could be set for the public-sector deficit, with government expenditure and taxes being adjusted to keep the deficit at or within its target level. Box 30.1 looks at some examples of fiscal targets. Fiscal (and monetary) rules are examined in more detail in section 30.3.

30.2 MONETARY POLICY

Each month the Bank of England's Monetary Policy Committee meets to set interest rates. The event gets considerable media coverage. Pundits, for two or three days before the meeting, try to predict what the MPC will do and economists give their 'considered' opinions about what the MPC *ought* to do.

The fact is that changes in interest rates have gained a central significance in macroeconomic policy. And it is not just in the UK. Whether it is the European Central Bank setting interest rates for the eurozone countries, or the Federal Reserve Bank setting US interest rates, or any other central bank around the world choosing what the level of interest rates should be, monetary policy is seen as having a major influence on a whole range of macroeconomic indicators.

But is monetary policy simply the setting of interest rates? In reality, it involves the central bank intervening in the money market to ensure that the interest rate that has been announced is also the *equilibrium* interest rate.

The policy setting

In framing its monetary policy, the government must decide on what the goals of the policy are. Is the aim simply to control inflation, or does the government wish also to affect output and employment, or does it want to control the exchange rate?

The government must also decide where monetary policy fits into the total package of macroeconomic policies. Is it seen as the major or even sole macroeconomic policy instrument, or is it merely one of several?

A decision also has to be made about who is to carry out the policy. There are three possible approaches here.

In the first, the government both sets the policy and decides the measures necessary to achieve it. Here the government would set the interest rate, with the central bank simply influencing money markets to achieve this rate. This first approach was used in the UK before 1997.

The second approach is for the government to set the policy *targets*, but for the central bank to be given independence in deciding interest rates. This is the approach adopted in the UK today. The government has set a target rate of inflation of 2 per cent, but then the MPC is free to choose the rate of interest.

The third approach is for the central bank to be given independence not only in carrying out policy, but in setting the policy targets itself. The ECB, within the statutory objective of maintaining price stability over the medium term, has decided on the target of keeping inflation below, but close to, 2 per cent over the medium term.

Finally, there is the question of whether the government or central bank should take a long-term or short-term perspective. Should it adopt a target for inflation or money supply growth and stick to it come what may? Or should it adjust its policy as circumstances change and attempt to 'fine tune' the economy?

We will be looking primarily at *short-term* monetary policy: that is, policy used to keep to a set target for inflation or money supply growth, or policy used to smooth out fluctuations in the business cycle. It is important first, however, to take a longer-term perspective. Governments generally want to prevent an excessive growth in the money supply over the longer term. If money supply does grow rapidly, then inflation is likely to be high. Likewise they want to ensure that money supply grows enough and that there is not a shortage of credit, such as that during the credit crunch. If money supply grows too rapidly, then inflation is likely to be high; if money supply grows too slowly, or even falls, then recession is likely to result.

Control of the money supply over the medium and long term

In section 28.3 we identified two major sources of monetary growth: (a) banks choosing to hold a lower liquidity ratio; (b) public-sector borrowing financed by borrowing from the banking sector. If the government wishes to restrict monetary growth over the longer term, it could attempt to control either or both of these.

Liquidity of banks

The central bank could impose a statutory minimum reserve ratio on the banks, *above* the level that banks would otherwise choose to hold. Such ratios come in various forms. The simplest is where the banks are required to hold a given minimum percentage of deposits in the form of cash or deposits with the central bank.

The effect of a minimum reserve ratio is to prevent banks choosing to reduce their cash or liquidity ratio and creating more credit. This was a popular approach of governments in many countries in the past. Some countries imposed very high ratios indeed in their attempt to slow down the growth in the money supply.

A major problem with imposing restrictions of this kind is that banks may find ways of getting round them. After all, banks would like to lend and customers would like to borrow. It is very difficult to regulate and police every single part of countries' complex financial systems.

Nevertheless, attitudes changed substantially after the excessive lending of the mid-2000s. The expansion of credit had been based on 'liquidity' achieved through secondary marketing between financial institutions and the growth of securitised assets containing sub-prime debt (see Box 28.3). After the credit crunch and the need for central banks or governments to rescue ailing banks, such as Northern Rock and later the Royal Bank of Scotland in the UK and many other banks around the world, there were calls for greater regulation of banks to ensure that they had sufficient capital and operated with sufficient liquidity, and that they were not exposed to excessive risk of default.

Public-sector deficits

Government borrowing tends to lead to an increase in money supply. To prevent this, public-sector deficits must be financed by selling *bonds* (as opposed to bills, which could well be taken up by the banking sector, thereby increasing money supply). However, to sell extra bonds the government will have to offer higher interest rates. This will have a knock-on effect on private-sector interest rates. The government borrowing will thus crowd out private-sector borrowing and investment. This is known as financial crowding out.

If governments wish to reduce monetary growth and yet avoid financial crowding out, they must therefore reduce the size of public-sector deficits.

> **Definitions**
>
> **Minimum reserve ratio**
> A minimum ratio of cash (or other specified liquid assets) to deposits (either total or selected) that the central bank requires banks to hold.
>
> **Financial crowding out**
> Where an increase in government borrowing diverts money away from the private sector.

It is for this reason that, under the Stability and Growth Pact (see Box 30.1), eurozone countries are required to aim for a zero government deficit over the business cycle, so that in times of economic slowdown the deficit will not exceed 3 per cent: the limit set for deficits under the Pact.

Similarly, in the UK, the Labour government adopted the 'golden rule' of fiscal policy. This was that, over the course of the business cycle, the government would borrow only to invest. In other words, leaving investment aside, there was a long-term target for government borrowing of zero. It is expected that the Coalition government will adopt a similar rule once the deficit has been brought back down.

Short-term monetary measures

Inflation may be off target. Alternatively, the government (or central bank) may wish to alter its monetary policy. What can it do? There are various techniques that could be used. These can be grouped into three categories: (a) altering the money supply; (b) altering interest rates; (c) rationing credit. These are illustrated in Figure 30.3, which shows the demand for and supply of money. The equilibrium quantity of money is initially Q_1 and the equilibrium interest rate is r_1.

Assume that the central bank wants to tighten monetary policy in order to reduce inflation. It could (a) seek to shift the supply of money curve to the left: e.g. from M_s to M'_s (resulting in the equilibrium rate of interest rising from r_1 to r_2), (b) raise the interest rate directly from r_1 to r_2, and then manipulate the money supply to reduce it to Q_2, or (c) keep interest rates at r_1, but reduce money supply to Q_2 by rationing the amount of credit granted by banks and other institutions.

Credit rationing was widely used in the past, especially during the 1960s. The aim was to keep interest rates low, so as not to discourage investment, but to restrict credit to more risky business customers and/or to consumers. In the UK, the Bank of England could order banks to abide by such a policy, although in practice it always relied on persuasion. The government also, from time to time, imposed restrictions on hire-purchase credit, by specifying minimum deposits or maximum repayment periods.

Such policies were progressively abandoned around the world from the early 1980s. They stifle competition and prevent efficient banks from expanding. Hire-purchase controls may badly hit certain industries (e.g. cars and other consumer

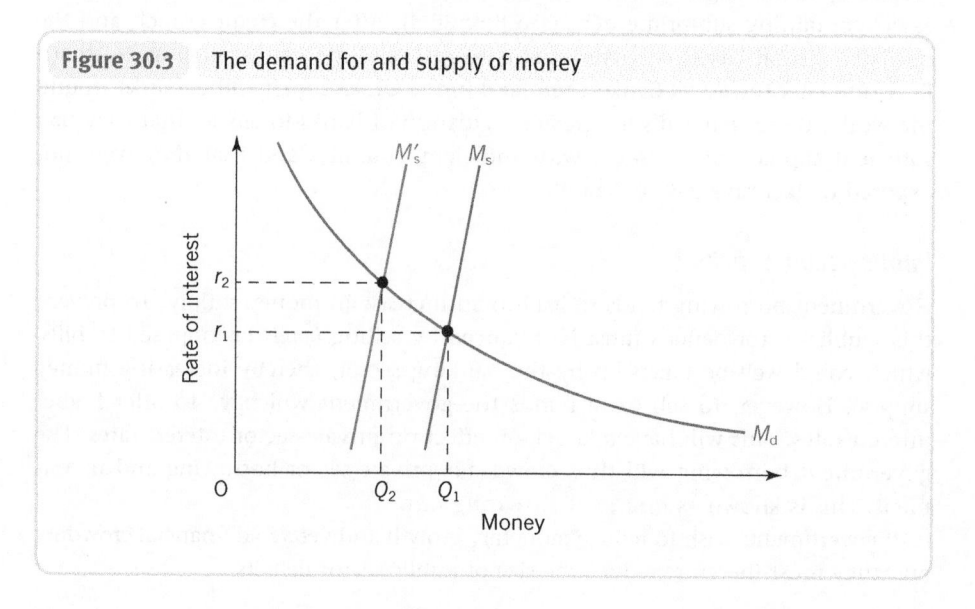

Figure 30.3 The demand for and supply of money

durables), whose products are bought largely on hire-purchase credit. What is more, with the deregulation and globalisation of financial markets up to 2007, it had become very difficult to ration credit. If one financial institution was controlled, borrowers could simply go elsewhere.

With the excessive lending in sub-prime markets that had triggered the credit crunch of 2007–9, there were calls around the world for tighter controls over bank lending. But this was different from credit rationing as we have defined it. Tighter controls would be used to prevent reckless behaviour by banks, rather than to achieve a particular level of money at a lower rate of interest. We thus focus on controlling the money supply and controlling interest rates.

Techniques to control the money supply

There are four possible techniques that a central bank could use to control money supply. They have one major feature in common: they involve manipulating the liquid assets of the banking system. The aim is to influence the total money supply by affecting the amount of credit that banks can create.

Open-market operations. Open-market operations are the most widely used of the four techniques around the world. They alter the monetary base. This then affects the amount of credit banks can create and hence the level of broad money (M4 in the UK).

Open-market operations involve the sale or purchase by the central bank of government securities (bonds or bills) in the open market. These sales (or purchases) are to fund additional (or reduced) government borrowing, and are best understood, therefore, in the context of an unchanged PSNCR.

If the central bank wishes to *reduce* the money supply, it sells more securities. When people buy these securities, they pay for them with cheques drawn on banks. Thus banks' balances with the central bank are reduced. If this brings bank reserves below their prudent ratio (or statutory ratio, if one is in force), banks will reduce advances. There will be a multiple contraction of credit and hence of (broad) money supply.

> **Definition**
>
> **Open-market operations**
> The sale (or purchase) by the authorities of government securities in the open market in order to reduce (or increase) money supply.

> **Pause for thought**
>
> *Explain how open-market operations could be used to increase the money supply.*

Central bank lending to the banks. The central bank in most countries is prepared to provide extra money to banks (through gilt repos, rediscounting bills or straight loans). In some countries, it is the policy of the central bank to keep its interest rate to banks *below* market rates, thereby encouraging banks to borrow (or sell back securities) whenever such facilities are available. By cutting back the amount it is willing to provide, the central bank can reduce banks' liquid assets and hence the amount of credit they can create.

In other countries, such as the UK and the eurozone countries, it is not so much the amount of money made available that is controlled, but rather the rate of interest (or discount). The higher this rate is relative to other market rates, the less will banks be willing to borrow, and the lower, therefore, will be the monetary base. Raising this rate, therefore, has the effect of reducing the money supply.

In response to the credit crunch of 2007–9, central banks in several countries extended their willingness to lend to banks. As we saw in Box 28.4, under its 'Special Liquidity Scheme', the Bank of England was willing to swap, on a temporary basis, banks' mortgage and other debt (an illiquid asset) for special 12-month Treasury bills (a liquid asset). The Bank was effectively lending Treasury bills against the

BOX 30.2 THE DAILY OPERATION OF MONETARY POLICY

What goes on at Threadneedle Street?

The Bank of England (the 'Bank') does not normally attempt to control money supply directly. Instead it seeks to control interest rates by conducting open-market operations (OMOs) through short-term and longer-term repos and through the outright purchase of high-quality bonds. These operations, as we shall see, determine short-term interest rates, which then have a knock-on effect on longer-term rates, as returns on different forms of assets must remain competitive with each other.

Let us assume that the Monetary Policy Committee (MPC) of the Bank of England forecasts that inflation will fall below target as a result of a low level of aggregate demand. At its monthly meeting, therefore, it decides to reduce interest rates. What does the Bank do?

The first thing is that it will announce a cut in Bank Rate. But it must do more than this. It must back up the announcement by using OMOs to ensure that its announced interest rate is the equilibrium rate.

Short-term open-market operations

Central to the process is banks' reserves with the Bank of England. Banks are paid at Bank Rate on these reserves. The Bank of England conducts short-term OMOs every week (on a Thursday) at Bank Rate. In other words, if banks start running short of reserves, as they may well do if lower interest rates encourage customers to spend more from their accounts, they can borrow at Bank Rate through short-term repos (with a one-week maturity).

The size of the weekly OMO is adjusted to help banks maintain reserves at the target level and reflect variations in the amount of cash withdrawn or deposited in banks. Fluctuations in banknotes in circulation, and hence in banks' reserves, are accepted *within* the week as the reserve target is a weekly *average*.

Although there is usually a shortage of liquidity in the banking system, in some weeks there may be a surplus. To prevent this driving market interest rates down too far, the Bank will invite banks to bid for outright purchase of short-dated Treasury bills (i.e. ones part-way through their life) at prices set by the Bank to reflect Bank Rate: i.e. in this case, at prices *lower* than the market would otherwise set. At such prices, the Bank has no difficulty in selling them and hence in 'mopping up' the surplus liquidity.

At the end of the monthly period between MPC interest rate decisions, the Bank of England conducts a 'fine-tuning' OMO. This is conducted on a Wednesday – the day before the MPC decision on interest rates. The idea is to ensure that banks meet their reserve targets as closely as possible. This OMO could expand or contract liquidity as appropriate.

Longer-term open-market operations

Normally once per month – on a Tuesday at 10 a.m. mid-month – the Bank of England conducts longer-term OMOs. This involves repos at 3-, 6-, 9- and 12-month maturities. In other words, the Bank of England lends money to banks to provide longer-term liquidity.

The rate of interest is market determined. Banks bid for the money and the funds are offered to the successful bidders. The bigger the demand for these funds by banks and the lower the supply by the Bank of England, the higher will be the interest rate that banks must pay. By adjusting the supply, therefore, the Bank of England can influence longer-term interest rates.

Since 2006, the Bank of England has also been willing to make outright purchases of gilts and high-quality foreign-currency government bonds. This was used as a means of offsetting the drying up of liquidity in the credit crunch of 2007–9. Such purchases are normally made monthly on a Monday.

In January 2009, as part of a second bank rescue plan (see Box 28.4) the Treasury agreed that the Bank of England could purchase up to £75 billion of high-quality assets, such as corporate bonds and assets backed under the Credit Guarantee Scheme. This was extended to £125 billion in May, to £175 billion in August and to £200 billion in November 2009. These open-market purchases would have the effect of injecting extra narrow money into the economy. This massively extended the scope of OMOs to boost liquidity in the economy. This deliberate injection of additional narrow money is known as 'quantitative easing' and is examined in Box 30.4.

Assume that the Bank of England wants to raise interest rates. Trace through the process by which it achieves this.

---

security of mortgage and other debt. Normally banks could sell these mortgage assets on the money markets as a means of raising finance. With the credit crunch, however, such markets dried up as lenders became more cautious.

Funding. Rather than focusing on controlling the monetary base (as in the case of the above two techniques), an alternative is for the central bank to alter the overall liquidity position of the banks. An example of this approach is a change, by the central bank, in the balance of funding government debt. To reduce money supply the central bank issues more bonds and fewer bills. Banks' balances with the central bank will be little affected, but to the extent that banks hold fewer bills, there will be a reduction in their liquidity. Funding is thus the conversion of one type of government debt (liquid) into another (illiquid).

Variable minimum reserve ratios. In some countries (such as the USA), banks are required to hold a certain proportion of their assets in liquid form. The assets which count as liquid are known as 'reserve assets'. These include assets such as balances in the central bank, bills of exchange, certificates of deposit and money market loans. The ratio of such assets to total liabilities is known as the minimum reserve ratio. If the central bank raises this ratio (in other words, requires the banks to hold a higher proportion of liquid assets), then banks will have to reduce the amount of credit. The money supply will fall.

> **Definitions**
>
> **Funding**
> Where the authorities alter the balance of bills and bonds for any given level of government borrowing.
>
> **Minimum reserve ratio**
> A minimum ratio of cash (or other specified liquid assets) to deposits (either total or selected) that the central bank requires banks to hold.

Difficulties in controlling money supply

Targets for the growth in broad money were an important part of UK monetary policy from 1976 to 1985. Money targets were then abandoned and have not been used since. The European Central Bank targets the growth of M3 (see Box 30.3), but this is a subsidiary policy to that of setting interest rates in order to keep inflation under control. If, however, a central bank did choose to target money supply as its main monetary policy, how would the policy work?

Assume that money supply is above target and that the central bank wishes to reduce it. It would probably use open-market operations: i.e. it would sell more bonds or bills. The purchasers of the bonds or bills would draw liquidity from the banks. Banks would then supposedly be forced to cut down on the credit they create. But is it as simple as this?

The problem is that banks will normally be unwilling to cut down on loans if people want to borrow – after all, borrowing by customers earns profits for the banks. Banks can always 'top up' their liquidity by borrowing from the central bank and then carry on lending. True, they will have to pay the interest rate charged by the central bank, but they can pass on any rise in the rate to their customers.

The point is that as long as people *want* to borrow, banks and other financial institutions will normally try to find ways of meeting the demand. In other words, in the short run at least, the supply of money is to a large extent demand determined. It is for this reason that central banks prefer to control the *demand* for money by controlling interest rates.

Techniques to control interest rates

The approach to monetary control today in most countries is to focus directly on interest rates. Normally an interest rate change will be announced, and then open-market operations will be conducted by the central bank to ensure that the money supply is adjusted so as to make the announced interest rate the *equilibrium* one. Thus, in Figure 30.3 (on page 690), the central bank might announce a rise in interest rates from r_1 to r_2 and then conduct open-market operations to ensure that the money supply is reduced from Q_1 to Q_2.

Let us assume that the central bank decides to raise interest rates. What does it do? In general, it will seek to keep banks short of liquidity. This will happen automatically on any day when tax payments by banks' customers exceed the money

BOX 30.3 MONETARY POLICY IN THE EUROZONE

The role of the ECB

The European Central Bank (ECB) is based in Frankfurt and is charged with operating the monetary policy of those EU countries that have adopted the euro. Although the ECB has the overall responsibility for the eurozone's monetary policy, the central banks of the individual countries, such as the Bank of France and Germany's Bundesbank, were not abolished. They are responsible for distributing euros and for carrying out the ECB's policy with respect to institutions in their own countries. The whole system of the ECB and the national central banks is known as the European System of Central Banks (ESCB).

In operating the monetary policy of a 'euro economy' roughly the size of the USA, and in being independent from national governments, the ECB's power is enormous and is equivalent to that of the Fed. So what is the structure of this giant on the European stage, and how does it operate?

The structure of the ECB

The ECB has two major decision-making bodies: the Governing Council and the Executive Board.[1]

The Governing Council consists of the members of the Executive Board and the governors of the central banks of each of the eurozone countries. The Council's role is to set the main targets of monetary policy and to take an oversight of the success (or otherwise) of that policy.

The Executive Board consists of a president, a vice-president and four other members. Each serves for an eight-year, non-renewable term. The Executive Board is responsible for implementing the decisions of the Governing Council and for preparing policies for the Council's consideration. Each member of the Executive Board has a responsibility for some particular aspect of monetary policy.

The targets of monetary policy

The overall responsibility of the ECB is to achieve price stability in the eurozone. The target is a rate of inflation below, but close to, 2 per cent over the medium term. It is a weighted average rate for all the members of the eurozone, not a rate that has to be met by every member individually.

The ECB also sets a reference value for the annual growth of M3, the broad measure of the money supply. This was set at $4\frac{1}{2}$ per cent at the launch of the euro in 1999 and was still the same value in 2008. The reference value is not a rigid target, but is used as a guide to whether monetary policy is consistent with long-run price stability. In setting the reference value, three things are taken into account: the target for inflation, assumptions about the rate of growth of GDP (assumed to have a trend growth rate of 2 to $2\frac{1}{2}$ per cent per year) and the velocity of circulation of M3 (assumed to be declining at a rate of between $\frac{1}{2}$ and 1 per cent per year). The reference value is reviewed in December each year.

---

[1] See www.ecb.int/ecb/orga/decisions/govc/html/index.en.html

---

they receive from government expenditure. This excess is effectively withdrawn from banks and ends up in the government's account at the central bank. Even when this does not occur, sales of bills by the central bank will effectively keep the banking system short of liquidity.

This 'shortage' can then be used as a way of forcing through interest rate changes. Banks will obtain the necessary liquidity from the central bank through repos (see pages 620–1) or by selling it back bills. The central bank can *choose the rate of interest to charge* (i.e. the repo rate or the bill rediscount rate). This will then have a knock-on effect on other interest rates throughout the banking system. (See Box 30.2 for more details on just how the Bank of England manipulates interest rates on a day-to-day basis.)

The effectiveness of changes in interest rates

Even though central bank adjustment of the repo rate is the current preferred method of monetary control in most countries, it is not without its difficulties. The problems centre on the nature of the demand for loans. If this demand is (a) unresponsive to interest rate changes or (b) unstable because it is significantly affected by other determinants (such as anticipated income or foreign interest rates), then it will be very difficult to control by controlling the rate of interest.

On the basis of its inflation target and M3 reference value, the ECB then sets the rates of interest. In January 2010, the rates were as follows: 1 per cent for the main 'refinancing operations' of the ESCB (i.e. the minimum rate of interest at which liquidity is offered once per week to 'monetary financial institutions' (MFIs) by the ESCB); a 'marginal lending' rate of 1.75 per cent (for providing overnight support to the MFIs); and a 'deposit rate' of 0.25 per cent (the rate paid to MFIs for depositing overnight surplus liquidity with the ESCB).

Interest rates are set by the Governing Council by simple majority. In the event of a tie, the president has the casting vote.

The operation of monetary policy

The main instrument for keeping the ECB's desired interest rate as the equilibrium rate is open-market operations in government bonds and other recognised assets, mainly in the form of repos. These repo operations are conducted by the national central banks, which must ensure that the repo rate does not rise above the marginal overnight lending rate or below the deposit rate.

The ECB uses four types of open-market operation:

Main refinancing operations. These are short-term repos with a maturity of one week. They take place weekly and are used to maintain liquidity consistent with the chosen ECB interest rate.

Longer-term refinancing operations. These take place monthly and have a maturity of three months. They are to provide additional longer-term liquidity to banks as required at rates determined by the market, not the ECB.

Fine-tuning operations. These can be short-term sales or purchases of short-term assets. They are designed to combat unexpected changes in liquidity and hence to keep money-market rates at the ECB's chosen rate.

Structural operations. These are used as necessary to adjust the amount of liquidity in the eurozone. They can involve either the purchase or sale of various assets.

ECB independence

The ECB is one of the most independent central banks in the world. It has very little formal accountability to elected politicians. Although its president can be called before the European Parliament, the Parliament has virtually no powers to influence the ECB's actions. Also, its deliberations are secret. Unlike meetings of the Bank of England's Monetary Policy Committee, the minutes of the Council meetings are not published.

What are the arguments for and against publishing the minutes of the meetings of the ECB's Governing Council and Executive Board?

Problem of an inelastic demand for loans. If the demand for loans is inelastic (i.e. a relatively steep M_d curve in Figure 30.3), any attempt to reduce demand will involve large rises in interest rates. The problem will be compounded if the demand curve shifts to the right, due, say, to a consumer spending boom. High interest rates lead to the following problems:

- They may discourage investment and hence long-term growth.
- They add to the costs of production, to the costs of house purchase and generally to the cost of living. They are thus cost inflationary.
- They are politically unpopular, since the general public do not like paying higher interest rates on overdrafts, credit cards and mortgages.
- The necessary bond issue to restrain liquidity will commit the government to paying high rates on these bonds for the next 20 years or so.
- High interest rates encourage inflows of money from abroad. This drives up the exchange rate. A higher exchange rate makes domestically produced goods expensive relative to goods made abroad. This can be very damaging for export industries and industries competing with imports. Many firms in the UK have suffered badly in recent years from a high exchange rate, caused partly by higher interest rates in the UK than in the eurozone and the USA.

Evidence suggests that the demand for loans may indeed be quite inelastic. Especially in the short run, many firms and individuals simply cannot reduce their borrowing commitments. What is more, although high interest rates may discourage many firms from taking out long-term fixed-interest loans, some firms may merely switch to shorter-term variable-interest loans.

Problem of an unstable demand. Accurate monetary control requires the central bank to be able to predict the demand curve for money (in Figure 30.3). Only then can they set the appropriate level of interest rates. Unfortunately, the demand curve may shift unpredictably, making control very difficult. The major reason is *speculation*. For example, if people think interest rates will rise and bond prices fall, in the meantime they will demand to hold their assets in liquid form. The demand for money will rise. Alternatively, if people think exchange rates will rise, they will demand the domestic currency while it is still relatively cheap. The demand for money will rise.

It is very difficult for the central bank to predict what people's expectations will be. Speculation depends so much on world political events, rumour and 'random shocks'.

If the demand curve shifts very much, and if it is inelastic, then monetary control will be very difficult. Furthermore, the central bank will have to make frequent and sizeable adjustments to interest rates. These fluctuations can be very damaging to business confidence and may discourage long-term investment.

> **Pause for thought**
>
> *Assume that the central bank announces a rise in interest rates and backs this up with open-market operations. What determines the size of the resulting fall in aggregate demand?*

The net result of an inelastic and unstable demand for money is that substantial interest rate changes may be necessary to bring about the required change in aggregate demand. For example, central banks had to cut interest rates to virtually zero in their attempt to tackle the global recession of the late 2000s. Indeed, as we see in Box 30.4, central banks took to other methods as the room for further interest rate cuts simply disappeared.

Using monetary policy

It is impossible to use monetary policy as a precise means of controlling aggregate demand. It is especially weak when it is pulling against the expectations of firms and consumers and when it is implemented too late. However, if the authorities operate a tight monetary policy firmly enough and long enough, they should eventually be able to reduce lending and aggregate demand. But there will inevitably be time lags and imprecision in the process.

An expansionary monetary policy is even less reliable. If the economy is in recession, no matter how low interest rates are driven or however much the monetary base is expanded, people cannot be forced to borrow if they do not wish to. Firms will not borrow to invest if they predict a continuing recession.

A particular difficulty in using interest rate reductions to expand the economy arises if the repo rate is nearly zero but this is still not enough to stimulate the economy. The problem is that (nominal) interest rates cannot be negative, for clearly nobody would be willing to lend in these circumstances. Japan was in such a situation in the early 2000s. It was caught in what is known as the liquidity trap.

Despite these problems, changing interest rates can be quite effective. After all, they can be changed very rapidly. There are not the time lags of implementation that there are with fiscal policy. Indeed, since the early 1990s, most governments

> **Definition**
>
> **Liquidity trap**
> When interest rates are at their floor and thus any further increases in money supply will not be spent but merely be held in idle balances as people wait for the economy to recover and/or interest rates to rise.

BOX 30.4 QUANTITATIVE EASING

Rethinking monetary policy in hard times

As the economies of the world slid into recession in 2008, central banks became more and more worried that the traditional instrument of monetary policy – controlling interest rates – was insufficient to ward off a slump in demand.

Running out of options?

Interest rates had been cut at an unprecedented rate. Typically central banks have changed interest rates by just a quarter of a percentage point at a time. But in November 2008 the Bank of England cut Bank Rate from 4.5 to 3 per cent and in December to 2 per cent and then by half a percentage point each month to stand at 0.5 per cent by March 2009. The ECB too was making large cuts: from 3.25 to 2.5 per cent in December, to 2 per cent in January. By May it was just 1 per cent.

Central banks were reaching the end of the road for interest rate cuts. The Fed was the first to be in this position. It had cut the target federal funds rate (the overnight rate at which the Fed lends to banks) from 2 to 1.5 per cent in October, to 1 per cent in November and to a range between 0 and 0.25 per cent in December. But you cannot cut nominal rates below zero – otherwise you would be paying people to borrow money, which would be like giving people free money.

The problem was that there was an acute lack of willingness of banks to lend, and firms and consumers to borrow, as people saw the oncoming recession. Banks were more cautious about mortgage lending as the prices of houses fell and unemployment rose, and more cautious about lending to business as the recession deepened. Firms did not want to invest and consumers tried to rein in debt. So the cuts in interest rates were not having enough effect on aggregate demand.

Increasing the money supply

So what were central banks to do? The answer was to increase money supply directly, in a process known as quantitative easing. This involves an aggressive version of open-market operations, where the central bank buys up a range of assets, such as securitised mortgage debt and long-term government bonds. The effect is to pump large amounts of additional cash into the economy in the hope of stimulating demand and, through the process of credit creation, to boost broad money too.

In the USA, in December 2008, at the same time as the federal funds rate was cut to a range of 0 to 0.25 per cent, the Fed embarked on large-scale quantitative easing. It began buying hundreds of billions of dollars worth of mortgage-backed securities on the open market and planned also to buy large quantities of long-term government debt. The Federal Open Market Committee (the interest rate setting body in the USA) said that 'The focus of the committee's policy going forward will be to support the functioning of financial markets and stimulate the economy through open-market operations and other measures that sustain the size of the Federal Reserve's balance sheet at a high level.'

The result was that considerable quantities of new money were injected into the system. This also had the effect of reducing interest rates on the assets purchased by the Fed, thereby stimulating aggregate demand.

In the UK, in January 2009, the government authorised the Bank of England to embark on a programme of quantitative easing. This would entail it purchasing from the private sector on the secondary market a range of high-quality assets, including existing government bonds and various private-sector assets, to help increase the amount of credit available to business.

At its March 2009 meeting, the Bank of England's Monetary Policy Committee decided that it would buy, over the coming months, up to £75 billion of such assets. Given the extent of the economic downturn, however, this target was increased to £125 billion at the May meeting of the MPC; then to £175 billion at the August meeting; then to £200 billion at the November meeting. By January 2010, some £190 billion of assets, mainly government bonds, had been purchased under the scheme.

The aim was directly to increase money supply. In addition, the Monetary Policy Committee was given the power to use asset purchases as an additional means of meeting the inflation target.

The danger of this approach is that in the short run little credit creation may take place. People need to have the confidence to borrow. In the equation $MV = PY$, the rise in (narrow) money supply (M) may be largely offset by a fall in the velocity of circulation (V) (see Chapter 29, page 652). There is also the danger that if this policy is conducted for too long, the growth in money supply may then prove to be excessive, resulting in inflation rising above the target level. It would thus be important for central banks to foresee this and turn the monetary 'tap' off in time.

Would it be appropriate to define the policy of quantitative easing as 'monetarist'?

Definition

Quantitative easing
A deliberate attempt by the central bank to increase the money supply by buying large quantities of securities through open-market operations. These securities could be securitised mortgage and other private-sector debt or government bonds.

or central banks in OECD countries have used interest rate changes as the major means of keeping aggregate demand and inflation under control.

In the UK, the eurozone and many other countries, a target is set for the rate of inflation. As we have seen, in the UK the target is 2 per cent; in the eurozone it is 'close to' 2 per cent. If forecasts suggest that inflation is going to be above the target rate, the government or central bank raises interest rates. The advantage of this is that it sends a very clear message to people that inflation *will* be kept under control. People will therefore be more likely to adjust their expectations accordingly and keep their borrowing in check.

30.3 ATTITUDES TOWARDS DEMAND MANAGEMENT

Debates over the control of demand have shifted ground somewhat in recent years. There is now less debate over the relative merits of fiscal and monetary policy. There is general agreement that a *combination* of fiscal and monetary policies will have a more powerful effect on demand than either used separately.

The debate today is much more concerned with the extent to which governments ought to pursue an active demand management policy or adhere to a set of policy rules.

Those in the Keynesian tradition prefer discretionary policy – changing policy as circumstances change. Those in the monetarist tradition prefer to set firm rules (e.g. targets for inflation, public deficits or growth in the money supply) and then stick to them. The financial crisis of the late 2000s helped to fuel the debate about the *type* and *flexibility* of policy rules and the extent to which governments should have discretion over policy.

The case for rules and policy frameworks

Why should governments commit to rules or design policy frameworks which may involve them giving up control of economic instruments? Well, there are two important arguments against discretionary policy.

Political behaviour. The first concerns the motivation of government. Politicians may attempt to manipulate the economy for their own political purposes – such as the desire to be re-elected. The government, if not constrained by rules, may over-stimulate the economy some time before an election so that growth is strong at election time. After the election, the government strongly dampens the economy to deal with the higher inflation which is now beginning to accelerate, and to create enough slack for another boost in time for the next election.

When politicians behave in this way, they may lose *credibility* for sound economic management. This can lead to higher inflationary expectations, uncertainty and lower long-term investment.

Time lags with discretionary policy. Both fiscal and monetary policies can involve long and variable time lags, which can make the policy at best ineffective and at worst destabilising. Taking the measures before the problem arises, and thus lessening the problem of lags, is no answer since forecasting tends to be unreliable.

By contrast, setting and sticking to rules, and then not interfering further, the government can provide a sound monetary framework in which there is maximum freedom for individual initiative and enterprise, and in which firms are not cushioned from market forces and are therefore encouraged to be efficient. By the government setting a target for a steady reduction in the growth of money supply, or a target for the rate of inflation, and then resolutely sticking to it, people's expectations of inflation will be reduced, thereby making the target easier to achieve.

This sound and stable monetary environment, with no likelihood of sudden contractionary or expansionary fiscal or monetary policy, will encourage firms to take a longer-term perspective and to plan ahead. This could then lead to increased capital investment and raise long-term growth rates.

The optimum situation is for all the major countries to adhere to mutually consistent rules, so that their economies do not get out of line. This will create more stable exchange rates and provide the climate for world growth.

The case for discretion

Many economists, especially those in the Keynesian tradition, reject the argument that rules provide the environment for high and stable growth. Demand, they argue, is subject to many and sometimes violent shocks: e.g. changes in expectations, domestic political events (such as an impending election), world economic factors (such as the world economic recession of 2008–9) or world political events (such as a war). The resulting shifts in injections or withdrawals cause the economy to deviate from a stable full-employment growth path.

Any change in injections or withdrawals will lead to a cumulative effect on national income via the multiplier and accelerator and via changing expectations. These effects take time and interact with each other, and so a process of expansion or contraction can last many months before a turning point is eventually reached.

Since shocks to demand occur at irregular intervals and are of different magnitudes, the economy is likely to experience cycles of irregular duration and of varying intensity.

Given that the economy is inherently unstable and is buffeted around by various shocks, Keynesians argue that the government needs actively to intervene to stabilise the economy. Otherwise, the uncertainty caused by unpredictable fluctuations will be very damaging to investment and hence to long-term economic growth (quite apart from the short-term effects of recessions on output and employment).

Difficulties with choice of target under a rules-based policy

Assume that the government or central bank sets an inflation target. Should it then stick to that rate, come what may? Might not an extended period of relatively low inflation warrant a lower inflation target? The government must at least have the discretion to *change* the rules, even if only occasionally.

Then there is the question of whether success in achieving the target will bring success in achieving other macroeconomic objectives, such as low unemployment and stable economic growth? The problem is that something called Goodhart's Law is likely to apply. The law, named after Charles Goodhart, formerly of the Bank of England, states that attempts to control an *indicator* of a problem may, as a result, make it cease to be a good indicator of the problem.

Goodhart's law. Controlling a symptom (i.e. an indicator) of a problem will not cure the problem. Instead, the indicator will merely cease to be a good indicator of the problem.

Definition

Goodhart's Law
Controlling a symptom of a problem, or only part of the problem, will not cure the problem: it will simply mean that the part that is being controlled now becomes a poor indicator of the problem.

Targeting inflation may make it become a poor indicator of the state of the economy. If people believe that the central bank will be successful in achieving its inflation target, then those expectations will feed into their inflationary expectations, and not surprisingly the target will be met. But that target rate of inflation may now be consistent with both a buoyant and a depressed economy. As we saw for the UK in Figure 29.7, it is possible that the Phillips curve may become *horizontal*.

In extreme cases, as occurred in the first part of 2008, the economy may slow down rapidly and yet cost-push factors cause inflation to rise. Targeting inflation in these circumstances will demand *higher* interest rates, which will help to deepen the recession. Thus achieving the inflation target may not tackle the much more serious problem of creating stable economic growth and an environment which will therefore encourage long-term investment.

Use of a Taylor rule. For this reason, many economists have advocated the use of a Taylor rule,[1] rather than a simple inflation target. A Taylor rule takes *two* objectives into account – (1) inflation and (2) either the rate of economic growth or unemployment – and seeks to get the optimum degree of stability of the two. The degree of importance attached to each of the two objectives can be decided by the government or central bank. The central bank adjusts interest rates when either the rate of inflation diverges from its target or the rate of economic growth (or unemployment) diverges from its sustainable (or equilibrium) level.

Take the case where inflation is above its target level. The central bank following a Taylor rule will raise the rate of interest. It knows, however, that this will reduce economic growth. This, therefore, limits the amount that the central bank is prepared to raise the rate of interest. The more weight it attaches to stabilising inflation, the more it will raise the rate of interest. The more weight it attaches to maintaining stable economic growth, the less it will raise the rate of interest.

Thus the central bank has to trade off inflation stability against real income stability.

Constrained discretion in the UK

Many countries have, in recent times, been operating economic policy within a framework of rules. This is known as constrained discretion.

On being elected in 1997 the UK Labour government set about reforming the frameworks within which fiscal and monetary policies operated.

Fiscal policy. The Labour government set targets for government expenditure, not for just one year, but for a three-year period. It also adopted two operational rules: the golden rule and the sustainable investment rule. These were examined in Box 30.1.

Monetary policy. As far as monetary policy is concerned, this involved granting operational independence to the Bank of England.

> **Definitions**
>
> **Taylor rule**
> A rule adopted by a central bank for setting the rate of interest. It will raise the interest rate if (a) inflation is above target or (b) economic growth is above the sustainable level (or unemployment is below the equilibrium rate). The rule states how much interest rates will be changed in each case.
>
> **Constrained discretion**
> A set of principles or rules within which economic policy operates. These can be informal or enshrined in law.

---

[1] Named after John Taylor, from Stanford University, who proposed that for every 1 per cent that GDP rises above sustainable GDP, real interest rates should be raised by 0.5 percentage points, and that for every 1 per cent that inflation rises above its target level, real interest rates should be raised by 0.5 percentage points (i.e. nominal rates should be raised by 1.5 percentage points).

Figure 30.4 Fan chart of CPI inflation and GDP growth projections (made in 2010 Q3), based on market interest rate expectations

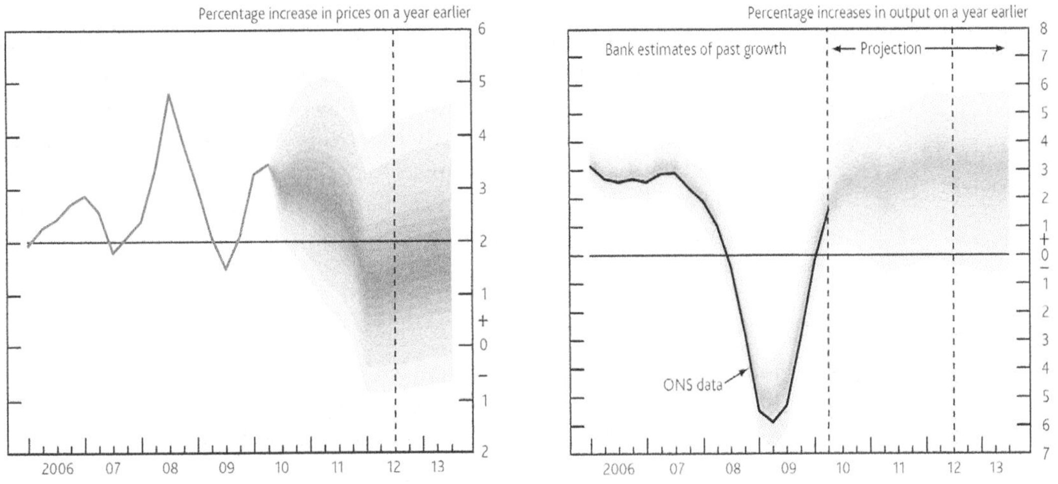

(a) CPI inflation

(b) Real GDP growth

Note: The projections are based on the assumption that the £200 billion made available under the Asset Purchase Programme will be fully used and remain so throughout the period.
Source: *Inflation Report*, August 2010 (Bank of England)

Operational independence for the Bank of England means that it sets interest rates in order to meet a government-set inflation rate target. Since December 2003, the target has been that CPI inflation should be 2 per cent in 24 months' time.

To achieve this target two years in the future, the Bank of England publishes a quarterly *Inflation Report*, which contains projections for inflation for the next three years. These projections assume that interest rates follow market expectations. They form the basis for the Monetary Policy Committee's monthly deliberations. If the projected inflation in 24 months' time is off target, the MPC will change interest rates accordingly.

Two key projections of the MPC are shown in the Bank of England's *Inflation Report*, which is published each quarter. These are shown in Figure 30.4. They are known as 'fan charts'. The first plots the forecast range of inflation. The second plots the forecast range of real GDP growth. In each case, the darkest central band represents a 10 per cent likelihood, as does each of the eight subsequent pairs of lighter areas out from the central band. Thus inflation or GDP growth are considered to have a 90 per cent probability of being within the fan. The bands get wider as the time horizon is extended, indicating increasing uncertainty about the outcome. Also, the less reliable are considered to be the forecasts by the MPC, the wider will be the fan. The dashed line indicates the two-year target point. Thus in quarter 3 of 2010, the 2 per cent inflation target was for quarter 3 of 2012.

Although projections are made for GDP growth, these are to help inform the forecast for inflation. GDP growth is not itself an explicit target.

Another aim of central bank independence is to enhance transparency in policy making. In the UK, transparency is enhanced by the publication of the minutes of the monthly meetings of the MPC, at which interest rates are set. One of the main purposes of transparency is to convince people of the seriousness with which the

Pause for thought

If people believe that the central bank will be successful in keeping inflation on target, does it matter whether a simple inflation rule or a Taylor rule is used? Explain.

Bank of England will adhere to its targets. This, it is hoped, will keep people's *expectations* of inflation low: the lower expected inflation is, the lower will be the actual rate of inflation.

In both fiscal and monetary policy, therefore, rules appeared to have replaced discretion. There was, however, a new form of fine tuning: the frequent adjustment of interest rates, not to smooth out the business cycle, but to make sure that the inflation rule is adhered to. Nevertheless, with automatic fiscal stabilisers still operating, and with interest rate changes to stabilise inflation also having the effect of stabilising aggregate demand, cyclical fluctuations had become less pronounced – at least until 2007. In the 12 years to 2007, annual economic growth did not fall below 1.8 per cent or rise above 3.8 per cent.

Response to the credit crunch

The global crisis, which started in 2007 with the credit crunch and then developed into the worldwide recession of 2008–9, highlighted differences between countries in their monetary and fiscal frameworks. It also raised the question of whether rules should be abandoned – at least in exceptional circumstances.

Monetary policy responses. In 2007–8, many countries were faced with a possible return of stagflation (low or no growth accompanied by rapidly rising prices). World food and other commodity prices were rising rapidly. This supply-side shock meant that inflation rates rose. For example, in the UK by September 2008, the annual CPI inflation rate had reached 5.2 per cent while general food prices were rising at an annual rate in excess of 10 per cent. To meet their inflationary target, central banks were under pressure to raise interest rates. But, to avert a recession they were under pressure to cut them.

Eventually, with confidence in the banking system plummeting and inter-bank markets virtually frozen, the Bank of England (along with several other central banks) began cutting interest rates. At least now the rate of inflation was forecast to be below 2 per cent in 24 months' time. The Bank of England reduced the Bank Rate from 5 per cent by September 2008 to just 0.5 per cent in March 2009. In addition, as we saw in Box 28.4, massive amounts of liquidity and capital were pumped into the banking system to stimulate lending and hence aggregate demand.

But despite general agreement that both inflation and GDP were falling, the extent and speed of the interest rates cuts varied across countries. In part, this reflects differences in the frameworks within which central banks operate.

Fiscal policy responses. The extent of the downturn put governments under pressure to give their economies a fiscal stimulus. In the UK, with the current budget already in deficit (see Box 30.1), the government was in danger of breaching its golden rule and thus would seem to have limited scope for increased expenditure or tax cuts to stimulate aggregate demand.

But the problem was seen to be too serious to stick to rules for rules sake. The golden rule would have to be abandoned – at least temporarily. As Box 30.1 illustrates, fiscal policy was relaxed with a package of tax cuts and increases in government expenditure, though increases in taxes further down the line were pre-announced. Therefore, the golden and sustainable investments rules were to be temporarily abandoned. They were replaced with more general principles, known as temporary operating rules, for both budget balances and the stock of government debt, which would apply once the economy had emerged from the downturn.

While the economic downturn of the 2000s did not lead to the total abandonment of rules, it did lead many countries to soften their implementation of constrained discretion. In the UK there has been considerable debate about how quickly firm constraint should be reintroduced. The Coalition government wants to reduce the deficit quickly through substantial cuts in government expenditure and some rise in taxation, arguing that this is necessary to avoid a loss of confidence by international financiers. The Labour opposition argues that rapid and large-scale cuts risk driving the economy back into recession, with too little aggregate demand from the private sector and exports to compensate for the reduction in demand from the public sector

SUMMARY

1a The government's fiscal policy will determine the size of government budget deficits or surpluses.

1b Automatic fiscal stabilisers are tax revenues that rise and benefits that fall as national income rises. They have the effect of reducing the size of the multiplier and thus reducing cyclical upswings and downswings.

1c Discretionary fiscal policy is where the government deliberately changes taxes or government expenditure in order to alter the level of aggregate demand. Changes in government expenditure on goods and services will have a full multiplier effect. Changes in taxes and benefits will have a smaller multiplier effect as some of the tax/benefit changes will merely affect other withdrawals and thus have a smaller net effect on consumption of domestic product.

1d There are problems in predicting the magnitude of the effects of discretionary fiscal policy. Expansionary fiscal policy can act as a pump primer and stimulate increased private expenditure, or it can crowd out private expenditure. The extent to which it acts as a pump primer depends crucially on business confidence – something that is very difficult to predict beyond a few weeks or months. The extent of crowding out depends on monetary conditions and the government's monetary policy.

1e There are five possible time lags involved with fiscal policy: the time lag before the problem is diagnosed, the lag between diagnosis and new measures being announced, the lag between announcement and implementation, the lag while the multiplier and accelerator work themselves out, and the lag before consumption fully responds to new economic circumstances.

1f In recent years, many governments preferred a more passive approach towards fiscal policy. Targets were set for one or more measures of the public-sector finances, and then taxes and government expenditure were adjusted so as to keep to the target.

1g Nevertheless, in extreme circumstances, as occurred in 2008/9, governments were prepared to relax rules and give a fiscal stimulus to their economies.

2a Control of the growth of the money supply over the longer term will normally involve governments attempting to restrict the size of the budget deficit. This will be difficult to do, however, in a period of recession.

2b In the short term, the government can use monetary policy to restrict the growth in aggregate demand in one of three ways: (a) reducing money supply directly, (b) reducing the demand for money by raising interest rates, or (c) rationing credit. Credit rationing has not been used in recent years.

2c The money supply can be reduced directly by using open-market operations. This involves selling more government securities and thereby reducing banks' reserves when their customers pay for them from their bank accounts. Alternatively, the central bank can reduce the amount it is prepared to lend to banks (other than as a last-resort measure). Or it could use funding, by increasing the sale of bonds relative to bills, thereby reducing banks' liquid assets. Finally, it could operate a system of variable minimum reserve ratios. Increasing these would force banks to cut back on the amount of credit they create.

2d The money supply is difficult to control precisely, however, and even if it is successfully controlled, there then arises the problem of severe fluctuations in interest rates if the demand for money fluctuates and is relatively inelastic.

2e The current method of control involves the Bank of England's Monetary Policy Committee announcing the interest rate and then the Bank of England bringing this rate about by its operations in the repo and discount markets. It keeps banks short of liquidity, and then supplies them with liquidity largely through gilt repos, at the chosen interest rate (gilt repo rate). This then has a knock-on effect on interest rates throughout the economy.

2f Nevertheless there are problems with this approach too. With an inelastic demand for loans, there may have to be substantial changes in interest rates in order to bring the required change in aggregate demand. What is more, controlling aggregate demand through interest rates is made even more difficult by fluctuations in the demand for money. These fluctuations are made more severe by speculation against changes in interest rates, exchange rates, the rate of inflation, etc.

2g Nevertheless, controlling interest rates is a way of responding rapidly to changing forecasts, and can be an important signal to markets that inflation will be kept under control, especially when, as in the UK and the eurozone, there is a firm target for the rate of inflation.

3a The case against discretionary policy is that it involves unpredictable time lags that can make the policy destabilising. Also, the government may *ignore* the long-run adverse consequences of policies designed for short-run political gain.

3b The case in favour of rules is that they help to reduce inflationary expectations and thus create a stable environment for investment and growth.

3c The case against sticking to money supply or inflation rules is that they may cause severe fluctuations in interest rates and thus create a less stable economic environment for business planning.

3d Although perfect fine tuning may not be possible, Keynesians argue that the government must have the discretion to change its policy as circumstances demand.

3e The UK Labour government, elected in 1997, enshrined in law monetary and fiscal frameworks which involved constraining some of its discretion over economic policy. This included making the Bank of England independent. This now targets a 2 per cent rate of inflation, and adjusts interest rates in order to meet that target. To meet its Code for Fiscal Stability, the UK government set a golden rule to balance its current (as opposed to capital) budget over the course of the business cycle.

3f Many countries have pursued a policy of constrained discretion. This came under increasing pressure in 2008 with rising inflation and falling growth. Given the changing economic environment in which we live, rules adopted in the past may no longer be suitable for the present.

REVIEW QUESTIONS

1 'The existence of a budget deficit or a budget surplus tells us very little about the stance of fiscal policy.' Explain and discuss.

2 Adam Smith remarked in *The Wealth of Nations* concerning the balancing of budgets, 'What is prudence in the conduct of every private family can scarce be folly in that of a great kingdom.' What problems might there be if the government decided to follow a balanced budget approach to its spending?

3 What factors determine the effectiveness of discretionary fiscal policy?

4 Why is it difficult to use fiscal policy to 'fine tune' the economy?

5 When the Bank of England announces that it is putting up interest rates, how will it achieve this, given that interest rates are determined by demand and supply?

6 How does the Bank of England attempt to achieve the target rate of inflation of 2 per cent? What determines its likelihood of success in meeting the target?

7 Imagine you were called in by the government to advise on whether it should adopt a policy of targeting the money supply. What advice would you give and how would you justify the advice?

8 Imagine you were called in by the government to advise on whether it should attempt to prevent cyclical fluctuations by the use of fiscal policy. What advice would you give and how would you justify the advice?

9 What do you understand by the term 'constrained discretion'? Illustrate your answer with reference to the UK and the eurozone.

10 Is there a compromise between purely discretionary policy and adhering to strict targets?

11 Under what circumstances would adherence to an inflation target lead to (a) more stable interest rates, (b) less stable interest rates than pursuing discretionary demand management policy?

Chapter 31

Supply-side policy

Business issues covered in this chapter

- How can supply-side policy influence business and the economy?
- What types of supply-side policy can be pursued and what is their effectiveness?
- What will be the impact on business of a policy of tax cuts?
- How can the government encourage increased competition?
- What is the best way of tackling regional problems and encouraging business investment in relatively deprived areas?
- What is meant by 'industrial policy' and what forms can it take?

31.1 SUPPLY-SIDE PROBLEMS

In considering economic policy up to this point we have focused our attention on the demand side of the economy, where unemployment and slow growth are the result of a lack of aggregate demand, and where inflation and a balance of trade deficit are the result of excessive aggregate demand. Many of the causes of these problems, however, lie on the *supply side* and, as such, require an alternative policy approach.

If successful, **supply-side policies** will shift the aggregate supply curve to the right, thus increasing output for any given level of prices (or reducing the price level for any given level of output).

Effective supply-side initiatives increase an economy's *potential output*: the economy's output when firms are operating at normal levels of capacity utilisation.

> **Definition**
>
> **Supply-side policies**
> Government policies that attempt to influence aggregate supply directly, rather than through aggregate demand.

But, more than this, economists and policy-makers are interested in how supply-side policies can raise the rate at which the level of potential output grows over time. Therefore, supply-side policies can be evaluated on their ability to affect an economy's long-run economic *growth*.

The quantity and productivity of factors of production

The aggregate supply curve is fundamentally related to an economy's factors of production (i.e. its resources, such as labour and capital). Therefore, policies which influence the *quantities* of factors employed and their *productivity* constitute supply-side policies. The quantity and productivity of factors of production are key supply-side variables.

The labour market

> **Pause for thought**
>
> *How can increasing the effectiveness of labour improve both the productivity of labour and the productivity of capital?*

Consider first the labour market. Can policies be designed, for instance, which over time will raise the productivity or effectiveness of the labour force? Can policies be put in place which will make workers more responsive to job opportunities? And how long will it take for such policies to be effective?

Supply-side policies can also be used to reduce unemployment. In section 26.3 we introduced the concept of equilibrium unemployment: the difference between those who would like to work at the current wage rate and those willing and able to take a job. We saw how this is caused by various rigidities or imperfections in the market. There is a mismatching of aggregate supply and demand, and vacancies are not filled despite the existence of unemployment. Perhaps workers have the wrong qualifications, or are poorly motivated, or are living a long way away from the job, or are simply unaware of the jobs that are vacant. Generally, the problem is that labour is not sufficiently mobile, either occupationally or geographically, to respond to changes in the job market. Labour supply for particular jobs is too inelastic.

Supply-side policies might look to increasing labour market flexibility, to providing better job information or to supporting retraining. Alternatively, they may aim to make employers more adaptable and willing to operate within existing labour constraints.

Investment

For decades, the UK has had a lower level of investment relative to national income than other industrialised countries. This is illustrated in Table 31.1. In particular, investment by the private sector has been weak by international standards: a trend that seems to have persisted over four decades.

> **Pause for thought**
>
> *How can the UK's low level of investment relative to national income be explained?*

To some extent the UK's poor investment performance has been offset by the fact that wage rates have been lower than in competing countries. This has at least made the UK relatively attractive to inward investment, especially by Japanese, Korean and US companies seeking to set up production plants within the EU.

The poor performance of UK manufacturing firms has resulted in a growing import penetration of the UK market. Imports of manufactured products have grown more rapidly than UK manufactured exports, and since 1983 the UK has been a net importer of manufactured products.

Table 31.1 Gross fixed capital formation as a percentage of GDP: 1970–2009

	1970s		1980s		1990s		2000s	
	General govt	Private	General govt	Private	General govt	Private	General govt	Private
Belgium	4.3	19.0	3.2	15.8	1.8	18.1	1.7	19.0
Canada	3.6	19.1	2.9	18.8	2.6	16.5	2.9	18.1
Denmark	3.5	11.9	2.2	17.3	1.8	16.9	1.8	18.4
Germany	4.0	18.8	2.8	17.7	2.3	19.7	1.6	17.0
Netherlands	4.5	19.4	3.5	17.9	3.1	18.6	3.4	16.5
UK	4.2	15.7	2.2	16.3	1.8	15.4	1.8	14.8
USA	2.6	16.5	2.3	17.0	2.4	15.3	2.8	15.2

Note: Figures for 2009 are based on forecasts; figures for Germany are for West Germany prior to 1991.
Source: based on data in the annual macro-economic database [AMECO] of the European Commission's Directorate General for Economic and Financial Affairs

Of course, it might not be just the *quantity* of investment that matters, but also the *type* and *quality* of that investment. Increasingly the debate concerning the drivers of economic growth has been concerned with what influences the rate of technological progress. For instance, can countries achieve higher rates of growth by investing in 'cutting-edge' technologies or by raising the shares of national income devoted to education, training and research and development? Some economists argue that under certain conditions new innovations and new ideas will result in further new innovations and ideas. A key question is what policies can best achieve the conditions for the most effective propagation of innovation and technological progress.

Some economists believe that the UK's low-investment economy highlights the need for more government intervention, especially in the fields of education and training, research and development, and the provision of infrastructure. This has been the approach in many countries, including France, Germany and Japan.

Inflation and supply-side policies

Supply-side policies can impact on prices too. For instance, if inflation is caused by cost-push pressures, supply-side policy can help to reduce these cost pressures in at least two ways:

- by encouraging more *competition* in the supply of labour and/or goods and services – perhaps through reducing the power of unions and/or firms (e.g. by anti-monopoly legislation);
- by encouraging increases in *productivity* through the retraining of labour, or by investment grants to firms, or by tax incentives, etc.

Types of supply-side policy

Supply-side policies can take various forms. Section 31.2 examines *market-orientated* supply-side policies. These policies focus on ways of 'freeing up' the market, such as encouraging private enterprise, risk taking and competition; policies that provide incentives and reward initiative, hard work and productivity.

Then, in section 31.3, we look at *interventionist* supply-side policies. These focus on means of counteracting the deficiencies of the free market.

BOX 31.1 GETTING INTENSIVE WITH CAPITAL

How quickly does it grow?

Do we really understand what is meant by capital? Do we really know what a country's capital stock includes?

In this box we take a look at two issues relating to capital. First, we consider what counts as capital in a country's national accounts. Second, we compare the growth of the capital stock in the UK and France and then see how this compares with the rates of economic growth in the two countries.

What is capital?

In a country's national accounts, capital consists of non-financial *fixed assets*. It does not include goods and services transformed or used up in the course of production; these are known as *intermediate goods and services*.

By focusing on the purchase of fixed assets, capital in the national accounts may be seen by some as being quite narrowly defined. For instance, some expenditures relating to staff development and to research and development are excluded. On the other hand, capital stock figures value parts of the country's infrastructure, such as its road, rail and telecommunications network. Further, it values the country's social capital, such as its school buildings, libraries and hospital building.

A country's stock of fixed assets can be valued at its replacement cost, regardless of its age: this is its *gross* value. It can also be valued at its written-down value, known as its *net* value. The net value takes into account the *consumption of capital* which occurs through wear and tear (depreciation) or when capital becomes naturally obsolescent.

The table shows that the estimated *net* capital stock of the UK in 2008 was £3.01 trillion. To put this into context, this is roughly 2.1 times the value of GDP.

The table shows that there are five broad categories of fixed assets. The largest of these by value is *dwellings*, which includes houses, bungalows and flats. You might question why we include dwellings, but residential housing does yield rental incomes for landlords and, more generally, provides all of us with important consumption services, most notably shelter.

The second largest component by value is *other buildings and works*. This includes buildings, other than dwellings, and most civil engineering and construction work. It will include structures such as factories, schools and hospitals and the country's railway track.

The third largest component is *plant, machinery and cultivated assets*. It includes electricity and telephone lines as well as tractors and fork-lift trucks, while cultivated assets include livestock and forests. The next smallest component by value is *vehicles*. This includes lorries for haulage, buses and railway rolling stock for transportation and all civil aircraft. But the smallest component of all is *intangible assets*. This includes computer software, original works of literature or art and mineral exploration.

UK net capital stock, 2008

Type	£ billions	% of fixed assets	Ratio to GDP
Dwellings	1,126.9	40.4	0.84
Other buildings and works	1,150.1	38.2	0.80
Plant, machinery and cultivated assets	508.9	16.9	0.35
Vehicles	83.0	2.8	0.06
Intangible assets	51.9	1.7	0.04
All fixed assets	3,010.8	100.0	2.08

Source: based on data from *Capital Stocks Tables for Publication* (National Statistics) and *UK Output, Income and Expenditure* (National Statistics)

Regional imbalances. It is all too easy to view supply-side policies and initiatives solely in terms of *national* objectives. But, there are often marked differences in incomes, unemployment rates and other measures of economic and social well-being *within* a country. Therefore, both national governments and international bodies, such as the EU, may adopt supply-side projects and initiatives that help to tackle regional inequalities. We look at regional policy in the final section of this chapter.

> **Pause for thought**
>
> Why might it take time for the benefits of supply-side policies to become evident?

Net capital per person employed in France and the UK

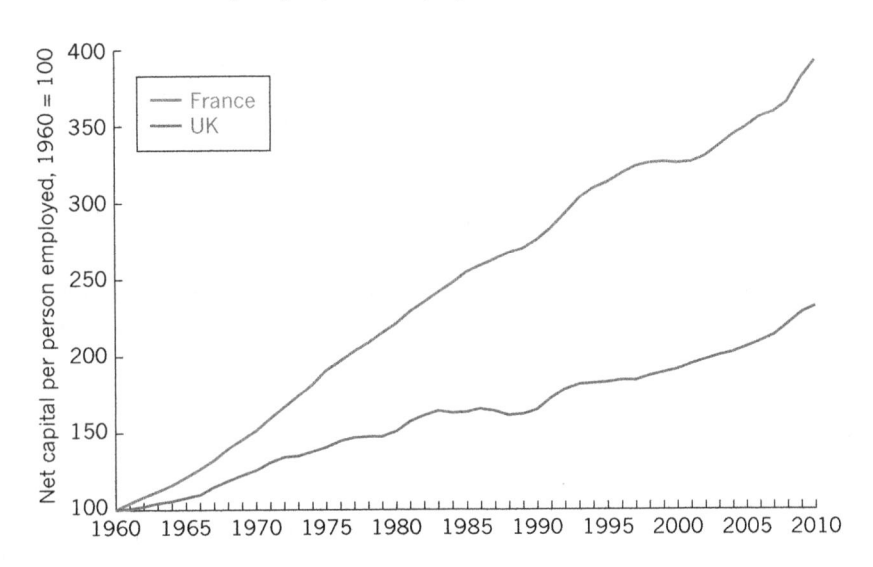

How does capital grow? The UK and France compared

In models of economic growth an important measure of how much capital is being used is the amount of capital per person employed (per worker). This is also known as *capital intensity*. In the chart we plot the amounts of capital per worker in the UK and France since 1960. The series for each country is presented as an index (1960 = 100) so that we can compare across the two countries without worrying about local currencies. In both countries capital intensity has increased. Therefore, there is capital accumulation in both the UK and France.

The rate of capital accumulation in the two countries is, however, very different. If we compare the amount of capital per worker in 2009 with that in 1960, it is 3.75 times higher in France but only 2.25 times higher in the UK.

Generally, the higher the level of capital per worker, the greater will be the level of output (real GDP) per worker. If we compare the amount of output per worker in France and the UK in 2009 with that in 1960, we find that it is 3.6 times higher in France compared to 2.6 times higher in the UK.

A note of caution is necessary at this point. While there appears to be a statistical association between capital accumulation and economic growth, it is the role of economic theory to explore the relationship between the two. As you will see in this chapter, there is considerable debate about this relationship!

1 How does human capital (the skills and expertise of the workforce) fit into a national account's definition of capital?
2 Does the composition of a country's capital affect its long-run economic growth?

MARKET-ORIENTATED SUPPLY-SIDE POLICIES

Radical market-orientated supply-side policies were first adopted in the early 1980s by the Thatcher government in the UK and the Reagan administration in the USA, but were subsequently copied by other right and centre-right governments around the world. The essence of these supply-side policies is to encourage and reward individual enterprise and initiative, and to reduce the role of government; to put

Reducing government expenditure

The desire of many governments to cut government expenditure is not just to reduce the size of the public-sector deficit and hence reduce the growth of money supply; it is also an essential ingredient of their supply-side strategy.

In many countries the size of the public sector, relative to national income, grew substantially over the last century. For instance, in the UK it rose from around 10 per cent at the start of the century to around 50 per cent in the early 1980s (see Table 31.2). A major aim of many governments throughout the world has been to reverse this trend. The public sector is portrayed by some as more bureaucratic and less efficient than the private sector. What is more, it is claimed that a growing proportion of public money has been spent on administration and other 'non-productive' activities, rather than on the direct provision of goods and services.

Two things are needed, it is argued: (a) a more efficient use of resources within the public sector and (b) a reduction in the size of the public sector. This would allow private investment to increase with no overall rise in aggregate demand. Thus the supply-side benefits of higher investment could be achieved without the demand-side costs of higher inflation.

In practice, governments have found it very difficult to cut their expenditure without cutting services and the provision of infrastructure.

> **Pause for thought**
>
> *Why might a recovering economy (and hence a fall in government expenditure on social security benefits) make the government feel even more concerned to make discretionary cuts in government expenditure?*

Tax cuts

The imposition of taxation can distort a variety of choices that individuals make. Changes to the rates of taxation can lead individuals to substitute one activity for another. Three commonly referred to examples in the context of aggregate supply are:

- taxation of labour income and its impact on labour supply (including hours worked and choice of occupation);

Table 31.2 Total general government expenditure as a percentage of GDP

	1970–4	1975–9	1980–4	1984–9	1990s	2000s
Belgium	42.4	51.3	59.4	55.5	52.3	50.1
Canada	36.9	40.9	45.3	46.6	48.3	40.4
Denmark	41.9	46.5	56.3	54.8	57.6	53.4
Germany	41.2	47.7	46.8	44.5	47.5	46.5
Netherlands	44.7	51.6	57.7	56.7	51.6	45.8
UK	43.3	47.3	50.0	43.2	42.3	43.3
USA	32.3	33.2	35.7	36.6	36.7	37.3

Note: Figures for 2009 based on forecasts; total expenditure in this table includes transfer payments as well as expenditure on final goods and services.
Source: based on data in the annual macro-economic database *[AMECO]* of the European Commission's Directorate General for Economic and Financial Affairs

- taxation of interest income earned on financial products (savings) and its impact on the funds available for investment;
- taxation of firms' profits and its impact on capital expenditure by firms.

Over time, the UK has witnessed a decline in the marginal rates of taxation associated with each of these cases. For example, in 1979, the standard rate of income tax in the UK was 33 per cent and the top rate was 83 per cent. In 2009 the standard rate was only 20 per cent and the top rate was only 40 per cent. In 1983 the main rate of corporation tax in the UK stood at 52 per cent. By 2009 this was 28 per cent.

Substitution effects of tax cuts. The argument for reducing tax rates on incomes and profits is that it contributes to higher levels of economic output. Specifically, it encourages an increased supply of labour hours, more moneys invested with financial institutions and more capital expenditure by firms than would otherwise be the case. The reason is that tax cuts increase the return on such activities. In other words, there is a *substitution effect* inducing more of these beneficial activities. In the case of labour, people are encouraged to substitute work for leisure as their after-tax wage rate is now higher.

Income effects of tax cuts. However, in each case there is a counteracting incentive. This is the *income effect*. Tax cuts increase the returns to working, saving and undertaking capital expenditure. This means that less of each activity needs to be undertaken to generate the same income flow as before. Take the case of labour, if a tax cut increases your hourly take-home pay, you may feel that you can afford to work fewer hours.

Because economic theory offers no firm conclusions as to the benefit of tax cuts, economists and policy-makers often look to empirical evidence for guidance. In the case of whether or not tax cuts encourage people to work longer hours, the evidence suggests that the substitution and income effects just about cancel each other out. Anyway, for many people there is no such choice in the short run. There is no chance of doing overtime or working a shorter week. In the long run, there may be some flexibility in that people can change jobs.

> **Pause for thought**
>
> *If taxes as a proportion of national income have risen since 1979, does this mean that there can have been no positive incentive effects of the various tax measures taken by first the Conservative and then the Labour governments?*

Reducing the power of labour

The argument here is that if labour costs to employers are reduced, their profits will probably rise. This could encourage and enable more investment and hence economic growth. If the monopoly power of labour is reduced, then cost-push inflation will also be reduced.

The Thatcher government took a number of measures to curtail the power of unions. These included introducing the right of employees not to join unions, preventing workers taking action other than against their direct employers, and enforcing secret ballots on strike proposals (see pages 374–5). It set a lead in resisting strikes in the public sector.

As labour markets have become more flexible, with increased part-time working and short-term contracts, and as the process of globalisation has exposed more companies to international competition, so this has further eroded the power of labour in many sectors of the economy (see section 18.7).

Reducing welfare

New classical economists claim that a major cause of unemployment is the small difference between the welfare benefits of the unemployed and the take-home pay of the employed. This causes voluntary unemployment (i.e. frictional unemployment). People are caught in a 'poverty trap': if they take a job, they lose their benefits.

A dramatic solution to this problem would be to cut unemployment benefits. A major problem with this approach, however, is that, with changing requirements

---

BOX 31.2 PRODUCTIVITY AND ECONOMIC GROWTH

The key to a better standard of living?

A country's potential output depends on the productivity of its factors of production. There are several commonly used measures of productivity. One measure is output per worker. This is the most straightforward measure to calculate. All that is required is a measure of total output and employment.

A second measure is output per hour worked. This has the advantage that it is not influenced by the *number* of hours worked. So for an economy like the UK, with a very high percentage of part-time workers on the one hand, and long average hours worked by full-time employees on the other, such a measure would be more accurate in gauging worker efficiency.

The chart shows comparative productivity levels of the G7 group of leading industrialised economies in 2008 using GDP per worker and GDP per hour worker. Using GDP per worker, productivity is highest in the USA (32 per cent higher than the UK) and lowest in Japan (12 per cent lower than the UK). When GDP per hours worked is used, productivity is again highest in the USA (21 per cent higher than the UK), and lowest in Japan (15 per cent lower). Note on this measure, however, that both France and Germany score relatively higher than on the output per worker measure as the working week is shorter in these two countries. The USA is not so high on this measure as Americans work relatively long hours. Nonetheless, on both measures the UK is somewhat below the average for the G7.

Whilst there remains a productivity gap between the UK and the G7 group, this gap is closing. The following table shows that the UK has experienced the fastest productivity growth of all G7 countries. Between 1990 and 2008 GDP per worker grew by 39 per cent and GDP per head by 49 per cent.

Productivity in selected countries, 2008 (UK = 100)

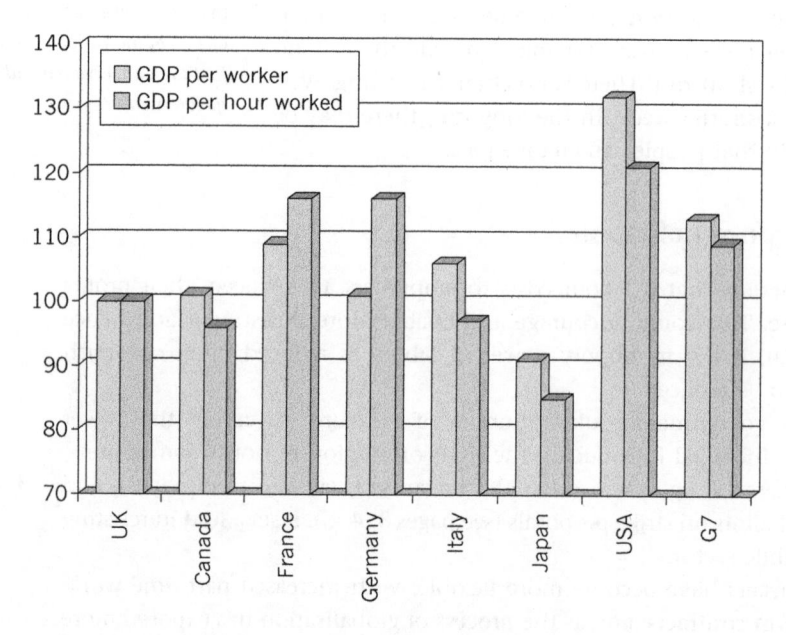

Source: based on data in *International Comparisons of Productivity* (National Statistics)

for labour skills, many of the redundant workers from the older industries are simply not qualified for new jobs that are created. What is more, the longer people are unemployed, the more demoralised they become. Employers would probably be prepared to pay only very low wages to such workers. To persuade these unemployed people to take low-paid jobs, the welfare benefits would have to be slashed. A 'market' solution to the problem, therefore, may be a very cruel solution. A fairer solution would be an interventionist policy: a policy of retraining labour.

Productivity growth since 1990, percentage

	GDP per worker	GDP per hour worked
UK	39	49
Canada	23	25
France	20	31
Germany	25	35
Italy	16	20
Japan	20	35
USA	35	37
G7	30	37
G7 excl. UK	29	36

Source: based on data in *International Comparisons of Productivity* (National Statistics)

The two measures of productivity considered so far focus solely on the productivity of labour. In order to account directly for the productivity of capital, we need to consider the growth in *total* factor productivity (TFP). Total factor productivity (TFP) tries to measure that part of output growth not caused by changes in the quantity of factors used. Changes in total factor productivity over time provide a good indicator of technical progress.

The importance of productivity

The faster the growth in productivity, the faster is likely to be the country's rate of economic growth. Any government seeking to raise the long-term growth rate, therefore, must find ways of stimulating productivity growth.

On what does the growth of productivity depend? There are seven main determinants:

- private investment in new physical capital (machinery and buildings) and in research and development (R&D);
- public investment in education, R&D and infrastructure;
- training and the development of labour skills;
- innovation and the application of new technology;
- the organisation and management of factors of production;
- the rate of entry of new firms into markets: generally such firms will have higher productivity than existing firms;
- the business environment in which firms operate. Is there competition over the quality and design of products? Is there competitive pressure to reduce costs?

Identify some policies a government could pursue to stimulate productivity growth through each of the above means.

But what are the mechanisms whereby productivity growth feeds through into growth of the economy?

- The capacity of the economy to grow will increase as productivity improvements extend potential output.
- Productivity improvements will drive prices downwards, stimulating demand and actual growth.
- With high returns from their investment, investors might be prepared to embark upon new projects and enterprises, stimulating yet further productivity growth and higher output.
- Some of the returns from firms' investments, such as from innovations in products and processes, may be captured by other firms. In turn, these firms may look to further develop these products and processes, perhaps in order to gain a competitive advantage over their rivals. In so doing, they stimulate technological progress and productivity growth.
- As labour productivity rises, so wages are likely to rise. The higher wages will lead to higher consumption, and hence, via the multiplier and accelerator, to higher output and higher investment, thereby stimulating further advances in productivity.
- In the longer term, businesses experiencing higher productivity growth would expect their lower costs, and hence enhanced competitiveness, to allow them to gain greater market share. This will encourage further investment and productivity growth.

It is clear that the prosperity of a nation rests upon its ability to improve its productivity. The more successful it is in doing this, the greater will be its rate of economic growth.

What could explain the differences in productivity between the countries in the chart? What do you think governments can do to help businesses raise productivity levels?

Another alternative is to make the payment of unemployment benefits conditional on the recipient making a concerted effort to find a job. In the jobseeker's allowance introduced in the UK in 1996, claimants must be available for and actively seeking work and must complete a Jobseeker's Agreement, which sets out the types of work the person is willing to do and the plan to find work. Payment can be refused if the claimant refuses to accept jobs offered. Similarly, under the employment and support allowance, which replaced incapacity benefit in 2006, those assessed as 'capable of work with help' are assisted in finding work by employment advisers. Anyone refusing such help has their benefits reduced.

Policies to encourage competition

If the government can encourage more competition, this should have the effect of increasing national output and reducing inflation. Five major types of policy were pursued under this heading.

Privatisation. If privatisation simply involves the transfer of a natural monopoly to private hands (e.g. the water companies), the scope for increased competition is limited. However, where there is genuine scope for increased competition (e.g. in the supply of gas and electricity), privatisation can lead to increased efficiency, more consumer choice and lower prices.

Alternatively, privatisation can involve the introduction of private services into the public sector (e.g. private contractors providing cleaning services in hospitals, or refuse collection for local authorities). Private contractors may compete against each other for the franchise. This may well lower the cost of provision of these services, but the quality of provision may suffer unless closely monitored. The effects on unemployment are uncertain. Private contractors may offer lower wages and thus may use more labour. But if they are trying to supply the service at minimum cost, they are likely to employ less labour.

Deregulation. This involves the removal of monopoly rights: again, largely in the public sector. The deregulation of the bus industry in the 1980s, opening it up to private operators, is a good example of this initiative. An example in the private sector was the 'Big Bang' on the Stock Exchange in 1986. Under this the monopoly power of 'jobbers' to deal in stocks and shares on the Stock Exchange was abolished. In addition, stockbrokers now compete with each other in the commission rates they charge, and online share dealing has become commonplace.

Introducing market relationships into the public sector. This is where the government tries to get different departments or elements within a particular part of the public sector to 'trade' with each other, so as to encourage competition and efficiency. The best-known examples are within health and education.

The process often involves 'devolved budgeting'. For example, in the UK, under the local management of schools scheme (LMS), schools have become self-financing. Rather than the local authority meeting the bill for teachers' salaries, the schools have to manage their own budgets. The objective is to encourage them to cut costs, thereby reducing the burden on council tax payers. However, one result is that schools have tended to appoint inexperienced (and hence cheaper) teachers rather than those who can bring the benefits of their years of teaching.

Another example is in the National Health Service. In 2003, the UK government introduced a system of 'foundation trusts'. Hospitals can apply for foundation trust status. If successful, they are given much greater financial autonomy in terms of purchasing, employment and investment decisions. By 2009, there were 120 foundation trusts. Critics argue that funds have been diverted to foundation hospitals away from the less well-performing hospitals where greater funding could help that performance.

The Private Finance Initiative (PFI). This is where a private company, after a competitive tender, is contracted by a government department or local authority to finance and build a project, such as a new road or a prison. The government then pays the company to maintain and/or run it, or simply rents the assets from the company. The public sector thus becomes a purchaser of services rather than a direct provider itself.

The aim of these 'public–private partnerships' (PPPs) is to introduce competition (through the tendering process) and private-sector expertise into the provision of public services (see Web Case K.13). It is hoped that the extra burden to the taxpayer of the private-sector profits will be more than offset by gains in efficiency. Critics, however, claim that PPPs have resulted in poorer quality of provision and that cost control has often been poor, resulting in a higher burden for the taxpayer in the long term.

Free trade and capital movements. The opening up of international trade and investment is central to a market-orientated supply-side policy. One of the first measures of the Thatcher government (in October 1979) was to remove all controls on the purchase and sale of foreign currencies, thereby permitting the free inflow and outflow of capital, both long term and short term. Most other industrialised countries also removed or relaxed exchange controls during the 1980s and early 1990s.

The Single European Act of 1987, which came into force in 1993, was another example of international liberalisation. As we saw in section 25.3, it created a 'single market' in the EU: a market without barriers to the movement of goods, services, capital and labour.

INTERVENTIONIST SUPPLY-SIDE POLICIES 31.3

The basis of the case for government intervention is that the free market is likely to provide too little research and development, training and investment.

There are potentially large external benefits from research and development. Firms investing in developing and improving products, and especially firms engaged in more general scientific research, may produce results that provide benefits to many other firms. Thus the *social* rate of return on investment may be much higher than the *private* rate of return. Investment that is privately unprofitable for a firm may therefore still be economically desirable for the nation.

Similarly, investment in training may continue yielding benefits to society that are lost to the firms providing the training when the workers leave.

Investment often involves risks. Firms may be unwilling to take those risks, since the costs of possible failure may be too high. When looked at nationally, however, the benefits of investment might well have substantially outweighed the costs, and thus it would have been socially desirable for firms to have taken the risk. Successes would have outweighed failures.

Even when firms do wish to make such investments, they may find difficulties in raising finance. Banks may be unwilling to lend. Alternatively, if firms rely on raising finance by the issue of new shares, this makes them very dependent on the stock market performance of their shares. This depends largely on current profitability and expected profitability in the near future, not on *long-term* profitability.

Types of interventionist supply-side policy

Nationalisation. This is the most extreme form of intervention, and one that most countries had tended to reject, given a worldwide trend for privatisation. Nevertheless, many countries have stopped short of privatising certain key transport and power industries, such as the railways and electricity generation. Having these industries under public ownership may result in higher investment than if they were under private ownership. Thus French governments have invested heavily in the state-owned railway system. This has resulted in fast, efficient rail services, with obvious benefits to rail users and the economy generally.

Then with the financial crisis of 2007–9, many countries resorted to nationalising some of their financial institutions in order to rescue them from bankruptcy and to ensure the stability of the financial system.

Direct provision. Improvements in infrastructure, such as a better motorway system, can be of direct benefit to industry. Alternatively, the government could provide factories or equipment to specific firms.

Funding research and development. Around about one-third of UK R&D is financed by the government, but around half of this has been concentrated in the fields of defence, aerospace and the nuclear power industry. As a result, there has been little government sponsorship of research in the majority of industry. Since the mid-1970s, however, there have been several government initiatives in the field of information technology. Even so, the amount of government support in this field has been very small compared with Japan, France and the USA. What is more, the amount of support declined between the mid-1980s and the late 1990s.

The UK operates a system of tax credits for small and medium enterprises (SMEs) and for other companies. Companies can claim tax credits on expenditures incurred in carrying out R&D. These credits either take the form of a tax relief, with the credits used to reduce the amount of profit liable for taxation, or for SMEs take the form of a cash sum.

In 2007, the 850 largest UK corporate spenders in R&D invested £21.6 billion, equivalent to around $1^{1}/_{2}$ per cent of GDP. Across the UK's 850 largest firms, the ratio of R&D to sales averaged 1.7 per cent as compared with 4.4 per cent for the largest US investors in R&D.

Training and education. The government may set up training schemes, or encourage educational institutions to make their courses more vocationally relevant, or introduce new vocational qualifications (such as GNVQs, NVQs and foundation degrees in the UK). Alternatively, the government can provide grants or tax relief to firms which themselves provide training schemes. The UK invests little in training programmes compared with most of its industrial competitors. Alternative approaches to training in the UK, Germany, France and the USA are examined in Case Study K.14 on the book's website.

Assistance to small firms. UK governments in recent years have recognised the importance of small firms to the economy and have introduced various forms of advisory services, grants and tax concessions. For example, in 2009 small firms paid a 21 per cent rate of corporation tax compared with 28 per cent for larger companies. In addition, small firms are subject to fewer planning and other bureaucratic controls than large companies. Support to small firms in the UK is examined in Case Study K.15 on the book's website.

Advice and persuasion. The government may engage in discussions with private firms in order to find ways to improve efficiency and innovation. It may bring firms together to exchange information, so as to coordinate their decisions and create a climate of greater certainty. It may bring firms and unions together to try to create greater industrial harmony.

Information. The government may provide various information services to firms: technical assistance, the results of public research, information on markets, etc.

BOX 31.3 A NEW APPROACH TO INDUSTRIAL POLICY

Industrial policy attempts to increase investment and halt or slow the shrinking of the industrial sector. As with many other areas of economic policy, industrial policy throughout most of the world has undergone a radical reorientation in recent years. The government's role has shifted from one of direct intervention in the form of subsidies and protecting industry from competition, to one of focusing upon the external business environment and the conditions that influence its competitiveness.

The reasons for such a change are both philosophical and structural:

- The rise of the political right in the 1980s led to a shift away from interventionist and towards market-based supply-side policy.
- Growing government debt, and a desire to curb public expenditure, acted as a key incentive to reduce the state's role in industrial affairs. This was argued to be one of the driving forces behind the European privatisation process in the 1980s and 1990s.
- During the 1980s, industry became progressively more global in its outlook. As such, its investment decisions were increasingly being determined by external environmental factors, especially the technology, productivity and labour costs of its international competitors.

The new approach to industrial policy, being widely adopted by many advanced countries, is to focus on improving those factors which shape a nation's competitiveness. This involves shifting away from particular sectors to targeting what are referred to as 'framework conditions for industry'. Policies include the following:

- The promotion of investment in physical and human capital. Human capital in particular, and the existence of a sound skills base, are seen as crucial for attracting global business and ensuring long-run economic growth.
- A reduction in non-wage employment costs, such as employers' social security and pension contributions. Many governments see these costs as too high and as a severe limitation on competitiveness and employment creation.
- The promotion of innovation and the encouragement of greater levels of R&D.
- Support for small and medium-sized enterprises. SMEs have received particular attention due to their crucial role in enhancing innovation, creating employment and contributing to skills development, especially in high-tech areas (see Chapter 16).
- The improvement of infrastructure. This includes both physical transport, such as roads and railways, and information highways.
- The protection of intellectual property by more effective use of patents and copyright. By reinforcing the law in these areas, it is hoped to encourage firms to develop new products and commit themselves to research.

These policies, if they are to be truly effective, are likely to require coordination and integration, since they represent a radical departure from traditional industrial policy.

1. In what senses could these new policies be described as (a) non-interventionist; (b) interventionist?
2. Does globalisation, and in particular the global perspective of multinational corporations, make industrial policy in the form of selective subsidies and tax relief more or less likely?

In addition to adopting supply-side measures that focus on the economy as a whole, governments might decide to target specific regions of the economy, or specific industries for policy initiatives. Such initiatives are often more interventionist in nature, as the next section shows.

31.4 REGIONAL POLICY

Within most countries, unemployment is not evenly distributed. Take the case of the UK. Northern Ireland and parts of the north and west of England, parts of Wales and parts of Scotland have unemployment rates substantially higher than in the south-east of England.

Similarly, countries experience regional disparities in average incomes, rates of growth and levels of prices, as well as in health, crime, housing, etc. In the UK, these disparities grew wider in the mid-1980s as the recession hit the north, with its traditional heavy industries, much harder than the south. In the recession of the early 1990s, however, it was the service sector that was hardest hit, a sector more concentrated in the south. Regional disparities therefore narrowed somewhat. Disparities are not only experienced at regional level. They are often more acutely felt in specific *areas*, especially inner cities and urban localities subject to industrial decline.

Within the European Union differences exist not only within individual countries, but between them. For example, in the EU some countries are much less prosperous than others. Thus, especially with the opening up of the EU in 1993 to the free movement of factors of production, capital and labour may flow to the more prosperous regions of the Union, such as Germany, France and the Benelux countries, and away from the less prosperous regions, such as Portugal, Greece and southern Italy. With enlargement of the EU in 2004 to include ten new members, mainly from central and eastern Europe, and then two more, Romania and Bulgaria, in 2007, regional disparities within the EU have widened further.

Causes of regional imbalance and the role of regional policy

If the market functioned perfectly, there would be no regional problem. If wages were lower and unemployment were higher in the north, people would simply move to the south. This would reduce unemployment in the north and help to fill vacancies in the south. It would drive up wage rates in the north and reduce wage rates in the south. The process would continue until regional disparities were eliminated.

The capital market would function similarly. New investment would be located in the areas offering the highest rate of return. If land and labour were cheaper in the north, capital would be attracted there. This too would help to eliminate regional disparities.

A similar argument applies between countries. Take the case of the EU. Labour should move from the poorer countries, such as those of eastern Europe, to the richer ones and capital should flow in the opposite direction until disparities are eliminated.

In practice, the market does not always behave as just described. There are three major problems.

Labour and capital immobility. Labour may be geographically immobile. The regional pattern of industrial location may change more rapidly than the labour market can adjust to it. Thus jobs may be lost in the depressed areas more rapidly than people can migrate.

Similarly, the existing capital stock is highly immobile. Buildings and most machinery cannot be moved to where the unemployed are! *New* capital is much more mobile. But there may be insufficient new investment, especially during a recession, to halt regional decline, even if some investors are attracted into the depressed areas by low wages and cheap land.

Regional multiplier effects. The continuing shift in demand may in part be due to regional multiplier effects. In the prosperous regions, the new industries and the new workers attracted there create additional demand. This creates additional output and jobs and hence more migration. There is a multiplied rise in income. In the depressed regions, the decline in demand and loss of jobs causes a multiplied downward effect. Loss of jobs in manufacturing leads to less money spent in the local community; transport and other service industries lose custom. The whole region becomes more depressed.

> **Definition**
>
> **Regional multiplier effects**
> When a change in injections into or withdrawals from a particular region causes a multiplied change in income in that region. The regional multiplier is given by $1/(1 - mpc_r)$, where mpc_r is the marginal propensity to consume products from the region.

Externalities. Labour migration imposes external costs on non-migrants. In the prosperous regions, the new arrivals compete for services with those already there. Services become overstretched; house prices rise; council house waiting lists lengthen; roads become more congested, etc. In the depressed regions, services decline, or alternatively local taxes must rise for those who remain if local services are to be protected. Dereliction, depression and unemployment cause emotional stress for those who remain.

Approaches to regional policy

Market-orientated solutions

Supporters of market-based solutions argue that firms are the best judges of where they should locate. Government intervention would impede efficient decision taking by firms. It is better, they argue, to remove impediments to the market achieving regional and local balance. For example, they favour either or both of the following.

Locally negotiated wage agreements. Nationally negotiated wage rates mean that wages are not driven down in the less prosperous areas and up in the more prosperous ones. This discourages firms from locating in the less prosperous areas. At the same time, firms find it difficult to recruit labour in the more prosperous ones, where wages are not high enough to compensate for the higher cost of living there.

Reducing unemployment benefits. A general reduction in unemployment benefits and other welfare payments would encourage the unemployed in the areas of high unemployment to migrate to the more prosperous areas, or enable firms to offer lower wages in the areas of high unemployment.

The problem with these policies is that they attempt initially to widen the economic divide between workers in the different areas in order to encourage capital and labour to move. Such policies would hardly be welcomed by workers in the poorer areas!

> **Pause for thought**
>
> 1 Think of some other 'pro-market' solutions to the regional problem.
> 2 Do people in the more prosperous areas benefit from pro-market solutions?

Interventionist solutions

Interventionist policies involve encouraging firms to move. Such policies include the following.

Subsidies and tax concessions in the depressed regions. Businesses could be given general subsidies, such as grants to move, or reduced rates of corporation tax. Alternatively, grants or subsidies could be specifically targeted at increasing employment (e.g. reduced employer's national insurance contributions) or at encouraging investment (e.g. investment grants or other measures to reduce the costs of capital).

The provision of facilities in depressed regions. The government or local authorities could provide facilities such as land and buildings at concessionary, or even zero, rents to incoming firms; or spend money on improving the infrastructure of the area (roads and communications, technical colleges, etc.).

The siting of government offices in the depressed regions. The government could move some of its own departments out of the capital and locate them in areas of high unemployment. The siting of the vehicle licensing centre in Swansea is an example.

> **Pause for thought**
>
> *If you were the government, how would you set about deciding the rate of subsidy to pay a firm thinking of moving to a less prosperous area?*

It is important to distinguish policies that merely seek to *modify* the market by altering market signals, from policies that *replace* the market. *Regulation* replaces the market, and unless very carefully devised and monitored may lead to ill-thought-out decisions being made. *Subsidies* and *taxes* merely modify the market, leaving it to individual firms to make their final location decisions.

Regional policy in the EU

An interesting case study of the use of regional policy is the European Union. Indeed, the EU has allocated around 35 per cent of its total budget to regional policy over the period 2007–13, spending some €346 billion.

So why does it need a regional policy? The overriding reason, as it is for individual countries, is the existence of *economic and social disparities*. The EU estimated prior to the programme starting that about 154 million inhabitants (one in three EU citizens) had a GDP per head below what it terms the 'convergence level' – defined as under 75 per cent of the EU-27 average. These disparities had grown with the accession of ten new members in 2004 and two more in 2007.

The 2007–13 programme was designed to focus primarily on the poorest member states and regions of the EU: i.e. those below the convergence level of GDP per head. But the programme also promoted the themes of jobs, growth and innovation across the EU. The programme allocated a quarter of resources for projects related to research and innovation.

In order to allocate these vast resources, the EU operates a series of interrelated funds, which are collectively known as the Structural and Cohesion Funds. These are illustrated in Figure 31.1 along with the overall *objectives* for regional policy.

The European Regional Development Fund (ERDF). This fund is managed by the Directorate-General for Regional Policy. It allocates grants for projects designed to aid development in poorer regions of the EU. In particular it focuses upon:

- investment in companies – especially SMEs – to create and maintain employment;
- investment in infrastructure, particularly research and innovation, transport and the environment;

Figure 31.1 Objectives and EU Structural and Cohesion Funds, 2007–13

Objectives	Structural Funds and Instruments		
Convergence = €282.8 billion	European Fund for Regional Development	European Social Fund	Cohesion Fund
Regional Competitiveness and Employment = €55 billion	European Fund for Regional Development	European Social Fund	
European Territorial Cooperation = €8.7 billion	European Fund for Regional Development		

Source: European Union

funds to support regional and local development and to foster cooperation between regions.

The European Social Fund (ESF). The ESF is managed by the Directorate-General for Employment and Social Affairs. It allocates funds to help workers and businesses adapt to industrial change, to encourage the social integration of disadvantaged people, to help the unemployed into work, and to strengthen the stock of human capital: i.e. the skills and knowledge base of the workforce.

Cohesion Fund. This fund is aimed at members states whose national income per head is less than 90 per cent of the EU average. Its aim is to support the development of infrastructure projects, particularly transeuropean transport networks, and enhance measures that help protect and improve the quality of the environment: for example, improving the quality of water supply and the treatment of waste.

As Figure 31.1 shows, resources are allocated to projects in order to meet three broad objectives for EU regional policy. The 2007–13 programme saw the largest share of the moneys set aside for the 'convergence regions' of the EU (those with GDP per head less than 75 per cent of the EU average). All three funds meet, in one way or another, this objective. The amount available under the convergence objective was €282.8 billion.

Outside of the convergence regions, funds were allocated according to the regional competitiveness and employment object. This objective emphasises the concepts of innovation, human capital, the promotion of a 'knowledge society' and job creation. The amount available under this objective was €55 billion. The European Fund for Regional Development and the European Social Fund were the funds designed to meet this objective.

The European territorial cooperation objective is met by the European Fund for Regional Development. The objective focuses on developing economic and social *cross-border* activities and *transnational* cooperation, including the sharing of ideas and experiences.

SUMMARY

1a Supply-side policies, if successful, will shift the aggregate supply curve to the right. Supply-side policies look to influence the quantity and productivity of factors of production.

1b The UK has had a lower rate of investment than most other industrialised countries. This has contributed to a historically low rate of economic growth and a growing trade deficit in manufactures.

2a Market-orientated supply-side policies aim to increase the rate of growth of aggregate supply and reduce the rate of unemployment by encouraging private enterprise and the freer play of market forces.

2b Reducing government expenditure as a proportion of GDP is a major element of such policies.

2c Tax cuts can be used to encourage people to work more and more efficiently, and to encourage investment. The effects of tax cuts will depend on how people respond to incentives. The substitution effect will result in greater output; the income effect in lower output.

2d Reducing the power of trade unions and a reduction in welfare benefits, especially those related to unemployment, may force workers to accept jobs at lower wages, thereby decreasing equilibrium unemployment.

2e Various policies can be introduced to increase competition. These include privatisation, deregulation, introducing market relationships into the public sector, the Private Finance Initiative, and freer international trade and capital movements.

3 Interventionist supply-side policy can take the form of grants for investment and research and development, advice and persuasion, the direct provision of infrastructure and the provision, funding or encouragement of various training schemes.

4a Regional and local disparities arise from a changing pattern of industrial production. With many of the older industries concentrated in certain parts of the country and especially in the inner cities, and with an acceleration in the rate of industrial change, so the gap between rich and poor areas has widened.

4b Regional disparities can in theory be corrected by the market, with capital being attracted to areas of low wages and workers being attracted to areas of high wages. In practice, regional disparities persist because of capital and labour immobility and regional multiplier effects.

4c EU states work together to reduce regional economic imbalances. Regional policy is underpinned by a series of Structural and Social Funds. The 2007–13 programme of funding focused these funds on reducing economic and social inequalities in the poorest regions of the EU and, more generally, on promoting jobs, innovation and economic growth.

REVIEW QUESTIONS

1 Define demand-side and supply-side policies. Are there any ways in which such policies are incompatible?

2 Outline the main supply-side policies that have been introduced in the UK since 1979. Does the evidence suggest that they have achieved what they set out to do?

3 What types of tax cuts are likely to create the greatest (a) incentives, (b) disincentives to effort?

4 Compare the relative merits of pro-market and interventionist solutions to regional imbalances.

5 Is the decline of older industries necessarily undesirable?

6 In what ways can interventionist supply-side policy work with the market, rather than against it? What are the arguments for and against such policy?

Chapters from Adams
Part Two

chapter 2
HOW THE LAW IS MADE

Introduction

This chapter explains where English law comes from and how it is made. There are currently three important sources of law:

1 European law;
2 Parliament;
3 The courts.

Parliament and the European Union are the primary sources, but the courts also have a minor (though important) law-making role. The courts also have a crucial role in the interpretation of legislation.

Learning Objectives

When you have studied this chapter you should be able to:

- Name the sources of English law
- Distinguish between the functions of the institutions of the European Union
- Differentiate between EC regulations, directives and decisions
- Explain the application of the doctrine of precedent in the English courts
- Describe the differing judicial approaches to interpreting statutes
- Appreciate the effect of the Human Rights Act 1998 on the development of English law.

Photo: STOCKFOLIO®/Alamy

European law

The law of the European Community has been a source of UK law since 1973, when the UK became a member of what was then called the European Economic Community (EEC). The 1992 Treaty on European Union (the Maastricht Treaty) officially changed the name to European Community to signify that the objectives of the Community are not just economic. The Maastricht Treaty also created the European Union (EU), which consists of three 'pillars'. In the middle pillar are the three existing Communities, i.e. the European Coal and Steel Community (ECSC), the European Atomic Energy Treaty Community (EURATOM) and the Economic Community. These three Communities are known collectively as the European Community. On either side of this central pillar are the Common Foreign and Security Policy (CFSP) and Police and Judicial Co-operation in Criminal Matters (PJCCM). These three pillars support the overarching constitutional order of the Union. However, only the central pillar, the EC, is governed by Community law. The CFSP and the PJCCM pillars are governed by intergovernmental co-operation. This means that they are outside the jurisdiction of the Community institutions, particularly the Court of Justice. Also, none of the articles of the outside pillars are enforceable, or challengeable, in national courts. Thus, although the Union is wider than the European Community, it has its roots within it. EC law is an important source of business law and you will notice its impact in a number of topic areas in this book, such as product safety and employment law. The European Community (EC) is currently composed of 27 member states.

Under the European Communities Act 1972 (ECA 1972), s 2, EU law is part of UK law. In the event of conflict, EU law takes priority. Disputed points of EU law must be referred by the domestic courts for interpretation to the Court of Justice of the European Communities, or be decided in accordance with principles found in its existing decisions.

The institutions of the European Union

The Councils

The Council of Ministers

(Note that rather confusingly this may also be referred to as the 'Council of the EU' or sometimes just 'the Council'. It must *not* be confused with the European Council, which is entirely separate.) The **Council of Ministers** is the main legislative organ of the Community and within it the interests of member states find direct expression. It is made up of 'a representative of each Member State at ministerial level, authorised to commit the government of that Member State' (Treaty of Nice, Article 203). The representatives vary according to the subject matter under discussion. For General Council meetings, a member state's representative is generally its foreign minister; otherwise, meetings are attended by the ministers of state with the relevant portfolio. So, for example, a meeting will be made up of agriculture ministers when the common agricultural policy is under discussion. It is chaired by the President. The presidency rotates every six months between the heads of state or heads of government of the member states.

The European Council

In 1974, Community leaders agreed to hold regular meetings at the highest political level within what became known as a '**European Council**'. This European Council met regularly on an informal basis, until it was given a legal basis by Article 2 of the Single European Act. Article 4 of the Maastricht Treaty states its composition and functions. It is composed of the heads of state or of government of the member states. It meets at least twice a year in order to discuss major Community issues in a less formal atmosphere than that which prevails at the Council of Ministers (Council of the EU). It is chaired by the current President of the Council of Ministers, assisted by the minister of foreign affairs of each of the member states and a member of the Commission. The European Council's function is to provide the Union with the necessary impetus to define the general political guidelines for its development.

The European Commission

The Commission is composed of one nominee from each member state and is an executive and policy-making body with legislative powers. Most major decisions taken by the Council must be made on the basis of proposals from the Commission. Currently there are 27 Commissioners, but once appointed they represent Community interests rather than national interests.

The European Parliament

The **European Parliament** consists of 785 members directly elected by people with the right to vote in each member state (the UK returns 78 MEPs). Parliament exercises democratic supervision over the Commission, with the appointment of the President and members of the Commission subject to its approval. The Commission is thus politically answerable to the Parliament, which can pass a 'motion of censure' calling for its resignation. Together with the Council, Parliament formulates and adopts legislation proposed by the Commission.

The European Court of Justice (ECJ)

The **European Court of Justice** is made up of 25 judges and eight advocates-general. If the court so requests, the Council may, acting unanimously, increase the number of advocates-general. The judges and advocates-general are appointed by common agreement of the governments of the member states and hold office for a renewable term of six years. They are chosen from legal experts whose independence is beyond doubt and who possess the qualifications required for appointment to the highest judicial offices in their respective countries or who are of recognised competence. The judges select one of their number to be President of the court for a renewable term of three years. The President directs the work of the court and its staff and presides at hearings and deliberations of major formations of the court.

The advocates-general assist the court in its task. They deliver independent and impartial opinions in all cases in open court, where a case does not raise any new points of law, unless the court decides otherwise. Their duties should not be confused with those of a public prosecutor or similar body.

The court has two functions:

1 to interpret any point of EU law referred by the courts of member states. It is mandatory for the highest appeal court of any member state to make a referral, if the meaning of a principle of EU law is unclear;

2 to decide the outcome of cases alleging breaches of EU legal obligations, brought by EU institutions, member states or individuals.

Once the court has reached its decision, this is immediately effective. It takes precedence over any conflicting domestic legislation. Individual states have responsibility for implementing the court's decisions by changing the relevant domestic law. Reluctance to comply may result in pressure from other member states. Since the Maastricht Treaty, a state which does not comply with a judgment may be subject to a penalty payment. With the passage of time it became apparent that too many demands were being placed on the court, which is why the Single European Act 1987 introduced the Court of First Instance (CFI). The CFI is currently composed of 25 judges, at least one from each member state. The judges are appointed for a renewable term of six years by common accord of the governments of the member states. There are no permanent advocates-general attached to the CFI. All cases heard at first instance by the Court of First Instance may be subject to a right of appeal to the Court of Justice on points of law only.

The sources of European law

The treaties

A number of treaties impose legal obligations on member states, including the Treaty of Rome 1957, the Single European Act 1987, the Maastricht Treaty 1992, the Treaty of Amsterdam 1997 and the Treaty of Nice 2003. Some of these obligations are directly enforceable by individual citizens, regardless of whether the relevant member state has taken legislative action to implement them. Such directly enforceable obligations include those under Article 119 (now 141) of the Treaty of Rome, which relates to the equal treatment of men and women in employment.

Regulations

Regulations are intended to impose uniformity of law throughout the Community. They take effect in all member states immediately on being issued.

Directives

Directives comprise the most prolific source of law in the EC. Directives apply to all member states and are intended to lead to harmonisation of law between member states, making it similar but not identical. Directives set the aims which must be achieved but leave the choice of the form and method of implementation to each member state. Thus, they have to be implemented by national parliaments. Implementation legislation may reflect the legal and social conventions of each member state.

States are required to implement Directives within specified time limits, but sometimes drag their heels if a particular Directive is unpopular. The Court of Justice may permit claims by individuals against an organ of a member state (though not an individual) for breaches of a Directive which has not yet been implemented, provided that the wording of the Directive is sufficiently clear and unconditional.

Decisions

A **decision** affects only particular member states, companies or individuals. It may empower the party to whom it is issued to do something, or prevent it from doing something.

The impact of EU membership on English law

The main impact so far has been felt in the areas of trade, industry, employment, the environment and provision of financial services. Membership of the EU has, therefore, had considerable influence in many areas of business law. A number of references to such developments will be found throughout this book.

As the scope of European law expands through new treaties, its impact on English law, politics and society at large increases. The Treaty of Amsterdam, which came into force on 1 May 1999, aims to place employment and citizens' rights at the heart of the Union, to remove the last remaining obstacles to freedom of movement within the Union and to strengthen security. This had a considerable impact on human rights. It required the widening of the existing principles of non-discrimination legislation in employment with regards to gender, race and ethnic origin to include religious belief, age and sexual orientation. Directives on all these issues were issued to member states and implementation has taken place. (For details see pages 378–90)

The Treaty also seeks to promote privacy of citizens' personal data. The security issues within the Treaty will also have an impact on criminal law and procedure, since the Treaty requires the police and the judiciary of all member states to co-ordinate action on terrorism, offences against children, drug trafficking, corruption and fraud. It also requires member states to co-operate more closely in the fight against racism and discrimination in general, while promoting equality before the law and social justice.

Parliament

Most English law is currently made by, or with the authority of, Parliament. **Direct (parliamentary/primary) legislation** comprises Acts of Parliament, created by the passage of a Bill through certain prescribed processes in the House of Commons and the House of Lords. Indirect **(delegated) legislation** is created by a body (usually a government department or local authority) which has been given the power to legislate by Parliament under an *enabling* Act.

How an Act of Parliament is created

Most legislation is proposed by government ministers, but backbench MPs have limited opportunities to put forward **Private Members' Bills**. These usually relate to non-party-political issues. In practice, few Private Members' Bills become Acts because of the limited amount of parliamentary time available to them.

The pre-legislative stage

A government Bill is usually preceded by the issue of a **Green Paper** which sets out the legislative proposals for discussion. Consultation with relevant interest groups may take place. A **White Paper** is then issued, which lays down the principles on which the draft Bill is based.

Parliamentary procedure

The first stage of a Bill's journey through Parliament is *the introduction and first reading*. Most Bills are initially processed in the House of Commons and then go through the same procedures in the House of Lords. All important and controversial Bills, including all money Bills, must start off in the Commons. The first reading is a formality to announce the existence of the Bill and to set down a date for the second reading.

The *second reading* involves a full debate which starts with a speech from the minister who is proposing the Bill. This is answered by the relevant shadow minister. After contributions from any interested member, a vote is taken. Provided that a majority is in its favour, the Bill passes on to the committee stage.

At the *committee stage* a standing committee of 25–45, appointed in proportion to party representation, usually examines the Bill clause by clause. Amendments may be proposed. (Some Bills require consideration by a committee of the whole House. They do not have a report stage, but progress straight to the third reading.)

Following the committee stage the committee reports on its findings (the *report stage*), debate takes place on proposed changes, and further amendments may be proposed to the Bill.

At the *third reading* of the Bill, a short debate concentrates on the main points of the Bill. In the Commons, only superficial changes (to grammar or syntax) will be made, though greater changes may take place in the House of Lords.

The processes discussed above are repeated when the Bill reaches the House of Lords (*transfer to the other House*). Note that, under the Parliament Acts 1911 and 1949, the House of Lords cannot reject a Bill outright, although it may delay any Bill except a money Bill for up to a year: a money Bill can be delayed only for a month. The power to delay may give the Lords considerable power, as the government is likely to seek a compromise to enable it to pursue its policies.

Before the Bill can become an Act of Parliament and pass into law, it must receive the *Royal Assent*. By convention this is just a formality: hundreds of years have passed since the Crown took an active legislative role.

The date of implementation of the whole or any part of an Act of Parliament is usually specified in it.

Delegated legislation

This is indirect or secondary legislation made by bodies outside Parliament, through the exercise of legislative power delegated to them by Act of Parliament. You will come across examples of delegated legislation in later chapters of this book in connection with, for example, the Health and Safety at Work etc. Act 1974.

In practice, the bulk of law created every year is delegated, rather than direct. Such legislation is the means by which both central and local government agencies administer their policies. Over 2,000 such regulations are enacted annually. These may, for example, limit benefit entitlements, raise the required hygiene standards in a fast-food business, and help to keep local parks free from noise pollution.

There are four main types of delegated legislation:

1. *Orders in Council*. The Emergency Powers Acts 1939 and 1984 give law-making powers to the Privy Council in times of national emergency.

2. *Statutory instruments*. These are created by government departments to execute general principles of policy set out in the enabling Act of Parliament. The Consumer Credit Act 1974 empowers the Secretary of State to make rules to safeguard users and potential users of credit facilities.

3. *Regulations to implement law from the EU*. The European Communities Act 1972, s 2, empowers ministers and government departments to implement directives and treaty provisions. For example, the Unfair Terms in Consumer Contracts Regulations 1999 were created under this power.

4. *Bye-laws*. These are made by local authorities and other bodies with statutory powers, like London Underground and Network Rail, to regulate the facilities which they provide.

The use of delegated legislation is somewhat controversial. In general, however, its practical advantages outweigh its disadvantages. The advantages of delegated legislation are:

1. *Saving of parliamentary time*. The parliamentary legislative process is slow and protracted. Parliament finds it difficult to complete its annual legislative schedule and does not have time to debate the fine details of the regulations necessary to execute government policy.

2. *Specialist knowledge*. The creation of many regulations requires specialist knowledge not enjoyed by the average MP. They are, for example, unlikely to understand the finer points of abattoir management, or appreciate the appropriate levels of pork to be found in a sausage.

3. *Flexibility*. Such rules may be easily and quickly introduced, altered or extinguished, as and when appropriate.

4. *Legislation can take place when Parliament is not sitting*. This assists the smooth running of central and local government outside parliamentary sessions.

The disadvantages of delegated legislation are:

1. *Loss of parliamentary control*. Since details of policy administration are determined by the relevant government department, Parliament may be deprived of the opportunity to

question and debate them. Scrutiny of most delegated legislation is negligible. It is laid before Parliament, but most of it is subject to a 'negative resolution' procedure. This means that it will be implemented as it stands unless an objection is sustained within the specified time limit. Exceptionally, the enabling Act may require Parliament positively to approve the regulations.

2 *Bulk and frequent change*. The huge quantity of delegated legislation which is produced every year makes it very difficult – even for lawyers – to keep abreast of all changes. Adapting to changes may considerably add to the burdens of running a business, even where publicity materials are circulated by the regulating body.

The courts

Creative powers

The law made by the courts is case law, sometimes described as common law. Until the nineteenth century the courts were the primary law-makers, but were superseded by Parliament since social conditions required a different style of law-making. Case law evolves slowly and haphazardly, when relevant cases come before the courts with facts which justify further legal development. A point of case law may be very narrow in its effect since the courts can legislate only with regard to things that have already happened; they cannot legislate for what is to happen in future cases with different facts. This makes case law an inadequate form of law-making in a sophisticated industrial society, where blanket legislation is needed to regulate possible future problems.

Today the bulk of both civil and criminal law is statutory. New principles are most commonly developed in this way and much of the common law has been *codified* (converted into statutory form). The senior courts retain some limited creative powers, mainly in tort and contract law which are still not predominantly statutory. For example, the law of negligence, which is described in Chapters 13–14, has been, and mainly continues to be, developed by judges.

Interpretative powers

Since most law is now statutory, the courts are mainly concerned with the interpretation and application of points of law derived from Acts of Parliament and delegated legislation. When exercising this function the courts must respect the sovereignty of Parliament as a superior law-making body. A judge interpreting a statute will therefore aim to give such meaning to a disputed point of legislation as to reflect what Parliament seemed to have intended.

The words used in the statute are the main focus of the interpretation exercise and limit the freedom of the court. If the statute has an apparent gap and consequently an injustice exists, the court is not necessarily free to create the law to fill that gap, unless the context gives the necessary scope. Otherwise, all that the court can do is to recommend that Parliament amends the legislation.

Judges have a number of resources and tools which may assist their interpretative function.

1 Intrinsic aids

These are found within the statute itself. It is common for an interpretation clause to be included which explains any special meaning to be given to words within the statute. For example, the Occupiers' Liability Act 1957 defines 'premises' as any 'fixed or moveable structure' (see Chapter 15).

2 External aids

These are materials which are not part of the statute itself. They include the following:

(a) The Interpretation Act 1978. This gives guidance on terms and phrases commonly found in legislation.

(b) Reports of the Law Commission or government inquiry. These may indicate why legislation is needed and thereby indicate its meaning.

(c) Parliamentary Reports. Until 1993 the courts refused to admit evidence from *Hansard* Reports of parliamentary proceedings relating to the passage of the statute. There were three main objections:

- the legislative and judicial functions of the state would be confused;
- the cut and thrust of parliamentary debate was unlikely to provide objective explanations;
- the research required to check *Hansard* would also add considerably to the cost of litigation.

Pepper v Hart (1993, HL)

Held (by majority): *Hansard* may be consulted by the courts if all the following circumstances exist:

- the disputed legislation is ambiguous or obscure, or the words taken at their face value produce an absurd result; and
- the *Hansard* extract consists of statements made by the relevant minister or other sponsor of the Bill; and
- the meaning of the extract is clear.

Pepper v *Hart* has been followed in a number of cases, but it is doubtful how far it is useful. The disputed section of an Act may not have been debated. Even if it was, any comments made may, in themselves, be ambiguous and confusing.

3 Judicial principles of statutory interpretation

The judiciary has developed the following practices to assist the interpretative process:

(a) *The contextual approach*. Any disputed words must always be interpreted within the context of the statute as a whole (a **contextual approach**). The significance of a vague, obscure or even apparently meaningless word may become crystal clear when scrutinised in relation to the surrounding text. The ***ejusdem generis* rule** forms part of the contextual approach. General words, like 'other animals', 'other person', or 'other thing' are meaningless in themselves. Their meaning may be clarified by reference to any specific words which precede them. Thus, if the words 'other animals' were preceded by the words 'cats, dogs and guinea pigs', it would be reasonable to assume that they include any animal commonly kept as a domestic pet. Generous interpretations are sometimes made to assist the perceived purpose of the statute. Thus in *Flack* v *Baldry* (1988) an electric shock from a stun gun was held to come within the definition of 'any noxious liquid, gas or other thing' under the Firearms Act 1968.

(b) *The literal rule*. A **literal rule** approach requires the court to take words at their face value where there is no ambiguity and the meaning is clear, even if this produces an absurd result.

Fisher v *Bell* (1961)

The defendant shopkeeper displayed a 'flick knife' (knife with a retractable blade) in his shop window and was charged with offering for sale an offensive weapon in breach of the Restriction of Offensive Weapons Act 1959, s 1(1).

Held: he was not guilty since, in contract law, a display of goods is an 'invitation to treat' and not 'an offer for sale' (see Chapter 4).

The application of the rule in such a case has been justified by the courts on the ground that it is for Parliament to correct any practical problems arising from the statute. Any action by the courts is an unjustifiable interference with parliamentary sovereignty.

(c) *The golden rule*. The **golden rule** developed as a means of blunting the worst excesses of the literal rule. If the statute is ambiguous, the court will apply the least ridiculous meaning in order to avoid an absurd result.

Adler v *George* (1964)

A CND demonstrator who invaded a sentry post at an army base was charged with obstructing a member of HM Forces 'in the vicinity of a prohibited place' under the Official Secrets Act 1920. It was argued that since she had actually entered the base she was on it when the obstruction took place rather than in its vicinity.

Held: to dismiss the charge on the basis of a literal interpretation would produce an absurd result; 'vicinity' must be interpreted as including the place itself, not just its environs.

Smith v *Hughes* (1960)

A prostitute who, from her window, encouraged gentlemen passing in the street to avail themselves of her services was successfully prosecuted for 'soliciting in the street'.

Held: the purpose of the legislation was to prevent annoyance to people arising from the activities of prostitutes in public places. Since the effects of the defendant's conduct were felt by people in the street, that conduct clearly fell within the purpose of the Street Offences Act 1959.

(d) *The mischief rule.* The **mischief rule** is a sixteenth-century rule that allows the court to adopt a meaning which will enable the statute to fulfil its intended purpose. The court examines the law before the Act to discover the problem (mischief) which the statute was intended to correct; then the statute can be given the meaning which resolves the problem.

This rule largely fell into disfavour with the rise of the literal rule, which dominated judicial decision-making in the nineteenth century and for approximately the first 70 years of the twentieth century.

(e) *The purposive approach.* The **purposive approach**, which is somewhat similar to the mischief approach, but broader in its effect, has come into use since the UK's entry into the EC. The courts of other member states have traditionally used this approach, as does the European Court of Justice. It requires the court to interpret the statute by looking beyond its words to determine the general purpose behind it. To do this the court may examine relevant extrinsic documentary evidence such as government reports proposing the reform. The next case is a good example of this.

Royal College of Nursing v *DHSS* (1981, HL)

Section 1(1) of the Abortion Act 1967 states that an abortion is legal only if carried out by a 'registered medical practitioner'. A change in abortion methods after the Act was passed meant that the procedure was largely carried out by nurses, subject to some supervision by a doctor. The courts had to decide whether abortions carried out by this procedure were legal under the Act.

Held by the Court of Appeal (adopting a literal approach): the practice was unlawful since nurses do not have the necessary qualifications.

Held by the House of Lords (by majority): a purposive approach should be used and that no illegality had occurred. Lord Diplock said: '*The approach of the Act seems to me to be clear. There are two aspects of it: the first, to broaden the grounds on which an abortion may be obtained; the second is to ensure that the abortion is carried out with proper skill and in hygienic conditions.*'

(Before the Act legalised abortion in certain circumstances, many women died at the hands of backstreet abortionists.)

The House of Lords' decision in *Pepper* v *Hart* (see above at page 25) may be seen as enabling and encouraging this approach. While the literal rule is still used today, a purposive approach is common where this assists a just outcome in the public interest. The court may use it to complement the literal rule: looking at the purpose of the statute will assist correct choice of meaning of an ambiguous word or phrase. It may be more radically used to correct an anomaly or fill a small gap.

Although called 'rules', it is more accurate to describe these judicial principles as 'tools' of interpretation. As *Royal College of Nursing* v *DHSS* (above) illustrates, they represent differing possible approaches to the interpretation process. They are not in any way superior or inferior to each other. Judges will choose what they view as the approach likely to produce the interpretation most beneficial to the public interest and which reflects current constitutional developments.

Real Life

Horace is enjoying the spring sunshine and bird song in his local park when Wayne and Waynetta settle down on the grass nearby and entertain themselves by playing their phone radio very loudly. Horace is not charmed by their taste in music (heavy metal) and points out the park bye-laws notice. This states a list of noise prohibitions, including 'singing or playing music', breach of which may be punished by fine. Wayne, who fancies himself as a bit of a barrack room lawyer, says: 'We ain't playing nothing mate, you'd better prosecute the radio station.'

It would probably be wise of Horace to admit defeat at this point and find somewhere quieter to sit. However, he probably has the law on his side. If a court were to consider the issue, it might well conclude that Wayne had breached the bye-laws. 'Playing music', even literally interpreted, is capable of including a radio transmission, so by using the golden rule approach an absurd result could be avoided by choosing the meaning of play as in 'a radio was playing music'. As the object of the bye-laws is to prevent noise pollution, a purposive approach would also include broadcast music.

4 Judicial presumptions

The courts will presume in the absence of clear evidence to the contrary that a statute will not:

(a) impose strict liability, i.e. where it is not necessary to prove that the accused intended to commit the offence;

(b) operate retrospectively, i.e. be said to apply to offences committed before the statute came into force;

(c) change the common law.

These presumptions may be contradicted (rebutted) only by express wording in the statute, or by clear implication to that effect.

Sweet v *Parsley* (1969, HL)

Miss Sweet let out a house which was raided by the police, who found cannabis in the possession of the tenants. Miss Sweet was charged with a statutory offence of 'being concerned in the management of premises' where the drugs were found.

Held: in the absence of a clear indication in the statute that she could be liable without reasonable knowledge of what was happening on her property, Miss Sweet was not guilty without proof of guilty knowledge. Strict liability was presumed not to have been intended.

The law of binding precedent

When exercising either their creative or interpretative functions, judges are bound by the law of binding precedent. This is a distinctive feature of the English legal system. In mainland European countries judges tend to follow each other's decisions in a similar way but are not obliged to do so. Their fellow judges' decisions are all **persuasive** but they are not **binding**. Under English law judges are not necessarily entitled to make their own decisions about the development or interpretation of the law. They may be bound by a decision reached in a previous case.

Two factors are crucial to determining whether a precedent (previous judicial decision) is binding:

1. the position in the court hierarchy of the court which decided the precedent, relative to the position of the court trying the current case. Inferior courts are bound by the decisions of superior courts (the letters HL, CA and PC following the name of a case indicate that it involves an appeal in one of the higher courts);

2. whether the facts of the current case come within the scope of the principle of law in the previous decision.

The court hierarchy

1 The House of Lords

This is the final court of appeal in the English court system. Its decisions are binding on all courts below. Before 1966, in the interests of preserving certainty, the House of Lords followed its own decisions unless a previous decision was found to have been reached **per incuriam**. Translated literally, this means 'through lack of care' caused by a failure by counsel to draw the attention of the court to crucial statutory or case law, preventing a correct decision from being reached. Since 1966 it has indicated that it is prepared to depart from existing decisions, if this is necessary to prevent injustice or unreasonable restriction of development of the common law.

Worth thinking about?

In what circumstances do you suppose that the House of Lords would find a previous decision unjust or restrictive?

Suggested solutions can be found in Appendix 2.

2 The Court of Appeal

(a) The *Civil Division* of the Court of Appeal is bound by the decisions of the House of Lords, and its decisions bind all the civil courts below. Subject to three exceptions laid down in *Young* v *Bristol Aeroplane Company* (1944), it is supposed to follow its own previous decisions. The exceptions are:

- two of its own previous decisions are in conflict: it must then choose which to follow; the one which is not chosen ceases to be good law;
- a previous decision conflicts with a decision of the House of Lords: the decision of the House of Lords must be followed;
- the previous decision was reached *per incuriam*.

(b) The *Criminal Division* of the Court of Appeal is bound by the decisions of the House of Lords, and its decisions bind all the criminal courts below. It may depart from its own decisions where such flexibility is in the interests of justice.

3 The Divisional Courts

These are all bound by the House of Lords and Court of Appeal decisions. The decisions of the Divisional Courts are binding on those courts from which they hear appeals. They follow their own decisions subject to the same exceptions as the Civil Division of the Court of Appeal.

4 The High Court

Judges in the High Court are bound by the decisions of the House of Lords and Court of Appeal, but not by the decisions of their fellow judges. High Court decisions are binding on the Crown Court, county courts and magistrates' courts.

Decisions made in the Crown Court, the county courts and magistrates' courts are not binding in other cases or in other courts. Such courts, of course, are bound by the decisions of the relevant superior courts.

The relevance of the previous decision: the scope of the *ratio decidendi*

When judges have heard cases in the High Court or any of the courts above, they may deliver lengthy judgments. These explain their reasons for deciding in favour of one party rather than the other.

This statement of reasons, which refers both to relevant proven facts and to the applicable principles of law, is called the **ratio decidendi** (the reason for the decision). It is the *ratio decidendi* which forms the potentially binding precedent for later cases.

A later court, when hearing a case, has to decide whether that case's facts are sufficiently relevant to the principle of the *ratio decidendi* of a previous case. If so, the previous decision must be applied, provided it was decided by a relevant court. If there are material differences, the later case can be *distinguished* on its facts and the previous decision is not applicable.

Reversing and overruling decisions

An appeal court may decide to overturn a decision reached by a lower court. This may be on the ground that the case was incorrectly decided in the light of the current law. The lower court's decision is then said to be *reversed*. The victor at the previous trial is now the loser.

Reversing a decision does not in itself affect the validity of any precedent applied in the case. If the appeal court believes that a precedent, which bound the lower court, no longer represents the law, it may (subject to the rules explained above) **overrule** that precedent and restate the legal principle.

The importance of the law reporting system

No system of precedent can work unless there is an accurate and comprehensive collection of the key decisions of the superior courts readily accessible to all who have need of them. Authoritative reports compiled by legally qualified law reporters are produced primarily by the Council of Law Reporting. The courts may refuse to allow a non-authoritative report to be quoted in court.

Persuasive precedents

While a court may be bound to apply a precedent, other decisions called persuasive precedents are influential only. The court can choose to apply them. Persuasive precedents include:

1 *Obiter dicta*. In a judgment it is quite common to find statements of law relating to hypothetical facts. These are not part of the ***ratio decidendi*** and are called ***obiter dicta*** (***obiter dictum*** in the singular). These indicate how the judge thinks the law should develop in the hypothetical circumstances. They are highly persuasive if they come from the House of Lords or Court of Appeal, but a court still has a choice about applying them in a future case. Once applied, the *obiter dicta* become binding principles of law. Some important principles of law have originated from *obiter dicta*. See *Central London Property Trust* v *High Trees House* (Chapter 5).

2 *The decisions of the Judicial Committee of the Privy Council*. The Privy Council, which is staffed by members of the House of Lords, hears appeals from the courts of some Commonwealth countries. As the decisions do not involve English cases they are of persuasive influence only, despite the status of the judges. The rules relating to remoteness of damage in negligence are derived from a case called *The Wagon Mound*, an appeal from the Australian courts (see Chapter 14).

The advantages and disadvantages of the binding precedent doctrine

Conflicting opinions exist about the value of the binding precedent system. The advantages are said to be:

1 *Certainty*. The system promotes valuable certainty in the law. A party can generally be given a reasonably clear prediction of the outcome of its case.

2 *Flexibility*. The necessarily firm rules are tempered by the ability of the higher courts to overrule their own decisions. A court's ability to distinguish or reconcile decisions on their facts also promotes flexibility.

3 *Practical nature*. Principles of pure case law can be developed in response to actual problems and tailored to solve them.

4 *Speed*. The law can be developed without waiting for Parliament to legislate in a new area.

The disadvantages of the system often appear correlative to the perceived advantages:

1. *Uncertainty*. The powers of the courts to distinguish and reconcile binding precedents often lead to confusing hairline distinctions and distorted applications of case law.

2. *Rigidity*. Certainty is preserved by rigid rules which arguably inhibit development of the law.

3. *Retrieval problems*. The vast amount of case law makes it easy for relevant precedents to be overlooked during preparation for litigation, and increases the time and, therefore, the cost to the client.

4. *Haphazard development*. A change in the law depends on a case with relevant facts reaching the appropriate court. This usually means the Court of Appeal or the House of Lords; litigants do not necessarily have the means to take their cases that far.

5. *Undemocratic*. The development of pure case law by judges (not interpreting statutes) is not appropriate since they are not democratically appointed and law-making conflicts with parliamentary sovereignty.

The Human Rights Act 1998 (HRA 1998)

This important statute, which came into force in October 2000, makes most of the rights in the European Convention on Human Rights directly enforceable in the English courts. It has the potential directly and indirectly to be highly influential on the content and interpretation of legislation and on the way case law is developed.

The legal and political background to the Act

The **European Convention on Human Rights** (the Convention) was drafted by the Council of Europe and came into force in 1953. It now has over 40 signatories, including the UK. It requires signatory states to uphold a number of fundamental civil rights, including the rights to liberty and security (Article 5), freedom of thought, conscience and religion (Article 9), freedom of expression (Article 10), and freedom of assembly and association (Article 11). The rights to life (Article 2), a fair trial (Article 6) and privacy and family life (Article 8) are also included. There is a right to manifest your religion under Article 9 and a right to access to religion (Protocol 1, Article 2). Until the HRA 1998, none of these was directly and specifically enforceable in the UK courts. Individuals had to take claims that the UK had breached its duties under the Convention to the **European Court of Human Rights (ECtHR)** at Strasbourg, if no remedy had been found to exist in their case by the UK courts under domestic law.

The Convention, even when not directly binding on the English courts, was always used as an aid to statutory interpretation and to determine the scope of the common law. Decisions of the ECtHR were used as persuasive precedents.

The Convention and the ECtHR must not be confused with the law and institutions of the EU. They are different in their origins, signatories and operations. However, the European Court of Justice, based at Luxembourg, which is responsible for upholding the law of the European Union, tends to reflect the principles of the Convention in its decisions.

The operation of the HRA 1998

Section 6 of the HRA 1998 requires 'public authorities' to act compatibly with the Convention. Public authorities include central government departments and local authorities, as well as the courts, tribunals and police forces. A breach of the Convention by a **public authority** is therefore now actionable in the domestic courts.

The judges' functions

Interpretation of Convention rights (s 2)

When the court is deciding any issue which has 'arisen in connection with human rights' it must take into account the case law of the ECtHR.

Interpretation of legislation (s 3)

The court must, 'so far as it is possible to do so', interpret legislation so that it is compatible with Convention rights. Note that the duty under s 3 is not an absolute one. To preserve parliamentary sovereignty, the Act does not permit the court to override a statute found to be incompatible with the Convention. Instead, the court has the power (s 4) to issue a declaration of incompatibility to the relevant minister, who may then at his or her discretion ask Parliament to amend the legislation. In the first year of the operation of the Act only three such declarations were issued in a total of 56 claims under the Act.

R (on the application of Pearson) v Secretary of State for the Home Department and Martinez; Hirst v Attorney-General (2001)

It was held that the Representation of the People Act 1983, which states that prisoners do not have the right to vote, was not incompatible with Article 10 of the Convention (right to freedom of expression). The Convention right is not absolute and proportionate restrictions can be imposed by the state.

Judicial remedies (s 8)

Where a breach of the Convention is proved the court has the power to grant a number of remedies, including damages and injunctions and other orders.

The impact of the Act

The Act has both a **direct** and **indirect** effect on the way domestic law is interpreted and applied.

Direct effect

The HRA 1998 introduces an entirely new right of action for alleged breaches of Convention rights, though only against a 'public authority'. Such an action cannot be brought against a private institution or individual.

Contrary to many people's belief prior to implementation, the direct impact of the Act on domestic law has not generally been a dramatic one. This is not surprising. Apart from the innate conservatism of the English judiciary, Convention rights are very broadly worded, giving judges flexibility to find compatibility. Almost all Convention rights are not absolute, but instead are hedged around with qualifications. For example, the right to life (Article 2) may not be breached if a person dies while being lawfully arrested. The right to liberty (Article 5) may be limited in the interests of protecting the public through lawful arrest. Similarly, a person with mental illness may be detained against their will if necessary for their own or the public's safety.

R (on the application of Laporte) v Chief Constable of Gloucestershire Constabulary (2007, HL)

Jane Laporte (and 26 other anti-war protestors) claimed that their rights to freedom of expression and freedom of assembly (ECHR, Articles 10 and 11) had been breached when the police prevented them from attending a lawful demonstration at RAF Fairford, just before the base was used to launch bombing raids on Iraq. The police stopped their coach, searched the passengers and then sealed it and escorted it back to London. The police argued that it was necessary to do so in order to prevent a breach of the peace, given the past history of some of the demonstrators and some items found on the coach (e.g. a can of spray paint). Only the three main speakers were allowed to proceed to Fairford.

Held (unanimously): the police's entirely disproportionate conduct had breached the applicants' Convention rights. They had also been unlawfully detained. At the point that the police intervened there was no reason to view them as other than '*committed and peaceful*' demonstrators. It was irrelevant that a breach of the peace might occur some time in the future. The HRA 1998 had created a '*constitutional shift*' and created a right to peaceful protest. The right to freedom of expression was '*an essential foundation of a democratic society*' (Lord Bingham).

The court, when determining a human rights claim, has to attempt to balance the interests of the parties to ensure neither suffers an undue limitation of their Convention rights. This is sometimes described as 'proportionality'. For example, a claim to protect a right of privacy (Article 8) must not be decided in a way that unduly curtails freedom of expression of the other party or which will unreasonably interfere with the public's right to information (Article 10). 'In the News' (opposite) provides a case example of rights to family life being compromised for public benefit.

The Act has not directly generated large numbers of claims and most of those which have been brought have not been successful. Between October 2000 and December 2001, 297 claims were heard and only 56 of them were upheld. However, the challenge under the Act affected the outcome, reasoning or procedure in 207 of them, which indicates that the Convention was at least highly influential.

In the News

Austin v Commissioner of Police of the Metropolis (2009, HL)

Ms Austin took part in a large May Day demonstration against global capitalism in Oxford Street in London involving about 3,000 people in 2001. The police, who had not been informed that the demonstration would take place, decided that the only workable strategy to prevent injury, damage and violence was to form a cordon round a large crowd of demonstrators near Oxford Circus and then disperse them in an orderly fashion. The dispersal took seven hours due to the behaviour of a large minority of the demonstrators who became obstructive and violent. Some prised up paving stones and hurled lumps of the masonry at the police. Others obstructed arrest of violent demonstrators and refused generally to co-operate with the police.

Ms Austin claimed that by detaining her in the cordon the police had deprived her of her liberty in breach of Article 5(1) of the ECHR. Her claim was unsuccessful in the lower courts and she appealed to the House of Lords.

Held: measures by the police which impacted on an individual's liberty must be proportionate to the situation and done in good faith, in order to maintain the fundamental principle that detention must not be arbitrary. The crowd control undertaken by the police was done in the public interest with the intention of enabling orderly dispersal of the demonstrators as soon as reasonably possible. The size and behaviour of the crowd had made controlled dispersal unusually difficult and slow. Consquently, the detention of the demonstrators had not amounted to a breach of the ECHR and Ms Austin's appeal must be dismissed.

R (on the application of Begum) v *Headteacher and Governors of Denbigh High School* (2006, HL)

Begum's school, while accommodating Muslim dress, only permitted girls to wear the *shalwar kameez*. Begum was happy with this initially but after two years insisted on wearing the *jilbab*. For the next two years she was excluded from the school. There were other schools nearer her home which permitted the *jilbab*. She claimed that Denbigh High School had deprived her of her right to manifest her religion (Article 9) and her right to access education (Protocol 1, Article 2) of the ECHR.

Held (by majority): her right to religious expression had not been breached. The school had acted with proportionality in devising a dress code which 'respected Muslim beliefs but did so in an inclusive, unthreatening and uncompetitive way'.

Held (unanimously): she had not been deprived of access to education. Her absence from school was due to her refusal to comply with a reasonable rule and her failure to obtain a place at a school which would have accommodated her religious beliefs.

Indirect effect

As indicated above, a court as a public authority is obligated under s 6 to act compatibly with the Convention. This, combined with its duties to take ECtHR judgments into account (s 2) and to interpret statutes compatibly (s 3), means that since 2000 Convention law has been influential on the outcome of a number of cases which were not brought under the Act. In *A v B sub nom Garry Flitcroft* v *Mirror Group Newspapers Ltd* (2002, CA), the court refused to grant an injunction for breach of confidence to a professional footballer to prevent publication of the story of his extramarital exploits. The court in its decision balanced the claimant's right to privacy against the rights to freedom of expression and the public interest and found that these outweighed the claimant's rights. (More detail on this and other similar cases below at pages 531–2.)

The Human Rights Act 1998 has clearly already had a significant impact on the development of the law and a human rights culture is beginning clearly to emerge. You will find a number of examples of relevant decisions in later chapters.

Chapter summary

Sources of English law
EU, British Parliament, and English courts.

EC institutions
The Council of Ministers, the European Council, the European Commission, the European Court of Justice and the European Parliament.

European legislation
Regulations, Directives, Decisions.

British parliamentary legislation
Direct: Acts of Parliament. An Act starts life as a Bill, which must successfully pass through three readings and a committee stage in each House before receiving the Royal Assent.
Delegated: Orders in Council, statutory instruments, rules and regulations, bye-laws.

The courts
Case law: created by judges, e.g. much of contract and tort law on a case-by-case basis.

Statutory interpretation of direct and delegated legislation using literal/golden/mischief/purposive approach.

The law of precedent: judges have regard to previous decisions and must apply those which are binding.

A precedent is binding if (a) *ratio decidendi* relevant to the current case, and (b) it comes from a higher court in the hierarchy, *or* (c) the case is being heard in the House of Lords or Court of Appeal which follow their own decisions.

Note: Crown/county/magistrates' court decisions are not binding on other courts nor on themselves.

The Human Rights Act 1998
Direct effect: ECHR rights directly enforceable by individuals against a 'public authority'.
Indirect effect: The court must act compatibly with the Convention. Therefore, its content and case law may be influential in shaping the judge's decision in any case.

Key terms

Binding precedent: a judicial decision which a court must follow.

Council of Ministers: Consists of the government minister from each EU state whose portfolio reflects the business of the meeting (e.g. Internal Affairs).

Contextual approach: vague words in a statute take their meaning from their immediate/general context.

Decision: EU legislation binding in one state only.

Key terms (Continued)

Delegated legislation: law made by a body authorised to do so by Act of Parliament.

Direct effect: under the HRA 1998 the ECHR can be enforced in cases against a public authority in an English court.

Direct legislation: law made by Parliament/Acts of Parliament.

Directive: EU legislation aimed at harmonising law of member states which becomes effective once domestic law is passed to implement it.

Ejusdem generis **rule:** 'of the same class'. If a class of people/things is specified by the Act any person/thing within that class comes within the Act.

European Council: an EU institution composed of the foreign ministers from each member state.

European Convention on Human Rights: the fundamental freedoms to be expected by the citizens of a democratic state and binding on its 54 state signatories. (*Not* EU legislation.)

European Court of Justice: EU institution which hears cases from/against member states and the EU.

European Court of Human Rights: hears cases concerning alleged breaches of the ECHR by citizens against their home state. (*Not* an EU institution.)

European Parliament: EU institution, members of which are elected by citizens of each member state.

Golden rule: Rule of statutory interpretation stating that if two literal meanings exist the least ridiculous be adopted.

Green Paper: discussion paper containing proposals for new legislation.

Indirect effect: the HRA 1998 makes the ECHR influential on the outcome of cases not brought under the Act as the court must act compatibly with ECHR and take account of ECtHR judgments.

Literal rule: the words of a statute must be taken at face value.

Mischief rule: a statute must be interpreted to remedy the gap in the law which it was intended to correct.

Obiter dictum/obiter dicta: a judicial statement indicating how the judge would interpret the law in different circumstances.

Overrule: the court declares an existing binding precedent to be no longer good law.

Per incuriam: a case decision found later to have been incorrectly reached, because the court did not have the opportunity to consider potentially relevant law.

Persuasive decision: a non-binding but influential precedent.

Private Member's Bill: proposed by a backbench MP, as opposed to a minister (Government Bill).

Purposive approach: the court interprets a statute in the way which will implement its purpose.

Public authority: HRA 1998, s 6 includes the courts and any body with public functions.

Ratio decidendi: the reasons in law and fact why a judge reached a decision.

Regulation: EU legislation which is directly effective in UK.

Reversing a decision: on appeal the party who won becomes the loser.

White Paper: details of proposed legislation with explanation of what it is intended to achieve.

Quiz 2

1. Name the three main sources of English law.
2. Distinguish between EU regulations and directives.
3. Name the stages through which a Bill will pass in Parliament.
4. Name two kinds of delegated legislation.
5. Explain the difference between the literal rule and the mischief rule.
6. Explain how the *ejusdem generis* rule works.
7. When may a precedent be binding?
8. What is the difference in the potential effect of a *ratio decidendi* and an *obiter dictum*?
9. Why might the status of a decision by the Judicial Committee of the Privy Council be described as an anomaly in the law of precedent?
10. In what circumstances may a right of action be brought under the Human Rights Act 1998?

Answers to all quizzes can be found in Appendix 2.

Take a closer look

The following cases provide important examples of how the law you have studied in this chapter has developed. They are primary sources illustrating the law in action and give you more detail about their facts, as well as helping you to understand the law and to appreciate how the judges reached their decisions.

Try looking them up in the law reports or accessing them via a database, e.g. Bailli (www.bailii.org/databases.html). LexisNexis or Westlaw may be available in your university or college library, or you may find extracts in a case book. (See Appendix 1: Additional resources.)

Adler v *George* [1964] 1 All ER 628
R (on the application of Begum) v *Denbigh High School* [2006] 2 All ER 487, HL
Royal College of Nursing v *DHSS* [1981] AC 800, HL
Sweet v *Parsley* [1969] 1 All ER 347, HL

Web activity

Please go to:

www.yourrights.org.uk/

Click on 'The Human Rights Act' to get more information about the ECHR and the HRA 1998. There is a lot of interesting information on this site that you also might wish to explore.

Assignment 1

With reference to decided cases, discuss the impact of the Human Rights Act 1998 on the rights of claimants.

mylawchamber

Visit **www.mylawchamber.co.uk/adams** to access multiple choice questions and glossary flashcards to test yourself on this chapter. You'll also find weblinks to the web activity in this chapter.

Use Case Navigator to read in full some of the key cases referenced in this chapter:

Central London Property Trust v *High Trees House* [1947] KB 130

chapter 4
THE LAW OF CONTRACT:
offer and acceptance

Introduction

A contract is a legally binding agreement concerning a bargain which is essentially commercial in its nature and involves the sale or hire of commodities such as goods, services or land. Such contracts are known as **simple** or **parol** contracts, since they are usually enforceable without having to be put into writing. You probably make literally hundreds of contracts every year when doing everyday things like shopping, getting your hair cut, or getting your DVD player repaired. None of the legal paraphernalia that the words 'forming a contract' may bring to mind are involved in such transactions. They are legally binding without documents, signatures or witnesses. If the goods or services provided to you are defective, you have legal rights arising from the contract you made with the shop. To enforce those rights you will, of course, need to prove the existence of the contract. The receipt is handy evidence of this. However, if you have lost this, other evidence – like a credit card docket, or a cheque stub, or the word of your Aunt Ada who was with you at the time – will be perfectly adequate. In this chapter we shall examine how contracts are formed.

Learning Objectives

When you have studied this chapter you should be able to:

- List the essential requirements for a binding contract
- Define offer and acceptance
- Distinguish between an invitation to treat and an offer
- Appreciate the importance of reasonable expectation in determining intention in offer and acceptance
- Demonstrate how offer and acceptance may be effectively communicated.

Photo: uk retail Alan King/Alamy

The essentials of a binding contract

No contract can come into being unless the following features exist:

1 an **offer**;

2 an **acceptance**;

3 **consideration** (each party will contribute something of material value to the bargain);

4 **intention to create legal relations**.

Writing is not usually essential

As indicated above in the Introduction, writing is not a legal requirement for the great majority of contracts, though it may well be useful proof of the contents of a complex contract. While the law does not require a building contract to be in writing, most clients would not be very happy to have settled complicated terms by word of mouth only.

A minority of contracts *must* be written in order to be valid. These include contracts to sell land under the Law of Property (Miscellaneous Provisions) Act 1989, and contracts to obtain credit which are governed by the Consumer Credit Act 1974. Where such regulation applies, the written document comprises the contract. Without the contractual document the law will treat the transaction as if it does not exist, regardless of other available evidence.

Under the Statute of Frauds 1677, contracts of guarantee – under which one party agrees to guarantee the debt of another party for the benefit of a creditor – will be unenforceable without written evidence.

Some transactions will be legally valid only if put in the form of a deed. You need not be concerned with these, which do not necessarily involve bargains at all and do not come within the scope of the law of parol contract.

The offer

This may be defined as a clear statement of the terms on which one party (the **offeror**) is prepared to do business with another party (the **offeree**). An offer may be bilateral or unilateral.

Most offers are **bilateral**, i.e. such an offer consists of a promise made in return for a promise. In a sale of goods contract, for example, the offeror promises to take and pay for goods and the offeree promises to supply goods of an appropriate description and standard. A **unilateral offer** is a promise made in return for the completion of a specified act. An offer of a reward for the return of lost property falls into this category.

A legally binding offer will include:

1 clearly stated terms;

2 intention to do business;

3 communication of that intention.

These must all exist for a valid offer to have been made.

Clearly stated terms

A statement may be held to be too vague to comprise a valid offer.

Guthing v Lynn (1831)

The buyer of a horse promised to pay the seller an extra £5 'if the horse is lucky for me'.

Held: this was too vague to be enforceable. No indication was given of what the promise really meant.

An apparently vague offer may be capable of clarification by reference to:

1 *The parties' previous dealings and the nature of the relevant trade.*

2 *Statutory implied terms.* For example, an offer to sell goods is valid even if no price is mentioned. Under the Sale of Goods Act 1979, s 8, if no price is stated, a reasonable price is payable.

3 *Arbitration clauses.* Sometimes the parties may purposely state terms vaguely and include provision for arbitration to settle disputes if and when they arise. This allows for later variations to take into account future needs, availability or price. Since the lack of clarity may be resolved, a binding offer exists.

Hillas v Arcos (1932, HL)

A contract to supply wood for one year contained an option permitting the buyer to buy more wood the next year, but it did not specify the terms on which the supply would be made.

Held: this was a valid offer. Clarification of this rather vague option could readily be gleaned from the previous business dealings of the parties, as well as from custom and practice in the timber trade.

Foley v Classique Coaches (1934, CA)

The arbitration clause in a long-term contract stated that F would supply petrol to the coach company 'at a price to be agreed in writing and from time to time'.

Held: the contract was binding as the arbitration clause would enable any lack of clarity about the price to be resolved when and if necessary.

Intention to do business

An offer represents the parties' 'last word' prior to acceptance. A statement which does not indicate commitment to be bound by its terms (if accepted) will not be interpreted as a binding offer.

Problems arise where a party, who believes that a binding offer has been made, communicates an 'acceptance'. The party then believes that a contract exists. However, if the original statement is not a binding offer, there will as yet be no contract, since a valid contract requires both binding offer and acceptance.

There are two types of statement which may be confused with a legally binding offer:

1 **invitation to treat**;

2 negotiation.

An invitation to treat

Most advertisements for the sale of goods, land or services are not usually treated by the courts as indicating the necessary intention to form an offer. Such statements invite potential customers to make an offer. It is then up to the business proprietor to decide whether or not to accept. Without acceptance, no contract exists; therefore, buyers have no rights to the goods, etc. they want to purchase.

Catalogues, price lists, menus and circulars advertising so-called 'cheap offers' at local businesses are interpreted this way. In *Partridge* v *Crittenden* (1968, HL) it was held that a magazine advertisement saying 'Bramble finch cocks and hens 25 shillings each' was an invitation to treat. Any offers came from those responding to it and asking to buy the birds.

A display of goods in a shop, with or without a price tag, is merely an invitation to treat.

Fisher v *Bell* (1961, CA)

The defendant exhibited a flick knife in his shop window and was prosecuted under the Restriction of Offensive Weapons Act 1959, s 1(1), for 'offering for sale' an offensive weapon.

Held: the defendant was not guilty since he had not made an offer. Goods in a shop window, even those bearing a price tag, represent an invitation to treat, not an offer. Customers make offers by saying that they are prepared to do business at the price shown. Sellers then decide if they want to accept; only if they do does any contract result.

As new methods of marketing develop the law needs to be interpreted to fit the new circumstances. Self-service shopping, which is the norm today, did not start to appear in the UK until the 1950s.

Pharmaceutical Society (GB) v *Boots Cash Chemists (Southern) Ltd* (1953, CA)

Boots introduced self service including its patent medicines and was prosecuted by the Pharmaceutical Society under the Pharmacy and Poisons Act 1933 which made it illegal to sell certain drugs 'without supervision of a registered pharmacist'.

Held: no offence had been committed. The medicines on display were merely an invitation to treat. The customer made an offer when handing the goods to the checkout operator. A pharmacist was present at this point and could be refuse the customer's offer if appropriate.

Electronic contract making became an important feature of marketing in the late twentieth century – Amazon sells a lot of copies of this book! So far, there is little case law (but see 'In the News' below at page 69 in relation to email communication).

The courts support the principle of invitation to treat in the interests of business efficiency. In practice, this may mean what is efficient for the sellers rather than for the disappointed buyer whose request the shopkeeper is able to refuse. However, if statements currently treated as invitations to treat were interpreted as offers, shopkeepers for example, would, be forced to demolish their window displays to remove goods which customers had contracted for simply by expressing their wish to buy them. Equally, the customer would be committed to buying something which did not look so good when more closely inspected.

(The Race Relations Act 1976 and the Sex Discrimination Act 1975 aim to prevent abuses of the right of a business to refuse a customer's offer. Similarly misleading pricing notices may be a criminal offence under Part III of the Consumer Protection Act 1987.)

Negotiation

Lengthy negotiations may lead up to the formation of a contract. Problems may occur where one party assumes that a statement represents the other party's offer and claims to have accepted it. The court will have to decide whether the alleged offeror had by that point indicated a sufficient intention to be bound. In a potentially complex contractual situation where protracted negotiations would normally be expected, a statement made early in the negotiations is unlikely to be held to be a valid offer.

Harvey v Facey (1893)

The claimants were interested in buying land which the defendant had not advertised for sale. They sent a telegram asking the defendant to state the lowest price he would accept. When the defendant replied with a mere statement of price, the claimants attempted to accept.

Held: no contract had been formed, since the statement of price was merely an early step in negotiations and did not amount to a valid offer.

However, it all depends on the facts; in the next case sufficient intention was found to exist:

Bigg v Boyd Gibbons (1971, CA)

In the course of negotiations, the claimant wrote to the defendants: 'For a quick sale I would accept £20,000.' The defendant wrote back accepting and the claimant then sent another letter in reply thanking the defendant 'for accepting my offer'.

Held: a binding offer was made in the claimant's first letter. Russell LJ said: '*I cannot escape the view having read the letters that the parties would regard themselves at the end of the correspondence ... as having struck a bargain for the sale and purchase of this property.*'

The offer must be communicated to the offeree

The offeror must know of the offer to be able legally to accept. The communication of an offer may be written or spoken, but it may often be by conduct, such as taking goods to the supermarket checkout, or putting money into a vending machine. An offer is most commonly made to an individual, but a unilateral offer may be made to the world at large. In such a case, a contract will be made with all the people who can and do fulfil the terms of the offer.

Carlill v *Carbolic Smoke Ball Co. Ltd* (1893, CA)

The defendants published an advertisement which claimed that their product would prevent influenza, and promised that they would pay £100 to any person who, having used the product correctly, still caught influenza. The advertisement also stated that £1,000 had been placed in a separate bank account to 'show their sincerity in the matter'.

Miss Carlill bought a smoke ball from her local chemist. When she became ill with influenza despite regularly sniffing her smoke ball as instructed, she claimed £100 from the manufacturers.

Held: the advertisement was a unilateral offer by the manufacturers to the world at large, which would be accepted by any person who knew of it and who contracted influenza after using the product as directed. The £1,000 bank deposit showed intention to enter a contract and was evidence that the advertisement was not just puffing the goods.

The offeree must, therefore, know of the offer in order legally to be able to accept it. Coincidental performance of the terms of an offer, made in ignorance of its existence, does not create a binding contract.

Bloom v *American Swiss Watch Co.* (1915)

The claimant gave evidence to the authorities which led to the arrest of some jewel thieves. He then discovered that the defendant had previously advertised a reward for such information. The defendant refused payment.

Held: the defendant was not legally obliged to pay as no contract to do so existed between the parties, since the offer of the reward had not been communicated to the claimant prior to his giving the information.

> ### In the News
>
> #### *J. Pereira Fernandes SA* v *Mehta* (2006)
>
> In this case Judge Pelling QC implicitly accepted that email offer and acceptance is a potentially valid form of communication, but gave no indication of any special rules concerning when communication is effective.
>
> The defendant by email agreed to guarantee the debts of a company of which he was a director. Under the Statute of Frauds 1677, contracts of guarantee require 'a written note or memorandum' including the main terms and signature of the guarantor to indicate intention to be bound by it.
>
> Held: the email was capable of being a sufficient note or memorandum, but as the defendant's name did not appear anywhere except in the address in the header, this was insufficient to fulfil the statutory requirement.

Tenders

A **tender** is a competitive offer to provide goods or services. Many businesses and other organisations will invite tenders to ensure that they get the best value for money. Some publicly funded bodies may be required to do so by law.

Although the request for tenders is an invitation to treat, it may also be an offer by the advertisers to *consider* any offer submitted to them.

Blackpool & Fylde Aero Club v *Blackpool Council* (1990, CA)

The Aero Club was invited by the council to tender for a concession to provide pleasure flights for the summer tourist trade. Although the club delivered its tender before the deadline, the council, due to an oversight, failed to clear its letter box and so the tender did not reach the appropriate committee in time to be considered.

Held by the Court of Appeal: as well as inviting tenders, the council's request also implicitly contained a unilateral offer to consider any tender submitted by the deadline. The council was therefore in breach of this contract with the Aero Club which had been deprived of its chance to be the successful bidder.

Bingham LJ said:

> He [the tenderer] *need not accept any tender ... but where as here the tenders are solicited from selected parties all of them known to the invitor, and where a local authority's invitation prescribes a clear, orderly and familiar procedure ... the invitee is protected at least to this extent: If he submits a conforming tender before the deadline, he is entitled ... as ... of contractual right to be sure that his tender will after the deadline be considered ... The law would I think be defective if it did not give effect to that.*

The termination of offers

An offer, if not accepted, can be brought to an end in a number of different ways.

Death

If the offeree dies, the offer dies too. The death of the offeror terminates the offer if its terms require personal performance. An offer may survive if it can be performed by personal representatives.

Bradbury v *Morgan* (1862)

During his life the deceased had made a standing offer to guarantee another man's debt. The debtor failed to pay the creditor, who, not knowing of the death of the guarantor, wrote to claim his money.

Held: the guarantor's obligations could be satisfied out of his estate, because at the time he accepted the offer the creditor could not reasonably have known of the offeror's death.

Refusal and counter-offer

If an offer is rejected it ceases to exist. If offerees then change their minds and try to accept, they will in contractual terms be making a new offer. The same result is achieved by a **counter-offer**. This is an attempt to vary the terms of the existing offer to get more favourable terms, like a price reduction.

Hyde v *Wrench* (1840)

The defendant offered to sell his farm for £1,000. The claimant at first said that he would pay only £950, but after a few days said he would pay the full price. He heard nothing from the defendant.

Held: there was no contract between the parties: the defendant had not accepted the offer from the claimant, who had destroyed the defendant's original offer by his counter-offer of a reduced price. The claimant's subsequent statement that he would pay the asking price could not revive the original offer. It was a new offer which the defendant never accepted.

If the offeree, while not accepting an offer, asks for further information, or tests out the ground to see if further negotiation is possible, this is not treated as a counter-offer; it, therefore, does not destroy the offer. Therefore, in *Stevenson* v *McLean* (1880) an offer to sell iron at a certain price was not destroyed when the offeree enquired whether delivery and payment might be made in instalments. This was not a counter-offer of different terms, merely an enquiry as to whether the terms might be varied, which therefore did not destroy the original offer.

Lapse of time

An offer will cease to exist if not accepted within any specified time limit. Otherwise it will lapse if not accepted within a reasonable time.

Ramsgate Hotel Co. Ltd v *Montefiore* (1866)

The defendant applied to buy some shares in June but heard nothing more until November when the company informed him that the shares were his.

Held: the company's delay in notification of the allotment of the shares had made the defendant's offer lapse and the acceptance came too late to result in a contract.

Revocation

Offerors are entitled to change their minds and withdraw offers at any time right up to the moment of acceptance. If, at an auction sale, you place the highest bid and the auctioneer is saying 'going, going …', you still have time to shout that you are withdrawing your offer, as it will not be accepted until the auctioneer's gavel hits the table (Sale of Goods Act 1979, s 57). However, if you do choose to do this, it might be a good idea to leave the auction room immediately.

Notice of revocation is crucial; it is not effective unless the offeree knows of it. Personal notification is usual, but is not essential as long as the offeree knew or reasonably should have known that the offer had been withdrawn. In *Dickinson* v *Dodds* (1876, CA) Dodds made an offer to sell property to Dickinson, but sold it to a third party (Allan) before Dickinson responded. A mutual acquaintance of the buyer and Dodds told Dickinson of the sale and this was held to be adequate notice of revocation. A reasonable person would have realised that since the property had been disposed elsewhere the offer was no longer open. James LJ said: *'It is to my mind perfectly clear that before there was any attempt at acceptance by the plaintiff, he was perfectly well aware that Dodds had changed his mind, and that he had in fact agreed to sell the property to Allan. It is impossible, therefore, to say that there was ever that existence of the same mind between the two parties which is essential in point of law to the making of an agreement.'*

Real Life

Horace offered to sell his grand piano to his neighbour Hilda, who said she was really interested but needed to think about whether she could afford it. Later on that day Frederick, a friend of Horace, came to visit and, hearing that the piano was for sale, said he would buy it and collect it the next day. In the morning Frederick came back with the money, a van, and a burly assistant. With Horace's help, they got the piano onto a trolley and wheeled it down to the van and loaded it up. Emmeline, Horace's next-door neighbour, who is somewhat inquisitive, asked Horace what was going on and he told her. That evening Emmeline bumped into Hilda and told her what she had heard.

As *Dickinson* v *Dodds* indicates, Horace's offer to Hilda has been revoked, since reliable information even from a third party, not acting on the offeror's instructions, is sufficient notice.

A *promise to keep an offer open* for a certain time or to give someone 'first refusal' will not be legally binding unless the offeree gave some payment to the offeror in return for the favour. Otherwise the offeror is making only a gratuitous promise: giving something for nothing. Such a promise is not a contractual one, since it lacks consideration (see Chapter 5). In the scenario above, Horace might have lost a sale to Frederick if he had waited for Hilda to make up her mind, and then she might have come back and said she was not interested after all. The offeror is therefore free to withdraw (revoke) the promise at any time before the offer is accepted. In *Routledge* v *Grant* (1828) the defendant offered to buy the claimant's house, promising that he would keep the offer open for six weeks. It was held that he could withdraw the promise at any time before the offer was accepted, as his promise was merely gratuitous.

If the offeree does pay for the offer to be held open, a legally binding **option** is created. This means that the offeree has a contract that allows time to choose whether or not to accept the offer. This is different from putting down a deposit on goods or land. An option agreement gives you time to choose *whether* or not to buy, whereas the deposit is evidence that a contract to purchase has been made.

It would obviously be unjust to apply the ordinary rules of revocation to *unilateral offers*, for two reasons:

1 Notice. A unilateral offer is often made to the world at large. If the offeror decides to revoke such an offer, it would be impossible to notify everyone who saw it. Provided the offeror takes reasonable steps to give notice, this will be sufficient. Putting another advertisement in the same newspaper which carried the offer would clearly be adequate.

2 Incomplete acceptance. Acceptance of a unilateral offer always involves the performance of an act. If an offeree has begun but not completed the acceptance of a unilateral offer, it would be unjust to allow the offeror to revoke the offer. Therefore, revocation may not be effective if the offeree is already in the process of accepting a unilateral offer.

Errington v Errington & Woods (1952, CA)

A father bought a house and promised his son and daughter-in-law that it would become theirs if they paid all the mortgage instalments.

Held: although his offer would technically be accepted only when the last payment had been made, the father's promise was irrevocable as long as the payments were kept up. While the payments continued it would be unjust for the offer to be revoked.

The acceptance

The offeree, by acceptance, agrees to be bound by all the terms of the offer. To be legally binding, such acceptance must fulfil three rules:

1 it must be a 'mirror image' of the offer;

2 it must be firm;

3 it must be communicated to the offeror.

Acceptance must be a 'mirror image' of the offer

The offeree must be agreeing to all the terms of the offer and not trying to introduce new terms. In *Jones* v *Daniel* (1894) the offeree responded to an offer by submitting a draft contract which included some new terms. This response was held to be a counter-offer, not an acceptance.

Where two businesses are negotiating a contract, they may each wish to contract on their own standard terms (pre-set terms not open to negotiation). The offerors present their standard terms, but the offerees, instead of accepting on those terms, reply with their own set of standard terms. This is sometimes called 'the battle of the forms'.

Butler Machine Tools Ltd v *Ex-Cell-O Ltd* (1979, CA)

The claimants, on their standard terms, offered to sell machine tools to the defendants. These terms named a price but allowed the claimants to vary this on delivery. The defendants replied with their terms, which specified a fixed price and required the claimants to return an attached acknowledgement slip indicating that they were prepared to supply the defendants' order on these terms. The claimants did so, but when the goods were delivered, they tried to claim that the price could be increased.

Held: the claimants' offer had not been accepted by the defendants: their reply was a counter-offer accepted by the claimants when they returned the slip. The contract was on the defendants' terms and only the fixed price was payable.

Acceptance must be firm

Conditional acceptance is not binding. An acceptance containing the words '**subject to contract**' is not generally a valid acceptance and use of this phrase is normal practice in sales of land. The parties will not be legally bound to each other until exchange of contracts takes place. This is meant to assist buyers by giving them time to carry out surveys and searches before deciding to commit themselves. It can also mean that the seller is free to sell to another buyer who is prepared to offer more money in the meantime. Such 'gazumping' may cause financial loss to the first buyer, who may have spent money on legal and survey fees and is then left without means of redress against the seller, since there is as yet no binding contract with the seller. However, the intention of the parties is paramount and exceptionally the court may decide that, despite its provisional appearance, it is outweighed by other factors and valid acceptance has taken place. In *Branco* v *Cobarro* (1947, CA) a written agreement described as 'a provisional agreement until a fully legalised contract is drawn up' was held to be a valid acceptance, since it completely reflected all the terms already agreed between the parties.

Acceptance must be communicated

The law relating to communication involves a number of different rules.

Communication is effective only if made by an authorised person

Powell v Lee (1908)

The claimant was notified that his job application had been successful by a member of an appointments board, which then decided to give the job to someone else.

Held: the person who had told the claimant of his success had not been authorised to do so and therefore acceptance had not been effectively communicated.

Methods of communication

Conduct

Brogden v Metropolitan Railway Co. (1877, HL)

Mr Brogden had supplied coal to the railway company for some time, when the company suggested that they should regularise their arrangements with a new contract. The draft contract was sent to Brogden who added certain terms, including the name of an arbitrator. He then marked it 'approved' and sent it back to the company. He heard no more but the company continued to order coal, which Brogden supplied on the terms of the draft agreement.

Held: Brogden's amendments to the draft contract amounted to a counter-offer which had been accepted. The company's intention to assent was in itself insufficient to be acceptance. It became sufficient only once Brogden knew of it. Here the company's conduct evidenced acceptance, either when it placed the first order, or when it accepted the first delivery.

Communication is, therefore, effective only when it reaches the offeror or the offeror's place of business. Commercial practice may enable the court to interpret conduct in relation to the making of offer and acceptance. Thus, in *Confetti Records* v *Warner Music UK* (2003) the sending of an invoice together with a music track was deemed to be an offer by Confetti to sell the material to Warner to be marketed. By producing an album containing the track Warner accepted the offer.

However, only unequivocal conduct will make the acceptance binding:

Inland Revenue Commissioners v Fry (2001)

Ms Fry owed the Revenue £113,000 and sent a cheque for £10,000, with an accompanying letter stating that this was all that she could raise and that it should be regarded as full and final settlement of the debt. The Revenue cashed the cheque on receipt and the case worker to whom the letter was forwarded subsequently phoned Ms Fry to tell her that the sum could either be treated as part payment of her debt, or she could have the money back.

Held: the Revenue had not made a valid acceptance. Cashing the cheque gave rise to no more than a rebuttable presumption of acceptance and here the presumption had clearly been rebutted by the case worker's subsequent phone call. No reasonable person would believe that banking the cheque indicated intention to be bound by the terms of the offer. The Revenue's administration system would not be likely to permit a contract, under which it gave up its rights to substantial sums of money, to be concluded in this way.

Verbal communication

Acceptance is effectively communicated only when the offeror has received notice of it. In a face-to-face situation it will usually be immediately evident if any communication problems have occurred. However, if the parties cannot see each other this may be more problematic; acceptance by *telephone* is held to be effective only on being heard by the offeror. The courts have extended this principle to *telex* transmissions. In *Entores Ltd* v *Miles Far East Corp.* (1955, CA) the Court of Appeal made it clear that acceptance by telex should be treated like acceptance by telephone: instantaneous and effective on being received.

Brinkibon Ltd v Stahag Stahl und Stahlwarenhandels GmbH (1982, HL)

The House of Lords suggested (*obiter dicta*) that telex messages transmitted when the receiver's office was closed would be effective only once the office had reopened.

The *Brinkibon* ruling was applied in *Mondial Shipping and Chartering BV* v *Astarte Shipping Ltd* (1995) where it was held that a telex message sent just before midnight on a Friday was communicated at 9 a.m. the following Monday when the receiver's office opened for business.

When developing such rules the courts are guided by the '**reasonable expectations of honest men'** in the context of accepted commercial practice. In *Entores* it was stressed that if it were the fault of the offeror that the message was not received (due perhaps to lack of ink in the teleprinter), the offeror would still be bound, as the offeree would reasonably expect successful receipt. This principle, generally applied by the courts, enables objective assessment of the parties' behaviour from which it can be determined whether the intention to offer or accept is adequately demonstrated.

Electronic communications

As yet, there are no reported cases involving communication via fax, or answerphone. Using the reasonable expectations approach, *faxes* are likely to be treated like telex messages.

It can probably be successfully argued that messages left on *answering machines* are not communicated until, like any telephone message, the recipient actually hears them. It is, after all, immediately evident to the sender that the message is not going to be transmitted at once.

Emails have implicitly been accepted by the courts as a valid means of communication of acceptance but without any ruling on when communication becomes effective (see *Pereira Fernandes SA* v *Mehta* (2006), above at page 69). It may be reasonable to argue that since, once they have been sent, arrival may well be instantaneous but delays may occur in transmission via the server, perhaps here communication should be deemed to exist once the message is capable of being downloaded to the receiver's mailbox.

Internet sales are covered, though not in detail, by the Electronic Commerce (EC Directive) Regulations 2002 (which implement the E-Commerce Directive 2000/31/EC). Regulation 11 states that electronic orders/acknowledgements of orders 'are deemed to be received when the parties to whom they are addressed are able to access them'. This suggests that when a contract is made on the *Internet,* the website details of goods are an invitation to treat. Presumably, the customer communicates the offer by placing the order, entering name, address and credit card details and transmitting this information to the seller with a click on the relevant button. The seller will not be deemed to have accepted until it communicates acceptance by sending a message confirming that the order has been placed successfully. This will happen only after it has successfully accessed the customer's credit or debit card.

The post rule

The **post rule** provides an exception to the usual communication rule. In the nineteenth and early twentieth centuries the only method of communication for parties contracting at a distance from each other was the post. In the milestone case of *Adams* v *Lindsell* (1818), it was held that once a letter of acceptance is posted, a contract comes into existence immediately. The postal rules were later extended to cover telegrams. The rules were clarified further by *Household Insurance* v *Grant* (1879, CA) which held that communication of acceptance by post is effective even if a letter is delayed in the post or fails to reach the offeror, as long as this is not due to some fault of the offeree's: for example, an incorrect address.

Worth thinking about?

Judges always have a reason for changing the law.

Why do you think the post rule was developed?

Suggested solutions can be found in Appendix 2.

Only postal acceptance produces an instantaneous legal effect: a postal offer or revocation is effective only on receipt.

Byrne v *Van Tienhoven* (1880)

1 October:	The defendant posted an offer from Cardiff to the claimant in New York.
8 October:	The defendant changed his mind and posted a letter of revocation.
11 October:	The defendant's offer arrived and the claimant sent a telegram of acceptance.
15 October:	The claimant affirmed his acceptance by letter.
20 October:	The letter of revocation was received by the claimant.

Held: a contract was formed on 11 October when the claimant mailed his telegram of acceptance. The revocation was not communicated to the claimant until 20 October and was, therefore, too late to be effective.

> It has always been possible for offerors to avoid the postal rules either by specifying a different means of communication, or by stating that they would not be bound until receipt of an acceptance letter. Even where an offeror specifies nothing to this effect, the courts may be prepared to imply such an intention.

Holwell Securities v Hughes (1974, CA)

The offeror had granted an option to the offeree concerning the purchase of some land, which had to be exercised by 'notice in writing'. The claimant's letter of acceptance was posted before the deadline but failed to reach the offeror before the deadline expired, though this was not the claimant's fault.

Held: no contract resulted from the postal acceptance. The postal rule was implicitly excluded by the offeror, who, by requiring notice in writing, had indicated that for communication to be effective it must actually receive the letter of acceptance.

> Today the postal rules do not play an important part in the law of contract, though they continue to feature in exam papers. Parties contracting at a distance now generally have much faster and more reliable means of communication available to them. Even where the parties choose to use the post, it is very common for offerors to state that no contract will result until they receive an acceptance.

The offeror cannot waive the communication rule

In a bilateral contract situation offerors cannot bind offerees by saying that they will assume acceptance unless the offerees tell them differently. The communication rule ensures that an offeree is not pressurised into acceptance.

Felthouse v Bindley (1862)

The claimant offered to buy a horse from his nephew, John, who was selling up all his farm stock. The claimant said that he would assume John's acceptance unless told otherwise. Intending to accept, John instructed the auctioneer to withdraw the horse from the sale, but by mistake the auctioneer sold it. The claimant sued the auctioneer in tort.

Held: the claimant's action failed because he was unable to prove that he was the horse's owner. Since John had not communicated his intention to accept to the claimant, there was no contract under which ownership of the horse could pass. The auctioneer had not disposed of the claimant's property. When the sale took place the horse still belonged to John.

In a unilateral contract acceptance and performance constitute the same act, so no prior communication of acceptance is practicable. If you see a notice offering a reward for the return of lost property, you will be able to accept only if you find it and actually return it, thereby performing the act for which the reward was promised. You cannot be refused it because you have not given advance notice.

The offeror may expressly require a particular method of communication

The court will usually be prepared to treat any reasonable method of communication as effective. Where no mode is specifically requested, the mode of offer and the nature of the subject matter of the contract may indicate suitable methods of response. For example, a telephone offer of perishable goods would necessitate a swift means of communicating acceptance.

Chapter summary

Formation of a simple contract requires the following factors to be present:
Agreement (offer and acceptance).
Bargain (consideration).
Intention to create legal relations.
Writing not essential unless required by statute.

Offer
The *final* terms on which the offeror is prepared to contract which becomes effective once received by the offeree.
An offer may be bilateral (a promise in return for a promise) or *unilateral* (a promise in return for an act).
An invitation to treat or merely negotiating statement is not an offer because it does not indicate finality or intention to be bound.

An offer may be revoked up until the time of acceptance.
An offer will lapse unless accepted within a stipulated or reasonable time.

Acceptance
Acceptance is only binding in law if it is firm and completely reflects the offer terms. Any attempt to vary the terms may amount to a counter-offer.
It must be communicated. This usually requires receipt by the offeror, but exceptionally a letter of acceptance is binding once posted.
Determining the legal existence of offer and acceptance: the court interprets the behaviour of the parties objectively in accordance with 'the expectations of reasonable men'.

Key terms

Acceptance: unconditional assent to the terms of an offer.

Bilateral offer: a contractual promise of performance of an act in return for the other party's promise of performance.

Consideration: money/goods/services/land representing the bargain element of the contract.

Counter-offer: an offer made in response to an existing offer.

Intention to create legal relations: the parties' intention to make their agreement legally binding.

Invitation to treat: encouragement to make an offer, usually by advertisement of some kind.

Key terms (Continued)

Offer: a full clear statement of terms on which the maker is prepared to do business with the person(s) to whom the offer is communicated.

Offeree: the recipient of the offer.

Offeror: the maker of the offer.

Option: a promise to allow an offeree time to consider doing business on the terms of a pre-existing offer.

Parol: see simple/parol contract (below).

Post rule: the default rule governing acceptance by post which is that the acceptance is binding from the moment of posting.

Reasonable expectations of honest men: the objective standard by which the court decides whether a party's conduct evidences sufficient intention to be contractually bound.

Simple/parol contract: a contract that does not need to be in the form of a deed to be valid.

Subject to contract: a provisional acceptance, prior to a contract being drawn up.

Tender: a competitive offer (bid) to provide goods or services.

Unilateral offer: an offer of a promise in return for the performance of an act.

Quiz 4

1. Does an offer exist in the following circumstances?
   (a) Joshua puts a teddy bear wearing a price ticket in his shop window.
   (b) Ruth distributes flyers stating 'Cheap Offer: 10% off the cost of all our pizzas'.
   (c) Mary advertises a reward of £50 for the return of her lost bracelet.
   (d) Martha returns Mary's bracelet and then discovers that a reward was offered.
   (e) Peter offered to sell his car to Esther for £3,000; Esther told him she would pay only £2,500.
   (f) Elizabeth offered to sell her fridge-freezer to Paul for £100. He asked her to give him three days to decide. The next day she sold the freezer to Jacob.

2. Has a valid acceptance resulted in the following situations?
   (a) John offers to sell potatoes to Thomas, who replies that he will take them if he can raise the money.
   (b) Eve offers to sell apples to Matthew and tells him that she will assume that he wants to buy them unless he tells her to the contrary by 10 o'clock on Saturday morning. The deadline has now passed but Matthew has not been in touch.
   (c) Luke sent a letter to Michael offering to sell an antique clock. Michael replies accepting, but his letter is lost in the post.
   (d) Susanna offered by telephone to rewire Antony's house. He accepted, but Susanna did not hear because the line went dead.

Answers to all quizzes can be found in Appendix 2.

Take a closer look

The following cases provide important examples of how the law you have studied in this chapter has developed. They are primary sources illustrating the law in action and give you more detail about their facts, as well as helping you to understand the law and to appreciate how the judges reached their decisions.

Try looking them up in the law reports or accessing them via a database, e.g. Bailli (www.bailii.org/databases.html). LexisNexis or Westlaw may be available in your university or college library, or you may find extracts in a case book. (See Appendix 1: Additional resources.)

Carlill v *Carbolic Smoke Ball Co. Ltd* [1893] 1 QB 156, CA

Blackpool & Fylde Aero Club v *Blackpool Council* [1990] 3 All ER 25, CA

Entores Ltd v *Miles Far East Corporation* [1955] 2 All ER 493, CA

Holwell Securities v *Hughes* [1974] 1 All ER 161, CA

Web activity

Please go to:

www.carbolicsmokeball.co.uk

to read the law report, see a full colour reproduction of the famous advertisement with testimonials and find out what a smokeball actually looked like.

Assignment 3

Iris made an offer to sell her piano to Diana for £500 on Monday. Diana replied: 'I will buy it if I can raise the money.' Iris promised that she would not sell to anyone else before Saturday, and added that Diana could collect the piano any time before noon on Saturday. On Wednesday, Diana phoned and left a message with Iris's daughter, Athena, saying that she had got the money and would come to collect the piano on Saturday morning. Athena forgot to pass on the message. On Thursday, Iris was visited by Juno who said that she would pay £600 for the piano. Iris accepted this offer. Later that day Iris posted a letter to Diana telling her that she could not have the piano. Mercury, the postman, delivered it to the wrong address and Diana, who never received the letter, appeared with a hired van to collect the piano at 10 o'clock on Saturday morning.

Advise Iris of her legal position.

(*Some hints on answering problem questions, including an analysis of the above assignment, can be found in Chapter 26.*)

mylawchamber

Visit **www.mylawchamber.co.uk/adams** to access multiple choice questions and glossary flashcards to test yourself on this chapter. You'll also find weblinks to the web activity in this chapter.

Use Case Navigator to read in full some of the key cases referenced in this chapter:

Brinkibon v *Stahag Stahl und Stahlwarenhandels GmbH* [1982] 1 All ER 293
Butler Machine Tools Ltd v *Ex-Cell-O Ltd* [1979] 1 All ER 965
Carlill v *Carbolic Smoke Ball Co. Ltd* [1893] 1 QB 256

chapter 5
THE LAW OF CONTRACT:
consideration, intention and privity

The Law of Contract: Consideration, Intention and Privity **395**

Introduction

Contracts are essentially commercial agreements: they are about striking bargains, or achieving what is sometimes called '**mutuality**'. Both parties stand to gain materially from the transaction: each receives a '**consideration**'. Where one party agrees to do something for the other without anything being promised in return, that party is said to be making a '**naked**' or '**gratuitous**' promise. A legally binding contract cannot result from such a promise, only a moral obligation.

It is quite possible to find agreements in which the elements of offer, acceptance and consideration can be identified, but the agreement will not be binding as a contract unless that is deemed to be the parties' intention. When they entered into the agreement, they may not have intended that failure to perform the agreement would make them liable to legal sanctions for breach of contract.

A contract may be made for the benefit of a third party who does not contribute consideration but the common law rule of **privity of contract** generally prevented him or her from enforcing it. This is now mitigated by the Contracts (Rights of Third Parties) Act 1999.

Learning Objectives

When you have studied this chapter you should be able to:

- Define consideration
- Recognise the circumstances when valid consideration exists
- Describe the operation of the promissory estoppel doctrine
- Appreciate the characteristics of agreements which demonstrate intention to create legal relations
- Explain how the Contracts (Rights of Third Parties) Act 1999 has impacted on the doctrine of privity of contract.

Photo: redsnapper/Alamy

Consideration

Consideration has been defined by the courts in different ways. In *Currie* v *Misa* (1875) it was held to constitute a benefit to one party or a detriment to the other. Generally, it is easy to analyse contracts on this basis. When you buy a DVD recorder from a shop, the benefit you receive is the DVD recorder, and the detriment is the money you pay the shop. The shop clearly enjoys a corresponding benefit, and suffers a corresponding detriment in taking your money and parting with the DVD recorder.

In *Dunlop* v *Selfridge* (1915, HL), the House of Lords defined consideration in terms of the price by which one party bought the other party's act or promise. This is also clearly reflected in the example of the sale of the DVD recorder.

Executory and executed consideration

Executory consideration

A binding contract may be formed by the exchange of promises to be carried out at a later date. If you order goods which are to be paid for on delivery, a binding contract results on your order being accepted. Failure to deliver the goods to you would be a breach of contract. The consideration in such a contract consists of the mutual promises and is described as **'executory'** because the promises have not yet been **executed** (performed).

Executed consideration

Sometimes no obligation to pay arises unless or until another party has executed their consideration. For example, if someone advertises a reward for the safe return of a lost cat, that person is making a unilateral promise to pay money that will become binding on the performance (execution) of an act (the return of the cat). The consideration provided by the person who returns the cat is called 'executed consideration'.

The rules governing consideration

Consideration must not be past

The act claimed to represent consideration for another party's promise to pay must not precede that promise, or it will be treated as past consideration and the promise will be merely gratuitous.

Real Life

Horace, knowing that his elderly neighbour, Bertie, is concerned about the state of his garden, offers to clear it up for him. This occupies Horace for most of the day, and Bertie is so pleased with the result that he promises to pay Horace £15 for his trouble. If Bertie fails to pay, Horace will not be able to sue for breach of contract as Bertie's promise to pay was made after the work was completed. The work represents past consideration and, therefore, the promise to pay is merely gratuitous.

To be contractually binding, it must be shown that a promise to pay preceded the act so that the promise and act form one undivided transaction. The principle is clearly illustrated in the following case:

Re McArdle (1951, CA)

A house was left by Mr McArdle to his wife for life. On her death it was to be sold and the proceeds divided equally between the children of the marriage. The wife of one of the children paid for home improvements at a cost of £488. When the work had been done all the children agreed that she should recover this sum from the proceeds of the eventual sale. After Mrs McArdle died the validity of this agreement was disputed.

Held: no valid contract existed since the home improvements were past consideration; they had been carried out before any promise to pay had been made.

There is an exception to this rule when a subsequent promise is enforceable. Valid consideration may be held to exist in the absence of an express prior promise to pay provided that:

1 the act was done in response to a specific request; and
2 the situation was one where payment would normally be expected.

Re Stewart v Casey (Casey's Patents) (1892, CA)

An employee contributed many hours of his own time to the development of an invention for his employers at their request. When the work was completed, the employers promised that they would pay him a share of the profits once the invention was patented.

Held: the employers were bound by the promise as the employee had done the work at their request, and the nature of their relationship implied that future payment would be made.

The subsequent explicit promise to pay in such situations is seen as an affirmation of an implied promise which accompanied the request that the work be carried out.

Consideration must move from the promisee

This rule prevents a party from enforcing a contract unless he or she has contributed consideration. However, a number of exceptions exist under common law and statute and further reform has resulted from the Contracts (Rights of Third Parties) Act 1999 (see below at page 94).

Consideration must be sufficient

Consideration must be of material value, capable of assessment in financial terms. Usually the financial nature of the consideration is obvious where goods, land or money is involved. Any legal right has a financial value. Settling a case out of court involves a contract under which one party agrees not to exercise their legal right to sue the other, provided that the other pays an agreed sum of compensation. The consideration for the promise of compensation is the promise not to sue. In *Alliance Bank v Broome* (1864) a bank was held to have provided consideration, for the defendant's promise to give security for a loan, by promising not to take action to recover it.

White v Bluett (1853)

A son agreed not to bore his father by nagging him to make a will in his favour and in return his father agreed to release him from a debt.

Held: the father was not bound by his promise as the son had not provided valid consideration. He had no right to dictate how his father disposed of his property, so he had not given up anything of material value by stopping nagging his father.

Note that consideration *may be sufficient without being adequate*. Provided the alleged consideration is of financial value, it is irrelevant that it is not an adequate return. The courts are not interested in whether the parties have made a *good* bargain, but only in whether they have made a *bargain* at all. Therefore, proof of financial value, however minute, will be enough to make consideration sufficient.

Thomas v Thomas (1842)

A widow was promised a house in return for a ground rent and promising to keep the property in good repair.

Held: an annual rent of £1 was held to be sufficient consideration for the promise.

Advertising campaigns frequently offer to supply goods in return for wrappers, packet tops or vouchers cut from relevant product wrapping. If you comply with what is asked, then a binding contract results and you are entitled to the tea towel, cuddly toy or other delight being offered. So in *Chappell v Nestlé & Co. Ltd* (1960, HL) three chocolate wrappers were held to constitute valid consideration entitling the sender to pop music recordings. Nestlé derived a clear economic benefit from an increase in sales. It was irrelevant that the wrappers would be thrown away on arrival.

Sufficiency usually involves taking on some *new obligation* in return for the other party's promise of payment. Performing an existing legal duty does not generally amount to sufficient consideration.

Collins v Godefroy (1831)

The claimant was a key witness at a trial and was under a court order to attend. Failure to do so would have made him guilty of the crime of contempt of court. The defendant was a party to the proceedings; because the claimant's attendance was important to him, he promised to pay the claimant if he would attend.

Held: the defendant's promise of payment was not contractually binding. The claimant had not provided sufficient consideration merely by promising to perform his existing legal duty.

In a case like this the claimant is effectively promising the defendant that if the claimant pays him money he will not commit a criminal offence, and such agreements are treated as being against *public policy* (not in the public interest).

Similarly, where two parties have made a contract, a subsequent promise of additional payment to encourage performance is not a binding contractual promise. The promisee is already contractually bound to perform and is therefore providing no fresh consideration.

Stilk v *Myrick* (1809)

Two sailors deserted from a ship in the course of a voyage. The captain promised the remainder of the crew that he would pay a bonus to each man if they got the ship home to England from Scandinavia.

Held: this promise was not binding. Crew members were required by their contracts to cope with the normal difficulties of a voyage, which in those days included crew shortages of this kind. Therefore, there was insufficient consideration to make the captain's promise enforceable.

The court's unwillingness to enforce promises of this kind generally results from a concern that the promisee has exerted **economic duress** – blackmailed the promisor into offering extra payment. This topic is explained in Chapter 7.

The court may take a more generous attitude if satisfied that the public interest is not adversely affected and that enforcing the promise would produce the fairest outcome. The court may justify such a decision in one of three ways:

1 By finding that the promisee has exceeded the scope of his or her legal duty. The excess represents the consideration or

Hartley v *Ponsonby* (1857)

The facts of this case are similar to those in *Stilk* v *Myrick*, but here the depletion of the crew and the length of the journey were so great that the crew's existing contract of employment was discharged.

Held: by getting the ship home, the crew effectively were taking on a new set of duties and thus providing sufficient consideration for the captain's promise of more pay.

2 Or by finding that the promisee, in carrying out the legal duty, has actually conferred a new benefit on the promisor

Glasbrook Bros v *Glamorgan County Council* (1925, HL)

The defendant mine owners, fearing vandalism of their premises during an industrial dispute, promised that if the police authority provided a full-time guard, they would make a donation to a police charity.

Held: this promise was binding, as the police could have fulfilled their legal duty by periodic inspection of the premises: the full-time guard exceeded this and was therefore sufficient consideration.

3 Or by deciding that the act of the promisor enabled the promisee to *avoid* some material *disadvantage*.

Williams v Roffey Bros (1990, CA)

Roffey was a builder who had a contract to refurbish a building for a housing association. This contract contained a delay clause under which Roffey was required to pay substantial sums if the work was not finished on time. Roffey sub-contracted carpentry work to Williams, who later ran into financial difficulties and told Roffey that because of this he would be unable to continue. Roffey promised him payment of extra money to complete the contract on time. He then refused to honour this undertaking arguing that Williams was merely doing what he had originally contracted to do.

Held: Roffey's promise was binding, since by securing the completion of the contract he was obtaining a benefit, or at least avoiding a burden. He avoided having to pay the delay costs to the housing association. He had freely entered into the agreement and not been forced by economic duress.

In making this decision the Court of Appeal was breaking new ground judicially, but the ruling reflects current commercial practice.

Note that *Stilk* v *Myrick* is not overruled by *Williams* v *Roffey Bros*. There are clear distinguishing features. It must be decided on the facts of a case which decision will apply.

Worth thinking about?

In what ways can *Williams* v *Roffey* be distinguished from *Stilk* v *Myrick*?

Suggested solutions can be found in Appendix 2.

The *Williams* v *Roffey* principle was limited and clarified by the Court of Appeal in the following case:

Re Selectmove (1995, CA)

Selectmove owed arrears of tax to the Inland Revenue which threatened to start liquidation proceedings. Selectmove negotiated with a tax inspector and stated that it would pay all future tax as and when it fell due and that it would pay off all arrears of tax at £1,000 a month. The tax inspector said that if Selectmove heard nothing more it could assume that this plan was agreeable to the Revenue. Later, the Revenue then started liquidation proceedings.

Selectmove claimed that the Revenue was bound by the tax inspector's agreement since, under the *Williams* v *Roffey* principle, it obtained a benefit or at least avoided a disbenefit. If the company went into liquidation the Revenue might not acquire full repayment of the tax arrears and would not get the benefit of future tax payments.

Held: promising to carry out an existing duty can only be binding under *Williams* v *Roffey* if the duty is to perform *an act*, not just to *pay money*. The rule in *Pinnel's* case (below) applies to part payment of debt.

Part payment of debt is not sufficient consideration

The rule in Pinnel's Case (1602)

A promise by a creditor to accept less than the full sum owed does not discharge the debtor from the legal obligation to pay the balance.

The rule in *Pinnel's* case is illustrated by the following example:

Real Life

Horace owes Josephine £50, but he is so hard up that he can pay her only £35 when the date of repayment arrives. She can still pursue him later for the £15 even if she agrees that she will take the £35 in full settlement. This looks unfair, but if you analyse Josephine's promise in terms of the rules of consideration you can see the legal logic, if not the moral justice, of the outcome. Horace, by repaying only part of what he owes, obtains a benefit (£15) but gives nothing to Josephine in return. Josephine loses £15 from their agreement. Horace provides no consideration and so Josephine's new promise is not contractually binding; it is merely a gratuitous promise.

There are some exceptions to this rule. The debt will be discharged by part payment if the creditor requests:

1 part payment at an earlier date; or

2 part payment at a different place; or

3 some goods or other material benefit to accompany the part payment.

In these situations the debtor is providing some consideration by doing something different at the creditor's request. For example:

Real Life

Horace did building work at James's delicatessen for £1,000. When payment was due James was unable to pay in full, so Horace agreed to take £900 plus £100's worth of smoked salmon for his parents' forthcoming silver wedding anniversary celebration.

Part payment by a third party in return for a promise from the creditor not to pursue the original debtor for the balance also discharges the whole debt. An agreement (**composition**) between creditors has a similar effect. It is common business practice for the multiple creditors of a debtor to agree that they will each accept a proportionate repayment of their debts. An individual creditor cannot renege on this contract to pursue the balance of his or her debt as this would be a fraud on the other creditors.

A form of such an agreement, commonly known as an Individual Voluntary Arrangement (IVA) was introduced and regulated by the Insolvency Act 1986. These are brokered by finance businesses for a commission and allow debtors to repay a proportion of their debt to their creditors over a specified period which is usually five years. In recent years the number of people dangerously in debt has grown and IVAs have become very popular as an alternative to bankruptcy. (See 'In the News'.)

In the News

IVA controversy

Accountants KPMG said that there has been a huge growth in the use of IVAs since 1998 when there were under 5,000. The annual total in 2006 was 45,000, with the average IVA debtor owing £52,000 but seeking to repay only 39% of this sum. Setting up these arrangements has become an industry, with many firms getting involved at an average fee of £7,000.

Some providers have been heavily criticised for making unrealistic promises about the performance of their products. Some portray IVAs as a universal panacea for debt, failing to point out that they adversely affect credit records, and that inability to maintain payment can still result in bankruptcy. Concerns about mis-selling led the Office of Fair Trading to order 17 firms selling IVAs to review their advertising in January 2007 and to produce evidence of conformity with OFT guidelines within four weeks. Thirty-eight more warning and advisory letters were issued by the end of December 2007.

James Ketchell from the Consumer Credit Counselling Service (CCCS) stressed that IVAs are not the only answer for people struggling with debt and are not generally suitable for the huge majority of people in financial difficulty. CCCS advised 70,000 people in 2006, but in only 3% of these cases was an IVA the most appropriate option. The remainder were better served by a debt management scheme or an application for bankruptcy.

(Sources: press releases from: KPMG, 5/5/2006; OFT, 17/1/2006; Consumer Credit Counselling Service, 30/1/2007; Guardian article, 30/1/2007; and OFT press releases 17/1/07 and 17/12/2007.)

The cases of *Re Selectmove* (1995) (above) and *Re C (A Debtor)* (1994), indicate that the Court of Appeal is not prepared to allow the principle in *Williams* v *Roffey* to validate agreements to pay *less* than the agreed sum, rather than *more*. This would otherwise undermine the rule in *Pinnel*'s case.

Promissory estoppel

Promissory estoppel is an equitable defence which may be relevant in part-payment situations. Under this principle, parties who gratuitously promise that they will not enforce existing contractual rights may lose their entitlement to do so if it would be unfair to allow them to go back on their promise; they are prevented (*estopped*) from breaking the promise. This defence was developed in the following case:

Central London Property Trust v High Trees House (1947)

The defendants owned a block of flats on land leased to them by the claimants. By September 1939, many flats had become vacant due to outbreak of war. Consequently, the defendants were having difficulties paying their ground rent. The claimants agreed that they would accept reduced payments. The defendants continued to pay the reduced rent even when the flats refilled and the war was over.

The claimants brought a test case claiming arrears of rent for the last two quarters of 1945 (by which time the war had ended).

Held: the claimants were found to be entitled to the arrears they claimed, but it was also held (*obiter dictum*) that had they claimed for arrears prior to the end of the war this would have been refused. It would be unfair to allow them to go back on their promise on which the defendants had naturally relied. The claimants' gratuitous promise operated to suspend their rights to full payment while the extenuating circumstances in which the promise had been made continued to operate.

This *obiter dictum* (persuasive ruling) from a then youthful Mr Justice Denning has been applied by the House of Lords. In *Tool Metal Manufacturing Co. Ltd* v *Tungsten Ltd* (1955) a gratuitous promise, to suspend rights to royalty payments on a patent during the war, was held to be a good defence to a subsequent claim for such payments.

However, although the doctrine of promissory estoppel has been much discussed by the Court of Appeal and the House of Lords in subsequent cases, it has been used very little and its scope is far from clear. Two elements are certain:

1 *It can operate only as a defence*. Denning LJ clarified this aspect of the doctrine in *Combe* v *Combe* (CA, 1951). Describing it as a '*shield and not a sword*', he emphasised that the doctrine '*should not be stretched too far*' and the principle '*did not create new causes of action where none had existed before*' and that '*the doctrine of consideration is too firmly fixed to be overthrown by a side wind.*'

Therefore, if we apply this reasoning to *High Trees*, it is clear that the defendants could not have sued on the claimants' promise, but it would have been a good defence against the claimants if they had tried to enforce their original contract rights for the period in which they had been suspended.

2 *It is an equitable principle*. The court will not grant an equitable remedy unless it will produce a just result for both parties; parties seeking such a remedy must show that they have behaved morally as well as legally.

D & C Builders v *Rees* (1965, CA)

Mrs Rees persuaded the builders, whom she knew to be in financial difficulties, to accept payment of £300 in full settlement of a debt of almost £483, by telling them that they would otherwise get nothing.

Held: it would not be equitable to allow their promise to be used as a defence against them, given that Mrs Rees had effectively '*held the builders to ransom*' (Denning LJ) forcing them to accept the smaller sum.

Intention to create legal relations

In determining whether the parties intend their agreement to be legally binding, the courts are guided by two presumptions concerning the parties' **intention to create legal relations**):

1. parties to a domestic or social agreement do not intend to be legally bound;
2. parties to a business agreement intend to be legally bound.

These are presumptions only and can be rebutted (disproved) by sufficient evidence to the contrary.

Domestic and social agreements

The courts believe that family members and friends do not generally intend agreements, made merely for their mutual convenience, to be legally enforceable. Property rights between family members are generally adequately covered by other areas of the law. Unless there is clear evidence of a commercial transaction – for example, the sale of a car between family members – an intention to be contractually bound will not be presumed.

Balfour v *Balfour* (1919, CA)

Held: no intention to create legal relations existed in an agreement under which a husband working abroad promised to pay maintenance to his wife in England.

The courts take a different view if the couple do not intend to continue in the marriage. In *Merritt* v *Merritt* (1970, CA) a contractual relationship was held to arise from a post-separation maintenance agreement.

Car pool agreements may involve the necessary intention:

Albert v *Motor Insurers Bureau* (1971, HL)

Held: if lifts are provided on a regular and systematic basis under which drivers anticipate payment, an intention to create a legally binding relationship is present.

Even a 'fun' transaction may implicitly contain a more formal intention.

Simpkins v *Pays* (1955, CA)

The claimant lodged in the defendant's boarding house. Every week she, the defendant and the defendant's granddaughter entered a fashion competition in a Sunday newspaper. They took it in turns to pay the entry costs and postage and agreed that any winnings should be divided equally. One week their entry, sent in the defendant's name, won £750 but she refused to pay the claimant her share. The claimant sued in breach of contract and the defendant argued that no legally binding relationship had been intended in the transaction.

Held: the claimant should succeed since the parties demonstrated sufficient intention to be legally bound. This was more than just a friendly agreement. It was a joint enterprise to which each of the parties contributed financially in the expectation of sharing prize money.

> A clearly defined agreement must exist before evidence of intention to be bound can be deduced

Wilson and Anor v *Burnett* (2007, CA)

The claimants organised a girls' night out to the local bingo hall with the defendant, a workmate. The defendant won substantial prizes totalling £101,354. The claimants alleged that at the start of the evening that they had all agreed to share equally any prize over £10. The defendant disputed this. At the trial Judge Nelligan said: '*I accept the defendants' evidence that there was chat or talk about sharing winnings which went no further than discussion or chat, and did not cross and cannot be inferred to have crossed that line which exists between talk and "meaning business", or an intention to create a legal relationship, that is to share the prize money*'. He therefore held that the claimants were not entitled to share the money. The claimants appealed.

Held: Judge Nelligan had been justified in coming to his decision. In agreements between friends it was presumed that there was no intention to be legally bound, though every case must be examined on its facts. Although there had been discussion about sharing winnings, there was insufficient evidence of any clear agreement sufficient to prove the existence of such intention, so the claimants lost their case.

> It is easy to see clear differences between the facts in the two cases above. In *Simpkins v Pays* the parties had regularly entered the competition together following the same process each time and each party contributed to it and had a stake in the outcome. In *Wilson v Burnett* the parties were engaged in a one-off outing and the evidence of any potential agreement was conflicting.

Exam tip

If the question describes parties in a problem as friends or family members, this may be to nudge you into mentioning the issue of intention to create legal relations.

Business agreements

In the world of business, the presumption that agreements are intended to have legal consequences means that an *explicit* indication of lack of intention to create legal relations is necessary.

Rose & Frank Co. v J.R. Crompton & Bros (1925, HL)

The claimant was a US company, selling carbon paper, and it agreed to permit the defendant, an English company in the same line of business, to market its product in the USA. The wording of the agreement stated that it was not 'a formal legal agreement and shall not be subject to legal jurisdiction in the law courts either of the United States or England, but it is only a definite expression and record of the purpose and intention of the parties concerned to which they each honourably pledge themselves'.

The defendant subsequently breached the agreement and claimed that it did not amount to a binding contract.

Held: this clause was effective to exclude intention to be legally bound as it was clear and specific.

Next time you see an advertisement for a competition, check the small print and you will usually find that it contains similar words. In *Jones* v *Vernons Pools* (1938) it was held that no legally binding contract was created between punter and pools company: the entry coupon stated clearly that the relationship between the parties was 'binding in honour only'.

Privity of contract

Sometimes a contractual situation may arise where one party (**promisor**) agrees with another (the **promisee**) to provide a benefit for a third party. From your study of consideration earlier in this chapter, you may remember that the common law rule is that parties who have not contributed consideration to a contract cannot sue on it if it is breached. This is because they are not full parties to the contract: in the rather archaic language still used by lawyers, they are not *privy to the contract*, or there is no *privity of contract* between the parties. Thus, the beneficiary cannot sue if the contract is breached.

Tweddle v Atkinson (1861)

William Tweddle was engaged to marry Miss Guy. The fathers of the happy couple contracted that they would each put up a sum of money when the marriage took place, but Mr Guy died before making payment.

Held: William had no right to sue Mr Guy's estate for the money since he had provided no consideration for the promise and was merely a beneficiary of the contract. As a mere beneficiary, William was not *privy to the contract*: he was not truly a party to it because he was not contributing to the consideration.

Similarly, the burdens of a contract cannot be enforced against a party to whom no consideration has been promised.

Dunlop Rubber Co. Ltd v *Selfridge* (1915, HL)

Dunlop supplied tyres at a discount (less than list price) to Dew & Co., who agreed not to resell below list price to trade buyers unless those buyers also agreed not to resell below list price. Dew supplied Selfridge, who breached the resale price agreement. Dunlop tried to take action against Selfridge.

Held: Dunlop could not sue Selfridge, as there was no privity of contract between them: Dunlop had given no consideration to Selfridge in return for the promise to stick to the resale price. (Any action could only be taken against Selfridge by Dew for breach of the contract between them.)

Exceptions to the rule of privity

To prevent injustice, a number of exceptions to the rule have been acknowledged to enable beneficiaries to enforce their rights.

1 *Agency*. Where agents make contracts on behalf of their principals with third parties, the principals may sue or be sued on those contracts as if they had made them themselves. (See Chapter 10.)

2 *Third-party insurance*. A third party may claim under an insurance policy made for their benefit, even though that party did not pay the premiums (for example: life assurance and third-party motor insurance).

3 *Assignment of contractual rights*. The benefits (but not the burdens) of a contract may be assigned to a third party, who may then sue on the contract (for example: selling debts). The original debtor may be sued by the new creditor to whom the rights to collect the debt have been assigned. The duty to perform a contract cannot be assigned.

4 *Trusts*. This is an equitable concept by which one person transfers property to a second person (the trustee), who holds it for the benefit of others (beneficiaries). The party who created the trust, which is often done by a will, lays down the rules under which it is to be administered. If these are not complied with, the beneficiaries have the right to ask the court to enforce the trust for their benefit.

5 *Collateral contracts*. The performance of one contract between A and B may indirectly bring another into being between A and C.

6 *Contracts for the benefit of a group*. Where a contract to supply a service is made in one person's name but is intended to benefit a group of people, the members of the group have no rights to sue at common law if the contract is breached; there is no privity of contract between them and the supplier of the service. The court, however, may take some of their losses into account when awarding damages to the buyer.

Shanklin Pier Ltd v Detel Products Ltd (1954)

Detel advised Shanklin Pier Ltd that their paint was suitable for maritime use and would last for at least seven years. Shanklin Pier Ltd contracted with a decorating firm to paint the pier; a term of the contract required the decorators to buy Detel's paint for the purpose. The paint began to peel off within three months.

Held: Shanklin Pier Ltd could successfully sue Detel Products on a collateral contract which was linked to the main contract between Shanklin Pier Ltd and the decorating firm. Detel had made promises about the quality of their paint and Shanklin Pier had provided consideration for this promise by requiring their decorators to use it.

Jackson v Horizon Holidays Ltd (1975, CA)

Horizon provided such a poor level of service that the Jackson family holiday was ruined.

Held: Mr Jackson, who had made the contract, was the only party who could sue but the damages he was awarded took into account the loss to the whole family resulting from Horizon's failure to deliver a holiday of the promised quality.

Statutory reform of the privity rule

In 1996, the Law Commission (Report No. 242) stated that reform was needed since the law at that time:

(a) prejudiced third parties who may have relied on contracts which they had no power to enforce;

(b) caused problems in commercial life;

(c) was out of step with other EU members and much of the common law world, including New Zealand and the USA.

As a result, reforming legislation was introduced.

Contracts (Rights of Third Parties) Act 1999

Section 1 gives a third party the right directly to enforce any contract which expressly permits this or where the contract is intended to benefit them. This gives the third party the same remedies as any other party to a breach of contract action. They must be expressly identified in the contract by name or class or description, but need not be in existence when the contract is made. Thus, a contract to provide an ongoing benefit to 'all my children' could benefit any children born after formation of the contract.

Section 2 further protects third parties by preventing cancellation or variation of the contract without their permission unless the contract *expressly* provides for this. Generally, a third party's rights cannot be withdrawn or varied without their consent if: they have communicated agreement by words or conduct to the terms, or the promisor is aware that they have relied on the terms, or the promisor should have reasonably foreseen that they would rely on the term and they have in fact done so. In exceptional circumstances (e.g. mental incapacity of the third party) the court may dispense with the right of consent.

Section 5 protects the promisor from double liability. If the promisor fails to perform the duty owed to the third party, they will not be liable to the third party for any losses that the promisee has already recovered from the promisor. This prevents the third party from recovering twice for the same losses. Third-party rights cannot be enforced in some contract situations. Section 6 specifies some exceptions: for example, a third party cannot enforce any term against an employee in an employment contract; in a contract for carriage of goods, a third party has no enforceable rights except for the protection of any exclusion or limitation clause in the contract.

Note that the 1999 Act does not abolish the privity doctrine: it just introduces a new right. Section 7 specifies that existing third-party rights and remedies remain unchanged.

Chapter summary

Consideration
The bargain element which distinguishes a contract from any other sort of agreement, legally binding or otherwise.
Definition: material benefit gained/detriment arising from performance of a contract.
Price paid for the other party's promise or act. Benefit/detriment.

The rules of consideration
It must not be past: not precede the promise to pay.
It must be sufficient: represent some detriment/benefit though not necessarily an adequate price.
Generally, only a party who provides consideration may enforce the contract (see Privity, below).
Part payment of a debt does not generally discharge it (*Pinnel's* case).
Promissory estoppel may provide a defence for a defendant sued for breach of contract, if he or she can prove that the claimant had previously gratuitously varied the contract in the defendant's favour so that it would be unjust to let them go back on their word.

Intention to create legal relations
The parties to a contract must intend it to be legally binding or it will not be enforceable in the courts. Two rebuttable presumptions operate here. An agreement between friends or family members is presumed not to reflect that intention, while business agreements are.

Privity of contract
Generally, the doctrine of privity of contract prevents anyone except a party who contributes to the bargain from enforcing it.
The Contracts (Rights of Third Parties) Act 1999 enables a contractual beneficiary to sue for breach of a contract that was clearly made for their benefit, even though they have not provided any consideration.

Key terms

Composition (with creditors): a legally binding agreement between creditors that they will each take only a proportion of what the debtor owes, in full settlement of the entire debt.

Consideration: money/goods/services/land representing the bargain element of the contract.

Economic duress: an attempt to obtain favourable contract terms by threatening financial loss to a contracting party.

Executed consideration: a contractual promise which has been performed.

Executory consideration: a contractual promise which has not yet been performed.

Gratuitous promise: a promise which is not supported by consideration.

Intention to create legal relations: the parties' intention that their agreement be binding in law, not just morally.

Mutuality: both parties support their promises by consideration.

Naked promise: see gratuitous promise above.

Privity of contract: exclusivity of contractual rights and duties to parties who contribute consideration.

Promisee: a party making a promise.

Promisor: a recipient of a promise.

Promissory estoppel (*High Trees* doctrine): an equitable defence which a party may use when a contract has been gratuitously varied for their benefit and the other party seeks to enforce it in its original form.

Quiz 5

1. Are the following promises legally binding or merely gratuitous?

    (a) Red returned Brown's lost tortoise. Brown promised him £5.

    (b) Green agreed to sell his vintage sports car to Black for 10p.

    (c) Scarlet promised her employee, Orange, that she would give him a £10 bonus if he arrived at work on time for a week.

    (d) Blue was owed £50 by Yellow, but agreed to take £45 in full settlement if Yellow made the repayment a week early.

    (e) Pink agreed that his tenant, Turquoise, might pay a reduced rent while he was out of work.

2. White told his tailor to make a wedding suit for White's nephew, Grey, who chose the style and material. The cost was to be charged to White's account. When the suit was finished it did not fit Grey, who had to hire one. Has Grey any rights against the tailor?

Answers to all quizzes can be found in Appendix 2.

Take a closer look

The following cases provide important examples of how the law you have studied in this chapter has developed. They are primary sources illustrating the law in action and give you more detail about their facts, as well as helping you to understand the law and to appreciate how the judges reached their decisions.

Try looking them up in the law reports or accessing them via a database, e.g. Bailli (www.bailii.org/databases.html). LexisNexis or Westlaw may be available in your university or college library, or you may find extracts in a case book. (See Appendix 1: Additional resources.)

Re McArdle [1951] Ch 669
Williams v *Roffey Bros* [1990] 1 All ER 512, CA
Simpkins v *Pays* [1955] 3 All ER 10, CA
Jackson v *Horizon Holidays* [1975] 3 All ER 92, CA

Web activity

Please go to:

www.clearstart.org/index.php

Click on IVA to find out more about how these work.

Assignment 4

(a) Is it true to say that the doctrine of privity of contract is redundant since the Contracts (Rights of Third Parties) Act 1999?

(b) Arthur rents a house to his friend Brian for £400 a month in January. In May, hearing that Brian is in financial difficulty, Arthur offers to reduce the rent to £250 'until things pick up for you again'. In October, Cathy, Brian's wife, is left £20,000 by her uncle. In December, Arthur finds out about this windfall and asks for full rent from October onwards.

Advise Arthur.

mylawchamber

Visit **www.mylawchamber.co.uk/adams** to access multiple choice questions and glossary flashcards to test yourself on this chapter. You'll also find weblinks to the web activity in this chapter.

Use Case Navigator to read in full some of the key cases referenced in this chapter:
Central London Property Trust v *High Trees House* [1947] KB 130
Williams v *Roffey Bros* [1990] 1 All ER 512

chapter 6
THE TERMS OF THE CONTRACT

Introduction

A contract is made up of terms, offered by one party and accepted by the other. This chapter contains three topics concerning terms:

1. *The difference between **express** and **implied** terms*. The parties may be bound by terms which they have not expressly agreed.

2. *The relative importance of contractual terms*. Some terms are crucial to the existence of the contract; others are more trivial, and therefore different legal consequences flow from breach of them.

3. *Exclusion of liability*. Even if a party is in breach of contract, it may be protected from liability by an exclusion clause.

Learning Objectives

When you have studied this chapter you should be able to:

- Distinguish between conditions, warranties and innominate terms
- Explain the purpose of exclusion clauses and the common law rules governing them
- Demonstrate the differences in scope of the Unfair Contract Terms Act 1977 and the Unfair Terms in Consumer Contract Regulations 1999.

Photo: Manor Photography/Alamy

Express and implied terms

The terms of a contract fall into three categories: **conditions**, **warranties** and **innominate terms** (explained fully below). These terms may be expressed or implied. Express terms are specifically communicated by the offeror. Other terms may be implied by statute, custom or the courts.

The sources of implied terms

Statute: the Sale of Goods Act 1979

This is the most important source of implied terms. Parliament safeguards the consumer by implying certain terms concerning the standard and quality of goods in most sale of goods contracts. The seller is in breach if the goods do not meet these standards, regardless of whether the seller gave any undertakings expressly to the buyer.

This statutory protection means that if you buy an MP3 player from a shop you can assume that it will work. If it is faulty, the shop cannot avoid liability by claiming that it never promised you that the MP3 player would work. These terms are fully explained in Chapter 11 below.

Trade custom and practice

In many trades it is customary for certain practices to prevail in performance of a contract, or for risks to be allocated between the parties in a particular way. For example, in crane and plant hire contracts, it is generally implied that any damage to the equipment occasioned during the hire period will be the financial responsibility of the hirer, not the owner.

Business efficacy

The court is not generally sympathetic to parties who assume that they have rights under a contract which were not expressly promised to them. Exceptionally, though, a term may be implied to give '**business efficacy**' to the contract. The court will do this if the contract lacks a term so obvious that the parties are considered (*deemed*) to have intended to include it in the contract. For example, if you asked the dairy to deliver you 'two pints of milk', it is unlikely that you would feel the need to specify that the milk must be in a container rather than left in a puddle on your doorstep. In *The Moorcock* (1889) a party who hired docking space at the defendant's wharf was entitled to assume that the ship's bottom would not be damaged by the state of the river bed adjacent to the dock. This strategy prevents a party from avoiding contractual liability on a technicality and gives effect to the obvious common but unspoken intention of the parties.

The relative importance of contractual terms

The terms of a contract are not necessarily equally important. Breach of contract, therefore, gives rise to different rights according to the importance of the breached term. Generally, terms can be classified as conditions or warranties. Whether terms are to be classified as conditions or warranties is determined by the parties' apparent intentions when they made the contract. An apparently trivial matter like a sea view from the hotel bedroom may be elevated to the status of a condition of the contract if its necessity is stressed before acceptance takes place.

Conditions

Conditions are the most important terms which form the main structure of the contract. For example, when you are booking hotel accommodation, the dates of your stay and the type of room (single/double) are some of the most crucial requirements. If particular details are crucial to one party, this must be pointed out to the other party before the formation of the contract is completed. If you are booking a double room, this may result in your being given single or double beds unless you stipulate which you prefer.

Breach of a condition gives the injured party the right to treat itself as free of any further contractual duties and to claim compensation.

Warranties

Warranties are more minor terms; they are *ancillary* to the contract rather than crucial to it. For example, when you are booking hotel accommodation, the promise of tea- and coffee-making facilities and colour TV will not be vital to the performance of the contract. Their absence does not stop you from getting most of the enjoyment that you expect from the holiday.

Breach of a warranty does not entitle the injured party to refuse to perform its side of the contract. That party is entitled only to compensation for consequential loss, i.e. loss *resulting* from the breach.

The next two cases illustrate the distinctions between these two types of term.

Poussard v Spiers & Pond (1876)

An actress was employed for a season, but was delayed by illness from taking up her role until a week after the opening night.

Held: her employers were entitled to terminate the contract: her presence on the opening night was crucial to the contract.

Bettini v Gye (1876)

A singer, engaged for a season, failed to turn up for the first three of the six prescribed rehearsal days.

Held: given the length of the contract and because no performances were missed this amounted only to a minor breach; the employer was not entitled to repudiate.

Innominate terms

Not all terms are clearly and immediately identifiable as conditions or warranties. Some, described by the courts as 'innominate', are worded broadly to cover a variety of possible breaches, some more serious than others. The court then has to decide whether a particular breach is to be treated as one of condition or warranty.

Hong Kong Fir Shipping Co. Ltd v Kawasaki Kisen Kaisha (1962, CA)

A contract stated that a ship would be 'in every way fitted for cargo service'. This term was capable of including many types of breach, from a large hole in the hull to a missing life raft which was unlikely ever to be required. Due to the incompetent engine room crew and a malfunctioning engine, the ship broke down and 20 weeks' use of the ship was lost from a two-year charterparty (hire contract). The defendants who had hired the ship abandoned the contract and the claimant owners sued them for breach.

Held: the breach of the term relating to the ship's fitness was not sufficiently serious to permit the defendants to terminate the contract. The importance of the term must be judged in relation to the actual damage resulting from it. The damage caused did not strike at the root of the contract (the ship was still available for more than 18 months of the hire period), and therefore no breach equivalent to a breach of condition had occurred.

Diplock LJ stated that the judge's task in cases of this kind was *'to look at the events which had occurred as a result of the breach at the time which the charterers purported to rescind the charterparty and to decide whether the occurrence deprived the charterers of substantially the whole benefit which it was the intention of the parties as expressed in the charterparty that the charterers should obtain'* (from the performance of the contract).

Hong Kong Fir was a controversial decision since it was argued that the so-called 'damage test', would promote uncertainty, since parties to a contract would not be aware of the importance of a term until it was breached. Although the test has survived, a later Court of Appeal decision puts it last in the criteria by which the courts may interpret the status of an innominate term (*Cehave NV* v *Bremer Handelsgesellschaft* (*The Hansa Nord*) (1975, CA):

1 The express intention of the parties is paramount: if the contract specifies that a particular breach will entitle a party to opt out of the contract, that is conclusive.

Lombard North Central plc v Butterworth (1987, CA)

A contract for the lease of a computer stated that prompt payment of instalments was of the essence of the contract and that failure to comply would entitle the hire company to terminate the agreement. The defendant paid the third, fourth, and fifth instalments late and the sixth became six weeks overdue. At this point the claimant repudiated the agreement and sued for damages for breach of contract.

Held: late payment in such circumstances would not normally be grounds for repudiation of the contract, but here the term had been elevated to the status of a condition, because the supplier had specifically made the time factor crucial. The supplier was entitled to repudiate even if payment was minimally late.

Mustill LJ stated:

A stipulation that time is of the essence, in relation to a particular contractual term, denotes that timely performance is a condition of the contract. The consequence is that delay in performance is treated as going to the root of the contract, without regard to the magnitude of the risk.

2 The use of the words 'condition' and 'warranty' to describe a term is of evidential value only – it is not conclusive in itself.

Schuler AG v Wickman Machine Tool Sales (1974, HL)

Wickman was given sole selling rights for Schuler's products for four-and-a-half years. A term of the contract stated that it was 'a condition of the contract' that Wickman would send its representative weekly to solicit orders from the six largest UK manufacturers.

Held (by majority): this term was not a condition in the sense that a single breach, however trivial, would entitle the innocent party to terminate the contract.

The reasonableness or otherwise of treating a term as a condition was crucial to deciding whether the parties intended breach of the term to give rise to repudiation rights.

Lord Reid said:

We are seeking to discover intention as disclosed by the contract as a whole. Use of the word 'condition' is an indication – even a strong indication – of such an intention but is by no means conclusive.

3 If a party has a statutory right to terminate the contract if a term is breached, the term is a condition (for example, Sale of Goods Act implied conditions: see Chapter 11).

4 Consistently established commercial practice will determine the status of a term. In *The Mihalis Angelos* (1970, CA) it was held that an 'expected readiness to load' term in a **charterparty** was, as a matter of commercial practice, always to be treated as having the force of a condition, if the party in breach had given the undertaking untruthfully or without reasonable grounds for believing that it could be fulfilled.

5 If the damage resulting from the breach is so extensive that it substantially deprives the innocent party of the benefits bargained for, that party may repudiate their obligations. The damage test is, in practice, used as a last resort.

> ### Reardon Smith Line v Hansen-Tangen (1976, HL)
>
> A vessel built for a buyer fulfilled all its contractual specifications except that it was built at a different shipyard from that named in the contract.
>
> Held: this term should be treated as innominate; no damage had resulted so there was no right to repudiate.

The court, when applying these criteria, is seeking to do justice between the parties, as well as acting in the public interest. Taking these considerations into account can help to make the cases above more accessible.

In *The Mihalis Angelos* (1970) the Court of Appeal sought to avoid bringing uncertainty into an area of the law which underpinned an important part of the national economy and which had been formed from the custom and usage of international traders with whom a good business relationship was crucial. Edmund-Davies LJ said: *'It would be regrettable to … disturb an established practice.'* Megaw LJ (stressing the need for predictability) stressed that: *'In commercial law there are obvious and substantial advantages of having, where possible, a firm and definite rule for a particular class of legal relationships.'*

In the *Reardon Smith* case, when the buyer entered the contract he wanted to increase his fleet of ships for charter because of a boom in trade. At the point when the ship was ready for delivery, however, a recession had occurred and the buyer tried, by repudiation of the contract, to avoid paying for a vessel which was now surplus to requirements. The damage test was a useful device to prevent the buyer from unfairly avoiding contractual responsibility on a technicality.

Limitation and exclusion of liability

Many contracts include a term by which one party seeks to limit financial claims against it in the event of loss or damage to the other party, or to exclude itself from legal liability altogether. For example, by a **limitation clause** a holiday firm's contract may restrict customers' claims in the event of delay, postponement and cancellation of flights to specified sums for meals and overnight accommodation. When you pay to use a car park, it is usual for the contract to include an **exclusion clause** stating that the proprietors have no legal liability for damage to or theft of or from your vehicle.

Such limitation of or exclusion from liability may be a perfectly reasonable business practice, but is subject to control, both by the courts and statute, to prevent abuses. Without such regulation a business could avoid liability for flagrant negligence, or for gross and irresponsible breach of contract.

Before any exclusion clause can be effective it must satisfy three criteria:

1 it must be incorporated within the contract;

2 it must be clear and unambiguous;

3 it must not be rendered ineffective by statute.

Incorporation

In order for a term to be incorporated in the contract (form part of it), the party to be bound by it must have sufficient notice of it. Two factors are crucial to the issue of notice: timing and sufficiency.

1 **Timing**: *The term excluding liability must be notified to the other party prior to that party's acceptance.*

   Notice may be given by a written sign of some kind displayed at the place of business, or in a contractual document. It should be clearly evident to customers before they commit themselves to the contract.

Olley v *Marlborough Court Hotel* (1949, CA)

A notice in Mrs Olley's bedroom stated that the hotel proprietor would not be liable for theft of guests' property. Later jewellery and furs were stolen from her room.

Held: the contract between Mrs Olley and the hotel had been concluded at the reception desk when Mrs Olley booked in, before she read the notice, which consequently did not form part of the contract. The hotel was therefore not exempt from liability for the theft.

Thornton v *Shoe Lane Parking* (1971, CA)

A notice inside a car park stated that the proprietors would not be liable for injuries to customers. This was also printed on the ticket dispensed from the automatic barrier at the car park entrance.

Held: the exemption clause did not form part of the contract: by driving alongside the machine at the car park entrance from which the ticket was dispensed, the claimant had already communicated acceptance of the defendant's offer to supply parking space.

Chapelton v *Barry UDC* (1940, CA)

The claimant, who wished to hire a deckchair at the beach, took one from a pile beside which there was a notice. This stated that payment of the specified hire charge should be made to the attendant. When he paid, the claimant was given a ticket that stated that the council would not be liable for accidents arising from use of the chairs. Later the claimant was injured when the chair collapsed because it had been negligently maintained.

Held: the ticket was not a contractual document but merely a receipt, which the claimant did not receive until after he had accepted the offer by taking the chair from the pile.

> Note that a party may be *deemed* to have implied notice from past contractual dealings where the court is satisfied that these have occurred on the same terms, sufficiently regularly, over a sufficient length of time.

Kendall v Lillico (1968, HL)

The parties had contracted 100 times in the previous three years on consistent terms for delivery of goods including a sales note which contained an exemption clause. The next delivery was defective, but was not accompanied by the sales note and the buyer claimed that the seller was not protected by the exemption clause.

Held: the buyer had adequate notice, since the notification had been consistently supplied throughout the long course of previous dealings.

However, such an implication is unlikely to be made in a consumer contract.

McCutcheon v David McBrayne Ltd (1964, HL)

The claimant had shipped his car on a number of occasions on the defendant's ferry. Sometimes he had been been asked to sign a risk note with a clause exempting the ferry company from liability for damage to goods. On one occasion, when a note had not been supplied, the ferry sank due to the defendant's negligence and the claimant's car was lost.

Held: the exclusion clause did not protect the defendant; the claimant had not had notice of the exemption. The previous dealings between the parties had not been sufficiently consistent, as risk notes had not been supplied regularly.

2 **Sufficiency**: *Generally a clause will not be binding unless the offeror has taken reasonable steps to draw it to the customer's attention.*

The more onerous the term, the greater is the degree of notice required. Exclusion clauses contained in the body of a document should be printed in clear type, which may need to be underlined or otherwise highlighted.

Interfoto Picture Library Ltd v Stiletto Productions (1988, CA)

(Although this case did not relate to an exemption clause, the principle is relevant to any contractual term.) In a contract for hire of photographic transparencies there was a clause imposing a penalty of £5 per transparency per day. It was contained in the delivery note which comprised the contract.

Held: this was not binding as the supplier had not done enough to draw the attention of the hirer to the clause. A special cover note was needed, or at least bold type on the delivery note.

The sufficiency rule does not cover signed documents. Customers have constructive notice of the contents of any contractual document which they sign; this means that they are deemed to have notice of its contents, whether they have read it or not. There is no obligation to alert the signer to the presence of an exclusion clause. In *L'Estrange v Graucob* (1934) the claimant signed a 'sales agreement' for a vending machine without reading it but was held to be bound by an exemption clause in the agreement.

It is useless for customers to claim that they misunderstood the effect of the clause, unless the seller helped to cause the misunderstanding.

Curtis v *Chemical Cleaning & Dyeing Co.* (1951, CA)

The claimant took her wedding dress to be cleaned and was asked to sign a note exempting the cleaners from liability for damage to the dress. She queried this, but signed it when told not to worry as it was there only to protect the company if beads or sequins were damaged. The dress was returned to her badly stained. She sued for breach of contract and the defendant cited the exemption clause in its defence.

Held: the defendant was liable. The exemption clause was not effective as the customer had been misled about its scope.

An exclusion clause is not effective if it is ambiguous

Where its wording is unclear, the court may apply the ***contra proferentem*** rule to restrict the effects of an exclusion clause. The clause is construed *contra* (against) *proferentem* (the party who offered it); the meaning least favourable to the offeror is therefore adopted.

Andrews v *Singer* (1934)

A contract expressly stated that new cars would be supplied. An exemption clause stated that the supplier would not be liable for breach of any condition or warranty implied by statute. When the cars were delivered one was secondhand.

Held: the buyer could reject the secondhand car: breach of an express term of the contract had occurred. The exemption clause referred only to *implied terms*.

Liability for fundamental breach

Where a breach of contract is so serious that it defeats the whole purpose of the contract (**fundamental breach**), the courts may still be prepared to allow an exclusion clause to protect the party in breach. The nature of the contract and the type of breach will be evidence of what the parties are deemed to have intended. For example, in a travel contract the provider promises to take the customer to a particular destination at a particular time; such contracts usually include a clause to limit or completely exclude the liability of the provider in the event of cancellation of services in bad weather. Failure to transport the customer on time is not the fault of the provider in such circumstances, though it may defeat the customer's purposes completely. Such exclusions are likely to be treated as effective. The customer is deemed to have intended to accept the risk.

Issues of insurance are also relevant, and an exclusion clause will protect a provider where the court believes that insurance responsibilities were intended to remain with the other party.

Photo Production Ltd v Securicor Transport Ltd (1980, HL)

While on duty at the claimant's premises, Securicor's employee intentionally started a fire. The contract stated that there would be no liability for such damage unless Securicor was negligent; the claimant did not allege negligence. It was clearly a fundamental breach: Securicor was the cause of the destruction of the property which it had promised to keep safe. The only issue was whether the exemption clause was effective.

Held: the clause protected Securicor from liability for fundamental breach; the parties had bargained on equal terms that periodical visits should be made by a patrolman for a modest charge (26p) per visit. It was reasonable to leave the risk for fire damage with the claimant, who would be the most appropriate party to insure against such damage.

The 'Real Life' example below should help your further understanding of how the common law rules apply.

Real Life

Horace goes shopping by car to the Buymore-Stuff shopping centre. A notice near the entrance to the underground car park states:

> Parking: 70 pence per hour. Please pay at machines inside car park and display ticket on your vehicle windscreen. Buymore-Stuff will not be liable for death or injury to any person using these premises, nor for any damage to any vehicle or other property however caused.

After displaying his ticket, he shuts the car door with a loud bang, which triggers a fall of masonry from the badly maintained roof above. This damages the car and a piece of masonry crushes his foot.

If the notice is clearly displayed so that people can see it before they are committed to entering the car park, the exclusion clause forms part of Horace's contract with Buymore. (See *Thornton v Shoe Lane Parking*, above.) However, Buymore may not be relieved of liability. If the roof fall is caused by Buymore's negligence in failing adequately to maintain its premises, then, applying the *contra proferentem* rule, a court would be likely to hold that since the wording of the clause does not precisely specify exclusion from negligence liability, this is not covered. So Horace should get compensation for harm to himself and the car. However, there are now simpler statutory remedies.

(Continued below at page 111.)

Statutory controls on exclusion clauses

Unfair Contract Terms Act 1977

The scope of the Act

The Unfair Contract Terms Act 1977 (UCTA) applies almost exclusively to contracts giving rise to *business liability* (s 1(3)). Thus, it is primarily concerned with sellers or suppliers who seek to limit or exclude liability incurred in the course of business. Private sellers or suppliers are generally not restricted in the use of exclusion clauses. (See s 6, below.)

Certain types of contract are *expressly excluded*: for example, contracts of insurance and contracts for the sale or lease of land.

Although the title of the Act refers to 'contract terms', the Act also regulates non-contractual notices which attempt to restrict liability for negligence. For example, a notice, outside premises, stating that people enter at their own risk is covered by UCTA 1977.

The substance of the Act

Negligence liability (s 2)

Under s 2(1), liability cannot be excluded if death or personal injury is caused by negligence. Damage to property through negligence is addressed by s 2(2). Under that provision, negligence liability may be excluded if this is *reasonable* in the circumstances (see below). Note that under s 7(2) of the Contracts (Rights of Third Parties) Act 1999 (see above at page 000) the reasonableness defence is not effective against a claim by a third party beneficiary.

Real Life *(Continued from page 110)*

The outcome if Horace uses UCTA is likely to be the same as by claiming under common law principles. However, UCTA can resolve the problem more quickly and simply.

If negligence is proved against Buymore, their liability for Horace's physical injuries is indisputable (UCTA, s 2(1)). As regards the damage to the car, it is very likely that it would not be regarded as reasonable (UCTA s 2(2)) to allow Buymore to avoid liability for failure to properly maintain public premises, which are clearly in a condition which endangers people as well as property, so it will probably be liable for the car damage too.

Note that Horace has rights under the UTCCR 1999 (see below at page 116), but again UCTA is the simplest route to success.

Breach of contract (s 3)

Liability for breach of contract may not be excluded where a party enters into a contract made on the other party's **standard terms** (when no negotiation will have been possible), or where the party deals as a consumer, unless the exclusion is *reasonable*. (See page 116 below for guidance on how the term 'reasonable' is interpreted.)

Breach of implied terms in contracts for sale/hire purchase/supply/hire of goods (ss 6–7)

Certain conditions are implied under the Sale of Goods Act 1979, Supply of Goods (Implied Terms) Act 1973 and the Supply of Goods and Services Act 1982 to protect a buyer or hirer of goods. Full details can be found in Chapter 11, but the implied terms may be summarised as follows.

The supplier implicitly promises that it has title to the goods (rights of ownership) and is authorised to transfer it and that the goods:

1 match their description; and

2 are of satisfactory quality (in sales by way of business); and

3 are suitable for their purpose; and

4 correspond to any sample which has been provided.

UCTA 1977, s 6 restricts the extent to which such conditions may be excluded in sale of goods and hire-purchase contracts. Section 7 operates similarly regarding contracts for the sale and supply of goods. Consumers enjoy special protection in a commercial contract; and none of these conditions can be effectively excluded against them. A **consumer** is defined as someone not contracting in the course of a business (UCTA 1977, s 12) and this has been interpreted generously.

Thus, in *R & B Customs Brokers Co Ltd* v *United Dominions Trust* (1988, CA) 'consumer' was held to include anyone obtaining goods for use in their business, as long as these are not integral to the course of the business, or regularly bought for incidental purposes. A contract to buy a car for private and business use made by a company owned by a husband and wife was therefore deemed to be made by a consumer. This reasoning was affirmed by the Court of Appeal in *Feldaroll Foundry plc* v *Hermes Leasing (London) Ltd* (2004) on the grounds that it furthered the intention of UCTA, which was to safeguard a buyer's protection under the terms implied under relevant sale and supply legislation.

A buyer who is *not a consumer* does not enjoy such comprehensive protection. The condition regarding title (under ss 6–7) can never be excluded; the others may be excluded if the clause is 'reasonable' in any contract with a non-consumer buyer.

Note that a *private seller* is free to exclude liability for breach of any of the relevant terms above in a sale of goods or hire-purchase contract (s 6(4)). In practice, this is not as generous as might first appear. In effect, it covers only implied terms regarding title, description and sample, since the term regarding satisfactory quality is implied only in contracts where the seller/supplier is a business. Furthermore, while private sales of goods are common, private hire-purchase contracts are probably extremely rare.

What is 'reasonable' for the purposes of UCTA 1977?

Section 11 of UCTA 1977 provides guidance as to what is 'reasonable' for the purposes of the Act:

1 a contract term will satisfy the requirement of reasonableness if it is fair and reasonable with regard to all the circumstances which should have been considered by the parties when they entered the contract (s 11(1));

2 if the claim relates to a non-contractual notice, reasonableness is judged with reference to all the circumstances prevailing when the damage was caused (s 11(3)).

Schedule 2 to the Act offers further guidelines:

1 *Imbalance of bargaining power*. The parties to a contract may not enjoy equal bargaining power. In a standard terms contract, one party is presented with a set of terms and given no opportunity to negotiate existing terms or add others. The buyer of goods or services may be heavily reliant on the technical knowledge and expertise of the seller, and that ignorance produces power imbalance.

2 *Inducements and choices*. If a customer is given an unfair inducement to accept the exclusion clause, this may make it unreasonable. If that party could have made a similar

contract with another party without being subject to such a term, this may make the exemption reasonable.

3 *Prior knowledge.* If the customer should reasonably have been aware of the existence and extent of the term, taking into account previous dealings between the parties and trade custom, it may be reasonable to impose the exclusion.

4 *Special requirements.* If the goods were made or adapted to meet the customer's special requirements, an exemption may be binding.

The courts have also taken other factors into account, including the issue of insurance and whether the customer should have taken independent advice.

The following cases illustrate the approach of the courts to the interpretation of reasonableness.

Smith v Eric S. Bush (1989, HL)

The claimant bought a house in reliance on a surveyor's report, prepared on the instructions of the building society. The report stated that it was issued without any guarantee of accuracy or acceptance of any legal liability. The surveyor negligently overlooked some serious defects which led to the chimney collapsing into Mrs Smith's bedroom, and resulted in a large bill for structural repairs.

Held: the exclusion of liability was not effective as it was unreasonable:

1 *The parties did not have equal bargaining power.* Mrs Smith could not be expected to know whether or not the surveyor's report was correct, because of her lack of special knowledge.
2 *The financial resources of the claimant.* It was not reasonable to expect Mrs Smith to go to the expense of getting a second opinion. She was a first-time buyer of a modest property and, like most such purchasers, pushed to her financial limits.
3 *The surveyor had failed in a simple task.* Any reasonably competent surveyor ought to have spotted the defects.
4 *Insurance cover.* This was readily available at modest cost to the surveyor, while the purchaser was unlikely to enjoy such protection.

Green v Cade Bros (1978)

A standard terms contract, which complied with the requirements of the National Association of Seed Potato Merchants, restricted the right of rejection of potato seed to three days from delivery; any compensation was limited to the return of the contract price. The potato seed supplied to the buyer was infected by a virus which was not detectable until the growing process had started.

Held: the three-day time limit was not reasonable given the type of damage suffered. The limit on compensation was reasonable: it was usual in the trade, the parties enjoyed equal bargaining power, and the buyer had received no inducement to accept the limitation. The buyer could have bought guaranteed seed for a higher price.

George Mitchell v Finney Lock Seeds Ltd (1983, HL)

The claimant ordered cabbage seed from the defendant which did not match its description. It was also inferior in quality. The claimant lost his entire crop, sustaining a £61,000 loss. The contract limited liability for breach to replacement of the goods or a refund of the price.

Held: this was not reasonable because:

1. the breach arose from the seller's negligence;
2. the seller could have insured against crop failure at a modest cost;
3. in the past the seller had settled claims in excess of the limitation sum; this indicated that the seller did not always consider the clause fair and reasonable.

St Albans City and District Council v International Computers Ltd (1996, CA)

Computer software, supplied and installed by the defendant company to provide a database facility for the local authority, was defective. It caused errors in the estimation of the number of eligible poll-tax payers, and as a result the local authority lost substantial funds. A limitation clause in the contract restricted the defendant's liability to £100,000.

Held: the limitation clause was unreasonable because:

1. the defendant was a multinational company with substantial resources;
2. the defendant carried product liability insurance of £50 million and the limitation of liability was too small relative to the possible risk and the loss actually suffered;
3. the claimant's specialist needs greatly limited its choice of providers;
4. it was fairer to put the risk on the defendant who stood to make a profit on the contract. If the risk lay with the local authority, its taxpayers would be unjustly burdened by the loss.

> As should be evident from the above examples, the facts of each case are crucial to its outcome. The issues of the knowledge and resources of both parties are crucial to determining bargaining power. Issues of policy may also play a part. For example, compare the *St Albans* case, where, in effect, losses would have fallen on council taxpayers, with the *Watford Electronics* case below, where the claimant was a private company and bespoke software was involved.

Watford Electronics v Sanderson (2001, CA)

A specially designed computer software package was provided by the defendant under a contract that excluded liability for indirect and consequential losses and limited any general liability to the value of the contract price (£104,600). Due to defects in the software the claimant suffered £4.5 million losses from lost profits, replacement of the system and increased working costs.

Held: each clause was reasonable, as the clauses were negotiated between parties of appropriate experience representing equally substantial companies. There was equal bargaining power between the parties.

Chadwick LJ commented:

> *Where experienced businessmen representing substantial companies negotiate an agreement, they may be taken to have had regard to matters known to them. They should be taken to be the best judge of whether the terms of the agreement are reasonable. The court should not assume that either is likely to commit his company to an agreement which he thinks is unfair or which he thinks included unreasonable terms. Unless satisfied that one party has in effect taken unfair advantage of the other or that a term is so unreasonable that it cannot properly have been understood or considered the court should not interfere.*

The issue of one party seeking to use a clause to take unfair advantage is illustrated by *Overseas Medical Supplies* v *Orient* (1999) where an exclusion clause stating that the defendant would not be liable for loss of goods in transit was held to be unreasonable given that another term in the contract required the defendant to insure the goods, which had not been done. The existence of an alternative remedy may make what would appear to be an unreasonable term acceptable.

Regus UK Ltd v *Epcot Solutions Ltd* (2008, CA)

Regus (R) were IT trainers who rented accommodation for their courses from Epcot (E). The air conditioning system broke down, making work conditions on the premises very difficult for R's employees and customers. E failed to rectify the situation after a number of requests by R who then refused to pay the rent. E sued R for breach of contract and R counterclaimed for their losses. E claimed that it was protected by a clause 23(3) which stated that it would not be liable 'in any circumstances' for any loss of business or profits, third-party claims and any consequential loss. Clause 23(4) stated that in any event R's losses would be limited to 125% of the fees or £50,000 whichever was higher.

R successfully claimed in breach of contract in the High Court which held that clause 23 was unreasonable under UCTA, s 3 because it deprived R of any remedy at all and covered intentional acts because it was to operate 'in any circumstances'.

E appealed.

The CA dismissed the appeal and held: clause 23 was not unreasonable because it did not leave R without a remedy as it was still entitled to claim for diminution in value of the services provided. 'In any circumstances' could not be construed as excluding liability for fraud/wilful/reckless/malicious damage. However, this argument was irrelevant since E had not refused to repair the air conditioning from a wish to harm R's customers but from a desire to save money.

It was not unreasonable for E to restrict liability for breach of contract. There was no inequality of bargaining power between the parties and E had made it clear that customers should make their own insurance arrangements to protect themselves against business losses.

Unfair Terms in Consumer Contracts Regulations 1999 (UTCCR 1999)

The scope of the regulations

These regulations implement an EC Directive (91/13/EC) and replace the 1994 Regulations of the same name. They protect *consumers* who have entered a contract containing a *non-negotiable term* imposed by the *seller or supplier*, which is deemed to be unfair according to criteria laid down in the regulations. Such a term is voidable by consumers, i.e. they are not bound by it unless they choose to comply, but the rest of the contract remains binding.

The substance of the regulations

The relevant contracts

The regulations apply to unfair terms in a contract between a consumer and a seller or supplier (r 1).

Consumers

Consumers are defined as human beings, making contracts for non-business purposes (r 3(1)).

Seller/supplier

The contract must be made by the seller or supplier in the course of its business. The business may be publicly or privately owned (r 3(1)).

Non-negotiable terms

These will have been stated before the contract is finalised and the consumer will have had no influence on their contents (r 5(2), (3)). It is up to the seller or supplier to prove that such terms were not individually negotiated (r 5(4)).

Unfairness

A term is unfair if it fails to fulfil the requirements of **good faith** and this causes a **significant imbalance** in the parties' contractual relationship, which is prejudicial to the consumer's interests (r 5(1)). In assessing whether the seller or supplier acted in good faith, the court must have regard to all the circumstances relevant to formation of the contract (r 6(1)).

Worth thinking about?

The language used to describe unfairness in the UTCCR 1999 is very vague and woolly. You might well ask why it is not more precise. Can you think of any reasons why such imprecise language is used?

Suggested solutions can be found in Appendix 2.

Core terms

Provided it is clearly worded, a term relating to 'the definition of the main subject matter of the contract', or to the adequacy of 'price or remuneration', is not covered by the regulations (r 6(2)).

Written contracts

The seller or supplier must ensure that clear, intelligible language is used in the contractual documents (r 7(1)). Any ambiguity is resolved in favour of the consumer (r 7(2)).

The effect of an unfair term

The consumer is not bound by an unfair term. The rest of the contract remains effective as long as it is capable of existing without the problem term (r 8).

Interpreting the 1999 Regulations

The wording of the 1999 Regulations has permitted the courts to apply them to contracts that have not traditionally been regarded as consumer contracts. In *R (on the application of Khatun)* v *Newham London Borough Council* (2004, CA) it was held that contracts concerning land came within the 1999 Regulations, which therefore covered the terms under which Newham let accommodation to homeless people. Granting tenancies for rent was an economic activity that might be carried on for profit by a private business.

The courts appear to be prepared to interpret 'consumer' quite liberally where this best serves the interests of justice.

Evans v Cherry Tree Finance Ltd (2008, CA)

The claimant Mr Evans (E) obtained a loan from the defendant finance company (CTF) which he stated was to pay off the mortgage on premises which were used for both home and residential purposes and to comply with a divorce settlement. The loan agreement included an early redemption penalty. When E defaulted on the loan repayments CTF sold the premises and took the penalty sum in addition to the remainder of what was owed. E argued that he was protected by the Unfair Terms in Consumer Contract Regulations 1999 and that the redemption term was unfair. CTF argued that he was not protected because he was not a consumer, since he ran a business from the premises.

Held by the CA (affirming the decision of the High Court): the size of the early redemption penalty made it unfair. E was a consumer, for the purposes of this transaction. Enabling E to continue to trade from the premises was not the only purpose of the loan. It was evident to CTF, from the address and other details in the paperwork, that the loan was also for residential purposes.

The courts have tended to give a restrictive interpretation to what comes within the scope of 'price or remuneration' to prevent consumer protection from being undermined. This was stressed by the House of Lords in *Director General of Fair Trading* v *First National Bank* (below), which held that the disputed term which related to payment of interest was not excluded from the court's jurisdiction. This approach was followed in *Bairstow Eves London Central Ltd* v *Smith* (2004), where an escalating commission rate charged by an estate agent was deemed not to come within the core terms exclusion.

Schedule 2 to the 1999 Regulations contains an illustrative list of potentially unfair terms. This includes terms which:

1 permit a seller unfairly to retain a deposit or to impose a penalty on the consumer in the event of non-performance;

2 bind a consumer who has not had sufficient time to study the term's implications before entering the contract;

3 permit the seller unilaterally to alter the terms of the contract or the characteristics of the relevant goods or service;

4 oblige consumers to perform all their obligations, while not placing a reciprocal responsibility on the other party.

The list is not intended to be comprehensive. It is up to the consumer to prove that the term was unfair, taking into account the nature of the subject matter of the contract, the legal and commercial context in which the contract was made and the reasonable expectations of both parties; and all the circumstances surrounding the contract are relevant to determining any imbalance.

The concept of good faith appears rather nebulous and hard to define. The House of Lords' decision in *Director General of Fair Trading* v *First National Bank* (below) assists in developing an understanding of how it may be interpreted. Lord Bingham said that good faith was reflected by 'good standards of morality and commercial practice' and would be evidenced by 'fair and open dealing'. Just because a term is not beneficial to the consumer and may come, as their Lordships commented, as 'a nasty surprise' does not necessarily indicate unfairness or breach of good faith.

Director General of Fair Trading v *First National Bank* (2001, HL)

Under the Consumer Credit Act 1974 (CCA 1974), if a borrower defaults on a loan and judgment is obtained against him or her, the lender's full rights to interest on the future instalments are lost.

First National's loan terms stated that in such circumstances the Bank could claim remaining interest at the original contract rates. The DGFT claimed that this was an unfair term.

Held: the term did not amount to a breach of good faith. The CCA 1974, despite being enacted to protect borrowers, did not forbid such agreement; without it the bank would suffer an unreasonable loss. There was nothing unbalanced or detrimental to the borrowers in the term.

Non-beneficial terms were also judged to be fair in:

R (on the application of Khatun) v *Newham London Borough Council* (2004, CA)

Held: a term which required an applicant for housing to accept an offer of accommodation without viewing it in advance, and on pain of losing his bed and breakfast accommodation if he refused, was deemed in the circumstances not to be 'oppressive, perverse, or disproportionate'.

A different result occurred in the following case:

Munkenbeck & Marshall v *Michael Harold* (2005)

Held: terms in a standard form contract for architectural services were unfair. They were unduly onerous and had not been drawn to the consumer's attention before the contract was made. There was an imbalance between the parties that breached the good faith requirement.

In *Baybut & Others* v *Eccle Riggs Country Park* (2006) it was held that only express terms are governed by the regulations, since regulation 4(2) specifically excluded terms implied by statute from the effect of the regulations and also because the list of potentially unfair terms in Schedule 2 contained nothing which could be regarded as implied.

Enforcement of the regulations

The regulations may be used by consumers directly to enforce their contractual rights. The role of the Office of Fair Trading (OFT) is also crucial, since the 1994 Regulations empowered it to investigate complaints about allegedly unfair terms from consumers and trading standards departments. If the complaint is upheld, the OFT by legal action may require the offending business to change or withdraw the term. Recent cases involving intervention by the DGFT include the *First National Bank* case (above) and *The Office of Fair Trading v Foxtons* (2009) where the Court of Appeal held that an injunction should be granted to prevent the enforcement of unfair terms in an estate agent's contract. See also *Abbey National PLC and Others* v *Office of Fair Trading* (2009) below.

By the end of 1998, the OFT had investigated 3,000 complaints, of which 1,200 had been upheld. Other 'qualifying bodies' received enforcement powers under the 1999 Regulations. They include trading standards departments, the Director General of Water, Gas and Electricity Supply, and the Consumers' Association.

In the News

Bank charges for unarranged overdrafts

The Court of Appeal in *Abbey National PLC and Others* v *Office of Fair Trading* (2009) decided on 26 February 2009 that bank charges for unarranged overdrafts on personal accounts may be assessed for unfairness by the OFT under the Unfair Terms in Consumer Contracts Regulations 1999. The banks argued unsuccessfully that the charges were part of the core terms and therefore excluded from any consideration for unfairness under the regulations. The Court of Appeal decided however that the charges were not part of the essential bargain between the bank and the customer, since the charges were contingent (would be imposed only if a customer became overdrawn without previous agreement with the bank) and the relevant terms not specifically negotiated.

The OFT announced that it would now go ahead with its investigation and publish the results in due course.

However, it may be too early for bank customers to celebrate as the House of Lords (31/3/09) gave permission for the claimants to appeal.

(Sources: OFT press release of 26/2/09 and case transcript.)

A comparison of UCTA 1977 and the Unfair Terms in Consumer Contracts Regulations 1999

UCTA 1977	The regulations
Scope Renders ineffective certain types of exclusion clauses in a contract or non-contractual notice if the exclusion was issued in the course of business.	May render any non-negotiable term in a relevant contract voidable by a consumer buyer, if the seller was acting in the course of business.
Protected parties Not necessarily consumers or contracting parties. Includes corporations.	Human consumers only: must be contracting parties.
Extent of protection Some exclusions are automatically ineffective: for example, negligently caused death or personal injury. Some liabilities can be excluded or limited if 'reasonable': for example, breach of a standard terms contract, or of any non-consumer contract	An *unfair* term is one which does not fulfil the requirement of *good faith* by causing a significant imbalance of power between the parties *to the detriment of the consumer*.
Burden of proof On the seller. The seller must prove reasonableness where relevant.	On the buyer. The consumer must prove that the term was unfair.

Reform of unfair contract terms legislation

Having studied the table above, you may well be thinking that the law in this area is anomalous, inconsistent and confusing. When answering questions on the topic you have to be very careful to work out which piece of legislation is applicable and not get confused about the amount of protection provided, or the criteria relevant to establishing proof and its onus. You are not alone in finding this difficult. The Department of Trade and Industry recently asked the Law Commission to investigate the legislation with a view to its reform. Its report of March 2005 (Law Com. No. 292) stated that 'A law that affects ordinary people in their everyday lives has been made unnecessarily complicated and difficult'. Furthermore, 'the combination of legislation has led to widespread confusion among consumers, businesses and their advisers'. The Law Commission has produced a draft Unfair Contract Terms Bill which combines both the Act and the regulations, rewritten in order to make them clearer and easier to understand. It also provides some extra protection for consumers and small businesses.

The draft Unfair Contract Terms Bill

The draft Bill makes the following provision:

1 covers all the terms within the scope of the regulations (not just exclusion clauses);

2 includes negotiated as well as standard terms clauses in consumer contracts (not previously covered by the regulations);

3 places the burden of proof on the business in a claim by a customer (the OFT will still have to prove that a term is unfair);

4 continues to make ineffective any exclusion of liability for death or personal injury, or quality or fitness for purpose of goods;

5 gives additional powers to the OFT to prevent the display of notices including ineffective terms;

6 gives extra protection to 'micro businesses' (nine employees maximum and not part of a group). Although enjoying a degree of protection from unfair exclusion clauses by UCTA, small businesses, through lack of expertise, knowledge and bargaining power, are still vulnerable to the imposition of other standard terms by much larger businesses. The Bill enables a small business to challenge any standard term, provided it has not been varied by negotiation, in most types of contract. Contracts for more than £50,000, and those already covered by sufficient statutory protection, are excluded.

At the time of writing, this Bill has not yet been laid before Parliament.

Chapter summary

A contract is composed of promises called 'terms'. These may be express or implied.

Classification of contract terms
Conditions.
Warranties.
Innominate terms.

Exclusion clauses
Use is controlled by the common law and statute.

Common law controls of exclusion clauses
Incorporation of the terms requires timely and sufficient notice unless a party signs the contract.

The *contra proferentem* rule protects a vulnerable party from being disadvantaged by ambiguous language.

Statutory controls of exclusion clauses
This legislation seeks to prevent misuse of exclusion clauses by businesses.

UCTA protects consumers and non-consumers against attempts to avoid liability for breach of contract or tort. It gives special protection to consumers in contracts for sale, supply and hire of goods contracts. Exclusions which breach the terms of the Act are ineffective and cannot be enforced.

UTCCR 1999 protects consumers only. The regulations make terms voidable if they breach good faith by unfairly exploiting an imbalance of power between the parties.

Key terms

Business efficacy: the obvious common but unspoken intention of the contracting parties.

Charterparty: a contract to hire a fully crewed ship.

Condition: a major contractual term crucial to its existence. If breached, the innocent party may refuse further performance and sue for breach.

Consumer: in general, this means a human buyer who purchases goods/services etc. for personal use, but UCTA includes companies contracting for accessories for the business.

***Contra proferentem* rule:** any ambiguity of a contract term is resolved against the party who would most benefit from it.

Express term: a contractual term specifically stated to be part of the contract.

Exclusion clause: a contractual term which attempts to limit or exempt a party's contract/tort liability against another. Sometimes called an exemption clause.

Fundamental breach: so serious a breach of a condition, that it completely defeats the entire object of the contract.

Good faith: general honest dealing. Under the UTCCR 1999 a term's failure to evidence this makes that term voidable.

Implied term: a term which was not specified in the contract, but may be implied into it by statute or common law.

Innominate term: a term capable of giving rise to a variety of breaches of different degrees of seriousness.

Limitation clause: a contractual term which seeks to restrict the amount of damages payable to the innocent party in the event of a civil action.

Significant imbalance (UTCCR 1999): a lack of equal bargaining power, which may evidence unfairness.

Standard terms: contract terms on which a business always trades and which are not open to negotiation.

Warranty: a minor contractual term, breach of which entitles the innocent party to damages.

Quiz 6

1. Distinguish between conditions and warranties.
2. What is an innominate term?
3. Are exclusion clauses incorporated in a contract when notified in the following ways:
   - (a) in a notice on the counter of a shop?
   - (b) in a signed document?
   - (c) in a hotel bedroom?
   - (d) in a receipt?
4. To what extent may negligence liability be excluded under UCTA 1977?
5. What special protection is given to consumers by UCTA 1977?
6. State the main differences between the effects of UCTA 1977 and the Unfair Terms in Consumer Contracts Regulations 1999.

Answers to all quizzes can be found in Appendix 2.

Take a closer look

The following cases provide important examples of how the law you have studied in this chapter has developed. They are primary sources illustrating the law in action and give you more detail about their facts, as well as helping you to understand the law and to appreciate how the judges reached their decisions.

Try looking them up in the law reports or accessing them via a database, e.g. Bailli (www.bailii.org/databases.html). LexisNexis or Westlaw may be available in your university or college library, or you may find extracts in a case book. (See Appendix 1: Additional resources.)

Interfoto Picture Library Ltd v *Stiletto Productions* [1988] 1 All ER 348, CA
Lombard North Central plc v *Butterworth* [1987] QB 527, CA
Smith v *Eric S. Bush* [1989] 2 WLR 790, HL
Watford Electronics v *Sanderson* [2001] 1 All ER (Comm) 696, CA.

Web activity

Please go to:

www.oft.gov.uk/

Click 'Search' and then type 'Unfair terms in Consumer Contracts Regulations' in the 'keywords' box. Choose 'unfair terms guidance' from the list you are offered. Then choose any of the guidance topics that come up for practical examples, e.g. Guidance on Unfair Terms in Package Holiday Contracts.

Assignment 5

Widgets plc entered into a three-year contract with Crankit plc under which Crankit agreed to service Widgets' production line machinery. Widgets signed a document headed 'Service Agreement' consisting of 150 terms, including the following:

10. It shall be a condition of the contract that Crankit will attend in response to any call-out request by Widgets within 24 hours.

36. Crankit will not be responsible to Widgets for any defect in quality of any spare parts supplied by Crankit when servicing customers' machinery.

142. Widgets agree to indemnify Crankit against any claims by Widgets or any other third party who may suffer damage to person or property arising from any failure properly to perform this service agreement.

Advise the parties how these terms will affect the outcome of a claim in the following circumstances:

(a) When carrying out the first annual service, Crankit fits a new fuel pump. This malfunctions 48 hours later, causing an explosion. Injuries result to Jeremy, who lives next door to the factory and the explosion also causes business interruption for three weeks.

(b) Twenty months into the contract, Crankit is called upon by Widgets, which reports that a major mechanical failure has brought its production line to a halt. Crankit replies that due to a lack of staff, it will be unable to attend for three days. Next day, Widgets tells Crankit that it is opting out of the contract as immediate servicing is obtainable from Best and Sons Ltd.

mylawchamber

Visit **www.mylawchamber.co.uk/adams** to access multiple choice questions and glossary flashcards to test yourself on this chapter. You'll also find weblinks to the web activity in this chapter.

Use Case Navigator to read in full some of the key cases referenced in this chapter:

Director General of Fair Trading v *First National Bank* [2001] 1 All ER 97
Hong Kong Fir Shipping Co. Ltd v *Kawasaki Kisen Kaisha* [1962] 1 All ER 474
Interfoto Picture Library Ltd v *Stiletto Productions* [1988] 1 All ER 348

chapter 13
TORT LIABILITY FOR DEFECTIVE GOODS

Introduction

In previous chapters contractual rights and remedies have been explained, but it is important to remember that these rights are not sufficient to protect *all* consumers. The law of contract protects only the *buyer* of the defective goods. Other people harmed by the goods will not generally be able to sue in contract because of the lack of privity of contract between themselves and the seller. Even a buyer may not be adequately protected, should the seller have gone out of business.

A tort is a civil wrong independent of contract. The law of tort imposes duties at civil law in respect of a wide range of behaviour relevant to business activity. This area of the law has a particular importance for consumers and those doing business with them.

Both the buying and non-buying consumer may be protected by the law of tort. This chapter is concerned with situations where parties suffer loss or damage due to defective products, and explains their rights in negligence and under the Consumer Protection Act 1987 (CPA 1987).

Learning Objectives

After studying this topic you should be able to:

- Appreciate the relationship of the law of contract to tort liability for defective products
- Understand the scope of duty of care in negligence relating to defective products
- Grasp the difference between consequential and pure economic loss
- Envisage the circumstances where liability in negligence and/or the CPA 1987 may arise.

Photo: ©Richard Klune/Corbis

Negligence liability

The tort of negligence gives rights to persons who have suffered damage to themselves or to their property, against a party who has failed to take reasonable care for those persons' safety. Negligence is the commonest tort claim and is relevant to the whole gamut of accidental injury situations: for example, road accidents, illness and injuries caused by workplace conditions and harm arising through medical treatment. It also plays an important part in product liability: a person who suffers damage because of defects in a product, caused by the carelessness of the manufacturer or other party responsible for the state of the goods, may have a right to sue in negligence.

To be successful in a claim of negligence, the claimant must prove that:

1 the defendant owed the claimant a **duty of care**; and

2 the defendant failed to perform that duty; and

3 as a result, the claimant suffered damage.

1 The duty of care

The claimant must be able to show that he or she is someone who, in the circumstances, the defendant should have had in mind when embarking on the course of conduct which led to the alleged damage. This concept was established by the House of Lords in the following key case.

Donoghue v Stevenson (1932, HL)

Mrs Donoghue and a friend stopped for refreshment at a café one hot afternoon. The friend purchased from the proprietor some ginger beer manufactured by the defendant. This was supplied in stone bottles which were opened at the table. Having happily consumed a glassful, Mrs Donoghue tipped the bottle to make sure nothing was left; to her horror what appeared to be the decomposing remains of a snail slithered into her glass. She consequently became ill with gastro-enteritis and sued Stevenson (the manufacturer) in negligence.

Held (by a majority): the manufacturer did owe Mrs Donoghue a duty of care. As she was the user of its product, she was somebody who reasonably foreseeably would be affected by the way the manufacturer processed its product.

Lord Atkin stated:

> *A manufacturer of products, which he sells in such a form as to show that he intends them to reach the ultimate consumer in the form in which they left him, with no reasonable possibility of intermediate examination and with the knowledge that the absence of reasonable care in the preparation or putting up of the products will result in an injury to the consumer's life or property, owes a duty of care to the consumer to take reasonable care.*

In these consumer conscious days it comes as a surprise that prior to the decision in *Donoghue* v *Stevenson* a person in Mrs Donoghue's position had no rights in tort. Before 1932, liability in negligence was restricted to harm caused by defective products which were dangerous in themselves, such as guns or explosives. *Donoghue* v *Stevenson* established a general principle of product liability in negligence known sometimes as the '**neighbour principle**'. This is because Lord Atkin said that a duty was owed only to one's neighbour, which in law means: *'persons who are so closely and directly affected by my act that I ought reasonably to have them in my mind as being so affected when I am directing my mind to the acts or omissions called into question'*.

The scope and influence of Lord Atkin's judgment

Lord Atkin's judgment has had a huge impact on the civil law. The 'neighbour principle' has enabled successive judges to use it as a springboard for the development of negligence in all its forms. To understand its influence, it is necessary to analyse some of the terms used by Lord Atkin and see how they have been interpreted in later case law.

Manufacturer

The duty was soon extended from the maker of goods to those delivering services such as fitting and installing or repairing goods (see *Stennet* v *Hancock* (1939) below at page 260), and defendants with responsibility to check the goods prior to sale. Today it covers the whole range of products and service industries. This aspect of duty is covered in greater depth in Chapter 14.

Product

Case law illustrates that liability in negligence covers a huge variety of products in normal daily use for example, cars (*Herschtal* v *Stewart & Ardern* (1940)), computer software (*St Albans City Council* v *International Computers* (1996)), and including some less likely items such as tombstones (*Brown* v *Cotterill* (1934)), and itchy underpants (*Grant* v *Australian Knitting Mills* (1936)).

Lord Atkin referred to the *'preparation or putting up of the products'* so the duty of care extends to the packaging and any instructions accompanying the product. The goods may be perfectly safe in themselves but become dangerous because inappropriately packaged, or because they do not carry correct instructions or a warning (e.g. medicines, weed-killer).

The ultimate consumer

Mrs Donoghue is the perfect example of an **ultimate consumer** – the actual user of the defective goods who is harmed by the defects, but who is not necessarily the buyer.

'Consumer' in this context has a very wide meaning, which extends beyond mere users of the goods or service. A consumer may be defined as someone reasonably likely to be affected by the goods in question. Consumers will be owed a duty, since the supplier should have taken their needs into account.

Barnett v Packer (1940)

A shop assistant laying out chocolates for display was injured by a wire protruding from one of them.

Held: the manufacturer owed a duty of care to the shop assistant, as well as to people who ate the goods, as anybody handling the chocolates could have suffered injury from this foreign body.

> Even a bystander with no relationship to a party to the original transaction may come within the neighbour principle.

Stennett v Hancock (1939)

The claimant, a pedestrian, suffered a leg injury when he was hit by part of a wheel which came off a passing lorry.

Held: the garage which had recently negligently fitted the wheel owed a duty to the claimant, since it was reasonably foreseeable that any road user in the vicinity of the lorry could be harmed if a wheel became detached.

The limits of the duty of care

Marc Rich & Co. AG v Bishop Rock Marine (1995, HL)

The House of Lords held that, when deciding whether a duty of care exists in any negligence action, the court must take into account whether the following criteria are satisfied:

1 reasonable foreseeability;
2 proximity;
3 public interest taking into account fairness, justice and reasonableness.

> These factors are interlinked and interdependent.
>
> 1 *Reasonable foreseeability*. No duty of care will exist unless it is **reasonably foreseeable** that the particular claimant was vulnerable to the risk created by the defendant. For example, in *Stennett* v *Hancock* (above) it was reasonably foreseeable that, if the lorry wheel was not securely fitted, an accident endangering any pedestrian in the vicinity might result.
>
> 2 *Proximity*. There must be a close enough relationship of **proximity** between the defendant's acts and the claimant at the time of the wrong complained of. Lord Atkin (*Donoghue* v *Stevenson*) stated that proximity was not restricted to 'mere physical proximity, but [should] be used ... to extend to such close and direct relations that the act complained of directly affects a person whom the person bound to take care would know would be directly affected by his careless act'. The claimants in *Barnett* v *Packer* and *Stennett* v *Hancock* above provide good examples of such proximity. They both lacked close physical proximity but nonetheless stood to suffer from the negligence of the defendant.

In the following circumstances such *proximity* is lacking.

(a) *The goods are no longer under the defendant's control.* The defendant ceases to have control if, prior to use, the goods have been tampered with or examined by a third party or claimant, in such a way as would probably cause or reveal a defect. Remember that in *Donoghue* v *Stevenson* the ginger beer was supplied to Mrs Donoghue in an opaque bottle which was opened in Mrs Donoghue's presence. There was no possibility that its unwanted inhabitant could have got there through the intervention of a third party. The bottle arrived at the table in the same state as when it left the manufacturer. The stone bottle prevented the hazard from being evident until its contents were removed.

(b) *Too much time has elapsed since the product left the defendant.* Whether the goods have been used or not, it would be unfair to place the manufacturer under a duty for an indefinite time.

Evans v *Triplex Glass* (1936)

Mr Evans bought a new Vauxhall car fitted by the manufacturer with a windscreen made of toughened safety glass manufactured by Triplex. One year later, he and his family were injured during a car journey when the windscreen shattered.

Held: Triplex did not owe Evans a duty of care because:

- any weakness in the glass might have been caused by Vauxhall when fitting the windscreen;
- a defect might have been detectable on inspection by Vauxhall prior to fitting;
- too much time had elapsed between the product leaving their control and the accident – the glass could have been weakened in use.

(c) *The claimant has failed to take reasonable precautions prior to or when using the product.* A claimant must be able to show that the product has been used appropriately, in accordance with instructions.

3 *Public interest.* This criterion covers a wide range of circumstances involving what may be described as policy or **public interest** issues. A duty of care will not be acknowledged unless it is fair, just and reasonable and not damaging to the interests of the public at large, however beneficial it might be to the individual claimant. The court may refuse to develop the scope of negligence to provide a right of action already covered by an existing area of the law, or to develop the law so as to discourage people from taking reasonable precautions, such as insurance, to protect their own interests. A duty may be developed because it will actively promote the *public interest*. In *Donoghue* v *Stevenson*, public health considerations made it desirable to impose a duty, as well as the fact that Mrs Donoghue had no other legal rights to pursue. It was fair to put the loss on the manufacturer who stood to profit in general from his product.

Pure economic loss rarely gives rise to a duty of care

The courts have not usually regarded it as just and reasonable to impose a duty of care where the defect results in **pure economic loss**. Such loss, which is derived from the goods being defective rather than dangerous, merely causes the claimant to be out of pocket. The courts treat such losses as contractual only as they relate only to the *quality* of the goods rather than any actively dangerous fault, which causes damage. However, this limitation is not helpful to a party who did not buy the goods from the defendant in the first place.

> **Real Life**
>
> Horace was given an electric blanket for Christmas by his Aunt Betty, who bought it from Flash Electricals plc. The blanket was manufactured by Cosiwarm Ltd. Due to a production defect, it set fire to his bedroom on Christmas night with resulting damage to carpets and furniture. Horace was made ill due to smoke inhalation. He is entitled to claim damages from Cosiwarm plc which made the blanket for:
>
> 1 the pain and suffering caused by the smoke inhalation;
> 2 any loss of earnings while he recuperated and the cost of replacing furnishings and decorating his bedroom.
>
> These are the knock-on costs of the damage caused by the defendant's negligence and are described as *consequential economic loss*.
>
> Horace would not be entitled to recover the cost of replacing the defective electric blanket, which is categorised as *pure* economic loss; *the defect* does not of itself give rise to liability of the manufacturer in negligence. It is *the physical damage to person or other property* which imposes the duty. The lack of *quality* in the goods does not in itself give rise to negligence liability.

This difference between pure and **consequential economic loss** is also illustrated by the following case.

Muirhead v Industrial Tank Specialities Ltd (1986)

The claimant, who ran a lobster farm, was supplied with oxygen pumps manufactured by the defendant through a contract with a third party. They proved to be unsuitable for use with the English electricity system and kept cutting out. The claimant's lobsters died and he was unable to restock for a substantial period of time while he attempted to work out what was wrong.

Held: the claimant was entitled to recover the consequential cost of restocking the lobsters and for the loss of profits on those that died. He was not entitled to recover for profits lost during the time that lobster production was suspended, or the cost of replacing the pumps, since these were pure economic losses only.

Exceptionally, the claimant may be able to claim for pure economic loss if it can be shown that the claimant obtained the goods after having personally and directly consulted the manufacturers and placed reliance on their expertise. This creates a high degree of proximity between the parties, which is deemed to make it fair, just and reasonable to impose the duty.

Junior Books v *Veitchi* (1982, HL)

Junior Books made a contract for the construction of a warehouse. They told the building contractor that they wanted flooring to be supplied by the defendant, who was consequently a nominated sub-contractor. The flooring was so defective that the warehouse was unusable until the floor was replaced causing considerable expense.

Junior Books had no claim in contract as, by nominating Veitchi, Junior Books had relieved the building contractor of responsibility for the appointment, and no contract had been formed between Junior Books and Veitchi. Consequently, Junior Books claimed in negligence.

Held: the claimant's reliance on the defendant's expertise was sufficient to bring the parties into close proximity, and so a duty of care existed for the pure economic loss.

Veitchi was not applicable in the *Muirhead* case as Muirhead had not nominated the manufacturer to his supplier. The court usually takes the view that a contract between the claimant and supplier provides the appropriate route to compensation. The supplier should have been able to negotiate terms to give himself or herself adequate protection, or, if this is not workable, to insure against possible pure economic losses, such as business interruption. The issue of duty of care for pure economic loss is explored further in Chapter 14.

2 The claimant must prove breach of duty

It is not enough for the claimant to prove that the defendant owed them a duty of care. The claimant must prove that by objective standards the defendant failed to take reasonable care, i.e. did not provide a reasonable level of protection against reasonably foreseeable accidents. This includes taking into account the particular needs of a target group and giving adequate warning or instructions about the use of the product. For example, a soft-toy manufacturer must consider that baby and toddler users of its teddy bears may indeed literally try to consume them. Thus, it must ensure that non-toxic materials are used and that the bears' eyes and noses are very firmly attached. In the next chapter we will examine breach of duty in more detail and with regard to negligent service delivery.

3 The claimant must prove consequential damage

The claimant must also prove that it was the defendant's breach of duty which actually caused the damage suffered. In the story of Horace and the electric blanket outlined earlier, Horace would not be successful, despite proof of a defect in the blanket making it a fire risk, if there was evidence that the fire was actually caused by defective wiring in Horace's house.

Defendants are not necessarily liable for all the consequences of their behaviour: some may be deemed *too remote* from their original act. In negligence a defendant is generally liable for all reasonably foreseeable damage, but not for highly improbable or fluke results.

The issues of breach and consequential damage are explored in greater depth in Chapter 14.

The Consumer Protection Act 1987 (Part I)

The Consumer Protection Act 1987 (CPA 1987), which was enacted to implement the EC Product Liability Directive (85/374/EC), has introduced a measure of **strict liability** for defective products into English law.

The difference between fault and strict liability

Most torts, including negligence, are based on **fault liability**. The claimant has to prove not only that the defendant's behaviour broke the law and caused damage, but also that the defendant either intended to cause harm to the claimant, or was blameworthy in overlooking the risk to the claimant.

Strict liability is exceptional in tort. Where it exists the claimant is relieved of the need to prove any intent or carelessness on the part of the defendant; the claimant merely has to prove the causal link between the defendant's tortious behaviour and the damage suffered. This may increase the claimant's chances of a successful claim, as proof of failure to take care is often problematic.

Cases involving injuries caused by the side-effects of drugs like Thalidomide, which caused serious injuries to many unborn foetuses during 1960s, raised public perception of the problems caused by fault liability and encouraged recommendations for reform from the Pearson Commission of 1978, as well as from judges and pressure groups. Successive governments ignored these recommendations, and change came only after intervention by the EC prompted the enactment of the CPA 1987.

The main provisions of Part I of the Consumer Protection Act 1987

Who may sue? s 2(1)

Any person suffering damage giving rise to liability under the Act to their person or property and resulting from defective goods resulting from defective goods.

Methods of supply: s 46

The goods may have been supplied by way of sale, barter, hire, prize or gift provided that the supplier was acting in the course of business.

Potential defendants: s 2

Section 2(1) provides that 'where any damage is caused wholly or partly by a defect in a product', the following persons shall be liable:

1 **The producer**. This includes the manufacturer and persons responsible for winning or abstracting a product, for example, mineral water or electricity.

2 *The self-branding supplier* 'who, by putting his name on the product or using a trade mark or other distinguishing mark in relation to the product has held himself out as the producer of the product'.

So where goods are marketed under an 'own brand' label (like many supermarket goods), the business whose name appears on the label is likely to be treated as the producer. If the label indicates that the goods were manufactured by another producer ('produced for Sainsburys by X plc'), it may be arguable that the supplier is not the producer as they are not 'holding themselves out as the producer'.

3 **The importer**. The party who *initially* imported the product *into the EU* may be liable. (This is not necessarily the party responsible for the goods entering the UK.)

4 *The supplier*. Suppliers are liable only if they fail, on request from the injured party, to identify the manufacturer, producer or importer.

The meaning of 'product': s 1

'**Product**' includes packaging and instructions and potentially covers a huge variety of manufactured and other goods and utilities.

1 *Manufactured products*. This includes components of another product. Although buildings are not goods, building components which become fixtures to the land like window frames or girders are 'products' under the Act.

2 *'Substances won or abstracted'*. This includes things like electricity and water.

3 Things which owe their 'essential characteristics' to an 'industrial or other process'. In *A and Others* v *National Blood Authority* (2001) blood and blood products supplied by the defendant were 'products' within the meaning of s 1 because they had been subject to an industrial process. Anti-coagulants are mixed with blood on collection and it may be subject to other processes before storage.

4 Agricultural products like growing crops and game, which were not originally included have been covered since 2000 when the Act was amended by the CPA 1987 (Product Liability Modification Order 2000 to implement Directive 1999/34/EC).

It is unclear how far goods conveying information such as books and computer programs are covered by the Act. It would be possible for information transmitted in this form to cause harm through its defects. A book on fungi might incorrectly describe a species as edible, with disastrous consequences. There is medical evidence which suggests that some computer games may trigger fits and migraine. Unless and until such matters are conclusively determined by the courts, this will remain an uncertain area.

Defective means dangerous: s 3

The CPA is not concerned with the *quality* of the product but with its *safety*. Therefore, a product is not **defective** under the Act unless it is unsafe: there is no liability unless it actually causes damage to the consumer or the consumer's other property. The standard of safety under the Act is that which people 'generally are entitled to expect' which is actually set by the court rather than necessarily reflecting public expectation, which may be regarded as unreasonably high. The case of *Bogle* v *McDonalds Restaurants* (below) aptly illustrates this point. Some products do have inherent risks attached to their use which cannot be entirely prevented, like power tools. Other products would require disproportionate expenditure to eliminate or reduce risk which would make them over expensive. Risk/benefit analysis is necessary in such cases to determine a reasonable standard.

The Act specifies the following factors to be relevant in deciding whether this standard has been met:

1 *The packaging and any warnings or instructions*. A medicine may be perfectly safe in and of itself, but rendered dangerous because it lacks clear instructions or a warning that it is unsuitable for people with certain medical conditions.

2 *The normal uses of the product*. The needs of the relevant class of consumer must be taken into account in deciding whether the manufacturer has rendered the product safe. Toys marketed for use by small children require different safety standards, in relation to things like sharp edges, non-toxic materials and the size of removable parts, than goods for the entertainment of adults. If the consumer is harmed by use of the product for purposes which are not normal, liability does not arise. By indicating the purpose of a product and the age group for which it is intended, the manufacturer may limit the 'normal use' of the product.

3 *The time when the product was issued*. This is relevant to issues like shelf life, or situations where the product met appropriate standards of safety when issued but current research now indicates that those standards were not high enough.

The next case provides a useful example of how the issue of defectiveness is determined by the court.

Bogle & Others v *McDonalds Restaurants Ltd* (2002)

This case concerned a number of child litigants who had sustained scalding injuries after tea and coffee purchased from McDonalds had been spilt on them. Many of the injuries were serious involving severe pain and the need for skin grafts. However, in no case was the spillage directly caused by McDonalds' staff but resulted from other restaurant users, or the claimant dropping or knocking over the drink.

The claimants argued that the hot drinks, a product of McDonalds, were defective because of the temperature at which they had been served and the mode of delivery, including the nature of the cups, lack of appropriate staff training and failure to give warning of the likelihood of scalding.

Held by Field J: McDonalds had not supplied a defective product under the CPA because:

1 Staff obtained very thorough training, with supervision in their first six months of training and regular assessment after that. This training included ensuring that tops were firmly attached to cups before handing them over to customers and giving a tactful warning about the danger of spillage where appropriate. The drinks were served at a temperature which customers would expect. Buyers of tea and coffee were usually people old enough to appreciate such risks and take precautions against them.

2 The cup design did not encourage spillage. A standard cup would only tip over at an angle of 20 degrees and a large one at 18 degrees. With the lid on, the contents would not spill if knocked over or dropped. Even if the lid was removed (to add sugar, for example), it was still effective when replaced.

3 '*Persons generally expect tea or coffee purchased to be consumed on the premises to be hot. Many prefer to consume a hot drink from an unlidded cup rather than through a spout in the lid. Persons generally know that if a hot drink is spilled onto someone, a serious scalding injury can result. They accordingly know that care must be taken to avoid such spills, especially if they are with young children. Given that the staff were trained to cap the drinks securely and given the capabilities of the cups and lids used, I am satisfied that the safety of the hot drinks served by McDonald's was such as persons generally are entitled to expect*'.

The claimant must prove that the defendant was responsible for the defect. This may be problematic if as in *Piper* v *JRI (Manufacturing) Ltd* (2006) the product was handled by a third party who could have caused the defect, enabling the defendant to argue that on the balance of probability the third party caused the defect.

In the News

Piper v *JRI (Manufacturing) Ltd* (2006)

Mr Piper had a total hip replacement using a prosthesis made by JRI. Not long after it had been implanted it sheared in two and had to be removed and replaced, causing him increased loss of mobility, as well as the additional pain and suffering of undergoing more surgery.

He claimed that the prosthesis was defective under the CPA 1987. JRI argued that they were protected by s 4 as the defect was not present at the point the goods were released from the factory.

Held: Mr Piper's claim must fail as he was not able to prove that the defect occurred during the production process. Any defects arising during manufacture which might have weakened the prosthesis would most probably have been picked up by the scanning process used by the defendant to check the goods.

Worth thinking about?

Who else might Mr Piper consider claiming from?

Which tort would his claim be based on?

What problems might he have in proving the case?

Suggested solutions can be found in Appendix 2.

Actionable damage: s 5

This covers death, personal injuries and damage to property (including land) which the claimant is *not* using for business purposes. A claim for property damage must be for at least £275.

Since pure economic loss is not recoverable, the cost of replacing or repairing the defective item cannot be claimed. The same principles apply here as in negligence.

Causation and liability: s 2

The claimant must prove that the defect was the cause of the damage claimed. Since liability is strict the claimant does not have to prove that the defendant was careless, merely that the product comes within the statutory meaning of defective.

Defences

Under s 4 of the Act, the defendant will have a defence if able to show the following:

1 The goods comply with EC or UK safety standards and the defect is attributable to compliance with those standards.

2 The goods became defective after they were supplied. The defendant is liable only if the defect is present when the goods are put in circulation. If it arises later due to use or abuse by the consumer or a third party, the defendant is not liable.

3 The 'state of the art/developments risk' defence. This is a special defence under the Act which potentially undermines the strict liability element. The defendant will not be liable if it can be shown that when the product was released the defendant had done all that was required to fulfil safety standards in accordance with current research and technological expertise, and in consequence the defect was not discoverable.

This defence is meant to be a safeguard for manufacturers of new products. It is argued that without it manufacturers fearful of litigation might restrict important new product development of great potential benefit to the public. However, this remains a controversial subject. The Directive does not prohibit such defences and the approach of other EU countries varies but, prior to the Act both the Law Commission (Law Com. 82) and the Pearson Commission rejected exemption from liability on the grounds of development risk. It is highly arguable that a drug like Thalidomide could slip through the liability net through the use of this defence. No such defence is available under the law of contract and it can be argued that with appropriate insurance a manufacturer can protect itself against liability.

4 The defendant did not at any time supply the product to another in the course of business.

Contributory negligence and consent are also relevant. These are examined at the end of Chapter 15.

Area of law	Contract	Tort	Tort
	Sale of Goods Act 1979 (SGA 1979) Supply of Goods and Services Act 1982 (SGA 1982)	Negligence	Consumer Protection Act 1987
Who can sue?	Buyer only	Injured party (ultimate consumer)	Injured party
Who can be sued?	Seller	Manufacturer of goods Servicer of goods Supplier – if duty to inspect	Producer of product Manufacturer Own-brand labeller Importer Supplier
What must be proved?	Goods – breach of SGA 1979, ss 13, 14, 15 Goods and services – breach of CPA 1987, ss 4, 5 Goods – like SGA 1979 SGSA 1982 Services – lack of reasonable care and skill, reasonable timeliness, reasonable charging	(i) Duty of care (ii) Breach of duty (iii) Consequent damage	(i) Product defective and unsafe (ii) Damage suffered as a result
Damage compensated	Any loss or damage to buyer as long as not too remote, including purchase price	Any loss or damage to injured party as long as not too remote; excluding purchase price and other pure economic loss	Death/personal injury Damage to land, goods (over £275)
Liability	Goods – strict Services – fault Civil only	Fault Civil only	Strict Criminal liability also possible under CPA 1987, Part II

Figure 13.1 Liability for defective products

Time limits

Under the Limitation Act 1980, s 11A, claimants must take action within three years of the date when they first became aware of the damage, the defect, and the identity of the defendant. There is a final cut-off date of 10 years from the date on which the product was supplied to the claimant and no action can be started after that time.

Real Life

Horace was injured and suffered damage to his property when an electric blanket, manufactured by Cosiwarm and which was a present from his Aunt Betty, caught fire on its first use. As well as a claim in negligence, Horace also has a claim under the CPA 1987, as his losses certainly exceed the £275 minimum.

Cosiwarm, the manufacturer, is liable as producer under the CPA 1987 if the blanket is proven to be defective. Even if Cosiwarm is not clearly identifiable as producer of the blanket, it may still be best to claim under the CPA, as this may give Horace more flexibility in his choice of defendant.

Flash Electricals, from which Aunt Betty bought the blanket, would be the 'marker', if the blanket was marketed as Flash's own brand. If there is no label saying who the producer is, Flash may still be personally liable as 'supplier' unless it identifies the producer. Even if Flash merely imported the blanket, it could still be sued as 'importer' if it obtained the goods directly from any country outside the EU.

As long as he can prove that the electric blanket was defective and actually caused the fire, he will be successful and will not have to prove failure to take reasonable care as the CPA 1987 imposes strict liability.

The impact of the Consumer Protection Act 1987

As cases emerged some commentators perceived that the way in which the law was being interpreted seemed to provide no more protection for claimants than an action in negligence. This was a concern since the Product Liability Directive had indicated that its purpose was to enable claimants to avoid the need to prove fault by the defendant, thus overcoming one of the main obstacles to a successful claim. The Act (s 1) stated that it was intended to comply with the Directive.

European Commission v UK (1997, ECJ)

The Commission claimed that the UK was failing in its obligations to implement the purpose of the Directive with respect to the concept of a defective product and the scope of the state of the art defence.

Held: it was essential that the Act be construed in accordance with the purpose of the Directive and that the Directive must prevail in the event of conflict.

Two subsequent judgments since this case clearly reflect this approach.

Abouzaid v Mothercare (UK) Ltd (2000, CA)

The claimant, who was 12 years old, was blinded in one eye while attempting to attach the defendant's product (a Cosytoes sleeping bag) to his little brother's push chair. An elastic fastening strap sprang from his hand and the attached buckle struck his eye.

Held: the product was defective under s 3, since the reasonable expectations of the public that the product was safe to use were not satisfied, given the vulnerability of the eye and potential seriousness of such injuries. There was a risk attached to use of the product but no warning was given to the user to avoid the risk.

The fact that no injuries had previously been reported, and that serious damage to the face were unlikely, indicated that the defendants were not negligent. However, this was irrelevant to a claim under the Act where only proof that the product was defective was needed to establish liability.

> In the next case the judge constantly referred to the Directive for assistance in interpreting the meaning of defective product and the scope of the state of the art defence.

A and Others v National Blood Authority (2001)

The claimants contracted Hepatitis C after being given transfusions of contaminated blood products supplied by the defendant.

Held: the product was defective under the Act. The claimants did not have to prove fault or negligence, merely that the product did not meet the reasonable expectations of the public to be safe for any foreseeable use. A reasonable person would expect that blood used for transfusion would not be infected.

Both the Act and the Directive required the court to take into account 'all the circumstances attendant upon the reasonable person's expectations of safety'. These did not include the questions of whether the defendant could have avoided the danger, nor whether this would have been impracticable, costly or difficult.

The state of the art defence should be narrowly interpreted in order to avoid defeating the purpose of the Directive. It only protects the defendant against unknown risks in the context of the most advanced available knowledge which should have been accessible to them.

> These cases provide a more level playing field for the consumer, the party which the Directive was aiming to assist. It can also be seen as a sensible loss distribution system since the losses of the claimant are made the responsibility of the manufacturer which sought to make a profit from its product. The manufacturer is not unreasonably burdened as the losses are insurable and that cost is passed on to the consumers.

Chapter summary

A person harmed by a defective product may claim in:
(a) **breach of contract** against the seller (provided claimant purchased the goods); or
(b) **tort** (*negligence/CPA 1987, Part 1*).

Negligence
Defendant: the manufacturer.
Claimant must prove: duty (owed by manufacturer to ultimate consumer of the goods), breach (failure to take reasonable care), resulting damage.

Liability: based on fault: proof of failure to take reasonable care.
Compensation covers personal injury and all consequential economic loss. Generally, pure economic loss cannot be recovered.

The CPA
Claimant: any person harmed by the product.
Defendant: producer/'own brand' provider/supplier/importer.

Chapter summary *(Continued from page 271)*

Liability: strict. Claimant must prove that the product is dangerous (does not conform to reasonable public expectation of safety) and caused the relevant damage.

Claims are limited to those over £275. Pure economic loss is never recoverable.

Key terms

Consequential economic loss: financial loss resulting from injury to the claimant and/or damage to some property *other than* the defective product.

Duty of care: a person undertaking an activity or course of behaviour owes a duty not to harm any person reasonably expected to be caused loss/damage as a result.

Fault liability: most tort actions require the claimant to prove that the defendant was at fault, i.e. acted intentionally, carelessly or without reasonable foresight.

Neighbour principle: formulated in *Donoghue* v *Stevenson* by Lord Atkin indicating that the defendant only owes a duty of care to persons with sufficient proximity to him or her.

Proximity: a sufficiently close relationship must exist between claimant and defendant at the time the dangerous behaviour occurred for a duty of care to exist.

Public interest: benefit of people in general. Influential on the court's decision to permit/refute a duty of care.

Pure economic loss: loss of money alone, not arising from personal injury to the claimant or damage to other property.

Reasonable foreseeability: limits the scope of duty of care as this is owed only when it is reasonable to anticipate damage to the claimant.

Strict liability: exceptionally (as in claims under the CPA 1987) the claimant can succeed merely on proof that the tortious behaviour occurred and that damage resulted.

Ultimate consumer: any person directly or indirectly harmed by a defective product or service.

CPA 1987 terms

Defective: goods *dangerous physically* to person/property.

Importer: first party to import the product into an EU country from a non-EU country.

Producer: manufacturer/processor.

Product: covers a wide variety of goods, including agricultural produce, utilities like water and gas, and even blood.

Quiz 13

1. What must a claimant in an action for negligence prove?

2. In an action for negligence, what factors are important to proof of duty of care?

3. What circumstances may bring a duty of care for defective goods to an end?

4. Basil buys a pork pie from Tarragon Stores. The pie was manufactured by Marjoram Foods. Basil shares the pie with Rosemary and they both become ill. What are the civil law rights of Basil and Rosemary?

5. What are the main differences between liability for negligence and liability under the Consumer Protection Act 1987?

Answers to all quizzes can be found in Appendix 2.

Take a closer look

The following cases provide important examples of how the law you have studied in this chapter has developed. They are primary sources illustrating the law in action and give you more detail about their facts, as well as helping you to understand the law and to appreciate how the judges reached their decisions.

Try looking them up in the law reports or accessing them via a database, e.g. Bailli (www.bailii.org/databases.html). LexisNexis or Westlaw may be available in your university or college library, or you may find extracts in a case book. (See Appendix 1: Additional resources.)

Donoghue v *Stevenson* [1932] AC 32, HL
Junior Books v *Veitchi* [1983] 2 All ER 301, HL
A v *National Blood Authority* [2001] 3 All ER 289

Web activity

Please go to:

http://en.wikipedia.org/wiki/Donoghue_v._Stevenson

Scroll down to find links to a full law report, an interesting article (Mrs Donoghue's Journey) giving some background information to the case, with photographs, and even a music video inspired by the case from YouTube.

Assignment 12

Florence visits a supermarket with her daughter Daisy, aged eight. A promotion for Funny Mug face paints is taking place and children are being offered a free make-over. Florence lets Daisy take part. Florence buys some frozen puff pastry and a bag of mixed salad leaves that bears a notice saying 'Wash thoroughly before consumption'. Then she visits the deli counter to buy some ham for Edwina, her elderly next-door neighbour. When she gets home an hour later she immediately delivers the ham to Edwina and puts the puff pastry in her freezer in accordance with the instructions on the packet. She uses the leaves to make a salad for tea for herself and her husband, Gordon.

That evening, Florence and her husband, Gordon, become ill from bacteria in the salad.

Next day, Daisy develops an allergic rash, which her doctor says is caused by the face paints.

Later in the week, Edwina contracts salmonella poisoning which is traced to the ham.

A month later, Florence retrieves the puff pastry from the freezer and defrosts it. When she rolls it out, she discovers that it smells strongly of petrol and is therefore unusable.

Discuss the remedies available to Daisy, Edwina, Florence and Gordon.

mylawchamber

Visit **www.mylawchamber.co.uk/adams** to access multiple choice questions and glossary flashcards to test yourself on this chapter. You'll also find weblinks to the web activity in this chapter.

Use Case Navigator to read in full some of the key cases referenced in this chapter:

Abouzaid v Mothercare (UK) Ltd [2000] 1 All ER (D) 2436

chapter 14
TORT LIABILITY FOR DEFECTIVE SERVICES

Photo: TRIP/Art Directors & TRIP Photo Library

Introduction

This chapter is divided into two parts. The first part is concerned with duty of care in negligence for defective services and includes analysis of some problematic duty of care situations outside the traditional scope of negligence liability. The second part is concerned with breach of duty and causation.

As indicated in the previous chapter, under Donoghue v Stevenson principles, any third party reasonably likely to be affected by the workmanship of a service provider is clearly owed a duty of care in negligence if he or she directly suffers personal injury or damage to property. A central heating engineer, therefore, will owe a duty to people in a building who suffer carbon-monoxide poisoning from the system which the engineer negligently installed.

Sometimes there may be a large pool of potential claimants. The garage which services your car owes a duty of care to carry out the work safely not only to you, but to your passengers as well as other road users and pedestrians in the vicinity of your vehicle when it is in use. However, the law is unwilling to make defendants vulnerable to every possible claim of damage resulting from their negligent behaviour. Liability in negligence is greatly restricted by the courts in some situations. The problem of recovering pure economic loss caused by defective goods was mentioned in the preceding chapter. There are also a number of other problematic duty situations relevant to the delivery of services relating to pure economic loss, negligent statements, shock-induced injuries, liability for damage caused by third parties and the exercise of statutory discretion by public authorities.

Proof of duty alone does not guarantee a successful claim. In a negligence action, the claimant must also prove that the defendant breached the duty by failing to take reasonable care and that damage which is not too remote resulted to the claimant.

Learning Objectives

After studying this chapter you should be able to:

- Recognise the relationship from which a duty of care for pure economic loss may arise
- Appreciate the scope of nervous shock liability
- Describe when a duty exists for omissions and third-party acts
- Understand when a public authority may be liable in negligence when exercising statutory discretion
- Explain the circumstances when a breach of duty of care may occur
- Distinguish between causation in fact and in law.

Part 1 – problematic duty situations

As can be seen from Chapter 14, the tort of negligence has traditionally covered claims for death, personal injury and consequential damage to property. In claims of this sort the existence of duty of care is not in doubt. In *Caparo* v *Dickman* (1990, HL) (below at page 285) Lord Oliver . . . said: *'the existence of a nexus of duty between the careless defendant and the injured plaintiff can rarely give rise to any difficulty'*, and in *Sandhar* v *Department of Transport* (2004) May LJ affirmed this: *'Personal or physical injury directly inflicted is the first building block of negligence ... it will almost always be a component of breach of duty of care owed by the person inflicting the injury to the person or owner of the material object injured'*.

However, the law of negligence today embraces liability for less traditionally recognised types of damage and their cause, but the courts are wary of imposing liability in these less traditional areas. The criteria relevant to existence of duty (reasonable foreseeability, proximity, justice and reason) may be stringently applied. In order to limit the scope of duty to make it just and reasonable, the court may take a very restricted view of what is reasonably foreseeable and require proof of a very close relationship of proximity. Issues of policy also (whether it is just and reasonable to impose a duty) often underpin such judgments even if not expressly mentioned by the judge.

Pure economic loss

Negligence liability does not usually arise from the poor *quality* of a service, but from the *physical damage* to people and property caused by it. Any purely financial loss arising from defective performance is not generally recoverable, as indicated by the decisions in *Spartan Steel Alloys* v *Martin* (1972, CA) and *Murphy* v *Brentwood Council* (1990, HL) (below).

Students initially studying this area often find it difficult to tell consequential from pure economic loss. Judges usually just talk about 'economic loss' without clearly indicating what sort they mean and leave you to work it out from the context. It may help you to think about this in terms of the cost of the damage to the claimant and their goods caused by the defendant's product or service (consequential economic loss) as opposed to a loss of money alone, which is often related to future and possibly notional future income (pure economic loss). Thus, in *Pride & Partners* v *Institute for Animal Health* (2009) the defendant was not liable for the financial loss to the claimant who was unable to send his stock to market due to the movement restriction orders arising from a foot and mouth disease outbreak caused by the virus escaping from the Institute. The claimant's stock was unharmed by the virus and had not been culled so the claimant's only damage was to his bank account.

The next case provides a helpful example of the difference between the two different types of economic loss.

Spartan Steel Alloys v *Martin Ltd* (1972, CA)

Early one morning the negligent operation of a power shovel outside the claimant's steelworks resulted in a power cut which put its furnace out of action for the rest of that day. The metal, which had been in the furnace when the power was cut off, was spoilt and no further consignments could be processed that day.

Held: the claimant was entitled to damages for the cost of the spoilt metal and for the profit which would normally have been made on its sale in good condition as this was a directly consequential loss. However, the claim for the lost profits on the melts which could not be processed that day must fail, as it concerned pure economic loss and did not result from any damage to the claimant's property.

Lord Denning said: '*at bottom I think the question of recovering economic loss is one of policy. Whenever the courts draw a line to mark out the bounds of duty, they do it as a matter of policy so as to limit the liability of the defendant*'.

Lord Denning held that no duty of care existed concerning the unprocessed melts because:

1 It would be unfair to impose a duty on the defendants since statutory providers of electricity and other utilities enjoy exemption from liability for pure economic loss arising from interruption of supply.
2 Such interruption is well known and commonplace. Most people temporarily deprived of electricity supply '*do not go running round to their solicitor*'. They may insure against possible losses or install a back up generator as a precaution '*or make up the economic loss by doing more work the next day. This is a healthy attitude which the law should encourage*'.
3 A huge number of claims would arise if a duty existed in this situation '*some might be genuine, but many might be inflated or even false … it would be well nigh impossible to check the claims*'.
4 It would place an unreasonable burden on the contractor. '*The risk of economic loss should be suffered by the community who suffer the losses, usually many but comparatively small losses rather than … on the contractor on whom the total of them … might be very heavy*'.
5 '*The law provides for deserving cases*', i.e. where physical damage results to the claimant or material property.

> While you may sympathise with the claimant in *Spartan Steel*, it is important to understand that in many cases of pure economic loss insurance plays a part, as Lord Denning indicates. Business interruption insurance is readily available to the likes of Spartan Steel. No doubt Martin carried insurance too, but the court tends to take the view that the claimant should carry the risk in situations where it expects them to be insured. Something else to bear in mind is that prior to litigation the claimant will often have made a successful claim on their own insurance and then their insurers take the case in the insured's name to recover what was paid out. The court is unlikely to feel that it is fair to allow the insurers to recoup a loss that may well have been more than covered by insurance premiums.

Murphy v Brentwood Council (1990, HL)

The claimant's newly built house subsided when the foundations turned out to be defective. As a result, he had to sell the house for £35,000 less than its proper market value. He claimed that the local authority building inspection department had been negligent in its checks on the foundations.

Held by the House of Lords: the house was defective, but no personal injuries had been caused to Mr Murphy and none of his property had been damaged. Therefore, the local authority did not owe a duty of care to the claimant, since his only loss was purely economic: only the diminution on the value of the house was affected.

There was insufficient proximity between the parties, since it was not reasonably foreseeable to the council that Mr Murphy would place reliance on its checks which were carried out in order to comply with the building regulations to safeguard public health rather than protect the financial position of future home owners. No liability in tort would rest on a builder for damage to someone like Mr Murphy who had no contractual relationship or other sufficiently proximate relationship and it would be unfair to impose liability on the council which was less directly involved. It also was not just and reasonable to burden local taxpayers with homeowners' financial losses in such circumstances. Lord Oliver said: '*I am not sure that I see why the burden should fall on the community at large rather than be covered by private insurance*'.

Again in *Murphy* the issue of policy is extremely influential and insurance is relevant to determining what is fair, just and reasonable. Many of us would rather see our council tax being used on services rather than assisting individual home owners. However, as consumer groups afterwards pointed out, normal buildings insurance does not cover structural problems which arise from defective materials or workmanship, but only those caused by natural phenomena like drought or geological features.

Home owners may have other remedies. They may be able to sue under the Defective Premises Act 1972 (DPA). Section 1(1) imposes a duty on *'any person taking on work in connection with the provision of a dwelling ... to see that the work is done in a workmanlike ... or professional manner ... so that the dwelling will be fit for human habitation when completed'*. This covers pure economic loss but was no to help Mr Murphy as his claim arose after the six-year limitation period had elapsed.

Property bought subject to a transferable guarantee from the builder who constructed or substantially renovated is also protected. Such compensation schemes provide more generous terms than the DPA. Claims can be made by the buyer and subsequent purchasers for the lifetime of the guarantee, so no contractual relationship with the builder is required.

In *White* v *Jones* (1995, HL) (below) the claimants were successful as the House of Lords acknowledged that there was a very close relationship between them and the defendant.

White v *Jones* (1995, HL)

An elderly man, after a quarrel with his two daughters, cut them out of his will. Three months later he forgave them and informed his solicitor that he wished to make a new will under which the daughters were each to be given a legacy of £9,000. Two months after giving his instructions he died, before the solicitor completed the necessary work. Due to this negligent delay, the daughters did not receive their inheritance. They successfully sued the solicitor.

Held: the solicitor was brought into a special relationship of close proximity with the sisters. By agreeing to draft the will, he was deemed voluntarily to have accepted the responsibility for ensuring the creation of a valid will. It was reasonably foreseeable that any potential beneficiary would suffer pure economic loss if the will was invalid.

Note the different but equally valid criteria applied by the House of Lords for determining proximity in these cases:

- *Murphy v Brentwood Council*: reasonable reliance by the *claimant*;
- *White v Jones*: voluntary assumption of responsibility by the *defendant*.

In some cases both factors may be present (see, for example, *Hedley Byrne v Heller*, below). The *White v Jones* approach is more realistic, where the defendant is asked by a third party to do something which affects the well-being of a claimant, who is unaware of the request and so cannot realistically be said to be placing reliance on the defendant.

In the News

West Bromwich Albion Football Club Ltd v *El-Safty* (2007)

Michael Appleton damaged his knee during a training session with the claimant club. His contract required him to be treated by one of the medical advisers employed by the club's insurance scheme. The defendant was a service provider to the insurers and his fees in respect of the treatment were settled by that company. The defendant negligently recommended reconstructive surgery and as a result Appleton became unable to play professional football. Had the appropriate conservative treatment been carried out, he would have been match fit within four months.

As a result, the club claimed that they had lost millions for the loss of Appleton's services, including the expense of finding a replacement and covering the costs of his lost salary.

Held: the defendant did not owe a duty of care to the claimant for these losses. No special relationship existed between the claimant and defendant as the defendant had not assumed responsibility to the claimant for this type of loss. Also it was not fair, just and equitable to impose a duty in these circumstances.

Negligent statements

In principle, there is no difference between liability arising from negligent statements and from negligent acts. A party may suffer physical damage by reliance on incorrect advice just as he or she may be injured by other negligent conduct. In *T v Surrey County Council*, T was injured by the actions of a childminder negligently recommended to his mother by the defendant council. The council owed a duty of care to T, as, by advising his mother, the council had been brought into close relationship to T, and it was reasonably foreseeable that he would be affected by the quality of the advice acted upon by his mother.

In practice, the duty is generally limited because a negligent statement has the potential to have more far-reaching effects than a negligent act. One snail-infested bottle of ginger beer will poison only one or two people, but a negligent statement may affect thousands and its effects may be long-lasting. The courts are not willing to make the defendant liable to potential claims from a large and unidentifiable class of persons, for an indefinable period of time.

In exceptional cases where a duty is deemed to exist between the parties, there is liability for all forms of damage including pure economic loss. The duty arises from the claimant's close relationship to or reliance on the defendant. In *Hedley Byrne* (below) the relationship was described variously as a '**special relationship**', or '**quasi-fiduciary**' in character and 'akin to contract'.

Hedley Byrne v *Heller* (1963, HL)

A firm called Easipower entered into a contract with the claimant, an advertising agency to book advertising on TV and the national newspapers on terms which made the claimant personally liable for the cost if their client defaulted. Satisfied by an initial reference from Easipowers's bank the claimant went ahead. Three months later it sought further reassurance asking whether Easipower could be relied on 'to the extent of £100,000 pounds per annum.' The bank replied repeating its initial statement that it believed Easipower '*to be respectably constituted and good for its normal business engagements*', but adding '*your figures are larger than we would normally expect to see*'. The reference was headed '*Confidential. For your private use and without responsibility on the part of this bank or its officials.*' Reliant on this, the claimant continued to work for Easipower, but lost over £17,000 when it went into liquidation. The claimant sued the defendant bank for giving negligent advice.

Held: the defendant did not owe a duty of care to the claimant because of the disclaimer. However, in the absence of an effective disclaimer, a duty not to make a careless statement which causes pure economic loss might exist, provided that a special relationship of close proximity 'akin to contract' existed between the parties.

The criteria determining existence of a 'special relationship'

This relationship which is essential to success in *all* pure economic loss claims in negligence must satisfy certain criteria.

Proximity

The parties must have been brought sufficiently into a close relationship of proximity with each other. A high degree of trust will be involved. This relationship may arise in a number of ways:

1 *The statement may be made directly to the claimant by the defendant.*

This is illustrated by the facts of *Hedley Byrne* v *Heller*.

2 *The statement may be made to a third party who passes it on to the claimant.*

Smith v *Eric S. Bush* (1989, HL)

The defendant surveyors' valuation report prepared for a building society was shown with their knowledge to the claimant buyer. In reliance on this Ms Smith bought the property.

Held: the defendant owed a duty of care to the claimant since she could reasonably be expected to rely on the advice.

(For more detail see page 113 above.)

---

3 The statement may be made to a third party who relies upon it thus causing consequent loss to the claimant.

Spring v *Guardian Assurance* (1994)

The claimant had worked for the defendant insurance company but was made redundant. He applied for a job with Scottish Amicable. LAUTRO (the regulatory organisation for insurance companies) requires a reference from a previous employer for applicants to such jobs. The reference was described by the trial judge as *'so strikingly bad as to amount to … the kiss of death to his career in insurance. Scottish Amicable wanted no truck with the man it described.'* This slur on his character was completely unwarranted so the claimant sued the defendant in negligence in preparation of the reference.

Held by the House of Lords (by majority): the defendant owed a duty of care to the claimant under the *Hedley Byrne* principle. It had special knowledge of the claimant's character, skill and diligence evidenced by the way he had worked while employed by it. The defendant had assumed responsibility to the claimant by giving the reference to Scottish Amicable and the claimant had relied upon it to compose the reference with reasonable care and skill.

Reasonable reliance and assumption of responsibility

These are usually two sides of the same coin but note *White* v *Jones* (above), which indicates that the circumstances may be such that the defendant will be assumed to have taken responsibility even though the claimant may not at that time have placed reliance upon it. It must have been reasonable for the claimant to rely on the statement and thus reasonably foreseeable to the defendant that reliance would be placed. The defendant will then be taken to have responsibility.

In *Hedley Byrne* v *Heller* (1963), the House of Lords indicated criteria helpful to establishing when reliance can reasonably be placed.

1 *The defendant's ability to give reliable advice.* Specialist knowledge, professional qualifications or other expertise are all relevant.

2 *The circumstances in which the advice was given.* Specialist advice cannot reasonably be relied on when given off the cuff, or on a purely social occasion. Even if given in a business context, it may not be reasonable to rely on it if it is given without proper checks on relevant data.

3 *Disclaimer or condition.* If the defendant indicates expressly or impliedly that the advice should not be relied upon, this may make the claimant's reliance unreasonable and, therefore, not reasonably foreseeable. In *Hedley Byrne* v *Heller* a **disclaimer** by the bank

was a factor preventing imposition of a duty of care. Today the Unfair Contract Terms Act 1977 s 2(1) makes it impossible to exclude liability for negligence for death or personal injuries so specific disclaimer is not necessarily effective protection for the defendant. However, liability for negligence may be excluded for other damage or loss if reasonable (UCTA, s 2(2)). (See above at page 110.)

Even if no disclaimer is given, any doubt raised by the way the advice is worded – for example, statements like 'as far as I know', or 'if performance reflects last year', or 'without checking my figures', or 'you might want a second opinion' – may make it unreasonable for the claimant to rely upon the defendant.

Restriction of the *Hedley Byrne* principle

In *Hedley Byrne* and the other cases we have so far examined, the only person likely to be harmed was the claimant him or herself. In *Caparo v Dickman* (1990) (facts below) the court was confronted for the first time by a statement issued to the public. This necessitated restriction of the *Hedley Byrne* principle to prevent a defendant from being potentially liable to a large and unascertainable group of people. The House of Lords held that no duty of care will arise unless the following conditions are satisfied:

1 when the advice was given the defendant must reasonably have anticipated what it would be used for (e.g *Caparo Industries plc v Dickman* (1990, HL);

2 the defendant must reasonably have known the destination of that advice – a specific (not necessarily named) individual, or a member of a clearly ascertainable group (e.g *Caparo Industries plc v Dickman* (1990, HL));

3 the defendant must reasonably have anticipated that the advice would be acted upon without the claimant seeking further clarification or independent advice (e.g *McNaughten (James) Paper Group Ltd v Hicks Anderson & Co.* (1991, CA).

It must be just and reasonable to impose a duty

You may find some case decisions in this area conflicting. This is because the courts may interpret the concepts of proximity and foreseeability more strictly in some cases than others in order to prevent the duty of care from developing in ways that are perceived not to be in the public interest. While glad to assist a vulnerable consumer like Ms Smith (see above, at page 282) without many financial resources, the courts do not wish to encourage a lack of responsibility in economically powerful parties with access to independent advice, particularly those pursuing a speculative deal with high stakes, as in *Caparo v Dickman* (1990) (see below).

Similarly, if alternative legal remedies are available, a right of action in negligence may be perceived to be redundant, even though the other remedies may not be applicable to the particular claimant due to the particular circumstances of the case.

The following cases illustrate the operation of some of the *Caparo* criteria.

Caparo Industries plc v Dickman (1990, HL)

The claimant company owned shares in Fidelity plc. The defendants were the accountancy firm which had audited the annual accounts. These negligently stated that Fidelity had profits of £1.3 million; it had actually made a loss of over £465,000. The claimant increased its shareholding and later made a successful takeover bid. It then discovered that its acquisition was much less valuable than it had been led to believe by the accounts.

Held: no duty of care was owed to the claimant. The purpose for which the information was given was crucial here. The accounts were to enable shareholders to decide how to vote at the annual general meeting, not to give them personal investment advice.

If a duty was imposed, it would protect not only the shareholders but potential buyers on the open market, thus creating potential liability to a diffuse group of people which would not be appropriate.

McNaughten (James) Paper Group Ltd v Hicks Anderson & Co. (1991, CA)

No duty was owed by accountants to a company director for whom they prepared draft accounts for consideration prior to a takeover bid.

Held: the defendant was not liable because it was not reasonably foreseeable that the claimant would rely on the draft accounts, particularly as he had access to expert advice to evaluate them. The defendant was also aware that the accounts had been swiftly compiled in draft form, providing a guide to the company's financial health rather than a definitive statement.

Compare the two decisions above with the following:

Morgan Crucible Co. plc v Hill Samuel Bank (1991, CA)

The claimants' takeover bid was made in reliance on a profit forecast issued to them by the defendant company. The defendant accountants and bank stated that this had been made in accordance with the company's accounting procedures, after full and careful enquiry.

Held: the defendants were liable. They had intended the claimants to rely on the information when making the bid, which they had done. The claimants' reliance was reasonable since, although they had independent advice, much of the information was available only to the defendants and could not be independently verified.

See also *Smith* v *Eric S. Bush* (1989), which is described at page 282, above.
Most of the reported cases on negligent statement concern pure economic loss; the next one concerns a personal injuries claim.

T v Surrey County Council (1994)

T was a small baby. His mother consulted the council to check on the suitability of a registered childminder. The council failed to tell T's mother that previously a small baby had been brain-damaged while in the minder's care and, although there was no conclusive evidence against her, it had been suggested that she should in future only look after children over two years old. T subsequently suffered severe brain damage when shaken violently by the childminder.

Held: the council owed a duty of care to T since it had given advice directly relevant to his safety and thus created a relationship of sufficient proximity. The council should reasonably have foreseen that the advice, which came from one of their professional officers with special knowledge, would be relied upon. If incorrect, it would clearly jeopardise T's safety.

Although the judge in the above case said that a *Hedley Byrne* relationship existed in this case, where physical rather than pure economic loss has occurred it is sufficient that *Donoghue* v *Stevenson* principles are satisfied. In *Clay* v *Crump* (1963) the defendant architect was held liable to workers on a demolition site injured after a wall, which he had negligently stated was stable, collapsed on to them. It was held that it was reasonably foreseeable to the defendant that if his advice was incorrect the labourers would be endangered.

Interesting and as yet unsolved questions of liability are raised by specialist information on financial and legal issues broadcast to the public on radio and TV programmes and published in some periodicals. There are also books which claim to help you to do your own conveyancing, or to make a will. Here the large class of potential claimants which exists might make the courts unwilling to entertain claims. On the other hand, such publications often encourage reliance on the given information by offering help and suggesting that this will be provided by experts. The more focused such information is (e.g. one-to-one on a radio phone-in), the greater the likelihood of a duty arising unless an appropriate and effective disclaimer is given.

Real Life

Horace is an enthusiastic computer user and reads a lot of computer magazines. When he meets Florence at a party she is impressed by his apparent knowledge, and asks him if he will help her buy a computer for her new design business. Horace tells her that he knows where to find her a bargain and the following week takes her to the premises of Mouse Technology, where on his advice she buys a model which he assures her will do everything she needs. However, within a couple of weeks' use it becomes evident that it is entirely unsuitable for the sort of programs that she needs to use and she has to buy a different machine which puts her £1,500 out of pocket.

Horace may unwittingly have made himself liable to Florence by taking her under his wing. Although he is not an expert in the relevant technology, he has held himself out as having that knowledge and a *Hedley Byrne* relationship has been held to exist in non-business relationships. In *Chaudhry* v *Prabhakar* (1988) amateur advice on buying a secondhand car gave rise to liability. However, unlike Ms Chaudhry, Florence was present when the computer was purchased and could have checked the advice with a shop assistant, so her reliance on Horace might well not be regarded as reasonable.

Nervous shock (psychiatric harm)

A duty of care readily exists where the claimant has suffered physical injury from the defendant's careless behaviour. It may be harder to establish a duty of care when the claimant suffers illness induced by acute shock or distress caused by the defendant. Damages are *not* recoverable for the *actual shock or distress*, but liability may arise from the *medically recognisable* illness or condition triggered by it. Such illness could be physical, like a heart attack, but most recent claims concern psychiatric conditions like post-traumatic stress syndrome.

In *Page* v *Smith* (see below) the House of Lords held that the rules determining duty of care for **nervous shock** are different according to whether the claimant is categorised as a **primary** or a **secondary victim** of the accident caused by the defendant. Primary victims were defined as those directly involved in the accident, who, as a result, have been physically hurt or reasonably put in fear for their own safety.

Dulieu v *White* (1901)

The defendant negligently failed to control his horse and cart, which demolished the wall of the pub, where the claimant was working as a barmaid. She managed to shelter from the shower of masonry and was not directly hurt. Later, however, she suffered a miscarriage from the shock.

Held: the defendant was liable because it was reasonably foreseeable that the claimant would suffer shock from fear for her own physical safety in the dangerous situation created by the defendant's negligence.

Secondary victims are not so closely involved since they merely witness the accident. Stricter rules are therefore necessary to limit the duty to them, as large numbers might claim and it would not be fair, just and reasonable to make the defendant responsible for them all.

Primary victims

Since the defendant has caused a dangerous situation to arise, the duty is largely based on basic negligence principles. A duty of care arises because there is reasonable foreseeability of some physical or psychiatric injury to the claimant.

Page v *Smith* (1995, HL)

The defendant's negligent driving caused his car to collide with that of the claimant. Minor damage resulted to the vehicles but the claimant appeared unhurt. Shortly afterwards, however, he suffered a recurrence of ME (myalgic encephalomyelitis, then perceived as a psychiatric condition) from which he had enjoyed a lengthy remission.

Held: the defendant owed the same duty of care to the claimant as he would to any other fellow road user, since it was reasonably foreseeable that he might suffer personal injuries if the defendant drove negligently. It was not necessary for the claimant to prove that psychiatric damage might result. The distinction between physical and psychiatric injury was irrelevant in these circumstances.

The House of Lords indicated the limits of *Page* v *Smith* in *Johnston* v *NEI International* (*and other conjoined claims*) (2007, HL) which comprised four claims by various employees who had developed pleural plaques as a result of exposure to asbestos by their employers.

In the News

Johnston and Others v *NEI International* (2007, HL)

The claimants were all diagnosed with pleural plaques (hardening of lung tissue), which indicate exposure to asbestos. While harmless in themselves, they show that asbestosis, which is often fatal, may develop in the future. Diagnosis occurred years after the employer's negligent behaviour. Fear that they might develop asbestosis resulted in Mr Johnston and two others suffering anxiety and distress and one (Mr Grieves) developing clinical depression and irritable bowel syndrome.

Held by the House of Lords: all the claims failed.

1. Mr Johnston and the two other claimants, who argued that the defendants were liable for the pleural plaques and their consequent anxiety and distress failed, because legal liability requires some actual injury recognised by law. The plaques were just a simple physical change, not the cause of illness. They were harmless in themselves and neither they nor the fear of future illness amounted to actionable damage. Even when combined, they did not amount to actionable harm.
2. Mr Grieves' claim failed because it was not reasonably foreseeable that a person of reasonable fortitude would develop a medically recognised disease as a result of the fear of future illness.

His other argument that he was a primary victim and therefore owed a duty because physical harm, i.e. asbestosis, was a reasonably foreseeable result of asbestos exposure, also failed because the principle in *Page* v *Smith* was limited to injury resulting directly and immediately from the negligence of the defendant where the claimant's injury was '*an immediate response to a sudden and alarming incident of which the plaintiff had no opportunity to prepare himself*' (Lord Hope). Twenty years had passed between exposure to the asbestos and the diagnosis of pleural plaques and, therefore, there was no causative link between them.

The *Johnston* case is controversial as until this point insurers had paid out for this sort of claim. The Scottish government promptly legislated: the Damages (Asbestos-Related Conditions) (Scotland) Act 2009 which in effect reverses the *Johnston* decision in Scotland from the date of the judgment. The Damages (Asbestos-Related Conditions) Bill 2008–9 is a private member's bill and, at the time of writing, is passing through the English parliament. If passed, it will have a similar effect to the Scottish government's provision, and asymptomatic pleural plaques will be again be treated as actionable damage in themselves.

Involuntary participants

The claimant, an **involuntary participant** is made to feel responsible for the accident although it is the defendant's conduct which is the real cause, may also be treated as a primary victim.

Dooley v Cammell Laird (1951)

The claimant was operating a crane which had been negligently maintained by his employer. The crane cable snapped and he saw the heavy crate attached to it hurtle into the hold. His shock at the anticipated fate of his workmates (who miraculously escaped injury) induced an acute nervous breakdown.

Held: the employer was liable since the claimant's response was prompted by his feelings that he had helped to cause the accident, and fear for his colleagues was reasonably foreseeable.

> It is not easy to persuade the court that sufficient foreseeability exists in this area. In *Monk v Harrington Ltd and Others* (2008) (see below), Mr Monk's genuine belief that he was responsible for the accident, which had aggravated his trauma, was not justified in the circumstances and he lost his claim because it was held that it was not reasonably foreseeable that anyone in his situation would suffer psychiatric injury.
>
> #### Rescuers
>
> Until the House of Lords' decision in *White* (below) rescuers were automatically deemed to be primary victims, provided they had a sufficient degree of involvement in the accident. The rationale of this principle was that it was in the public interest to encourage people to act humanely in an emergency.

Chadwick v British Rail (1967)

The claimant became acutely clinically depressed after spending a gruelling night giving first aid and comfort to severely injured and dying victims within the compacted wreckage of a horrific train crash.

Held: it was reasonably foreseeable that volunteers would render assistance and might suffer psychiatric injury as a result and, therefore, a duty of care was owed to the claimant.

> The duty of care to rescuers was restricted by the House of Lords in *White v Chief Constable of South Yorkshire*, which held that a duty of care to rescuers exists only if the rescuer was actually in danger or reasonably believed that they were.

White v Chief Constable of South Yorkshire (1999, HL)

At Hillsborough football stadium 95 people were killed and hundreds injured in the crush resulting from the failure of senior police officers adequately to control admission to the stadium. The claimants, who were junior police officers, claimed for post-traumatic stress syndrome resulting from the harrowing scenes in which they had been heavily involved for many hours as rescuers.

Held: these claims must fail, since the claimants had not been exposed to or put in fear of danger and therefore no duty of care was owed to the claimants by their employers.

> This decision can be justified on policy (public interest) grounds. The House of Lords was concerned to limit the increasing number of claims for compensation from members of the emergency services whose employment as a matter of course involves potential exposure to

harrowing, though not necessarily dangerous, situations. The cost of settling such claims could, if not checked, undermine the provision of the services themselves and put an unreasonable burden on the taxpayer. However, someone like Mr Chadwick might not win his case today unless the court were prepared to acknowledge sufficient danger or reasonable fear. This point is well illustrated by the next case.

Monk v Harrington Ltd and Others (2008)

During the building of the Wembley stadium an accident was caused by the negligence of the defendant construction firm. Two of Mr Monk's workmates fell 60 feet when a platform collapsed. One died shortly afterwards and the other broke a leg. M tried to help both men. Subsequently, as a result of what he had seen, he began to suffer from post-traumatic stress disorder and depression.

Held: When M rendered assistance, it was unlikely that he believed himself to be in danger and there were no reasonable grounds for his subsequent belief that he had caused the accident. Therefore, he was not a primary victim and no duty of care was owed to him.

This case illustrates the problems caused by the limitation of the rescuer category. By so doing, their Lordships have effectively barred the courts from assisting other litigants in areas where policy might well suggest that liability should be imposed. The construction industry, although better regulated than it used to be, is still well known for a poor accident record. While it is questionable that imposing liability necessarily drives up safety standards, at least deserving claimants like Mr Monk would be entitled to compensation for the loss of their livelihood as result of their acting humanely.

Negligent statements and nervous shock

Liability may arise from statements as well as acts. There is a duty of care to deliver bad news with sufficient sensitivity to prevent reasonably foreseeable psychiatric damage (*AB* v *Tameside & Glossop Health Authority* (1997)). Similarly, there is a duty to deliver news accurately. In *Allin* v *City & Hackney Health Authority* (1996), it was held that the defendant was liable for nervous shock suffered by the claimant when she received the sensitively delivered but *inaccurate* news that her baby was dead. Where negligent statements are involved duty may be based more on a *Hedley Byrne* relationship than the normal rules relating to nervous shock.

Liability to primary victims may be costly for service providers. This is evidenced by the Kings Cross fire, where London Transport was liable for multiple successful claims, including firefighters. A mass claim was brought by traumatised victims and relatives of the 193 people who drowned when the *Herald of Free Enterprise* ferry to Zeebrugge capsized in 1987. The sinking of *The Marchioness* pleasure boat on the Thames in 1989, with 51 dead, is another case in point.

Secondary victims

These merely witness the accident or, if involved, are *not* in danger or reasonable fear of it. The next case was the first **secondary victim** claim and laid down most of the basic principles governing such claims today.

Hambrook v Stokes (1925, CA)

A mother saw the defendant's driverless lorry careering down the hill in the direction of her two daughters who had just disappeared round the corner of the road. Although she did not see the accident, she heard the impact when the vehicle crashed through a wall after mounting the pavement close to her daughters. Miraculously, the girls were unhurt, but their mother suffered a fatal heart attack due to the shock resulting from fear for her children's safety.

Held: the defendant was liable. A duty of care was owed to a person who suffered nervous shock from directly witnessing an accident caused by the defendant's negligence, where such trauma was *reasonably foreseeable in a person of reasonable fortitude. The shock might result from the claimant witnessing the build-up to the accident and/or the immediate aftermath, but without seeing the accident itself.* The shock must be a product of what the claimant actually witnessed *with their own senses*, not what was reported to them by a third party.

> In a later case the House of Lords further developed the law, stressing the need for proximity of the claimant both physically and temporally to the accident and imposed limits on the concept of immediate aftermath.

McLoughlin v O'Brian (1982, HL)

The claimant suffered acute depression and personality change resulting from the shock of witnessing serious injuries caused to her husband and children by the defendant's negligent driving.

Held: her claim was successful. Although she was not present when the accident occurred, the harrowing scenes she witnessed at the casualty department an hour afterwards were horrific enough to make her sufficiently proximate, and her response reasonably foreseeable.

> In *Alcock* v *Wright* the House of Lords rationalised the criteria determining duty of care to secondary victims.

Alcock v Wright (1991, HL)

The 16 claimants had loved ones who had perished in the horrific occurrences at the Hillsborough stadium. (See Web activity on page 313.) None was successful because they did not fulfil the necessary criteria laid down by the House of Lords, which restrict the concepts of reasonable foreseeability and proximity applicable in such circumstances.

Held: claimants must be able to prove the following:

(a) *They have suffered some medically recognised illness or condition as a result of a* '**sudden and immediate attack**' *upon their senses*. This rules out claimants who do not suffer a quick and sudden trauma, but whose illness is caused by a build-up of stress and fear.
(b) *It was reasonably foreseeable that they would react in this way: there must be a* '**close bond of love and affection**' *between them and the accident victim*. This is presumed only between spouses and

parents and children; all other claimants must prove that the bond exists in the relevant circumstances. (Not all the *Alcock* claimants could satisfy this test.)

(c) Their reaction was that of a *reasonably brave person* given the level of trauma that they witnessed.

(d) *They were* **sufficiently proximate** *to the accident.* Proximity is measured both in terms of time and space. The claimant must usually be present at the scene when the accident occurs, although seeing the build-up to it and/or the immediate aftermath may be sufficient. The claimant must have witnessed the accident directly with his or her own senses and not have had the scene interpreted for him or her by a third party. (This ruled out some of the *Alcock* claimants, who had seen events unfold through a simultaneous TV broadcast, or who had identified a body at the mortuary eight hours after the accident.)

Worth thinking about?

Why do you think the House of Lords in *Alcock* (above) insisted that secondary victims must witness the accident directly and ruled that TV transmitted pictures did not count?

Suggested solutions can be found in Appendix 2.

The *Alcock* criteria make a very useful checklist for you to refer to, particularly when answering problem questions on this topic. Their application is usefully illustrated by the next two cases.

Taylorson v *Shieldness Products* (1994, CA)

The claimants were the parents of a 14-year-old boy who died three days after being crushed by a lorry driven by the defendant's negligent employee. The parents, who did not witness the accident, only briefly glimpsed their son after initial treatment when he was transferred to a second hospital. They were not present while he was being treated. The father visited on the night of the accident but the mother did not see him until the next day. They both remained with him for the next two days while he was on a life support system. They claimed that they suffered clinical depression as a result of the experience.

Held: no duty of care existed, as there was insufficient proximity of the parents in time and space to the accident. It was also probable that the damage to the claimants was more the result of grief than shock.

The only successful reported claim from a Hillsborough victim was that of John McCarthy (*McCarthy* v *Chief Constable of South Yorkshire* (1996)) who received over £200,000 damages for his ongoing post-traumatic stress. His half-brother, Ian, died from asphyxiation in one of the grandstands. John satisfied the *Alcock* criteria as he was at the ground though in a different stand with a view of the events as they unfolded. He was therefore deemed to be sufficiently proximate, and the close nature of his relationship to Ian evidenced a close bond of affection.

In practice, very few claims by secondary victims have succeeded.

Palmer v Tees Health Authority (1999, CA)

The claimant's daughter was abducted and murdered by a psychiatric patient. The claimant suffered acute post-traumatic stress disorder and alleged that the defendant authority were negligent in failing to diagnose that the patient was a risk to children. She claimed that within 15 minutes of discovering that her daughter had disappeared she was told that she had been abducted and this produced an immediate shock to her nervous system. When the child's body was discovered three days later, the claimant was within the vicinity of the patient's house but was not allowed to see her daughter's body at that point. She claimed that the psychiatric illness was caused by her presence at the scene and the immediate aftermath of the abduction and the search for and discovery of the body, which she later identified.

Held: her claim must fail on two counts:

(a) she had not witnessed the abduction, nor the murder, nor the discovery of the body, nor was she involved in the immediate aftermath, so she was not sufficiently proximate;
(b) what she had witnessed and experienced did not amount to a sudden and shocking event within the scope of *Alcock*.

Her situation was similar to that of unsuccessful Hillsborough claimants who went through a period of acute anxiety before their worst fears were realised. Her imagination of what had happened was not the same as 'the sudden appreciation by sight or sound of the horrifying event'.

> Recently, however, the Court of Appeal has been prepared to interpret the *Alcock* principles more generously to deal with extreme circumstances.

Walters v North Glamorgan NHS Trust (2002)

Due to the negligence of the Health Trust, the claimant's son died of liver failure. During the 36 hours leading up to his death, the claimant witnessed a number of traumatic events after the child had been admitted to the hospital, starting with her waking to find her son having a violent epileptic fit and vomiting blood all over his cot and ending when he died in her arms when life support was eventually terminated. She was given conflicting information about the likely outcome for her son. In effect, she was on an emotional roller coaster throughout: '*her hopes were lifted and then dashed and finally destroyed*' (Ward LJ). As a result, she suffered a pathological grief reaction.

Held: these circumstances must be treated as one entire 'horrifying' event and, therefore, the *Alcock* criteria were satisfied and a duty of care was owed to her.

> This is a complex and controversial area of the law of negligence. The rules often seem arbitrary and may sometimes produce apparently unjust results. In 1998 a Law Commission Report (No. 249, *Liability for Psychiatric Damage*) was published which proposed statutory reform of the duty of care regarding secondary victims to replace the *Alcock* rule. The Report included the following recommendations:
>
> (a) *The class of persons presumed to have a close bond of love and affection should be extended* to include siblings and cohabitees of at least two years' standing (including same-sex partners).

(b) *The claimant's illness need not be caused by a sudden shock* but might arise from a build-up of anxiety and stress over a period of time.

(c) *The claimant's proximity to the accident or its aftermath should be irrelevant.*

(d) *If physical injury were reasonably foreseeable, there would be liability* even if only psychiatric injury resulted.

So far, none of these proposals has been implemented by Parliament.

Omissions to act and liability for damage caused by third parties

Omissions

The law of tort is concerned with compensating acts by a defendant which have actively damaged the claimant (*misfeasance*), rather than with the defendant's failure to act for the claimant's benefit (*nonfeasance*). Consequently, it is rare for a duty of care to result from an omission to act. In *Stovin* v *Wise* (1996) Lord Goff said: *'There are sound reasons why omissions require different treatment from positive conduct. It is one thing for the law to say that a person who undertakes some activity shall take reasonable care not to cause damage to others. It is another thing for the law to require that a person who is doing nothing in particular shall take steps to prevent another from suffering harm.'* He went on to say that there are political, moral and economic reasons for this approach. Imposing liability would unduly restrict personal freedom. There is no moral justification in making one person bear the economic burden of compensating a claimant when he or she may be one of a number who might morally be expected to intervene. *'Liability to pay compensation for loss caused by negligent conduct acts as a deterrent ... But there is no similar justification to require a person who is not doing anything* [wrong] *to spend money on behalf of someone else.'*

As Lord Goff indicates, it is important to distinguish between moral and legal duties as the two do not necessarily overlap. For example, you would not be liable in negligence or any other tort if you failed to stop a blind person from walking into a road in front of an oncoming bus, if you had no previous legal responsibility for their safety.

'False omissions' may give rise to a duty of care

There are situations where a failure to act does give rise to a duty, though if we examine them closely, we see that the omission was not an isolated failure to act but was part of a chain of events already giving rise to liability or that the claimant was in a dependent relationship with the defendant. In both these situations a duty of care already exists between the parties. For example, you will be liable for harm to any pedestrian you knock down with your car, if the accident happened because you omitted to use your brakes, or to keep a proper lookout. If you choose to help a blind person across the road, you will by intervening create a duty of care and may be liable to that person if you bungle the rescue operation. Similarly, a school teacher may be liable for failing to stop a pupil from climbing into the bear pit on a visit to the zoo, as might a doctor who harms patients by failing to warn them that the drug prescribed cannot be safely combined with certain foods.

Acts of third parties

There is a presumption in law that we are all responsible for our own behaviour, therefore, it is rare to find cases where one party is liable for the tort of a third party (apart from circumstances giving rise to vicarious liability, see below at page 339).

Smith v Littlewoods Organisation (1987, HL)

Littlewoods bought a disused cinema with a view to opening one of its stores on the land. While the cinema was being demolished, at a time while no contractor or Littlewoods employees were present, vandals entered the premises and started a fire. This spread to Smith's adjoining premises. Smiths alleged that Littlewoods were in breach of a duty to prevent this damage, by making the premises secure against trespassers. Both parties agreed that only a twenty-four-hour guard could have prevented entry by trespassers.

Held: although occupiers of premises have a duty to take reasonable care that their premises are not a source of danger to neighbouring landowners, Littlewoods did not owe a duty of care as there were no special circumstances indicating that such vandalism was reasonably foreseeable.

Lord Griffiths stated: '*I do not say that there will never be circumstances in which the law will require an occupier to take special precautions against such a contingency, but they would have to be extreme indeed ... there was nothing inherently dangerous ... stored on the premises, nor can I regard a cinema stripped of its equipment as likely to be any more alluring to vandals than any other recently vacated building in the centre of a town. No message was received ... from the local police, fire brigade or any neighbour that vandals were creating a danger on any premises.*' To require a twenty-four-hour guard would be '*an intolerable burden*' in the circumstances.

> The *Littlewoods* case is a good example of the court taking a restricted view of what is reasonably foreseeable. Vandalism is a well known problem in urban areas. However, in cases involving property damage the court expects a claimant to be insured, so it is usually unsympathetic to claims for negligent omissions and third party damage. The aim of this policy is to encourage property owners to be prudent and to prevent insurance companies from fronting a successful action to recover their losses.
>
> Occupiers do not generally have a duty to secure their premises in order to safeguard neighbouring premises unless alerted by evidence that they represent a risk. If the defendant's premises have previously been subject to trespass and vandalism, this would be more likely to make the court take the view that the damage to the claimant was reasonably foreseeable.
>
> *A duty may arise in the following circumstances*:
>
> 1 The defendant had a responsibility to control the third party's behaviour because of a pre-existing relationship with the party.

Home Office v Dorset Yacht Co. Ltd (1970, HL)

The Home Office was held liable when the claimant's yacht was damaged by improperly supervised Borstal trainees who had escaped from a nearby work camp.

2 The defendant's pre-existing relationship to the claimant makes the defendant responsible for preventing the damage.

Stansbie v *Troman* (1948, CA)

Stansbie was a decorator who was left in sole charge of Mrs Troman's house. He left it unlocked when going out to buy wallpaper and was held liable for the loss arising from the burglary which took place in his absence.

Public authorities and statutory discretion

Public service providers, such as the fire brigade, the police and local authorities, operate in the context of statutory duties and powers. Such duties are mandatory but often widely drafted, leaving a large element of discretion to the authority about how it is implemented. For example, a local authority must provide full-time education for children in its catchment area, but how it does so is left largely to its discretion. The authority decides, for example, whether single-sex education shall be an option and determines the selection methods, if any, for transfer to secondary schools. Some local authorities provide special schools for pupils with some acute physical disabilities and learning difficulties, while others choose to place such students in mainstream schools. Such choices are made with regard to the perceived needs of the particular community and may be limited by budgetary concerns.

The statutory duty exists to benefit the public at large through the provision of services relevant to local needs. The courts have traditionally been unwilling to permit a duty of care in negligence to be owed by a public authority to individual members of the public who claim to be harmed by the way the authority has used its **statutory discretion** in performing its public duties. Usually, such claims arise where an omission to exercise the power is allegedly the cause of the damage or where a third party is actually responsible for the harm. These factors combined with the desire of the courts not to fetter discretion derived from Parliament makes them particularly reluctant to impose a duty of care. Policy plays a very important role in such circumstances.

The fire brigade and ambulance services owe a limited duty

Capital and Counties Bank plc v *Hampshire Fire Brigade* (1997, CA)

Here the brigade fought a fire on the claimant's premises, but left having turned off sprinklers in the roof area, which was still smouldering. Later it reignited and the building was destroyed.

Held: a fire brigade was under no duty at civil law to attend a fire. Duty of care was to be limited to situations where acts of the fire brigade directly worsened the claimant's problems. The defendant fire brigade was liable, as its intervention had increased the damage to the claimant.

Remember that the court's decision in cases like this will be influenced by the expectation that the claimant will have insurance against fire damage. Maybe if a case concerning death or physical injury occurs we may see a different approach.

Ambulance services, because their remit involves medical care, owe a greater duty than other emergency services and must provide a timely service once a caller has been told that an ambulance will be dispatched.

Kent v Griffiths and Others (No. 3) (2001, CA)

The claimant had an acute asthma attack and suffered severe brain damage when delay caused by negligence by the ambulance service prevented her from receiving timely treatment.

Held: provided an ambulance was available and a caller was told that it would be sent, it should attend within a reasonable time. The ambulance service was part of the health service. It was therefore appropriate to regard it as providing services of the same kind as those provided by hospital services rather than being equivalent to those of the fire brigade and police.

The police

While the police authority will be liable in the same way as any other employer for negligent driving by its officers or failure to protect a person in custody from coming to harm, the court has refused to hear cases where the police were apparently negligent in preventing crimes from occurring. It was perceived that this would unduly restrict discretion in an area where much flexibility was needed and could lead to defensive behaviour by the police which would be prejudicial to the public.

Osman v Ferguson (1993, CA)

A schoolmaster who became obsessed with a pupil, harassed him and his family, carried out acts of vandalism against their property and tried to ram their car while it was being driven. The police were informed and interviewed the man but did not take steps to arrest him. He continued his campaign of harassment which culminated in his shooting both father and son, killing the former and injuring the latter. An action in negligence was taken against the police.

Held: the action must be struck out. Arguably, there was sufficient proximity between the police and the victims of the shooting to give rise to a special relationship. However, it was not fair, just and reasonable to impose a duty of care by the police to the victims of crime. It would not improve standards and could dangerously divert police resources from the general investigation and suppression of crime necessary to protect the public.

This case seemed to indicate that the police enjoyed complete immunity from litigation concerning policing discretion.

The courts have been compelled to take a less prescriptive approach since *Osman* v *UK* (1999), where the European Court of Human Rights held that giving the police immunity was in effect a breach of Article 6 of the ECHR (right to a fair trial). The House of Lords (*Barrett* v *Enfield Borough Council* (1999)) subsequently held that any claim where immunity of any public authority is in question must be tried to determine whether a duty of care exists. This, of course, does not mean that a duty will necessarily be held to exist, but it gives the claimant the opportunity to have his or her own case considered, thus enabling his or her right to a fair trial.

Given the House of Lords' decision (below), it seems almost impossible to persuade the court that a duty of care in negligence or liability by the police for breach of Article 2 of the ECHR exists.

Chief Constable Hertfordshire v *Van Colle and Smith* v *Chief Constable of Sussex* (2008, HL)

These two cases involved claims against the police for failing to intervene to protect a party in danger of alleged violent attack. The first case concerned a witness who was murdered days before he was due to give evidence at a trial for theft by a party later convicted for X's murder. In evidence, it was alleged that X had been subjected to a number of threats and intimidation by Y which the police had known about.

Smith repeatedly told the police that A (his former partner) had threatened to kill him and provided sufficient evidence to justify his arrest. For example, he had received over 130 text messages from A. Some contained very explicit threats such as: '*U are dead*'; '*Look out for yourself psycho is coming*'; '*I am looking to kill you and no compromises*'; '*I was in the Bulldog last night with a carving knife. It's a shame I missed you*'. However, the police chose to ignore Mr Smith's complaints. Eventually, A attacked him with a claw hammer causing serious injury. X's representative claimed breach of the ECHR, Article 2 (right to life) and Mr Smith claimed in negligence.

Held: both appeals must be dismissed.

X's claim: under *Osman* v *UK* the test of liability stipulated that the court should not acknowledge a breach unless 'at the time' the police should have known of a 'real and immediate risk to life of an identified individual from criminal acts of a third party'.

Y was a seriously 'disturbed and unpredictable individual'. Therefore, it could not be said that the police by involving X as a witness and making him a member of a special class separate from the public at large, should have anticipated that Y was a sufficient risk to X's safety. The *Osman* test did not impose an invariable standard and the particular facts were relevant to determining whether or not it was satisfied.

Mr Smith's claim (Lord Bingham dissenting): under the rule in *Hill* v *Chief Constable West Yorkshire* (1989, HL) the police owed no common law duty of care to protect individuals from attacks by criminals, unless there were very special circumstances justifying departure from the principle which protected the public interest. A specific and evident threat would have to exist for the police to owe a duty. It had not existed here.

While this can look unjust, bear in mind that the victims of such crimes as these do have alternative means of dispute resolution, such as the Criminal Injuries Compensation Board and the formal complaint systems.

Education and social services

The courts in the past generally refused to allow claims to proceed in negligence against a local authority's education and social services departments, on the ground that this would fetter executive discretion in the use of resources, and interfere with social policy. In *X v Bedfordshire County Council* (1995) the House of Lords struck out two claims concerning allegedly negligent decisions by local authorities in failing to take children into care. It was held that no duty of care existed in such cases or social services departments would be unduly constrained. They might be inclined to act defensively and unnecessarily take children into care.

As indicated above, this attitude has had to change since the ECtHR decision in *Osman*. This was evidenced by the House of Lords decision in (*Barrett v Enfield Borough Council* (1999) (above)).

A case of failing to take a child into care may now succeed (*Pierce v Doncaster Metropolitan Borough Council* (EWHC 2968)). However, a claim by a parent that their child was wrongly taken into care is still unlikely to be successful. In *Lawrence v Pembrokeshire County Council* (2007, CA) the claimant's children were mistakenly put on the at risk register when Ms Lawrence was wrongfully suspected of abusing them. Her action was struck out since no duty of care was deemed to exist. The claimant appealed, arguing that application of Article 8 (right to family life) of the ECHR in domestic law since implementation of the HRA 1998, should result in an incremental change in the law of negligence. The Court of Appeal held that the House of Lords (*JD v East Berkshire Community Health NHS Trust and Ors* (2005)) had already decided (albeit prior to implementation of the HRA) that no duty of care in negligence was owed to parents wrongly suspected of abuse provided the local authority had acted in good faith. An extension in the scope of duty of care would be a step too far. There was a lack of proximity between Ms Lawrence and the council. It would also militate against the public interest, which required that a child protection authority should be able to exercise its discretion freely during the investigation and prevention of abusive behaviour, without being inhibited by threat of potential litigation.

In such cases, alternative remedies are often available. Ms Lawrence had already received compensation after an ombudsman investigation and an action under the HRA was also possible.

The impact of the Human Rights Act 1998

Since 2000, an action under the Human Rights Act 1998 for breach of the Convention is now possible in cases against a public authority. This may well be more appropriate than an action in negligence and more likely to be successful, where the claim involves omission to act, failure to prevent damage by a third party or negligent exercise of a statutory discretion. In *Z and A v UK* (2002) the claimants (two of the child claimants involved in *X v Bedfordshire County Council* (1995)) successfully claimed that the council had breached its duty under Article 3 (the right not to be subjected to inhuman or degrading treatment) by failing to protect them from prolonged and serious ill-treatment and abuse. Article 8 (right to respect for family life) was breached in respect of another child who was wrongly taken into care. Her mother also succeeded with an Article 8 claim. Such claims can now be brought in the English courts, which must have regard to decisions of the European Court of Human Rights (see Chapter 3 page 41, above).

In conclusion: duty criteria are guidance only

From your study of all the various problematic duty situations examined in this chapter, you will now be aware that judges determining the existence of duty of care often refer to such criteria as reasonable foreseeability, proximity and justice and reason (policy). Students often ask their lecturers to tell them what exactly these words mean in the hope that this will provide a magic key to unlock a secret door to understanding. Be warned that this is a fruitless quest. Such words cannot be defined as legal terms and in themselves, do not provide certain answers to the question of whether a duty of care exists in a particular case. The context in which they are applied, i.e. the circumstances of the particular case, heavily influences their definition and limits, so that apparently conflicting decisions are made. As May LJ said in *Merret v Bubb* (2001): it would be *'reaching for the moon … to expect to accommodate every circumstance which may arise within a single short abstract formulation'*.

It may help you to keep in mind that a duty is unlikely to be acknowledged for any case which is not concerned with physical damage directly caused to the claimant or their property if the claimant had some alternative available remedy, or could be expected to insure against the loss. The courts are wary of creating a duty owed to an indefinable class and take an incremental approach to the development of duty within the problem. Therefore, any change will be a small step at a time rather than a leap into the dark.

Part 2 – breach of duty

It is up to the claimant to prove that the defendant failed to take reasonable care in performing the duty of care. What is reasonable is measured objectively against the standards of the so-called '**reasonable man**' in the circumstances of the particular case. Certain criteria exist to guide the court.

The likelihood of an accident happening

The greater the likelihood of an accident the more care the defendant may need to take. The court will need to be satisfied that the incidence of risk was reasonably reduced. It need not be completely removed for the standard to be met.

Bolton v Stone (1951)

The claimant was injured by a cricket ball hit from the cricket club grounds controlled by the defendant. The boundary fence was 17 feet high and the ball had travelled over 80 yards from the wicket. There was evidence to show that such a hit was a very rare occurrence.

Held: the defendant was not liable as reasonable care had been taken to reduce the chances of such an occurrence, given the height of the fence and the distance from the wicket and the previous history of balls rarely escaping from the ground.

However, a similar accident occurring in different circumstances gave rise to liability for the defendant since the chances of an accident were very likely.

Hilder v Associated Portland Cement (1961)

Children were often known to play football on some land belonging to the defendant company which was close to a road and bordered by a wall less than three feet high. A motorcyclist was killed when a ball was kicked into the road.

Held: the defendant was liable since it had not taken reasonable care to reduce the chances of a very likely accident. It had neither prevented the children from playing on its land nor provided a boundary fence sufficient to prevent footballs escaping into the highway.

The extent of the potential harm

The greater the extent of the likely damage the more the defendant is expected to do to reduce its risk.

Paris v Stepney Council (1951)

The claimant was employed in a manual job by the defendant company. He had only one eye and was then blinded in his good eye in an accident at work.

Held: the defendant had failed to act with reasonable care by failing to supply goggles to the claimant. It was irrelevant that the work he was doing would not necessitate use of goggles by a normally sighted person. The consequence of injury to his eyes was much more serious than to other employees.

The practicability of taking precautions: risk–benefit analysis

The court when determining reasonable care seeks to impose a standard of care that gives reasonable protection to the claimant while not unduly burdening the defendant. This may be described as a **risk–benefit analysis**. A risk-free environment can never be fully guaranteed.

Withers v Perry Chain Ltd (1961)

The claimant, who was employed in a factory where contact with grease was involved at every stage of the production process, became allergic to grease and developed a skin condition. Her employer moved her to the most grease-free job that fitted her capabilities but the allergy persisted.

Held: the defendant company had done everything that it could reasonably be expected to do to prevent harm to the claimant and was therefore not in breach of its duty and Ms Withers' claim must accordingly fail.

Latimer v AEC (1953)

A factory floor was slippery after a flash flood. The defendant spread sawdust over most of the walkways in the factory and issued warnings to employees. The claimant, who was injured when he slipped in an area which had not been sawdusted because it was less often used, argued that the building should have been closed until it had dried out.

Held: the extent of the risk and likely injury did not justify this extreme response. The precautions taken were all that was practicable in the circumstances.

The defendant's resources and the nature and size of the business may be relevant factors for the court to take into account. However, the greater the risk and extent of damage the less relevant the cost factor to the defendant. This is an area of the common law where standards have been influenced by statutory developments in health and safety regulation (see Chapter 16 at page 359, below). This commonly requires prior risk assessment for certain activities. Evidence that this process was sufficiently comprehensive and resulted in relevant precautions is often sufficient to discharge the duty of care. Risk assessment is becoming accepted practice even where it is not statutorily required.

Skilful claimants

If a claimant has a skill which should make him or her aware of an inherent danger, the defendant will not be expected to take steps to protect him or her from it.

Roles v Nathan (1963)

Two sweeps died when they were overcome by fumes while attempting to seal a hole in a flue while the boiler on the defendant's premises was still alight.

Held: the defendant was not negligent. The sweeps were experienced tradesmen and knew that the boiler should have been extinguished before work was started. It was not up to the defendant to put it out or issue warnings.

The qualifications claimed by the defendant

Defendants will be held liable if they fail to act with the reasonable degree of care and skill to be expected from a person with the qualifications which the defendants claim to have – *Bolam* v *Friern Hospital Management Committee* (1957) (see below).

Phillips v William Whitely (1938)

The defendant jeweller who pierced the claimant's ears was not liable for the abscess which resulted.

Held: the defendant was not negligent. He had acted in accordance with the level of care and skill to be expected from a person with his training. The standards of a surgeon could not be expected of him.

Only the level of qualification is relevant. Lack of experience is not taken into consideration: the same standards are expected of a newly qualified professional or craftsperson as of one with considerable experience. In *Wilsher* v *Essex Area Health Authority* (1986) the Court of Appeal held that it was irrelevant that the doctor who treated the claimant was newly qualified and had been working excessively long hours when she treated the claimant (facts below, at page 306).

This extends to learner drivers, who are required to demonstrate the same standard of care as those who have passed a driving test (see *Nettleship* v *Weston* (1971, CA)). This is to prevent insurance companies avoiding liability to third parties.

A defendant claiming no special training or skill is expected to take such care as can reasonably be expected in the circumstances. In *Perry* v *Harris* (2008) the Court of Appeal held that the defendant was not liable for the injuries sustained by a child hurt when using a bouncy castle at a children's birthday party. She had acted as a responsible adult in her supervision of the children at the time and constant supervision was not required as serious injury was not reasonably foreseeable. Similarly, the standard required of an amateur carpenter's repairs is not as high as that required of a professional tradesperson (*Wells* v *Cooper* (1958, CA)).

Children are expected to exercise a level of skill commensurate with their age. In *Orchard* v *Lee* (2009), the Court of Appeal decided that a 13-year-old boy, who seriously injured a dinner lady on colliding with her in the playground when he was playing tag, had not breached his duty of care. A reasonable 13-year-old would not have reasonably foreseen that such harm would be likely to result from his conduct.

Good practice

Conformity with accepted and current good practice may be indicative of reasonable care. Thus, in *Thompson* v *Smiths Ship Repairers Ltd* (1984) the defendant employer's failure to provide ear protectors was held not to amount to a failure to take reasonable care until they had been alerted to the necessity by government circular.

There may be more than one type of good practice: both claimant and defendant may produce expert witnesses with conflicting views. The judge does not have the relevant professional skill to decide whose procedure was correct. The claimant must prove that on the balance of probability the defendant was in breach. If there is proof that what the defendant did would also have been done by another similar professional in compliance with good practice then the claimant fails.

Bolam v *Friern Hospital Management Committee* (1957, CA)

The claimant, who suffered a fractured pelvis when undergoing electro-convulsive therapy, brought expert evidence that his limbs should have been restrained during treatment.

Held: on the balance of probability there was no proof of a failure to take reasonable care. The hospital was able to prove that its practice of cushioning limbs was equally well accepted in respected medical circles.

The House of Lords approved the *Bolam* principle in *Bolitho* v *City and Hackney Area Health Authority* (1997), but stressed that it is not enough to show that other professionals subscribe to the practice: an expert witness must be able to justify its use in the circumstances of the particular case, having weighed up its risks and benefits.

Unhappy outcomes

In *Bolam* v *Friern Hospital Management Committee* Lord Justice Denning neatly summarised the nature of reasonable care when he said *'the doctor does not promise to cure the patient nor the lawyer to win the case'*. All reasonable care may be taken but the claimant may still suffer damage. Proof of damage to claimant or even proof of a mistake by the defendant does not necessarily prove that the defendant has failed to take reasonable care.

Luxmoore May v *Messenger May Bakers* (1990, CA)

The defendant auctioneers claimed to be expert picture valuers. They failed to judge correctly the potential of two paintings owned by the claimant, who consequently obtained only a tiny fraction of their true value when they were sold.

Held: the claimants had failed to prove that the defendants acted without reasonable care. Evidence from the defendant indicated that a competent valuer could have made the same mistake.

Encoding the standard of care

The Compensation Act 2006

Section 1 states that when a court is deciding whether a defendant has taken reasonable care it may

have regard to whether a requirement to take those steps might –

(a) *prevent a desirable activity from being undertaken at all, to a particular extent or in a particular way, or*

(b) *discourage persons from undertaking functions in connection with a desirable activity.*

From what you have read earlier, you will see that this statute merely reflects current judicial practice, so may appear to be a redundant piece of legislation. Parliament's intention was presumably to improve awareness of this aspect of the law and to attempt to ensure that normal activities are not inhibited by fear of litigation and excessively risk-averse behaviour. There does appear to be an increase in such behaviour of late, encouraging the popular belief that life should be risk free, and that, since any and every accident is preventable somebody must be legally liable.

Reflecting this legislation, the Health & Safety Executive published (August 2006) proposals for a code of principles for risk management which states that, while the safety of workers and members of the public should be properly protected, sensible risk management is not about *'creating a totally risk free society'* or *'stopping important recreational and learning activities'* or *'scaring people by exaggerating or publicising trivial risks'*.

Proving consequent damage

The claimant must prove the link between the defendant's failure to take reasonable care and the damage which the claimant has suffered. Two elements are involved: the claimant must first prove that but for the defendant's behaviour the damage would not have occurred (*causation in fact*) and secondly that the damage is a reasonably foreseeable result (*causation in law*).

1 Causation in fact: the 'but for' rule

The defendant's failure to take care must be the material cause of the damage. A claimant must show that he or she would not have been injured **but for** the defendant's act or failure to act.

Barnett v Chelsea & Kensington Hospital Management Committee (1969)

A man died from arsenic poisoning which the hospital negligently failed to detect.

Held: the hospital was not liable, as according to expert evidence he would still have died even if the hospital had diagnosed the problem and treated him appropriately.

McWilliams v Arrol (1962)

The claimant's husband fell from a roof that he was repairing; he had not been wearing a safety belt. There was evidence that, although belts were normally available, on the day of the accident, the shed where they were stored was locked. The claimant argued that if the belts had been available her husband would not have fallen.

Held: she must lose her case since the defendant employer was able to prove that her husband did not usually bother to wear a belt.

Multiple causes

The 'but for' principle works well as long as there is only one likely cause of the damage. Where there are multiple causes, the claimant may be unable to prove on the balance of probability that it was the defendant's behaviour which was a material cause of the accident.

Wilsher v Essex Area Health Authority (1988, HL)

Failure by the hospital to give the claimant, a premature baby, the correct oxygen mixture was alleged to be the cause of his becoming visually impaired.

Held: the claimant could not succeed since the 'but for' test had not been satisfied, as he was suffering from a number of other conditions, any of which could have caused the same damage. It had not been proved on the balance of probability that the oxygen mixture was a material cause.

> In a previous case the House of Lords had adopted a different approach.

McGhee v National Coal Board (1972, HL)

The claimant worked in very hot and dirty conditions in a brick kiln. No showers were provided and he could not get clean until he had cycled home from work. He contracted dermatitis. He could not prove on the balance of probability that showering before leaving work would have prevented the dermatitis.

Held: the NCB was liable as the medical evidence indicated that lack of showers greatly increased his chances of developing the condition.

> In *Wilsher* v *Essex Area Health Authority* the House of Lords described the *McGhee* approach as 'robust and pragmatic': correct on its facts but not a principle of law. This cast doubt on the standing of *McGhee*, and produced a puzzling distinction for many students. However, in 2002 the House of Lords clarified the law:

Fairchild v Glenhaven Funeral Services (2002, HL)

The claimants in this case all contracted mesothelioma (a form of invariably fatal cancer) from being exposed to asbestos fibres at work. There was clear evidence of flagrant breach of safety standards by all the employers. Causation was problematic, however, as all the claimants had been employed by more than one employer. Each employee could only have contracted the disease during one period of employment, and it was impossible for them to prove which one was the source of the disease.

Held (unanimously): given the impossibility of proof, the claimants should succeed. It was fair and just to use the less stringent *McGhee* rule here, as by breaching safety standards all the employers had materially increased the claimants' chances of contracting the condition. The facts could clearly be distinguished from those in *Wilsher* where a number of possible causes, apart from the oxygen, could have led to the claimant's disability. In *Fairchild*, asbestos was the only possible cause. The House of Lords in *Wilsher* was incorrect in failing to acknowledge *McGhee* as establishing a new principle of law.

The defendants were jointly and severally liable. Therefore, the claimants were entitled to full compensation from the employer who was being sued, since that employer could seek contribution from any other employer who had exposed the claimant to the risk.

> The *Fairchild* decision is important as it firmly establishes the *McGhee* approach as a principle of law. It is also a good example of a public interest or 'policy' decision. Had the

employers escaped liability, others would have been encouraged to ignore safety standards in similar situations, secure in the knowledge that the causative link could not be established. Insurers, too, would have unjustly profited.

Four years later in *Barker* v *Corus UK Ltd, Murray* v *British Shipbuilders Ltd, Patterson* v *Smiths Docks Ltd* (2006, HL) a differently constituted House of Lords decided three cases in which the facts were subtly different from *Fairchild*. This resulted in the principle in *Fairchild* being both expanded in one respect and restricted controversially in another.

The expansion

Mr Barker had been exposed to the risk of mesothelioma not only by his employers but also during a period of self-employment, but this was held to be irrelevant to his employers' liability. It was held that, provided there was evidence of negligence by the defendant which materially increased the risk of contracting mesothelioma, it was irrelevant that the claimant had also been exposed to the risk from another source. It was irrelevant that that other exposure might have been caused by tortious or non-tortious behaviour or some natural cause.

The restriction

In *Barker*, etc. the House of Lords by majority held that joint and several liability could only be imposed if the defendants had actually *caused the claimants to contract* the disease. It also held that only a minority of the House of Lords in *Fairchild* had actually decided that the defendants had done so. The majority (three out of five) had merely held that the defendant had exposed the claimants to the *risk of contracting* the disease. Therefore, their Lordships restated the decision in *Fairchild* holding that each defendant could only be held liable severally (only for the damage it had personally caused) and so would pay compensation proportionately to the period of time the claimant had been employed by them. This impacted unfavourably on the current claimants as all previous employers bar the current defendants were insolvent and, as mentioned above, Mr Barker had been self-employed for a time.

This was a very controversial decision as regards the several liability issue. Lord Hoffmann said that it would '*smooth the roughness of the justice which a rule of joint and several liability creates*'. It certainly would have pleased the defendant insurers and those involved in other pending claims. However, it may be argued that it roughened the justice for the claimants and their dependants, as Lord Rodger clearly indicated in his dissenting judgment where he called upon Parliament to come to their assistance. Richard Leyton (president of the Association of Personal Injury Lawyers) declared that it was '*an insult to the victims*' families' and Parliament was quick to intervene.

The Compensation Act 2006, s 3

Section 3 in effect imposes joint and several liability for negligence and breach of statutory duty arising from the circumstances of exposure covered by the *Fairchild* and *Barker* decisions but s 3(5) expands this to cover liability for failure to protect from exposure.

The Act received Royal Assent assent in July 2006 and s 3 has retrospective effect, which means that all future cases must be decided in accordance with it, even if the damage occurred before the section came into force. It also means that the outcomes of some past claims may need to be varied.

This was a very welcome parliamentary intervention for those of us who agree with the House of Lords in *Fairchild*, that perfect justice cannot be obtained in this problematic causation situation and that any injustice should be borne by a party who is culpably in breach of their duty of care, rather than their innocent victims.

The *Barker* decision no longer reflects the law as regards the issue of liability. However, we should not completely disregard the *Fairchild* and *Barker* cases in future. Section 3 clearly reflects them pretty precisely as regards exposure issues. Parliament has in effect made that part of those decisions statutory so they will presumably still be regarded as factually persuasive in future cases by courts interpreting and applying s 3.

Lost chances

The more liberal approach to causation in *Fairchild* has not been extended to claims for a lost chance. Although damages may be award for such losses the claimant must as usual in civil cases, establish that the defendant was on the balance of probabilities the material cause of the loss.

In *Hotson* v *East Berkshire Health Authority* (1987) the claimant fractured his hip and the hospital negligently failed to spot that he had associated nerve damage which resulted in long-term damage to his hip joint, severely reducing his mobility. He claimed that he had been deprived of his mobility by the hospital's failure to treat the condition. He lost his claim because he was unable to prove that but for the defendant's negligence he would have been cured, since expert evidence showed that treatment was only successful in 25% of cases. Therefore, he could not prove that on the balance of probability he would have regained full mobility, because he was unable to prove that treatment was successful in at least 51% of cases. This principle was affirmed by the House of Lords in 2005 in *Gregg* v *Scott*. Due to the defendant's negligence, Mr Gregg's cancer was diagnosed late, reducing his chance of a cure to 25%. Prompt diagnosis would have increased this chance to 46%. His claim failed since even swift intervention would not on the balance of probability have resulted in his cure.

2 Causation in law (remoteness of damage)

The damage must not be too remote. The defendant is not held legally responsible for all the results of the breach.

The law treats intentional and unintentional torts differently as regards determining remoteness. We are presumed to intend all the direct consequences of our intentional acts, so in a tort like trespass the defendant will be liable for all the direct consequences regardless of whether they could reasonably have been foreseen (*Re Polemis* (1921, CA)). However, it was decided in *The Wagon Mound* (1961) (below) that damage caused to the claimant by a non-intentional tort like negligence or nuisance must be of a reasonably foreseeable type.

Overseas Tankships & Engineering v *Morts Dock & Engineering Ltd (The Wagon Mound (No. 1))* (1961, PC)

Fire damage was caused to the claimant's dock when a spark from a welding torch being used on the claimant's dock ignited oil which the defendants had negligently discharged into the harbour.

Held: the chance of fire breaking out in such circumstances was not reasonably foreseeable by the defendants who were therefore not liable.

> In *Corr* v *IBC Vehicles Ltd* (2008) the House of Lords held Mr Corr's employer (IBC) liable for his death. The acute clinical depression arising from the disfigurement and post-traumatic stress which resulted from the negligence of his employers made it reasonably foreseeable that he would commit suicide.
>
> Provided that the *type of damage* is reasonably foreseeable, the defendant will be liable. It is irrelevant that the defendant might not have been able to foresee its cause or its severity.

Hughes v *Lord Advocate* (1963, HL)

The defendant telephone engineers left an inspection hole for the night, covered only by a tent and surrounded by lighted paraffin lamps. The child claimant was severely burned when he fell down the hole carrying a lamp which exploded as it hit the ground, producing a fireball.

Held: the defendants were held liable as it was reasonably foreseeable that a child would be attracted by the lamps and might be burned when playing with them. It was irrelevant that the explosion and the severity of the burn damage were not reasonably foreseeable.

> Their Lordships reaffirmed this principle in the following case:

Jolley v *London Borough of Sutton* (2000, HL)

The defendant council failed to remove an abandoned boat from its land. The claimant (aged 14) was seriously injured when it fell on him after he had jacked it up to try to repair it.

Held: the council was liable, as the precise circumstances causing the accident did not have to be foreseeable. The boat was a safety hazard and likely to attract children.

Intervening acts

Sometimes subsequent behaviour of the claimant or a third party may lead to an aggravation of the damage set in train by the defendant. The question for the court to decide is whether that **intervening act** breaks the chain of causation and thus prevents the defendant from being liable for the resulting damage. However, if the act is reasonably foreseeable and/or the defendant has a duty to prevent it then liability remains with the defendant, as the damage is not too remote.

McKew v *Holland & Cubitts Ltd* (1969, HL)

The defendant negligently injured the claimant's leg. As a consequence, it would quite often give way. In full knowledge of this, the claimant attempted to descend a steep stairway without using the hand rail. His leg gave way and he fell down the stairs, sustaining further injuries.

Held: the defendant was not liable for the injuries sustained in the fall; the claimant's descent of the stairs was an intervening act which was not reasonably foreseeable to the defendant. It was unreasonable of the claimant to behave as he had.

A different result was reached in *Wieland* (below) due to the claimant being unaware of the full effects of her previous accident.

Wieland v *Cyril Lord Carpets* (1969)

Due to negligence of the defendant, the claimant suffered injuries. She was sent to hospital and was fitted with a surgical collar. This impeded her head movement and, consequently, use of her bifocal spectacles. The next day when she was returning home from a checkup at the hospital, she felt so unwell that she called in at the defendant's show rooms where her nephew worked, to get him to take her home. Unable to see properly, she fell down some steps and hurt herself.

Held: the defendant was liable for all the claimant's injuries since its negligence had left her unable to cope with the normal necessities of life. Descending the stairs was not unreasonable and did not break the chain of causation. She had not had time to adjust to the effects of her treatment and was still suffering from some residual shock at the time of the second accident.

When a third party is involved, the issue of whether the defendant had a duty to control them or to prevent such acts is relevant to determining liability.

Reeves v *Commissioner of Police for the Metropolis* (1999, HL)

Reeves committed suicide while in police custody. He was known at the time to be in a mentally unstable condition.

Held: the police were liable for his death as it was their negligence, in failing to supervise him appropriately, which enabled him to end his life. His intervening act was both reasonably foreseeable and the very thing that they were meant to prevent.

The 'eggshell skull' rule

The **'eggshell skull'** rule is an exception to the *Wagon Mound* principle. If the claimant has some particular weakness that makes him or her susceptible to a type of harm which is not reasonably foreseeable, the defendant will nevertheless be liable.

Smith v *Leech Brain & Co. Ltd* (1962)

Due to the defendants' negligence, an employee suffered a minor burn to his lip which would normally have caused only superficial damage. However, pre-cancerous cells in his lip which might otherwise have remained dormant were activated and he died. It was held that the defendants were liable for their employee's death although such serious damage was not foreseeable.

In *Page* v *Smith* (1995) the House of Lords held that the eggshell skull principle applied to both mental and physical conditions. The principle has also been held to apply to a claimant whose financial situation makes him or her more vulnerable to the damage caused by the defendant.

Mattocks v *Mann* (1993)

The claimant's car was damaged by the negligence of the defendant. When it had been repaired, there was a delay before she could recover it, as the garage refused to part with it until the insurance company came up with the money. The claimant did not have the funds to pay the bill herself.

Held: the defendant (in reality, his insurers) was liable for the cost of her hiring a car until she could recover her own.

Chapter summary

Problematic duties of care
The requirements for proof of duty of care in these problematic areas are rigorous and based on a high degree of foreseeability and proximity and public interest.

Pure economic loss
A special relationship of close proximity between the parties is essential, involving reliance by the claimant on the defendant's expertise and/or assumption of responsibility by the defendant. A disclaimer or conditional undertaking by the defendant prevents creation of the relationship.

Liability may result from negligent advice as well as other negligent behaviour.

Nervous shock
Shock causing physical/psychiatric injury which must be medically recognised.
Primary victims: if duty for physical harm exists it includes nervous shock.
Secondary victims: for a duty to exist the claimant must satisfy the *Alcock* criteria:
(a) sudden shock causing medically recognised condition;
(b) reasonable foreseeability of this reaction;
(c) claimant's reaction that of a reasonably brave person;
(d) claimant close to the accident in time and space.

Omissions/third-party acts
The defendant must generally owe a duty of care to the claimant/have a duty to control the third party.

Public authority exercise of statutory discretion
Duty of care is very rarely upheld.
Limited duty: fire and ambulance services.
Human rights action may be more viable.

Breach of duty of care
The claimant must prove that the defendant failed to take reasonable care taking into account:
(a) seriousness of the risk arising from the defendant's conduct;
(b) the extent of the reasonably foreseeable damage to the claimant;
(c) any relevant skill of the claimant; and
(d) the skill/qualifications of the defendant.

Causation: the link between the breach and the damage to the claimant must exist:
(a) *in fact*: the damage must be the result of the breach ('but for' test);
(b) *in law*: the damage must not be too remote from the breach of duty.

Test for remoteness: damage must be of a reasonably foreseeable kind in unintentional torts like negligence and nuisance.
Intervening acts make damage too remote unless they were reasonably foreseeable to the defendant.

Key terms

'But for' principle: damage to the claimant must be a result of the defendant's breach.

Close bond of love and affection: the required relationship between claimant and accident victim in nervous shock claims.

Disclaimer: a statement by which a party seeks to avoid liability for the consequences of negligent advice or behaviour.

'Eggshell skull' rule: exception to remoteness rule, which makes the defendant liable for unforeseeable damage to a claimant arising from a pre-existing medical condition or weakness.

Intervening acts: events aggravating the claimant's damage which occur between the defendant's act and resulting damage.

Involuntary participants: a primary nervous shock victim, who, though blameless, feels implicated in an accident caused by the defendant's negligence.

Nervous shock: psychiatric or physical harm caused by the shock of being involved in or witnessing an accident caused by the defendant's negligence.

Primary victim: nervous shock victim directly endangered by the defendant's negligence.

Reasonable man: the standard by which reasonable care is judged. This is said to reflect the behaviour of the average person in the given circumstances.

Risk–benefit analysis: a balancing exercise to determine the required level of care relating to an activity to determine what precautions are necessary, without unreasonably inhibiting its beneficial effects.

Quasi-fiduciary: describes a relationship involving a high degree of trust, though not a fiduciary relationship as such.

Secondary victims: a claimant in a nervous shock claim who sustains damage as a result of directly witnessing the accident caused by defendant's negligence.

Special relationship: essential to liability for pure economic loss claims in negligence. The claimant reasonably places a high degree of reliance on the defendant's knowledge or expertise.

Statutory discretion: flexibility in implementation of a statutory duty derived from the wording of the relevant Act of Parliament.

Sudden and immediate attack: the nature of the trauma which may give rise to nervous shock liability.

Sufficiently proximate: describes the required degree of connection between a secondary victim and the accident scene in a nervous shock claim.

Quiz 14

1 May a duty of care exist in the following circumstances?

(a) To Ruby, who was wrongly advised by Turquoise on the value of her antique clock?

(b) To Sapphire, by Beryl Electrical Appliances, the manufacturer of an electric kettle which was given to her for Christmas and which did not work?

(c) To Emerald, who witnesses a horrific accident caused by Diamond in which Emerald's daughter Crystal was killed?

(d) To Amber, who suffered theft from her premises; the thieves gained access to her premises through a hole in the next-door fence which belongs to Garnet?

Quiz 14 (Continued)

2 What is the relevant standard of care against which the defendant will be judged in a negligence action?

3 What is the eggshell skull rule?

Answers to all quizzes can be found in Appendix 2.

Take a closer look

The following cases provide important examples of how the law you have studied in this chapter has developed. They are primary sources illustrating the law in action and give you more detail about their facts, as well as helping you to understand the law and to appreciate how the judges reached their decisions.

Try looking up the law report or accessing it via a database, e.g. Bailii (www.bailii.org/databases.html). LexisNexis or Westlaw may be available in your university or college library, or you may find extracts in a case book. (See Appendix 1: Additional resources.)

Hedley Byrne v *Heller* (1963) 2 All ER 575, HL
Alcock v *Wright* (1991) 4 All ER 907, HL
Fairchild v *Glenhaven Funeral Services* [2002] 3 All ER 305, HL
Overseas Tankships & Engineering v *Morts Dock & Engineering Ltd* (*The Wagon Mound* (*No. 1*)) (1961) 1 All ER 404

Web activity

Please go to:

www.bbc.co.uk

Then type 'Hillsborough' into the search facility. Scroll down the results until you reach 'Liverpool – Local History – Hillsborough disaster'. First click on this link to read the BBC report of this tragic accident. Then click on 'Audio Slideshow: Remembering Hillsborough' a collection of photographs accompanied by personal accounts from people at the scene.

Assignment 13

Alice bought a small bakery business. It was surveyed by George, for Happy Homes Building Society, which provided Alice with the mortgage. Alice paid Happy Homes for a summary report from George. This stated that there were no major structural problems and that the premises were worth the asking price. It concluded: 'This report is for valuation purposes only and will not give rise to any legal liability.'

Alice contracted with Industrial Kitchen Fitters Ltd (IKF) to refit the kitchen. They installed a new oven manufactured by Cinders plc.

On moving in, Alice discovered severe and large-scale dry rot when she fell through a storeroom

Assignment 13 *(Continued from page 313)*

floor and broke her leg. Her injuries and the eradication of the dry rot delayed the opening of the premises for several months.

A week after the business eventually opened, the new oven malfunctioned. As a result, a wedding cake was badly burnt, leading to a claim for damages for breach of contract against Alice, by the bride's father.

IKF have gone out of business.

Advise Alice of the possible liability in negligence of George and Cinders.

mylawchamber

Visit **www.mylawchamber.co.uk/adams** to access multiple choice questions and glossary flashcards to test yourself on this chapter. You'll also find weblinks to the web activity in this chapter.

Index

A

abnormal profit, 98
Abortion Act 1967, 361
accelerationist theory, 288–290
accelerator theory, 296, 298
acceptance, contract law, 384–388
   communication methods
      conduct, 386–387
      electronic communications, 387–388
      post rule, 388
      requirement of particular method, 390
      verbal communication, 387
      waiving communication rule, 389–390
   firm, 385
      'subject to contract,' 385
      'mirror image' of offer, 385
acid rain, 173, 216, 218, 235
Act of Parliament
   creation of
      parliamentary procedure, 356
      pre-legislative stage, 356
   public corporations and, 10
ACTS, 206
actual growth, 245–249
   and business cycle, 245–249
   causes of fluctuations in, 250
   defined, 245
   and potential growth, 245
   in UK/France, 248–249
advertising campaign, 132, 150, 156
aggregate demand (*AD*), 250, 252, 258
   business cycles and, 295–299
   inflation/unemployment and, 282–295
   for labour curve, 258, 259
   money supply and, 280–282
aggregate expenditure line (E), 277
aggregate supply of labour curve, 258–259
agreement (composition), 402
air pollution, 180, 219, 224
allocative efficiency, 164
Amazon.com, 110, 379
ambient-based standards, 219
Apple, 117, 152
Armani, Giorgio, 86
asymmetric information, 6
Austin Rover, 10
Austin v Commissioner of Police of the Metropolis (2009, HL), 369
average cost (*AC*), 71, 73
   fixed cost (*AFC*), 71, 72
   and marginal cost, 73–74
   pricing, 133
   variable cost (*AVC*), 71, 73
average physical product (*APP*), 67–68
average revenue (*AR*), 90, 91–92

B

balance of payments, 244, 264
'bandwagon' effects, 297
Bank of England, 10, 244, 268, 281, 293, 314, 316, 318
Barcelona Summit of the Council of Ministers, 206
Barclays, 9
barometric firm price leadership, 132–133
battle of forms, 385
BBC, 10
'B2C' (business-to-consumers), 110
behavioural theories
   defined, 157
   organisational slack, 157–158
   'stakeholder economy,' 158
   target setting, 157
Berle, A. A., 5
Bertrand, Joseph, 135
Bertrand model, 135
bilateral offer, 376
binding precedent, 363
   advantages/disadvantages of, 365–366
   court hierarchy, 363
      court of appeal, 364
      divisional courts, 364
      high court, 364
      House of Lords, 363
   persuasive precedents, 365
      decisions of Judicial Committee of Privy Council, 365
      Obiter dicta, 365
   reporting system, 365
   reversing and overruling decisions, 364–365
   scope of *ratio decidendi,* 364
BIOMED, 206
Body Shop, 186
bounded rationality, 10–11
BP, 9, 53, 56, 129
Bradford and Bingley, 10
Branson, Sir Richard, 121
breach of duty, 482–493
   encoding standard of care, 486
      Compensation Act 2006, 486–487
   extent of potential harm, 483
      Paris v *Stepney Council* (1951), 483
   good practice, 485
      Bolam v *Friern Hospital Management Committee* (1957, CA), 485–486
   likelihood of accident happening, 482
      Bolton v *Stone* (1951), 482–483
      Hilder v *Associated Portland Cement* (1961), 483
   precautions: risk–benefit analysis, 483
      Latimer v *AEC* (1953), 484
      Withers v *Perry Chain Ltd* (1961), 483

proving consequent damage, 487
   causation in fact: 'but for' rule, 487–489
   causation in law (remoteness of damage), 490–493
  qualifications claimed by defendant, 484
   Phillips v William Whitely (1938), 484–485
  skilful claimants, 484
   Roles v Nathan (1963), 484
  unhappy outcomes, 486
   Luxmoore May v Messenger May Bakers (1990, CA), 486
Bridgestone, 198
British Aerospace, 10
British Gas, 10, 239
BSkyB, 9
budget deficit, 306
budget surplus, 306
Bush, G. W., 222
business activity, employment and inflation
  business cycles
   and aggregate demand, 295–296
   aggregate demand and course, 296–298
   aggregate supply and 'real business cycles,' 299
  determination of
   circular flow of income, 276
   identifying equilibrium level of GDP, 277–278
   multiplier, 278–279
   principle of cumulative causation, 276
  inflation targeting and unemployment, 292–295
  relationship between money and GDP
   aggregate demand and money supply, 280–282
   aggregate demand and output/prices, 282
   equation of exchange, 280
  unemployment and inflation
   effect of expectations, 287–290
   expectations of output and employment, 291
   Phillips curve, 285–287
   rational expectations, 290–291
   at same time, 284–285
   simple Keynesian model, 282–284
business agreements, 406
business cycles
  and actual growth, 245–247
  and aggregate demand, 295–296
   fluctuations in stocks, 296
   instability of investment, accelerator, 295–296
  aggregate demand and course, 296–298
   accelerator, 297
   'bandwagon' effects, 297
   booms and recessions, 297–298
   ceilings and floors, 297
   changes in government policy, 297
   echo effects, 297
   random shocks, 297
   time lags, 297
  and aggregate supply, 299
   supply-side effects, 299
   turning points, 299
  defined, 246
  and macroeconomic objectives, 269
business efficacy, 414

business organisations (firms), 2–16
  defined, 3
  internal structure of, 10–15
   flat organisation, 12
   M-form, 11–12
   multinationals, 12–15
   U-form, 10–11
  legal structure of, 7–10
   companies, 9
   consortia, 9
   cooperatives, 9–10
   partnerships, 7–8
   public corporations, 10
   sole proprietor, 7
  nature of, 2–7, 14
   complex production process, 3–4
   goals, 4–5
   principal–agent relationship, 5–6
   survival, 6–7
'but for' principle, 487

C

Camelot, 120–121
'cap and trade' scheme, 220, 223
capital expenditure, 307
capital intensity, 335
car pool agreements, 404
car tax, 231
'carbon tax,' 218
carbon-based fuels, 217
Cardiff Bus, 197
cartels, 131, 198–199
causation in fact: 'but for' rule, 487–493
  Barnett v Chelsea & Kensington Hospital Management Committee (1969), 487
  lost chances, 490
  McWilliams v Arrol (1962), 487
  multiple causes, 487–490
   Compensation Act 2006, s 3, 486–487
   expansion, 489
   Fairchild v Glenhaven Funeral Services (2002, HL), 488–489
   McGhee v National Coal Board (1972, HL), 488
   restriction, 489
   Wilsher v Essex Area Health Authority (1988, HL), 488
causation in law, remoteness of damage
  'eggshell skull' rule, 492
   Mattocks v Mann (1993), 493
   Smith v Leech Brain & Co. Ltd (1962), 492–493
  Hughes v Lord Advocate (1963, HL), 491
  intervening acts, 491–492
   McKew v Holland & Cubitts Ltd (1969, HL), 491–492
   Reeves v Commissioner of Police for the Metropolis (1999, HL), 492
   Wieland v Cyril Lord Carpets (1969), 492
  Jolley v London Borough of Sutton (2000, HL), 491
  Overseas Tankships & Engineering v Morts Dock & Engineering Ltd (The Wagon Mound (No. 1)) (1961, PC), 490–491

central government, deficits/surpluses
    general government, 306
    whole public sector, 306–307
        public sector deficits, 315–316
        total public expenditure, 307–308
change in demand, 21, 25, 33
change in quantity supplied, 29, 49
change in supply, 21, 29, 36
change in quantity demanded, 25
Channel Tunnel, 9
charterparty, 417
'cheap offers,' 378
child benefit, 271, 309
Chrysler, 136
circular flow of income
    injections, 272
    inner flow, 270–271
    and macroeconomic objectives, 272–273
    withdrawals, 271–272
claimant unemployment, 254
Clayton Act of 1914, 201
Climate Change and Sustainable Energy Act (2006), 224
Climate Change Programme (2006), 224
Cline, W. R., 221
'close bond of love and affection,' 473
CO_2 emissions, 221
Coase, Ronald, 3
Coase theorem, 174
Coca-Cola, 129
Cohesion Fund, EU, 347
collusive oligopoly, 130–133
    cartels, 131
    favourable factors, 133
    tacit collusion, 131–132
collusive tendering, 196
command-and-control (CAC) systems, 219–220
Common Foreign and Security Policy (CFSP), 352
communication methods
    conduct, 386–387
    electronic communications, 387–388
    post rule, 388
    requirement of particular method, 390
    verbal communication, 387
    waiving communication rule, 389–390
companies, legal structure of, 9
    private limited, 9
    public limited, 9
Compensation Act 2006, 486–487, 489–490
Competition Act (1998), 194, 195
Competition Appeal Tribunal (CAT), 137, 196
Competition Commission (CC), 136–137, 177, 195, 200, 236, 240
competition for corporate control, 118
competition policy, 106
    advantages, 191–192
    cartel cases, 198
    EU policy, 192–194
        merger policy, 193–194
        monopoly policy, 193
        restrictive practices policy, 192–193
        and UK policy, assessment of, 200–201

UK policy, 194–200
    and EU policy, assessment of, 200–201
    merger policy, 200
    monopoly policy, 197–200
    restrictive practices policy, 196–197
complementary goods, 25
composition (with creditors), 402
conduct, 386–387
consequential economic loss, 444
consideration, contract, 376, 396
    Central London Property Trust v High Trees House (1947), 403
    Collins v Godefroy (1831), 398–399
    D & C Builders v Rees (1965, CA), 404
    executed consideration, 396
    executory consideration, 396
    Glasbrook Bros v Glamorgan County Council (1925, HL), 399–400
    Hartley v Ponsonby (1857), 399
    promissory estoppel, 403
    Re McArdle (1951, CA), 397
    Re Selectmove (1995, CA), 400–401
    Re Stewart v Casey (Casey's Patents) (1892, CA), 397
    The rule in Pinnel's Case (1602), 401
    rules governing consideration, 396–401
    Stilk v Myrick (1809), 399
    Thomas v Thomas (1842), 398
    White v Bluett (1853), 398
    Williams v Roffey Bros (1990, CA), 400
consortia, legal structure of, 9
constrained discretion, 326–329
consumer cooperatives, 10
Consumer Credit Act 1974, 357, 376, 430
Consumer Credit Counselling Service (CCCS), 402
consumer, defined, 424
consumer prices index (CPI), 263, 293
Consumer Protection Act 1987, 379, 439, 446
    A and Others v National Blood Authority (2001), 447
    Abouzaid v Mothercare (UK) Ltd (2000, CA), 452–453
    Bogle & Others v McDonalds Restaurants Ltd (2002), 448–459
    defences, 450–451
    European Commission v UK (1997, ECJ), 452
    fault and strict liability, difference, 446
    impact, 452
    main provisions of, 446–449
    Piper v JRI (Manufacturing) Ltd (2006), 449
    time limits, 451
consumer surplus, 169
consumption of domestically produced goods and services (Cd), 275
contestable markets, theory of, 118–121
    assessment of, 119–121
    case study, 120–121
    costless exit, 119
    and monopolies, 119
    perfectly contestable, 118
    potential competition, 118
contextual approach, statutory interpretation, 360
contra proferentem rule, 421

contract, law of
  acceptance, 384–390
  Bigg v Boyd Gibbons (1971, CA), 379–380
  Blackpool & Fylde Aero Club v Blackpool Council
    (1990, CA), 381
  Bloom v American Swiss Watch Co. (1915), 380
  Bradbury v Morgan (1862), 382
  Carlill v Carbolic Smoke Ball Co.
    Ltd (1893, CA), 380
  Errington v Errington & Woods (1952, CA), 384
  essentials of binding contract, 376
  Fisher v Bell (1961, CA), 378
  Foley v Classique Coaches (1934, CA), 377
  Guthing v Lynn (1831), 377
  Harvey v Facey (1893), 379
  Hillas v Arcos (1932, HL), 377
  Hyde v Wrench (1840), 382
  offer, 376–390
  Pharmaceutical Society (GB) v Boots Cash Chemists (Southern) Ltd
    (1953, CA), 378–379
  Ramsgate Hotel Co. Ltd v Montefiore (1866), 383
Contracts (Rights of Third Parties) Act 1999, 397,
    408, 409, 423
contractual terms
  express and implied terms, 414
    business efficacy, 414
    sources, 414
    Statute: Sale of Goods Act 1979, 414
    trade custom and practice, 414
  importance of, 415–418
    Bettini v Gye (1876), 416
    conditions, 415
    George Mitchell v Finney Lock Seeds Ltd (1983, HL), 426
    Green v Cade Bros (1978), 425
    Hong Kong Fir Shipping Co. Ltd v Kawasaki Kisen Kaisha
      (1962, CA), 416
    innominate terms, 416–418
    Lombard North Central plc v Butterworth
      (1987, CA), 417
    Poussard v Spiers & Pond (1876), 415
    Reardon Smith Line v Hansen-
      Tangen (1976, HL), 418
    Schuler AG v Wickman Machine Tool
      Sales (1974, HL), 417
    Smith v Eric S. Bush (1989, HL), 425
    St Albans City and District Council v International Computers
      Ltd (1996, CA), 426
    warranties, 415
    Watford Electronics v Sanderson
      (2001, CA), 426–427
  limitation and exclusion of liability, 418–431
    Andrews v Singer (1934), 421
    Chapelton v Barry UDC (1940, CA), 419
    comparison of UCTA 1977 and UTCCR 1999, 432
    Curtis v Chemical Cleaning & Dyeing Co. (1951, CA), 421
    draft Unfair Contract Terms Bill, 422–423, 432–433
    exclusion clause, 421
    fundamental breach, 421–422
    incorporation, 419–421
    Interfoto Picture Library Ltd v Stiletto Productions (1988,
      CA), 420–421
    Kendall v Lillico (1968, HL), 420
    McCutcheon v David McBrayne Ltd (1964, HL), 420
    Olley v Marlborough Court Hotel (1949, CA), 419
    Photo Production Ltd v Securicor Transport
      Ltd (1980, HL), 422
    reform of unfair terms legislation, 432–433
    Thornton v Shoe Lane Parking (1971, CA), 419
    Unfair Contract Terms Act 1977, 422–423
    Unfair Terms in Consumer Contracts
      Regulations 1999 (UTCCR 1999), 428–431
Cooperative Bank, 185
cooperatives, legal structure of, 9–10
  consumer, 10
  producer, 10
Cornwall, 262
corporation tax, 271, 337, 343, 346
costs
  long-run cost, 82–86
    average cost, 82–83
    economies of scale, 84–85
    and short-run average cost, relationship
      between, 83
  long-run production, 74–82
    changes in, 65–66
    industry size, 77
    location, importance of, 77, 78–79
    scale of, 74–76
    techniques, 77, 80–81
    time periods, decision making in, 81–82
  opportunity costs, 63–65
    measuring factors, 64–65
  short-run cost, 69–74
    average/marginal cost, 71–74
    and inputs, relationship between, 69–70
    and long-run average cost, relationship
      between, 83
    total cost (TC), 70–71
  short-run production, 65–69
    average/marginal product, 67–69
    changes in, 65–66
    diminishing returns, 66
    total product, 66–67
cost–benefit analysis, 229
cost-push inflation, 267
Council of Ministers, 352
counter-offer, 382
countervailing power, 139
Cournot model, 134–135
courts
  Adler v George (1964), 360
  binding precedent, 363
    advantages and disadvantages, 365–366
    court hierarchy, 363
    importance of law reporting system, 365
    persuasive precedents, 365
    reversing and overruling decisions, 364–365
    scope of ratio decidendi, 364
  creative powers, 358
  external aids, 359
  Fisher v Bell (1961), 360
  interpretative powers, 358–359

external aids, 359
intrinsic aids, 359
judicial presumptions, 362
judicial principles of statutory interpretation, 360
contextual approach, 360
golden rule, 360
literal rule, 360
mischief rule, 361
purposive approach, 361
Pepper v Hart, 359
Royal College of Nursing v DHSS (1981, HL), 361–362
Smith v Hughes (1960), 361
Sweet v Parsley (1969, HL), 362–363
court hierarchy, 363–364
court of appeal, 364
divisional courts, 364
high court, 364
House of Lords, 363
court of appeal, 364
Court of First Instance (CFI), 354
credible threats/promises, 142
Credit Guarantee Scheme, 318
Criminal Injuries Compensation Board, 480
cross-price elasticity of demand, 48, 49
crowding out, 309
cumulative causation, 276
current expenditure, 307

D

'damage test,' 416
Damages (Asbestos-Related Conditions) (Scotland) Act 2009, 470
deadweight welfare loss, 171
DealTime, 110
decision, 363
decision tree, 144
deflationary gap, 283–284
delegated legislation, 357–358
advantages/disadvantages, 357–358
bye-laws, 357
defined, 357
orders in council, 357
regulations to implement law from EU, 357
statutory instruments, 357
demand curve, 24
demand management, 324–329
case for discretion, 325–326
choice of target under rules-based policy, 325–326
Goodhart's law, 325
Taylor rule, 326
case for rules and policy frameworks
political behaviour, 324–325
time lags with discretionary policy, 324–325
constrained discretion in UK, 326–329
CPI inflation and GDP growth projections, 327
fiscal policy, 328–329
monetary policy, 326–328
response to credit crunch, 328–329

demand schedules, 23–24
demand-deficient/cyclical unemployment, 259–260
demand-pull inflation, 266–267
demand-side policy
attitudes towards demand management, 324–329
fiscal policy, 305–314
monetary policy, 314–324
Denning, Justice, 403
destabilising speculation, 54–55
direct effect, 368
direct (parliamentary/primary) legislation, 355
Directives, 354–355
discretionary fiscal policy, 308–309
diseconomies of scale, 76
disequilibrium unemployment, 259–260
defined, 259
demand-deficient/cyclical unemployment, 259–260
real-wage, 259
divisional courts, 364
domestic and social agreements, 404–405
Albert v Motor Insurers Bureau (1971, HL), 404
Balfour v Balfour (1919, CA), 404
Simpkins v Pays (1955, CA), 405
Wilson and Anor v Burnett (2007, CA), 405
dominant firm price leadership, 132
dominant strategy games, 140–141
Dunlop Oil & Marine/Continental, 198
duopoly, 134
duty of care, 440
limits of duty of care, 442–443
and pure economic loss, 444
scope and influence of Lord Atkin's judgment, 441
duty situations (problematic), 460–482
negligent statements
Caparo Industries plc v Dickman (1990, HL), 467
Hedley Byrne v Heller (1963, HL), 464
just and reasonable, 466
McNaughten (James) Paper Group Ltd v Hicks Anderson & Co. (1991, CA), 467
Morgan Crucible Co. plc v Hill Samuel Bank (1991, CA), 467
proximity, 464
reliance and responsibility, 465–466
restriction of *Hedley Byrne* principle, 466
Smith v Eric S. Bush (1989, HL), 464–465
'special relationship,' 464
Spring v Guardian Assurance (1994), 465
T v Surrey County Council (1994), 468
nervous shock (psychiatric harm), 469
Alcock v Wright (1991, HL), 473–474
Chadwick v British Rail (1967), 471
close bond of love and affection', 473–474
Dooley v Cammell Laird (1951), 471
Dulieu v White (1901), 469
Hambrook v Stokes (1925, CA), 473
involuntary participants, 470
Johnston and Others v NEI International (2007, HL), 470
McLoughlin v O'Brian (1982, HL), 473
Monk v Harrington Ltd and Others (2008), 472
negligent statements and nervous shock, 472
Page v Smith (1995, HL), 469–470

Palmer v Tees Health Authority (1999, CA), 475
   primary victims, 469–472
   secondary victims, 472
   'sudden and immediate attack,' 473
   sufficiently proximate, 474
   Taylorson v Shieldness Products (1994, CA), 474
   Walters v North Glamorgan NHS Trust (2002), 475
   White v Chief Constable of South Yorkshire (1999, HL), 471–472
omissions to act and liability for damage caused by third parties
   'false omissions' may give rise to duty of care, 476
   Home Office v Dorset Yacht Co. Ltd (1970, HL), 477–476
   omissions, 476–477
   Smith v Littlewoods Organisation (1987, HL), 477
public authorities and statutory discretion
   Capital and Counties Bank plc v Hampshire Fire Brigade (1997, CA), 478–479
   Chief Constable Hertfordshire v Van Colle and Smith v Chief Constable of Sussex (2008, HL), 480
   education and social services, 480–481
   fire brigade and ambulance services, 478
   impact of Human Rights Act 1998, 481
   Kent v Griffiths and Others (No. 3) (2001, CA), 479
   Osman v Ferguson (1993, CA), 479–480
   police, 479
pure economic loss, 460–463
   Murphy v Brentwood Council (1990, HL), 461–462
   Spartan Steel Alloys v Martin Ltd (1972, CA), 460–461
   West Bromwich Albion Football Club Ltd v El-Safty (2007), 463
   White v Jones (1995, HL), 462–463

E

eBay, 110–111
e-commerce, 110–111
Economic Community (EC), 352
Economic duress, 399
economic growth
   actual growth, 245–246
   defined, 245
   output gaps, 248
   policies, 252
   potential growth, 245, 252
economic profit, 98
economies of scale, 75–76
   as barrier, 112
   defined, 75
   reasons of, 75–76
   survey, 84, 85
economies of scope, 76, 112
'effective ownership,' 5
'eggshell skull' rule, 492
ejusdem generis rule, 360
elasticity of demand
   defined, 40, 42
   measurement of, 46–47

Electronic Commerce (EC Directive) Regulations 2002, 388
electronic communications, 387–388
electronic road pricing (ERP), 232
e-mail and management information systems, 12
Emergency Powers Act 1939/1984, 357
Emerson, M., 84
Emissions Trading Scheme (ETS), 220
employees' national insurance contributions, 271
Enterprise Act (2002), 194
envelope curve, 83
Environment Act (1995), 224
environmental policy, 214–224
   defined, 215
   intervention problems, 215–216
   Kyoto Protocol, 222–223
   options, 216–224
      command-and-control systems, 219–220
      taxation, 216–219
      tradable permits, 220–224
   and production, 215
   Stern Review, 221
   UK/EU policy, 224
Environmental Policy Review (2007), 224
environmental scanning, 181
equation of exchange, 292
equilibrium, 20
equilibrium price, 20, 32
equilibrium/natural unemployment, 260–262
   defined, 258
   frictional (search), 261
   seasonal, 262
   structural, 261–262
equity, 164–165
Ethical Investment Research Service, 187
Ethisphere, 186
EU policies
   competition policy, 192–194
      merger policy, 193–194
      monopoly policy, 193
      restrictive practices policy, 192–193
      and UK policy, assessment of, 200–201
   environmental policy, 220, 222–223, 224
   technology policy/R&D, 203–206
European Atomic Energy Treaty Community (EURATOM), 352
European Central Bank (ECB), 312, 314
European Coal and Steel Community (ECSC), 352
European Commission, 192, 194, 353
European Communities Act 1972 (ECA 1972), 352, 357
European Convention on Human Rights, 366–367
European Council, 353
European Court of Human Rights (ECtHR), 366
European Court of Justice (ECJ), 353–354
European Fund for Regional Development, 347
European law
   impact of EU membership on English law, 355
   institutions
      Council of Ministers, 352
      Councils, 352–353
      European Commission, 353

European Council, 352, 353
European Court of Justice (ECJ), 353–354
European Parliament, 353
  sources
    decisions, 355
    directives, 354–355
    regulations, 354
    treaties, 354
European Parliament, 353
European Regional Development Fund (ERDF), 346–347
European Social Fund (ESF), 347
European Strategic Programme for Research in Information Technology (ESPRIT), 206
European System of Central Banks (ESCB), 320
European Union, institutions
  Council of Ministers, 352
  Councils, 352–353
  European Commission, 352
  European Council, 352, 353
  European Court of Justice (ECJ), 353–354
  European Parliament, 353
excess burden of taxes, 175
excess capacity, 127
exchange rates, 244
exclusion clause, 418
executed consideration, 396
executory consideration, 396
expectations-augmented Phillips curve, 287
expenditure method (GDP measurement), 278–279
explicit costs, 64
express term, 414
external benefits, 165
external costs, 165
external diseconomies of scale, 77
external economies of scale, 77
externalities, 165–167, 172, 178, 345

F

Facebook, 117
factor market, 22
'fan charts,' 327
fault liability, 446
FBI, 198
Federal Open Market Committee, 323
Fiat, 136
final expenditure, 307
financial crowding out, 315
fine tuning, 306
firms
  defined, 3, 180
  and social responsibility, 180–188
    economic performance and, 184–188
    views of, 180–181
    virtue matrix, 181–184
first-mover advantage, 144
fiscal policy, 305–309, 311
  deficits and surpluses
    central government, 306–308
    general government, 306
  defined, 305
  discretion back into, 311–313
  effectiveness, 309–314
  fiscal rules, 311–314
  problems of magnitude, 309–310
    crowding out, 309
    predicting effect of changes in government expenditure, 309
    predicting effect of changes in taxes, 309–310
    predicting resulting multiplied effect on national income, 310
    pure fiscal policy, 309
    random shocks, 310
  problems of timing, 310–311
  use of fiscal policy, 308–309
    automatic fiscal stabilisers, 308
    discretionary fiscal policy, 308–309
fixed cost, 70
fixed factors, 65
flat organisation, 12
food retailing, 97
Ford, 20
formal complaint systems, 480
franchising, 239
free market, 20
  advantages of, 179–180
free-rider problem, 168
frictional (search) unemployment, 261
FTSE 100 (Financial Times Stock Exchange), 34
fuel taxes, 231
full-employment level of GDP, 283
fundamental breach, 421
funding, 318–319
future price, 57
futures/forward markets, 57–59
  buyers, 58–59
  price determination, 59
  sellers, 57
  speculators, 59

G

game theory, 140–145
  advantage of, 144–145
  defined, 140
  multiple-move games, 142–145
    credible threats/promises, 142
    decision tree, 144
    timing, importance of, 142–144
  prisoner's dilemma, case study, 143
  single-move games, 140–142
    complex games with no dominant strategy, 141–142
    dominant strategy games, 140–141
Gap, 184
Garnaut Climate Change Review, 221
General Motors, 2, 204, 205
General National Vocational Qualifications (GNVQs), 208
Giorno, C., 248
global sourcing, 15
global warming, 166, 170, 214, 218, 219, 221

good faith, 428
Goodhart, Charles, 325
Goodhart's law, 325
goods market, 22
Google, 117
Gössling, T., 185
government and individual firms, 191
   competition policy, 191–201
      advantages, 191–192
      case study, 198–199
      in European Union, 192–194
      EU/UK policy, assessment of, 200–201
      UK policy, 194–200
   technology policy/R&D, 201–206
      change and market failure, 202
      forms of intervention, 203
      stages, 201–202
      in UK/EU, 203–206
   training policies, 207–212
      approaches, 207
      and economic performance, 207
      Leitch review, 210–211
      UK policy, 208–212
      in various countries, 207–208
government and whole market, 214–241
   environmental policy, 214–224
      defined, 215
      intervention problems, 215–216
      options, 216–224
      UK/EU policy, 224
   privatisation, 234–235
      advantages/disadvantages of, 234–235
   regulation, 235–240
      competition in privatised industries, 239–240
      identifying short-run optimum price/output, 235–236
      in practice, 236–237
      in UK, 238–239
   transport policy, 225–234
      road space allocation, 225–227
      road usage, socially efficient level of, 227–229
      traffic congestion, solutions to, 229–234
government intervention, 163–189
   drawbacks of, 178–179
      bureaucracy and inefficiency, 179
      lack of individuals' freedom, 179
      lack of market incentives, 179
      poor information, 178
      shifts in government policy, 179
      shortages and surpluses, 178
   firms and social responsibility, 180–188
      economic performance and, 184–188
      views of, 180–181
      virtue matrix, 181–184
   forms of, 172–178
      direct provision of goods and services, 177–178
      information provision, 177
      price controls, 177
      prohibition laws, 176–177
      property rights, 174
      taxes/subsidies, 172–174
   and market failure, types of, 165–171
      externalities, 165–167
      ignorance/uncertainty, 171
      immobility/time-lags, 171
      market power, 168–171
      protecting people's interests, 171
      public goods, 167–168
   objectives, 163–165
      equity, 164–165
      social efficiency, 163–164
   vs. free market, 179–180
      advantages of capitalism, 179
      automatic adjustments, 179
      competitive forces, 179–180
government surplus, 175
grandfathering, 220
gratuitous promise, 395
Green Paper, 356
green taxes, 217, 218
gross domestic product (GDP) 245, 298
growth maximisation, 155–156

H

Hall, R. L., 135
Health and Safety at Work Act 1974, 357
H-form enterprises, 12
high court, 364
historic cost, 64, 65
Hitch, C. J., 135
holding company, 12
House of Commons, 355, 356
House of Lords, 356, 361
Human Rights Act 1998 (HRA 1998) 366–370, 382
   impact, 367–368
      defective services, 481
      direct effect, 368
      indirect effect, 369–370
   judges' functions
      Interpretation of Convention rights (s 2), 367
      Interpretation of legislation (s 3), 367
      Judicial remedies (s 8), 367
   legal and political background to Act, 366–367
      European Convention on Human Rights, 366–367
   operation of HRA 1998, 367–370
      judges' functions, 367
   R (on the application of Begum) v *Headteacher and Governors of Denbigh High School* (2006, HL), 369
   R (on the application of Laporte) v *Chief Constable of Gloucestershire Constabulary* (2007, HL), 368
   R (on the application of Pearson) v *Secretary of State for the Home Department and Martinez; Hirst* v *Attorney General* (2001), 367
hysteresis, 293

I

imperfect competition
   defined, 106
   game theory, 140–145

advantage of, 144–145
multiple moves, 142–145
prisoner's dilemma, case study, 143
single move, 140–142
monopolistic competition, 125–129
assumptions of, 125
case study, Britain's 'eating-out' sector, 128–129
limitations of, 126–127
perfect competition/monopoly, comparison with, 127–129
short/long-run equilibrium, 125–126
oligopoly, 129–140
collusive, 130–133
and consumers, 139
and contestable markets, 139–140
features of, 130
non-collusive, 133–138
imperfect competition, 106
implicit costs, 64–65
implied term, 414, 423
importer, 447
incapacity benefit, 254, 340
income effect, 23, 337
income elasticity of demand, 48–49
income tax, 257, 271, 337
incorporation, 419–421
sufficiency, 420
timing, 419
independence, 125
Individual Voluntary Arrangement (IVA), 402
indivisibilities, 75
industry's infrastructure, 77
inferior goods, 25
infinitely elastic demand, 45
inflation
aggregate demand/supply/level of prices analysis, 265–266
causes of, 266–268
coping with low rates, 268
costs of, 264–265
defined, 244, 264
inflation targeting and unemployment
changes in equilibrium unemployment, 293–294
hysteresis, 293
structural unemployment, 292–293
inflation targeting, 292–295
inflationary gap, 284
injections (J), 272
innominate term, 414, 416–418
Insolvency Act 1986, 402
integrated international enterprise, 15
intention to create legal relations, 404
business agreements, 406
Rose & Frank Co. v *J.R. Crompton & Bros* (1925, HL), 406
domestic and social agreements, 404–405
Albert v *Motor Insurers Bureau* (1971, HL), 404–405
Balfour v *Balfour* (1919, CA), 404
Simpkins v *Pays* (1955, CA), 405
Wilson and Anor v *Burnett* (2007, CA), 405

interdependence, 130
Intergovernmental Panel on Climate Change, 221, 222
intermediate goods and services, 334
International Labour Organisation (ILO), 254
Internet, 201
Interpretation Act 1978, 359
intervening acts, 491–493
interventionist supply-side policies, 341–344
advice and persuasion, 343
approach to industrial policy, 343
assistance to small firms, 343
direct provision, 342
funding research and development, 342
information, 343–344
nationalisation, 342
training and education, 342
invitation to treat, 378–379
involuntary participants, 470
IVA controversy, 402

J

J. Pereira Fernandes SA v *Mehta* (2006), 381
Jackson, Thomas Penfield, 116
Japan Fair Trade Commission, 198
joint-stock company, 4
just-in-time methods, 158

K

Kelkoo, 110
Ketels, C. H. M., 78
Keynes, John Maynard, 259, 277
'Keynesian 45° line diagram,' 277
Keynesians, 260, 325
KFC, 128
kinked demand theory, 135, 138
'knowledge economy,' 14
Kyoto Protocol, 222–223

L

labour force, 254
Law Commission (Report No. 242), 1996, 408
Law Commission Report (No. 249, *Liability for Psychiatric Damage*), 1998, 475
law of demand, 23
law of diminishing (marginal) returns, 66
Law of Property (Miscellaneous Provisions) Act 1989, 376
Learndirect, 209
Learning and Skills Council (LSC), 208
legally binding option, 384
Leitch Committee, 209, 210–211
Leitch, Lord, 209
Lenin, Vladimir, 58
level of prices, aggregate demand/supply, 265–269
Liability Act 1957, 359
Limitation Act 1980, 451
limitation clause, 418, 426

Linux, 117
liquidity trap, 322
literal rule, 360–362
local management of schools scheme (LMS), 340
Locally negotiated wage agreements, 345
London Stock Exchange, 34
long run, time period, 66
long run under perfect competition, 108, 115
long-run average cost (*LRAC*) curves, 82–86
   assumptions, 83
   and short-run, relationship between, 83–84
long-run profit maximisation, 151, 154, 156
long-run shut-down point, 99
L'Oréal, 186

M

Maastricht Treaty in 1992, 311, 352, 353
macroeconomic objectives
   aggregate demand/supply/level of prices analysis, 265–266
   balance of payments, 244
   business cycle and, 269
   and circular flow of income, 270–273
   economic growth, 244, 245–252
   inflation, 244, 263–268
   unemployment, 244, 253–262
Major, John, 234
managerial utility maximisation, 152–154
Manchester United football club, 9
Manuli, 198
marginal cost (*MC*), 71–73
   and average cost, 73–74
marginal physical product (*MPP*), 67–69
marginal revenue (*MR*), 90, 92
marginal social benefit (*MSB*), 164–167, 172, 215, 227–229
marginal social costs (*MSC*), 172, 215
markets
   demand, 23–26
      curve, 23–24
      curve shifts, 25–26
      determinants of, 24–25
      and price, 23
   operation of, 19–22
      demand/supply changes, 21–22
      interdependence of, 21–22
      price mechanism, 20–21
   power, 20
   price and output determination, 29–36
      demand/supply curves, 32–33
      demand/supply curve shifts, 33–36
   structure
      categories/features, 104
      concentration ratios, 105
   supply, 26–29
      curve, 27–28
      curve shifts, 29
      determinants of, 28–29
      and price, 26–27

market clearing, 32
market demand schedule, 23
market failure, types of, 165–171
   and environment protection, 170
   externalities, 165–167
      benefits of consumption (*MSB>MB*), 167
      benefits of production (*MSC<MC*), 166
      costs of consumption (*MSB<MB*), 166
      costs of production (*MSC>MC*), 165–166
   ignorance/uncertainty, 171
   immobility/time-lags, 171
   power under monopoly, 168–171
      deadweight loss, 169, 171
      effect on total surplus, 169–171
   protecting people's interests, 171
   public goods, 167–168
market price elasticity, 39–60
   adjustment, time period and, 51–56
      expectations and speculation, 52–56
      short-run and long-run adjustment, 51–52
   of demand, 40–43
      and decision-making, 43–47
      defined, 41–42
      determinants of, 42–43, 48–51
   futures/forward markets, 57–59
      buyers, 58–59
      price determination, 59
      sellers, 57
      speculators, 59
   of supply
      defined, 49
      determinants of, 50–51
   uncertainty, risk and, 56–59
market-orientated supply-side policies, 335–341
   policies to encourage competition, 340–341
      deregulation, 340
      free trade and capital movements, 341
      market relationships into public sector, 340–341
      Private Finance Initiative (PFI), 341
      privatisation, 340
   productivity and economic growth, 338
   reducing government expenditure, 336
   reducing power of labour, 337
   reducing welfare, 338–339
   tax cuts, 336–337
      income effects of, 337
      substitution effects of, 337
   total general government expenditure, 336
Markets and Policy Initiatives Division (MPI), 195
Marks & Spencer, 9
Martin, Roger L., 181
mass rail transit (MRT) system, 232
maximax, 141
maximin, 141
McDonald's, 125, 128, 184, 449
Means, G. C., 5
menu costs of inflation, 263
merger policy, 193–194, 200
merit goods, 171
M-form business organisation, 11–12
Microsoft, 116–117, 152–153

minimum efficient plant size (*MEPS*), 84
minimum efficient scale (*MES*), 84
minimum reserve ratio, 315, 319
Mintel, 128, 153
mischief rule, 361
'monetary financial institutions' (MFIs), 321
monetary policy, 314–324
    control of money supply over medium/long term, 315–317
        liquidity of banks, 315
        public-sector deficits, 315–316
    daily operation of monetary policy, 318
    effectiveness of changes in interest rates, 319
    monetary policy in Eurozone, 320–321
        role of ECB, 320–321
    policy setting, 314–315
    quantitative easing, 323
    rethinking monetary policy in hard times, 323
    short-term monetary measures, 316–317
    techniques to control interest rates, 319–322
        effectiveness of changes, 321
        problem of inelastic demand for loans, 321–332
        problem of unstable demand, 322
    techniques to control money supply, 317–319
        central bank lending to banks, 317–318
        difficulties in controlling money supply, 319
        funding, 318–319
        open-market operations, 317
        variable minimum reserve ratios, 319
    using monetary policy, 322–324
Monetary Policy Committee (MPC), 314, 318, 321, 327
money and GDP, relationship between
    aggregate demand and output/prices, 282
    change in aggregate demand/output and prices, 282
    equation of exchange, 280
    money supply and aggregate demand, 280–282
        long run, 281–282
        short run, 280–281
    velocity of circulation, 280
monopolistic competition, 104, 125–129
    assumptions of, 125
    case study, Britain's 'eating-out' sector, 128–129
    equilibrium of, 125–126
    limitations of, 126–127
    perfect competition/monopoly, comparison with, 127–129
monopoly, 112–121
    case study, 116–117
    defined, 103–104, 112
    entry barriers, 112–113
    equilibrium price/output, 113–114
    EU policy, 193
    UK policy, 197
    vs. perfect competition, 114–118
multinationals
    H-form, 12
    integrated international enterprise, 15
    transnational association, 15
multiplier
    defined, 278
    effect, 276
    formula, 279
mutuality, 395

N

naked promise, 395
Nandos, 128
Nash equilibrium, 135, 141, 143, 144
Nash, John, 135
National Health Service, 309, 340
National Lottery Commission (NLC), 120–121
National Vocational Qualification (NVQ), 208
nationalised industries, 10, 234, 235
natural monopoly, 112
natural rate of unemployment or non-accelerating inflation unemployment (NAIRU), 290, 292, 293
negative equity, 30
negligence liability, 423–427
    Barnett v *Packer* (1940), 442
    duty of care, 440
        limits of duty of care, 442
        pure economic loss, 444
        scope and influence of Lord Atkin's judgment, 441
Neighbour principle, 441
Neighbourhoods and Environment Act (2005), 224
nervous shock (psychiatric harm), 469
    Alcock v *Wright* (1991, HL), 473–474
    Chadwick v *British Rail* (1967), 471
    close bond of love and affection, 473–474
    Dooley v *Cammell Laird* (1951), 471
    Dulieu v *White* (1901), 469
    Hambrook v *Stokes* (1925, CA), 473
    involuntary participants, 470
    Johnston and Others v *NEI International* (2007, HL), 470
    McLoughlin v *O'Brian* (1982, HL), 473
    Monk v *Harrington Ltd and Others* (2008), 472
    negligent statements and nervous shock, 472
    Page v *Smith* (1995, HL), 469–470
    Palmer v *Tees Health Authority* (1999, CA), 475
    primary victims, 469–472
    secondary victims, 472
    'sudden and immediate attack,' 473
    sufficiently proximate, 474
    Taylorson v *Shieldness Products* (1994, CA), 474
    Walters v *North Glamorgan NHS Trust* (2002), 475
    White v *Chief Constable of South Yorkshire* (1999, HL), 471–472
Nestlé, 184, 186, 398
Netscape Communications, 116
Network Rail, 120, 236, 357
'new classical' economists, 290
Nike, 184
Nintendo, 129, 152–153
noise pollution, 219, 357, 362
'nominal ownership,' 5
non-collusive oligopoly, 133–138
    assumptions about rivals' behaviour, 134–138
    breakdown of collusion, 133–134
    defined, 130
non-excludability, 167–168
non-rivalry, 167–168

normal goods, 25
normal profit, 97–98
normal-form game, 140, 146
Northern Rock, 10, 315
number unemployed, 253

O

Obama, Barack, 222
obiter dictum (persuasive ruling), 365, 403
Occupiers' Liability Act 1957, 359
offer
   bilateral, 376
   clearly stated terms, 377
   death, 382
   intention to do business, 378
      invitation to treat, 378–379
      negotiation, 379
   lapse of time
      counter-offer, 382
   offer/offeree, communication, 380
   tenders, 381
   termination of
      death, 382
      lapse of time, 382
      refusal and counter-offer, 382
      revocation, 383–384
   unilateral, 376
offeree, 376
offeror, 376
Office for Gas and Electricity Markets (Ofgem), 236
Office of Communications (Ofcom), 236
Office of Fair Trading (OFT), 177, 194, 236, 238, 431
Office of Rail Regulation (ORR), 236
Office of Water Services (Ofwat), 236
Official Secrets Act 1920, 360
oligopoly, 104, 129–140
   case study, industrial sectors, 136–137
   collusive, 130–133
      cartels, 131
      favourable factors, 133
      tacit collusion, 131–132
   and consumers, 139
   and contestable markets, 139–140
   features of, 130
   non-collusive, 133–138
      assumptions about rivals' behaviour, 134–138
      breakdown of collusion, 133–134
open-market operations (OMOs), 317, 318
opportunity cost, 64–65
   case study, 64
   defined, 63
   explicit costs, 64
   historic cost, 65
   implicit costs, 64–65
   replacement cost, 65
   sunk cost, 65
Organisation for Economic Co-operation and Development (OECD), 254
organisational slack, 157–158, 157–159
Organization of Petroleum Exporting Countries (OPEC), 54

output gap, 245
overhead costs, 76
overrule, 365
own-brand 'value' products, 137
ownership and separation of control, 4–5
ozone layer, depletion of, 170, 216, 219

P

Parker ITR, 198
parliament
   Act of Parliament, creation of
      parliamentary procedure, 356
      pre-legislative stage, 356
   delegated legislation, 357–358
      advantages/disadvantages, 357–358
      bye-laws, 357
      orders in council, 357
      regulations to implement law from EU, 357
      statutory instruments, 357
   direct (parliamentary/primary) legislation, 355
   private members' bills, 356
Parliament Acts 1911/1949, 356
partnerships, legal structure of, 7–8
'peculiar economies of scale,' 120
Penfield, Thomas, 116
pensions, 9, 58, 158, 253, 264, 271, 309, 343
The People's Lottery, 121
Per incuriam, 363
perfect competition, 106–112
   assumptions, 106–107
   defined, 103
   e-commerce, 110–111
   economic efficiency, 110–111
   incompatibility with economies of scale, 109–110
   long run equilibrium, 108–109
   market structures, 103–106
   short run equilibrium, 107–108
   vs. monopoly, 114–118
perfectly competitive market, 20
perfectly contestable markets, 118
persuasive decision/precedents, 365
   decisions of Judicial Committee of Privy Council, 365
   Obiter dicta, 365
Peugeot, 198
Pharmacy and Poisons Act 1933, 378
Phillips, A. W., 285
Phillips curve, 285–287
plant economies of scale, 76
Police and Judicial Co-operation in Criminal Matters (PJCCM), 352
pollution taxes, 216–219
Porter, M. E., 78
post rule, 388
potential growth, 245, 249, 252
   availability of resources, 250–251
   productivity of resources, 252
   in UK/France, 252–253
potential output, 245–247
Pratten, C. F., 84
price benchmarks, 133

price controls, 177
price discrimination, 193, 197, 201
price elasticity of demand, 40–43
   and decision-making, 43–47
   defined, 41–42
   determinants of, 42–43, 48–51
price elasticity of supply
   defined, 49
   determinants of, 50–51
price mechanism, 20
price taker, 20, 90
price-cap regulation, 237
primary stock markets, 34
primary victims, nervous shock (psychiatric harm), 469
principal–agent problem, 5–6
   asymmetric information in, 6
prisoner's dilemma
   case study, 143
   defined, 141
Private Finance Initiative (PFI), 341
private limited companies, 9
private members' bills, 356
privatisation and regulation, 234–240
   advantages/disadvantages of privatisation, 234–235
   case study, UK railways, 236–237
   competition in privatised industries, 239–240
   identifying short-run optimum price/output, 235–236
   in practice, 236–237
   in UK, 238–239
privity of contract
   Dunlop Rubber Co. Ltd v *Selfridge* (1915, HL), 407
   exceptions to rule of privity
      agency, 407
      assignment of contractual rights, 407
      collateral contracts, 407
      contracts for benefit of group, 407
      third-party insurance, 407
      trusts, 407
   Jackson v *Horizon Holidays Ltd* (1975, CA), 408
   Shanklin Pier Ltd v *Detel Products Ltd* (1954), 408
   statutory reform of privity rule, 408
      contracts (Rights of Third Parties) Act 1999, 408–409
   Tweddle v *Atkinson* (1861), 406–407
producer
   defined, 446
   cooperatives, 10
   surplus, 169–170
product
   defined, 447
   differentiation, 125
production function, 67
profit maximisation
   case study, 98
   defined, 97–98
   long-run, 97
   long-run shut-down point, 98
   and minimising loss, 98

   short-run
      using average/marginal curves, 95–97
      using total curves, 94–95
   short-run shut-down point, 98
profit satisficers, 151, 154
profit-maximising rule, 95
profit-maximising theories
   alternative theories, 151–156
      case study, video games war, 152
      and consumers, 156
      growth maximisation, 155–156
      long-run profit maximisation, 151–152
      managerial utility maximisation, 152–154
      sales revenue maximisation (short run), 154–155
   multiple aims, 156–159
      behavioural theories, 157–158
      and consumers, 159
      organisational slack, 157–158
      predictions, 159
      satisficing/target setting, 156–157
   traditional theories, problems with, 149–151
      lack of/alternative aims, 150–151
      maximising profit, difficulties in, 149–150
prohibition laws, 176–177
   advantages/disadvantages of, 176
   regulatory bodies, 176–177
promisor, 406
Promissory estoppel (*High Trees* doctrine), 403
proving consequent damage, 487
   causation in fact: 'but for' rule, 487–490
   causation in law (remoteness of damage), 490–493
proximity, 442, 464
public authority, 367
public corporations, legal structure of, 10
public goods, 167–168
public interest, 443
public limited companies, 9
public–private partnerships (PPPs), 341
Public-sector net cash requirement (PSNCR), 307
pure fiscal policy, 309
pure profit, 98
purposive approach, 361

Q

quantitative easing, 323
quantity demanded, 23
'quasi-fiduciary,' 464
quota (set by cartel), 131

R

Race Relations Act 1976, 379
Railways Act (1993), 236
ratio decidendi, 364
rational expectations, 290–291
rationalisation, 76
real business cycle theory, 299

real growth values, 263
real-wage unemployment, 259–260
'reasonable expectations of honest men,' 387
reasonable foreseeability, 442
reasonable man, 482
recessionary or deflationary gap, 283
rectangular hyperbola, 46
regional multiplier effects, 345
regional policy, supply-side policy, 344–347
  approaches, 345–346
    interventionist solutions, 346
    locally negotiated wage agreements, 345
    market-orientated solutions, 345
    provision of facilities in depressed regions, 346
    reducing unemployment benefits, 345
    siting of offices in depressed regions, 346
    subsidies/tax concessions in depressed regions, 346
  causes of regional imbalance and, 344–345
    externalities, 345
    labour and capital immobility, 345
    regional multiplier effects, 345
  regional policy in EU, 346–347
    European Regional Development Fund (ERDF), 346
    European Social Fund (ESF), 347
    objectives and EU structural and cohesion funds, 347
Regulations, 354
Regulations (1999), 432
regulatory capture, 238
repeated games/extensive-form games, 142
replacement cost, 65
Representation of the People Act 1983, 367
resale price maintenance, 196
Research and Technology Programme, 206
'reserve assets,' 310
restrictive practices policy
  EU, 192–193
  UK, 196–197
returns to scale, 74–75
revenue, 89–94
  average revenue (AR), 90
  curves, price is unaffected by firm's output, 90–91
  curves, price varies with output, 91–93
  marginal revenue (MR), 90
  and profit maximisation, 94–99
  shifts in revenue curves, 93–94
  total revenue (TR), 89–90
reversing decision, 364
risk, 56
risk–benefit analysis, 483
road pricing, 231–233
  area charges, 231–232
  variable electronic, 233
Roddick, Anita, 186
Royal Bank of Scotland, 315
RPIX (retail prices index), 293
rule of privity, exceptions
  agency, 407
  assignment of contractual rights, 407
  collateral contracts, 407
  contracts for benefit of group, 407
  third-party insurance, 407
  trusts, 407
rules governing consideration
  move from promisee, 397
  not be past, 396–397
  part payment, 401
  sufficient consideration, 397–401

S

Sainsbury's, 136
Sale of Goods Act 1979, 377, 414, 423
sales revenue maximisation (short run), 154–155
satisficing/target setting, 156–157
scale of production, 74–76
  diseconomies of scale, 76
  economies of scale, 75–76
seasonal unemployment, 262
secondary stock markets, 34
secondary victims, nervous shock (psychiatric harm), 469, 472
self-fulfilling speculation, 53
Seventh Framework Programme, 206
Sex Discrimination Act 1975, 379
Sherman Act of 1890, 201
short run, time period, 66
short run under perfect competition, 107
short-run production cost, 65–69
  average and marginal product, 67–69
  diminishing returns, 66
  and long-run changes, 65–66
  total product, 66–67
short-run shut-down point, 98
significant imbalance (UTCCR 1999), 428
simple/parol contracts, 375
Single European Act of 1987, 341, 353
Sixth Environment Action Programme (2002–(2012), 224
Skype via VoiP (voice internet protocol), 239
small and medium-sized enterprises (SMEs), 137
Smith, Adam, 198
social benefit, 165
social costs, 164–165
social efficiency, 163–164
social responsibility and firms, 180–188
  defined, 180
  economic performance and, 184–188
    access to capital, 187–188
    case study, Body Shop, 186
    employee attraction/retention, 187
    enhanced brand image, 185–187
    improved performance, 185
  views of, 180–181
    classical, 180
    socioeconomic, 180–181
  virtue matrix, 181–184
    civil foundation, 182
    frontier, 182–183
    globalisation, 184
    pressures on companies, 183–184

social security benefits, 309, 336, 343
social-impact standards, 219
sole proprietor, legal structure of, 7
Sony, 2, 152–153
South Korean Federal Trade Commission, 199
Special Liquidity Scheme, 317
special relationship, 464
specialisation and division of labour, 75
speculation, 52–56
   case studies, 54–55, 58
   defined, 52
   destabilising effect, 54–56
   self-fulfilling, 53
   stabilising effect, 53–54
spot price, 57
stabilising speculation, 53–54
Stability and Growth Pact (SGP), 313, 316
stakeholders, 157, 158, 181, 183–184
standard terms, 423
standardised unemployment rates, 254
Statute of Frauds 1677, 376, 381
statutory discretion and public authorities, 478
statutory reform of privity rule, 408
Stern, N., 221
Stock Exchange, 9, 34, 54, 56, 340
stock markets, 34–35
Strategic Rail Authority (SRA), 237
Street Offences Act 1959, 361
strict liability, 446
Structural and Cohesion Funds, 346–347
structural unemployment, 261–262
'subject to contract,' 385
subsidised public transport, 233–234
substitute goods, 25
substitution effect, 23
sudden and immediate attack, 473
sufficiency, 420
sufficiently proximate, 474
Sugal and Dumani UK Ltd, 121
sunk costs, 65, 119
Superdrug, 200
supernormal profit, 98
supply curve, 27
Supply of Goods and Services Act 1982, 423
Supply of Goods (Implied Terms) Act 1973, 423
supply schedule, 27
supply-side policy
   defined, 331
   interventionist, 333, 341–344
   market-orientated, 335–341
   problems, 331–345
   regional imbalances, 334
   regional policy, 344–347
supply-side problems
   getting intensive with capital, 334
   inflation and, 333
   quantity and productivity of factors of production
      investment, 332–333
      labour market, 332
Sweezy, Paul, 135

T

tacit collusion, 131–132
   average cost pricing, 133
   barometric firm price leadership, 132–133
   dominant firm price leadership, 132
   price benchmarks, 133
takeover bid, 135
tax cuts, 336–337
   income effects of, 337
   substitution effects of, 337
taxes and subsidies, 172–174
   advantages/disadvantages of, 173–174, 175
taxes, road, 231
Taylor rule, 326
technical or productive efficiency, 80
technology policy/R&D, 201–206
   change and market failure, 202
      duplication, 202
      monopolistic/oligopolistic market
         structures, 202
      R&D free riders, 202
      risk and uncertainty, 202
   defined, 201
   forms of intervention, 203
      Cooperative R&D, 203
      diffusion policies, 203
      other policies, 203
      patent system, 203
      public provision, 203
      R&D subsidies, 203
   R&D Scoreboard, 204–205
   stages, 201–202
   in UK/EU, 203–206
technology-based standards, 219
temporary operating rules, 328
tenders, 381
Tesco, 9, 34, 35, 136, 137
Thames Barrier, 9
Thatcher, Margaret, 234, 259, 335, 337, 341
tie-in sales, 200
tit-for-tat strategy, 142
tort liability for defective goods
   Consumer Protection Act 1987 (Part I)
      defences, 450–451
      difference between fault and strict liability, 446
      impact of, 452
      main provisions of, 446–450
      time limits, 451
   negligence liability
      Barnett v *Packer* (1940), 442
      breach of duty, 445
      consequential damage, 445
      Donoghue v *Stevenson* (1932, HL), 440–441
      duty of care, 440
      Evans v *Triplex Glass* (1936), 443
      Junior Books v *Veitchi* (1982, HL), 445
      Marc Rich & Co. AG v *Bishop Rock Marine*
         (1995, HL), 442
      Muirhead v *Industrial Tank Specialities Ltd* (1986), 444

'neighbour principle,' 441
   Stennett v Hancock (1939), 442
tort liability for defective services
  breach of duty, 482–493
  problematic duty situations, 460–482
total cost (*TC*), 70–71
  total fixed cost (*TFC*), 70
  total variable cost (*TVC*), 71
total factor productivity (TFP), 339
total physical product (*TPP*), 66
total revenue (*TR*), 43, 89–90
totally inelastic demand, 45
toxic waste, 170, 175, 182
tradable permits, 220
trade cycle, 246
trade unions, 158, 183, 259, 267, 287
traditional theories, problems with, 149–151
  lack of/alternative aims, 150–151
  maximising profit, difficulties in, 149–150
train operating companies (TOCs), 236
'Train to Gain,' 212
Training and Enterprise Councils (TECs), 208
transaction costs, 3–4
  defined, 3
transfers, 307
transfer payments, 271, 309
transnational association, 15
transport policy, 225–234
  case study, in Singapore, 232
  road space allocation, 225–227
    demand, 225–227
    supply, 227
  road usage, social cost/benefit of, 227–229
  traffic congestion solutions, 229–234
    direct provision, 229–230
    price mechanism, 231–234
    regulation/legislation, 230
Treaty of Amsterdam 1997, 192, 354, 355
Treaty of Lisbon, 192
Treaty of Nice 2003, 352
Treaty of Rome 1957, 354
Treaty on European Union (1992), 352
Trelleborg, 198

U

U-form enterprises, 10–11
UK environmental policy, 224
UK house prices, 30–31
UK National Lottery, 120–121
UK policies
  competition policy, 194–200
    assessment of, 200–201
    industrial clusters, 78–79
    merger policy, 200
    monopoly policy, 197–200
    restrictive practices policy, 196–197
  environmental policy, 224
  fiscal/monetary policies, 326–329
  privatisation, 236–237
  regulation, 238–239
  technology policy/R&D, 203–206
  training policy, 208–212
ultimate consumer, 440
uncertainty, 56–59
unemployment
  cost of, 257
  defined, 244, 253–254
  disequilibrium, 258–260
  duration of, 254–256
  equilibrium/natural, 260–262
  and labour market, 258–259
  measures of, 254
  rates, 254, 256–257
unemployment and inflation
  effect of expectations, 287–290
  expectations of output and employment, 291
  Phillips curve, 285–287
  rational expectations, 290–291
  at same time, 284–285
    accelerationist theory of inflation, 288–290
    effect of expectations, 287–290
    long-run Phillips curve and natural rate of
      unemployment, 290
    Phillips curve, 285–287
    rational expectations, 290–291
  simple Keynesian model, 282–284
    deflationary gap, 283–284
    'full-employment' GDP, 282–283
    inflationary gap, 284
  unemployment and inflation at same time, 284–285
Unfair Contract Terms Act 1977
    (UCTA), 422, 466
  scope of, 422–423
  substance of
    Breach of contract (s 3), 423
    negligence liability (s 2), 423
    purposes of UCTA 1977, 424–425
Unfair Contract Terms Bill, 432
unfair contract terms legislation, reform
    of, 432–433
  draft Unfair Contract Terms Bill, 432–433
Unfair Terms in Consumer Contracts
    Regulations 1999 (UTCCR
    1999), 357, 428–432
  enforcement of, 431
  interpretation
    Baybut and others v Eccle Riggs Country Park
      (2006), 431
    Director General of Fair Trading v First National Bank
      (2001, HL), 430
    Munkenbeck & Marshall v Michael Harold
      (2005), 430–431
    R (on the application of Khatun) v Newham London
      Borough Council (2004, CA), 430
  scope of, 427
  substance of, 428
    consumers, 428
    core terms, 428
    effect of unfair term, 429
    non-negotiable terms, 428
    relevant contracts, 428

seller/supplier, 428
   unfairness, 428
   written contracts, 429
unilateral offer, 376
unit elastic demand
   defined, 42
   and revenue, 46–47
US Antitrust Division, 198
US Sentencing Commission, 198

V

van Beurden, P., 185
variable cost, 70
variable factors, 65
VAT, 257, 271, 313
velocity of circulation, 280
verbal communication, 387
Vernons Pools, 120
vertical price-fixing agreements, 196
vertical restraints, 200

virtue matrix, 181–184
   civil foundation, 182
   frontier, 182–183
   globalisation, 184
   pressures on companies, 183–184

W

The Wagon Mound, 365, 490, 492
waiving communication rule, 389–390
Walt Disney Company, 12
   organisational structure of, 13
Warranty, 415, 416, 417, 421
Waste and Emissions Trading Act (2003), 224
water pollution, 219
White Paper, 356
'Winner's Curse,' 121
withdrawals (W)/leakages, 270–272
Wolf, Martin, 221
working tax credit, 271
World Trade Center, 310